The Friends of Liberty

The Friends of Liberty

The English Democratic Movement
in the Age of the French Revolution

Albert Goodwin

Harvard University Press
Cambridge, Massachusetts
1979

Library of Congress Cataloging in Publication Data

Goodwin, Albert.
  The friends of liberty.

  Bibliography: p.
  Includes index.
  1. Great Britain – Politics and government – 1789–1820.
  2. Radicalism – Great Britain. I. Title.
DA520.G6   320.9′41′073   78–15673
ISBN 0–674–32339–4

To Ethelwyn

Contents

Appendices

Abbreviations

AAE	Archives du Ministère des Affaires Étrangères, Paris
AN	Archives Nationales, Paris
BL	British Library
BN	Bibliothèque Nationale, Paris
EHR	*English Historical Review*
Parl. Hist.	*Parliamentary History* (ed. Cobbett)
PRO	Public Record Office
ST	*State Trials* (ed. T. B. and T. J. Howell)
TRHS	*Transactions of the Royal Historical Society*
TS	Treasury Solicitor's Papers
WWM	Wentworth Woodhouse Muniments, Central Library, Sheffield

List of illustrations

Acknowledgements

For permission to reproduce the illustrations in this volume, the
author is grateful to the National Portrait Gallery, London; the
Trustees of Dr Williams's Library, London; the City of
Manchester Art Galleries; Dr Kenneth Garlick; the Trustees of
the British Museum; and Norwich Central Public Library.

Preface

The English reformers of the reign of George III liked to call themselves the 'Friends of Liberty'. It was a defiant, but justified description. After all, they had backed John Wilkes in his struggle for the rights of the Middlesex parliamentary electors flouted by the unrepresentative House of Commons; had supported the constitutional claims of the American colonists against the legal and fiscal supremacy of the imperial Parliament; and had campaigned for the abolition of the Negro slave trade and the removal of the political and religious disabilities of the Dissenters under the obsolescent Test and Corporation Acts. As 'Citizens of the World', the members of the London Revolution Society in 1789 despatched messages of congratulation to the French National Assembly on the overthrow of Bourbon 'despotism' and proclaimed their millenary hopes in the emancipating effects of the Declaration of the Rights of Man. In 1792, both the Society for Constitutional Information and the London Corresponding Society demonstrated in support of, and did their best to assist, the beleaguered Parisian *sans-culottes* against the combined forces of European reaction. In the same spirit the metropolitan and provincial reform societies vindicated the right of national self-determination, laid claim to universal male suffrage and annual parliaments as part of a lost but recoverable inheritance, assimilated and disseminated the political radicalism, but not the republicanism, of Thomas Paine, pioneered the concept of social justice, exercised the right of association, public meeting and remonstrance, and did not shrink, in defence of such constitutional liberties, from head-on confrontation with legislature and executive. In the effort to achieve parliamentary reform by extra-parliamentary pressure, the 'friends of liberty' encouraged the formation of working-class political societies and promoted the growth of the popular or democratic movement in Scotland and Ireland, as well as in England

and Wales, and kept alive their radical faith and aspirations in the darkest days of repression and reaction.

After 1789, in an age increasingly dominated by fear and rampant French republicanism, their opponents sought to denigrate and ostracize such reformers by labelling them 'English Jacobins'. The contemporary use of such rival epithets in fact mirrored opposing attitudes to constitutional 'innovation' and egalitarian principles whose clash did so much to accelerate the formation of English conservatism, and, in the long run, of working-class political consciousness. Thomas Walker, the prosperous and influential Manchester cotton merchant, who sacrificed fortune and friends by his commitment to radicalism, felt the compulsion to record for posterity the vicissitudes of that conflict, even at the local level, in the conviction that 'the struggles of the Friends of Liberty, on the one hand, and the abettors of ancient errors and sacred abuses, on the other, form the most instructive part of the history of mankind'[1] – a large claim, but not without relevance to, and bearing on, our own times. The demand for 'participation' in civic affairs, from which they were excluded by the Corporation Act, was raised by lay Dissenters in the last decade of the eighteenth century because 'natural right' doctrines taught them that without it, they were, at best, second-class citizens. Similarly the 'right to protest' is not a newly won political privilege or tactical device first exploited by the campaigners for nuclear disarmament, it was jealously defended and repeatedly exercised by popular societies and trade unions against the repressive legislation of 1795 and 1799. Nor is the welfare state solely the brain-child of the late Lord Beveridge, for its blue-print is contained in Part II of Paine's *Rights of Man*. The insistence on human rights is not a diplomatic lever invented by President Carter for use against totalitarian oppression; it stems from the French Declaration of the Rights of Man of 1789, as re-echoed by the English 'friends of liberty'.

It is now over half a century ago since I first became interested in this theme after reading Robert Birley's Oxford University Prize Essay on *The English Jacobins from 1789 to 1802*[2]. A latter-day persuasion that I too could perhaps fill in some of the gaps in

1. *A Review of some of the Political Events which have occurred in Manchester during the last Five Years*. . . . (London, 1794), p. 3.

2. 1924. My thanks are due to Sir Robert Birley, as he now is, for his kindness in lending me *The Spirit of Anti-Jacobinism for 1802* – a rare item from his collection of pamphlet materials on the period.

existing accounts was prompted by a not untypical combination of accident and personal experience.[3] I was born and educated in Sheffield, an urban centre which had played a vital part in the evolution of provincial radical politics, as will be shown later. My father, as I first remember him, was an edge-tool forger, working for one of those 'small masters', whose existence had seemed almost anachronistic even a century earlier. Then he would have been a radical, but in the late 1890s, he was a Conservative Unionist. For years he was secretary and treasurer of an Oddfellows Sick and Benefit Society. He had hoped to become an engraver and, like Thelwall, he was a collector of prints, water-colours and oil paintings. I could well understand how Sheffield cutlers a century before had been so independent and ingenious in the administration of their own political affairs and so well aware of what was at stake in the wider world of national and international politics.

By accident also my first academic appointment was at the University of Liverpool on the staff of the late Professor G. S. Veitch, whose pioneering and classic work, *The Genesis of Parliamentary Reform*, showed that the English radical movement of the 1790s could not be properly understood without a detailed study of its relations with the French revolutionary assemblies and popular clubs. It is only by having access to the Treasury Solicitor's papers in the Public Record Office, which he did not, and by the use of other material from the French archives that I have, I hope, been able to supplement, and in matters of minor detail, perhaps to correct, his invaluable analysis. Without his guidance I should, for the most part, have been groping in the dark.

My main teaching life was spent at Oxford where I specialized in the history of the late eighteenth century in Europe and the French revolution. It was, however, my move to the University of Manchester, as successor to the late Sir Lewis Namier, which finally enabled me to combine French revolutionary studies with a growing interest in the history of English provincial radicalism. There I was able to profit from the researches of Professor Arthur Redford and Dr W. H. Chaloner into the municipal and economic history of Manchester and its region in its formative period of industrialization. At the John Rylands Library the late Mr Ronald Hall placed at my disposal the Spencer tracts, the Hamilton Rowan pamphlets and the

3. For other typical examples of historical specialization determined by accident rather than by choice, see R. Cobb, *A Second Identity: Essays on France and French History* (London, 1969), pp. 1, 46–7.

unrivalled collection of French revolutionary journals deposited by the Earl of Crawford and Balcarres.[4]

I was able to undertake the initial research for this study in the archives of the French Foreign Office and the French National Archives thanks to a leave of absence granted by the Council of the University of Manchester and renewed financial assistance from the Leverhulme Trustees, for which I have much pleasure in offering this grateful, if belated, acknowledgement. After my retirement in 1969 it was my good fortune also to be elected to a Visiting Research Fellowship at All Souls College, Oxford. This enabled me to continue work at the Public Record Office and British Library and to complete my investigations into English provincial radicalism. It was a memorable and profitable year for which I shall always be indebted to the Warden and Fellows of the College.

I would like also to acknowledge the help I have received from the staff of the following libraries, record offices and research institutions: the British Library, the Public Record Office, the London Library, the Institute of Historical Research, The Royal Commission on Historical Manuscripts, and Dr Williams's Library in London; the John Rylands University Library, the Central Reference and Chetham's Libraries in Manchester; the Central Library and the Norfolk and Norwich Record Office in Norwich; the Central Library at Sheffield (where my use of the Fitzwilliam and Burke papers was by kind permission of Earl Fitzwilliam, the Trustees of the Wentworth Woodhouse Estates Co. and the City Librarian; the Library of the University of Nottingham and the Duke of Portland for permission to quote from the Portland Mss. on deposit there; the Bodleian, the Codrington and Nuffield College Libraries in Oxford; the Cambridge University Library; and the Archives Nationales, the Archives du Ministère des Affaires Étrangères and the Bibliothèque Nationale in Paris.

My warmest thanks are due to my friend Professor Marcel Reinhard of the Sorbonne for drawing my attention to Pétion's file of correspondence with the English radicals in the Archives Nationales, and to Dr A. Hassell Smith of the Centre of East Anglian Studies, Mr C. B. Jewson of the Norfolk Record Society, Dr J. K. Edwards, and Miss P. J. Corfield of the Department of History, Bedford College, London for their interest in, and practical help with my work on Norwich radicalism. Professor M. A. Jones, of

4. For my article on the French revolutionary collections in the library see *Bulletin of the John Rylands Library*, vol. 42 (Sept. 1959), pp. 8–14.

University College, London, very kindly read Chapter 2, and closed a vital gap in my bibliographical knowledge, while Professor I. R. Christie, also of University College, read the whole book in typescript, made several valuable suggestions for its improvement, corrected not a few factual errors, and drew my attention to some recently published works which had escaped my notice. I hope the changes made as a result of his meticulous and scholarly comments will indicate how much I have appreciated his assistance.

Finally, I should like to thank the research students whose work I have either supervised or examined for their criticisms, stimulus and encouragement.

1 Introduction: The influence of the French revolution on the movement for parliamentary reform and on the evolution of British working-class radicalism

Historians of British radicalism in the last decade of the eighteenth century have not, perhaps, been very successful in assessing the complex influence of the French revolution on the character and content of the movement for parliamentary reform which had its origins in the time of Chatham and Wilkes.[1]

The difficulty of interpretation arises, in the first place, because English parliamentary reformers before 1789 were diverse in their political objectives and commitments and made, therefore, divergent responses to the formidable challenge from across the Channel which admitted no such evasions or compromises as had hitherto formed the substance of English eighteenth-century politics.[2] Secondly, the revolution itself was far from being a 'bloc' and went through more than one social and political metamorphosis in its progression from liberal constitutional reform to the republican extreme of Jacobin 'revolutionary government'. It was not surprising, therefore, that some of its initial sympathizers and supporters in Britain, such as Wordsworth and Mackintosh, became its latter-day opponents. Nor have historians paid sufficient attention to the political effects of the nation-wide celebrations of the centenary of the English revolution of 1688. Owing to the illness of George III, these celebrations had to be muted and postponed, with the result that in 1788 they were overshadowed by Whig preoccupation with the Regency issue and in 1789 by the outbreak of the French revolution. Yet it was this centenary that first dissipated the public apathy on the question of parliamentary reform which had followed the defeat of Pitt's proposals in 1785, rather than the French revo-

1. For the latest attempt to do so see J. Cannon, *Parliamentary Reform, 1640–1832* (Cambridge, 1973), pp. 140–3.
2. G. S. Veitch, *The Genesis of Parliamentary Reform* (London, 1965 reprint), p. x.

lution, the effects of which on English politics were considerably delayed. Until recently, moreover, it was not so evident as it now is that the ardent reformers of the Marquess of Lansdowne's 'Bowood circle' welcomed the French revolution, not only because they thought it would strengthen their case in England, but even more because they saw an opportunity for themselves to influence the course of legal and constitutional reform in France.[3] Bentham's aspirations in this respect were also complicated by his critical attitude to the whole theory of 'natural rights'.[4]

Though the cause of parliamentary reform could only benefit in the long run from the discussion of fundamental political problems, which the revolution provoked between Edmund Burke and his critics, in the more immediate future radicalism was undoubtedly hampered and ultimately crushed by the repressive policies of a government obsessed by the bogey of 'English Jacobinism' – a phenomenon which was not entirely a figment of the over-heated imaginations of the Alarmists.[5]

Then, too, the divisions in the Whig party, which finally culminated in the Portland schism of July 1794, were partly due to personal antagonisms and jealousies dating back to the debacle of 1784 and the Regency debates of 1788.[6] These had debilitated the party long before it had to face a momentous crisis of conscience over the revolution in France.[7] The 'new Whigs' of Grey's 'Association of the Friends of the People' merged into the Foxite remnant of the old Whig party after the schism without ever persuading Charles James Fox formally to join their society or to become, despite his general support, a convinced parliamentary reformer.[8] For so committed a champion of the French revolution this stance was, to say the least, a peculiar one.

3. D. Jarrett, *The Begetters of Revolution: England's involvement with France, 1759–1789* (London, 1973), ch. 10.

4. E. Halévy, *Growth of Philosophical Radicalism* (London, 1928), pp. 176, 187. See also J. H. Burns, 'Bentham and the French Revolution', *TRHS*, 5th series, vol. 16 (1966), pp. 95–114 and C. Blount, 'Bentham, Dumont and Mirabeau', *University of Birmingham Historical Journal*, vol. 3 (1952), pp. 153–67.

5. R. R. Fennessy, *Burke, Paine and the Rights of Man* (The Hague, 1963) and R. Birley, *The English Jacobins from 1789 to 1802* (Oxford, 1924), pp. 23–33.

6. F. O'Gorman, *The Whig Party and the French Revolution* (London, 1967), and L. G. Mitchell, *Charles James Fox and the Disintegration of the Whig Party, 1782–1794* (Oxford, 1971).

7. J. W. Derry, *The Regency Crisis and the Whigs, 1788–9* (Cambridge, 1963), ch. 4.

8. I. R. Christie, 'C. J. Fox', *History Today*, vol. 8 (1958), pp. 110–18.

Nor were the attitudes of the radical parliamentary reformers to the revolution any more monolithic. Their ranks contained militant enthusiasts prepared to dabble in treason in collusion with the French on the eve of, and even after the outbreak of war.[9] There were, however, others, such as Thelwall, who combined provocative and seditious exhortations in private with a scrupulous observance of legal and constitutional forms in public, and also Horne Tooke, who while dominating the rejuvenated Society for Constitutional Information in its Painite and Gallic phase, was yet the quintessence of caution and deliberation when it came to the resort to extra-parliamentary methods of political pressure or to indulgence in the evocative terminology of French democracy.[10] Though the British working-class radicals erupted on to the political stage almost simultaneously with their counterparts, the Parisian *sans-culottes*, in the summer and autumn of 1792, and though their social origins were not dissimilar from those of the Paris *sectionnaires*,[11] their instinctive reaction, in the face of embattled Loyalist opinion, was to defend the case for parliamentary reform in terms of dubious Anglo-Saxon 'liberties' rather than of French democracy, and to pose as champions of the recovery of constitutional privileges more nearly related to the needs of the seventeenth than of the eighteenth century.[12] These were the ancestral rights which they claimed as 'free-born Englishmen' and did not form part of any package importation of 'natural rights' from France. In self-defence against the accusations of the Reevites the radicals were also compelled to define their views on equality. By this they meant, not a redistribution of wealth or property, but equality of opportunity and equal civic rights.[13] In other words they were neither seventeenth-century Levellers, nor converts to any French notions of agrarian communism.

Nevertheless the French revolution had initially provided a much needed stimulus for the revival of reform movements of various

9. Most of these 'traitors' had American, Irish or Scottish associations, e.g. Paine, Joel Barlow, John Oswald, Lord Edward Fitzgerald, William Duckett, Nicolas Madgett, Dr Maxwell and Thomas Muir. Most of them at one time or another found political refuge in Paris.

10. *ST*, vol. 25, cols. 87, 318, 421, 488.

11. Gwyn A. Williams, *Artisans and Sans-Culottes: Popular Movements in France and Britain during the French Revolution* (London, 1968), p. 5.

12. *Address of the London Corresponding Society*, 6 August 1792, *ST*, vol. 24, cols. 382–7.

13. *Manchester Herald*, 8 December 1792.

kinds which had either recently forfeited strong public support or which had already encountered firm resistance from vested interests.[14] The centenary celebrations of the English revolution of 1688 had also supplied a similar incentive – especially for those members of the Dissenting interest who had committed themselves to the agitations for the abolition of the slave trade and the repeal of the Test and Corporation Acts.[15] The renewed but fruitless application of these reformers to the legislature in 1789 and 1790 naturally deepened and sharpened their existing interest in parliamentary reform, and it was to some extent under their middle-class and moderate auspices that new recruits were, between 1791 and 1792, drawn into the ranks of reform – in the shape of working-class members of the metropolitan and provincial radical societies.[16]

A new dimension was, thereby, added to the movement for parliamentary reform, for these new allies were, unlike their predecessors of the 1780s,[17] unenfranchised and were already strongly Painite in their political sympathies. They were also quick to assert their independence of middle-class leadership, to develop their own forms of organization and to elaborate new techniques of applying political pressure on Parliament. Owing to this new basis of popular support, the kind of parliamentary reform that came to be demanded after 1791 was for fully effective and equal representation of the people in the House of Commons. Before 1789 more than one variety of moderate reform had been designed to limit rather than extend the scope of electoral concessions to the disfranchised.[18] Earlier schemes, such as those advocated by Chatham and the Younger Pitt, which had involved tampering with electoral constituencies or the transference of seats from the rotten boroughs to the counties, were now recognized as totally inadequate. Though the radicals chose as their model of parliamentary reform the scheme for universal male suffrage and annual elections advocated by the

14. Veitch, ch. 5; P. A. Brown, *The French Revolution in English History* (London, 1965 reprint), ch. 3.

15. R. W. Davis, *Dissent in Politics, 1780–1830: The political life of William Smith, M.P.* (London, 1971), pp. 48–9, 56. U. Henriques, *Religious Toleration in England, 1787–1833* (London, 1961), pp. 56–67.

16.   See below, Chapter 5.

17. I. R. Christie, *Wilkes, Wyvill and Reform* (London, 1962), p. 226.

18. C. B. Cone, *The English Jacobins: Reformers in Late Eighteenth Century England* (New York, 1968), p. 70. A. G. Olson, *The Radical Duke: Career and Correspondence of Charles Lennox, Third Duke of Richmond* (Oxford, 1961), p. 55.

Duke of Richmond in 1780,[19] it was clearly intended by them to ensure an effective redistribution of political power between the governing class and the governed, in a way that even the 'radical duke' had not contemplated.

In more than one way also the French revolution strengthened the radical case for universal suffrage and annual parliaments by the appeal which it made to natural rights against the rights of property,[20] by its experiments with the principle of the rotation of annually elected representatives,[21] and, indirectly, in consequence of the political education of the masses, resulting from the debate on Burke's *Reflections.* The better recognition of their political rights and responsibilities could, thus, be held to vindicate the radicals' claim to universal suffrage, which earlier critics had condemned as synonymous with an inevitable increase in electoral bribery and corruption.

As Paine himself commented, the French revolution also refocused attention on the surviving relics of feudalism in Britain – the game laws, the tithe system, the Scottish feudal land laws, the prevalence of primogeniture and the outworn manorial organization of justice and police in local government. In doing so it pointed the way to a radical reform of Parliament as a means of overthrowing what Cobbett was later to call 'Old Corruption'. The attack on these evils associated with the whole structure of government and society would, it was expected, unite a wide section of public opinion behind the radicals, who were primarily concerned to use parliamentary reform in order to rectify their social and economic grievances as victims of the industrial revolution.[22] It was because they were attracted by Paine's prophetic sketch of the social benefits which might become available in a future welfare state that working men

19. Olson, ch. 2. *ST*, vol. 24, col. 383.

20. But see A. Lincoln, *Some Social and Political Ideas of English Dissent, 1763–1800* (Cambridge, 1938), p. 2, where the existence in England before 1789 of an 'indigenous and mature school of natural right politics' is emphasized.

21. Those radicals who, like Thomas Cooper of the Manchester Constitutional Society, defended the feasibility of annual Parliaments on this basis probably did so, however, as much on the strength of American experience as on French precedents. Rotation of members was commonly practised in New England both before and after the break with Britain was advocated by both Paine and Joel Barlow. On the indebtedness of the English radicals to the American colonists, see Colin Bonwick, *English Radicals and the American Revolution* (Chapel Hill, N.C., 1977), chs. 6–8.

22. See G. Whale, 'The influence of the industrial revolution on the demand for Parliamentary reform', *TRHS*, 4th series, vol. 15 (1922), pp. 130 ff.

in the provinces became such avid readers of the cheap editions of Part II of *The Rights of Man*, which were published and circulated by their own radical societies.[23] Thus parliamentary reform became the concern, not so much of the county freeholders as in the 1780s, as of the urban and working-class radicals.[24] Little or nothing was now heard, except from interested party politicians, of the need to preserve that constitutional balance between the executive and legislative powers which had once seemed so important to those who had pressed for 'economical' or parliamentary reform between 1780 and 1783.[25]

Apart from Paine's blue-print of revolutionary financial, legal, and political change, there was, however, at this period, a relative dearth among radical publicists of constructive ideas for the reform of the Poor Laws, the redistribution of wealth or land nationalization.[26] This was partly because poverty was not then regarded as the consequence of the economic process, but rather as the result of the burden of the national debt and the unfair incidence of taxation.[27] A further reason for this deficiency was, however, precisely that parliamentary reform was itself regarded as a panacea. Once achieved, so the radicals thought, it would automatically ensure fiscal reform (and with it Poor Law reform), the closer scrutiny and restriction of enclosure acts, the limitation of exclusive monopolies, aristocratic privilege, ministerial abuses and official pensions.[28] Popularly elected representatives would be held to the performance of these tasks of purification by the sanction of annual elections. Once the fortress of privilege had been breached, however, it was generally anticipated that further resistance to the popular will would prove to be impossible.

Although the radical advocates of parliamentary reform did not propose to infringe the royal prerogatives, or to compromise the

23. Paine, *The Rights of Man*, ed. H. Collins (Harmondsworth, 1969), p. 37.
24. Cannon, p. 142.
25. Christie, *Wilkes, Wyvill and Reform*, p. 1.
26. P. Colquhoun, *Treatise on the Wealth, Power and Resources of the British Empire* (1814) – the chief contemporary text on the distribution of wealth – and Thomas Evans, *Christian Policy the Salvation of the Empire*, 2nd ed. (London, 1816) – a Spencean tract on land nationalization – were both published towards the end of the Napoleonic wars. For the social and economic utopianism of the English Jacobins, see below, Chapter 12.
27. Patricia Hollis, *The Pauper Press: A Study in Working-Class Radicalism in the 1830s* (Oxford, 1970), pp. 204–5.
28. *Ibid.*, p. 205.

constitutional position of the House of Lords, their attack on the borough influence of the nobility in elections to the lower house, Paine's prescription of 'representative democracy', and criticisms of the established church by Priestley, Robinson, Cooper and Freud were easily misrepresented by their opponents as 'subversive' of the constitution, especially when they were construed as the imported by-products of French revolutionary principles. Hence, whereas the pre-revolutionary parliamentary reformers had not encountered any violent or strongly organized opposition, the radical reformers provoked a virulent and well-orchestrated movement of conservative reaction from the Burkian 'Alarmists' and Reevite Loyalists.[29] These enemies of the reformers now questioned their motives and methods and depicted them as anarchists, Levellers, atheists, and in general, as the ignorant dupes of French republican propaganda.

Despite (or perhaps because of) the insistence of radical leaders like Thomas Hardy, Thelwall and Place that one of the primary tasks of radicalism was the political education of the masses; despite Godwin's teaching that opinion, not violence, would prove to be the effectual solvent of the old regime; and in the face of repeated disclaimers of radical pamphleteers that political equality would not involve social levelling, ministerial opponents maintained that radical parliamentary reform was only a specious subterfuge intended to conceal the existence of a Jacobin conspiracy for the violent overthrow of established institutions in church and state. This accusation had first been levelled by Burke against the London Revolution Society and the Society for Constitutional Information, both pillars of middle-class respectability, in his *Appeal from the New to the Old Whigs* in August 1791.[30] It became the parrot-cry of the Association for the Preservation of Liberty and Property against Republicans and Levellers in late 1792 and the subject, subsequently, of Gillray's cartoons and Canning's jibes in the *Anti-Jacobin*. It was given official sanction in successive reports of the secret committees of both houses of Parliament in 1794 and 1799.

Though Britain was not, in the autumn of 1792, on the verge of revolution, and though the radicals were reformers not anarchists, the public expression of their feelings of sympathy for, and solidarity

29. E. C. Black, *The Association: British Extraparliamentary Political Organization, 1769–1793* (Cambridge, Mass., 1963), ch. 7.
30. E. Burke, *Select Works*, ed. E. J. Payne, vol. 3 (1878), p. 7.

with, the beleaguered Parisian democrats, their attempts to supply them with money, arms and shoes, and their provocative congratulatory addresses and deputations to the French Convention as the republican armies swept through Belgium in November, gave colour and verisimilitude to the strictures of the Anti-Jacobins.[31] Special attention will be given to the effects of these radical addresses in deluding the French Executive Council and Convention as to the probability of a revolution in Britain as soon as open war ensued[32] and in enabling ministerialists, in the spring of 1793, to discredit parliamentary reform when it was moved by Grey in the House of Commons with the backing of petitions from the metropolitan and provincial radical societies.[33]

Once war with republican France had broken out the members of the popular societies became an isolated and alienated minority powerless to achieve their political objectives even in temporary association with the aristocratic Whig splinter group of the Friends of the People. A sense of frustration gave way to one of desperation and some of the provincial radicals began to express their determination to look elsewhere than to Parliament for the reform which they had repeatedly been denied.

In this situation, and while the metropolitan radical leaders were still discussing alternative methods of procedure, the initiative passed, in the summer of 1793, to the Scottish reformers who were exasperated by the failure of the movement for Burgh reform, by the political reaction organized by the Dundas ascendancy, and by the monstrous injustice of the trials of Muir and Palmer on charges of sedition.[34] The British Convention held at Edinburgh in late November 1793, although short-lived, was, in reality, a landmark in the history of British radicalism. It was organized by the Scottish societies of the Friends of the People, who now dissociated themselves from their parent society in London and committed themselves to the full programme of radical reform – universal suffrage and annual parliaments. Its meetings were remarkable for the unity and solidarity of the Scottish, Irish and English democrats, the uncom-

31. See particularly the Reevite publication, *Collection of Addresses transmitted by certain English clubs and societies to the National Convention of France*, 2nd ed. (1937).

32. See below, Chapter 7.

33. Speech of Lord Mornington, 6 May 1793, *Parl. Hist.* vol. 30, col. 864.

34. H. W. Meikle, *Scotland and the French Revolution* (Glasgow, 1912), chs. 2, 4, 7.

promising nature of its resolutions and its adoption of French revolutionary jargon and procedures. It was, however, the English delegates of the London Corresponding Society – Margarot and Gerrald – and Sinclair of the Society for Constitutional Information who dominated the assembly, devised its organization and dictated its policies. With the exception of Sinclair, who turned King's evidence, they too became the most notable victims of further Scottish judicial intemperance.[35]

The attempted summons of an English Convention in the spring of 1794 followed directly from the dissolution of the Edinburgh convention and the consequent radical confrontation with the government occurred, at least partly, on the recommendation of the English delegates imprisoned at Edinburgh.[36] The challenge was readily accepted by the government as a means of stopping the radical movement in its tracks and demonstrating to the country, now in danger of invasion, if not the treasonable nature, at least the reality and extent of the radical threat to established institutions and social order. Though there were technical reasons why the Attorney General decided to prosecute the radical leaders on charges of high treason, rather than for sedition, the real motivation of the state trials of 1794 was political.[37]

When English juries, thanks to the brilliant advocacy of Erskine and Gibbs, acquitted Hardy, Horne Tooke and Thelwall, and when the government released the rest of the accused without trial, a crisis in the history of British liberty was safely surmounted. Not, however, without loss or damage to the intended victims or to the societies which had supported them in adversity. The back of the democratic movement was broken. The Society for Constitutional Information, so long the mainspring of radical organization and propaganda and the early protector of so many popular societies in the provinces, virtually collapsed. The links between the London Corresponding Society and the northern centres of urban radicalism were severed and the persecuted leaders either withdrew from active participation in politics or emigrated to the United States. Though the official theory of a Jacobin conspiracy was disproven, it was not wholly discredited – just as the main defendants in the State Trials were

35. Lord Cockburn, *Examination of the Trials for Sedition in Scotland* (2 vols., Edinburgh, 1888).

36. Margarot to Hardy, 22 December 1793. PRO TS11/954/3498.

37. *Lord Eldon's Anecdote Book*, ed. Anthony L. J. Lincoln and Robert L. McEwen (London, 1960), pp. 55–8.

acquitted but not wholly vindicated. Windham was, indeed, far from being the only one who regarded them as 'acquitted felons'.[38] If they had been, like their colleagues in Edinburgh, charged with sedition, rather than treason, it is doubtful whether they would have been acquitted.

In the famine year of 1795, although the London Corresponding Society attempted to fill the void left by the extinction of the Society for Constitutional Information by expanding its circulation of reform pamphlets, its continued pleas for universal suffrage and annual parliaments increasingly lacked conviction. The promotion of public remonstrances and petitions for the redress of grievances, the end of hostilities and the removal of ministers, even when supported by the new device of large-scale open-air meetings of the society, failed to intimidate and only antagonized the government. Widely scattered food riots in the provinces, in which local units of the militia were sometimes implicated, and crimping riots in the capital undoubtedly gave the administration greater cause for concern. Thus, though the mass public meeting was to become a potent political weapon in the nineteenth century, its initial use by the London Corresponding Society only brought down on its head further repressive legislation in the form of the Pitt and Grenville 'Gagging Acts' of November–December 1795.

This legislation provided an effective answer to two of the most potentially damaging forms of propaganda so far devised by the radicals – the large public meetings for protesting against government policy and the political lecture as exploited by Thelwall.[39] It put an end to the remarkable recovery in strength and numbers of the London Corresponding Society and its provincial associates since the treason trials and forced the democratic movement on to the defensive. A complete reorganization of the administrative structure of the society in the metropolitan area in response to the newly imposed restrictions failed to check falling attendances at meetings of the general delegate committee and of the local divisions. The promotion of missionary tours in 1796 by specially commissioned

38. For this, see the debate on 5 January 1795 in the House of Commons on the extension of the suspension of Habeas Corpus. *Parl. Hist.*, vol. 31, cols. 1062–130.

39. The only mass public meeting organized by the London Corresponding Society after 1795, although summoned according to the regulations of the Seditious Meetings Act, was easily dissolved by local magistrates assisted by a strong show of military strength. See below, p. 412.

delegates, in order to re-establish the society's contacts with the provincial clubs and to revive the flagging spirit of reform in sensitive areas such as the Midlands, only involved its most active members in further political trials, which in turn overstretched the London society's finances.[40] Internal schisms and the increasing tensions between moderates and extremists initiated a further and final stage of decline. Apathy about the practical prospects of parliamentary reform now became widespread. Accumulating signs of the imminence of national disaster led many disillusioned supporters to consider, in Godwinian terms, that reform would arise phoenix-like from the ashes and that patience rather than continued political pressure was all that was now needed.[41] This was certainly the prevailing mood in 1797 when the suspension of cash payments at the Bank of England indicated the financial straits to which the government had been reduced, when the naval mutinies at Spithead and the Nore for a time compromised national security, and when ministerial hopes of a negotiated peace with France proved illusory. But, just as the millennium which the 'friends of liberty' had anticipated in the first flush of their enthusiasm for the French revolution had never materialized, so the national calamity, which the later radicals had forecast as the inescapable consequence of the protracted struggle with France, never happened. Even to the end political realism was a faculty which seemed to have escaped these eighteenth-century democrats. Hard experience and repeated disappointments had not affected their Micawber-like attitude to their political prospects even when these were already desperate.

As the final decade of the century drew to its close the submerged and alienated remnants of British radicalism at length assumed the conspiratorial, treasonable and republican character which had been so vigorously repudiated by its former leaders.[42] This was partly the result of governmental repression, but it was also necessitated by the co-operation of the extremists with the United Irishmen and by their hesitant willingness to envisage, if not to accept, the prospect of armed assistance from the French. This clandestine movement

40. Much of the time and energy of the LCS in 1796 were spent in fund-raising for the legal defence of John Gale Jones and John Binns after their arrest at Birmingham in March for seditious speeches.

41. *Reply of the Friends of the People in Sheffield . . . respecting a General Meeting, 15 May 1797.* BL, Place collection of newspaper cuttings, vol. 38, fo. 67.

42. See below, Chapters 11 and 12.

was probably never as highly organized, nor as extensive in its ramifications, as the secret committee of the House of Commons reported in 1799, nor as shadowy and insubstantial as some modern historians have supposed.[43] It relied for support mainly on the Irish ghettos in London and Lancashire and, to some extent, on the still simmering discontent in Scotland.[44] Perhaps its most significant aspects were in the way in which it penetrated the opposition to the government's new Combination Acts in the industrial North-West and its revelation of the assistance, and indeed leadership, which nineteenth-century radicalism was to draw from the alien Irish populations of the urban industrial areas. To government spies it appeared as a conspiracy directed not only against British supremacy in Ireland and the English Crown, but also against organized religion – for the insidious influences of French metaphysics and Painite propaganda were still thought to be at work as the democratic movement foundered.[45] The 'United English' were also involved by their Irish counterparts in tampering with the loyalty of the armed forces and their efforts culminated in the forlorn conspiracy of the unfortunate Colonel Despard.[46] Its immediate result, however, was government intervention to suppress the little that still remained of the radical societies by Act of Parliament in 1799.

Such, in brief retrospect, is the familiar outline of the rise and decline of the British democratic movement in the age of the French revolution. What has not been sufficiently emphasized, perhaps, by some historians is that the direction of this movement was from time to time diverted and its fortunes virtually decided by events in France, Scotland and Ireland. Equally significant was the solidarity of interest displayed by radicals across national or provincial frontiers in an age when the idea of Fraternity was as real and evocative a political motive as the concepts of Liberty and Equality. The London Revolution Society, by its messages of goodwill to the

43. Veitch, p. 338, obviously underrated the extent of the movement, relying on the evidence of Francis Place. Thompson was perhaps the first to treat the subject seriously. *Making of the English Working Class* (London, 1965), p. 172.

44. Most of the English evidence is contained in the Privy Council records: PRO PC 1/41/A 136; 143; 144; 150.

45. Report of W. Barlow on Liverpool radicals (August 1799). PRO PC 1/44/A 161.

46. Sir Charles Oman, *Colonel Despard and other studies* (London, 1922), ch. 1. A. W. Smith, 'Irish rebels and English radicals, 1798–1820', *Past and Present*, no. 7 (April 1955), pp. 78–85. M. Elliott, 'The "Despard conspiracy" reconsidered', *Past and Present*, no. 75 (May 1977), pp. 46–61.

French National Assembly, by its efforts to promote the prospects of universal peace through an alliance between Britain, France and America, and by its reception of deputations from French Jacobin societies and of Girondin leaders like Pétion, may well have contributed not a little to the idea of a federated association of freedom-loving peoples – a concept which at a later stage aroused the enthusiasm of William Skirving, the Scottish reformer.[47] The solidarity (and it was no more than that) which certain radical societies expressed with the French in the autumn of 1792 earned them the description of 'English Jacobins', but they themselves had assumed and came to merit the proud title of 'friends of liberty'. In doing so they were vindicating their claims to the recovery of a lost, but not irrecoverable, heritage of ancestral liberties, but in 1792 they were also defending the French revolutionary assertion of the right to self-determination, the claim of the Irish Catholics to political emancipation, and in 1793 the demands of the Scottish radicals for long-overdue reforms in local government and criminal law procedure. English radicalism at this period cannot, in other words, be properly studied except within the larger framework of Anglo-American, Anglo-Scottish, Anglo-Irish and, above all, Anglo-French affairs. It is the main purpose of this study to present these varied and inter-locking 'dimensions' as dynamic factors in the early history of English radical democracy.

47. W. Skirving to Thomas Hardy, 17 May 1793. *ST*, vol. 24, col. 410.

2 The radical tradition in the eighteenth century

A man may be a patriot without being an antiquary.

w. HAZLITT, Essay on Sir Francis Burdett in *The Spirit of the Age*

It is not because we *have been* free, but because we *have a right to be free* that we ought to demand freedom.

Sir James Mackintosh, *Vindiciae Gallicae*

On the whole William Hazlitt saw no reason to dissent from the popular view of that old-fashioned, unpretentious and plain-spoken radical and parliamentary reformer – Sir Francis Burdett MP. He described him as 'a very honest, a very good-tempered, and a very good-looking man', the darling of his Westminster constituents and 'a prodigious favourite of the English people'. In this political paragon, however, Hazlitt detected two flaws, both inherited from Burdett's mentor and patron – the eccentric, one-eyed parson – philologist, John Horne Tooke. Burdett, fortunately, unlike Tooke, grew out of an 'early tendency to petulance and caustic sententious- ness', but never overcame a more deeply rooted disposition 'to go back to the early times of our Constitution and history in search of the principles of law and liberty'.[1] Hazlitt did not himself see the need in the nineteenth century for English radicals to be antiquar- ians, and, indeed, perhaps few of them were. But, in this failing, if it was one, Burdett was not unique – for it was characteristic of whole generations of eighteenth-century English radicals, just as it had been of their seventeenth-century predecessors.[2] Burdett, indeed, came at the end of a long line of 'progressive' reformers, the modern- ity and enlightenment of whose political views derived partly from

1. W. Hazlitt, *The Spirit of the Age*, ed. E. D. Mackerness (London, 1969), p. 230.
2. H. Butterfield, *The Englishman and his History* (Cambridge, 1945), Zera S. Fink, *The classical Republicans: An essay in the recovery of a pattern of thought in seventeenth-century England* (Evanston, Ill., 1945). J. G. A. Pocock, *The ancient constitution and feudal law: English historical thought in the seventeenth century* (Cambridge, 1957).

a scholarly, partly from a popular, interpretation of the historical origins of English liberty.

In the 1790s radical publicists and even popular demagogues nevei tired of invoking the hallowed names and political doctrines of Milton, Algernon Sydney, Harrington and Locke in support of their protests and remonstrances against clerical intolerance, Loyalist reaction and ministerial repression.[3] Alternatively they appealed to the bogus but strongly held historical myth that English popular liberties and the forms of democratic government had been of Anglo-Saxon origin and had been cherished and carefully nurtured by Alfred the Great.[4] These responses and attitudes were, to some extent, self-consciously adopted by the radicals in the effort to rebut the charges of political and social 'innovation' levelled against them by their opponents, and also to disprove the even more damaging slur that they had assimilated and hoped to spread French revolutionary notions of popular sovereignty. In their recourse, however, to seventeenth-century constitutional precedents and to the 'undefiled' pre-Conquest sources of English freedom, the radicals of the revolutionary era were also harking back, often consciously, to the behaviour and political attitudes of the 'real Whigs' or 'eighteenth-century Commonwealthmen' of almost a century before.[5]

These were a small group of Irish and English intellectuals prominent in scientific and philosophical inquiry, the earliest exponents of deism, free-thinking and materialism and, in politics, defenders of the classical seventeenth-century 'republican' tradition. Repelled by the contemporary trend towards absolutism in the Europe of Louis XIV, critical of the increasingly conservative policies adopted by the main body of the Whigs after 1694, and champions of a wider religious toleration than that advocated by either Milton or Locke, they set themselves the task of defending the popular liberties or ideals which appeared to have been diminished or set aside by the political compromises of the revolution of 1688.[6]

3. Cf. Henry Redhead Yorke's citations from Locke's *Second Treatise on Civil Government* at the open-air meeting of reformers at Sheffield on 7 April 1794. Sheffield Central Reference Library, Local Pamphlets, vol. 80 (3), p. 21.

4. Joseph Gerrald's *Address of the British Convention assembled at Edinburgh, November 19, 1793, to the People of Great Britain* contained a succinct summary of this popular myth.

5. C. Robbins, *The Eighteenth-Century Commonwealthman* (Cambridge, Mass., 1959), Introduction.

6. J. H. Plumb, *The Growth of Political Stability in England, 1675–1725* (London, 1967), pp. 134–5. Robbins, p. 11.

By their efforts to accommodate their political principles to an age in which republicanism had become no more than a memory, they did, however, succeed in transforming the seventeenth-centuiy republican tradition into 'a new vision of political liberty'.[7] We may, therefore, regard them as the first generation of the eighteenth-century 'friends of liberty'.

The nucleus of the group was formed by a trio of Irish politicians and publicists, of whom the most influential was Robert, first Viscount Molesworth, the most radical and cosmopolitan in outlook was the deist John Toland, and the most 'patriotic' was the early champion of Irish legislative independence, William Molyneux. All of these, however, were closely associated either on terms of personal friendship, or by way of literary collaboration, with the other members of the group – Walter Moyle, John Trenchard and Anthony Ashley Cooper, third Earl of Shaftesbury.[8] Though the contemporary impact and long-range significance of the group lay chiefly in the realm of ideas, most of its members had had some experience of the realities of practical politics. Molesworth had served on William III's Irish Privy Council and in 1692 had been an envoy to the court of Denmark. Molyneux had sat in the Irish House of Commons as one of the representatives of Trinity College, Dublin, between 1692 and 1698, while Moyle, Trenchard and Cooper had represented Saltash, Taunton and Poole respectively between 1695 and 1698 in the English lower house.

Their main controversial publications were related to contemporary political issues, such as their resistance to the maintenance of standing armies in time of peace, their defence of the Hanoverian succession or the advocacy of the legislative independence of the Irish parliament.[9] Their lasting political significance, however, derives from their persistent assertion of what they regarded as the

7. Franco Venturi, *Utopia and Reform in the Enlightenment* (Cambridge, 1971), p. 53.

8. For a sympathetic appreciation of the influence of these publicists both at home and on the Continent, see Venturi, ch. 2.

9. Cf. Moyle and Trenchard, *An Argument showing that a Standing Army is inconsistent with a Free Government, and absolutely destructive to the Constitution of the English Monarchy* (1697), and Toland's *Anglia Libera* (1701) – a defence of the Act of Succession – and Molyneux's famous *Case of Ireland's being bound by Acts of Parliament in England stated* (1699). The latter had been prompted by an act of the English Parliament in 1698 forbidding the export of Irish woollen goods. It provided the American colonists with their slogan condemning taxation without representation. E. M. Johnston, *Ireland in the Eighteenth Century* (Dublin, 1974), pp. 60–3.

prerequisites for the maintenance of fundamental private and public liberties. When the Whig aristocracy, after 1694, began to strengthen rather than restrict monarchical authority – by opposing the reduction of the standing army, by negotiating the Act of Union with Scotland, by reducing the democratic franchise of the City of London and by forcing through the Septennial Act – the minority of 'real' or 'independent' Whigs ignored the war emergency and the danger from Jacobitism which had prompted some of these measures; they saw England as already on the slippery slope that, on the Continent, had led to despotism.[10] Molesworth had seen at first hand the warning signals of a new resurgence of state tyranny in Denmark after his expulsion from the country in 1692, and in 1711 he had republished the sixteenth-century Calvinist philippic against French monarchical despotism, Francis Hotman's *Franco-Gallia*, with a brilliant preface that came to serve as the group's political manifesto.[11] When the Whig Junto made clear its intention of consistently exploiting both the electoral system and royal patronage as a means to political domination, the 'real Whigs', along with the emerging Tory country party, stressed the need for reviving such seventeenth-century radical constitutional panaceas as the separation of the executive and legislative powers, the total exclusion of placemen from the House of Commons, the rotation of offices, and shorter or even annual parliaments.[12] In this context Toland, who had precipitated the deist controversy by the publication in 1696 of his *Christianity not Mysterious*, had strengthened the appeal to such radical solutions by his editions of the prose works of Milton (1698) and Harrington's *Oceana* (1700), under the patronage of Molesworth and subsequently of the Earl of Shaftesbury.[13]

Even while advocating the continued relevance of such securities against the encroaching powers of centralized state supremacy, these early eighteenth-century Commonwealthmen were compelled by

10. Plumb, pp. 134–5.

11. It was reprinted in 1775 and continued to act as a stimulus to reformers in the latter part of the century. Hotman's emphasis on the 'elective' origins of the French monarchy, the primitive popular assemblies of the Merovingians and his praise of the 'mixed' form of government no doubt evoked a strong response from those English reformers who liked to believe in the Anglo-Saxon origins of British democracy. M. Göhring, *Weg und Sieg der Modernen Staatsidee in Frankreich* (Tübingen, 1946), pp. 87–8.

12. Plumb, pp. 140–1.

13. Toland regarded the *Oceana* as 'the most perfect form of popular government that ever was'. Venturi, p. 59.

circumstances to disavow republicanism, realizing that it had ceased to be practical politics. Instead they came to glorify English liberty and to attribute it to the 'mixed' form of government that had resulted from the revolution of 1688. But the republican tradition, divorced from the historical forms it had taken in the past, achieved the status of an ideal Utopia which seemed to have relevance to the future. In fact none of the 'real Whigs' were democrats and none of them wished to extend the franchise beyond the circle of the propertied classes. Even so characteristic a member of the group as John Trenchard, although a Whig with strong popular sympathies, was by no means a republican and, though an assailant of High Church principles, was certainly no deist.[14]

Nevertheless, the 'real Whigs', already in the first decades after the 'Glorious Revolution' of 1688, had detected the dangers which might in the future threaten the balanced British constitution from any considerable extension of Crown influence under monarchs who were or had been Dutch Stadholders or German Electors. Molyneux, at least, had also identified the actual or potential conflict between the legal supremacy of the British Parliament and the concept of fundamental law which could be, and later was, invoked by subordinate or colonial legislatures.[15] Finally, the Interregnum's legacy of republican experiment had been transformed into a new-style Whig opposition creed which had little or nothing to do with notions of social or political equality, but which re-emphasized the right of collective resistance, the need to extend the scope of religious toleration and the necessity of continued vigilance against the menace of a Jacobitism allied to popery and French despotism.

Molesworth's conviction that 'good learning . . . is a great antidote against tyranny' also inspired a second generation of English Commonwealthmen who, in the middle years of the eighteenth century, did even more for the preservation and republication of seventeenth-century republican texts than their immediate predecessors. A lead in this respect was given by an artless and obscure hack journalist Richard Baron, who between 1737 and 1740 had been a pupil of Francis Hutcheson, the famous Glasgow professor of moral philosophy.[16] A friend of Thomas Gordon, author of the

14. *Dictionary of National Biography.* Article on Trenchard.

15. Robbins, p. 10.

16. Hutcheson, before his appointment at Glasgow, had been a member of Molesworth's philosophic coterie in Dublin. J. C. Beckett, *The Making of Modern Ireland, 1603–1923* (London, 1971), p. 184.

Independent Whig (1724), Baron earned the reputation of being a republican by his editions of Algernon Sydney's *Discourses concerning Government* and Ludlow's *Memoirs*, both published in 1751, Milton's prose works in 1753 and Needham's *Excellency of a Free State* of 1656 in 1757. Before his death in 1766 Baron had been befriended and encouraged by a more notable figure – Thomas Hollis V of Lincoln's Inn, the 'strenuous Whig' of Boswell's acquaintance, and as 'professional' a 'friend of liberty' as any of his generation, not excluding John Wilkes himself or Parson Horne Tooke.[17]

Although Hollis would have 'given his right hand' to have become a Member of Parliament, once he had completed his political education by extensive Continental travels, he steadfastly refused repeated suggestions that he should become a candidate because he could not tolerate the exercise of political patronage on his behalf or the expenditure of vast sums on electoral bribery.[18] Such indeed was his undisguised contempt for contemporary political chicanery that he himself never cast a vote in a parliamentary election. Instead of an active parliamentary career, Hollis decided to devote his considerable wealth, his undoubted talents and artistic flair to a lifelong campaign of philanthropy and propaganda. He himself provided a personal link between the colleagues and disciples of Molesworth and the third generation of eighteenth-century Commonwealthmen – the political coterie associated with the Price–Priestley group of Rational Dissenters.[19]

Born in 1720 of a northern Dissenting family which had already distinguished itself by its philanthropic work, Hollis concentrated his attention from 1754 to 1763 on an ambitious scheme for the collection, production and dissemination of books, coins, medals and prints illustrative of the history and principles of English liberty.[20] The spur to this crusade was his conviction that English civil liberty

17. Archdeacon Francis Blackburne (ed.), *Memoirs of Thomas Hollis* (2 vols., London, 1780): Robbins, *The Eighteenth-Century Commonwealthman*, pp. 384–5; also 'The strenuous Whig: Thomas Hollis of Lincoln's Inn', *William and Mary Quarterly*, 3rd series, vol. 7 (1950), pp. 406–53; A. T. P. Cooper, 'The good Mr Hollis: Dorset's greatest democrat', *The Dorset Year Book, 1964–65* (Weymouth), pp. 11–21.

18. He refused to stand for Dorchester in 1760 and 1763 and for Westminster in 1769. Robbins, 'The strenuous Whig', p. 431.

19. Although never professedly a Dissenter, Hollis had many friends among the clerical leaders of the earliest Unitarian congregations, such as Theophilus Lindsey and John Disney.

20. Robbins, 'The strenuous Whig', p. 430.

was once more under threat from the spread of popery and that, both at home and abroad, monarchy seemed to be challenging with success the legal and constitutional restraints on its authority. He was a generous benefactor of colleges and universities in England, Europe and the North American colonies, particularly those, such as Cambridge, Harvard, Berne and Zurich, where the influence of Protestant Dissent was marked.[21] Between 1763 and 1765 Hollis edited Toland's biography of Milton and the works of Algernon Sydney and Locke and took a prominent part in the negotiations which led to the acquisition of a Thomason collection of civil war tracts by the British Museum.[22] As a connoisseur he used the talents of Cipriani in the design of commemorative coins and medals and the skills of the bookbinder Mathewman in the production of those elaborately bound presentation copies of the English seventeenth-century republican classics in green, blue, red or brown leather, which were provocatively embossed with the emblems of ancient republican virtue – daggers, flails or caps of liberty.[23] When, in the 1760s, Horace Walpole's 'Dame Thucydides', the celebrated and fashionable Mrs Catherine Macaulay, undertook, as a Whig counterblast to Hume's recent Tory history of the seventeenth century, to chronicle the 'shameful' misdeeds of the Stuart tyranny in several volumes, Hollis gave her both sympathetic encouragement and practical assistance.[24] He not only designed the frontispiece for her history, provided material for her account of the Irish Massacres and other episodes, but also saw several volumes through the press and presented the whole work to the library of Harvard College.[25]

His own political views were by no means original, being derived more immediately from Molesworth, and indirectly from Harrington. Like his cousin Timothy, Hollis held no brief for the political

21. Cooper, p. 15. He presented the well-known portrait of Oliver Cromwell by Cooper to Sidney Sussex College in 1764 and another of Sir Isaac Newton to Trinity College in 1761.

22. Robbins, 'The strenuous Whig', p. 424. The collection of printed books published between 1640 and 1661, made by George Thomason, was presented to the Museum in the name of George III in 1762. British Museum, *The Catalogues of the Printed Books* (1952), pp. 38–9.

23. Robbins, 'The strenuous Whig', p. 425.

24. The first volume of Mrs Macaulay's work, *History of England from the accession of James I to that of the Brunswick Line* appeared in 1763. The eighth and final volume was published in 1783.

25. L. M. Donnelly, 'The celebrated Mrs. Macaulay', *William and Mary Quarterly*, 3rd series, vol. 6 (1949), p. 182.

education or enfranchisement of artisans or agricultural workers, and did not conceal his patrician belief that 'all commonwealths were founded by gentlemen'. He seems to have taken over from Richard Baron an idea that was later adopted by the advocates of moderate parliamentary reform – the suggestion for the increased parliamentary representation of the counties – which he probably passed on to his friend the Earl of Chatham.[26] Like Chatham he cherished the ideal of a state devoid of political factions but led by great men, willing to execute the wishes of the independent and propertied classes formulated in frequently held but not popularly elected assemblies – a dream which had also occupied the thoughts of Andrew Marvell and Henry Neville.[27]

Between 1763 and 1770, when he retired from London to his country estate at Corscombe in Dorset, Hollis extended his services to liberty by espousing the cause of the American colonists and by disseminating in England the controversial writings of the colonial leaders relayed to him by his friends, the Dissenting clergy of Boston – the Rev. Dr Jonathan Mayhew and the Rev. Dr Andrew Elliot.[28] By correctly interpreting 'the true sentiments' of the colonists to his countrymen he strove persistently to bring about mutual understanding.

In this context his previous and continuing literary benefactions to Princeton and Harvard assumed an even larger significance since the political doctrines they had enshrined – such as the need for the separation of executive and legislative powers, and of church and state, the rotation of offices, the appeal to natural rights and the provision for judicial review – found acceptance and consecration in the state or federal constitutions of the independent United States.[29] Hollis himself did not live to see either the outbreak of the colonial conflict, which he had sought to avert, or its consummation in American independence, which he would no doubt have welcomed as a defeat for royal, ministerial and parliamentary 'usurpation'. He died early in 1774. After 1770, in retirement in Dorset, he remained an unrepentant 'true Whig'. At Urless farm at

26. Robbins, 'The strenuous Whig', p. 448.
27. *Ibid.*, p. 447.
28. *Ibid.*, p. 410.
29. Robbins, *The Eighteenth-Century Commonwealthman*, p. 385. Mrs Macaulay, in commenting on the American federal constitution, nevertheless regretted its over-centralization, and that more use had not been made of the Harringtonian device of rotation of office and deplored the adoption of a bicameral system. Donnelly, p. 195.

Corscombe he tilled the fields which he named Republic, Revolution, Toleration, Boston and Geneva, and in one of them, at his own request he was buried in an untitled grave ten feet deep which was immediately ploughed over.[30] Though this may have procured him the decent oblivion he had sought in Dorset, it did not prevent his memory being gratefully and rightly preserved at Harvard or his significance in the origins of American independence being recognized by transatlantic historians.[31]

Just as many of the characteristic political attitudes assumed by the radical reformers of the 1790s may thus be traced back to the 'archaic and academic whiggism' of the first half of the eighteenth century, so the origins of that metropolitan radicalism that was to culminate in Thomas Hardy's London Corresponding Society go back, not only to the crisis over the Middlesex election issue in 1769–70, but even earlier to the period of the Seven Years War and its aftermath, when the City of London attained a new and growing political importance in opposition to the court and cabinets of George III.[32] It is, indeed, essential to appreciate that when radicalism thus first emerged as a factor in eighteenth-century politics, it did so, not on a national, or even regional basis, but within the relatively confined and artificial boundary of the City of London itself and the immediately surrounding metropolitan area.

This was because nowhere else at that time did there exist what Dame Lucy Sutherland has rightly designated 'the predisposing conditions for the development of Radicalism as a political force'.[33] If British radicalism in the age of the industrial revolution was essentially and fundamentally an urban phenomenon, this was first demonstrated in the greatest urban concentration of population in the country – London itself. Within its ancient boundaries the City of London had in 1750 an estimated population of 144,000 and a dependent population in the metropolitan area of 532,250. Fifty years later these figures were calculated at 134,300 and 765,700

30. Cooper, p. 20.

31. See particularly C. Bridenbaugh, *Mitre and Sceptre: Transatlantic Faiths, Ideas, Personalities and Politics, 1689–1775* (New York, 1962).

32. L. S. Sutherland, 'The City of London in eighteenth-century politics' in R. Pares and A. J. P. Taylor (eds.), *Essays Presented to Sir Lewis Namier* (London, 1959), p. 58, and L. S. Sutherland, *The City of London and the Opposition to Government, 1768–1774: A Study in the Rise of Metropolitan Radicalism* (London, 1959), p. 8.

33. *Ibid.*, p. 5.

respectively.[34] Although London was becoming not more but less industrialized as the century wore on, and thus escaped some of the worst evils associated with the progress of the industrial revolution in the North-West, a succession of bad harvests, rising prices and industrial recession in the wake of the Seven Years War had, nevertheless, induced in the capital and its environs economic dislocation and serious social unrest.[35]

A further prerequisite for the rise of radicalism as a political force was some form of direction from an organization at once independent and privileged enough to be capable, in the hands of its officials and representatives, of effective political intervention. This the City of London possessed in its ancient corporate institutions of municipal self-government – its Court of Aldermen, its Common Hall and Common Council and its high-ranking dignitaries – the Lord Mayor and Sheriffs.[36] The Corporation itself consisted of from 12,000 to 15,000 freemen by birth, apprenticeship or redemption, of whom two-thirds were also liverymen of the City Companies. The political ascendancy in this organization was exercised, not by the so-called 'monied interest' of the powerful city financiers, but by the 'middling' class of small merchants, tradesmen and master craftsmen who dominated the Common Council, elected the City's four Members of Parliament and played a great part in the election of the municipal officers.[37] Because the more wealthy citizens of the 'monied interest' had close social ties with the court and profitable financial connections with successive governments as favoured contractors, they provoked among the 'middling' mercantile classes in the City the same sort of social resentment and economic jealousy as did the increasingly exclusive group of Farmers-General among the members of the commercial Third Estate in Paris.[38] Politically this resentment showed itself in the way that City opinion tended after

34. For the detailed statistics, see M. D. George, *London Life in the Eighteenth Century* (Harmondsworth, 1966), p. 319.
35. Sutherland, *The City of London and the Opposition to Government*, p. 8. See also W. J. Shelton, *English Hunger and Industrial Disorders* (Toronto, 1973).
36. I. R. Christie, *Wilkes, Wyvill and Reform: The Parliamentary Reform Movement in British Politics, 1760–1785* (London, 1962), pp. 8–9.
37. The 'monied interest' consisted of the directors of the Bank of England, the main insurance societies and the South Sea and East India Companies, whose role was more significant in national than in City politics. G. Rudé, *Wilkes and Liberty: A Social Study of 1763 to 1774* (Oxford, 1962), p. 5.
38. G. T. Matthews, *The Royal General Farms in Eighteenth-Century France* (New York, 1958), pp. 241–2.

1763 to align itself with the various groups of the parliamentary Opposition. In time, however, City political leaders came to be dissatisfied with the tactics of influencing Parliament from within – through aristocratic Opposition groups which were usually factious and self-interested – and sought a more independent political role of bringing pressure to bear on Parliament and government from outside by means of petitions, remonstrances and instructions from the Common Council to the City representatives.[39] This more radical and separatist attitude was stimulated, formulated and finally symbolized, after the accession of George III, by the rise to power and influence, as City MP and Lord Mayor, of William Beckford, who, paradoxically, was the richest absentee West Indian sugar-planter of his generation and a large landowner in Wiltshire.[40] To some extent both a *parvenu* and an 'outsider' in City politics, Beckford, for sixteen years as City representative between 1754 and 1770, closely identified himself with his constituents, championed the cause of 'the middling classes of England' and signalized by his political leadership the existence in London of a progressive radicalism which had outgrown and transformed its former stance of traditional anti-ministerialism.

This form of political independence can legitimately be described as 'radical' because it involved the resort to extra-parliamentary pressure for the correction of popular grievances, because at times of crisis it could inspire the intervention of the London 'mob', and also because its main instigators were men of 'some education and independence of mind, who felt themselves ill served by, and were in consequence critical of their social and political environment'.[41] Beckford, whether as MP or as Lord Mayor, was prepared, and even glad, to act as their official spokesman. It is, however, ironic that his popular image is still that commemorated by his heroic statue in London Guildhall, inscribed with his celebrated but fictitious reply to George III after presenting the City's Middlesex election remonstrance in 1770 shortly before his death.[42] Beckford's

39. Sutherland in Pares and Taylor, p. 59.

40. Sutherland, *The City of London and the Opposition to Government*, pp. 9–12.

41. *Ibid.*, p. 5.

42. Thomas Cooper, the former radical member of the Manchester Constitutional Society, in a letter to John Fellows of New York, dated 9 November 1829 (reprinted by M. D. Conway in *The Athenaeum* for 16 April 1898), gave Horne Tooke's version of the incident: 'The party [Dunning, Glynn, Col. Barré, etc.] were waiting the return of Beckford, who was to deliver the address. . . . They were in great anxiety as to the result. Beckford was an honest, blunt, ignorant,

real importance as a leader of City opinion in his own right and as one of the earliest formulators of a progressive policy of parliamentary reform is, on the other hand, now almost wholly forgotten.[43]

Or perhaps his memory has been effaced by that most notorious of all eighteenth-century 'friends of liberty' – John Wilkes, who inherited, exploited and finally discarded that metropolitan radicalism, nurtured by Beckford, which blazed out into open resistance to the intransigent and unconstitutional behaviour of the House of Commons over the Middlesex elections of 1769. It is, however, easier to assess Wilkes's contribution to the cause of English popular liberties than to be confident that he was, in fact, as has been recently claimed, 'one of the principal founders of a mass radical movement in Britain'.[44] He did, it is true, temporarily overshadow as a metropolitan leader William Beckford, whose influence was confined to his own City constituency, whereas Wilkes's hold over radical opinion extended beyond Middlesex to Westminster, Southwark and parts of Surrey.[45] In that sense Wilkes's position in 1769–70 as elected, excluded and incarcerated representative of the most urbanized county constituency in England, attracting as it did the sympathy and riotous support of large masses of people in the capital, who were themselves unfranchised, foreshadowed, that bond of common purpose between the metropolitan constituencies which later inspired the so-called Quintuple Alliance of London

---

bold man, much given to swearing in his common conversation. They were at a tavern – I forget where – Beckford came in; and, after a short pause, one of the company said: "Well Beckford, come, tell us of your proceedings". "Why", says Beckford, "I presented the address, of course, and the king made some observations in reply". "Well, what did you say?" "Why, I was so damnedly confused, that I said something or other, but I cannot remember what". "Cannot you tell the substance of it?" "No; I was confused at the king saying anything, and I can give no account of the matter". Says Horne Tooke – "This will not do". He drew aside to a table, took pen, ink and paper, and wrote the reply. . . . He read it to Beckford and said "I know what you replied: you spoke thus". (He then read to Beckford the reply thus suddenly drawn up.) Beckford said, "I do not remember one word that I spoke: I said something, but what I said I cannot tell". "You have no objection to this as your reply", says Tooke. "None at all", answered Beckford. It was voted Beckford's reply, fathered by him, published next morning, and inscribed on his tombstone. Such is history.' See also G. H. Powell, *Table Talk of Samuel Rogers* (London, 1903), p. 102.

43. Sutherland, *The City of London and the Opposition to Government*, pp. 9–12.

44. Rudé, p. 196.

45. Sutherland, *The City of London and the Opposition to Government*, p. 18.

reformers.[46] There can be no doubt, either, that in 1771, Wilkes, as alderman for the ward of Faringdon Without, was primarily responsible for the successful deployment of the immunities and privileges of the City in the hard-fought struggle with the House of Commons over the printers' case for the right of newspapers to report the proceedings of Parliament – a victory which represented 'an important step towards the ultimate transference of political sovereignty from Parliament to the electorate at large'.[47] No other popular leader of the time had the charismatic appeal of Wilkes as an unrepentant and defiant victim of royal, ministerial and parliamentary persecution. He, above all, could command the allegiance of political groups in the City who resented their subordination to the whims and manoeuvres of the Opposition Whigs. He personified as no one else the successful defence of the legal, constitutional and civic liberties of the ordinary citizen. In that sense 'Wilkes and Liberty' was more than a mere political slogan; it was a powerful testimony to his past services and sacrifices since 1763, and, in 1769, a provocative challenge to those members of the aristocratic, magisterial or parliamentary establishment who sought to deprive him of his rightful status as MP, even though he had been elected four times in succession as a representative of Middlesex.[48]

On the other hand, even Wilkes himself admitted that he had been 'a patriot by accident', and later told George III that he had 'never been a Wilkite'. His intervention as a candidate in the General Election of March 1768 had been motivated, not so much by political ambition or reforming zeal, as by his pressing need to escape his creditors and to annul his convictions of 1764 by means of a royal pardon. It was only his election to the lucrative post of Chamberlain, after serving as Lord Mayor, which allowed him to retire from active City politics in 1779.[49] The popular enthusiasm which his candidature in Middlesex sparked off in the out-parishes of the

46. The Quintuple Alliance was a confederation of the radical reformers of London, Westminster, Southwark, Middlesex and Surrey formed in 1782 and organized by Dr John Jebb. E. C. Black, *The Association: British Extraparliamentary Political Organization, 1769–1793* (Cambridge, Mass., 1963), pp. 84–6.

47. P. D. G. Thomas, 'John Wilkes and the Freedom of the Press, 1771', *Bulletin of the Institute of Historical Research*, vol. 33 (1960), p. 86.

48. Wilkes's final victory on 13 April 1769 over the court nominee, Henry Lawes Luttrell, was by 1143 votes against 296. Rudé, p. 70.

49. This sinecure was worth £1500 a year. It enabled Wilkes to pay off his debts and involved him in conferring the Freedom of the City on Pitt and Nelson. W. P. Treloar, *Wilkes and the City* (London, 1917), pp. 193–205.

county to the east and north of London among the lesser forty-shilling-freeholders of both urban and rural districts, and the over-heated loyalty to 'Wilkes and Liberty' on the part of the Spitalfields weavers and the coal-heavers of East London were greeted by Wilkes with the cynical unconcern of a political mountebank.[50] He also displayed profound indifference to some of the wider political issues which his more thoughtful supporters wished to bring before the public, because he thought their ventilation would divert attention from his own personal grievances. The Wilkite movement itself evoked little interest or sympathy outside the metropolitan area, except in remote industrial or commercial centres such as Norwich or Bristol.[51] 'It was, as has been well said, significant more for what it anticipated than for what it accomplished.'[52] It collapsed as suddenly as it had begun, and did so long before Wilkes was able, by his motion of 3 May 1782, to secure that the Commons resolution of 17 February 1769, declaring his incapacity to be elected, should be expunged from the journals of the House, as 'subversive of the Rights of the whole body of Electors of this Kingdom'.[53]

This, however, is not meant to underrate the significance of the Middlesex election controversy in the eighteenth-century radical tradition. The action of a government majority in the Commons – in expelling from its midst a repeatedly elected candidate, in finally awarding his seat to his rejected and discredited opponent and in declaring Wilkes 'incapable of being elected to the present parliament' on grounds unknown to the law – administered a formidable shock to the credibility of the whole representative system and raised the issue of the whereabouts of political sovereignty.[54] This flagrant violation of the right of electors had, moreover, occurred in a *county* constituency, where the eighteenth-century electoral machinery was usually supposed to be immune from the grosser forms of influence or governmental interference.[55] The public response was a determined and prolonged resistance from Whig

50. Rudé, ch. 5, and Sutherland, *The City of London and the Opposition to Government*, p. 13.
51. *Ibid.*, p. 30.
52. Black, p. 14.
53. Rudé, p. 194.
54. J. Cannon, *Parliamentary Reform 1640–1832* (Cambridge, 1973), p. 61.
55. Christie, p. 32. Veitch, *The Genesis of Parliamentary Reform* (London, 1965 reprint), p. 15, and 'The early English Radicals' in F. J. Hearnshaw (ed.), *Social and Political Ideals of some representative thinkers of the Revolutionary Era* (London, 1931), p. 30.

Opposition magnates, the outraged freeholders of Middlesex, the liverymen of London and those who in parliamentary and municipal elections had hitherto been only indifferent spectators – the unenfranchised craftsmen and journeymen of the metropolis. The inability of these various sections of anti-ministerial opinion to work together effectively or to sink their own internal differences at first stultified and subsequently stimulated metropolitan radicalism in the period 1769–74.

In the effort to launch a nation-wide petitioning movement of protest, the City radicals, led by Beckford, felt it necessary in May 1769 to try to secure the support of the English counties by a political compact with the aristocratic magnates of the Grenville and Rockingham Opposition groups. For this they had to sacrifice their plans for an instalment of parliamentary reform and, on the insistence of the Whig leaders, they confined the agitation to the grievances of the Middlesex electors.[56] These plans, designed by the Opposition to overthrow the ministry and to compel the dissolution of Parliament, misfired completely. The country gentry did not respond to the political directives of the Whig magnates or to the attempts of the Wilkites to create a network of local corresponding societies, whilst the grievances of the Middlesex electors proved wholly inadequate as a rallying cry in the provincial county constituencies.[57] The government naturally treated the handful of petitions from eighteen counties and a dozen boroughs with contempt. Though Grafton resigned early in 1770, he was replaced as First Lord of the Treasury by a more resilient upholder of the status quo and a much stronger King's minister in the person of Lord North. The consequent breach between the Rockingham party and the City illustrated what was to prove a perennial difficulty for the radicals – how to secure the co-operation of Opposition groups inside Parliament in any campaign involving pressure on Parliament from outside – a problem which was only finally solved in 1832 with the passage of the great Reform Bill.[58]

Released by this fiasco from his commitments to the Rockingham Whigs, Beckford reverted to his plans for parliamentary reform and sought to advance them by closer ties with the Wilkite Society of

56. Sutherland, *The City of London and the Opposition to Government*, pp. 24–6.
57. *Ibid.*, pp. 27–9.
58. The split was further widened by the publication in April 1770 of Burke's pamphlet, *Thoughts on the Cause of the Present Discontents*, and Mrs Catherine Macaulay's rejoinder.

Supporters of the Bill of Rights. This organization, which had been started in February 1769 to promote Wilkes's electoral prospects in Middlesex and to defray by public subscription his accumulated debts and recent electoral expenses, also sought to defend 'the legal constitutional liberty of the subject'.[59] Whilst Wilkes was in prison, its members had become increasingly interested in the prospect of widening its political horizon to embrace more radical enterprises. Its guiding spirit and probable founder was a man who was destined to become, in consequence of a career of repeated frustration, a perverse but dynamic promoter of the radical cause in the 1790s – Parson John Horne, incumbent of New Brentford, who in 1782 assumed his more familiar name of Horne Tooke.[60] For 'Wilkes and Liberty', a cause which he had supported in print ever since it had first crystallized over the issue of the executive use of general warrants, Horne is said to have declared his willingness to 'dye his black coat red' – presumably because of his legal inability to divest himself of his clerical habit or profession.[61] His local knowledge of the county town of Middlesex – Brentford – and remarkable talents as an organizer and political strategist had already enabled him to serve as an impressive electoral agent for Wilkes. The most prominent members of this society were MPs with close personal or business links with the City – men like John Sawbridge, brother of the 'republican' historian Mrs Catherine Macaulay; James Townsend, son of Chauncy Townsend, a merchant and contractor; Frederick Bull, a leader of the Dissenting interest; Serjeant John Glynn, Wilkite MP for Middlesex; the West Indians Thomas Oliver and his cousin Richard; Sir Joseph Mawbey, malt distiller; Sir Cecil Wray, a Lincolnshire squire; and Samuel Vaughan, merchant of Mincing Lane.[62] Most of the members, though still in their thirties, were men of some professional standing, but with various

59. Rudé, pp. 61–2; Christie, pp. 33–5; Sutherland, *The City of London and the Opposition to Government*, p. 22. In all about £24,000 were raised to defray Wilkes's debts. Veitch, *Genesis of Parliamentary Reform*, p. 30.

60. The change was at the request of his friend William Tooke, whose estate at Purley, near Croydon, Horne had saved from the threat of enclosure in 1774 by attacking the partiality of the Speaker of the House of Commons, Sir Fletcher Norton.

61. In the eighteenth century it was legally impossible for a clergyman of the established church to resign his clerical status. Presumably Horne meant that he was a 'militant' Wilkite, not that he was a 'red' in the modern sense.

62. Sawbridge, MP for Hythe in 1769, represented the City in the Commons from 1774 till his death in 1795. Townsend was MP for West Looe, Mawbey for Southwark, Wray for East Retford and Oliver later MP for London.

reasons for dissatisfaction with the existing social or political order. For them the Middlesex election was only a symptom of more deeply rooted abuses of the body politic which called just as urgently for rectification as the personal grievances of Wilkes himself.

Wilkes's reluctance after his release from prison in April 1770 to approve these wider political pretensions, his growing personal rift with Horne, and his opposition to the use of part of the society's funds to assist the printers in their struggle over the reporting of parliamentary debates culminated, in the spring of 1771, in the secession of several of the more important members of the society, who joined Horne in the establishment of a short-lived Constitutional Society of their own.[63] The paradoxical result of this schism was that the remnant of the society, despite Wilkes's continued scepticism, adopted both the policies and tactics which they had hitherto opposed. On 11 June 1771, at a meeting presided over by Brass Crosby, the Wilkite Lord Mayor, the Supporters of the Bill of Rights not only approved the most comprehensive and radical catalogue of political grievances yet to be made public, but sought to enforce a succinct programme of reform upon prospective parliamentary candidates throughout the kingdom by means of specific electoral pledges.[64] The articles of this newly devised political 'test', drafted by an American, Dr Charles Lee, were intended to lead to a thorough-going parliamentary inquiry into the 'troubles and discontents' which had distracted the country since the accession of George III.[65] They envisaged a strict investigation into public expenditure and the conduct of judges in libel cases, the redress of the grievances of the Middlesex electors, compensation for the wrongful arrest of the Lord Mayor in the printers' case, close scrutiny of the whole range of maladministration in Ireland, and the virtual withdrawal of all the contentious imperial legislation affecting the American colonies since 1763. Candidates were also required to support legislation restoring annual parliaments, establishing 'full and equal representation of the people', and excluding all placemen without exception from the House of Commons.[66]

This was a curious mixture – an unexceptional and moderate programme of parliamentary reform, combined with the wildly impractical reversal of government policies, to be enforced through-

63. Christie, pp. 47–8. Little or nothing is known about this society.
64. *Ibid.*, p. 48.
65. Veitch, *Genesis of Parliamentary Reform*, p. 32.
66. Christie, pp. 48–9.

out the country on candidates who were expected to pledge themselves to the rectification of grievances in which the metropolitan area was alone really interested. It is significant that virtually the only candidates who took this highly contentious form of electoral pledge, for the first time in 1773 and in the General Election of 1774, came from constituencies in and around London and were either past or present members of the Society of Supporters of the Bill of Rights.[67] Yet this union of a political mandate with a binding electoral pledge on the part of parliamentary candidates – though vigorously repudiated by Burke as 'utterly unknown to the laws of this land' – was in time to become one of the most characteristic tenets of the future radical and Labour parties in the nineteenth and twentieth centuries.[68]

The schism in the Society of Supporters of the Bill of Rights may also have prompted Alderman Sawbridge, one of the secessionists, on 26 April 1771 to make the first of thirteen House of Commons motions for annual parliaments between then and 1786.[69] Such patient perseverance went entirely unrewarded – for ministers were content to 'conquer him by silence and by sleep', whilst leaving their followers to vote him down in the lobby.[70] This indifference, however, went some way to ensuring that the demand for annual parliaments should become one of the fundamental planks in the radical programme of the 1790s. Even from the effective beginning of the campaign for shorter parliaments this clearly stated preference for annual parliaments distinguished metropolitan radical leaders like Beckford and Sawbridge from those Opposition Whigs like Chatham, Shelburne and Junius, who would have been content with triennial parliaments.[71]

Nor did these contributions exhaust the political legacy of the Society of the Supporters of the Bill of Rights; for many of its

67. C. B. Cone, *The English Jacobins: Reformers in late Eighteenth-Century England* (New York, 1968), p. 50. See also I. R. Christie, 'The Wilkites and the General Election of 1774', in *The Guildhall Miscellany*, vol. 2, no. 4 (1962), reprinted in his *Myth and Reality in late eighteenth-century British politics and other papers* (London, 1970).

68. E. Burke, *Speech to the Electors of Bristol on the conclusion of the poll*, 3 November 1774.

69. B. Kemp, *King and Commons, 1660–1832* (London, 1957), p. 50.

70. G. S. Veitch, 'The early English radicals', p. 28.

71. Junius crystallized his objection to the Septennial Act by contending that under it MPs had 'six years for offence and one for atonement'. Veitch, *Genesis of Parliamentary Reform*, p. 36.

characteristic attitudes, panaceas and doctrines were, so to speak, codified and proclaimed in two publications which were quickly accepted as blue-prints for the future deployment of extra-parliamentary pressure in favour of widening radical objectives – Obadiah Hulme's *Historical Essay on the English Constitution* (1771) and James Burgh's *Political Disquisitions* (3 vols., 1774–5).[72]

The strength and progress of radical movements are often no less dependent on the propagation of popular myths than on the appearance of popular martyrs. If Wilkes had served his purpose at least as a pseudo-martyr, the obscure and originally anonymous author of the *Essay* provided the eighteenth-century radicals with their recurrent propaganda theme of the need for a return to the alleged primitive purity and democratic virtues of a largely unhistorical Anglo-Saxon 'free' constitution. Hulme and his disciples sought to confer respectability on their programmes of radical reform by contending that they would merely correct the inroads on the originally democratic forms of English self-government made by the feudal tyranny of the Norman Conquest and the aristocratic compromises of the revolution of 1688. According to the *Essay* the distinctive features of the Old English government were an elective Crown, the principle that the King must annually consult the national deliberative council or *witena gemot*,[73] local popular assemblies in the shape of the Hundred Courts, a system of regional defence based on the *fyrd* or popular militia, and above all a judicial system which made use of the jury. These 'free' institutions, it was suggested, had been originally introduced by the Saxons about AD 450, but they had only been brought to perfection by one of the greatest of all folk heroes, King Alfred.[74] Just as this 'Golden Age' of democratic and representative government had come to an end with the Norman Conquest, so, Hulme argued, the Triennial Act of

72. Little or nothing is known about Hulme though he is said to have been physician to the Charterhouse and of Yorkshire extraction. Robbins, *The Eighteenth-Century Commonwealthman*, p. 363. Burgh was a Scottish Unitarian, cousin of the historian William Robertson, who, after failure in business, had been employed by the printer to the House of Commons, William Bowyer, and had retired in 1771 after conducting his own school at Stoke Newington for a quarter of a century. *Ibid.*, pp. 364–5.

73. As F. M. Stenton noted, 'the democratic origin of this institution is contradicted both by the derivation of the word *witan* and the nature of the earliest recorded councils'. *Anglo-Saxon England* (Oxford, 1943), p. 546.

74. See C. Hill's stimulating essay on 'The Norman Yoke' in *Puritanism and Revolution*, paperback ed. (London, 1968), pp. 99–101.

1694, the Land Qualification Act of 1711 and the Septennial Act of 1716 had undermined the popular control of Parliament which had been regained at the Glorious Revolution of 1688.[75] On the basis of this naive form of historical folklore Hulme constructed an analysis of the 'decline and fall' of English popular liberties which had an immediate and lasting appeal for the radical reformers. Combined with the cult of Alfred as the exemplar of all 'patriot kings', this historical 'ideology' saturated much of the radical propaganda of the last decade of the eighteenth century and thus helped to shape the collective political mentality of the popular masses.[76]

More immediately, the *Essay* put forward a renewed plea for annual parliaments (which according to Hulme had already enjoyed a millenary existence in England), an extension of the franchise, a secret ballot and the elimination of rotten boroughs.[77] In order to enforce such reforms through the pressure of extra-parliamentary public opinion, Hulme advocated the establishment of 'associations' in every local constituency with a headquarters in London, and also reiterated the Wilkite demand for electoral pledges from parliamentary candidates. In so doing he helped to launch the concept of the 'association' on its successful career as 'the necessary vehicle for growing public participation in politics'.[78]

Virtually the same demands were also made in Burgh's *Political Disquisitions*, the first volume of which was intended to influence opinion in the General Election of 1774.[79] One recent scholar has described this work as 'perhaps the most important political treatise which appeared in England in the first half of the reign

75. The Triennial Act stipulated that parliaments should be held at least every three years and should not last more than three years. The Septennial Act allowed the life of Parliament to be extended to a maximum of seven years, while the Land Qualification Act laid down that knights of the shire must possess landed property worth £600 per annum and burgesses land worth £300 per annum. Much radical criticism of the two latter acts seems to have misfired, since the Septennial Act came to be regarded as an important guarantee of the Commons's independence of the Crown, in so far as the lower house thereby achieved 'A normal, regular and long life of their own', irrespective of the royal prerogative of dissolution and the Land Qualification Act could easily be circumvented by legal fictions which allowed the wealthy to qualify. Kemp, p. 42, and Plumb, p. 143.
76. The Sheffield *Patriot*, for example, serialized much of the *Essay* without acknowledgement in 1792–3. Vols. 1–3, *passim*.
77. Christie, pp. 52–3.
78. Black, p. 2.
79. Christie, p. 53. Vols. 2 and 3 appeared in 1774–5.

of George III'.[80] Its immediate purpose was to provide a convenient handbook of political information and argument, drawn from recent and past experience, which would 'teach the people a set of solid principles', thus saving those 'who would improve themselves in political knowledge, a great deal of time and labour'.[81] The principles in question were mainly those of the metropolitan radicals, of the so-called London Society of Honest Whigs, and of the Rational Dissenters.[82] Burgh not only delivered the same sort of uninhibited attack on governmental policy since the accession of George III as the Wilkites, but also provided the most elaborate and detailed indictment so far available of the corrupt nature of English parliamentary representation and its social and political consequences. His conclusion was that the constitution would need to be purged of its defects and abuses, public liberties re-established, and the independence of Parliament reasserted, if the state was to be saved from impending catastrophe.

Although Burgh did not support the idea of universal male suffrage, by advocating the extension of the franchise to all taxpayers, he made a significant breach with the contemporary and long-standing assumption that all who were not 'free agents' – that is, in the position of servants or in receipt of alms or parish relief – were not entitled to the vote. To maintain such a restriction would, he contended, deprive 'an immense multitude of the people . . . of all power in determining who shall be the protectors of their lives, their personal liberty, their little property'.[83] This line of argument was used by Wilkes in his motion in the House of Commons for a comprehensive reform of Parliament on 21 March 1776,[84] and it is significant that such incapacity as might have arisen from 'domesticity' or economic dependence on the public purse was always repudiated by the later eighteenth-century radicals.

Burgh's most fertile legacy to radical political activism was,

80. Robbins, *The Eighteenth-Century Commonwealthman*, p. 365.

81. Burgh, *Political Disquisitions* (3 vols., London, 1774–5), vol. 1, p. 12.

82. This was a select club of scientists, Dissenting clergymen, publicists and teachers which met fortnightly at St Paul's Coffeehouse and, after 1772, at the London Coffeehouse. Its American sympathies were partly the result of Benjamin Franklin's membership. James Boswell joined in 1769. Burgh himself was a member, along with Dr Price and Dr Priestley. V. W. Crane, 'The Club of Honest Whigs: friends of science and liberty', *William and Mary Quarterly*, 3rd series, vol. 23 (1966), pp. 210–33.

83. Burgh, vol. 1, p. 37.

84. *Parl. Hist.*, vol. 18, col. 1297.

however, the further elaboration he gave to the idea of a national association for the enforcement of a radical programme of reform upon a recalcitrant and corrupt Parliament.[85] This was clearly envisaged as an emergency measure only to be resorted to as a means of resolving the domestic crisis that loomed larger as the constitutional crisis with the American colonists deepened. Convinced that both the repeal of the Stamp Act in 1765 and the passage of the Irish Octennial Act of 1768 had been achieved by such extra-parliamentary pressure, Burgh called on all men of property, friends of liberty and even military commanders to assist in the establishment of a 'GRAND NATIONAL ASSOCIATION FOR RESTORING THE CONSTITUTION'.[86] This organization was to be based on an infrastructure of parochial and county committees, not only in England, Ireland and Scotland, but also in colonial America. The Association was designed to serve as a barometer of public opinion on the state of the nation, as a channel for petitions to Parliament in support of the whole reform programme of the metropolitan radicals, and as a weapon of ultimate resort 'in order to influence government and to prevent mischief'.[87] Though Burgh mentioned 'a Patriot King', or alternatively an 'independent nobility' (by which he meant the Rockingham Whigs), as possible heads of such an Association, political realism indicated that its best chance of success would derive from the more likely sponsorship of the City of London. These ideas were formulated in the third volume of his *Political Disquisitions* published in 1775 – and were, therefore, too late to influence the General Election of 1774. That election, which saw notable Wilkite victories in the metropolitan area, demonstrated, however, that the radical movement had made virtually no impact on the rest of the country.[88]

Though the prerequisites for a successful Association movement thus did not as yet exist in England, the conflict with the American colonists exemplified its merits and vindicated its future adoption by Burgh's disciples – Major John Cartwright and Dr John Jebb. Burgh also contributed to and reflected the views of the Price–Priestley group of Rational Dissenters, which did so much, in an

85. H. Butterfield, *George III, Lord North and the People, 1779–1780* (London, 1949), pp. 260–2.

86. *Ibid.*, p. 261.

87. Cone, p. 50.

88. Besides Wilkes, who was yet again elected for Middlesex and allowed to take his seat, five other of his supporters won metropolitan seats – out of a total of ten which were contested. Christie, p. 61.

Anglo-American context, to formulate and promote the speculative principles of a new type of radicalism whose appeal was not to City politicians but rather to the leaders of colonial opinion in America and to the enlightened mercantile and nonconformist elite in the urbanized centres of metropolitan and provincial England.[89]

A forcing-house of such political theory was the small society of eminent scientists and Dissenting 'friends of liberty' which met fortnightly, initially, from 1764 at St Paul's Coffeehouse and, after 1772, at the London Coffeehouse. This intimate supper club, regularly attended by Benjamin Franklin and called by him his club of 'Honest Whigs', consisted mostly of Dissenters – some like Burgh, being teachers and others, like Dr Richard Price or the Reverend Andrew Kippis, ministers in the metropolitan area.[90] Its most unlikely and uncommitted member was James Boswell, whose *Account of Corsica*, published in February 1768, had established his reputation by publicizing the protracted struggles of the island under its patriot hero, Pasquale Paoli, against Genoese rule and French invasion. His first mention of attendance at the club on 21 September 1769, at the height of the Middlesex election crisis, recalled the mixture of good cheer and political discussion on which its members thrived. 'We have', he wrote,

wine and punch upon the table. Some of us smoke a pipe, conversation goes on pretty formally, sometimes sensibly and sometimes furiously. At nine there is a side-board with Welsh Rabbits and Apple-Puffs, Porter and Beer. Our reckoning is about 18d. per Head. Much was said this night against the Parliament. I said that, as it seemed to be agreed that all members of parliament became corrupted, it was better to chuse men already bad, and so save good men.[91]

Like the rest of his companions Boswell was a reluctant Wilkite.

The Dissenting publicists of this society were perhaps the most influential of all the pro-American radical sympathizers. In turn Priestley, Burgh and Price each made his own contribution to the speculative principles proclaimed in the Declaration of Independence, but it is fair to add that they had been encouraged by Shelburne, as well as indoctrinated by their own clubmate 'the excellent Dr. Franklin'. Priestley's *Essay on the First Principles of Government* (1768) contained not only a variant of the sixteenth-century defence

89. H. W. C. Davis, *The Age of Grey and Peel* (Oxford, 1929), pp. 49–58.
90. Crane, pp. 210–33.
91. *Ibid.*, p. 229.

of tyrannicide, but also a specific vindication, where flagrant oppression was in question, of the right of revolution. It expressed in embryo the fundamental tenets of utilitarianism and borrowed from Rousseau's *Du Contrat Social* the doctrine of the natural, equal and inalienable rights of the individual.[92] Burgh's detailed exposure, in volume one of his *Political Disquisitions*, of the corrupt and unrepresentative character of the English Parliament confirmed the American resolve to reject its authority, and his merciless onslaught on ministerial incompetence encouraged the colonists to resist the policy of coercion.[93] As spokesman for Shelburne's policy of conciliation, Dr Richard Price, in his *Observations on the Nature of Civil Liberty* (February 1776), sustained the colonists' claim to the right of self-determination (the modern equivalent of what Price meant by 'civil liberty'), condemned the Declaratory Act as the enforcement of 'slavery' upon the colonial assemblies and advocated the relinquishment of English authority over colonial affairs, except for the regulation of imperial trade.[94] In effect this was to accept in advance the Americans' subsequent claim to complete independence.

Nor did the English radicals themselves emerge from the constitutional debate on the claims of the American colonists empty-handed.[95] This was foreseen by no less a person than Turgot, formerly French finance minister, when on 22 March 1778 he thanked Price for the latest edition of his *Observations on Civil Liberty*, presented to him through Dr Benjamin Franklin. 'Your misfortunes', he wrote,

92. Davis, p. 53. Priestley's assertion that the object of government was 'the good and happiness of the members, that is, of the majority of the members, of any state' had wide-ranging implications that became part of the eighteenth-century radical creed. On this assumption governments could be expected to subordinate foreign policy to domestic reform, to plan for social welfare and to place the needs of the majority of citizens before those of particular interest groups. D. Jarrett, *The Begetters of Revolution* (London, 1973), p. 131.

93. Burgh even stated that the ministry had caused the break with America 'all to get a few more places for their wretched dependents'. Burgh, vol. 2, p. 275.

94. G. H. Guttridge, *English Whiggism and the American Revolution* (Berkeley and Los Angeles, 1966), p. 87; Price, *Civil Liberty*, 6th ed. (London, 1776), pp. 105–7.

95. Professor E. C. Black's claim in *The Association*, p. 28, that 'Sustained American agitation probably contributed as much as any single factor to the direction of radical activity in Great Britain' seems excessive. See, however, the more recent study, C. Bonwick, *English Radicals and the American Revolution* (Chapel Hill, N.C., 1977), chs. 6–8.

may have the effect of a necessary amputation . . . And if they should terminate in the amendment of your constitution, by restoring annual elections, and distributing the right of voting in parliamentary elections so as to render it more equal and better proportioned to the interests of the represented, you will perhaps gain as much as America by this revolution; for you will preserve your liberty and by means of it, all your other losses will be speedily repaired.[96]

The contention and conflict with the Americans contributed to the radicals' reappraisal of the English constitution; it prompted the radical leaders to re-examine the basis of parliamentary representation, and it helped, also, to bring forward the case for universal suffrage. Though some radical publicists, like Major John Cartwright, reposed continued trust in the inherent virtues of the English constitution, others, like Price, came to agree with the colonists that the doctrine of parliamentary supremacy was outworn and that it should be either revised or rejected.[97] Price, Priestley and Cartwright all stressed the sovereignty of the people and were convinced of the need to restore the primitive 'Anglo-Saxon' purity of the constitution which eighteenth-century political factions and ministerial pretensions had debased. The radical stance in favour of parliamentary reform was also confirmed when the hollowness of the theory of 'virtual' representation had been exposed in the course of the American debate.[98] Nor did it escape observation that the colonial slogan, 'No taxation without representation', had its implications in the mother country itself. In March 1790, when moving in the Commons for his own version of moderate parliamentary reform, Henry Flood recalled with effect that 'this secret of inadequate representation was told to the people in thunder in the American war; which began with virtual representation, and ended in separation'.[99] Nor was it an accident that between 1776 and 1783 radical publicists in Britain committed themselves to the idea of universal male suffrage, using the same arguments based on natural justice and natural rights which the American colonists had borrowed from Price and Priestley and had wielded

96. Price, p. 126.

97. *Ibid.*, p. 15.

98. The argument that the colonists were 'virtually' represented in the Westminster Parliament in the same sense as the unenfranchised majority of people in Britain was clearly fraudulent. For the theory of 'virtual' representation see J. Cannon, pp. 31–2. For Price's criticisms of the theory see *Civil Liberty*, pp. 41–8.

99. *Parl. Hist.*, vol. 28, cols. 457–8.

with such success in their contest with the British Parliament.[100]

The man, however, who above all others succeeded in linking the American controversy with a fully fledged and, indeed, prophetic programme of radical parliamentary reform was Major John Cartwright.[101] Like Burgh, Cartwright argued in his *American Independence the Interest and Glory of Great Britain* (1775) that such plans could only be realized if reformers profited by American resistance. In the following year his more famous pamphlet *Take Your Choice* offered on its fly-leaf, as alternatives, 'Representation and Respect', coupled with 'Annual Parliaments and Liberty', or 'Imposition and Contempt', bracketed with 'Long Parliaments and Slavery'. Confronted by such a choice, who indeed could hesitate? What was, in fact, offered by Cartwright, who came of good Nottinghamshire country-gentry stock, and was himself a landed proprietor, was a blue-print for a 'New Deal', which proved to be generations ahead of its time. A disciple of both Obadiah Hulme and James Burgh, Cartwright rested his arguments also on 'the most well-known principles of the English constitution . . . the plain maxims of the law of nature and the clearest doctrines of Christianity'.[102] Personality, not property, was therefore to be the basis of political rights, so that all male adults who were not criminals or mentally deficient should have the electoral franchise, and the property qualification for parliamentary candidates should also be abolished. Parliamentary elections were to be, as in the past, annual; the vote was to be by secret ballot; MPs were to receive salaries; and the representative system was to be entirely reconstructed on the basis of equal, single-member constituencies.[103]

The mental reservations which Cartwright made in advancing these claims need, however, to be appreciated if his programme is to be properly understood. Universal suffrage he regarded as an

100. Staughton Lynd, *Intellectual Origins of American Radicalism* (London, 1973), ch. 2. See also J. H. Plumb, 'British attitudes to the American revolution' in *In the Light of History* (London, 1972), pp. 71–87; D. M. Clark, *British Opinion and the American Revolution* (New Haven, Conn., 1930), ch. 6; R. R. Palmer, *The Age of the American Revolution*, vol. 1: *The Challenge* (Princeton, N.J., 1959), ch. 6; and Bernard Bailyn (ed.), *Pamphlets of the American Revolution, 1750–1776*, vol. 1: *1750–1765* (Cambridge, Mass., 1965), introduction.

101. The latest study of this reformer is J. W. Osborne, *John Cartwright* (Cambridge, 1972).

102. F. D. Cartwright, *Life and Correspondence of Major Cartwright* (London, 1826), vol. 1, p. 65.

103. Cartwright, *Take Your Choice*, 2nd ed. (London, 1777), pp. 147–83.

ultimate ideal but, immediately, rather as a bargaining weapon in order to achieve more modest extensions of the franchise which might not otherwise be conceded. Similarly, the abolition of the property qualifications for MPs was intended to make eligible for election, not those devoid of property, but those who owned business assets or financial resources other than land. Nor was the payment of salaries to MPs thought of as facilitating the entry of working men to St Stephens, but rather as a means of rendering members independent of ministerial patronage or corruption.[104] Regarded in this way the proposals were neither as visionary nor as radical as they might seem to modern eyes. They were, indeed, originally intended as a draft programme for adoption by the Whig aristocracy. Forwarded in manuscript form to Shelburne in 1776, with the suggestion that Shelburne himself should assume the lead in Parliament, they were later circulated in printed form to all the Whig leaders, without evoking any sympathetic response except from the eccentric Duke of Richmond.[105] Though the choice offered by Cartwright only appealed to the most extreme of the metropolitan radicals at the time, it saturated the political views of the working-class reform societies in the 1790s and re-emerged as the political programme of the Chartists.

Not, however, until the crisis years of 1779–80 did the full impact of the American revolution on the evolution of British radicalism become apparent. As hopes of victory in America faded, as a quasi-revolutionary threat emerged in Ireland with the rise of the Volunteer movement, as French and Spanish fleets in the Channel brought invasion nearer, reformers gathered strength for an assault on the discredited administration of Lord North by the organization of extra-parliamentary opinion in both the provinces and the capital.[106] The result was an interlocking tripartite movement, whose leaders, while suspicious of the aims and methods of their auxiliaries, found it necessary to sink their differences in the vain effort to achieve a united Opposition front both in and out of Parliament.

104. Cone, pp. 58–9. According to Cartwright, universal suffrage could be justified because every Englishman had a share in the constitution by birthright and a secondary claim, if he had a wife and family, which gave him a stake in the country. J. Norris, *Shelburne and Reform* (London, 1963), p. 86.

105. A. G. Olson, *The Radical Duke: Career and Correspondence of Charles Lennox, third Duke of Richmond* (Oxford, 1961), p. 53.

106. The classic account of these struggles – interpreted, unconvincingly, as an English revolution *manquée* – is Butterfield, *George III, Lord North and the People*. See also Christie and Black.

The heavy financial burden of war expenditure, taxation, and sine-cure places and pensions induced the Chathamite wing of the Whig Opposition led by Lord Shelburne to unite with the main phalanx of the Whigs under Lord Rockingham to press for administrative or 'economical reform' in and through the existing Parliament.[107] These Whig magnates, prompted throughout by Edmund Burke, wished also, however, to take advantage of, and simultaneously to side-track, a movement for moderate parliamentary reform started with the support of the freeholders, landed gentry and Anglican and Dissenting clergy of Yorkshire by the Reverend Christopher Wy-vill.[108] This second, or Yorkshire Association, movement, though also aimed at financial retrenchment, was mainly concerned to achieve reform by shortening the duration of Parliament from seven to three years, by adding one hundred members to the county representation and by abolishing some of the rotten boroughs. The third group of reformers were the metropolitan radicals, now led by James Townsend and Brass Crosby, surviving members of the Society of Supporters of the Bill of Rights, Thomas Brand Hollis, heir to Thomas Hollis, Major John Cartwright and Dr John Jebb.[109] These were committed to the enfranchisement of the unrepresented population and were soon to endorse the whole gamut of constitutional reforms advocated by Cartwright in his pamphlet *Take Your Choice*.

All these reform movements were failures. The Shelburne and Rockingham Whigs fell apart, and the consummate parliamentary tactics of Lord North ensured, not only his own political survival for another two years, but also the virtual failure of Burke's legislative proposals for 'economical reform' in March 1780.[110] Wyvill's attempt to placate the Rockingham Whigs by sacrificing his initial support for annual parliaments only alienated the metropolitan

107. See I. R. Christie, 'Economical reform and the influence of the Crown, 1780', *Cambridge Historical Journal*, vol. 12 (1956).

108. Christie, 'The Yorkshire Association, 1780–4' in *Myth and reality in late eighteenth-century British politics*. N. C. Phillips, 'Edmund Burke and the county movement, 1779–1780' in R. Mitchison (ed.), *Essays in Eighteenth-Century History* (London, 1966), pp. 301–25.

109. John Jebb (1736–86), former fellow of Peterhouse and rector of Ovington (Norfolk), Oriental scholar. His Unitarian beliefs led him to resign his living and to study medicine at Edinburgh. Set up as a practitioner in London in 1778.

110. Burke's Civil Establishment Bill foundered on 20 March 1780 because it claimed for Parliament the right to interfere with the King's disposal of his civil list. Christie, *Wilkes, Wyvill and Reform*, pp. 86, 96.

radicals, while the 'speculative' projects of the latter aroused widespread scepticism or hostility. In the aftermath of the crisis, the General Election of September 1780 set the seal on the political discomfiture of both the 'economical' and parliamentary reformers.

Despite this, the crisis of 1779–80 formed a final and important link between the radicalism of the American and that of the French revolutionary period. The extra-parliamentary agitation of these years had certain novel features which differentiated it from its Wilkite origins.[111] The pressure exerted on government, it is true, took the form of a petitioning movement based mainly, but not exclusively, on the traditional county organization. The petitions for public economy, diminished taxation and the reduction of Crown influence in the Commons had been addressed, not as hitherto, to the King, but to Parliament itself. To organize these petitions, to continue the pressure on Parliament and to maintain connections with other counties and with the metropolis, regular county committees of correspondence had been established, following the example set in Yorkshire. Wyvill, moreover, had resorted to and popularized the principle of 'association', which the historian of the crisis, Sir Herbert Butterfield, described as 'perhaps the most curious device in extra-parliamentary organization that our history has ever known'.[112] Though the original sponsors of the county Association movement in Yorkshire had stressed its 'legal and constitutional methods', this concept had a suspect ancestry in America and Ireland, and its adoption, not merely on a county but on a national basis, had been canvassed by radicals like Burgh and Cartwright.[113] In 1779–80 a general or national association was advocated mainly by the most advanced of the metropolitan radicals. As in 1769, so in 1779, popular resentment in the metropolitan area against ministry and Parliament had arisen out of the latest, and this time the bogus, grievances of the Middlesex electors, and it was in his *Address to the Freeholders of Middlesex . . . 20 December, 1779* that Dr John Jebb set out in detail the plans for a national association or convention, which so alarmed and antagonized contemporaries. The scheme was realistically based on a distrust of the effectiveness of the petitioning method, since MPs did not then consider themselves bound by instructions from their constituents, and the House of Commons in its collective capacity would not bow to dictation from

111. Guttridge, p. 115.
112. Butterfield, *George III, Lord North and the People*, p. 185.
113. See above, p. 53.

particular constituencies. According to Jebb's ideas all the counties of England were to associate upon a uniform plan and their standing committees were to send deputies to a central representative body of the sovereign people. Such an assembly would, in Jebb's view, have the requisite authority, if necessary, to declare the corrupt and unrepresentative House of Commons dissolved and to 'new model the constitution'.[114]

In accordance with these ideas the call for a national delegate conference of reformers had gone out initially, in December 1779, from the Middlesex electors and, in February 1780, from the Westminster committee. Each county committee was invited by circular letter to send three deputies to London in March to consider plans for a national association and for 'public and constitutional reform'.[115] Though the response from the county committees was disappointing, the metropolitan area and the Home Counties were strongly represented by radical deputations.[116] Under the chairmanship of Wyvill, the conference assembled at the St Albans Tavern decided to establish a general association to press for a rigorous inquiry into the receipt and expenditure of public money, the addition of at least one hundred members to the county representation in the House of Commons and provision for annual parliaments. It was also resolved that legislation should be sought to reduce the crushing cost of electoral expenditure and bribery.[117]

When, however, on the insistence of the Rockinghamites, these plans were referred back to the county committees, and later to the full county meetings, only ten of the English counties, along with London, Westminster and Newcastle, agreed to associate.[118] To many of the county freeholders and provincial gentry, as well as to George III, 'association' smacked of colonial methods of insurrectionary resistance, while the delegate conference in London was roundly condemned by opponents of reform as a potential 'anti-Parliament'.[119] And, just as 'economical reform' was foundering in the Commons, and the Association movement was collapsing in the provinces, the Protestant association of Lord George Gordon, in June 1780, threw this new form of extra-parliamentary

114. Christie, *Wilkes, Wyvill and Reform*, pp. 78–9.

115. Butterfield, *George III, Lord North and the People*, pp. 274–5.

116. Among the more prominent delegates were, besides Wyvill, Jebb, Cartwright, Lord Mahon, J. Townsend, T. Brand Hollis and Brass Crosby.

117. C. Wyvill, *Political Papers* (6 vols., York, 1794–1806), vol. 1, pp. 427–38.

118. Phillips, p. 322.

119. R. Pares, *King George III and the Politicians* (Oxford, 1953), p. 53.

agitation into immediate and lasting disrepute by its riotous excesses in the capital.[120]

But, though much of the vigour of the county reformers was thus dissipated, and though support for parliamentary, as opposed to 'economical', reform declined sharply during the next decade, the crisis of 1779–80 had indicated ways and means of public agitation which could be exploited by the 'forgotten men' of the industrialized regions of the Midlands and the North-West when the time arrived for them to press for their own claims to representation. For the first time specific proposals for constitutional reform had been submitted to enfranchised public opinion in the provinces; new aristocratic 'friends of liberty' had emerged in the persons of Charles James Fox, the Duke of Richmond and Lord Mahon (later third Earl Stanhope), while the metropolitan radicals of the Westminster subcommittee had co-ordinated and published the extreme views of Burgh, Cartwright and Jebb, which were to endow later eighteenth-century radicals and nineteenth-century Chartists with a political legacy of their own.[121] It was thus that demands for manhood suffrage, annual parliaments, equal electoral districts, secret ballot, payment of members and the abolition of property qualifications

120. Memories of the Gordon riots did much to create that dread of popular demonstrations which affected the governing classes even before the outbreak of the French revolution. See G. Rudé, 'The Gordon Riots: A Study of the Rioters and their Victims', *TRHS*, 5th series, vol. 6 (1956), pp. 93–114.

121. Fox's emergence as the 'man of the people' (having been an anti-Wilkite earlier) owed less to his chairmanship of the Westminster committee than to his election for Westminster itself in the General Election of 1780, his candidature having been proposed by Dr Jebb. Like Fox, his uncle the Duke of Richmond represented a familiar type of aristocratic radicalism of which the political objectives were conservative. Both were descendants of Charles II. Olson, ch. 4. Lord Mahon, as chairman of the Kent committee, brought his brother-in-law, the young William Pitt, into the reform movement at this time. Mahon, too, entered Parliament in October 1780 as member for Shelburne's borough of Chipping Wycombe. His radical sympathies derived partly from his early education in Geneva and this was equally true of Richmond. His later prominence in radical politics as third Earl Stanhope (from 1786) arose from his chairmanship of the London Revolution Society in 1788–9, his unconcealed pro-French sympathies and his opposition in the Lords to the war with revolutionary France. The inventor of a microscope lens, a stereotyping process used by the Clarendon press and of two calculating machines, 'Citizen' Stanhope bequeathed some of his eccentricities to his famous daughter, Lady Hester Stanhope, the charming and devoted hostess of her bachelor uncle William Pitt in his declining years and the later recluse of Mount Lebanon. G. Stanhope and G. P. Gooch, *The Life of Charles, Third Earl of Stanhope* (London, 1914).

became part of the radical tradition of the future.[122] The immediate consequence, however, was that such extremism only alienated that limited popular sympathy for 'moderate' parliamentary reform which had been evoked and organized by the leaders of the Yorkshire Association movement.

It was partly a realization of this divergence between the expanding radical horizons of the metropolitan reformers and the more conservative objectives of the Yorkshire county freeholders which led Major John Cartwright to establish in April 1780 the Society for Constitutional Information.[123] This society sought

to supply, as far as may be, the want of those destroyed records (of our ancient constitution) and to revive in the minds of their fellow-citizens, THE COMMONALTY AT LARGE, a knowledge of their lost Rights; so that . . . they may restore Freedom and Independence to that branch of the legislature which originates from, represents, and is answerable to THEM-SELVES.[124]

This may have been, to some extent, an effort to disguise the radicalism of its metropolitan sponsors by antiquarian appeals to seventeenth-century, medieval, or even primitive Anglo-Saxon constitutional documents. The propagandist or educational role of the society was, however, also based on its members' objective calculation that the success of the movement for parliamentary reform could hardly be anticipated in the immediate future, given the existing divisions between its advocates and the limited response of the county electorate. Events between 1780 and 1783 amply confirmed this forecast.[125] Time and effort would clearly be required to ensure that future efforts to bring pressure to bear on a reluctant Parliament would receive support from the provincial nerve-centres of commercial and industrial growth, as well as from the metropolitan area and Yorkshire. From the start, therefore, the Society for Constitutional Information, though operating from London, gave considerable priority to the task of converting public opinion at large in the

122. Wyvill, *Political Papers*, vol. 1, pp. 228–43.
123. The founder members of the society, besides Cartwright, were the Rev. Edward Bridgen, Richard Brocklesby MD, the Rev. Edward Bromley, Thomas Day (author of *Sandford and Merton*), John Frost ('declined'), Thomas Brand Hollis, John Jebb MD, Capel Lofft, R. B. Sheridan, James Trecothick, John Vardy and Frederick Vincent. PRO TS. 11/1133/1 (minute-book of the SCI, vol. 1).
124. Cartwright, *Address to the Public* . . . (London, 1780), pp. 1–2.
125. See Christie, *Wilkes, Wyvill and Reform*, chs. 4–6.

provinces. This undertaking was rendered easier because the society, like its auxiliary, the London Revolution Society, came to include among its members a solid core of highly influential and well-endowed Dissenters.

3 From toleration to participation : The Dissenting interest and the campaign for the abolition of the Test and Corporation Acts, 1787–90

'Liberty' duly recognised in matters of religion breaks the people's chains; but toleration (which always necessarily implies a right to be intolerant) tends to rivet them.

LORD STANHOPE, July 1812[1]

Some radicals are, or have been, Utopian idealists; some seek to remedy what are, or appear to be, in their own grievances, the injustices or inadequacies of the existing establishment; yet others are motivated by materialist or secular ideologies. In the second half of the eighteenth century the English Protestant Dissenters came near to identifying themselves with the cause of radical reform for all these reasons.

It was they who provided both the stimulus for, and the impetus behind, the initial challenges to the unreformed regime of clerical privilege and civic inequality in church and state. The practical but incomplete toleration which they had inherited from the Whig revolution of 1688, their ability to lobby Parliament through their representative body of Dissenting deputies, their right not only to vote for, but also to sit as members of the House of Commons, the protection of powerful patrons such as Chatham and Shelburne, and their important positions in commerce and industry conferred on them all the advantages of an influential political and economic 'interest'.[2] The scientific achievements, the theological and philosophical learning and the moral independence of their leading ministers, the affluence, liberal outlook and charitable activities of

---

1. Ghita Stanhope and G. P. Gooch, *The Life of Charles, Third Earl Stanhope* (London, 1914), p. 212.

2. Only nineteen MPs, however, who are known to have been Dissenters, sat in the Commons between 1754 and 1790. J. Brooke, *The House of Commons, 1754–1790: Introductory Survey* (Oxford, 1968), p. 169. Mr Brooke's explanation that 'as artisans, small freeholders, or merchants', the Dissenters could not spare the time or money for a parliamentary life leaves something to be desired.

their congregations, and their intellectual affinities and personal connections with the leaders of progressive thought in America and on the Continent, gave them not only a unique and distinctive position in British eighteenth-century society, but also enabled them to sustain their proud claim to be 'citizens of the world'. In a century of protracted economic warfare, competitive imperialism and dynastic aggrandizement, the Dissenters were uncompromising pacifists – on moral, humanitarian and financial grounds.[3]

In one sense, the Dissenting cult of liberty in the eighteenth century derived from a search for a new and more positive motivation to replace its outdated devotion to Puritan ideals and its purely negative rejection of Anglican theology and church discipline.[4] Though for some, notably the Baptists, sectarianism provided a necessary substitute, the majority of Dissenters found a preferable spiritual ideal in the more embracing and comfortable concept of 'Catholic Christianity' and a more stimulating secular creed in their Whiggish worship of liberty. No one, indeed, in eighteenth-century England, could claim the title of 'friends of liberty' – which they passed on to the radicals – with more justification than the Dissenters, for they were enamoured, not only of their own liberty in matters of religious conscience but also of secular causes resting on the inherent rights of human personality, wherever they were in question. They risked their own cause for that of the American colonists, they made a pioneering and indispensable contribution to parliamentary reform, and they were among the earliest and most committed supporters of Negro emancipation. In an age of conservative reaction and repression, not a few, among whom Priestley, Benjamin Vaughan, Thomas Cooper, Joseph Gales, and J. H. Stone were only the most notable, preferred persecution and exile abroad to the surrender of their radical impulses and pro-French principles. A few, like Priestley, could rise above historic antipathies to champion the rights of Roman Catholics to the civil liberties which they themselves so long pursued but failed to achieve.

The vital significance of the Dissenting interest in the history of the British democratic movement at this period also lies in its

3. Much of the interest displayed by the Dissenters in Paine's *Rights of Man*, Part II, arose from its condemnation of the commercial and dynastic wars of the period.

4. For this see Russell E. Richey's stimulating analysis in 'The origins of British radicalism: the changing rationale for Dissent', *Eighteenth-Century Studies*, vol. 7 (1973–4), pp. 179–92.

formative impact on the evolution of provincial radicalism at the 'grass-roots' level. The Nonconformist leaders were deeply interested in the social and economic welfare of the local communities in which they lived, were critical of oligarchical or paternalist rule in the municipal governments from which they were excluded by the Corporation Act of 1661, and where, as in Norwich, they were not so debarred, they had set an enviable record of devoted service in local government.[5] The proceedings and activities of the provincial Literary and Philosophical Societies were also largely dominated by the Dissenting interest, and, as will be seen from a later chapter, Nonconformist merchants, industrialists and newspaper editors were to play a leading part in the formation of the earliest 'constitutional' societies in the rapidly expanding manufacturing towns of industrial Britain.[6] It was, indeed, no accident that in those industrialized regions of the Midlands and North-West, where the radical societies were to proliferate in the 1790s, the initiative and direction often came from a Nonconformist source. This was at least partly because the local Dissenters in these areas had suffered from the bigotry and prejudice exhibited by the Anglican clergy as resident magistrates during the campaigns for the abolition of the Test and Corporation Acts.

From that refusal to recognize the justice of the Dissenters' claims to civil and municipal office stemmed the highly orchestrated movement of 'Church and King' reaction in the localities which represented the first overt mobilization of ultra-conservative sentiment against the critics of the ecclesiastical and constitutional status quo.[7] In the final analysis, the Dissenters were to compromise rather than promote the prospects of their radical protégés, in so far as they rendered themselves so vulnerable to popular hostility and repression by their support of the American colonists, their attacks on the church establishment, their veneration for the republican and levelling doctrines of their seventeenth-century predecessors and by their public approval of the principles of the French revolution.[8] As

5. See below, pp 143, 147, 150.

6. See below, pp. 145 and 157.

7. For the activities of the Manchester 'Church and King' club, see A. V. Mitchell's 'Radicalism and repression in the north of England, 1791–1797', unpublished MA thesis, Manchester, 1958, and F. Knight, *The Strange Case of Thomas Walker: Ten Years in the Life of a Manchester Radical* (London, 1957), ch. 10.

8. For Priestley's attacks on the established church, see U. Henriques, *Religious Toleration in England, 1787–1833* (London, 1961), pp. 38–9.

Mackintosh noted in the concluding passages of his *Vindiciae Gallicae*, in artfully awakening the spirit of persecution against an unpopular sect, the votaries of the 'Church and King' clubs had insidiously planned to 'overwhelm as Dissenters', – 'the friends of freedom, whom it might be odious and dangerous professedly to attack'.[9] The lesson for those who, like Burke, dreaded the spread of popular radicalism, was clear – for it was to prove just as easy (and 'necessary') in 1792 to mobilize both loyalist sentiment against Painite principles and anti-Jacobin reaction against French revolutionary propaganda as it was to raise the cry of 'the church in danger' in 1790, when the Dissenters seemed intent on the abolition of ecclesiastical privileges.[10] Their claims to *liberty* of conscience in religious matters, to *equality* of civic status with the Anglicans, and their professions of *fraternity* with the French represented a set of principles which, in 1789–90, could plausibly be misrepresented by Burke as French in origin and revolutionary in implication.[11]

The Dissenting interest had, however, in the past century, undergone a number of changes – in doctrine, educational practice and political allegiances – which make its peculiar brand of 'native' radicalism on the eve of the French revolution more intelligible. A retrospective account of these changing horizons will also serve to set the Dissenters' claims, and the opposition they encountered, in their proper perspective.

The chief characteristic of English Dissent in the eighteenth century was the diversity of its sects and their divergent responses to the challenging doctrinal issues raised by biblical scholarship, scientific progress and philosophical speculation.[12] Of the three denominations of old Dissent, it was the Presbyterians who were the most flexible in allowing their theological doctrines to be reformulated in accordance with the findings of Socinian exegesis, Newtonian physics, and Locke's 'sensational' psychology.[13] Whereas the Independents (or Congregationalists) and the Baptists stilt continued to profess, in different degrees, the traditional Calvinisl

9. Sir James Mackintosh, *Miscellaneous Works* (London, 1851), p. 623.

10. See below, p. 264.

11. In the *Reflections* Burke decries the Rational Dissenters as 'smugglers of adulterated metaphysics'. *Works* ed. W. King, vol. 5 (London, 1826), p. 174

12. E. P. Thompson, *The Making of the English Working Class* (London, 1965), p. 51.

13. Olive M. Griffiths, *Religion and Learning* (Cambridge, 1935), pp. 153–4. R. W. Davis, *Dissent in Politics, 1780–1830: The political life of William Smith, M.P.* (London, 1971), p. 34.

doctrines of election and predestination, the Presbyterians (partly as a result of their contact with Dutch theologians) abandoned both these dogmas and the doctrine of the Trinity as irrational. Early in the eighteenth century they were converted to the Arian interpretation of the scriptures, according to which Christ himself was not regarded as divine, although divinely instructed.[14] These differences between the old sects were revealed in the Salters' Hall Synod of 1719, when a proposal to impose a Trinitarian test upon Dissenting ministers and their congregations in Devonshire and Cornwall was narrowly defeated by a majority of four.[15] In the second half of the century Arianism itself was abandoned by the majority of Presbyterians in favour of the more explicit theology of Socinianism or Unitarianism. Rejecting the Calvinist belief that humanity was by nature totally depraved, and claiming for all unrestricted freedom of speculation, the group of 'Rational Dissenters' – a Nonconformist intellectual elite – substituted for the doctrine of the Trinity the Socinian concept of the homogeneity of God.[16]

These heterodox views, and the political radicalism that often accompanied them, had been nurtured in the famous Dissenting academies which had won such general respect and prestige by the middle years of the eighteenth century.[17] Adequately endowed by their own denominational trust funds, ably staffed by tutors and ministers of wide culture and diversified scientific attainments, and closely connected with the Scottish universities, several of these academies, notably those of Daventry and Warrington, had devoted themselves not only to the training of Dissenting ministers, but had also attracted an elite of the aristocratic or professional laity, by

14. Davis, p. 36. The Arians believed that Jesus Christ was 'a mediator, subordinate to God, and not entitled to worship as part of the Divinity'. Griffiths, pp. 147–8.

15. C. Robbins, *The Eighteenth-Century Commonwealthman* (Cambridge, Mass., 1959), p. 235. The result of this acrimonious debate was announced by a spectator, Sir Joseph Jekyll, in the epigram: 'The Bible has it by four.' H. McLachlan, *The Unitarian Movement in the Religious Life of England* (London, 1934), p. 14.

16. By adopting the name of Unitarians, they incurred the risk of heavy legal penalties, as heresy against the doctrine of the Trinity had formed an exception to every Act of Toleration.

17. The authoritative treatment of this subject is H. McLachlan's *English Education under the Test Acts* (Manchester, 1931). The pioneer study was by I. Parker, *The Dissenting Academies in England* (Cambridge, 1914). See also A. Lincoln, *Some Political and Social Ideas of English Dissent, 1763–1800* (Cambridge, 1938), ch. 3.

offering their pupils a wide general education in modern subjects.[18] Designed in this respect to provide for the needs of those who would later occupy responsible positions in commerce or administration, as well as for the practical education of the landed gentry, their curricula included the study of science, English literature and *belles lettres*, modern languages, history, political theory and economics.[19] It was in these seminaries, particularly those of Hoxton (1701–85), Northampton (1729–51), Daventry (1752–89), Warrington (1757–86) and Hackney (1786–96), that the Dissenters' claim to reinterpret the scriptures in accordance with the dictates of reason were vindicated, that their rights to civic equality as well as religious toleration were expounded, and that the freest discussion of past and present systems of government was encouraged. These institutions trained the remarkable generation of distinguished theologians, scholars and scientists, headed by Dr Joseph Priestley and Dr Richard Price, collectively known as the Rational Dissenters, who paved the way for modern Unitarianism and won the contemporary repute of being the fomenters of modern English radicalism.[20] Their influence may also be detected in the growing alienation of the Dissenting interest from both the Hanoverian dynasty and the system of government of George III.

That was one of the changes which was to make the 'radicalism' of Dissent more probable as the Rational Dissenters in the reign of George III began to take a more active role in national politics. In the aftermath of the Hanoverian succession the Dissenters had demonstrated their loyalty to the new dynasty during the Jacobite rising of 1715 and had been well content, in the enjoyment of their re-established religious and constitutional liberties, to recede from the turmoil of opposition. They were conscious that George I was personally averse to persecution and were grateful to his ministers for repealing the Schism Act and the Act against Occasional Conformity in 1718.[21] Further relief came their way, in the following

18. Warrington Academy was exceptional in so far as the majority of its students consisted of the laity.

19. At Warrington Frenchmen were employed to teach their own language, but there is no evidence that Marat was ever on the staff. Priestley was instrumental in including history in the syllabus at Warrington.

20. Among those educated at these academies were two of Dissent's foremost parliamentary champions – Henry Beaufoy and William Smith. William Godwin was educated at Hoxton under Dr Alexander Kippis.

21. The Schism Act of 1712 had been intended to put an end to the Dissenting academies and to deprive Nonconformists of higher education, except those who

year, when an act 'for the quieting and establishing Corporations' indemnified those Dissenting members of municipal corporations who had omitted to take the sacramental test required under the Corporation Act of 1661 and provided, for the future, that such persons could only be deprived of office if prosecuted within six months of being elected.[22] Though only a grudging and strictly limited exemption from the penal laws had been conceded to the Protestant Dissenters under the Toleration Act of 1689, and though no further relief from their statutory civic disabilities was granted, the Nonconformists had yet remained content with Walpole's policy, after 1727, of passing annual Acts of Indemnity, suspending the operation of the penalties prescribed in the Test Acts.[23] Even when Walpole, at the height of the Excise Bill crisis in 1732, persuaded the London Committee of Dissenting Deputies to postpone its agitation for effective relief, and when its subsequent applications to Parliament in 1736 and 1739 met with crushing defeat, the Nonconformists had acquiesced.[24] Discomfited but not alienated from the Hanoverian establishment, the more ambitious and more pliant of the Dissenters obtained what they had vainly sought through agitation by seceding to the Anglican church. The more enterprising and well-endowed took a different course. After an education begun in the Dissenting academies and continued either in Scottish or Continental universities, and often completed at the Inns of Court or at Cambridge, such men turned their backs on politics and often achieved remarkable success in commerce or industry.[25] Failure to achieve a fuller toleration did not affect the fundamental loyalty of the Dissenters to the Hanoverian succession, as was shown yet again during the second Jacobite rising of 1745.[26]

In the reign of George III, however, this abstention from political agitation and acquiescence in their unequal civil status seemed to

---

could afford to attend Scottish or Continental universities. The aim of the Occasional Conformity Act of 1711 was to terminate the practice by which Dissenters occasionally received Communion in the Church of England and so defeated the provisions of the Test and Corporation Acts.

22. 5 Geo. I, c. 6.

23. For this see T. Bennett, 'Hallam and the Indemnity Acts', *Law Quarterly Review*, vol. 26 (1910), pp. 400 ff.

24. Davis, p. 31.

25. Examples were the Heywood family in Lancashire, the Milnes and Shore families in Yorkshire, the Strutts of Derbyshire, Benjamin Vaughan in London and John Hurford Stone, who settled in Paris in 1792.

26. Bogue and Bennett, *History of the Dissenters* (London, 1808), vol. 3, p. 176.

the Rational Dissenters, led by Dr Priestley and Dr Price, as no longer tolerable. In a new political departure the Dissenters became involved in extra-parliamentary opposition to government policies during the Wilkite crisis of 1769[27] and this new critical posture was confirmed when episcopal and royal opposition threw difficulties in the way of a widely supported movement to abolish compulsory subscription to the Articles of Religion in the 1770s. The Anglican Clerical Petition to Parliament in 1772 and the London Dissenting Ministers' Application of 1772–3, each based on a limited plea for the extension of the scope of the Toleration Act and on an appeal to 'candour', were both unsuccessful.[28] They were, nevertheless, significant episodes in the transition to the more universal claims and radical procedures of the later Dissenting campaign to repeal the Test and Corporation Acts.

The petition, promoted by a group of liberal-minded Anglican clergy in Cambridge, precipitated, by its failure, a series of resignations from the established church which reinforced the numbers, intellectual stature and driving force of the Rational Dissenters and especially of the Unitarian connection.[29] The application of the London ministers, by revealing the unsuspected divisions and animosities within Dissent, and the inadequacy of the appeal to 'candour', emphasized the need for the Nonconformists to press their claims on the basis of the more comprehensive and compulsive principle of natural rights and to extend any further campaign for

27. According to Priestley, 'the break came in the present reign at the time of the Middlesex Election'. *Works*, ed. J. T. Rutt (London, 1821), vol. 22, pp. 354–6.

28. According to John Aikin, 'Candour' consisted essentially in 'a disposition to form a fair and impartial judgment on questions and actions'. *Letters* (London, 1796), vol. 1, p. 91.

29. The most important resignations were those of Theophilus Lindsey (1723–1808), rector of Catterick, Fellow of St John's College, who had organized the Clerical (or Feathers Tavern) Petition and who founded the first avowedly Unitarian chapel at Essex St, London; John Jebb (1736–1786), mathematics tutor at Peterhouse, who resigned his livings in 1755 and, after graduation in medicine at Aberdeen, became a leading physician and radical publicist in London; Gilbert Wakefield (1756–1801), Fellow of Jesus College and subsequently tutor at Warrington Academy and Hackney College; Thomas Fysshe Palmer (1747–1802), Fellow of Queen's College, who resigned his Anglican orders in 1783 to become a Unitarian minister in Scotland; and William Frend (1757–1841), Fellow and tutor of Jesus College, who resigned his livings in 1787, was dismissed as tutor in 1788, and was banished and rusticated from the University in 1793 for publishing a pacificist pamphlet *Peace and Union* on the eve of the war with France. He had influenced Coleridge's conversion to Unitarianism as a Cambridge undergraduate.

the abolition of their civic disabilities from the metropolitan region to the country as a whole.[30] The Clerical Petition, though largely ignored by Dissent, showed that the Anglican church was, for the time being, totally averse to any practical extension of the Toleration Act, and enforced the lesson that Dissent should concentrate its attention on securing concessions from the state. The application of the Dissenting ministers to Parliament in 1772 and again in 1773 only resulted, however, in the defeat of remedial legislation, passed in the Commons, by the House of Lords, due largely to royal influence and the opposition of the bishops.[31] The mounting animus of the Dissenting interest against the established church and its growing alienation from the Crown were the inevitable consequences.

It had been in this spirit of frustration and aversion that the Rational Dissenters had championed the cause of the American colonists and had thrown their weight behind the movement for parliamentary reform.[32] The presence of a majority of influential metropolitan Dissenters in the Society of Honest Whigs, the London Revolution Society and the Society for Constitutional Information testified to the progressive liberalism of their views and the increasing activism latent in their political attitudes.[33] The close association of Price and Priestley with Shelburne's 'Bowood circle' of reformers between 1769 and 1779 also brought them into closer contact with French liberal thinkers of the period.[34] The main source of Priestley's materialism, apart from his own scientific research, was, however, English rather than French – David Hartley's theory of the automatic association of ideas and his reconciliation of materialism with Deism by the argument that God had endowed matter with the capacity for thought.[35] This led Priestley to propound the doctrine of 'philosophical necessity' on the assumption that all human action was prompted by motives, these being governed in turn by external impressions focused by the law of association. Since all matter obeyed natural laws, so human behavi-

30. Lincoln, pp. 224, 234.

31. Lincoln, pp. 226–7.

32. See above, p. 52.

33. See above, pp. 54 and 64.

34. For the Bowood circle see D. Jarrett, *The Begetters of Revolution: England's involvement with France, 1759–1789* (London, 1973), pp. 130–5; P. Brown, *The Chathamites* (London, 1967); J. Norris, *Shelburne and Reform* (London, 1963), ch. 14.

35. A. Cobban, *In search of Humanity: The role of the Enlightenment in Modern History* (London, 1960), p. 85.

our was determined by the same mechanical forces. Because these inexorable laws had been set in motion by God, man had a positive duty to conform to them, for this would itself assist the working of Divine Providence.[36] 'Necessarianism' was neither fatalism nor determinism. It assumed, on the contrary, that every man was the maker of his own destiny and enforced the injunction that human effort must help to hasten the coming of the millennium.[37] Such a concept was compatible with optimism, but not with inertia. Even though the influence of Priestley's philosophical writings did not extend much beyond the narrow confines of Shelburne's political coterie and a select group of Rational Dissenters, his 'necessarianism' was to provide a constituent element in the political thought of William Godwin and the early republicanism of William Words-worth.[38] More immediately, it formed part of the changed climate of opinion in which the Dissenters felt that action to relieve, rather than acquiescence in, their political disabilities would itself become a practical necessity. If toleration had failed, perhaps participation might succeed.

Among the developments which encouraged the Dissenters to launch a campaign for the repeal of the Test and Corporation Acts in 1787 was, however, the belated success in 1779 of their ministers in obtaining some of the concessions for which they had sought in vain in 1773. To some extent the grant was the counterpart to the act which had relieved the Irish Protestant Dissenters of their disabilities in 1778 and, like that measure, was an instalment of reform forced on the embattled administration of Lord North by the accumulating disasters in the American colonies. The relief bill which had been rejected by the Lords in 1773 was, with a few amendments, reintroduced and was passed by both houses with little or no opposition. Henceforth, in order to obtain the benefits of the Toleration Act, Protestant Dissenting ministers and teachers were merely required to take the oaths of allegiance and supremacy and to subscribe a declaration accepting Holy Scripture as the rule of their doctrine and practice.[39] This meant that the remaining

36. Priestley's *Doctrine of Philosophical Necessity* was published in 1777. For an analysis see Lincoln, pp. 155–7.

37. R. K. Webb, *Harriet Martineau: A Radical Victorian* (London, 1960), pp. 84–6.

38. *The Prose Works of William Wordsworth*, ed. W. J. B. Owen and J. W. Smysen (Oxford, 1974), vol. 1, pp. 35–44.

39. 19 Geo. III. c. 44. The terms of the declaration, in its final form, ran: 'I, A.B., do solemnly declare, in the presence of Almighty God, that I am a Christian

grievances of the Dissenters were substantially those of the laity. Nor did the laity consider themselves bound by the promises which their ministers had made in 1779 to refrain from further applications to Parliament if they were successful.[40] When the time was considered right nothing would, therefore, deter the laity from following the example set by their pastors. It was also inevitable that, however moderate their methods, their objectives would be more radical and have political rather than purely religious overtones. Nor were the Dissenting ministers themselves wholly satisfied with the scope of the concessions made in 1779. The memory of their earlier defeats at the hands of the bishops in the House of Lords still rankled: all attempts to throw open Oxford and Cambridge to the Dissenters had failed[41] and even the new scriptural declaration that had been substituted for subscription to the Articles of Religion, in its un-amended form, had clearly been aimed against the Socinians. It is not, therefore, wholly surprising that, after 1779, some Dissenting ministers such as the Baptist Robert Robinson and the Unitarian Joseph Priestley made the established church the target of their embittered and uncompromising attacks, thereby contributing to the defeat of the subsequent applications of their lay co-religionists.[42]

When, however, a general meeting of deputies of the three Dissenting denominations in London decided, early in 1787, to apply to Parliament for the abolition of the Test and Corporation Acts, there seemed, on the surface at least, reasonable grounds for cautious optimism. Almost a decade had elapsed since Dissent had importuned the legislature on the issue of further relief. During this interval, as Beaufoy was later to claim, not perhaps with complete candour, the Dissenters 'had not indulged the language of complaint, nor had they sought the aid of political alliances, or endeavoured to avail

---

and a Protestant; and as such that I believe that the Holy Scriptures of the Old and New Testaments as commonly received in Protestant churches, do contain the revealed will of God, and that I do believe the same as the rule of my Doctrine and Practice.' Henriques, p. 56.

40. In March 1790 Pitt accused the Dissenters of having broken the pledge given in 1773 not to renew their application to Parliament, in suggesting that they would not even be content with the repeal of the Test and Corporation Acts. This misrepresentation was, however, rebutted by Beaufoy. *Parl. Hist.*, vol. 28, cols. 412, 417–18.

41. The entire abolition of University tests was only carried in 1871 by Gladstone as a government measure. Partial repeal for matriculation and the taking of the bachelor's degree had come in 1858 – but MA candidates and elected College Fellows were still required to take the old subscription.

42. Henriques, pp. 39, 51.

themselves of party divisions'.[43] With perhaps even less justification Beaufoy contended that the Dissenters had also 'patiently awaited till the wisdom of a complete toleration should be generally acknowleged . . . and the experience of other nations should have proved that a toleration would strengthen the interest of the established church'.[44] In fact, even in 1787, there were few Anglicans who were prepared to accept the notion of a 'complete toleration' for Dissenters – except, perhaps, the man who had himself coined the phrase to fix the extent of their demands – Archdeacon William Paley. Nor had the French movement towards civil toleration for the Huguenots since 1775 been correctly assessed by its English sympathizers, who were more impressed by its potentialities than by its limitations.[45] The extent of the political emancipation likely to be won by the French Protestants in 1787 was undoubtedly exaggerated on this side of the Channel, and the encouragement thus given to English Dissenters to press on with their claims was consequently misplaced.[46] Moreover, events were also to betray the Dissenters' expectations in 1787 that the Younger Pitt, hitherto their supporter, and then firmly entrenched in office, would feel bound to honour the political obligation he had incurred when his survival as first minister had been virtually assured as a result of their desertion of the hated Fox–North coalition in the General Election of 1784.[47] No one could perhaps have been expected to foresee that events in France, so far from promoting, were, in fact, to postpone the final realization of the English Dissenters' political ambitions for over a generation.

Though Dissenting propaganda was able to expose many of the absurdities, anomalies and injustices involved by the continued retention of the Test and Corporation Acts on the statute book in the so-called 'Age of Enlightenment', it is, nevertheless, not easy to determine whether the legal disabilities and practical grievances

43. *Parl. Hist.*, vol. 28, col. 2 (8 May 1789).

44. *Ibid.*

45. Shelburne (or Lansdowne as he now was) was kept informed of the progress of the French movement towards civil liberty for the Protestants by his confidant, the abbé Morellet, and Price was in contact with the leading Protestant pastor Rabaut Saint-Étienne.

46. The edict of 19 November 1787 merely allowed French Protestants to register their births, marriages and deaths and thus recognized their civil status. All municipal, judicial and educational offices were still reserved for Catholics, who alone had the right of public worship. J. Égret, *La Pré-Révolution Française, 1787–1788* (Paris, 1962), pp. 139–44.

47. Henriques, p. 57.

of the Protestant Dissenters amounted, as they maintained, to actual persecution. By the Corporation Act of 1661, no one could enter upon a civic or municipal office unless he had taken the sacrament of the Lord's Supper according to the rites of the Church of England within a year previous to his election.[48] Under the Test Act of 1673 all who held offices or places of trust under the Crown, whether civil or military, were required to take the oaths of allegiance and supremacy, to sign a declaration repudiating the doctrine of transubstantiation, and to receive the sacrament according to the rites of the Church of England.[49] The widespread practice of 'occasional conformity', whereby Protestant Dissenters managed to evade the acts and the passage, after 1727, of virtually annual Acts of Indemnity under which the qualifying sacrament could be taken after, instead of before, election to a corporation, so mitigated the impact of this penal legislation that Nonconformity seemed to have been officially condoned. Chatham had even described these particular penal laws as so many 'bloodhounds held in leash'.[50]

It still remained true, however, that the mild administration, or virtual non-enforcement, of the penal statutes afforded no relief to strict Protestant Dissenters whose consciences forbade their taking the sacramental test, even on the easy basis of occasional conformity. The protection afforded by the Indemnity Acts was, moreover, by no means complete, since these acts always left intervals of time in which actions could be started against offenders.[51] Increasingly, in the reign of George III, Protestant lay Dissenters of wealth and ambition chose to accept municipal or Crown office 'with the hazard', that is to say without bothering to qualify themselves by taking the sacrament.[52] This 'hazard' under the Test Act was, technically, considerable – not only deprivation of office, but a fine of £500, coupled with legal inability to sue in any court of law or equity, incapacity to act as guardian or executor, and inability to inherit a legacy even from parents.[53] But neither the Dissenters nor

48. C. G. Robertson (ed.), *Select Statutes, Cases and Documents*, 4th ed. (London, 1923), p. 37.

49. *Ibid.*, pp. 81–4.

50. J. L. Le B. Hammond, *Charles James Fox: A Political Study* (London, 1903), p. 318.

51. T. Bennett, 'Hallam and the Indemnity Acts', *Law Quarterly Review*, vol. 26 (1910), p. 404.

52. Davis, p. 40.

53. S. Heywood, *The Right of Protestant Dissenters to a Compleat Toleration Asserted*, 2nd ed. (London, 1789), p. 45.

their opponents appear to have known how far the act imposing such a formidable list of legal disabilities was being implemented.[54] Some of the best-known Protestant Dissenters of the day, such as John Howard, the prison reformer, and Samuel Shore, of Norton Hall near Sheffield, had taken the office of High Sheriff of their respective counties, or served as local magistrates, without bothering to take the sacramental test, and this was true of others who served as elected members of civic or town corporations – both in the metropolitan area and in other important commercial centres such as Bristol, Norwich and Nottingham.[55] With the decline in occasional conformity which accompanied the growth of Unitarianism, 'risk-taking' in this sense, however, was a luxury more likely to be indulged in the sphere of municipal government where the only penalty was loss of office, than in respect of those civic or military offices which were covered by the heavy penalties under the Test Act. Exclusion of Dissenters from the direction of the great chartered companies – from the Bank of England, the East Indian, Russian or South Sea companies – seems to have been effective and to have been resented by the wealthy community of metropolitan Nonconformist merchants and business men.[56] In the provinces similar embargoes preventing Dissenters from holding responsible office in some local hospitals, alms-houses or work-houses, and prohibiting them from acting as trustees were contrasted with their unrestricted admission to those inferior 'offices of burthen' – as high and petty constables, tithingmen, overseers of the poor, church wardens and surveyors of the highway – the monopoly of which the Anglicans were quite willing to abandon to the sectaries.[57]

The two fundamental issues raised by the campaign against the Test and Corporation Acts were, therefore, the 'participation' of lay Protestant Dissenters in the so-called offices of 'trust' or 'profit', and their condemnation of the continued use of the sacramental test as the means of this exclusion. The first issue led the Dissenters to claim political equality with the Anglicans and in doing so to have recourse to neo-Lockian theories of natural rights. 'The grievance from which the Dissenters seek relief', explained one of their pamphleteers in 1789, 'is a *civil* and not an *ecclesiastical*

54. Henriques, pp. 83–4.
55. Davis, p. 41.
56. *The Case of the Protestant Dissenters* (1787), p. 5. This was the official submission of the Dissenters' Application Committee for repeal.
57. Heywood, p. 39.

oppression: they complain of being injured as *citizens*, of being wronged as *Englishmen*, and all they ask is a restoration of their civil rights'.[58] Convinced that the acid test of full citizenship was capacity for office, the repealers argued that exclusion involved a social and political stigma for all Dissenters.[59] The claim itself, however, represented the same direct and radical challenge to the existing establishment in church and state as the French revolutionary version of it – the 'career open to talent'. It meant, as Lord North noted, that the Dissenters had overstepped the demand for toleration and were urging their right to 'participation' in the Anglican monopoly of remunerative and responsible offices.[60] Pitt, in rebuttal of the same claim, elaborated a distinction between 'civil' liberty, the individual private rights which the Dissenters already possessed, and the 'political' liberty they were now demanding, which was a right to share political power and had no connection with natural rights.[61] Political offices were public trusts which the state had a discretionary right to confer on those who were competent to occupy them and whose political and religious views were above suspicion. The refusal of such offices would not, therefore, involve any stigma upon the Dissenters or brand them, in any sense, as second-class citizens.[62] Between such directly antagonistic views on the issue of Dissenting 'participation' there could hardly be any form of acceptable accommodation.

More unanswerable was the Dissenters' condemnation of the use of the sacrament as a test for the holding of secular offices. No one described its evil consequences with more telling effect than Henry Beaufoy when moving in the House of Commons on 8 May 1789 for its discontinuance.[63] At the end of a powerful speech on

58. *Half an Hour's Conversation Between a Clergyman and a Dissenter on the Test Laws* (1789), p. 2.

59. Henriques, p. 70.

60. Speech of 8 May 1789 opposing Beaufoy's motion. *Parl. Hist.*, vol. 28, p. 22. After reminding the House that the Dissenters enjoyed 'a free toleration', Lord North begged MPs to 'pause then, and pass not at one step from toleration to participation' – one of the earliest uses of what has now become a vogue word of modern politics. Pitt, however, had used it in the debates of 1787. *Parl. Hist.*, vol. 26, cols. 825–6.

61. *Parl. Hist.*, vol. 26, col. 825 (28 March 1787). Price and Priestley had used this distinction, but only to demonstrate that political liberty was essential to safeguard civil liberty.

62. *Ibid.*, col. 828.

63. Beaufoy (1750–1795), came of Quaker stock and had been educated at Hoxton and Warrington Dissenting academies. In 1790 he was MP for Great Yarmouth. Sir Lewis Namier and J. Brooke, *History of Parliament: The House of Commons, 1754–1790* (London, 1964), vol. 2, pp. 72–3.

behalf of the Dissenters, Beaufoy, as a member of the Church of England, deplored the degrading effect of the Test Act in compelling Anglican clergy, despite the injunctions of their religion, to administer the sacrament to men who might be notoriously unfit to receive it, just because they were seeking qualification for Crown office. 'If', he said,

in the records of human extravagance, or of human guilt, there can be found a law more presumptuous than this, I will give up the cause. And to what purpose is this debasement of religion? If it be thought requisite that dissenters should be excluded from the common privileges of citizens, why must the sacrament be made the instrument of the wrong; why must the purity of the temple be polluted; why must the sanctity of the altar be defiled; why must the most sacred ordinance of her faith be exposed to such gross, such unnecessary prostitution?[64]

The historical answer to this rhetorical question was, of course, that the Anglican sacrament had been the only effective means available to Parliament in 1673 for excluding, not the Dissenters, but the Roman Catholics from office.[65] Beaufoy did not himself use this additional argument in favour of its removal but, in conclusion, stressed the stupidity and blasphemy of its continued retention by the legislature.

'The Saviour of the world', he reminded the Commons,

instituted the Eucharist in commemoration of his death, an event so tremendous, that nature, afflicted, hid herself in darkness; but the British legislature has made it a qualification for gauging beer barrels, and soap boilers' tubs, for writing custom-house dockets and debentures, and for seizing smuggled tea. The mind is oppressed with ideas so misshapen and monstrous. Sacrilege, hateful as it always is, never before assumed an appearance so hideous and deformed.[66]

Even Burke, whose intervention in the parliamentary debate was so belated and yet so decisive, agreed with his former clients, the Protestant Dissenters, on this issue. In March 1790 he conceded that the sacrament ought not to be so prostituted and while, unwilling to abandon the penal laws as such, wished, if they were repealed, to

---

64. *Parl. Hist.*, vol. 28, col. 14 (8 May 1789).
65. G. M. Trevelyan, *The English Revolution, 1688–1689* (London, 1938), p. 28. Oaths and declarations were lightly taken and disregarded by members of all faiths, whereas Roman Catholics would never take part in an heretical sacrament.
66. *Parl. Hist.*, vol. 28, col. 15 (8 May 1789).

substitute for the sacramental test a declaration containing an oath not to subvert the constitution of the Church of England as by law established.[67] Most of the other opponents of repeal, however, preferred to smother this embarrassing issue in emotive protests against the removal of penal laws which were alleged to be the traditional bulwarks of church and state and part of the fundamental laws of the constitution.[68]

The campaign for the repeal of the Test and Corporation Acts between 1787 and 1790 has been viewed, like the earlier Association movement for parliamentary reform in 1779, as an English revolutionary movement which failed.[69] Though this interpretation was never entirely convincing, and has now passed into the limbo of frozen historiography, it did at least serve to underline the deep cleavage of opinion over the merits or dangers of the Dissenting application, not only in parliamentary circles but also in provincial affairs and in English society at large. The more apt French analogy, if one be sought, would be not so much with the social and political aspirations of the revolution of 1789 as with the social and political consequences of the *affaire Dreyfus*. The repeal agitation certainly afforded 'a first intimation' of the forthcoming conflict between church and state in nineteenth-century Europe, but more immediately it precipitated the emergence, particularly at local level, of High Tory conservatism and Dissenting radicalism. It provided the occasion in 1787 for the Younger Pitt's desertion of the cause of reform and of Burke's crossing to the Treasury benches in 1790. It was also the first reform issue to be vitally influenced by the outbreak and progress of the French revolution. If it did not in itself constitute a revolution, it marked the transition in England to an age which was dominated and shaped by revolution.

No less than three successive applications were made to Parliament – the first in March 1787 in the period of comparative political quiet between the General Election of 1784 and the Regency crisis of 1788; the second in May 1789 under the stimulus afforded by the centenary celebrations of the English revolution of 1688; and the third in March 1790 in the wake of the French revolution of 1789 and on the eve of a General Election. The first move was characterized by the studied moderation of the political strategy adopted by the Dissenters' Application Committee in London, and by the totally

67. *Ibid.*, col. 441 (2 March 1790).
68. Henriques, pp. 78–80.
69. Lincoln, p. 2.

unexpected but decisive opposition of the younger Pitt; the second phase was marked by the near success of Beaufoy's Commons motion for a parliamentary inquiry in May 1789; and the third by the Dissenters' more aggressive tactics of extra-parliamentary pressure, the heightening crisis of 'Church and King' alarmism in the provinces, the intervention of Edmund Burke in the parliamentary debate in opposition to Charles James Fox, and the final adverse vote against repeal under the impact of revolutionary events in France.

The moderation shown by the lay Dissenters in the initial stages of the repeal campaign was largely inspired by the ad hoc Application Committee appointed by the London deputies of the three denominations. This committee, chaired by Edward Jeffries, a well-known surgeon of St Thomas's Hospital, included the three MPs who were to be chiefly concerned in the parliamentary proceedings – Henry Beaufoy, MP for Great Yarmouth, who moved the applications in the Commons in 1787 and 1789; his seconder, Sir Henry Hoghton, a North-Country Dissenter, who had introduced the relief bills of 1772 and 1773; and William Smith, MP for Sudbury, who was soon to become the chief parliamentary advocate for the Unitarians.[70] Among other members of the committee were leading publicists, such as the lawyer Samuel Heywood, author of one of the most effective Repeal pamphlets, and wealthy representatives of provincial Dissent, such as Capel Lofft of Troston Hall, near Bury St Edmunds, and Samuel Shore of Norton Hall, near Sheffield, both members of the Society for Constitutional Information.[71] Though Beaufoy and Hoghton had been educated at Dissenting academies, the former was an Anglican and the latter was an independent country member, who, like Smith, usually supported the administration of Pitt. In its propaganda the committee repudiated the radical extremism of Priestley and concentrated on the exposition of the practical grievances of the Dissenting laity and the anomalies and futility of the Test and Corporation Acts. It also turned its back on politics by attempting to dissociate the application from the movement for parliamentary reform. The motion which Beaufoy was asked to propose in Parliament merely called on the Commons to consider the question of repeal in a committee of the whole house,

70. For a scholarly assessment of Smith's work as a reformer, see Davis.
71. Along with the Application Committee's *Case of the Protestant Dissenters*, Heywood's *The Right of Protestant Dissenters to a Compleat Toleration Asserted* was the best contemporary analysis of the Dissenters' grievances.

as a preliminary move towards the introduction of legislation at a later stage.[72]

Envisaging its task as essentially that of direct negotiation with the government, the committee appointed a delegation which interviewed Pitt in January 1787.[73] The Prime Minister's response was guarded and non-committal. The committee, however, made no attempt to work up a nation-wide agitation, though it maintained contact with leading Dissenters in the provinces and lobbied prominent politicians and divines. None of these preliminaries substantially eased the task of Beaufoy when, on 28 March 1787, he presented the case for relief in the Commons in a *tour de force* of parliamentary eloquence.[74] Despite his earlier sympathy with the Dissenters, Pitt had now changed his views. He appears to have been persuaded by Bishop Sherlock's *Arguments Against a Repeal of the Corporation and Test Acts*, republished in 1787 and 'read over to him' by his former tutor at Cambridge, Dr Pretyman, whom he had recently nominated to the see of Lincoln.[75] George III's own prejudices against the Dissenters and unwillingness to make concessions could hardly be disregarded, and when Pitt consulted the bishops, he found that, with two notable exceptions, they too were firmly against repeal.[76] The Prime Minister was no doubt also aware that the anxieties generated by the open hostility of Priestley and Robinson to the established church had not been effaced by the singular moderation displayed by the London Application Committee. The Commons debate on Beaufoy's motion on 28 March 1787 was thus mainly significant for Pitt's resolute opposition to the repeal of the penal statutes – an attitude correctly described by the Dissenting historian William Belsham as 'the first grand deviation in his conduct from the fundamental principles of Whiggism'.[77] While acknowledging that the Protestant Dissenters had collectively shown themselves 'the genuine and zealous friends of constitutional liberty' in

72. Though it was normal practice at the time for public bills to be considered in this way, this procedure was intended to be conciliatory. P. D. G. Thomas, *The House of Commons in the Eighteenth Century* (Oxford, 1971), p. 51.

73. Stanhope, *Life of William Pitt* (London, 1861), vol. 1, p. 337.

74. *Parl. Hist.*, vol. 26, cols. 781–817.

75. H. McLachlan (ed.), *Letters of Theophilus Lindsey* (Manchester, 1920), p. 64.

76. Only Watson of Llandaff and Shipley of St Asaph, both former nominees of Shelburne, favoured repeal. P. Brown, pp. 326, 336.

77. *History of Great Britain from the Revolution of 1688 to the conclusion of the Treaty of Amiens* (London, 1805), vol. 8, p. 135.

the General Election of 1784, and repudiating the specious objection that the Dissenters would only ask for further concessions if their present application were granted,[78] Pitt nevertheless strongly opposed their 'participation' in Crown or municipal office, as a matter of right, since, in his view, the state had the undoubted prerogative of confining such political privileges (as distinct from civil liberties) to those of whose loyalties it was assured.[79] If repeal were conceded the Dissenters might, he thought, 'acquire a dangerous ascendancy in corporations' and an exclusive corporation interest in the hands of the Dissenters was a very different thing from 'the liberty of sitting in that house on the free choice of the general mass of electors'.[80] Rejecting the argument that exclusion from civic or military office carried with it an unmerited stigma, Pitt could not see any reason to consider it 'more as a mark of infamy than any other distinction that upholds political government'.[81] Moreover, it was essential for the legislature to be on its guard against the small but dangerous minority of Dissenting extremists, who were committed to the policy of disestablishment. No means could be found of admitting the moderate part of the Dissenters and excluding the violent. 'The bulwark would need to be kept up against all.' What was at stake was the security, not only of the church, but of the state, for the two were indissolubly united.[82] Sir William Dobden, unrepentant member for the University of Oxford, found evidence for similar conclusions in Priestley's statement about 'a train of gunpowder' already laid for the demolition of the Anglican church, while Lord North reverted to the argument he had used in 1772 that repeal would jeopardize one of the fundamental laws of the constitution – the Act of Union with Scotland,[83] which he looked on as 'a most sacred compact'. Though Fox spoke up in its favour, the motion for an inquiry into the justice and consequences of repeal, lacking government support, was defeated by 176 votes to 98.[84]

Although the Dissenters were 'in the last degree astonished and chagrined' at what they regarded as Pitt's desertion,[85] the London

78. *Parl. Hist.*, vol. 26, col. 827.
79. *Ibid.*, col. 828.
80. *Ibid.*, col. 827.
81. *Ibid.*, col. 828.
82. *Ibid.*, col. 827.
83. *Ibid.*, col. 822.
84. *Ibid.*, col. 832.
85. Belsham, vol. 8, p. 135.

committee saw no reason to be discouraged and resolved to renew its application in the following session. In the interval it took the opportunity to change its tactics and to correct its previous mistakes in the effort to broaden the basis of its support both inside and outside Parliament. It began to lobby MPs to give promises of support for repeal at the next application; it saw the need not to separate the cause of Protestant from Roman Catholic relief and, by adding five more representatives from country districts to its membership, sought to associate provincial Dissenters more closely with the formulation of policy in London. It also negotiated a political reconciliation with Charles James Fox.[86] The cause of repeal, however, benefited most from the powerful stimulus it received at the time of the centenary celebrations of the English revolution of 1688.

The most significant of the ceremonies which were held throughout the country to mark this event was the anniversary meeting of the London Revolution Society on 4 November 1788 at the London Tavern in Bishopsgate St.[87] This society was one of the few survivors of a number of similar clubs formed at the beginning of the century to commemorate the 'glorious' Whig revolution of 1688. These societies had for some time continued to meet annually on the anniversary of the birthday of William III – 4 November.[88] As the Jacobite danger receded, most of these commemorative clubs had died out and even the meetings of the London Revolution Society had been suspended for a short period. According to an undated printed set of rules in Dr Williams's Library, the London Society had, however, been reconstituted as a body of exclusively Protestant Dissenters, meeting weekly at the Crown and Anchor Tavern as a social rather than a political club and with objects which were mainly recreational and charitable.[89] By 1788 the character of the society had changed again, for its membership had by then come to include members of the established church and 'many persons of rank and consequence from different parts of the kingdom', whereas

86. Henriques, pp. 61–2.
87. See *Abstract of the History and Proceedings of the Revolution Society in London* (1789).
88. 5 November, the date of William's landing at Torbay, might have been more appropriate, but it would have clashed with the anniversary of the 'Gunpowder plot' and with the Anglican commemoration.
89. MS 24.90(1). At quarterly meetings small gifts of two guineas were distributed to 'necessitous Dissenting Ministers' on the nomination of members.

originally, it had been confined to the inhabitants of the City of London.[90] At its annual anniversary meetings it had become the custom of the society to hold a religious service in the morning, followed later in the day by a more festive gathering at one of the London taverns. To mark the occasion of the centenary the members had observed these rites on a more impressive and dignified scale.[91] At the noonday service at the Old Jewry meeting-house, Dr Andrew Kippis, FRS, FSA, a well-known Unitarian minister and William Godwin's classical tutor at Hoxton Dissenting Academy, had been the preacher, and the evening dinner at the London Tavern, attended by about 300 members and guests, was presided over by Lord Stanhope. Among those present were the Duke of Portland, the Marquis of Carmarthen, the Lord Mayor of London, Henry Beaufoy and William Smith and two other MPs – Sir Watkin Lewes and Joshua Grigby.[92] As the members moved to dinner, the original standard of William III as flown at the Torbay landing was borne in the procession. In front of the tavern a painting 'emblematic of the glorious event' carried the legend 'A TYRANT DEPOSED AND LIBERTY RESTORED, 1688', and, after dark, the London Monument was illuminated. During dinner convivial songs were sung and forty-one toasts were drunk, calling attention to a comprehensive list of desirable reforms, including 'the repeal of all religious tests and penal laws regarding religion', the total abolition of the slave trade, the reform of the code of criminal law, the abolition of press gangs and the revision of the game laws.

After dinner, true to its title and the occasion, the society had unanimously approved the recommendation of its committee that a bill should be promoted in Parliament to declare the sixteenth of December – the day when the Bill of Rights had been carried – as a solemn day of national thanksgiving. Beaufoy agreed to move for leave to bring in the necessary bill in the Commons.[93] The despatch of routine business – election of new members to the committee and

90. *Abstract of the History and Proceedings of the Revolution Society*, p. 6.

91. For this meeting, see *An Abstract of the History and Proceedings of the Revolution Society*, pp. 7–15.

92. Sir Watkin Lewes (?1740–1821), MP for the City of London, had been a prominent Wilkite, and had supported Pitt's efforts at parliamentary reform. Namier and Brooke, vol. 3, p. 40. Grigby (?1731–98) sat for the county of Suffolk – 'a zealous advocate of civil and religious liberty'. *Ibid.*, vol. 2, p. 556.

93. Beaufoy's motion of 24 March 1789 was agreed to in the Commons but rejected on the first reading in the Lords on 23 July 1789. *Parl. Hist.*, vol. 27, col. 1332, and vol. 28, cols. 294–7.

of stewards for the ensuing year – was followed by the decision that the society should make a public profession of its political principles, as valid in 1788 as a century before. These were carried unanimously in the form of a tripartite declaration –

1 That all civil and political authority is derived from the people.
2 That the abuse of power justifies resistance.
3 That the right of private judgment, liberty of conscience, trial by jury, the freedom of the press and the freedom of election ought ever to be held sacred and inviolable.[94]

'These great principles of public freedom, of just and equal liberty' were further celebrated in a formal oration delivered by another Unitarian divine, Dr Joseph Towers, the friend and coadjutor of Dr Price in his pastorate at Newington Green. No doubt with recent memories of Anglo-French diplomatic friction in 1787 in mind, and with real concern over the dubious outcome of the contemporary reform crisis in France, Towers formulated, in conclusion, the society's earnest hope that

England and France may no longer continue their ancient hostility against each other; but that France may regain possession of her liberties; and that two nations, so eminently distinguished in arms, and in literature, instead of exhausting themselves in sanguinary wars for no valuable purpose, may unite together in communicating the advantages of freedom, science and the arts to the most remote regions of the earth.[95]

The message was to be prophetic of the society's future public commitments and it is not wholly fanciful to trace in it the influence of Dr Price, who had himself been invited to deliver the oration but who had been forced to decline, owing to illness.[96]

Though the Regency crisis of 1788 robbed the centenary celebrations of 1688 of much of their immediate religious relevance and distracted English attention from the outbreak and early progress of the revolution in France, the proceedings of the London Revolution Society at least created a more favourable climate for the prosecution of the Dissenters' second application for the removal of their civic disabilities.

94. *Abstract of the History and Proceedings of the Revolution Society*, p. 14.
95. *An Oration delivered at the London Tavern on the Fourth of November 1788 on the occasion of the Commemoration of the Revolution* (London, 1788), p. 24.
96. C. B. Cone, *Torchbearer of Freedom: The influence of Richard Price on Eighteenth-century Thought* (Lexington, Ky., 1952), p. 178.

Though the Commons debate on the second repeal motion on 8 May 1789 has been described by one historian as more 'impassioned' than that of 1787 and as 'a fitting prelude to the great agitation of 1790', this was mainly because of Beaufoy's invocation of natural rights and his withering condemnation of the sacramental test.[97] When Lord North and Pitt, however, stressed their fears for the security of church and constitution from the extremist opinions of the radical minority of the Dissenters, they did so without sounding any alarm bells, and the issue of repeal was discussed, not on the plane of principle, but on that of expediency.[98] Beaufoy himself gave a lead in this respect by coolly analysing the anticipated consequences of repeal on both church and state. He pointed out that, if their grievances were removed, the three denominations of Protestant Dissenters would lose their strength and solidarity. In the aftermath of their civil emancipation, the Nonconformists would be unlikely to threaten either the revenues or privileges of the church. As predominantly a commercial interest Dissent would not clamour for the abolition of ecclesiastical tithes, the burden of which fell mainly on the landed interest.[99] Nor was any substantial resentment felt by the Dissenters against the small voluntary contributions made towards the stipends of the Anglican clergy. The real threat to the power and influence of the church establishment would come, not from the holders of the subordinate offices of executive government, even if these were Dissenters, but rather from members of the legislature, of whom neither Commoners nor Lords were required to take the sacramental test.[100] Repeal would also increase rather than diminish the security of the state, in so far as it would strengthen the undoubted loyalty of the Protestant Dissenters to the Hanoverian dynasty and allow them to hold military offices in the defence of the country without the embarrassing necessity for the government to indemnify their infringement of the existing penal laws as had been done in 1715 and 1745.[101] It was only when Beaufoy summarized the provisions of article five of the Test Act of 1673 that he felt bound to complain that the 'pretended toleration of the Dissenters' was, in fact, 'a real persecution' – for the offender, under this statute, was 'robbed of his fortune, stripped of his inheritance, deprived of his

97. Lincoln, p. 247.
98. *Parl. Hist.*, vol. 28, cols. 17–27 and 38–40 (8 May 1789).
99. *Ibid.*, col. 8.
100. *Ibid.*, col. 9.
101. *Ibid.*, col. 11.

personal security and bereaved of the privileges which result from the natural relation of a father to his child'.[102]

Against these attacks Lord North replied that the heavy penalties for infringement of the Test Act had never been enforced in the eighteenth century, that the penal statutes did not involve discrimination or persecution, and that they formed the indispensable bulwarks of church and state.[103] Fox, supporting Beaufoy, shrewdly observed that 'those who attempted to justify the disabilities imposed on the Dissenters, must contend, if they argued fairly on their own ground, not that their religious opinions were inimical to the established church, but that their political opinions were inimical to the constitution'.[104] Taking his stand on expediency, and winding up the debate, Pitt did precisely that, suggesting that the real reason for the exclusion of the Dissenters from civil office was that their religious opinions might lead to 'civil inconveniences' from which the government had the responsibility to protect the public by the maintenance of the penal statutes.[105]

On this occasion the motion in support of the Dissenters' application was rejected by only 122 votes to 102.[106] The hopes of eventual success which this result inspired in the Dissenters were, however, to prove illusory. So far there had been no strongly pronounced reaction in the provinces to their demands, to which parliamentary opponents of their application could appeal in justification. So far Burke, soon to reveal himself as the arch-enemy of Rational Dissent, had not raised his voice in, or even been present at, the Commons debates. No reference either had yet been made in Parliament by opponents of relief to the course of events in France. A final reason for the closeness of the division in May 1789 was that Beaufoy's motion was only for a parliamentary inquiry into the operation and justice of the sacramental test, and not for the outright repeal of the Test and Corporation Acts.

The situation on 2 March 1790, when Charles James Fox rose in the Commons to champion the Dissenters' claims, was entirely different. As one of their historians later remarked, the elation of

102. *Ibid.*, col. 7.
103. *Ibid.*, cols. 17–20.
104. *Ibid.*, col. 30.
105. *Ibid.*, cols. 38–40.
106. *Ibid.*, col. 41. For the sources of the parliamentary voting strength of the Dissenters at this time see G. M. Ditchfield, 'The Parliamentary struggle on the repeal of the Test and Corporation Acts, 1787–1790', *English Historical Review*, vol. 89 (1974), pp. 551–7.

the Dissenters at their near success in May 1789 had been excessive and had betrayed them into 'gross and fatal indiscretions'.[107] The cautious tactics and conciliatory initiatives of the London Application Committee had been superseded by the extremist demands of organized provincial Dissent, often formulated by uncompromising and dedicated ministers. In the autumn of 1789 regional boards of deputies of the three denominations, established on the advice of the London committee in all the main centres of provincial Dissent where they did not already exist, had carried resolutions in favour of repeal and had adopted the forms and procedures of the earlier Association movement.[108] Radical Dissenters, such as Thomas Cooper of Bolton and Manchester, had also demanded the repeal, not only of the Test and Corporation Acts, but also of all penal statutes in matters of religion.[109] Such demands had clearly been put forward by, and in the interest of, the Socinians and Unitarians, who were popularly regarded as professed atheists and republicans. A grass-roots campaign for the abolition of ecclesiastical tithes and church rates, and Dr Price's pleas for the revision of the Anglican liturgy and articles were viewed as direct attacks on the finances and theology of the established church.[110] These aggressive and subversive moves had incited the anger and suspicion of local Anglicans and had led to the organization of two dozen meetings across the country in the course of January and February 1790 to promote counter-repeal resolutions and to portray the Dissenters in broadsheets and handbills as 'King-Killers' and Levellers.[111] The cry of 'the church in danger', which had not been heard since the days of Sacheverell, was echoed by local clerics and gentry who combined to organize a highly orchestrated movement of Alarmism – the immediate progenitor of High Tory reaction.[112] The first miscalculation of the Dissenters was, therefore, to have provoked such a powerful current of conservative and popular hostility, for their opponents not only did much to discredit the motivation of the repeal agitation, but also took their revenge by making them the

107. Belsham, vol. 8, p. 233.

108. Henriques, p. 63.

109. D. Malone, *The Public Life of Thomas Cooper, 1783–1839* (New Haven, 1926), p. 25.

110. R. Price, *A Discourse on the Love of our Country*, 4th ed. (London, 1789), pp. 16–18.

111. P. G. Barlow, *Citizenship and Conscience* (Philadelphia, 1962), pp. 257–60.

112. 'Party spirit at this period raged throughout England in a more violent degree than had been known since the days of Sacheverell'. Belsham, vol. 8, p. 396.

victims of what Thelwall called 'the petty tyranny of provincial persecution'.[113]

A second 'indiscretion' which gave a handle to their parliamentary opponents was the decision of the Dissenting activists, as the General Election drew nearer, to resort to the device of exerting political pressure through the exaction of electoral pledges from parliamentary candidates – an innovation that had been pioneered by the radical parliamentary reformers in 1779.[114] This step seemed to indicate that the London Application Committee's embargo on political activity was no longer valid and that the Dissenters were themselves prepared to adopt procedures which convention had not yet legitimized. This readiness to engage in current political controversy was further signalized by the Dissenters' reconciliation with Charles James Fox, which resulted in his agreement to move their application for repeal in Parliament, and by Dr Price's use of the pulpit at the Old Jewry, on the occasion of the commemorative gathering of the London Revolution Society of 4 November 1789, to celebrate not so much the English as the French revolution.[115]

This early and enthusiastic commitment of the Rational Dissenters to the principles of the French revolution was both more intelligible and less offensive to English prejudice than has been generally recognized. Both Price and Priestley, as former members of Lansdowne's 'Bowood circle', had been in contact with French liberal thinkers and administrators long before 1789 and had watched with sympathy and concern the progress of the movement for the civil emancipation of the French Protestants from the time of Turgot's ministry.[116] As 'citizens of the world' and 'friends of liberty' the Dissenters of the London Revolution Society were bound to welcome the overthrow of French despotism and the Declaration of the Rights of Man.[117] Among those rights, sanctioned under popular duress

113. J. Thelwall, *The Rights of Nature against the Usurpations of Establishments* (London, 1796), p. 20.

114. Henriques, p. 62.

115. Price, *Discourse*. See next chapter for analysis.

116. The main link with French affairs was through Lansdowne's confidant, the abbé Morellet, but Price corresponded with Turgot and Rabaut Saint-Étienne, the French Protestant leader, and Priestley's materialism had been affected by d'Holbach's theories. The best modern study of these Anglo-French contacts is Jarrett.

117. Cf. their message of congratulation to the French National Assembly on 4 November 1789 moved by Price. Price, appendix, p. 13.

by Louis XVI in the 'October days', was the principle of careers 'open to talent' for which the Dissenters were still contending in Britain, while the spectacle of Necker, as a Swiss Protestant, at the helm of French affairs earlier in the summer had seemed to demonstrate that religious obscurantism in France was already at an end.[118] It was clear also that the ancient Gallican church – the palladium of aristocratic priestcraft and privilege – would itself be reformed and that France would be endowed with representative institutions recruited by a semi-popular electoral system at both national and local levels. The Dissenters' approval of the downfall of 'Popish' superstition and Bourbon 'tyranny' in the winter of 1789 and the spring of 1790 was a sentiment shared by many others in England, who may, however, have welcomed these changes, partly for the same but partly also for different reasons.[119] Their 'Church and King' enemies in the provinces vilified the Dissenters, not so much as devotees of French democracy, but rather as the worshippers of their seventeenth-century forebears – the Levellers and Republicans of the Commonwealth period.[120] They could, indeed, hardly as yet be represented as English Jacobins.

Nevertheless, in the hands of Edmund Burke, these public demonstrations of the Dissenters' sympathies with the liberal reformers in France could be and were easily misrepresented as evidence of their sacrilegious designs against the established church and their subversive innovations in politics. He had already emphasized, in his speech on the Army Estimates on 9 February 1790, 'the danger of being led through an admiration of successful fraud and violence, to an imitation of the excesses of an irrational, unprincipled, proscribing, confiscating, plundering, ferocious, bloody and tyrannical democracy'.[121] When he intervened, at long last, in the debate on the Dissenters' third and final repeal application, Burke had already

118. Price himself referred to Necker's tenure of 'the first office in the state' in his sermon. *Ibid.*, p. 39. Article 6 of the Declaration of the Rights of Man specified that: '*Tous les citoyens . . . sont également admissibles à toutes dignités, places et emplois publics, selon leur capacité, et sans autre distinction que celle de leurs vertus et de leurs talents.*' J. M. Roberts, *French Revolution Documents* (Oxford, 1966), vol. 1, p. 172.

119. Some politicians welcomed the revolution because they thought it would paralyse French power in Europe.

120. The persecution to which the Dissenters were subjected by 'Church and King' mobs in 1791 marked the end of the eighteenth-century Commonwealthmen. Robbins, p. 321.

121. *Parl. Hist.*, vol. 28, col. 355.

determined to expose the Rational Dissenters as both atheists and anarchists.[122]

Even more significant for the eventual outcome of the debate was the attendance of a much larger body of MPs than in 1787 and 1789, many of whom had already been influenced by 'Church and King' propaganda in their constituencies, some of whom had been instructed by their constituents to vote against repeal in protest against the Dissenters' recourse to electoral pledges, and who were now becoming concerned at the possible repercussions of the French revolution on English politics.

The arguments on both sides on Fox's motion for a Commons committee of inquiry on 2 March 1790 took account of the altered political circumstances in both England and France and of the highly charged antagonism between the Dissenters and Anglicans in the localities. Fox, arriving in the Commons, 'booted and whip in hand from Newmarket', made one of the greatest speeches of his career, of which the keynote was his insistence on 'the principles of general toleration, and the universal rights of Mankind'.[123] Whereas Beaufoy and the London Application Committee had previously stressed the practical grievances of the Protestant Dissenting laity, Fox widened his brief to embrace the cause of the Roman Catholics and set aside both party political considerations and anti-French prejudices. Viewing any species of persecution, civil or religious, with 'horror and detestation', he considered that the conduct of the French in investigating the rights of men and applying them to the extinction of intolerance, well merited 'the esteem and applause of a great nation'. After reviewing the cruelties, absurdities and fallacies of past persecution, Fox urged that tests of political or religious opinions were absurd and that the only test or criterion of fitness for the tenure of civic office 'ought to be a man's actions'. 'Men,' he suggested, 'should be judged, "not from the imputations of their adversaries, but from their own conduct".'[124] The existing tests were unjust and oppressive, but the case for their repeal should be decided only on general principles.

Turning the tables on those who reprehended the political tactics

122. Writing to Philip Francis on 20 February 1790 Burke expressed his intention to expose Price, Priestley and the rest of the Bowood circle to the 'hatred, ridicule and contempt of the whole world'. *Correspondence*, ed. Cobban and Smith, vol. 6, p. 92.

123. *Parl. Hist.*, vol. 28, col. 402. The description of Fox's arrival from the races occurs in McLachlan, *Letters of Theophilus Lindsey*, p. 65.

124. *Parl. Hist.*, vol. 28, col. 392.

of the Dissenters, Fox strongly condemned the intervention of the resurgent High Church party in local and national politics as even more dangerous. The Dissenters were much less numerous, they had shown constant and much-tried loyalty to the house of Hanover, and their application for relief could not be ascribed to an imitation of any French example, for it had preceded, not followed, the revolution. The nationalization of church property in France was the result of the reign of ecclesiastical oppression after the revocation of the Edict of Nantes and, much as he condemned it, he thought it ought to serve as a caution to the Church of England. Priestley's condemnation of the establishment, he thought, was no more dangerous to the church than Pitt's former criticisms of parliamentary corruption had been to the constitution. Though approving the general principles of Dr Price as expressed at the anniversary meeting of the London Revolution Society in November 1789, he thought they should not have been ventilated from the pulpit – for politics and religion ought ever to be kept separate. Bishop Warburton's hallowed theory of the alliance of church and state, on which the opponents of repeal so much relied, had, in his view, resulted in the contamination, not the protection, of the church, and the corruption, not the security, of the state. The penal laws were not fundamental laws of the constitution and their repeal would not jeopardize the Act of Union with Scotland. In conclusion Fox warned the house that any decision to continue the test laws would not only 'serve to keep alive a spirit of animosity between the parties', but 'it might', also, lead to stronger exertions in defence of civil rights'.[125]

However effective in general Fox's presentation of the Dissenters' case may have been, it was bound to have antagonized Burke, for whom there is some hint that Fox intended it as a challenge. Emphasis on general principles, especially upon the 'rights of man', Fox well knew would be anathema to Burke. A reasoned view of the political and ecclesiastical reforms of the French National Assembly would not conciliate a man who had already condemned them as atheistical, confiscatory and anarchic;[126] while Fox's criticism of High Tory political intolerance and his tolerant disregard of the dangers to the church from Priestley's strictures showed that, in the crisis of their personal friendship, increasingly under strain from their divergent assessment of the situation in France, Fox was unrepentant in the views he had already expressed in the February debate on the

125. *Ibid.*, col. 402.
126. In the debate on the Army Estimates on 9 February 1790. *Ibid.*, col. 355.

Army Estimates, and was prepared to sacrifice everything for the sake of principle.

Pitt intervened early in the debate, not only to restate his former objections to repeal, 'with greater force and confidence', but also to differ with Fox on the extent to which toleration should be carried. Though the Dissenters had 'a right to enjoy their liberty and property; to entertain their own speculative opinions, and to educate their offspring in such religious principles as they approve', they had no right, in his view, to 'a full and complete equality of participation'.[127] Otherwise, even Papists, who acknowledged the supremacy of a foreign ecclesiastical prince, could only be excluded from office after the commission of some overt act against the constitution. Repeal, in that sense, would put an end to 'the wise policy of prevention'. 'The interest of individuals claiming pecuniary rewards and lucrative employment' was very different from the right to liberty of conscience, and 'the idea of right to civil offices, then, was highly absurd and ridiculous'.[128] The exclusion of Dissenters from offices of trust and profit under the Crown ought not, therefore, to be considered as a badge of second-rate citizenship.

Repeal could not be justified from the experience of America, where there was no establishment; from that of Scotland, where the security of the established Presbyterian kirk, though not protected by penal laws, was guaranteed by the Act of Union; nor from the example of the abolition of the test laws in Ireland, since the Anglican church there 'had a security in the superior numbers of the Catholics over the Dissenters'.[129] If the Dissenters were right to contend, as Fox had done, that the test laws were inefficacious and nugatory, since the legislature had been obliged to pass an Act of Indemnity every session, they could not maintain, at the same time, that they involved persecution, since it was obvious that the laws were not enforced. Non-enforcement of the acts when the church stood in no imminent danger did not mean that they would not need to be implemented in times of emergency.[130] Nor was the Application Committee logical in attempting to impose a political test on parliamentary candidates while claiming freedom from a religious test.

In reply Beaufoy defended the conduct of the Dissenters in their recent campaign from these aspersions and denied the validity of

127. *Parl. Hist.*, vol. 28, col. 406.
128. *Ibid.*
129. *Ibid.*, col. 413.
130. *Ibid.*, col. 414.

Pitt's reasons for rejecting the concept of 'complete toleration'.[131] Burke, however, seized on the opportunities he had been given by Fox to throw the whole weight of his authority against repeal. He delivered a frontal attack on abstract principles of natural right, 'which the dissenters rested on as their strong hold' as 'the most useless and most dangerous to resort to', rights which had no reality in society and which could only be recovered by its dissolution.[132] Accepting Fox's dictum that actions, not opinions, were the only valid test of any man's suitability for office, Burke proceeded to judge the Dissenters' conduct 'by their acts, their declarations, and their avowed intentions' – which was to strain the meaning of 'acts' somewhat beyond what is normally understood by the term.[133] He sought proofs for his concern at the dangers confronting the church by citing the *Catechisms* of Robert Robinson and Samuel Palmer, to show that the minds of young Dissenters were being prejudiced against the establishment;[134] he produced a letter from a Mr Samuel Fletcher, describing the proceedings of a recent meeting of Dissenting ministers at Warrington and inferred from it that their real and insidious objective was, not so much repeal of the Test and Corporation Acts, as the abolition of ecclesiastical tithes and the Anglican liturgy.[135] He quoted Priestley's declaration that 'he hated all religious establishments, and thought them sinful and idolatrous' and also referred to Priestley's confident prediction, in a letter to the Rev. Edward Burn of St Mary's, Birmingham, that the excesses of the friends of orthodoxy would only serve to ignite those 'grains of gunpowder', which had been for some time accumulating and which would certainly blow up the church at length – 'as suddenly, and completely, as the overthrow of the late arbitrary government in France'.[136] Burke also read some controversial extracts from Dr Price's sermon before the London Revolution Society. From this and other evidence Burke felt justified in concluding not only that 'the leading preachers among the dissenters were avowed enemies to the Church of England', but that 'possibly the dissenting preachers

131. *Ibid.*, cols. 415–27.
132. *Ibid.*, cols. 434–5.
133. *Ibid.*, col. 436.
134. The books to which Burke referred were Samuel Palmer's *The Protestant Dissenters' Catechism* (London, 1775) and Robinson's *Political Catechism* (London, 1782), which he appears to have confused with Robinson's *Plan of Lectures on the Principles of Nonconformity* (1778).
135. *Parl. Hist.*, vol. 28, col. 438.
136. *Ibid.*, col. 438.

were themselves recommending the same sort of robbery and plunder of the church as had happened in France'.[137] Though this latter insinuation could not have been sustained from the evidence Burke himself produced, it served its purpose. Enough suspicion had been sown in the minds of his audience for them to agree that an even greater danger had arisen to the Anglican church than the Dissenters' seventeenth-century Levelling principles, namely their adoption of French egalitarianism and their imputed design to remodel the English church on the same lines as the reconstituted and plundered church of revolutionary France. Though Burke had gone out of his way to defend Fox from some of the insinuations of Pitt, and had been scrupulously fair to his former clients the Dissenters in acknowledging the unsuitability and injustice of the sacramental test, the very excess of his mounting prejudices against what he regarded as the subversive tendencies of their ministers was decisive. At the conclusion of the debate, Fox's motion was negatived by 294 votes to 105.[138]

In the middle of May 1790 the London Application Committee in its *Address to the People of England* put a brave face on this renewed rebuff to its hopes of relief.[139] It complained of the manner in which the application had been rejected and the violent spirit which had been raised against it. It felt the defeat as an injury to itself and viewed what had happened as also discreditable to 'the character of a free and enlightened nation'. The allegations that the Dissenters were disloyal subjects and Republicans were once more refuted and the danger to the church from repeal was written off as 'an idle phantom'. On all these issues and also on the generous financial support given by the Dissenters to the Anglican church, the Application Committee had no qualms of conscience. It, therefore, felt entitled to hope that the 'generous nation' which had been 'misled by false alarms and insidious and bigoted misrepresentations' would speedily restore the Dissenters' rights when it returned to 'calmer feelings and more sober reflection'.[140] This confidence, even in the hour of defeat, in the inevitable consequences of the 'progress of truth, justice and sound policy' mirrored once again the naïveté and unreality of the Dissenters' political expectations. In fact the Test and Corporation Acts were not repealed until 1828.

137. *Ibid.*, cols. 436–7.
138. *Ibid.*, col. 452. The previous voting figures against repeal motions had been – in 1787, 176 to 98; in 1789, 122 to 102.
139. Printed in *New Annual Register* (1790), pp. 93–5.
140. *Ibid.*, p. 95.

Fox proved nearer the mark when he anticipated that the failure of 'participation' would involve renewed and harsher persecution for the Dissenters.[141] Henceforth, Priestley in particular was a marked man.[142] The rejection of this third application strengthened rather than weakened the determination of its opponents to maintain their advantages and to continue the policy of refusing all concessions. In the areas where Dissent had campaigned most vigorously, 'Church and King' clubs soon sprouted like mushrooms, not only to celebrate the delivery of the church in its hour of need, but also to ensure that the fruits of its victory over the Dissenters were not thrown away.[143] In this rejoicing and determination George III soon joined, and his birthday, as well as the date of the final rejection of the Dissenters' application, provided new anniversaries for the High Anglicans to celebrate. If, however, Anglican fears for the safety of the church were allayed by the defeat of repeal and the greater cohesion of conservative sentiment in the provinces, the more lasting and disquieting concern for the security of the state and society which Burke had voiced in Parliament, and was soon to reiterate in his *Reflections*, gave cause for revived popular suspicion and hatred of the Dissenters. This was because their leaders and spokesmen had publicly committed them to the approval of French revolutionary principles and had not stopped short of avowing their own 'subversive' intentions. This secular anxiety, moreover, seemed to be justified when the Dissenters, as a result of the rejection of their plea for civic equality, renewed their support for the cause of parliamentary reform and responded to the challenge of the 'Church and King' clubs by helping to organize new types of radical societies, of which the membership was open to working men and with objectives which appeared to be exclusively political. In this way the failure of the campaigns, for the repeal of the Test and Corporation Acts confirmed the inherent radicalism of Dissent and provided the new working-class reformers with the political leadership and intellectual stamina that enabled them in the years ahead to acquire political credibility and to develop unaccustomed powers of large-scale organization.

141. *Parl. Hist.*, vol. 28, col. 402.

142. Priestley himself, however, had nothing to do with suggesting the application of 1790 and 'very little in promoting it'. He 'purposely kept out of the way', knowing that many of the Dissenters disagreed with his views. *Familiar Letters addressed to the Inhabitants of the town of Birmingham* (Birmingham, 1790), Letter 8.

143. [Samuel Heywood], *High Church Politics* (London, 1792), p. 59.

4   The English friends of French liberty and Burke's *Reflections on the Revolution in France*

For he who values Liberty confines
His zeal for her predominance within
No narrow bounds; her cause engages him
Wherever pleaded. 'Tis the cause of man.

W. COWPER, *The Task*, Book 5

The political ideology of the new urban radicalism that erupted so abruptly in England in the course of 1792 was shaped by the antiquarian and Commonwealth traditions handed on by the Protestant Dissenters, by the pungent and practical propaganda of Thomas Paine, and by the example of the direct democracy practised by the Parisian *sans-culottes* at the time of the overthrow of the Bourbon monarchy. The English radicals, however, owed much, and they showed a malicious glee in acknowledging the debt, to the publication in November 1790 of Burke's conservative manifesto, *Reflections on the Revolution in France*; for this gave Paine the opportunity, for which he had been waiting since his return to Europe from America in 1787, to offer 'an address to the people of England on the subject of government'.[1] Burke's *Reflections*, although originating in a private correspondence with a young French friend on the future prospects of the revolution of 1789, was designed, in the first instance, to expose to public view the insidious and subversive objectives, as Burke saw them, of its English sympathizers. Like most major texts of political theory, Burke's pamphlet was an *oeuvre de circonstance*, reflecting his fears of the immediate impact of the French revolution on English society and politics rather than of its ulterior threat to the fabric of European civilization. In the

---

1. T. Paine, *The Rights of Man*, ed. H. Collins (Harmondsworth, 1969), vol. 2, p. 294. 'He [Burke] was the *flint* to Mr. Paine's *steel*; by the collision of one against the other, the *divine fire* of the Rights of Man was struck out for the benefit of all mankind, except Ministers and Placemen' (*Manchester Herald*, 28 April 1792).

event, as one of his major critics was quick to note, Burke's *Reflections* 'produced a controversy which may be regarded as the trial of the French revolution before the enlightened and independent tribunal of the English public'.[2] Above all, it provoked Paine's counter-manifesto, *The Rights of Man*, Part I of which vindicated both the revolution of 1789 and its English supporters, and Part II of which, 'combining Principle and Practice', provided the blueprint for the English democratic movement of the 1790s.[3]

In his *Reflections* Burke concentrated his attack on three distinct but overlapping groups of English friends of French liberty – some on the fringes, others at the centre of English politics. These were, firstly, the philosophic 'Bowood circle' of the Marquess of Lansdowne; secondly, the members of the London Revolution Society and the Society for Constitutional Information; and thirdly, those whom Burke himself designated as the 'New Whigs', because, in response to the intellectual challenges of 1789, they were beginning to stress the progressive rather than the conservative implications of the ambiguous Whig eighteenth-century political creed.[4] According to Burke's analysis of the contemporary situation, these various groups seemed to be fulfilling in English politics analogous roles to those already enacted in France by the French 'sect' of 'philosophers', the members of the so-called 'Patriot' party and the renegade Liberal aristocracy – the very 'conspirators' who had sapped the moral and religious foundations of French society, and had, according to Burke, not only sponsored but also organized the popular revolts which had overturned the *ancien régime*.[5] The importance which Burke attached to the attitudes and activities of these English Francophiles may be judged by his avowed intention in the *Reflections* to expose the members of Lord Lansdowne's coterie 'to the hatred, ridicule and contempt of the whole world';[6] by his later

2. Sir James Mackintosh, *Vindiciae Gallicae*, *Miscellaneous Works* (London, 1851), p. 622.

3. Paine noted in the Preface to Part II of *The Rights of Man* that 'Had he [Burke] not urged the controversy, I had most probably been a silent man.' *Rights of Man*, p. 175.

4. For the ambiguity of Whig principles in the eighteenth century see A. S. Turberville, *A History of Welbeck Abbey and its Owners* (London, 1939), vol. 2, p. 211.

5. E. Burke, *Correspondence*, ed. Earl Fitzwilliam and Sir R. Bourke (London, 1844), vol. 3, p. 176.

6. E. Burke, *Correspondence*, ed. A. Cobban and R. A. Smith (Chicago/Cambridge, 1967), vol. 6, p. 92.

reference, when the danger from English 'Jacobinism' had declared itself, to the London Revolution Society as 'that Mother of Mischief';[7] and by his condemnation, in his *Appeal from the New to the Old Whigs*, of the Whig leaders and magnates for their calm indifference to the spread of Painite doctrines and French principles.[8] To oppose the infiltration of French democratic principles through such channels Burke showed himself, indeed, prepared 'to abandon his best friends and to join with his worst enemies'.[9]

Burke's denunciation of 'the wicked principles and black hearts' of Lord Lansdowne's 'set' was clearly exaggerated.[10] Far from conspiring to smuggle French revolutionary principles into English politics, Lansdowne and his associates had attempted, but had conspicuously failed, to introduce English constitutional usages and procedures into the legislative processes of the French Constituent Assembly. Burke's execration both of Lansdowne and of his Bowood circle of speculative planners is, however, intelligible. Although Lansdowne had been a spent force in English politics after his resignation as First Lord of the Treasury in February 1783, his reputation for Machiavellian intrigue, his patronage of Dissenting extremists such as Priestley, his advocacy of legal and administrative 'innovation', and his close association with French Liberal thinkers such as the abbé Morellet and ministerial reformers like Turgot, had naturally aroused Burke's worst suspicions.[11] Lansdowne's political retirement had merely thrust him further into that 'curious limbo halfway between practical politics and intellectual day dreams', where he had given encouragement and support to the ill-assorted group of scientific, Utopian and Utilitarian 'projectors' which he had assembled at Bowood House, his Wiltshire country

7. This description was applied by Burke to the London Revolution Society in the debate on the third reading of the Traitorous Correspondence Bill on 9 April 1793. *Parl. Hist.*, vol. 30, col. 645. In his sketch of the History of the London Corresponding Society in the Place manuscripts, Thomas Hardy mistakenly claimed that Burke's epithet had referred to the London Corresponding Society and most historians have repeated the error. British Library, Add. MS. 27814, fo. 44.

8. *Appeal from the New to the Old Whigs* (London, 1826), vol. 6, pp. 248–50.

9. Speech on the Army Estimates, 9 February 1790. *Parl. Hist.*, vol. 28, col. 357.

10. Burke to Philip Francis, 20 February 1790, in Cobban and Smith, vol. 6, p. 92.

11. J. Norris, *Shelburne and Reform* (London, 1963), ch. 14. D. Jarrett, *The Begetters of Revolution* (London, 1973), ch. 10.

102 The Friends of Liberty

seat near Calne.[12] Between 1771 and 1789 Price, Priestley, Bentham, Romilly and the Genevan publicist Étienne Dumont had all, in turn, been drawn into the circle in various capacities – as members of Lansdowne's household staff, as experts in economics, law or science, or as tutors to Lansdowne's sons. In this way Bowood became a virtual centre for long-term forward planning modelled on that which Lansdowne had observed in the service of Trudaine de Montigny, the enlightened French administrator, in 1771.[13] Price no doubt contributed his views on sinking fund policy; Priestley, as nominal librarian, felt free to pursue his scientific discoveries; Bentham ventilated his schemes for universal legal codification and speculated on Utilitarianism; while Romilly, on the periphery of the group, emphasized the importance of criminal law reform. 'Brains' Trust'? 'Think Tank'? Or perhaps just paid companions of a lonely, frustrated and widowed politician? After 1782, however, Bowood had also been turned into a haven of refuge for exiled Genevan democratic leaders, such as Dumont, notorious French liberal publicists on the run from *lettres de cachet*, such as Linguet, Brissot and Mirabeau, and a recognized port of call for French notabilities visiting England.[14] These were the forerunners of the aristocratic and clerical *émigrés* who poured across the Channel to escape the September Massacres.

Besides having these dubious contacts with men who were to lead the Patriotic party in pre-revolutionary France, Lansdowne had exerted indirect political influence nearer home by patronizing religious, political or economic groups critical of the status quo. In the seventies he had been in touch with metropolitan radical politicians like James Townshend and Horne Tooke and it was significant that in 1776 Major Cartwright's radical blue-print for parliamentary reform, *Take Your Choice*, had been submitted in draft form to Shelburne, as he then was, for his approval and political backing.[15] He had also used his position as a borough proprietor in Buckinghamshire and Wiltshire to launch the parliamentary careers of

12. Jarrett, p. 134. For the Bowood circle see also E. Halévy, *The Growth of Philosophic Radicalism* (London, 1928), pp. 120–50; P. Brown, *The Chathamites* (London, 1967), and Norris, chs. 5, 14.

13. Jarrett, p. 129.

14. For Mirabeau's stay in England and his associations with Lansdowne and Romilly, see W. R. Fryer, 'Mirabeau in England, 1784–85', *Renaissance and Modern Studies* (University of Nottingham), vol. 10 (1966), pp. 34–87.

15. A. G. Olson, *The Radical Duke* (Oxford, 1961), p. 53. See also J. W. Osborne, *John Cartwright* (Cambridge, 1972), pp. 17–23.

Lord Stanhope, Henry Beaufoy and Benjamin Vaughan – all strong advocates of the claims of the Protestant Dissenters to civic equality and prominent members of the two reform societies which were to incur Burke's particular wrath, the London Revolution Society and the Society for Constitutional Information.[16] As one of the most skilled practitioners of the art of parliamentary lobbying, Lansdowne had placed his experience at the disposal of both the Protestant Dissenters and of industrial and commercial entrepreneurs in the Midlands who were pressing their claims for a more general representation of trade and industry in Parliament.[17] Above all, however, Lansdowne had given the stamp of his approval to Priestley's revolutionary idea that the object of government was 'the good and happiness of the members, that is, of the majority of the members, of any State'.[18] From this fundamental principle it followed that the essential task of government was domestic reform rather than the conduct of foreign affairs, that ministers should take positive action to remove abuses or injustices, and that nothing should be allowed to override the needs of the majority of citizens.[19] It was, however, left to Bentham to explain how the principle of utility could be used to justify resort to a purely democratic regime – a goal which was hardly less congenial to Lansdowne than it was to Burke.[20]

The general concept of utility and the more specific projects dear to the hearts of the Bowood philosophic circle did not have much appeal either to practising British politicians or to the British public.[21] This was apparent in 1788 when Benjamin Vaughan, one of Lansdowne's political henchmen, edited a short-lived radical journal called the *Repository* to set forward the ideas worked out at Bowood.[22] It was this failure and Bentham's inability to interest Continental enlightened despots in his schemes for legal codification which suggested that a more fruitful opening for the implementation

16. In October 1780 Shelburne had placed his pocket borough of High Wycombe at the disposal of Lord Mahon (who became Lord Stanhope in 1786); in March 1783 he arranged for Beaufoy to purchase a seat at Minehead and in 1792 he installed Benjamin Vaughan as his nominee for Calne.

17. J. Norris, 'Samuel Garbett and the early development of industrial lobbying in Great Britain', *Economic History Review*, 2nd series, vol. 10 (1957–8), pp. 450–60, and E. Robinson, 'Matthew Boulton and the art of parliamentary lobbying', *Historical Journal*, vol. 7 (1964), pp. 209–29.

18. J. Bentham, *Deontology*, vol. 1, p. 300.

19. Jarrett, p. 131.

20. Halévy, p. 147.

21. *Ibid.*, p. 149.

22. Jarrett, p. 259.

of the group's policies might be found in revolutionary France. Lansdowne's wide-ranging contacts among the French Liberal aristocracy and members of the Patriotic party were, in this connection, to prove invaluable. A few years earlier, when First Lord of the Treasury, Lansdowne had also extended his protection and patronage to a group of Genevan democratic leaders, belonging to the so-called faction of *Représentants*, who had been banished from the republican city state in 1782 by their aristocratic opponents with the support and encouragement of the French minister of foreign affairs, Vergennes. The failure to re-establish these Protestant refugees in Ireland, as colonists of a 'New Geneva' at Waterford, led them in the spring of 1789 to turn for rehabilitation and redress to their compatriot Jacques Necker, who was then at the helm of affairs in revolutionary France.[23]

In April 1789 Lansdowne allowed Étienne Dumont, a refugee Genevan pastor who had taken up a post at Bowood as tutor to his youngest son and who had already begun to collaborate with Bentham, to accompany Duroveray, a former influential Attorney General in Geneva, on an unofficial mission to Paris. Their object was, if possible, to secure from the French government the surrender of its rights, as protecting power, to veto legislation carried in the Genevan General Council or popular assembly, the confirmation of a decree of 10 February 1789 recalling the exiled democratic leaders and, finally, the restoration of those leaders to their former status and posts of authority in the city republic.[24] When Necker proved reluctant to authorize these concessions, the Genevans transferred their hopes to one of their former acquaintances – the renegade liberal aristocrat, Mirabeau, whom they assisted to gain influence in the Constituent Assembly as a leader of the embattled Third Estate against the reactionary manoeuvres of the court party.[25] Together with their colleagues Clavière and Reybaz, Duroveray and Dumont offered their services to Mirabeau as political advisers and technical experts in return for his assurances of support

23. The scheme for an Irish settlement had initially been suggested by Francis D'Ivernois, one of the Genevan expatriates, but though George III subsidized it to the extent of £50,000, the experiment failed owing to a deficiency of emigrants. J. Bénétruy, *L'Atelier de Mirabeau* (Geneva, 1962), pp. 44–54.

24. E. Dumont, *Souvenirs sur Mirabeau*, ed. J. Bénétruy (Paris, 1950), pp. 40–1.

25. Particularly important in this connection was Mirabeau's speech of 8 July 1789, calling on Louis XVI to withdraw the troops concentrated round Versailles. This was the joint work of Dumont and Duroveray. Dumont, p. 83.

for their objectives once he had forced his way into the ministry.[26] Their political collaboration was to prove both the making and undoing of Mirabeau. The advice of Duroveray on political tactics, the skill of Dumont as drafter of Mirabeau's impassioned speeches in the Assembly and as editor of his political journal, the *Courier de Provence*, and Clavière's financial expertise – all served to establish Mirabeau's reputation as a popular democrat, despite his aristocratic antecedents and unsavoury private life. The political programme canvassed by Dumont in the pages of Mirabeau's journal drew heavily on the constitutional and legal concepts which had been elaborated in the joint discussions of the pioneers of Utilitarianism at Bowood.[27] These well-meant efforts to smooth the path of legislative reform in France came, however, to be resented and were depicted as a covert conspiracy to force Anglo-Genevan constitutional doctrines upon the National Assembly.[28] Romilly's and Bentham's attempts, in concert with Mirabeau as their sponsor and with Dumont as their intermediary, to improve the haphazard and cumbrous legislative procedures of the Assembly and to revise the new French structure of judicial organization were thus frustrated and undoubtedly contributed to the defeat of Mirabeau's own political ambitions by provoking the passage of the famous decree of 7 November 1789, which excluded deputies from the ministry.[29] Even before Lansdowne prudently recalled Dumont from Paris in March 1790 the hopes of

26. Bénétruy, ch. 10.

27. For Bentham's contributions see J. H. Burns, 'Bentham and the French Revolution', *TRHS*, 5th series (1966), vol. 16, pp. 95–114. See also Bénétruy, *L'Atelier de Mirabeau*, pp. 271–2.

28. This alleged plot was 'exposed' by the journalist J. G. Peltier in a virulent pamphlet, *Domine salvum fac regem* (October 1789), in which Mirabeau's collaborators were cited by name, and the attack was continued in the reactionary journal, *Actes des Apôtres*.

29. Romilly's tract (composed with the help of his lawyer friends Wilson and Trail), was translated into French by the Comte de Sarsfield and Dumont as *Règlemens observés dans la Chambre des Communes pour débattre les matières et pour voter*. It was published, with an introduction by Mirabeau, in June 1789. J. Bénétruy, p. 277, *n* 2. When it was presented to the Assembly by Mirabeau late in June 1789 the deputies scornfully rejected it with the comment: *'Nous ne sommes pas Anglais et nous n'avons pas besoin des Anglais.' Ibid.*, p. 108. Bentham's elaborate treatise on *Political Tactics* was designed for the same purpose but delays in its translation in 1789 also raised doubts about its acceptability. Bentham's efforts to induce the Constituent Assembly to adopt his *Draught of a New Plan for the Organisation of the Judicial Establishment in France* (March 1790) were only abandoned in June 1790. His plans for a French Panopticon were terminated by the September Massacres.

the Genevan exiles had already faded. Romilly, if not Bentham, had accepted failure and Mirabeau had been forced to turn his ambitions in the direction of secret counter-revolution.

More prominent, however, in the pages of the *Reflections* than the secret intrigues and questionable designs of the Bowood circle (which Burke compared with those of the French *philosophes*) were the public activities and manifestos of the London Revolution Society early in November 1789. By then the enthusiasm generated by the centenary of 1688, dimmed by the illness of George III, had been rekindled by the fall of the Bastille and the emancipating decrees of the French National Assembly. The English Protestant Dissenters, as we have seen, were gathering strength for their final assault on the fortress of ecclesiastical privilege, stimulated by the consecration of the principle of careers open to talent in the Declaration of Human Rights.[30] The early draft of that charter of French and universal liberties and its preamble had been the work of Mirabeau and his Genevan collaborators.[31] But with the eclipse of Bentham's and Romilly's legislative aspirations and of Mirabeau's ministerial ambitions, the hopes of the English friends of liberty were concentrated, not on what Bowood could give to France, but on what the revolution of 1789 might do to make 'innovation' acceptable in England.[32] If the French legislators did not wish to borrow either parliamentary procedure or political experience from Bowood, it was still, as yet, not clear that French revolutionary precepts and principles would prove even more unacceptable in conservative Britain.

It was against this background of events and in this sanguine mood that the London Revolution Society had once more met to celebrate on 4 November the anniversary of England's own revolution of 1688 at the London Tavern. Once again, as in 1788, the formal proceedings and dinner were preceded by a sermon, delivered in the forenoon in the Meeting House at the Old Jewry by Dr Richard Price – friend and protégé of Lord Lansdowne and the Nonconformist divine who most soberly typified the modest hopes and eager expectations of the moderate reformers. Taking as his text Psalm

---

30. See above, p. 92. Article 6 of the Declaration, *French Revolution Documents*, vol. 1, ed. J. M. Roberts (Oxford, 1966) p. 172.

31. J. Bénétruy, pp. 190–2.

32. Not the least of Romilly's miscalculations in his *Thoughts on the probable influence of the French Revolution on Great Britain* (London, 1790) was that the great changes in France and their beneficial effects 'may diminish some of that horror at innovation, which seems so generally to prevail among us' (p. 13).

122:2–9, the Hebrew poet's salute to Jerusalem 'as a city, that is at unity in itself', Price delivered *A Discourse on the Love of our Country* which became historic, because it provoked the wrath of Burke and was singled out by him for ridicule and disparagement in the opening sections of the *Reflections*. From the outset of his address, Price, by his definitions and distinctions, innocently incited the hostility of the man who had once been, but was no longer, the friend and supporter of the Dissenters.[33] For the preacher 'love of our country' did not imply 'any conviction of the superior value of it to other countries, or any particular preference of its laws and constitution of government', and for him Christianity, as recommended by Christ and his Apostles, was no more than the 'Religion of Benevolence'.[34] 'Country' itself, he thought, should not be understood in purely geographical terms, but regarded as a corporate 'community' of persons associated together by the same civil polity and protected by the same laws.[35] Patriotism, much less chauvinism, was not enough, for we should, in loving our country, accept our wider obligations as 'citizens of the world' and in so doing 'take care to maintain a just regard to the rights of other countries'.[36] The promotion of Truth, Virtue and Liberty were the civic responsibilities in question. What Price inculcated by the first was the need for political education and for communicating 'just ideas of civil government'. This would afford protection from those usurped and tyrannical governments which 'like most of those now in the world, are usurpations on the rights of man, and little better than contrivances for enabling the *few* to oppress the many'.[37] Enlightenment of this kind would 'help to prepare the minds of men for the recovery of their rights and hasten the overthrow of priestcraft and tyranny'.[38] In recommending Virtue, Price had in mind, ultimately, 'a reformation of manners', but seized the occasion to state the case for 'a reformation of our established formularies' and thus aligned himself

33. Burke's sympathies for the Protestant Dissenters had been alienated by the support they had given Pitt in the General Election of 1784, by the democratic notions they had advanced in the Regency crisis and by their hypercritical attitude to C. J. Fox. U. Henriques, *Religious Toleration in England, 1787–1833* (London, 1961), pp. 111–17.

34. R. Price, *A Discourse on the Love of our Country* (London, 1790), pp. 2–5, 7–8.

35. *Ibid.*, p. 3.

36. *Ibid.*, p. 10.

37. *Ibid.*, pp. 12–13.

38. *Ibid.*, p. 14.

with the Dissenting extremists who were advocating the reform of the liturgy and articles of the Anglican church.[39]

Similarly, in describing Liberty as the coping-stone or, rather, 'glory of a community', and in coupling with it the Pauline injunction of obedience to magistrates, Price did not hesitate, in the same breath, to condemn 'the late addresses to George III on his recovery from illness' as unworthy of 'enlightened and manly citizens' or to describe a monarch, in a phrase which would have appealed to the recently deceased Frederick the Great, as 'no more than the first servant of the public'.[40] His own more candid formula for such an address would have honoured George 'as almost the only lawful King in the world, because the only one who owes his crown to the choice of his people'.[41] Political obligations to monarchs and civil magistrates should, however, never be 'blind or slavish' and there was a need for eternal vigilance if the trust reposed in the executive was not to be abused.[42]

One last duty imposed by the love of country remained – to offer prayers for its welfare and thanksgiving for events like the Glorious Revolution of 1688, which had conferred such lasting benefits on all sections of the community. 1688 marked the beginning of 'that aura of light and liberty by which we have been made an example to other kingdoms, and become the instructors of the world'.[43] In commemorating its centenary, the society had, 'as an instruction to the people', restated its principles and Price himself emphasized the tripartite doctrine which he regarded as fundamental:

First; the right to liberty of conscience in religious matters, secondly, the right to resist power when abused; And, thirdly, the right to chuse our governors; to cashier them for misconduct; and to frame a government for ourselves.[44]

The English revolution, however, had been 'by no means a perfect

39. *Ibid.*, pp. 15–17.
40. *Ibid.*, p. 23. Frederick had devised the formula that the King was 'the first servant of the state'.
41. *Ibid.*, p. 25.
42. *Ibid.*, p. 28.
43. *Ibid.*, p. 32.
44. The Declaratory principles approved by the Society in November 1788 had been '1. That all civil and political authority is derived from the people. 2. That the abuse of power justifies resistance. 3. That the right of private judgement, liberty of conscience, trial by jury, the freedom of the press and the freedom of election, ought ever to be held sacred and inviolable'. *Abstract of the History and Proceedings of the Revolution Society in London* (1789), p. 14.

work'. Its two main flaws were that, in conceding a limited religious toleration, it had postponed the achievement of liberty of conscience and, whilst bolstering private and public liberties, it had left the system of parliamentary representation both partial and corrupt. The latter defect Price stigmatized as the country's 'fundamental grievance' and he exhorted all real patriots to unite in procuring its redress.[45] His audience, however, must have noticed that he placed his main hopes of relief and reform on the example given by other countries. The campaign of the Protestant Dissenters for civil emancipation would, he considered, most probably succeed – but mainly because in France 'it had been declared an indefeasible right of all citizens to be equally eligible to public offices' and because a professed Dissenter (Necker) held the first office in the state.[46] The prospects for parliamentary reform, by comparison, seemed slight – public opinion could perhaps be again aroused by the occurrence of some great calamity or by some further unwarrantable abuse of power. A third and more likely contingency would be that 'the acquisition of a pure and equal representation by other countries (while we are mocked by the shadow) kindles our shame'.[47]

That Price was thinking of the probable effect of the French revolution upon English reform politics was evident from the famous *Nunc Dimittis* with which his sermon concluded. 'I have lived', he said,

to see a diffusion of knowledge, which has undermined superstition and error. I have lived to see the rights of men better understood than ever; and nations panting for liberty, which seemed to have lost the idea of it. – I have lived to see THIRTY MILLIONS of people, indignant and resolute, spurning at slavery, and demanding liberty with an irresistible voice; their king led in triumph, and an arbitrary monarch surrendering himself to his subjects. – After sharing in the benefits of one Revolution, I have been spared to be a witness to two other Revolutions, both glorious. – And now, methinks, I see the ardour for liberty catching and spreading; a general amendment beginning in human affairs; the dominion of kings changed for the dominion of laws, and the dominion of priests giving way to the dominion of reason and conscience.

Be encouraged, all ye friends of freedom, and writers in its defence! The times are auspicious. Your labours have not been in vain. Behold kingdoms, administered by you, starting from sleep, breaking their fetters,

45. Price, p. 41.
46. *Ibid.*, pp. 38–9.
47. *Ibid.*, pp. 41–2. British representation was described in a footnote as 'chosen principally by the Treasury, and a few thousand of the dregs of the people, who are generally paid for their votes'.

and claiming justice from their oppressors! Behold the light you have struck out, after setting America free, reflected to France, and there kindled into a blaze that lays despotism in ashes, and warms and illuminates EUROPE![48]

The reverend doctor, whom his French admirers were soon to proclaim 'The Apostle of Liberty', had for once been carried away by emotion, or perhaps by his sense of occasion. He had deplored the uncritical and prejudiced adulation of the British constitution, traditionally the envy of Continental observers; he had denied that the monarchy was based on the principle of hereditary descent; he had sponsored not only the application of the lay Protestant Dissenters for the repeal of the Test and Corporation Acts, but also the demands of their extremist ministers for the reform of the Anglican liturgy and articles. He had called for a union of the friends of liberty to press for parliamentary reform, invoked in its support the doctrines of the Declaration of the Rights of Man and of popular sovereignty and greeted the advent of the new millennium ushered in by the fall of despotism in France. The discourse took pride in the achievements of the European Enlightenment and had both Miltonic and Voltairian overtones. It was a summons to action and a recognition that the initiative in reform had passed to France. It reformulated the principles of 1688 so as to make it difficult to distinguish them from those of 1789.

When during the evening the society proceeded to formal business at the London Tavern under the chairmanship of Earl Stanhope, it elected Benjamin Cooper as its Secretary and Samuel Favell as its Treasurer, and admitted fifty new members, thus bringing its total to over 300. It also approved a resolution from its committee recommending the establishment throughout the kingdom of similar Revolution Societies, which by corresponding with each other, might form 'a grand concentrated Union of the true Friends of Public Liberty, in order the more effectually at all times to maintain its existence'.[49] Was this a defensive measure in anticipation of the 'Church and King' reaction in the provinces? a revival of the idea of association or a model for the radical societies of the future? It might well have been all three. In conclusion, the committee offered its congratulations to the members of the society, 'as Men, Britons and Citizens of the World' on 'the glorious success of the French Revolution' since their last meeting and expressed its ardent wishes

48. *Ibid.*, pp. 49–50.
49. *Abstract of the History and Proceedings of the Revolution Society* (London, 1789).

that its example would lead to the destruction of 'Tyranny and Despotism' throughout the world and the prevalence of 'Universal Liberty and Happiness'.[50] Practising what he had preached Price seized on the opportunity to transform these formal sentiments into a larger and more public gesture by moving his famous Address of Congratulation to the French National Assembly, which the society endorsed unanimously. This message echoed the views he had already ventilated in his sermon, but was also a demonstration of the society's solidarity with the French and a testimony to the hopes and expectations of the English reformers. Its generous and dignified phraseology strikes the modern reader as naive and innocuous; it was, however, in tune with the spirit of the times and struck a responsive chord in the hearts and minds of French liberal politicians and ordinary French citizens. It was one of the first public expressions of English sympathy with the ideas and ideals of the French revolution and led to a correspondence with Jacobin societies throughout France which lasted till the early months of 1792. It also set a precedent which was later followed by a number of English radical societies at a crucial stage of Anglo-French relations in the autumn of that year.[51]

'The society for commemorating the Revolution in Great Britain', ran the address,

disdaining national partialities, and rejoicing in every triumph of liberty and justice over arbitrary power, offer to the National Assembly of France their congratulations on the Revolution in that country, and on the prospect it gives to the first two kingdoms in the world, of a common participation in the blessings of civil and religious liberty.

They cannot help adding their ardent wishes of a happy settlement of so important a Revolution, and at the same time expressing the particular satisfaction, with which they reflect on the tendency of the glorious example given in France to encourage other nations to assert the unalienable rights of mankind, and thereby to introduce a general reformation in the governments of Europe, and to make the world free and happy.[52]

This resolution was despatched to France over the signature of Stanhope and was presented, at his request, in the National Assembly on 25 November 1789 by his friend, the duc de la Rochefoucauld.[53]

50. *History and Proceedings of the London Revolution Society*
51. See below, pp. 244–54.
52. Price, *Discourse.*
53. *Proceedings of the London Revolution Society* (4 November 1789), pp. 10–11. *Procès-Verbaux de l'Assemblée Nationale* (25 November 1789), p. 15.

Although Burke's main animus in the *Reflections* was directed against Price's sermon, there were other reasons why he came to feel 'a considerable degree of uneasiness' at the proceedings of the London Revolution Society.[54] The first was the exchange of goodwill messages between the society and the French National Assembly which followed. It was the form rather than the substance of the society's initial resolution of congratulation to which Burke took exception. In his view that communication was *ultra vires*, equivocal, fraudulent and premature.[55] Similarly, it was the continuity and consequences, rather than the content of the subsequent exchanges and the political prominence which the correspondence seemed to confer on an obscure 'club of dissenters' which caused Burke's disquiet. The letters of the duc de la Rochefoucauld to Price (2 December); of the president of the National Assembly, the archbishop of Aix, to Stanhope (5 December); Stanhope's note of acknowledgement in return (28 December); and, finally, the formal thanks of the society to the archbishop of Aix (6 January 1790) contained sentiments of mutual regard and testified to the spirit of Universal Benevolence which had prompted Price's gesture. Members saluted the condemnation of wars – 'those errors of government' – the prospect of Anglo-French concord opened up by the Assembly' control of French foreign policy, and 'the salutary instruction to monarchs' which the Revolution Society saw as one of the lessons exemplified in the limited monarchy so recently established in France.[56] Price's sermon and the cordial correspondence between the Revolution Society and the French Assembly, all of which were published before the end of 1789, seemed to Burke to betray 'the manifest design of connecting the affairs of France with those of England, by drawing us into an imitation of the conduct of the National Assembly'.[57]

A secondary reason why Burke was disturbed by the London

54. E. Burke, *Reflections on the Revolution in France*, ed. Conor Cruise O'Brien (London, 1969), p. 91.

55. *Ibid.*, pp. 88–91.

56. Extracts from these letters, printed in the *History and Proceedings of the Revolution Society*, were quoted by G. S. Veitch in his *Genesis of Parliamentary Reform* (London, 1965 reprint), pp. 123–4. The MS. originals (some in translation) are in the Archives Nationales in Paris, C.36 (307). G. Pariset's article, 'La Société de la Révolution de Londres dans ses rapports avec Burke et l'Assemblée Constituante', in *La Révolution Française*, vol. 29 (1895), pp. 297–325, is worth consulting for the society's contacts with the French Assembly.

57. Burke, p. 91.

Revolution Society was the close political association which now sprang up between it and the moribund Society for Constitutional Information. Although Burke affected in the *Reflections* to consider the latter as no more than a 'poor charitable club', circulating, 'at the expense of the members', tedious pamphlets which were a drug on the market, he soon became aware that its renewed activity, its Francophile sentiments, and its numerous contacts with provincial radicals might well constitute a new, and by no means negligible threat, to the ordered stability of the English political establishment.[58]

It is true that the fortunes of this society, since its foundation in 1780, had been chequered in the extreme. It had overstrained its meagre financial resources by flooding the country with its early *Addresses, Declarations of Rights* and volumes of *Constitutional Tracts:* it had nearly been ruined by the peculation and mismanagement of its first secretary, Thomas Yates, and further financial anxieties had resulted from the society's championship of the rights of juries to find the fact of libel as well as of publication in the case of the Dean of St Asaph.[59] Though its early extremism had been intended to counter the moderation of Wyvill's Yorkshire Association in 1780, the society had never subsequently departed from the full radical demands of the Westminster subcommittee's report, and its unwillingness to compromise had continued to restrict its membership which reached its peak as early as 1783.[60] The society's energies had, moreover, been diverted from its primary objective of parliamentary reform by its participation in the campaigns for the abolition of the slave trade, for prison reform and for the civic emancipation of the Protestant Dissenters, and also by its breach with the Foxite radicals after the Fox–North coalition.[61] The decline of public interest in parliamentary reform after Pitt's successive failures had led not only to declining membership, but also to

58. *Ibid.*, pp. 86–7.

59. For the early history of the Society of Constitutional Information see E. C. Black, *The Association: British Extraparliamentary Political Organization, 1769–1793* (Cambridge, Mass., 1963), ch. 5. The first two minute books of the society covering the period April 1780 to 7 October 1791 are in the Treasury Solicitor's papers at the Public Record Office (TS 11/1133/1 and TS 11/961/3057).

60. From an original membership of 14, the society had grown to a total of 130 in early March 1783; thereafter it declined, owing to discord over the Fox–North coalition. PRO TS. 11/1133/1.

61. Black, pp. 200–1. PRO TS 11/961 (15 August 1783 and 25 April 1788).

poorly attended meetings and, in 1787, to the suspension of all activity during the summer months.[62]

The society, however, if inanimate, was far from being a corpse, or even a mere charity. Ever since 1784 it had found an efficient and hard-working secretary in the person of Daniel Adams, a law clerk; it had built up a significant and well-distributed non-resident membership in the provinces and a system of country correspondents for the circulation of its addresses and publications; it had, since 1783, and thanks to the drive of Dr John Jebb, instituted a comprehensive inquiry into the state of parliamentary representation in England and Wales.[63] In the years immediately preceding the outbreak of the French revolution, as Cartwright, Jebb and other founder members withdrew or died, the society had also acquired a new political leadership which owed much to the personality and experience of the veteran John Horne Tooke.[64] The society's return to life had been announced by the support it had given, in the spring of 1788, to the Scottish movement for burgh reform and, later in the year, by the celebration of the centenary of the Glorious Revolution. In June 1789 it had resumed its inquiry into the state of parliamentary representation by a closely argued questionnaire addressed to its country correspondents on the abuses of the borough constituencies – research which resulted in the publication in 1792 of T. H. B. Oldfield's famous two-volume *History of the Boroughs*.[65] But, although the society had thus recaptured some of its former interest in parliamentary reform, it owed the newly found enthusiasm for French liberty, which was to characterize the next stage of its evolution, to the challenging gesture which had been made by the London Revolution Society.[66]

When the society held its first general meeting, after the summer recess, on 27 November 1789, only a dozen members were present,

62. Originally the society had met weekly throughout the year, then after 1784 fortnightly. The apparent lack of response to the early proceedings of the French Constituent Assembly was, no doubt, due to the fact that the membership of the society was dispersed at that period and out of London.

63. Black, p. 205.

64. Jebb died in March 1786 and Cartwright rarely attended. Horne Tooke had been elected a member of the SCI on 6 July 1781.

65. PRO TS 11/961/3507, fo. 199. *The State of the Representation in England and Wales* published by the Whig aristocratic Society of the Friends of the People in 1792 was an abridgement of Oldfield's work by George Tierney. Black, p. 286.

66. It is true to say, however, that the SCI had not met in the summer months of 1789.

but it was quick to follow the lead given by the London Revolution Society. It took notice of the 'exertions of a neighbouring kingdom for regaining to the community those Rights of Representation, the exercise of which had been long lost', it adopted 'with pleasure' the Revolutionary Society's message of congratulation to the French National Assembly, and expressed its hope and expectation of the early and progressive extension of a 'pure and equal representation' throughout Europe and, eventually, the whole world.[67] The grounds on which this confidence was based were expressed in resolutions passed at the dinner held at the London Tavern on 16 December 1789, to mark the centenary of the passing of the Bill of Rights. Among the twenty-six members present were four MPs, – James Martin, John Sawbridge, Sir Watkin Lewes and Joshua Grigby – Dr Price, J. H. Tooke, and his eccentric radical friend, the Venetian Count Zenobio.[68] Sixteen visitors included Monsieur St André (who was made an honorary member on the eve of hostilities with France in January 1793), Prince Gallitsin, Chevalier Lonza and Chevalier d'Aranjo.[69] In calling on the friends of freedom in all parts of the kingdom to make 'the most strenuous efforts for procuring a Parliamentary Reform', including the exaction of electoral pledges from candidates, the society expressed its confidence that 'the approaching expiration of the Term for which Parliament was chosen and the splendid efforts of several neighbouring nations for recovering their lost rights' would assist its countrymen to 'obtain from the *Apprehensions* of those who have hitherto opposed their reasonable desires what they have so often solicited in vain from their justice'.[70] A final resolution saluted

67. PRO TS 11/961/3507, fo. 202. It did not, however, transmit any similar message to the French National Assembly.

68. James Martin (1738–1810), MP for Tewkesbury, humanitarian reformer. Contrary to his own views, he voted against the repeal of the Test and Corporation Acts on 2 March 1790 in conformity with the instructions of his constituents. L. Namier and J. Brooke, *History of Parliament: the House of Commons, 1754–1790* (London, 1964), vol. 3, pp. 113–14. John Sawbridge (1732–95), MP for London 1774–95, succeeded Wilkes as Lord Mayor of London, 1775. Brother of Mrs Catherine Macaulay, the historian. Ever since 1771, had unsuccessfully moved annual motions in the Commons for shorter parliaments. *Ibid.*, vol. 3, pp. 409–11.

69. PRO TS 11/961/3507, fo. 203.

70. When introducing reform motions in the Commons in March 1790 for repeal of religious tests and the widening of parliamentary franchise, it may be that the reformers were counting as much on the sobering effects of the approaching General Election as on the influence of the French example.

the prospect of a complete emancipation of human society from political and intellectual servitude . . . and the concurrent disposition which, having been displayed in America, is now pervading Europe, of resisting all restraints on the Freedom of Enquiry, or exclusion from the exercise of any civil rights on account of religious opinion.[71]

Clearly the society anticipated that the days of the Test and Corporation Acts were numbered.

Among the twenty-six toasts proposed and drunk (one for each member of the society present) were the 'Liberties of Ireland', the 'States of Brabant' and the 'Scotch Convention' – each on account of their respective exertions in the cause of parliamentary reform. Two toasts only were reserved for France – the first congratulating her 'on the destruction of the Bastille – the Abolition of enslaving privileges, the co-operation of the Army in the cause of the People, and the exertion of the rights of national representation' and the second to 'the duc de la Rochefoucauld and the National Assembly', after Price had read the Duke's recent personal letter to him about the enthusiastic reception of the Revolution Society's message to the Constituent Assembly.[72]

This early euphoria at what had happened in France as an instance of the irresistible spread of Universal Benevolence, was, however, soon moderated when the reformers attempted to explain how the political interests of Britain would be affected. It is equally remarkable that the Society for Constitutional Information, which had hitherto adhered rigidly to its early radical extremism, when resuming its campaign for parliamentary reform early in 1790 began to exhibit both flexibility and moderation in its methods and immediate objectives. Despite its exhortations to the provincial friends of liberty, the metropolitan society adopted, in the run up to the General Election of 1790, what can only be described as a tentative and accommodating approach to the problem of remedying the inadequate popular representation at Westminster. This change of attitude may have been due to the political realism of Horne Tooke, who was now coming to be the dominating figure in the society, but also, no doubt, to the practical proposals for moderate parliamentary reform advanced by one of its most distinguished members, Henry Flood, MP. It seems likely, also, that the society may have responded in this way to the veiled attacks made on the reform societies by Burke – in his violent diatribe against the French

71. PRO TS 11/961/3507, fo. 204.
72. *Ibid.*, fo. 205.

revolution and its English sympathizers in his speech on the Army Estimates of 9 February 1790 – in which he adumbrated the views later elaborated in the *Reflections*.[73] Moreover, Flood himself, when moving for parliamentary reform in the Commons on 4 March 1790, may have been anxious to belie his previous reputation as the extremist who, in 1783, had pressed reform on the Irish legislature with the backing of the Armed Volunteers.[74]

It must also have been obvious that any suggestion of radical parliamentary reform, even remotely reminiscent of French principles, would be sure of rejection. In seeking to demonstrate the desirability, rather than the necessity, of an instalment of moderate reform, Flood therefore based his case on the lessons of past experience and only invoked the French revolution to defend the timeliness of his proposals. Timely and temperate reform would, in his view, have averted the evils which had befallen France and would render revolution in England unnecessary.[75] If France improved her constitution, as she undoubtedly would, she would rob us of the main advantage – our constitutional excellence – which had enabled us in the past to achieve superiority, despite the handicaps of an indifferent climate, restricted territory and a relatively small population. We would, therefore, need to regain that former advantage by remedying the undoubted flaws in our system of parliamentary representation.[76] France, moreover, had ceased to be either an actual or potential threat to our external security, since 'during her disturbances she cannot have the power; and after her liberty is established, she will not have the inclination to make ambitious war.'[77] Peace between the two nations would allow Parliament to pass reforms which even the threat of hostilities would inhibit or prevent.

Relying on the old argument that the constitutional balance, upset by the increased influence of the Crown and the House of Lords, needed to be redressed, and rejecting as exploded the concept of 'virtual' representation, Flood suggested the addition of one hundred

73. 'He was concerned to find that there were persons in this country, who entertained theories of government, incompatible with the safety of the state, and who were, perhaps, ready to transfer a part at least, of that anarchy which prevailed in France, to this kingdom, for the purpose of effectuating their designs.' *Parl. Hist.*, vol. 28, cols. 370–1.

74. J. Cannon, *Parliamentary Reform, 1640–1832* (Cambridge, 1973), p. 105.

75. *Parl. Hist.*, vol. 28, cols. 455–6.

76. *Ibid.*, col. 456.

77. *Ibid.*, col. 456.

members to the Commons – some representing Scotland – to be elected by the resident householders in every county. This would involve the addition of 'four hundred thousand responsible citizens from the middle ranks of the people to fortify the constitution, and to render it impregnable'.[78] If it were objected that the plan would render the House of Commons too large, Flood considered, though he did not himself propose it, that there were a hundred of the rotten boroughs that might be limited to the return of one member instead of two.[79] To implement these proposals all that would be needed would be a provision that elections should be held on the same day in each parish by the sheriff and his deputies.[80] The plan was intended to convert the House of Commons from being 'a second-rate aristocracy' into an assembly in which the people, but not 'the rabble', would be effectively represented. In effect what Flood was proposing was a tax-paying qualification for those resident householders in the counties who paid the national average of 50s. per annum in church rate and poor rate (scot and lot).[81] It was a far cry from the principle of universal suffrage.

Though Flood's main preoccupation was probably with the prospects opening up with the approaching General Election, and the chance of obtaining advance pledges from the party leaders on the issue of reform, the fate of his proposals was determined by the reaction of his opponents to the 'anarchy' and 'the dangerous and progressive spirit of innovation' which had overwhelmed France. Windham's famous but fatuous query, 'What, would he recommend you to repair your house in the hurricane season?',[82] though duly disposed of by Fox, nevertheless dominated the debate and convinced the audience, if it needed persuasion, that the timing of Flood's proposals was singularly inappropriate. Admittedly, Fox saw no reason why disruption in France should impede reform at home and even described Flood's outline proposals as 'the best of all which he had yet heard suggested'.[83] Pitt, impressed by the general fears of 'innovation', in asserting his intention of moving for reform at a later stage, suggested that Flood should withdraw his present motion. If not, he would himself move an adjournment of the question.

78. *Ibid.*, col. 476.
79. *Ibid.*, col. 463.
80. *Ibid.*, col. 464.
81. *Ibid.*, col. 461.
82. *Ibid.*, col. 467.
83. *Ibid.*, col. 472.

Flood refused to withdraw but his only consolation in defeat was his own unjustified conviction that Fox had given a clear and unequivocal pledge in favour of an amendment of the representation, and that even Pitt's sentiments on reform remained what they had been before 1789.[84] The 'alarmism' which had two days earlier rejected Fox's motion calling for the repeal of the Test and Corporation Acts now buried even moderate parliamentary reform.

Although the danger from the Society of Constitutional Information's renewed championship of parliamentary reform had thus been proved to be minimal, Burke's third and more acute form of anxiety had not been allayed but rather quickened by the recent parliamentary debates. Burke was now obsessed not only by the actual and anticipated repercussions of the French revolution on English politics in general, but also, and more particularly, by the vexed issue of the contemporary relevance of French revolutionary principles to the Whig political creed. The events of 1789 not only posed for the Whigs the problem of their future political strategy in Opposition, but also necessitated 'a fundamental re-examination of the intellectual basis of English Whiggery'.[85] Was the Whig creed fundamentally conservative or inherently liberal? Was the Whig party, as Burke believed, essentially an aristocratic connection, politically independent from either court or popular influence and, to that extent, a stabilizing element in the body politic? Or were its political attitudes and strategy capable of being deflected by the close social and intellectual bonds of its leaders before 1789 with the French liberal aristocracy?[86] The dilemma confronting the Whigs was all the more disturbing because their leaders were divided and because the Whig magnates were seemingly oblivious of, or indifferent to, the prospect that both party unity and their own dominance of the Whig power structure might be imperilled.[87]

Ever since its rout in the General Election of 1784, the party had been in disarray and the Regency crisis of 1788–9 had left a bitter legacy of dissension and personal animosities. Burke, in particular,

84. *Ibid.*, cols. 474–5.
85. L. G. Mitchell, *Charles James Fox and the disintegration of the Whig Party, 1782–1794* (Oxford, 1971), p. 153. See also F. O'Gorman, *The Whig Party and the French Revolution* (London, 1967) for a well-informed and critical discussion of these issues.
86. For Fox's long association with Lafayette, the vicomte de Noailles, and the duc d'Orléans see Mitchell, pp. 154–5.
87. Whig magnates like Earl Fitzwilliam were more aware of these dangers than Burke gave them credit for. O'Gorman, p. 52.

as an ageing politician, bereft of the support of his former patron
Lord Rockingham, felt himself increasingly isolated in the party
and was highly critical of both Fox and Sheridan for their virtual
abandonment of the impeachment proceedings against Warren
Hastings.[88] Apart, however, from an initial outburst of enthusiasm
at the fall of the Bastille, and his general approval of the dismantling
of the feudal regime and the proclamation of the Declaration of the
Rights of Man – which his friends de Noailles and Lafayette had
respectively sponsored and promoted – Fox had adopted a stance
of 'sympathetic detachment' from events in France.[89] He was indeed
far from being a democrat, though he had once been acclaimed as
'the Man of the People'. He would have been content to allow
parliamentary reform to remain 'a sleeping question' and saw no
reason why the French revolution should not also be regarded as an
issue on which the Whigs could agree to differ.[90] The animosity
which had grown up between Burke and Sheridan during the
Regency debates had, however, by 1790 festered, partly because
each was then attempting to impose his own highly individual views
of the significance of the French revolution on his Whig colleagues
and, also, because Sheridan, in Burke's estimation, had determined
to canvass a new line in Opposition political strategy.[91] When
Burke clashed with Sheridan in the Commons on 9 February 1790
over their radically opposed views of the French National Assembly
in the debates on the Army Estimates, their friendship finally
foundered.

What Burke found particularly disturbing was the tendency of
reformers of various shades of opinion, at this juncture, to coalesce
in some kind of 'popular front' and the disposition of Sheridan to
swing the progressive elements of the Whig club behind this new
departure as its potential leader.[92] One result of the failure of Flood's
reform motion was, in fact, to strengthen, rather than weaken, the
close political association which had recently developed between
the Society for Constitutional Information and the London Revo-

88. *Ibid.*, pp. 43–4.

89. Mitchell, p. 155.

90. O'Gorman, p. 47. Fox had referred to parliamentary reform as 'a sleeping
question' on 4 March 1790 in the debate on Flood's proposals. *Parl. Hist.*,
vol. 28, col. 471.

91. Mitchell, p. 155.

92. For Burke's fears of Sheridan's ambitions as a popular leader, see his son
Richard's letter to Earl Fitzwilliam, 29 July 1790, WWM A iv (f) 71 (a), extracts
of which are published in Cobban and Smith, vol. 6, p. 137.

lution Society. Taking the initiative, the Society for Constitutional Information resolved, on 26 March 1790, that a deputation of six of its members (including Flood and Horne Tooke) should consult their colleagues of the London Revolution Society on the submission of reform proposals to a joint general meeting of the two societies at the London Tavern.[93] Welcoming this overture the Revolution Society appointed a small subcommittee to concert action at the next meeting of the SCI on 9 April.[94] The joint general meeting thus fixed for the 16 April had, however, to be postponed till the twenty-third, and it is not wholly clear from the evidence whether this demonstration ever took place.[95] The resolutions approved at meetings of the Society for Constitutional Information on 9 and 16 April (at which delegates of the Revolution Society were present) give a clear idea, however, of the scope of the reform programme then canvassed by the metropolitan 'friends of liberty' and their determination to persist in their objectives until final victory. In effect, both societies reaffirmed their belief in the moderate policy previously advocated by Flood – namely, the tax-paying resident householders' franchise, the emphasis on the need to 'remedy the gross partiality of Borough Representation' and the reassertion that the time was ripe for such changes. Efforts were also made to resuscitate the metropolitan 'Quintuple Alliance' in support of these proposals.[96]

This perseverance, however, paid few, if any, dividends in the General Election towards the end of June 1790. Flood, Wilkes and William Smith all lost their seats, and Horne Tooke's renewed candidature at Westminster only had the effect of exposing the virtual disfranchisement of those independent electors who voted for him, and of embarrassing his opponents, Charles James Fox and the ministerialist Admiral Hood, the two elected candidates, who had previously agreed to divide the representation between them.[97] The

93. PRO TS 11/961/3507, fo. 212 (SCI minute-book, 1783–91).

94. *Ibid.*, fo. 214.

95. *Ibid.*, fo. 217. Cannon cites Wyvill, *Papers*, vol. 2, p. 564, as evidence that the meeting actually took place.

96. *Ibid.*, fos. 214, 217.

97. Tooke had stood as a parliamentary reformer in order to ensure a contest and prevent the disfranchisement of Westminster. He had refused to indulge in the bribery of the electors, 1679 of whom had, nevertheless, voted for him. For his petition against the return, see *Parl. Hist.*, vol. 28, cols. 921–5. Fox's action for costs, after the rejection of Tooke's petition, however, caused a national sensation.

election hardly affected the balance of forces in the Commons at all – the Opposition, with a net loss of three seats, found its numbers reduced to 141 in a house of 558.[98] This discomfiture did not, however, damp the enthusiasm of the reformers and it may have induced Sheridan to accept the invitation to members of the Whig club to attend the monster reform banquet held to celebrate the fall of the Bastille at the Crown and Anchor Tavern in the Strand on 14 July 1790.

The dinner, chaired by Lord Stanhope, was attended by 652 'friends of liberty', among whom the two London reform societies, Dr Price's Dissenting congregation at Newington Green, and the Whig club itself were strongly represented.[99] The pattern of proceedings followed closely those of the anniversary meetings of the London Revolution Society, with short preliminary invocations of the 'Supreme Being' by Dr Kippis and Dr Towers, speeches, resolutions and numerous 'patriot' toasts. The burden of the main speeches by Stanhope and Price was that France, by its emancipating reforms, had outdistanced its former preceptor Britain and had now set precedents worthy of our imitation in the fields of civil and religious liberty and foreign policy. Stanhope had no compunction in drawing attention to the French National Assembly's concession of full civic emancipation and its abolition of ecclesiastical tithes, and considered that the new French constitution would be 'hated only by the ill intentioned' – an obvious side-swipe at Burke.[100] He thought, too, that it 'would perhaps hasten the day when all men, even kings, will regard each other as brothers without regard to primogeniture'.[101] In proposing a toast to 'an Alliance between France and Great Britain for perpetuating peace, and making the world happy', Price commended the Constituent Assembly's decision to renounce all views of conquest and offensive war as opening up the prospect of a quadruple alliance of France, Great Britain, America and Holland, which would be able to arbitrate between contending nations and impose peace.[102]

Sheridan, acting in the name of the gentlemen of the Whig club,

98. O'Gorman, p. 248.
99. Veitch, pp. 149–50; C. B. Cone, *The English Jacobins* (New York, 1968), p. 90; G. Stanhope and G. P. Gooch, *Life of Charles, Third Earl Stanhope* (London, 1914), pp. 93–5.
100. Veitch, p. 149.
101. *Ibid.*
102. J. T. Rutt (ed.), *Life and correspondence of Joseph Priestley* (London, 1832), vol. 2, p. 79.

had drawn up and now moved a carefully worded resolution which alluded indirectly to the temporary differences between the English and French governments over the Nootka Sound dispute.[130] His motion was:

> That this meeting does most cordially rejoice in the establishment and confirmation of liberty in France: and that it beholds with peculiar satisfaction the sentiments of amity and goodwill which appear to pervade the people of that country towards this kingdom, especially at a time when it is the manifest interest of both states that nothing should interrupt the harmony that at present subsists between them, and which is so essential for the freedom and happiness, not only of both nations, but of all mankind.[104]

At this point Horne Tooke, noting that all the diners were wearing national cockades in their hats, and that a symbolic fragment of stone from the ruins of the Bastille assumed pride of place on the dining table, thought it prudent, in order to prevent misunderstanding, that the meeting should qualify its approval of the French revolution with a corresponding declaration of its attachment to the principles of the British constitution.[105] His attempt to move an amendment in this sense was greeted with hissing and such strong signs of disapproval that he withdrew it. This unruly demonstration, however, was a personal rebuke to Tooke from members of the Whig club who had been alienated by his opposition to Charles James Fox at the recent Westminster election.[106] When Tooke coolly stood his ground and reintroduced his proposal as a substantive motion, it passed without difficulty.[107] Harmony was restored by the drinking of the traditional toast of the Society for Constitutional Information to 'the Majesty of the People', and the evocation of the civic oath to 'The Nation, the Law and the King' which had been taken at the Festival of Federation in Paris earlier in the day by the massed battalions of the provincial National Guards. By comparison the pledge to the principle of 'Equal representation of the English people in Parliament' seemed somewhat tame, though it was no doubt drunk with equal fervour.

103. *ST*, vol. 25, col. 389.
104. *Ibid.*, col. 389.
105. *Ibid.*, col. 390.
106. *Ibid.*, col. 393.
107. Its final form was: 'We feel equal satisfaction that the subjects of England, by the virtuous exertions of their ancestors, have not so arduous a task to perform as the French have had; but have only to maintain and improve the constitution, which their ancestors have transmitted to them.' *Ibid.*, col. 391.

The significance of this festive occasion in the history of the reform movement can hardly be exaggerated. It confirmed Burke's apprehensions that Sheridan was undermining the unity of the Whig party in the effort to form an association of the 'friends of liberty' committed to the cause of parliamentary reform, and was abandoning the conventions of Whig Opposition laid down by Lord Rockingham.[108] It also convinced Burke that Fox's show of neutrality towards the events in France lacked credibility and that, although Fox himself had not attended the dinner, he would soon meekly submit to the democratic lead given by Sheridan.[109] It indicated that Dr Price and the Protestant Dissenters had switched their energies from repeal to parliamentary reform and were intent on establishing an *entente cordiale* with France. The festivity also established a new anniversary in the reformers' calendar, the celebration of which, against the background of rising popular hostility to French revolutionary principles, was to give a handle to the 'Alarmists' and an excuse for attacks on the lives and property of the so-called 'English Jacobins'.

More immediately it led to a resumption of the correspondence between the London Revolution Society, the French National Assembly and provincial Jacobin clubs, which was to continue intermittently till the spring of 1792. In communicating Sheridan's motion to his friend, the duc de la Rochefoucauld, with the request that it should be presented to the French National Assembly, Stanhope struck a note that was to be re-echoed throughout the ensuing correspondence. 'Soon', he wrote, 'we hope that men will cease to regard themselves under the odious aspect of tyrants and slaves, and that, following your example, they will look on each other as equals and learn to love one another as free men, friends and brothers.'[110] The formal interchange of goodwill messages between Stanhope and Treilhard, president of the National Assembly, was, however, less significant than the spontaneous response of

108. Lord Rockingham's practice in Opposition was to resist the bad measures of ministers, while maintaining 'both the form and substance of our present constitution'. R. Burke to Earl Fitzwilliam, 29 July 1790. WWM, A iv (f) 71 (a).

109. Fox, according to Burke's son, could not be counted on to dissociate himself from Sheridan's manoeuvres, because of his sympathy with the Dissenters and because his hopes in the present establishment were 'only reversionary and even then precarious'. *Ibid.*

110. The French MS. translation of Stanhope's letter is in AN C 42, bundle 379, fo. 25. Sheridan's resolution, in translation, is in fo. 26.

many local Jacobin clubs in many widely separated parts of France.[111] Calais, Montpellier, Paris, Chalon-sur-Sâone and Nantes led the way and so numerous were the letters and messages received by the Revolution Society's correspondence committee that, in some cases, replies were not despatched till the spring of 1791.[112]

The late Professor Veitch, to whom we are indebted for the first detailed analysis of this Anglo-French literary and political interchange, noted that it was entirely confined to the monarchical period of the French revolution; that the Jacobin societies, down to and beyond the royal flight to Varennes in June 1791, lived up to their official title of 'Friends of the Constitution' by never questioning, in either country, the principles of limited monarchy; and that the Jacobin club in Paris had, at this period, a membership as 'respectable', and even as 'aristocratic' as that of the London Revolution Society. He characterized the correspondence itself as an exchange of 'vague and high-flown sentiments' which could only be regarded as politically innocuous.[113] He recognized that, after Varennes, the monarchical views of the Jacobin societies were considerably eroded, that some clubs were more critical of the King's treasonable behaviour than the majority of the National Assembly, and also that, in consequence, the overthrow of the monarchy in August 1792 was hardly questioned by the provincial Jacobins.[114] He omitted to notice, however, that there had been a similar, but less drastic, evolution in the Revolution Society's attitude towards British political institutions over the same period. Nor did he draw attention to the solid core of political realism and calculation which often qualified the vague generalities and pious optimism expressed in the correspondence. These nuances emerge more clearly if we realize that the correspondence passed through three distinct phases, in which the attitude of the Revolution Society reflected changes not only in France but also in England.

The initial euphoria, which had been so admirably captured in Price's sermon on 'Love of our country' and his message to the French National Assembly, had been sparked off by the fall of

111. These were printed in the spring of 1792 as *The Correspondence of the Revolution Society in London with the National Assembly and with various Societies of the Friends of Liberty in France and England.*

112. The delay was occasioned partly by the comparative infrequency of general meetings of the society and also because the members of the correspondence committee lived in different parts of the country. *Ibid.*, p. 44.

113. Veitch, pp. 147, 159.

114. *Ibid.*, pp. 143–6.

Bourbon 'despotism' and had related to the reform of the manifold injustices of the *ancien régime* in accordance with the principles of the Declaration of the Rights of Man. The second phase of the correspondence, initiated by the Crown and Anchor dinner, was characterized by the feeling that the revolution in France had reached a successful conclusion and that the French Assembly's condemnation of aggressive war on 20 May 1790 would not only establish Anglo-French concord in foreign affairs, but would also initiate an era of universal peace. During this phase, the Revolution Society, so far from merely indulging in an Anglo-French exchange of vague and meaningless generalities, helped to avert the breakdown of good relations with France over the Nootka Sound dispute with Spain, and took an active and significant share in the formulation of the revolutionary doctrine of 'fraternity'.[115] From the spring of 1791 the mood of the correspondence committee of the Revolution Society changed yet again. By that time its extravagant hopes of the advent of the millennium had been clouded and the dream of universal peace had faded. The committee's correspondence with the Jacobin clubs then became much more outspoken in its criticism of the unreformed British political system, more conscious of the positive need to imitate the lead which had been given in France, and uneasily aware of the need for closer solidarity with the revolutionaries in order to stave off the growing danger of domestic reaction. This changed political emphasis in the third phase of the society's relations with its Jacobin counterparts may be ascribed to the realization that the prospects of reform in Britain were receding, to the strong personal contacts established with the Jacobin society at Nantes, and also to the publication of Burke's *Reflections on the Revolution in France* in November 1790.

A few examples of the changing significance of the Revolution Society's French correspondence may be chosen from its second and third phases. In the first place its early vision of universal peace had, by the spring of 1791, contracted to the more modest expectation

115. Differences between England and Spain over the latter's claim to dominion over the western coast of America from Cape Horn to Alaska came to a head in 1790 when several British vessels and their crews were apprehended as interlopers off Vancouver Island, near a small British settlement at Nootka. Until the French National Assembly denounced the Bourbon Family Compact with Spain as the basis of its foreign policy, there was some danger that France might be involved, as an ally of Spain, in hostilities with Britain. On 20 July 1790 Price made a speech at a general meeting of the Revolution Society which served to reassure the French Assembly and to calm its anxieties. Veitch, p. 151.

of continued Anglo-French harmony, while the concurrent French aspirations were countered by the reminder that '*general* Freedom must precede *Universal* peace', and that, even in Britain, 'important political changes' would be needed as a preliminary.[116] The society, therefore, considered it would be more realistic, in the interim, to seek a working agreement between the 'friends of liberty' in both countries, based on mutual self interest.[117] Between such groups, however, there could well be not only ties of sympathy and understanding, but the kind of political solidarity implicit in the idea of 'Fraternity'. One early indication of these sentiments had been the Anglo-French festival held at Nantes on 4 November 1790 in joint commemoration of the English revolution of 1688 and of the first popular assembly in the city on 4 November 1788.[118] This festival was a continuation of contacts already established between the Jacobin Society at Nantes and the London Revolution Society as a result of the Crown and Anchor dinner. That gesture by the English reformers had led, on 23 August 1790, to the organization at Nantes of an Anglo-French fête. A week later the local Jacobin club had deputed its president, Français, and one other member, Bougon, to convey in person to Lord Stanhope and the members of the London Revolution Society its fraternal greetings and a gift symbolical of Anglo-French union.[119] Although Lord Stanhope had resigned his membership of the London Society on 11 August, the two delegates had been warmly received and entertained to dinner at the London Tavern on 29 September by the committee of the society chaired by a future radical enthusiast – J. H. Stone.[120] On that occasion, Français, speaking in English, had claimed that 'universal brotherhood is not with us merely a speculative dogma' and as evidence had presented to the society a framed drawing of the tricolour borne at the recent fête at Nantes, inscribed '*À l'union de la France et*

116. *Correspondence of Revolution Society* (1792), p. 126.

117. Revolution Society to M. de Noailles, president of National Assembly and Jacobin club of Paris (undated), in reply to letter of 12 August 1790. *Ibid.*, p. 56.

118. *Correspondence of Revolution Society*, pp. 64–5. For French municipal demands for the double representation of the Third Estate in November 1788 see J. Egret, *La Pré-Révolution Française, 1787–1788* (Paris, 1962), pp. 355–8.

119. *Correspondence of Revolution Society*, p. 64.

120. Stanhope resigned because of resolutions passed at a general meeting of the society on 20 July 1790, binding members who had not been present to be responsible for what had been decided. Stanhope had himself not been present and disagreed with the resolutions. Stanhope and Gooch, p. 97.

d'Angleterre'.[121] It was partly in gratitude for this hospitality and in response to the contacts thus effected with the London society that the joint ceremony of 4 November had been organized at Nantes. Among the guests was Benjamin Vaughan, MP, former secretary of Lord Lansdowne and member of both the Society for Constitutional Information and the London Revolution Society. One of the proposals made on this occasion was that delegates from France and England should observe 4 November every year as a joint commemoration of the Glorious Revolution in England and the pre-revolution in France. It was also suggested that the delegates should be authorized 'to swear friendship and support to all Peoples who might wish, following their example, to recover their Liberty'.[122] This was a remarkable foreshadowing of the contentious Edict of Fraternity (19 November 1792) which did so much, in changed political circumstances, to plunge the two countries into bitter and prolonged hostilities. There are several indications in this correspondence that the London society had itself done something to encourage the formulation of this potent revolutionary principle, which is usually regarded as peculiarly French in origin. When, for example, on 20 July 1790, a general meeting of the London Revolution Society had reaffirmed its satisfaction with the correspondence which its committee had hitherto maintained with 'the Patriots of France', it had done so in the hope that its continuance would help to maintain Anglo-French amity and that it would animate 'the sons of Freedom to assert their rights – among all the Nations of the Earth'.[123] This perhaps did no more than underline what Price had said in the final paragraph of his congratulatory address to the National Assembly on 4 November 1789, but it was a forecast which the society felt justified in repeating on more than one occasion. In reply to a letter from the Jacobin club of Tours, the Revolution Society wrote on 5 April 1791 that despite the alarm it had created in some quarters, the publication of Burke's pamphlet

viciously reflecting on *your* heroic actions, and indecently abusing some of the most virtuous of our fellow Citizens, has produced a great number of well written refutations from persons of different ranks and connections, which have contributed very considerably to spread among the Inhabitants of this island a more accurate knowledge of the principles of *your* Revolution

121. For the proceedings at the dinner see *Correspondence of Revolution Society*, p. 65.
122. *Ibid.*, p. 104.
123. *Ibid.*, p. 42.

– adding significantly, 'which only want knowing to be imitated'.[124]

As its disillusionment with the prospects of reform deepened, the Revolution Society even dropped plain hints to its French correspondents that the English friends of liberty might, by their growing resentment or frustration, be provoked into imitating their example. Whereas, on 14 July 1790, the society had celebrated the consolidation of French liberties as, in some sense, derivative from the principles of 1688, by the spring of 1791 it had concluded that the correction of the admitted defects in the English revolution settlement might well depend on its countrymen's willingness to follow in the wake of the French reformers.[125] In its reply to the Jacobins of Vire on 5 April 1791 the society even asserted that

Royal prerogatives, injurious to the public interest, a servile Peerage, a rapacious and intolerant clergy, and corrupt Representation are grievances under which we suffer. But as *you*, perhaps, have profited from the example of our Ancestors, so shall we from *your* late glorious and splendid actions.[126]

In a letter of the same date to the Jacobin club at Tours, the society also noted how the French had

now given us such convincing practical instructions on the true formation of governments, that we are persuaded all our fellow citizens will soon be inspired with as ardent a desire of improving their own, as they formerly have been of *preserving* it.[127]

The wheel of political progress had now come full circle, and by February 1792, in one of its last letters to its French correspondents, the society hailed not England, but France, as 'the instructress of the world'.[128] Unfortunately for the reformers the majority of their compatriots proved as reluctant to take lessons from Paris as the members of the Constituent Assembly in 1789 had been to accept guidance from Bowood.

Meanwhile, once again, but for the last time, Price had caught the mood of the London Revolution Society at its anniversary dinner of 4 November 1790, when he had proposed, from the chair, or

124. *Ibid.*, p. 226.
125. *Ibid.*, p. 126.
126. *Ibid.*, p. 86.
127. *Ibid.*, p. 228. Hitherto the majority of the population had been attached to the forms of the English constitution and so had 'tolerated its faults, from affection to its excellencies'.
128. *Ibid.*, p. 184. The society's last letter, in reply to one from the Jacobins of Le Havre, was dated 3 March 1792. *Ibid.*, p. 233.

rather from a table on to which he had clambered, the toast – 'The Parliament of Britain – May it become a National Assembly'.[129] The meeting was well attended and the committee expressed its gratification not only with its growing correspondence with French Jacobin clubs but also with the formation of a number of local Revolution Societies in Britain, as it had suggested a year earlier.[130] The reforming impulse, however, was already on the wane and the Society for Constitutional Information now appeared in danger of imminent dissolution through loss of members, poor attendances and unpaid subscriptions.[131] Both the London reform societies were later to congratulate themselves that, at this point, their fortunes had been resuscitated and those of radicalism promoted by the publication, as Parliament reassembled in early November 1790, of Burke's *Reflections on the Revolution in France*.

At the time when Burke was writing this pamphlet in the spring and summer of 1790, he was, of course, only aware of the Revolution Society's French correspondence in its initial stages. Price's sermon, the message of congratulation to the French Assembly and the replies from the duc de la Rochefoucauld and the archbishop of Aix were, however, sufficient in themselves for his conclusion that 'its manifest design' was to draw us into 'an imitation of the conduct of the National Assembly'.[132] This is what Burke was determined at all costs to prevent. The *Reflections* were intended, in the first place, to ridicule the proceedings of the London Revolution Society as totally unrepresentative of the state of English public opinion and to discredit as dangerous 'innovation' the political maxims and Francophile sentiments expressed in Price's sermon.[133] Secondly, Burke's purpose in condemning the revolution of 1789 as metaphysical in origin, atheistical in tendency and anarchical in its consequences was to refute the reformers' contention that its principles were derivative from, or akin to, those of the conservative English revolution of 1688. Here again his object was to arrest growing English

129. C. B. Cone, *Torchbearer of Freedom: The influence of Richard Price on Eighteenth-Century Thought* (Lexington, Ky., 1952), p. 189.

130. *Correspondence of London Revolution Society*, pp. 105–7.

131. In the winter of 1790–1 the numbers attending meetings averaged half a dozen only. With annual subscriptions amounting to £75.15s.0d. and overhead expenses reckoned at £68.10s.0d. the society was operating on a shoe-string budget. PRO TS 11/961/3507, fo. 223.

132. Burke, *Reflections*, ed. C. C. O'Brien (London, 1969), p. 91

133. A. Goodwin, 'The political genesis of Burke's *Reflections on the Revolution in France*', *Bulletin of the John Rylands Library*, vol. 50 (1968), p. 350.

admiration for the aims and achievements of the French 'Patriotic' party. Thirdly, Burke was determined to issue a solemn warning to the Whig magnates against the dangers inherent in any attempt to imitate the conduct of the French liberal aristocracy by sponsoring, or conniving at, the new popular departure in Whig Opposition tactics canvassed by Sheridan.

The pride of place accorded in the *Reflections* to the transactions of the London Revolution Society and Price's political sermon was partly due to the specific queries raised by his correspondent de Pont in his letter of 29 December 1789.[134] It was, nevertheless, essential for Burke at the very outset to reject the interpretation which Price had put on the fundamental principles of the revolution of 1688. The reverend doctor had been candid in his criticisms of the eight-eenth-century British constitution which Burke, like most of his contemporaries, so much revered. He had implied, though perhaps not really meant, that the English throne was elective, when Burke had done so much to prove, ever since the Regency debates, that it was hereditary. He had also asserted that the Whig revolutionary settlement had been incomplete, because it had left a corrupt and' inadequate parliamentary representation as 'a fundamental grievance' of the reformers. All these unorthodox views ran counter to Burke's most cherished and inveterate political convictions, and had clearly been formulated in order to justify renewed attempts to redress the civil and religious disabilities of the English Protestant Dissenters and to impart a new incentive to the campaign for parliamentary reform.[135] Though repeal of the Test and Corporation Acts had failed miserably and though the General Election of 1790 had disillusioned the reformers, these defeats might be reversed if a fresh and more powerful stimulus came from France.

In the opening sections of the *Reflections*, Burke, therefore set out to slight the Revolution Society as an obscure 'club of dissenters' of 'undetermined denomination' which had only managed to attract public notice by the irregular, unrepresentative, 'fraudulent' and over-hasty 'sanction' which it had given to the proceedings of the National Assembly in France.[136] Dr Price – the most respected of

134. *Ibid.*, pp. 341–2. For biographical details of de Pont – a young magistrate of the *Parlement* of Paris, who had made Burke's acquaintance on a visit to England in 1785 – see Cobban and Smith, vol. 6, p. 31.

135. R. R. Fennessy, *Burke, Paine and the Rights of Man* (The Hague, 1963), p. 101.

136. Burke, pp. 88–90.

all English Dissenting ministers – was described as 'a man much connected with literary caballers and intriguing philosophers' – a clear allusion to his link with Lansdowne's Bowood circle – as, 'this archpontiff of the *rights of men*', 'the Apostle of Liberty' and, most unfairly, as the man who had rejoiced, in the peroration of his sermon, in the spectacle of Louis XVI being 'led in triumph' and an arbitrary monarch surrendering himself to his subjects'.[137] Commenting on Price's concluding remarks about 'the favourableness of the present times to all exertions in the cause of liberty', Burke asked what would, in fact, be involved if the example of France was followed in Britain.

Is our monarchy to be annihilated, with all the laws, all the tribunals, and all the ancient corporations of the kingdom? Is every landmark of the country to be done away in favour of a geometrical and arithmetical constitution? Is the house of lords to be voted useless? Is episcopy to be abolished? Are the church lands to be sold to Jews and jobbers; or given to bribe new-invented municipal republics into a participation in sacrilege? Are all the taxes to be voted grievances, and the revenue reduced to a patriotic contribution, or patriotic presents? Are silver shoe-buckles to be substituted in the place of the land-tax and the malt tax, for the support of the naval strength of this kingdom? Are all orders, ranks and distinctions to be confounded, that out of universal anarchy, joined to national bankruptcy, three or four thousand democracies should be formed into eighty three, and that they may all, by some sort of unknown attractive power, be organized into one? For this great end, is the army to be seduced from its discipline and its fidelity, first, by every kind of debauchery, and then by the terrible precedent of a donative in the increase of pay? Are the curates to be seduced from their bishops, by holding out to them the delusive hope of a dole out of the spoils of their own order? Are the citizens of London to be drawn from their allegiance, by feeding them at the expense of their fellow subjects? Is a compulsory paper currency to be substituted in the place of the legal coin of this kingdom?[138]

It was this kind of emotional exaggeration which laid the *Reflections* open to telling rejoinders.

Because Price had spoken of the defects of parliamentary repre-

---

137. *Ibid.*, pp. 93–6. In the fourth edition of his *Discourse* (1790), Price defended himself from this insinuation by noting that, in using these words, he had referred, not to the violent transference of the court from Versailles to Paris on 6 October 1789, but to the voluntary visit paid by Louis XVI to the capital immediately after the fall of the Bastille.

138. Burke, pp. 144–5.

sentation as vitiating 'all legitimate government' Burke read this as
a plea for the abolition of the House of Lords and even of the
monarchy.[139] Intent on the 'double ruin of church and state', the
Revolutionists had 'wrought under-ground a mine that will
blow up at one grand explosion all examples of antiquity, all
precedents, charters, and acts of parliament'.[140] This weapon
was, of course, 'the rights of men' – and this was the gravamen
of Burke's charges against the Protestant Dissenters in particular,
but also against all 'innovators' in general. Against such rights
no form of prescription would prevail, no agreement be valid
and no compromise be possible. In this sense, these abstract and
'pretended' rights were all extremes, and, in proportion as they
were 'metaphysically true' they were 'morally and politically
false'.[141]

Burke presented in the *Reflections* an interpretation of the revolution of 1789 that was highly individual, based not so much on
ignorance, prejudice or conscious misrepresentation as on his
overriding need, after the publication of Price's sermon, to differentiate it in its origins, methods and consequences from the English
revolution of 1688.[142] After an initial period of dispassionate appraisal, Burke's execration of the revolution had crystallized as a
result of his emotional response to the mob violence directed against
Marie Antoinette and Louis XVI in the October days, the seculari-
zation of the landed estates of the Gallican church and the rejection
of British constitutional practices in November 1789.[143] It was these
events which determined Burke's view of the whole revolutionary
process. Contemporary rumours and allegations that the events of
5 and 6 October were the result of Orleanist intrigue also helped to
shape his belief that the revolution itself had begun as a conspiracy
of Liberal aristocrats, traitors to their order and their country, who
had subverted the army and suborned the mobs. It had been the
union of men like the duc de la Rochefoucauld, the duc d'Aiguillon,
the vicomte de Noailles, the Lameth brothers and Lafayette, with
the leaders of the Tiers État – Barnave, Target, Mounier, Rabaut
de Saint-Étienne and Adrien Duport – to form the 'Patriotic party',
which had split the privileged orders and made possible the consti-

139. *Ibid.*, p. 147.
140. *Ibid.*, p. 148.
141. *Ibid.*, p. 153.
142. Mitchell, p. 155.
143. Goodwin, pp. 345–6.

tution of the National Assembly.[144] Similarly, Burke saw the nationalization of the church lands not only as an unjustifiable assault on the sacred institution of property held in trust and as the work of atheists, but also as an indirect attack on the nobles who filled the ranks of the upper clergy. The abolition of honorific and hereditary titles, the partial demolition of feudal rights, the dissolution of the provincial estates, the *Parlements* and the Gallican church – all bastions of aristocratic privilege – and the emigration of the nobility also convinced Burke that the chief motive of the revolutionaries was not so much the destruction of Bourbon despotism as the annihilation of the aristocracy.[145] Though critical of the nobility's Anglomania, its patronage of anti-Christian 'philosophy', the dissoluteness of its manners and its social exclusiveness, Burke rejected the accusation that it had 'any considerable share in the oppression of the people', and thought its tenacious defence of its privileges less than shocking. Such faults were, in his opinion, not incorrigible and did not necessitate the toppling of what he described as 'the Corinthian capital of polished society'.[146]

It was an interpretation of the revolution which fitted in with Burke's determination to distinguish the French from both the American and English revolutions, and it had the additional merit of vividly enforcing the solemn warnings which he and his son Richard had already addressed to their patron, Earl Fitzwilliam.[147] Burke's private correspondence with the Whig grandees suggests that he intended the *Reflections* to serve as a political manifesto for the instruction of the aristocratic leaders of the Whig party. What Burke feared in 1790 was that the independence of the Whig party from court or popular influence would be at an end if its leaders surrendered the political initiative to either the Protestant Dissenters or the parliamentary reformers. Just as the French nobility had been betrayed by the Liberal aristocrats, so, Burke thought, might the Whig aristocrats suffer a similar fate, if they were led astray by

144. For the French 'Patriotic party' see G. Lefebvre, *Quatre-Vingt-Neuf* (Paris, 1939), pp. 58–60.
145. 'Its great Object is not . . . the destruction of all absolute Monarchies, but totally to root out that thing called an *Aristocrate* or Nobleman and Gentleman'. Burke to Fitzwilliam, 21 November 1791. Cobban and Smith, vol. 6, p. 451.
146. Burke, pp. 244–5.
147. See particularly the full text of Richard Burke's letter to Fitzwilliam 29 July 1790, WWM, Milton MSS. Burke A iv(f) 71(a), photostat copy, portions of which are omitted in Cobban and Smith, vol. 6, p. 130.

political misfits like Lord Stanhope or intriguing 'speculators' like the Marquess of Lansdowne, or if they allowed Sheridan and Fox to create a new radical diversion in Whig politics.[148] In this sense the *Reflections* were concerned to plead the cause of English Grand Whiggery as the main preservative of the conservative principles of 1688 against infection from the French revolutionary doctrines of 1789. The book was, indeed, not so much an emotional lament for the demise of French nobility and the passing of the 'age of chivalry' as a Cassandra-like warning to the Whig aristocracy to shun all contact with English radical reformers and to repudiate the example set by their French liberal counterparts. Burke's doom-laden prophecies, however, related mainly to France, and this was so when he predicted that, along with 'its natural protectors and guardians' – the nobility and clergy – 'learning itself would be cast into the mire and trodden down under the hoofs of a swinish multitude'.[149] He could hardly have suspected, therefore, that English radicals would hug the unfortunate description to themselves and glory in it.[150]

Though eventually the *Reflections* turned the tide of conservative sentiment against the French revolution both in Britain and in Europe, in the short run it had to face much hostile criticism. The Whig magnates themselves refused to be stampeded – for the time being at least – and Burke's position inside the Whig party declined further. Even worse, the publication of the book did much to facilitate the advent of popular radicalism in Britain, by the controversy it provoked on the first principles of government.

148. Though Fox had adopted a position of studied neutrality towards the French reformers, Burke suspected that he would be overborne by Sheridan and therefore sought Fitzwilliam's help in checking his pro-French sympathies. R. Burke to Fitzwilliam, 29 July 1790. WWM, Milton MSS. Burke A iv(f) 71(a).
149. Burke, p. 173.
150. Burke's opponents always quoted him as having referred to '*the* swinish multitude', whereas he probably had in mind the excesses of the French mob on a particular occasion. *Ibid.*, p. 385.

5 The origins of provincial radicalism, 1790-2

Our business is with the people, and the people's business is to do their own business.

DR JOHN JEBB[1]

The present age will hereafter merit to be called the Age of Reason, and the present generation will appear to the future as the Adam of a new world.

THOMAS PAINE[2]

Much of the complexity of the history of English radicalism in the age of the French revolution arises from the need to depict its development concurrently in different contexts – in the provincial or regional settings that did so much to determine its social and economic objectives, in the metropolitan environment where the London reform societies were under constant surveillance, and in the larger dimension or framework of Anglo-French, Scottish or Irish politics. Both the friends and opponents of the English popular movement in the last decade of the eighteenth century were acutely aware of how changes in the tempo of radical activity in any one of these milieux might react on the political situation in either or both of the others. In framing their policies both radical activists and governmental security agencies had to keep the local, the metropolitan and the international aspects of reform politics constantly under review. The historian should, therefore, aim not only to keep all these three dimensions of evolving radicalism in focus, but also to gauge at each successive stage of development their relative importance.

The benefit of hindsight allows us to appreciate that the 1790s, when English working-class radicalism first emerged as a political force, formed a transitional stage between the pre-revolutionary age,

1. *Works*, ed. J. Disney (3 vols, London, 1787), vol. 1, pp. 199–200.
2. *Rights of Man*, Part II, ed. H. Collins (Harmondsworth, 1969), p. 290.

when most of the extra-parliamentary reform movements were generated in, or focused on, the metropolis, and the nineteenth century, when many of the reform agitations – for the extension of the parliamentary franchise, for the abolition of the Corn Laws, for currency reform or Chartism – were planned, financed and centred in the provinces. Nor was this relative shift of political activity due entirely to the displacement of economic forces and population consequent on the industrial revolution, even though recent research has characterized radical principles and attitudes at the earlier period as 'pre-political' and the society which produced them as pre-industrial'.[3] The greater emphasis given in the 1790s to the vital importance of provincial politics was however, also, the fruit of past experience. The early difficulties of metropolitan radicalism had shown that the acid test of the movement for parliamentary reform was whether or not it could command, not only a secure base of operations in the capital, but also the organized and sustained support of public opinion in the provinces. Experience had proved that the leadership of the Westminster or Middlesex radicals, whose political horizons did not extend much further than the ambit of the Quintuple Alliance,[4] or at most the Home Counties, could not expect to recruit the whole-hearted co-operation of the Yorkshire gentry or the other county 'associators'. The way in which the Rockinghamites had used 'economical reform' to stultify the prospects of effective parliamentary reform had also underlined the dangers of relying on the interested manoeuvres of parliamentary Opposition groups.[5]

These political lessons had first been assimilated by those who had come together to form the Society for Constitutional Information in 1780.[6] From the outset this society had elaborated a more extended concept of political association than that pioneered by Wyvill and both its founder, Major John Cartwright, and Dr Joseph Towers

3. 'Pre-political people' have been described as those 'who have not yet found, or only begun to find, a specific language in which to express their aspirations about the world' and hence lacking in political consciousness. E. J. Hobsbawm, *Primitive Rebels* (Manchester, 1959), p. 2.

4. The Quintuple Alliance was the political union of the cities and counties of the metropolis – London, Westminster, Southwark, Middlesex and Surrey – forged by the radicals in 1781.

5. N. C. Phillips, 'Edmund Burke and the County Movement, 1779–1780', *English Historical Review*, vol. 76 (1961), pp. 254–78.

6. For the formation of the society see C. Wyvill, *Political Papers*, vol. 2, pp. 463–516.

had put the case for bringing the unrepresented manufacturing towns of the Midlands and the North-West within the pale of the constitution.[7] The 'forgotten man' of the pre-reform era – the 'poor labourer and mechanic' – had in fact been remembered in the society's publications and in August 1783 the society had circularized its provincial correspondents, urging them to insert short essays in the country newspapers addressed to 'the collective body of the People descriptive of their primary rights as commoners' . . . 'in language adapted to the comprehension of the unlearned, and yet demonstrative to the most enlightened'.[8] It had gone even further by recommending its provincial supporters to combat the local powers of corporation monopolists and other vested interests and to form parochial societies in order to forward petitions for 'Parliamentary Reformation' to Westminster.[9] The intention not only to mobilize regional opinion, but also to deploy popular pressure on the nerve-centres of politics in the capital was evident.

The example set by the Constitutional Society had been followed by the London Revolution Society in 1789, when its committee had promoted the establishment of affiliated societies in provincial urban centres, whose union might be strengthened by correspondence.[10] After the narrow failure of Beaufoy's second motion for repeal of the Test and Corporation Acts in May 1789 the London Application Committee of the Protestant Dissenting Deputies, had also been at pains to encourage the formation of regional boards of deputies of the three denominations and, in 1790, it had afforced its own membership by delegates from the provinces.[11] The impressive body of political support which had thus been built up in the regions for the cause of repeal in 1790 had, unfortunately, produced a local backlash of High Anglican 'alarm' which, in the form of 'Church and King' clubs had sparked off the initial phase of Tory reaction. When, early in 1792, the Scottish shoemaker Thomas Hardy founded the first metropolitan society of working men – the London Corresponding Society – its very name indicated the priority it attached to the forging of links with similar reform societies which had already

7. E. C. Black, *The Association: British Extraparliamentary Political Organization, 1769–1793* (Cambridge, Mass., 1963), pp. 191–2.

8. SCI, *Constitutional Tracts*, vol. 1, pp. 57–8.

9. *Ibid.*

10. *Abstract of the History and Proceedings of the Revolution Society in London* (1789).

11. U. Henriques, *Religious Toleration in England, 1787–1833* (London, 1961), pp. 63–5.

made their appearance in the larger urban centres of industrial England.

These provincial societies owed their origin less to the stimulus of the French revolution than to the social and political tensions generated in their own local environments. Their rapid proliferation and political notoriety were initially due to Painite propaganda, orchestrated by the Society for Constitutional Information, but also to the subsequent attempt of the Royal Proclamation of 21 May 1792 against seditious writings and publications to depict their activities as subversive. Attention will, therefore, be concentrated, in this chapter, on the origins and organization of radical societies in the three regions dominated by Manchester, Sheffield and Norwich in the effort to ascertain whether they deserved their contemporary reputation as the 'pace-makers' of 'English Jacobinism'.[12]

When, after his acquittal in April 1794 on a trumped-up charge of conspiracy to subvert the constitution, Thomas Walker, leading Manchester cotton merchant and fustian manufacturer, looked back in wry dismay on the part he had played in local and national politics, he attributed the wreck of his private fortunes and the discomfiture of the radical cause in Manchester, among other reasons, to the 'want of a complete and universal system of public education'.[13] In his view this defect had made the mass of the local population and especially the ignorant and misguided handloom weavers not only 'the dupes of their oppressors' – the 'Church and King' reactionaries – but hostile to their real friends, the radical parliamentary reformers. It had also made 'the half-informed middling classes believe that their social superiors' – the local gentry, magistrates and Anglican clergy – had 'the exclusive monopoly of political knowledge', thus confirming their habitual attitude of deference to established authority and timid conformity. Lastly, it had discouraged 'the most ardent and enlightened men of the nation' from further political involvement because hard experience had convinced them that 'the seed of knowledge is sown upon barren ground; they doubt of its growth, they despair of seeing any effect from their exertions; and they are unwilling to become the victims of those, whom they are labouring to serve'.[14] It was, indeed, awareness of this

12. G. A. Williams, *Artisans and Sans-Culottes: Popular Movements in France and Britain during the French Revolution* (London, 1968), p. 64.

13. T. Walker, *A Review of some of the Political Events which have occurred in Manchester during the last five years* (London, 1794), p. 127.

14. *Ibid.*, p. 127.

serious obstacle in their way which induced middle-class critics of the status quo, like Walker, to establish provincial societies to press for radical parliamentary reform and ultimately to sponsor the growth of clubs of working men – largely as an experiment in their political education. Such men recognized in Paine's *Rights of Man* the astringent and challenging gospel ideally suited for a new type of democratic evangelism.

In considering the origins of Manchester radical politics in the 1790s, something must first be said of the town's special economic status in the opening years of the industrial revolution, the nature of its local government and the social, intellectual and religious attitudes of this rapidly expanding 'provincial metropolis'. By the last decade of the eighteenth century Manchester had, indeed, come to exercise in an extensive region of the North-West what T. S. Ashton rightly described as 'quasi-metropolitan functions'.[15] The region in question was wider than Lancashire alone and extended to Carlisle and Kendal in the north and to Macclesfield and Congleton in the south. Situated at the junction of the rivers Irk and Irwell – the latter a major tributary of the Mersey – Manchester was also, for geographical reasons, the chief road centre of south-east Lancashire and north-east Cheshire. Both road and river communications in this area had, moreover, been vastly improved and extended during the whole course of the century. The most vital development, however, had been the building by James Brindley of the third Duke of Bridgewater's canal (1759–64) between his coal mine at Worsley and Manchester, which by marginally increasing the town's supply of coal and halving its delivery costs, considerably benefited the poorer section of the community. The extension of this canal, in 1776, to Runcorn at the mouth of the Mersey, not only enabled West Indian and North American cotton to be imported more cheaply (after the War of Independence) to south-east Lancashire via Liverpool, but also linked the Manchester region to the Midlands market by way of the Grand Trunk canal running southwards from Runcorn (which was itself completed in 1777).[16]

Manchester's industrial and commercial importance in the late eighteenth century as the centre of this thriving regional economy arose partly from the fact that most of its textile manufacturers still

15. T. S. Ashton, *An Economic History of England: the Eighteenth Century* (London, 1955), p. 96.
16. W. H. Chaloner, 'Manchester in the latter half of the Eighteenth Century', *Bulletin of the John Rylands Library*, vol. 42 (1959), p. 46.

employed domestic workers over a wide area, supplying them with raw materials and yarns, partly because they themselves specialized in the finishing processes of bleaching, dyeing and calico printing, and in the production of fustians.[17] Ever since the early seventeenth century the weaving of woollens in Manchester had declined and had been replaced by the manufacture of mixed fabrics, known as smallwares and fustians, in both of which the warp was of linen yarn. Whereas in small wares – tapes, laces and garterings – the weft was usually worsted, in fustians – mostly stout hard-wearing cloth – the weft was regularly of cotton.[18] The fustian manufacture, however, was not by any means confined to Manchester, but extended over the central part of south Lancashire. From 1760 onwards its products had found remunerative export markets in Italy, Germany, the North American colonies, Africa, Asia Minor and even China.[19] These results had been achieved with the help of technological inventions in the carding, spinning and weaving processes which did not immediately require the application of steam power nor manufacture in urban-based factories.[20]

Just as, in the late 1780s, the manufacture of textiles in Manchester remained at the 'pre-industrial' level, so, in the larger economic region of the North-West, the industrial structure was considerably diversified. Despite the predominance of cotton in the textile industry, the manufacture of linen and silk in this area remained important, while the ascendancy of the textile trades over other industries was not as pronounced as it became in the nineteenth century. The town's main supplies of coal came, not from Worsley, but from widely dispersed coalfields on its periphery, near Oldham, Ashton, Hyde, Newton and Denton.[21] Iron foundries had been established by

17. The number of fustian manufacturers in Manchester and Salford rose from 81 in 1773 to 184 in 1788. A. P. Wadsworth and Julia de L. Mann, *The Cotton Trade and Industrial Lancashire, 1600–1780* (Manchester, 1931), p. 252.

18. G. H. Tupling, 'Medieval and Early Modern Manchester', in *Manchester and its Region* (Manchester, 1962), p. 124.

19. A. Redford, *Manchester Merchants and Foreign Trade*, vol. 1: *1794–1858* (Manchester, 1934), *passim*.

20. Both Hargreaves's 'spinning jenny' and Crompton's 'mule' were hand-operated and were used by domestic workers in their own cottages. In 1792 there were only two cotton-spinning mills in or near Manchester. By 1802 there were fifty-two. W. H. Chaloner, 'Robert Owen, Peter Drinkwater and the early factory system in Manchester, 1788–1800', *Bulletin of the John Rylands Library*, vol. 37 (1954–5), pp. 82–94.

21. J. Aikin, *A Description of the Country from thirty to forty miles round Manchester* (1795).

John Wilkinson, Priestley's brother-in-law, at Warrington, and both Oldham and Stockport had flourishing hat industries. As cotton spinning became mechanized the manufacture of textile machinery proliferated, along with engineering, paper-making, and the tin plate industry.[22] Glass and copper works were located at St Helens and the salt mines of Cheshire had long been famous. Some, if not all, of these trades used Manchester as a distributing centre.

This commercial and industrial expansion had been accompanied by a corresponding increase in Manchester's population. According to Dr Chaloner's calculations, the population of the civil township had risen from about 10,000 in 1717, to 17,000 in 1758, 24,000 in 1773, 42,821 in 1788 and 70,409 in 1801, at the time of the first national census.[23] This increase had been the product of short-distance migration from the surrounding countryside, improved food supplies and medical care, immigration from Scotland and above all Ireland, a high birthrate and the attractive power of high wages and steady employment.[24]

The town had yet another characteristic that had redounded to its economic advantage in the eighteenth century – its lack of corporate status. This meant that it had no oligarchical corporation exercising economic privileges denied to outsiders. As such it had attracted both French Huguenots, who 'had first introduced the cotton manufacture into Lancashire' and large numbers of industrious English and Scottish Protestant Dissenters and low-paid Irish, mostly from Ulster. In default of a municipal corporation, the town was dependent for its government on the relic of medieval private jurisdiction in the form of a Court Leet – itself an amalgamation of the Portmoot with the Court Baron.[25] This court was presided over by the steward of the lord of the manor – at that time a member of the Moseley family. This court met only twice yearly – after Michaelmas and Easter – when it was attended by the burgesses and resident householders. At each session twelve or more burgesses were designated by the steward to serve as the jury – in which was

22. W. H. Chaloner, 'The Birth of Modern Manchester', in *Manchester and its Region*, p. 134.

23. Chaloner, 'Manchester in the latter half of the Eighteenth Century', pp. 41–2.

24. A. Redford, *Labour Migration in England, 1800–1850* (Manchester, 1926); Chaloner, 'The Birth of Modern Manchester', p. 134. In 1792 the minimum wage paid to skilled workers in Manchester was said to be as high as 57s. or 58s. a week. Ashton, p. 232.

25. *Manchester and its Region*, p. 126.

vested the power of making by-laws to regulate the market, maintain highways, control traffic and settle civil disputes. Every October this jury also appointed numerous unpaid officers with picturesque titles but obsolete functions.[26] The chief officer was the borough reeve who alone could convene public meetings and who exercised mainly honorific quasi-mayoral duties with few executive powers. Together with the two chief constables, however, the borough reeve was responsible for public order and could enrol for this purpose large numbers of 'special' constables, sworn in by the county magistrates. He also had the disposal of certain charities.[27] Despite the creation of a body of Cleansing and Lighting Commissioners in 1765 empowered by act of Parliament to provide more satisfactory local services and a second Improvement Act in 1775, nothing effective was done either by the manorial jurymen or the statutory commissioners to provide Manchester with the sanitary or housing facilities so badly needed by its less fortunate inhabitants.[28]

The stirrings of discontent with the administrative inertia and Tory conservatism of the local governing hierarchy first became evident among a group of wealthier and more cultured merchants, doctors, lawyers, scientists and educationists, who, from 1781, had been conferring together weekly in the Manchester Literary and Philosophical Society.[29] This had been founded by Dr Thomas Percival, FRS – the first pupil to be enrolled at the famous Dissenting academy at Warrington – who, after studying medicine at the universities of Edinburgh and Leyden, had returned to Manchester in 1767. Here, as physician to Manchester Infirmary, he had taken an active interest in the welfare of the multiplying artisan population and had been mainly instrumental in the creation of the Manchester Board of Health. In its first phase the society was dominated by the friends and associates of Percival, mostly members of the medical profession.[30] From 1794, when Robert Owen introduced John Dalton to the society – as a former tutor in mathematics and natural

26. One of the few paid officers, the 'catchpole', collected fines imposed by the Court Leet. Several 'burleymen', or by-lawmen assisted the constables in seeing that the by-laws were observed.

27. Walker, p. 23.

28. A. Redford, *History of Local Government in Manchester* (London, 1939), vol. 1, p. 192.

29. W. H. Brindley, 'The Manchester Literary and Philosophical Society', *Journal of the Royal Institute of Chemistry* (1955), pp. 62–9.

30. At this early period, despite its title, the group formed what was virtually a medical club and served as the antecedent of the Manchester Medical Society.

philosophy at the recently founded Manchester Academy – it became mainly scientific in character. Its most distinguished honorary members were Benjamin Franklin, Lavoisier, Priestley and Volta. Among its comparatively restricted membership, the society found room, however, for local merchants, reformers and publicists of the stamp of Thomas Walker, Thomas Cooper, and Matthew Falkner who were to form the radical elite of the future. Just as the physicians and doctors in the society devoted themselves to the cause of public health and welfare, so the successful merchants and industrialists who were their associates turned their energies to the cause of municipal reform and in 1787 led the local crusade against Negro slavery. Improvement was on its way and reform was in the air.

The man who was to achieve notoriety as Manchester's leading radical, Thomas Walker, had won wide local popularity and national recognition as spokesman for the textile interest in Lancashire and had, incidentally, effected close personal friendships with the leading Foxite Whigs, by the important part he had played in the defeat of Pitt's proposed tax on fustians and his propositions for reciprocal trade with Ireland in the spring of 1785.[31] He had gained further political prominence by his chairmanship of the local anti-slavery committee in 1787 – an initiative which brought him election, along with his friends and associates, Thomas Cooper and Matthew Falkner, to the Society of Constitutional Information in the spring of 1788.[32] The Regency crisis of that year and the celebration by the Manchester Revolution Society of the centenary of 1688 reinforced Walker's Whig associations without in any way compromising his political independence or personal credit. Though not without enemies, his public activities had so far not involved him in any serious breach with other prominent figures in Manchester's community politics.[33]

The crucial controversy, however, which was to split the community into opposing political factions of die-hard conservatives and

31. F. Knight, *The strange case of Thomas Walker: Ten Years in the Life of a Manchester Radical* (London, 1957), ch. 3.
32. Cooper became a member on 8 February, Walker on 1 February and Falkner on 13 June 1788. PRO TS 11/961/3507.
33. In November 1790, while presiding over a festive dinner of the local Revolution Society as borough reeve, Walker fell foul of a Tory attorney, William Roberts, an American *émigré* barrister, who had settled in Manchester. A scurrilous handbill written by Roberts and printed by Harrop, the Tory printer, led to a libel action in which Walker was vindicated in March 1791. Knight, ch. 5.

determined reformers, was provoked by the agitation in support of Beaufoy's and Fox's motions for the repeal of the Test and Corporation Acts in 1789 and 1790. Nowhere in the country had that campaign been so highly organized or the claims of the Unitarians been formulated so uncompromisingly as in Manchester. Nowhere, perhaps, was repeal so stoutly resisted or, with the exception of Birmingham, was its failure so vociferously acclaimed. During the campaign both sides had resorted to tactics which only inflamed their mutual hostility – the Dissenters by exerting collective pressure through a regional board of deputies of the three denominations and the exaction of electoral pledges from parliamentary candidates; the Anglicans by political sermons, inflammatory handbills and public meetings to which their opponents were not invited and from which they were forced to retreat in confusion.[34] This hardening of attitudes persisted when the Anglicans celebrated the rejection of repeal in March 1790 by organizing a local 'Church and King' club and when the lay leaders of Dissent, by way of response, helped to establish the Manchester Constitutional Society in October 1790.[35] Henceforth the resentment of the lay Protestant Dissenters at their exclusion from the full range of individual liberties and their disillusionment with a corrupt Parliament and a conservative ministry made many of them change their priorities from 'participation' to parliamentary reform.[36] Their opponents were to entrench themselves in defence of the establishment in church and state and to interpret radical claims to effective citizenship as a challenge to their religion and an assault on the fabric of the constitution. 'Alarmism' – the tocsin of the conservationists – had thus already been sounded in the provinces while Burke's *Reflections* were still unpublished, and while the sectarians were still being portrayed in Anglican sermons and handbills as seventeenth-century King-killers

34. Walker was severe in his subsequent condemnation of political sermons: 'the doctrines delivered to an ignorant public from the pulpit are not to be repelled by opposite doctrines, like fair public or printed arguments, but are like wounds in the dark which become fatal before a remedy can be procured'. Walker, p. 15. After retreating from the Anglican meeting of 3 March 1790, Walker and his friends challenged its legality, since only the borough reeve had the right to summon a general meeting of the inhabitants. *Ibid.*, pp. 11–14.

35. The first meeting of the 'Church and King' club was held on 13 March 1790. Initially it was not much more than a dining club, meeting annually on the anniversary of the defeat of the repeal agitation.

36. R. W. Davis, *Dissent in Politics, 1780–1830: The Political Life of William Smith, M.P.* (London, 1971), pp. 51–2.

and Levellers rather than as Jacobin atheists and republicans.[37]

It was hardly surprising that the initiative in establishing the Manchester Constitutional Society should have fallen to Thomas Walker. His initial interest in parliamentary reform had been stimulated by his early perusal of Burgh's *Political Disquisitions*;[38] his conviction of the necessity for Manchester to have its own separate representation at Westminster had been confirmed by his difficulties in opposing the fustian tax, and his sense of the timeliness and, indeed, urgency of the question stemmed from the rejection of the Dissenting case for relief and the example of France. His most active assistant was his close friend Thomas Cooper, barrister, chemist and member of a Bolton calico-printing firm.[39] The Declaration of Principles, dated 5 October 1790, published by the society as a test for the admission of prospective members, reflected the views both of Walker, as a Foxite Whig with liberal sympathies, and of Cooper, as a Unitarian publicist with radical leanings. The organization of the society was also strongly reminiscent of that of the London Society for Constitutional Information, of which both had been members since 1788. Its subsequent repute as a fomenter of radicalism in Manchester should not mislead us as to its initial objectives, which were confined to moderate parliamentary reform. It is worth remembering that Walker had only recently been elected borough reeve for the ensuing year and would not have wished, as Manchester's chief citizen, to compromise the independence or dignity of the office by seeking reform by other than legal and constitutional methods. His position as an Anglican was also some guarantee that he would not sponsor some of the more extreme demands of the Dissenters. The declared political creed of the society was a characteristic blend of Lockian doctrines of consent, Utilitarian assumptions as to the ends of civil society and Foxite notions of the proper extent of the state's powers in the field of religious belief.[40] Its positive objective was stated briefly as the necessity of 'a full, fair, and adequate Representation', combined with the shortening of the duration

37. The standing toast of the society was, at this time, 'Church and King, and down with the Rump'. Walker, p. 15.

38. Walker referred to Burgh as 'an able writer, endeared to me, as the instructor of my youth'. *Ibid.*, p. 5.

39. D. Malone, *The Public Life of Thomas Cooper, 1783–1839* (New Haven, Conn., 1926). L. S. Marshal's *The Development of Public Opinion in Manchester, 1780–1820* (Syracuse, N.Y., 1946), is not very helpful.

40. Cf. Article 5: 'That *Actions* only, and not *Opinions*, are the proper object of civil jurisdiction.' Walker, p. 17.

of parliaments.[41] There was no mention of the radical panaceas of universal suffrage or annual parliaments.

Its constitution provided that the society was to meet once a month in the Bridgewater Arms in Manchester, and provided for the holding of an annual dinner every 14 July, which indicated its pro-French sympathies.[42] The conditions attached to membership were the payment of an annual subscription of half a guinea (which automatically excluded working men), election by ballot after being proposed and seconded at an earlier meeting, and assent to the society's Declaration of Principles. Meetings were chaired by a president, elected for each monthly session, though the secretary and treasurer were elected annually. The secretary was empowered to correspond in the name of the society 'with every similar institution in this, and, if need be, in any other kingdom' and could convene special meetings if requested to do so by twelve members.[43] Any publication sponsored by the society had to be approved by a majority of members at two successive meetings and signed by the secretary.

Though no firm figures are available, the evidence suggests that the society numbered between fifty and one hundred members once it had established itself.[44] They formed a remarkably homogeneous group – some were related to each other, others were close business associates or fellow members of the Manchester Literary and Philosophical Society, and there was a strong Dissenting element with a preponderance of Unitarians. Nearly half of the members can be identified as merchants – some, like the brothers Thomas and Richard Walker, being of considerable wealth. Over 20 per cent were manufacturers – including such local notabilities as Samuel Jackson and George Phillips. The remainder were professional men – barristers, attorneys, doctors, Dissenting ministers and schoolmasters. Two members – Matthew Falkner and Samuel Birch – were booksellers and printers.

The second regional capital in which working-class radicals were to step into the shoes of middle-class reformers was the ancient

41. *Ibid.*, Articles 6, 7. See also P. Handforth, 'Manchester Radical Politics, 1789–1794' in *Transactions of the Lancashire and Cheshire Antiquarian Society*, vol. 66 (1956), pp. 90–1.

42. *Rules and Orders of the Manchester Constitutional Society, Instituted October 1790* (Manchester, 1791). The celebration of the fall of the Bastille was, however, discontinued after July 1791.

43. *Ibid.*

44. A. V. Mitchell, 'Radicalism and repression in the north of England, 1791–1797'. Unpublished MA thesis (Manchester, 1958), p. 55.

cathedral city of Norwich. In the seventeenth century this had reputedly been the second largest city in the country. In the 1780s, however, its population of approximately 35,000 had ceased to expand and had already been outstripped by that of both Manchester and Liverpool.[45] Despite this, between the end of the war with the American colonies and the beginning of hostilities with revolutionary France, Norwich had reached a peak of industrial and commercial affluence as yet undimmed by the difficulties that were to compromise its continuance in the nineteenth century. Like Manchester, Norwich was a textile manufacturing centre on whose capitalist master combers the domestic spinners of the countryside for twenty miles around were dependent for the supply of their yarn.[46] Once the yarn had been spun it was sold by the master combers to the merchant-manufacturers who employed domestic workers both in the city and in the surrounding villages to weave it into cloth for piece-work wages. The finishing processes of dressing and dyeing were completed in the city and the final products were sold at home and particularly abroad by the merchant-manufacturers. The outstanding prosperity of the worsted trade of Norwich in the eighteenth century derived from several sources: the readily accessible supplies in Lincolnshire and Leicestershire of the long-staple wool needed for the manufacture of fine worsteds;[47] the relatively low wages earned in the first half of the eighteenth century by the Norwich weavers, which were often 40 per cent lower than those of weavers in the Exeter region;[48] the legislative embargoes placed on the export of wool and on the importation of printed cotton cloth; and the 'natural' protection afforded by the high quality of the heavy worsted cloth (camlets) and fine fabrics on which the reputations of the local manufacturers rested so securely.[49] It has been calculated

45. In 1801 the census returns put the population of Norwich at 36,832. J. K. Edwards, 'The decline of the Norwich textiles industry', *Yorkshire Bulletin of Economic and Social Research*, vol. 16 (1964), p. 34.

46. *Ibid.*, p. 35.

47. B. Green and M. R. Young, *Norwich: the Growth of a City* (Norwich, 1968), p. 26.

48. Partly for this reason, Norwich stuffs displaced Exeter serges in the first half of the eighteenth century in Spain, Portugal, Holland and Germany. W. G. Hoskins, *Industry, Trade and People in Exeter, 1688–1800* (Manchester, 1935).

49. Large quantities of fine camlets were bought by the East India Company for export to China and India. The main 'quality' products of the Norwich textile trade were calimancoes, camlets, camletees, crapes, satins and bombazines. The Norwich industry was also famous for its shawls and the superiority of its dyeing techniques.

that during the last two decades of the century these various processes gave employment directly or indirectly to about 100,000 persons in and around Norwich and produced goods to an annual value 'greatly in excess of £1 million'.[50]

Nevertheless, even on the crest of its achievement, the city's economy was doubly vulnerable. It was too dependent on a single dominant industry, and that industry's export trade with Continental Europe and the Far East was exposed to all the hazards of trade discrimination and the dangers presented by open warfare.[51] Though successful efforts were made at the time to diversify the city's economy by developing the local leather and brewing industries and by extending the scope of banking and insurance concerns,[52] Norwich's economic prospects were still too closely associated with a branch of manufacture the domestic demand for whose products had already been threatened, though not as yet seriously compromised, by machine-made cotton goods from Lancashire and cheaper woollens from Yorkshire.

Norwich differed from Manchester, however, administratively and politically, since it had both a municipal corporation and parliamentary representation at Westminster. These privileges and the existence in the city of several congregations of wealthy and influential Dissenters largely determined the character of its local politics before and after 1789. Eighteenth-century municipal corporations tended to be exclusively Anglican in composition, oligarchical in form and corrupt in the practices they exploited in parliamentary elections. Norwich was an exception to the rule. Bicameral in form – with a Court of Mayoralty balanced, and occasionally opposed, by a Court of Common Council – the corporation at this period reflected most shades of secular and religious opinion in the city. The Court of Mayoralty consisted of a mayor, chosen annually in May by the aldermen from their two most senior colleagues, two

50. Of those directly employed 60,000 were spinners and 8000 were weavers. Edwards, 'The decline of the Norwich textiles industry', p. 38.

51. The main European outlets were with Holland, Spain, Italy, Germany, Russia, Sweden and Norway.

52. The most famous banking firm was that started in 1775 by the Quaker family of Gurney, whose wealth was based on the worsted trade. J. K. Edwards, 'The Gurneys and the Norwich Clothing Trade in the Eighteenth Century', *Journal of the Friends' Historical Society*, vol. 50 (1963), pp. 134–52. The Norwich General Assurance Office (1792) and the Norwich Union Fire Insurance Society (1797) were both founded by a wine merchant and banker, Thomas Bignold, who had settled in the city in 1783.

sheriffs, one elected by the court and the other by the resident freemen in August, and twenty-four aldermen periodically elected for life by the resident freemen in their wards. The sixty members of the Court of Common Council were chosen annually in 'cleansing' or Passion Week in a process of indirect election by twelve 'nominees' who were themselves elected (three for each of the four wards) by the resident freemen.[53]

Although the members of the Court of Mayoralty were mainly Anglicans, they made no attempt before 1801, and then for the last time, to exclude known Dissenters from the Court of Common Council, under the terms of the Corporation Act.[54] Equally the local Dissenters, if and when elected, had no qualms about accepting office either as councillors or aldermen. Even before the abolition of the Test and Corporation Acts in 1828 several members of the Unitarian congregation of the Octagon Chapel in Norwich had served as mayor.[55] With religious differences excluded from municipal politics, church and Dissent had combined to support the same corporation candidate in parliamentary elections against a variety of Independent opposition candidates.

Norwich was one of the largest 'freeman' boroughs in the country, its wide franchise being vested in all its freemen, resident and non-resident, and since it also ranked as a county, in the forty-shilling freeholders.[56] In 1789 the city was represented at Westminster by William Windham and Henry Hobart. Windham, who later became a Burkian 'Alarmist' in reaction against the French revolution, had been one of the few Fox–North coalition candidates to obtain a parliamentary seat in the General Election of 1784.[57] Hobart had twice successfully contested the other Norwich seat against Sir Thomas Beevor in the by-elections of 1786 and 1787 – both of which had been fought on local issues. Though public

53. S. and B. Webb, *English Local Government from the Revolution to the Municipal Corporations Act* (1906–29), vol. 3, pp. 529–58. B. D. Hayes, 'Politics in Norfolk, 1750–1832'. Unpublished PhD thesis, Cambridge (1957), ch. 2.

54. Davis, p. 124.

55. R. K. Webb, *Harriet Martineau: A Radical Victorian* (London, 1960), p. 54. John and Edward Taylor, *History of the Octagon Chapel, Norwich* (London, 1808).

56. Davis, p. 120. Non-resident freemen were genuine freemen who had left the constituency to reside elsewhere.

57. William Windham (1750–1810) was elected as MP for Norwich on 5 April 1784. Re-elected in the General Election of 1790 and again in 1794 despite his acceptance of office as Secretary at War with a seat in Pitt's cabinet. He successfully defended his seat again in 1796.

interest in municipal and parliamentary elections had thus been sustained at a high level before 1789, it is remarkable that Norwich had displayed few signs of that early urban radicalism which had already shown itself not only in the metropolis but also in some of the other larger freeman boroughs, such as Worcester, Newcastle on Tyne, Bedford and Nottingham.[58] The abuse of the non-resident freeman vote, the ability of the corporation to multiply the number of honorary freemen with parliamentary voting rights, and the ruinous expense of contesting the local seats were, however, aspects of the electoral process which were increasingly to engage the attention of would-be reformers in Norwich.

The most potent force in the political and cultural life of Norwich towards the end of the eighteenth century was, however, Protestant Dissent. This was the influence which virtually shaped that type of intellectual Jacobinism for which the City was soon to be famous, which gave encouragement and practical assistance in the formation of working-class political clubs in and around Norwich in 1791 and 1792, and which proved to be the sheet anchor of unrepentant local radicalism in the age of conservative reaction and repression.[59]

In one sense, of course, the Dissenting elite of Norwich had reasonable grounds for satisfaction. They had a firm hold on positions of influence inside the municipal corporation, with a commanding voice in the management of the booming worsted industry and profitable banking concerns and an assured and respected place in the cultivated society in this East Anglian provincial capital. The close community of scholarly divines, distinguished scientists, literary innovators, agricultural improvers and attractive 'bluestockings' which nurtured the talents of George Borrow, Crabb Robinson and Harriet Martineau did not merit the latter's waspish aspersions on its alleged petty pretensions and ill-concealed provincialism.[60] The 'shallow men, pedantic women, and conceited lads'[61]

58. For the significance and limited objectives of this type of urban radicalism see J. Brooke, *The House of Commons, 1754–1790: Introductory Survey* (Oxford, 1968), p. 25.

59. Perhaps the best statement of the political and social attitudes of the Norwich Dissenting intelligentsia is R. Dinmore Jnr's *An Exposition of the Principles of the English Jacobins with strictures on the political conduct of Charles James Fox, William Pitt and Edmund Burke*, 3rd ed. (Norwich, 1797).

60. R. K. Webb, p. 56.

61. H. Martineau, *Autobiography*, vol. 1 (1877), p. 298. She wrote of Dr Enfield, the influential minister of the Octagon Chapel and founder of the Norwich Speculative Society, as a 'feeble and superficial man of letters'; Sir

of whom she later wrote in her *Autobiography* formed in fact a talented, earnest and brilliant coterie which came as near as any other in England (except perhaps the members of the Birmingham Lunar Society) to one of those provincial academies of contemporary France which did so much to endow the eighteenth-century Enlightenment with its humanity and social significance. A society in which Sir James Mackintosh, Robert Southey, Dr Parr, William Godwin and Mary Wollstonecraft could find pleasure and stimulus almost rivalled that other and more metropolitan Dissenting congregation of Dr Price at Newington Green.[62]

Although the Baptist congregations of St Paul's and St Mary's chapels were to acquire in 1788 and 1790 in the Reverend Mark Wilks and the Reverend Joseph Kinghorn notable ministers who were to leave a deep impression – the one on the political, the other on the religious life of the city[63] – the undoubted leadership of Norwich Dissent had fallen, since the mid century, to the Presbyterian ministers and deacons of that exquisite Octagon Chapel described by John Wesley as 'the most elegant one in Europe'.[64] Built between 1754 and 1756 by the gifted local architect, Thomas Ivory, for the Arian divine and Hebrew scholar, Dr John Taylor, the chapel had a succession of ministers who brought with them from Warrington Academy the cosmopolitan learning, the doctrines of materialism and necessity and the cult of seventeenth-century republicanism which were the distinguishing features of eighteenth-century rational Dissent. The most eminent of these ministers was Dr William Enfield, who from 1770 to 1783 had been Rector of the Academy and from 1774 tutor in natural philosophy and mathematics.[65] His ministry at the Octagon Chapel from 1785 to 1797 was marked by the cordial relations he established not only with other Dissenting ministers but with the Anglican bishop, Dr Bagot,

---

James Edward Smith, the eminent botanist, as 'weak and irritable'; and Dr Alderson, the father of Mrs Opie, as 'solemn and sententious'. Borrow was undoubtedly one of her 'conceited lads' and Mrs Barbauld one of her 'pedantic women'.

62. 'The worthies of Norwich', *Edinburgh Review*, vol. 150 (1879, July–October), pp. 41–76. Godwin, Mary Wollstonecraft and Mrs Barbauld were also habitués at Newington. C. Tomalin, *The Life and Death of Mary Wollstonecraft* (London, 1974), pp. 75–8.

63. Sarah Wilks, *Memoirs of the Rev. Mark Wilks* (London, 1821).

64. J. and E. Taylor.

65. H. McLachlan, *The Unitarian Movement in the Religious Life of England* (London, 1934), vol. 1, pp. 89–90.

and the cathedral clergy.[66] His colleague, from early 1787, was the Reverend Pendlebury Houghton, a former pupil and assistant tutor in *belles lettres* at Warrington, an eloquent preacher and able coadjutor.[67] Several of the most distinguished members of the congregation at the Octagon Chapel – the hymn-writer John Taylor, grandson of its founder, William Taylor, the noted Germanist, and Dr Francis Sayers, poet and author of *The Dramatic Sketches of Northern Mythology* (1790) – had also felt the influence of Warrington in their youth. The two latter had been pupils of the school at Palgrave in Suffolk conducted by the Reverend Rochemount Barbauld – a former Warrington student and husband of Anna Letitia, the gifted educationist and minor poet, herself the daughter of Dr John Aikin, one-time principal tutor at Warrington and personal friend of Priestley.[68]

A frequent visitor to Norwich, Mrs Barbauld was a devoted friend of the two chief literary hostesses of the day – both members of the Octagon congregation – Susannah, the charming and cultivated wife of John Taylor, the hymn-writer; and the vivacious Amelia Alderson, future wife of the Cornish painter Opie, poetess and sentimental novelist.[69] Mrs Barbauld's niece Lucy Aikin gives us a brief vignette of the group: 'My youth', she says,

was spent among the disciples or fellow labourers of Price or Priestley, the descendants of Dr. John Taylor, the Arian, or in the society of that most amiable of men, Dr. Enfield. Amongst these there was no rigorism. Dancing, cards, the theatres were all held lawful in moderation: in manners the Free Dissenters, as they were called, came much nearer the church than to their own stricter brethren, yet in doctrine, no sect departed so far from the Establishment.[70]

66. One of the ways in which Enfield consolidated his friendly contacts with the cathedral clergy was in the fortnightly tea-drinking sessions of the Norwich Speculative Society which he founded in November 1790. W. Taylor, *Collected Works of Dr. Francis Sayers* (Norwich, 1823), biographical introduction, p. lxii. See also A. D. Bayne, *A Comprehensive History of Norwich* (London, 1869), p. 299.

67. McLachlan, vol. 1, p. 90.

68. *Ibid.*, vol. 1, pp. 280–3. By September 1791, however, Sayers, under the influence of Burke, had come to the conclusion that 'a loyal subject should lean to the religion of the magistrate' and had become 'a frequenter of cathedral worship'. Taylor, *Collected Works*, p. lxvi.

69. For Mrs Opie, see Janet Ross, *Three Generations of Englishwomen* (London, 1888), and C. L. Brightwell, *Memorials of the Life of Amelia Opie*, 2nd ed. (Norwich, 1854).

70. McLachlan, vol. 1, p. 285.

Norwich Protestant Dissent, however, was more tolerant in religion than in politics. From being strenuous Foxites, its members were to become enthusiastic champions of the French revolution and committed patrons of local radicalism.

The first and parent reform society to be established in Norwich after 1789 – its local Revolution Society – was not, as at Manchester, the result of any polarization of opposing political groups engendered by the repeal agitation, nor can it be attributed, as it could be at Sheffield, to the economic discontents of artisans employed in depressed or dislocated local industries. The Norwich Revolution Society was indeed very properly so named, for it was either the aftermath of the East Anglian centenary celebrations of the English revolution of 1688, or the response to the first anniversary of the fall of the Bastille. In the absence of any specific documentary evidence as to the exact date of its foundation, some doubt remains whether 1688 or 1789 provided the initial impulse.[71] The society's Whiggish political principles and membership and its customary celebration of the fall of the Bastille in imitation of the London Revolution Society suggest, however, an English rather than a French derivation. An assertion to the contrary in the Home Office papers made at the height of the Alarmist scare in November 1792 can only be interpreted as an effort to discredit the society with the authorities.[72]

Coke of Norfolk and the strong Dissenting element in the Norwich corporation ensured, in fact, that the centenary of 1688 in East Anglia was observed with the proper solemnity and enthusiasm. At Holkam Hall a vast and magnificent evening fête was held by Mr and Mrs Coke on 5 November attended by 'a thousand persons of the first distinction'. A firework display on the lawn of the north front, a concert provided by Italian musicians, a ball commencing at 9 p.m., a supper for 360 guests served after 2 a.m. in the dining, audit and billiard rooms, and the illumination of the Egyptian hall provided suitable entertainment for the local Grand Whiggery. A splendid transparency over the door of the saloon proclaiming 'Liberty is our Cause' alluded perhaps to the constitutional liberties

71. Hayes, p. 236, takes the view that the society was not 'a survival of 1788' and that it was not in existence in 1790.

72. Robert Alderson to E. Nepean, endorsed 17 Nov. 1792. 'The original club which is now held at the Bell Inn on Hog Hill was instituted to celebrate the French Revolution.' It is fair to say, however, that by November 1792 the society had adopted virtually French revolutionary political principles. *Norfolk Chronicle and Norwich Gazette*, 10 Nov. 1792.

still to be won rather than those established or preserved one hundred years earlier.[73]

In Norwich the civic dignitaries, the 'populace' and a representative gathering of prominent citizens marked the occasion each in its own way. As the *Norfolk Chronicle and Norwich Gazette* of 8 November 1788 reported: 'The city guns and St. Peter's delightful bells ushered in the day; the Mayor accompanied by the Hon. Mr. Hobart and several of the aldermen, preceded by the regalia, attended divine service at the Cathedral.' In the evening a huge bonfire in the market-place, the illumination of the houses in the adjoining street, and musical parades through the main thoroughfares enabled the citizens to share in the general rejoicing. Meanwhile 'a large company of 102 gentlemen' sat down to a commemoration dinner at the Maid's Head Tavern under the chairmanship of a leading merchant-manufacturer, Thomas Barnard, and drank what the local newspaper succinctly described as 'numerous toasts'.[74]

A year later to the day 1688 was again celebrated by a Norwich 'revolutionary' dinner and, according to one contemporary, the following year, 1790, saw the foundation of the Norwich Revolution Society with more serious objects in view than mere annual indulgence.[75] The autumn of 1789 in Norwich, however, witnessed a significantly subdued and indeed almost perfunctory participation of the local Dissenters in the national campaign for the repeal of the Test and Corporation Acts. An initial meeting in October so provoked the indignation of a self-described anonymous 'Friend to the Rights of Man' in the *Chronicle and Gazette* on 7 November that he called on his fellow Dissenters in the county and the city to repent of their 'spiritless conduct' on that occasion by altering it at the next meeting.[76] In response to this challenge a Norfolk general meeting of Protestant Dissenters held at the Maid's Head Tavern on 25 November, with Elias Norgate in the chair, solemnly pledged itself to pursue with 'unabated zeal' the cause of repeal, appointed William Manning and Robert Alderson as its delegates to the London Application Committee and established a standing Committee

73. *Norfolk Chronicle and Norwich Gazette*, 8 Nov. 1788.
74. *Ibid.*
75. J. W. Robberds, *A Memoir of the Life and Writings of the late William Taylor of Norwich* (London, 1843), vol. 1, p. 66. 'A festive gathering to celebrate the centenary of 1688, repeated the following year led to the formation of a local Revolution Society after the London model.'
76. *Norfolk Chronicle and Norwich Gazette*, 7 Nov. 1789.

of Correspondence to assist them.[77] Their excellent relations
with the cathedral clergy and their unhampered participation in the
fruits and privileges of municipal office deprived the majority of
Norwich Dissenters, however, of any real zest in the prosecution of
the general cause of repeal. The exultation of the local Anglicans
at the final rejection of Fox's motion for repeal in the spring of 1790
was similarly muted and the pattern of mob violence against Dissenting celebrants of Bastille day in July 1791 was not repeated in
Norwich on any significant scale.[78]

Meanwhile, several of the leading members of the by now Unitarian congregation of the Octagon Chapel had demonstrated
another sort of enthusiasm, full of the millenary hopes inspired
by the destruction of despotism in France. A select party of Norwich
friends in the company of Dr Rigby had, in mid July 1789, witnessed
and shared in the wild enthusiasm of the Parisians at the fall of the
Bastille.[79] On its anniversary in 1790, Dr John Taylor, deacon of
the Octagon Chapel, had danced round a Tree of Liberty at Norwich
with his sprightly wife (later known to her friends as 'Madame
Roland') and the unpredictable Whig pedant Dr Parr, and was soon
turning his hymn-writing talents to a new use by composing his
rousing song 'The Trumpet of Liberty' with its evocative and
challenging refrain – 'Fall, Tyrants, Fall'.[80] Another Norwich
enthusiast, William Taylor Jnr, on a visit to Paris with letters of
introduction to Lafayette from Dr Price in the spring of 1790, felt
constrained immediately on landing at Calais to write back home
to say that at last he had 'kissed the earth on the land of liberty'.[81]
Other East Anglian visitors to Paris created a local precedent on
14 July 1790 by their celebration of the revolutionary anniversary
at the Star Tavern in Yarmouth. Among their toasts they remembered
the English, French and American champions of liberty and expressed the hope that the Parliament of England would become 'a true
National Assembly'.[82]

Although definite evidence of the Norwich Revolution Society's

77. *Ibid.*, 28 Nov. 1789.　78. *Ibid.*, 29 May 1790.

79. Dr E. Rigby, *Letters from France, etc. in 1789*, ed. Lady Eastlake (London,
1880), p. 62.

80. The full version of the song is quoted in BL, Add. MSS. 27818, fo. 2,
where it is said to have been first sung at Norwich on 4 or 5 November 1788. Its
date, however, is more probably 1791, and it was certainly sung at the Norwich
'Revolution' dinner on 14 July 1791.

81. Robberds, vol. 1, p. 67.

82. *Norfolk Chronicle and Norwich Gazette*, 17 July 1790.

existence does not much antedate its dinner in celebration of the fall of the Bastille on 14 July 1791 at the Maid's Head Tavern,[83] the society was probably formed in the second half of 1790. W. Taylor Jnr, who took a prominent part in its affairs, returned from his visit to Paris in June 1790 and it was 'shortly' afterwards that, according to his biographer, he translated the French National Assembly's decree of 22 December 1789 relating to its new representative system and read it with his own comments at one of the meetings of the Revolution Society.[84] But precisely how 'soon' after his return? The Revolution Society was undoubtedly the main sponsor and co-ordinator of the activity of the working-class clubs in and around Norwich, but the surviving evidence as to its origins dates from 1792 when it was soon to lose its middle-class leaders and, under the stress of worsening economic conditions, to exchange its original Foxite ideas for more democratic French revolutionary principles. Almost any statements made about the society's original membership, organization and political attitudes before the spring of 1792 must, therefore, remain somewhat conjectural.

As in Manchester, however, it seems clear that the lead was taken by a select group of merchant-manufacturers and professional men who were Dissenters in religion, Francophile in their political outlook, critical of Pitt's diplomacy because it endangered relations with Spain and Russia, and convinced of the need to educate the working-class in political knowledge as a means to their more effective participation in politics, but also in order to rid society of the turbulence and disorder which was then often inseparable from the ventilation of popular grievances.[85] In reply to a letter dated 12 July 1791 from the London Revolution Society 'soliciting the favour of its correspondence', the gentlemen of the Norwich Revolution Society insisted that 'their conduct will ever exhibit that they believe subordination to just Laws to be the basis of Freedom'. Their secretary, Charles Basham, wrote of their aims

to attack Falsehood with Truth – to dispel the mist of Ignorance, the foster parent of Tyranny – to enlighten the mind of the indigent labourer, and avert those evils which ever attend Tumults, excited by the hard hand of oppression, by directing them in the legal road for obtaining redress.[86]

83. *Ibid.*, 16 July 1791.
84. Robberds, vol. 1, p. 74.
85. A similar and more compelling motivation was expressed by the leaders of the Sheffield Constitutional Society.
86. Norwich Revolution Society to London Revolution Society, 18 July 1791. *Correspondence of the Revolution Society in London* (1792), pp. 225–6.

By the spring of 1792 the Revolution Society had ceased to be merely a select Whig dining club meeting twice yearly to celebrate 5 November and 14 July and was emerging as the regional hub of a quasi-federal organization of local popular societies committed to the idea of a national agitation for parliamentary reform. By the autumn it was acting in a tripartite role – firstly as a subscription book club and discussion group, secondly as a central caucus co-ordinating the activities of a number of subordinate but associated clubs which had sprung up in the city and the surrounding villages and, thirdly, as a channel of communication with the metropolitan reform societies.[87] Meeting twice monthly at the Bell Inn on Hog Hill, the Revolution Society included among its members a sprinkling of wealthy merchant-manufacturers, the Baptist minister and 'Norfolk farmer' Mark Wilks, Dr Edward Rigby, and a number of tradesmen and artisans.[88] A committee of correspondence, periodically elected by ballot, selected the books for purchase – among which figured prominently the main replies to Burke's *Reflections*, such as Mackintosh's *Vindiciae Gallicae* and Paine's *Rights of Man* – and arranged for their circulation among the confederated clubs. Regular contact with the latter was maintained through a committee of twelve nominated by acclamation to attend their meetings, which were held in local taverns or public houses.[89] Delegates from the individual clubs were also encouraged to attend the monthly meetings of the Revolution Society.

The polarization of political opinion in Manchester had stemmed from Anglican bigotry. The intellectual reformism of the Norwich Revolution Society reflected the liberalism of its merchant-manufacturers and the Francophile leanings of its Rational Dissenters. By contrast the more unvarnished popular radicalism of the Sheffield cutlers, filesmiths and razor-makers was rooted in their own more

87. The first contact had been made in reply to a letter from the London Revolution Society dated 12 July 1791. The new approach was made, this time to the London Society for Constitutional Information, by the Norwich Revolution Society on 26 April 1792. PRO TS 11/952/3496(ii). Contact with the London Corresponding Society was not effected till October 1792 at the time of the joint address to the National Convention. PRO TS 11/965/3510A2.

88. Both William Taylors – father and son – were, until 1791, prominent manufacturers, and at one time William Taylor Snr acted as secretary. Other 'considerable manufacturers' who were members of the society early in 1792 were W. Firth, Thomas Barnard, G. Watson and Edward Barron. PRO TS 11/952/3496(ii).

89. *Ibid.*

immediate and pressing economic grievances. It was, however, precipitated by the political doctrines of Thomas Paine. The Sheffield Constitutional Society – probably the first British working-class reform association of any consequence – erupted into political consciousness and fully fledged activity in the space of a few months late in 1791. Its growth was phenomenal. Its organization was to set the pattern for the urban popular movement throughout the country and, from the outset, without any prompting from the Society for Constitutional Information in London, it canvassed publicly the arguments and doctrines of Paine's *Rights of Man*, Part I.[90] The efforts of the society to allay public suspicion of its motives were inevitably unsuccessful, even though in its early public declarations it repeatedly emphasized its attachment to purely legal and constitutional methods,[91] its willingness to surrender the reform initiative to more 'respectable' and influential supporters,[92] and the fundamental moderation of its political objectives.[93] Despite these assurances, the Sheffield radicals soon won for themselves the local reputation of dangerous exponents of industrial combination in support of higher wages,[94] and a nation-wide notoriety as tumultuous and unruly democrats.[95] Before long they were suspected, not wholly without justification, of provoking economic and political unrest in town and countryside throughout the Midlands and the North-West

90. By mid January 1792 the society had arranged for the publication of a cheap edition of Part I of the *Rights of Man* at the price of 6d. and had obtained 1400 subscribers. J. Alcock (secretary) to the editor of the *English Chronicle*, 15 Jan. 1792. PRO TS 11/952/3496(ii).

91. *Address to the Public* (19 Dec. 1791). WWM, F 44a(31).

92. In a letter of 14 May 1792 its secretary, Samuel Ashton, wrote to the recently formed aristocratic Whig Association of the Friends of the People that 'it had so far refrained from specifying its detailed proposals' for parliamentary reform, 'believing that, in due time, men of more respectable characters and great abilities would step forward'. *ST*, vol. 24, col. 1026.

93. When, in June 1792, the society reprinted the Duke of Richmond's celebrated letter of 1783 to Lt.-Col. Sharman of the Belfast Volunteers, it commented that 'the principles laid down in that letter comprehend and include all and every object they have in view with respect to a reform in Parliament'. Sheffield Central Library, Local Pamphlets, vol. 184 (10).

94. 'The journeymen in Sheffield are now more than ever clamorous for an augmentation of their wages, conceiving themselves to have a right to prescribe for themselves. The same spirit begins to prevail elsewhere.' The Rev. H. Zouch to Earl Fitzwilliam, 5 April 1792. WWM, F 44a(9).

95. Earl Fitzwilliam conceived it his duty, as a self-professed 'Alarmist', to draw attention to the 'machinations' of the Sheffield radicals as publicly and frequently as he could. Letter to Rev. H. Zouch, 12 April 1792. *Ibid*. E 234/24.

and of sponsoring common political action by the proliferating popular societies. Thelwall, the peripatetic political lecturer of the London Corresponding Society later saluted 'these honest, intelligent manufacturers' as a veritable English *sans-culotterie* – high praise indeed from one who claimed to be a *sans-culotte* himself.[96] They had, in fact, all the political realism, resilience and common sense of their French counterparts, the Parisian *sectionnaires*.[97] Those who devised their organization, prompted their political initiatives, and conducted their correspondence did so in the full consciousness that they were setting the pace for the regional radicalism that sprang into existence in many different parts of the country in the early months of 1792. In one sense, however, they were responding to the long and patient efforts of the Society for Constitutional Information to evoke that effective provincial support without which no merely metropolitan campaign for parliamentary reform could hope for success. Paine and Horne Tooke between them had at last discovered how to make such an appeal irresistible, at least to men who had no part in the political process and who only dimly grasped the reasons for the precarious and pauperized condition of their existence.

The nature of this Sheffield radicalism was determined partly by the town's peculiar administrative institutions, the unusual substructure of its local craft industries, the bleak and bitter climate of industrial relations in its sharply divided community and the artisans' ingrained independence of outlook that helped to shape the local popular mentality.

Without either separate representation at Westminster or a municipal corporation, the township of Sheffield, itself a subdivision of the ecclesiastical parish, was still governed by an incongruous assortment of administrative bodies, partly manorial, partly royal and partly statutory in origin. The Duke of Norfolk, as lord of the manor, had long ceased to concern himself with the town's affairs, except as landlord. The Town Trustees, successors of the Free Tenants or Burgery of Sheffield, managed the town property and a number of charitable bequests; twelve Capital Burgesses provided for the endowment of clerical benefices under a charter of Queen Mary of 1554, while the Cutlers' Company of Hallamshire, incorporated by act of Parliament in 1624, regulated the affairs,

96. J. Thelwall, *The Rights of Nature against the Usurpations of Establishments* (London, 1796), p. 21.
97. A. Soboul, *Les Sans-Culottes Parisiens en l'an II* (Paris, 1958), pp. 407–57.

practices and membership of the cutlery industry.[98] By the end of the eighteenth century the Master Cutler had displaced the Town Collector as the leading town dignitary.[99] A number of non-resident county magistrates, two constables, police commissioners, overseers of the poor and the church wardens of the parish church made up the motley array of local government authorities, who were both conservatively paternalistic and narrowly provincial in outlook.[100] The few recent indications of a reforming impulse at work in the community had been its limited involvement in Wyvill's Yorkshire Association,[101] the successful launching of the Sunday School movement in 1785 by the Methodists[102] and, more significantly for the future prospects of provincial radicalism, the foundation in 1787 of Joseph Gales's newspaper the *Sheffield Register*, which strongly supported the local anti-slavery committee and sided with the cutlers in their wage disputes.[103] In the following year, however, no public dinners or official celebrations of the centenary of 1688 appear to have been held and, as at Norwich, little interest was shown in the campaign for the repeal of the Test and Corporation Acts.[104]

Despite the impetus given by Huntsman's invention of crucible steel in the forties and by Joseph Hancock's exploitation of the technique of silver-plating in the fifties, the main structure of the local metal-working industries was still, in the last decade of the eighteenth century, pre-industrial. In the cutlery trade the characteristic units of production were the numerous workshops of the

98. J. D. Leader (ed.), *Records of the Burgery of Sheffield, commonly called the Town Trust* (Sheffield, 1897), pp. xv–xvi; M. Walton, *Sheffield: Its Story and Achievements*, 4th edition (Wakefield, 1968), pp. 47, 72–3; R. E. Leader, *History of the Company of Cutlers in Hallamshire*, vol. 1 (1905); J. Hunter, *Hallamshire: the history and topography of the parish of Sheffield . . .*, ed. A. Gatty (Sheffield, 1869).

99. Walton, pp. 34, 151.

100. *Ibid.*, pp. 61, 145.

101. G. P. Jones, 'The Political Reform Movement in Sheffield', *Transactions of the Hunter Archaeological Society*, vol. 4 (1937), p. 57.

102. Walton, p. 138.

103. W. H. G. Armytage, 'The editorial experience of Joseph Gales, 1786–1794', *North Carolina Historical Review*, vol. 28 (1951), pp. 332–61.

104. The first year in which official celebrations of 1688 were held in Sheffield was 1792. Gales, however, did publish *Historical Facts relating to the Revolution* in 1788. It seems, however, that large crowds from Sheffield attended a commemoration of the secret meeting of the dukes of Leeds and Devonshire in November 1688 at the so-called Revolution House at Whittington, near Chesterfield – a public house called the Cock and Pynot (Magpie) – where they had concerted measures for the seizure of York and Nottingham. See *Gentleman's Magazine*, vol. 59 (1789), Pt. 1, pp. 124–6.

'little masters', who often worked by themselves or employed only a few journeymen.[105] So little capital was required to set up in business that a steady and industrious journeyman could quickly rise to the position of small employer – a prospect which only rein-forced the native independence of the cutlers. This attitude was reflected in the long struggle of the small masters to free themselves from the restrictive controls of the Cutlers' Company and in the formation of sick and benefit societies and the organization of strikes for higher wages by the journeymen.[106]

Despite this, however, the position of the small masters and of their skilled journeymen had become precarious. The former were feeling the competition of a number of manufacturers who, having successfully challenged the authority of the Cutlers' Company, had found it necessary in self-defence to amalgamate their concerns, in order to command greater capital resources, and to employ a larger work force.[107] These larger units found it easier to expand their operations when trade was good and to survive successfully the strains of economic recession.

By contrast, though technically freemen of their company, some of the small masters, in the face of this competition and rising costs, found themselves forced to revert to their former position as wage-earners, but in the larger firms, in preference to going out of business completely.[108] Similarly the status of the journeymen was threatened by their exclusion from the Cutlers' Company and by the tendency of the larger cutlery concerns to dispense with the system of appren-ticeship.[109] Both journeymen and apprentices were also at the mercy of the fluctuations in the fortunes of their employers and suffered from the effects of rising food prices. Economic trends inside the cutlery trade were thus creating crisis conditions for the skilled artisans who naturally felt that all the advantages were shifting to the side of the more aggressive larger employers.

One sign of the relative worsening of their situation was the

105. 'The manufacturers of this town are of a nature to require so little capital to carry them on that a man with a very small sum of money can employ two, three or four men.' Col. de Lancy to H. Dundas, 13 June 1792. PRO HO 42/20. See also G. I. H. Lloyd, *The Cutlery trades: an historical essay in the economics of small scale production* (London, 1913).

106. T. S. Ashton, *Iron and Steel in the Industrial Revolution*. 3rd ed. (Manchester, 1963), p. 206.

107. Walton, p. 135.

108. *Ibid.*

109. Mitchell, p. 49.

insistence of the masters in 1787 that the journeymen should make thirteen knives for the cost of a dozen, in compensation for the customary retention of surplus material by the workers.[110] This infringement of a long-standing perquisite, popularly attributed to the master cutler of the time, caused bitter resentment among the cutlers. This was voiced by the filesmiths' local song-writer Joseph Mather in his venomous rhyme 'Watkinson and his Thirteens', which is supposed to have brought the offending master cutler to the verge of a mental breakdown.[111] As a specimen of Mather's powers of vicious invective, which were often employed in defence of the Sheffield radicals, the song is worth quotation:

> That offspring of tyranny, baseness and pride,
> Our rights hath invaded and almost destroyed,
> May that man be banished who villany screens:
> Or sides with big W . . . and his Thirteens.
> And may the odd knife his great carcass dissect,
> Lay open his vitals for men to inspect,
> A heart full as black as the infernal gulph,
> In that greedy, blood-sucking, bone-scraping wolf.[112]

A further difficulty encountered by the cutlers was the growing determination of their employers to combine in resisting their strikes for higher wages. In 1777 the filesmiths and in 1787 the table-knife grinders had some temporary success with strikes but when, in August 1790, the manufacture of scissors was almost brought to a halt by a grinders' strike, the master scissorsmiths called a general meeting of the town's merchants and manufacturers 'to oppose the unlawful combination of the scissor grinders and the combinations of all other workmen'.[113] A week after the Cutlers' Feast early in September, a general meeting of manufacturers appointed a committee and raised a subscription to prosecute, not only the scissor grinders, but also all other workmen who should in future follow their example.[114] The only advantage secured by the grinders was the establishment of a scissorsmiths' sick and benefit society in

110. Walton, p. 140.
111. Joseph Mather (1737–1804) emerged as the champion of the artisan class in Sheffield at this period. To sell his songs in broadsheet form he would ride backwards on a donkey through the streets. W. H. G. Armytage, 'Joseph Mather: poet of the filesmiths', *Notes and Queries*, vol. 195 (1950), pp. 320–2.
112. J. Wilson (ed.), *The Songs of Joseph Mather* (Sheffield, 1862).
113. *Sheffield Register*, 27 Aug. 1790.
114. *Sheffield Local Register* (1830), p. 65.

April 1791.[115] At this stage industrial relations were clearly being conducted on a basis of confrontation.

A final source of class conflict in the town in the summer of 1791 was the dangerous conviction among those with common rights on the land that the Duke of Norfolk and the local gentry were exploiting a parliament of landed proprietors to promote their own sectional interests at the expense of the common people. The passing of a private enclosure act on 6 June relating to the manor of Sheffield and the prospect of a new general corn bill giving bounties to encourage the exportation of corn and imposing duties to restrain its importation, exacerbated popular resentment against the ruling local oligarchy to the point of actual violence. Under the terms of the act 6000 acres of common land and waste in Upper and Nether Hallam, Fulwood, Moorewood, Stannington, Storrs and Dungworth were to be enclosed and redistributed among the local landholders, tithe-owners and large freeholders. Village greens on the outskirts of the town at Fulwood, Heeley, Newfield, Owlerton and Rivelin were thus to pass into private hands, footpaths crossing the enclosed area were to be abolished and the poor were to be 'compensated' by the derisory allotment of two acres only.[116] The chief beneficiaries under the redistribution were the non-resident Duke of Norfolk as lord of the manor and the vicar of Sheffield, the Reverend James Wilkinson, the wealthy, fox-hunting squire of Broomhall.[117] Wilkinson was, moreover, named as one of the local enclosure commissioners, along with the Duke of Norfolk's agent, Vincent Eyre and the master cutler, Joseph Ward.[118] When, however, the commissioners attempted to receive and determine claims and to

115. *Ibid.*, p. 62.

116. Carolus Paulus (Charles Paul), *Some Forgotten Facts in the History of Sheffield and District* (Sheffield, 1907), pp. 75–9. Barbara Hammond, 'Two towns' enclosures', *Economic History* (1931), pp. 258–66.

117. Lived 1731–1805, vicar of Sheffield since 1754, Prebendary of Ripon and JP for the West and North Ridings of Yorkshire. Had supported Wyvill's Yorkshire Association movement in the 1780s. He was given some grudging respect by his parishioners as much on account of his broad dialect speech and pugilistic ability as because of his integrity. He had, however, recently incurred unpopularity among the townsfolk for allowing some graves in his churchyard to be disturbed for street-widening and had been made the victim of one of Mather's fiercest diatribes, 'The Black Resurrection'. Wilson, p. 44. Wilkinson's marble bust in Sheffield Cathedral is one of the early works of Chantrey. W. Odom, *Hallamshire Worthies* (Sheffield, 1926), pp. 56–7. R. E. Leader, *Sheffield in the Eighteenth Century* (Sheffield, 1901), p. 60.

118. PRO HO 42/19, fo. 54.

publish their awards they were repeatedly prevented from fulfilling their duties by disorderly mobs who also threatened the lives and property of the freeholders who had approved the enclosure. Writing on 23 July 1791 to the Home Secretary, Dundas, to ask for immediate military assistance, the commissioners drew his attention to the intimidation of 'the most respectable inhabitants', 'the many treasonable inscriptions daily repeated upon the walls and doors in several places in this town for several weeks past' and the recent intervention of 'incendiaries' fresh from the anti-Priestley riots in Birmingham, who had encouraged the townsfolk to redress their grievances by taking the law into their own hands.[119]

Though Dundas responded promptly to this request by ordering two troops of the Fifteenth Dragoons from Nottingham and two troops of the Fourth Dragoons from York to Sheffield, the arrival of the first detachments from Nottingham on 27 July only antagonized the mob further. The same night a crowd of many hundreds gathered and vented its resentment against the law's severity by breaking into the debtors' gaol in King Street and releasing the prisoners.[120] The rioters then converged on Wilkinson's residence at Broomhall, where they set the library and several hayricks on fire and did much other damage before being dispersed by the troops.[121] Although further disturbances appeared imminent, the arrival of the dragoons from York on 28 July allowed order to be restored and several arrests to be made. One hundred and fifty special constables were sworn in before magistrates specially summoned from the neighbourhood and the principal inhabitants found the necessary courage to pass resolutions condemning the riots. Although the mobs did not again assemble in force, on Friday 29 July the barn of Norwood Hall was mysteriously burnt down. The proprietor was the leading local attorney James Wheat – clerk to the Town Trustees, one of the Capital Burgesses and a prime mover of several recent enclosure acts.[122] By the 30th the riots were over, but cries of 'No King', 'No Corn Bill' and 'No Taxes' continued to be raised in the town and threats of further arson were

119. *Ibid.*
120. Leader, p. 60.
121. The popular ditty about the riots told how the crowd 'burnt his books, And scared his rooks, and set his stacks on fire'. *Ibid.*, p. 240.
122. Wheat lived in considerable style and 'rode to town in a chaise painted pea-green with touches of gold, arms, crests and cyphers'. R. Robson, *The Attorney in Eighteenth-century England* (Cambridge, 1959), pp. 69–70.

made for some time afterwards.[123] Of the thirteen rioters arrested, eight were set at liberty with a severe reprimand after examination before a local magistrate; five, all youths under nineteen years of age, were tried at York Assizes, in early August, four were acquitted and one – Bennett – was executed.[124] Two were colliers who had come into the town from nearby villages in quest of an evening's excitement. The others – a silversmith, a grinder and a steelburner – were Sheffield workmen who had, no doubt, been caught up in the popular movement of protest against what seemed to them acts of social injustice.[125]

Although the attack on Broomhall did not convert the resolute Wilkinson into an Alarmist, it certainly extinguished what little remained of his former interest in Parliamentary reform. The government, however, could not ignore the seriousness of the security situation which the riots had revealed at Sheffield – where one resident magistrate unsupported by any troops within easy call could not ensure the maintenance of public order in a community of well over 30,000.[126] It had no option, therefore, but to leave detachments of light dragoons quartered on the town.

When, against this general background of growing industrial malaise and economic and social unrest, '5 or 6 Mechanicks' began to meet in each other's houses in Sheffield in the latter part of 1791 to discuss 'the enormous high prices of Provisions' and the main causes of their current discontents, they were innovators of a far different and more significant kind than that imagined by their reactionary opponents. Their diagnosis of the nation's ills (and their own misfortunes) was that they derived from three types of private and public corruption – the depradations of the 'Monopolists' . . . of all Ranks from the King to the Peasant'; the plunder of public property by 'Placemen and Pensioners', and 'the Mock Representation of the People'. From this they concluded that 'nothing but darkness and Ignorance in the People could suffer the natural Rights of every free man to be thus violated'.[127] The diagnosis seems to indicate that the Sheffield artisans (or their leaders) were merely reverting to views expressed a decade earlier by the Yorkshire

123. V. Eyre to H. Dundas, Sheffield, 30 July 1791. PRO HO 42/19.

124. *Sheffield Register*, 5 Aug. 1791.

125. PRO Assize Papers 45/37.

126. The nearest other magistrate, Col. R. A. Athorne, resided at Dinnington Hall, near Worksop.

127. John Alcock (secretary) to the editor of the *English Chronicle*, Sheffield, 15 Jan. 1792. PRO TS 11/952/3496(ii).

County Associators, but the recognition of the need to persuade their benighted brethren to defend themselves against private and public exploitation by the assertion of their natural rights points towards their conversion to Painite solutions.

The role of political education thus espoused was later emphasized by one of the Sheffield Constitutional Society's founder members and subsequent secretary – the cutler, William Broomhead. When pressed by the prosecution, during the treason trials of 1794, to explain what the original purpose of the society had been, Broomhead replied:

To enlighten the people, to show the people the reason, the ground of all their complaints and sufferings; when a man works hard for thirteen or fourteen hours of the day, the week through, and is not able to maintain his family; that is what I understand of it; to show the people the ground of this; why they were not able.[128]

The argument from economic, social and financial injustice to political reform was, in no sense, novel, but it was now being advanced by working men with the independence and courage to establish reform societies of their own and on their own initiative.[129] When, however, the informal private discussion groups paved the way for the formation of a Sheffield Society for Constitutional Information in November 1791 and when this split into a number of associated smaller clubs meeting in public houses, their opponents were not slow to accuse the reformers of seditious and riotous intentions. As early as 1 December 1791 the committee of the society felt it, therefore, necessary to repudiate these allegations publicly and also to announce their willingness to defer to the political leadership of more respectable and experienced reformers. 'The sole purpose of these societies was', they maintained, 'to throw in their mites, at some proper opportunity, towards restoring by a peaceable reform a more equal representation in the House of Commons (whenever the people of property and consequence shall think fit again to come forward)'.[130] In a second *Address to the public,* dated

128. *ST*, vol. 24, col. 630.
129. Samuel Shore to C. Wyvill, 11 May 1792: 'The Society first originated with four or five persons, Mechanics, without having the business in the least suggested them by any one.' Wyvill, vol. 5, p. 43.
130. *Sheffield Register,* 2 Dec. 1791. The committee also invited their critics to attend the meetings of the society to see for themselves the 'order and regularity observed', though requesting them 'not to move any disputes which may be more properly discussed elsewhere'.

19 December 1791, the society reinforced this tentative attitude by soliciting 'the patronage of all parties' for a set of 'primary objects', which it obviously considered irreproachable.

FIRST, as our Constitution was, from the earliest periods, founded in Liberty, it should not be destroyed, as if it were the Government of Despotism. SECONDLY, That all our Political Evils, arising from the abuse of the Practice, and not from Defect of Principle, the Original Purity of its Spirit may be restored, without Violence to the body. THIRDLY, That as the corrupt state of the Representation originates with all Parties, its original Purity is only to be revived by the unanimous and disinterested efforts of every Rank and Degree in the kingdom. FOURTHLY, That as nothing but a Patriotic and disinterested Resolution in all, to recur to the first principles of our constitution, can restore us to the entire possession of our ancient liberties, it is not the fall of one party, or the rise of another, that should be the object of the public pursuit. And FIFTHLY, That as the restoration of our liberties is equally due to all, no difference of opinion, situation or circumstance, should prevent every individual peaceably uniting in the attainment of this invaluable blessing.[131]

Perhaps it was too much to ask a sceptical public to believe that such amateur politicians had solemnly rejected the example set by France, refused to entrust the task of purging Parliament to any of the existing political parties, and had also renounced their class antagonisms. Even when the *Address* went further and quoted the declaration imposed on all members of the society repudiating violence and enjoining support for a petition to Parliament in favour of moderate and unspecified reform, it did not allay the suspicions which the society's other activities were already arousing.[132]

For, no matter how the society might or might not disguise its real objectives, it could not conceal the extremely rapid growth in its numbers.[133] By the middle of March 1792 the Constitutional Society had mushroomed to a membership of nearly 2000.[134] Its missionary fervour, combined with the settled determination to avoid the dangers of tumultuous assemblies, had caused it to stumble on an effective and flexible formula for the organization of a large

131. Enclosed in J. Wheat's letter to the Rev. H. Zouch, 28 Dec. 1791. WWM, F 44a (31).

132. *Ibid.*

133. A. W. L. Seaman, 'Reform Politics at Sheffield, 1791–1797', *Transactions of the Hunter Archaeological Society*, vol. 7 (1957), p. 217.

134. MS draft statement of the aims and objects of the Sheffield Constitutional Society, 14 March 1792. WWM, MD 251. By mid May the society was claiming a ticket-holding membership of about 2400. *ST*, vol. 24, col. 1026.

and steadily increasing membership. The expedient was to hold several separate meetings, soon called 'divisions', in different public houses all on the same night at regular fortnightly intervals.[135] By mid January 1792 there were eight, and by February there were thirteen, such divisions, which also increased in membership – beyond the originally contemplated limit of ten, to as many as twenty or thirty. The unity of the society was maintained partly through an executive committee of elected delegates – one from each of the divisions – and partly by monthly general meetings of all the members. These arrangements were kept flexible, so that the attendance at the general meetings – which had reached 600 at the end of January 1792 – could be kept within reasonable bounds – again by the simple expedient of holding simultaneous meetings at different places.[136]

Although various suggestions were made from time to time for the further rationalization of this organization, it remained substantially unchanged until 1794.[137] It enabled the Sheffield reformers to achieve their dual objective of rapid expansion combined with the orderly conduct of business both at the divisional and general meeting level. It avoided the dangers of fragmentation and afforded real guarantees of democratic control – even though the method of election to the executive committee was indirect. The decisions of the executive committee were regularly reported by the delegates to the several divisional meetings, and the executive committee also made it a practice to report on its proceedings directly to the general meetings.[138] The admission of the general public to the latter on payment of a small fee gave the society's proceedings full publicity

135. In February separate divisions were meeting every other Monday at the Black Lion, The Bell, The Falcon, The Lion and Lamb, The Blue Pig, The Barrel (Sycamore St), The Bull's Head, The Gate, The Harrow, The Cock, The Barrel (Charles St) and the Old Hermitage. *Sheffield Register*, 24 Feb. 1972.

136. On 27 February 1792 the principal general meeting was held at the Freemasons' Hall in Paradise Square, while two overflow meetings were also held at the Fountain, Town-head Cross and the Tiger in New St. See advert in *Sheffield Register*, 24 Feb. 1792.

137. An elaborate plan for the formation of 200 'tythings' of ten members each, twenty groups of delegates and a 'Grand Council' of twenty suggested in January 1792 does not seem to have come to anything.

138. The abstracts of the proceedings of the general meetings in the first half of 1792 in the Wentworth Woodhouse Muniments at the Sheffield Central Library show that the executive committee was reporting its decisions accurately and regularly.

and obviated the need for its enemies to maintain spies in its midst.[139] The virtues and potentialities of this divisional organization, particularly in large urban areas, were quickly recognized by that most experienced of political manipulators – Horne Tooke, of the metropolitan Society for Constitutional Information – and it was on his recommendation that it was adopted by the recently instituted London Corresponding Society.[140]

The Norwich Revolution Society, the Leeds Constitutional Society, the Society of Friends of the People in Southwark, the Derby Society for Political Information, and possibly other societies in the Midlands and the North-West which the Sheffield leaders assisted with advice – made this organization their own. As will be seen later, Sheffield radicalism had other contributions to make to the English popular movement, but none exceeded this in significance.

139. 'Observers' were nevertheless reporting on proceedings to James Wheat, who passed on the information with critical comments to Earl Fitzwilliam, WWM, F 44a.
140. Horne Tooke to Sheffield Constitutional Society, 2 March 1792. PRO TS 11/951/3495.

6 The great debate:
the polarization of English politics and Painite radicalism. 1791–2

Hey for the new Jerusalem! The millennium! And peace and eternal beatitude be unto the soul of Thomas Paine.

THOMAS HOLCROFT[1]

I have been too long a farmer to be governed by anything but events; I have a constitutional abhorrence of theory, of all trust in abstract reasoning; and consequently I have a reliance merely on experience, in other words, on events, the only principle worthy of an experimenter.

ARTHUR YOUNG[2]

Several of the salient features which were to make 1792 the *annus mirabilis* of the English popular movement – the growth of Painite radicalism, the ever deepening significance of the French revolution in English politics, the proliferation of working-class reform societies, and their commitment to the cause of the beleaguered Parisian *sans-culottes* – were foreshadowed in 1791. That year was a transitional stage in the evolution of British eighteenth-century radicalism, for it was marked by the great debate on the principles of 1789, a series of emotive Anglo-French anniversary celebrations with unsuspected but important consequences, and the initial impact of Painite political theory.

The public controversy which James Mackintosh described as 'the trial of the French revolution before the enlightened and independent tribunal of the English public' flared up early in 1791 over Burke's *Reflections*.[3] Though the London Revolution

1. T. Holcroft to W. Godwin, on the publication of the first part of the *Rights of Man*. C. K. Paul, *William Godwin, his Friends and Contemporaries* (London, 1876), vol. 1, p. 69.

2. A. Young, *The Example of France a Warning to Britain*, 2nd ed. (London, 1793), pp. 2–4.

3. J. Mackintosh, *Vindiciae Gallicae*, in *Miscellaneous Works* (London, 1851), p. 622.

Society itself refused to be provoked and treated Burke's philippic with 'that silent disregard its futility deserves',[4] both it and its spokesman, Dr Price, found plenty of champions – from Dr Towers and Mary Wollstonecraft to James Mackintosh and Dr Priestley.[5] Similarly, the Society for Constitutional Information, the object of Burke's affected pity and derision rather than of his serious concern, was, nevertheless, stoutly defended by one of its non-resident members – Capel Lofft.[6] Though some of these and other replies to the *Reflections* raised fundamental political issues and precipitated a memorable debate on the first principles of government,[7] most were primarily concerned to explain and vindicate the welcome the reformers had given to the French revolution. It was partly in this way that the controversy became the stuff of British politics in the years which followed. A mere catalogue of the liberal reforms carried in the French National Assembly enabled Capel Lofft, for example, to extenuate, though in a somewhat rhetorical vein, their favourable reception by the English friends of freedom.

And, if the accession of an Army, so long the great instrument of Despotism, to the cause of rising Freedom; if sweeping from the earth that adamantine Fortress of insidious and most cruel tyranny, the BASTILE [*sic*]; if the abolition of LETTRES DE CACHET; the vindication of Liberty of Conscience; the Introduction of Liberty of the Press; the Trial by Jury, where Life, Liberty, or Reputation are concerned; the substitution of the Representative Will of a great People in the place of the Arbitrary Will of an individual or of secret Favouritism; the extinction of Seignorial Privileges, and particularly of the Game Laws, those oppressive and ignominious Badges branded on the sufferance of the Community by feudal Tyranny; – if the Recognition of the Natural and Civil Rights of

4. *Correspondence of the Revolution Society in London, with the National Assembly* etc. (London, 1792), introduction, p. iii.

5. J. Towers, *Thoughts on the commencement of a New Parliament* (London, 1790), appendix; M. Wollstonecraft, *A Vindication of the Rights of Man* (London, 1790); Mackintosh; J. Priestley, *Letters to the Rt. Hon. Edmund Burke*, etc. (Birmingham, 1791).

6. C. Lofft, *Remarks on the Letter of the Rt. Hon. Edmund Burke, concerning the Revolution in France* (London, 1790).

7. 'I have heard more talk about government, more discussion of the Rights of Man, more *sedition*, in Mr. Burke's sense of the term, since the publication of his book, than ever I heard in all my life, before.' T. Christie, *Letters on the Revolution of France* (London, 1791), pp. 47–8. See also A. Cobban (ed.), *The Debate on the French Revolution, 1789–1800* (London, 1950); R. R. Fennessy, *Burke, Paine and the Rights of Man* (The Hague, 1963); and B. T. Wilkins, *The Problem of Burke's Political Philosophy* (Oxford, 1967).

Mankind, and the progress made towards reducing them to Practice; if the Pledge of Peace and Amity tendered by the new Constitution as its First-Fruit and Perpetual Vow to the surrounding Nations; if the Diffusion of Light, Liberty and Happiness, which such an Expansion of the Human Powers, such an Emancipation of THIRTY MILLIONS of Men promises to Mankind; if these are not subjects of diffusive Joy, of rational Gratulation, of benevolent Triumph, I am at a loss what Event can take place, till the final Dissolution, at which a Friend of Liberty and Mankind can have cause to rejoice.[8]

It seemed fair comment.

The millenary hopes and aspirations of the English Rational Dissenters in the new age ushered in by the American and French revolutions, were, however, best mirrored by Priestley, one of the earliest and most distinguished victims of anti-Jacobin persecution. 'Such events as these,' he wrote,

teach the doctrine of *liberty, civil* and *religious*, with infinitely greater clearness and force, than a thousand treatises upon the subject . . . These great events, in many respects unparalleled in all history, make a totally new, a most wonderful, and important era in the history of mankind. It is . . . a change from darkness to light, from superstition to sound knowledge, and from a most debasing servitude to a state of the most exalted freedom. It is a liberating of all the powers of man from that variety of fetters, by which they have hitherto been held, so that, in comparison with what has been, now only can we expect to see what men really are, and what they can do.[9]

The same optimism was expressed by Thomas Paine in the first part of his *Rights of Man*, published on 16 March 1791, when quoting Lafayette's confident article of faith that: 'For a nation to love liberty, it is sufficient that she knows it; and to be free, it is sufficient that she wills it.'[10] For Paine, too, it was 'an age of Revolutions, in which everything may be looked for' – even 'a confederation of nations and an European Congress'.[11] The book was at once a scathing and destructive criticism of Burke's theory of prescription, an informed and sympathetic account of the origins and progress of the revolution of 1789, and an impassioned defence of the principles, personnel and constitutional innovations of the French National Assembly – all of which had been indiscriminately condemned by Burke. It was also the first instalment of that 'Address

8. Lofft, pp. 76–7.   9. Priestley, p. 141.
10. T. Paine, *The Rights of Man*, Part I, ed. H. Collins (Harmondsworth, 1969), p. 67.
11. *Ibid.*, p. 168.

to the English People' which Paine had been projecting for some time past.[12] Paine now called on the English radical reformers to abandon their reliance on dubious Anglo-Saxon precedents and seventeenth-century panaceas, and to base their political claims on the principles of natural rights.[13] Paine taught unenfranchised working men to throw off their habitual deference to the political views of their social superiors. He also overcame their reluctance to question their alleged blessings under the once vaunted British constitution, which Continental theorists had now ceased to admire, and whose existence he himself denied. He had no patience with the reformers' nostalgic reverence for the outmoded and conservative revolution of 1688.[14] He scouted the possibility of a corrupt Parliament being able to reform itself and demonstrated, from the examples of America and France, that the only rational way for a nation to fill a constitutional vacuum was 'by a general convention elected for the purpose'.[15] It would be well, he suggested, if the lead given by the French reformers were followed in England – if, for example, no ministers, placemen or pensioners were allowed to sit in a National Assembly, if the right of declaring war and peace were transferred from the monarch to the nation, if titles of nobility and the house of hereditary legislators were swept away and if the right of universal liberty of conscience, as opposed to mere toleration, were established.[16] Primogeniture, game laws and tithes should be consigned to a bonfire of feudal relics such as the French had lit on the night of the 4th of August 1789.[17] Finally, Paine proclaimed his own uncompromising faith in the superior merits of what he called completely 'representative governments' by which he meant, of course, republican institutions.[18]

Several items of this all-embracing 'revolutionary' programme were cautiously, or even indignantly, repudiated by the radical societies which, in other respects, accepted *The Rights of Man* as

12. Fennessy, pp. 160–7.
13. G. A. Williams, *Artisans and Sans-Culottes: Popular Movements in France and Britain during the French Revolution* (London, 1968), p. 14.
14. One of Paine's most telling criticisms of Burke's defence of the revolution of 1688 was his attack on the whole theory of prescription. 'I am contending for the rights of the *living*, and against their being willed away, and controlled and contracted for, by the manuscript assumed authority of the dead.' Paine, p. 64.
15. *Ibid.*, p. 95.
16. *Ibid.*, pp. 96–105.
17. *Ibid.*, p. 107.
18. *Ibid.*, conclusion.

their new political gospel. They rejected as absurd Paine's contention that, because it was unwritten and had not been drafted by a national convention, the British constitution did not exist. They did not agree that 'root and branch' reform was indispensable and they did not approve Paine's direct assault on the monarchy and the House of Lords.[19] They saw no reason to abandon the radical myth of Saxon constitutionalism or the Commonwealth ideals of the seventeenth century.[20] They also refused to follow Paine in belittling the contemporary relevance of the Glorious Revolution of 1688, which their French correspondents still venerated. Most of them preferred to seek redress of their grievances by the legal and constitutional method of petitioning Parliament rather than resort to the summons of a National Convention. Few were prepared to advance beyond the traditional radical plea for annual parliaments and universal male suffrage.[21] Little interest was, therefore, displayed in the details of French constitutional reform as models for imitation, though every sympathy was expressed for the revolutionary ideals of fraternity and international concord. Rational Dissenters, however, were delighted with Paine's denigration of 'priestcraft' as a pillar of Old Corruption, his renewed attack on ecclesiatical tithes, his pacifism and his demand for complete liberty of conscience.[22] *The Rights of Man* also proved its value as a stimulant of political discussion among the distressed artisans who were to form the bulk of the members of the new radical societies – its pungent phraseology and easily assimilated simplification of political theory making it a convenient and popular catechism.[23] Paine's emphasis

19. In its reply of 5 Feb. 1792 to a letter from the Jacobin society of Chartres, the London Revolution Society insisted: 'A reform in the Representation of the People is what we principally want, and that we shall peaceably obtain. For the noxious part of our Aristocracy are feeble out of their own corrupt mansion, and must, however unwillingly, yield quietly to the public voice.' *Correspondence of the Revolution Society*, p. 271.

20. It is worth noting that Paine himself was not above using the theory of the 'Norman yoke' on occasion. C. Hill, *Puritanism and Revolution* (London, 1968), p. 105.

21. The radical societies did not, as a rule, venture to prescribe detailed programmes of reform for fear of having their petitions rejected by the Commons.

22. Priestley, pp. 142–3.

23. Writing to Earl Fitzwilliam on 5 April 1792, the Rev. H. Zouch reported that at Sheffield even the children were taught to repeat Painite slogans. 'We are told that the children of Ancient Rome were taught to learn the Twelve Tables by heart: those at Sheffield are not less well instructed in repeating the political catechisms of P[aine].' WWM, F 44a(9).

on natural rights, his encouragement of independent radical initiatives and his cavalier attitude to all aspects of the establishment in church and state greatly stimulated working-class self-confidence. Provincial artisans, suffering from guild or craft restrictions, from the combined action of their employers to keep down wages, or from the enclosing activities of local landed proprietors, naturally relished Paine's attacks on local monopolists, borough proprietors and the beneficiaries of primogeniture. It is easy to understand why *The Rights of Man* was, from the outset, so popular in Sheffield and other centres of provincial unrest.

The most immediate impact made by *The Rights of Man* was, however, upon the Society for Constitutional Information – of which Paine himself had been elected an honorary member soon after his return to England in 1787.[24] Since the failure of Flood's motion for parliamentary reform and the disappointing results of the General Election of 1790, this society had once more gone into a decline. Meeting after meeting in the latter part of 1790 had been adjourned for lack of business and attendances had shrunk to a mere half dozen.[25] Burke's *Reflections* had contributed to the society's discomfiture and it seemed as if it too, like the London Revolution Society had been, in Horace Walpole's opinion at least, 'as much exploded as the Cock Lane ghost'.[26] Members had fallen behind with their subscriptions and the club's finances were in disarray.[27] At its meeting on 7 March 1791, attended by fifteen members only and five visitors, a committee was appointed to inquire into the society's affairs and to draw up 'such regulations as shall be necessary to continue its utility and to insure its permanence'.[28] The badly needed elixir however, was found shortly afterwards, not in minor administrative economies, or in measures to ensure the payment of subscriptions in arrear, but in the publication of Paine's *Rights of Man*. The society made haste, on 23 March 1791, to express its pride that the author was one of its members. In resolving that its thanks should be given to Paine 'for his most masterly book', it grounded its gratitude on 'the most important and beneficial political

24. Paine was admitted as honorary member on 7 December 1787. PRO TS 11/961/3507, fo. 168.
25. *Ibid.*
26. *Letters*, ed. Paget Toynbee (Oxford, 1903–5), vol. 14, p. 323. For the Cock Lane ghost see Birkbeck Hill, *Boswell's Johnson* (Oxford, 1887), vol. 1, pp. 406–8.
27. In March 1791 annual subscriptions amounted to £75.15s.0d. and overhead expenses to £68.10s.0d. PRO TS 11/961/3507.
28. *Ibid.*

truths' which opened up the prospect of 'usurping Borough sellers and profligate Borough buyers' being 'deprived of what they impudently dare to call their property – the choice of the representatives of the people'.[29] The society also expressed its sincere hope that 'the people of England will give that attention to the subjects discussed in Mr. Paine's Treatise which their manifest importance so justly deserves'. Suddenly the society found itself with a new and significant mission on its hands – the dissemination of Painite radicalism through press advertisements and the regular transmission of its own transactions 'to all our corresponding constitutional societies in England, Scotland and France'.[30]

There can be no doubt that the immense popular success of *The Rights of Man*, Part I, and its steadily mounting sales were partly the result of its energetic promotion by the Society for Constitutional Information and the provincial reform societies which it induced to follow its example – notably those in Manchester, Norwich and Sheffield. In the summer of 1791 the Manchester Constitutional Society commissioned Thomas Cooper to abridge the book for popular use,[31] while early in January 1792 the Sheffield newspaper editor Joseph Gales and the committee of the newly formed Sheffield Constitutional Society obtained Paine's permission to print the first cheap edition of *The Rights of Man* on condition that its sale was restricted to the society's own members.[32]

In committing itself to this extended campaign for the dissemination of *The Rights of Man*, the Society for Constitutional Information, while stressing its value 'as a masterly refutation of an audacious libel', took care to disavow Paine's republican principles.[33] In a statement for the newspapers the society explained that its political attitude remained unchanged.

29. PRO TS 11/631/3507, fo. 223.

30. *Ibid.* On 1 April it was also decided to publish the society's resolutions of thanks in the *General Evening Post*, the *Morning Post*, the *World* and the *English Chronicle*, as well as the local newspapers of Sherborne, Leeds, York, Bristol, Nottingham and Birmingham. *Ibid.*, fo. 224.

31. Cooper consulted Horne Tooke about the project, but as the latter did not reply, it seems to have fallen through. D. Malone, *The Public Life of Thomas Cooper, 1783–1839* (New Haven, 1926), p. 31.

32. Abstract of the proceedings at a general meeting, 26 March 1792. WWM, F 44a(6). Paine's own decision to publish a cheap edition of Parts I and II was clinched by the government's prosecution of Part II. General meeting of 28 May 1792. *Ibid.*, F 44a(16).

33. 28 May 1791. C. Wyvill, *Political Papers* (York, 1794–1806), vol. 5, pp. iv–v.

That we are not unfriendly to the real Constitution of this country, a reference to our publications will clearly demonstrate. We only contend, with a zeal suitable to the importance of the subject, for the revival of forms approved by experience, and derived from principles, the most simple and ancient. Defended by the shield of conscious integrity, we dread not the darts of loquacious calumny. It was never in our contemplation to extend a reform beyond the manifest corruptions of that part of it which the people at large have an undoubted right to create, and reflect with perfect satisfaction, on no other mode of address than what the established forms of the constitution may sanction.[34]

Commenting on this declaration, William Belsham, a contemporary Dissenting historian, noted that one of the main reasons why the society had wished to promote the circulation of *The Rights of Man* was precisely because it was the fullest and most decisive reply to the *Reflections*.[35] The radicals fully appreciated that Paine, as the author of *Common Sense* and citizen of a federal republic, could not be expected to repudiate his republican principles. The Society for Constitutional Information did not, however, endorse Paine's views on hereditary monarchy – opinions which, as Belsham suggested, were 'totally extraneous, or rather opposite to the main design of the work, as a vindication of the French revolution, the French nation having very wisely retained the monarchical form of government'.[36]

Such guarded constitutionalism, when combined with attempts to promote the sales of *The Rights of Man*, failed, however, to disarm opposition – especially when Paine, after Louis XVI's abortive flight to Varennes, tried to precipitate a republican movement in Paris early in July 1791.[37] Suspicion of, and hostility to, the reformers also crystallized when the 'friends of liberty' in London and the provinces met once more to celebrate the fall of the Bastille on 14 July. These celebrations provided the excuse for violent demonstrations of 'Church and King' bigotry directed against the Rational

34. W. Belsham, *Examination of an Appeal from the New to the Old Whigs* (London, 1792), p. 35.

35. *Ibid.*, p. 34.

36. *Ibid.*, p. 35.

37. On 1 July 1791, Paine, who had been in Paris since early April, published a manifesto translated and signed by his friend, Du Châtelet, advocating the proclamation of a French republic. The only notice taken of the manifesto by the National Assembly was to reject a motion for the prosecution of its author on the ground that he must be a madman! E. Dumont, *Souvenirs sur Mirabeau*, ed. J. Bénétruy (Paris, 1951), p. 176.

Dissenters, not only for religious, but also for political reasons. The climate of public opinion in England had, by this time, begun to veer sharply against any attempt at political 'innovation' and any expression of pro-French sentiment. The celebrations were, therefore, planned with considerable caution. Though the 'friends of liberty' met 1000-strong and dined at the Crown and Anchor Tavern in the Strand under the chairmanship of George Rous – one of Burke's most successful critics – it was only after the most careful preparations had been made to allay popular suspicion.[38] The Society for Constitutional Information had specifically recommended that no contentious resolutions should be proposed. Both Fox and Sheridan, under pressure from the Prince of Wales, had judged it wiser to stay away. On the chairman's suggestion, the diners dispersed quietly at nine o'clock in order to forestall further criticism.[39] The dinner took the form, as intended, of a ritual or formal celebration of the establishment of civil and religious liberty in France. The majority of the toasts merely re-echoed the expression of Anglo-French friendship by the London Revolution Society in November 1789.[40] A toast to the memory of the lamented Dr Richard Price – 'the apostle of liberty' and 'friend of the human race', who had died in the spring – and one of gratitude to his opponent Edmund Burke for having precipitated the great debate on the fundamental issues of government, could hardly be considered provocative. The only reference to Paine was indirect, in a general toast 'to the men of letters who had championed the rights of man'.[41] Half-way through the proceedings, an ode specially composed for the occasion by the dilettante Robert Merry was declaimed and sung, but it lacked the fervour and panache of Taylor's 'The Trumpet of Liberty', which, on the same evening, electrified the diners at the Maid's Head Tavern in Norwich.[42]

38. Rev. Theophilus Lindsey to Tayleur, 21 May 1791. H. McLachlan (ed.), *Letters of Theophilus Lindsey* (Manchester, 1920), p. 88.

39. L. G. Mitchell, *Charles James Fox and the Disintegration of the Whig Party 1782–1794* (Oxford, 1971), p. 172. Dr Robinet, *Danton Émigré* (Paris, 1887), p. 44.

40. 'Everything passed off in the way that every friend to the meeting could desire. About 500 were in the room we dined in . . . About 200 in an adjoining room. The toasts I enclose.' Rev. T. Lindsey to Tayleur. McLachlan, p. 16.

41. Robinet, p. 44.

42. There is a copy of the ode in the Bodleian Library at Oxford. G. Pamph. 1724 (20). Robert Merry (1755–1798), a former pupil of Dr Parr at Harrow and French revolutionary enthusiast.

At Manchester the Bastille dinner of the local Constitutional Society, held at the Bridgewater Arms, followed the London pattern closely. To avert possible dispute or disturbance celebrants had been warned against proposing motions with a party bias or on local issues, and against wearing cockades or badges of distinction.[43] Despite these precautions, on the morning of the 14th an inflammatory handbill had been circulated in the town with the message that 'if Englishmen had the spirit they used to have', they would demolish the reformers' meeting place and that 'the brains of every man who dined there would be much improved by being mingled with brick and mortar'.[44] Under the chairmanship of Thomas Walker, however, the dinner passed off quietly, mainly because it was well known that Walker, as borough reeve, could have called out the local police to deal with any mob violence.[45] The threat of the reformers had, nevertheless, been a real one and Walker himself did not rule out the possibility of future intimidation.

The situation in Birmingham was potentially much more dangerous, and the anti-Dissenting riots there, precipitated by the Bastille dinner, marked the high tide of religious bigotry and local reaction and cut short the prospective development of radicalism in the Midlands.[46] The main victim of the riots was Dr Joseph Priestley who, although not present at the dinner, had incurred a great deal of local spite and resentment by harping on the issue of church disestablishment in his *Familiar Letters addressed to the Inhabitants of the town of Birmingham* (1790), by his membership of the Birmingham Lunar Society, and by his efforts, in June 1791, to recruit members for the Warwickshire Constitutional Society, modelled on that of Manchester.[47] In his detailed study of these riots, Professor R. B. Rose, while giving due weight to the evidence indicating an

43. T. Walker, *A Review of some of the political events which have occurred in Manchester during the last five years* (London, 1794), pp. 22–3.

44. *Ibid.*

45. *Ibid.*, pp. 23–4.

46. For a first-hand account of the dinner see William Russell's article in the *Morning Chronicle* for 20 July 1791.

47. J. T. Rutt (ed.), *Life and Correspondence of Joseph Priestley* (London, 1832), vol. 2, p. 114. For the Lunar Society see R. E. Schofield, *The Lunar Society of Birmingham* (Oxford, 1963); E. Robinson, 'The Lunar Society: Its Membership and Organization', *The Newcomen Society*, vol. 35 (1962–3), pp. 153–77; also, by the same author, 'The Origins and Life-Span of the Lunar Society', *University of Birmingham Historical Journal*, vol. 11, no. 1 (1967), pp. 5–16.

organized coup of the local 'Church and King' establishment, concludes that 'we can hardly disregard the charged atmosphere and disruptive claims injected into English politics by the French Revolution, if we are to attempt a final explanation of the full fury of the Church & King Terror of 1791'.[48] There can be little doubt that the disturbances were originally prompted and later directed by three local magistrates – Dr Benjamin Spencer, vicar of Aston, Joseph Carles, of Handsworth, a Staffordshire JP and John Brooke, under-sheriff of Warwickshire.[49] In May 1792 Samuel Whitbread MP, in asking the Commons for a government inquiry into the riots, produced numerous affidavits to show that these magistrates had made no efforts to disperse the mob outside the Royal Hotel, where the anniversary dinner had been held, that they had later directed the rioters to the Unitarian New and Old Meetings, promising them protection so long as they did not attack private property, and that they had also refused an offer of assistance, when the mobs had got out of hand, from a recruiting party then in Birmingham.[50] The result was that for three whole days – until the arrival of various detachments of Dragoons from Nottingham, Manchester and Uxbridge late on Sunday 17 July – the Birmingham mob was allowed to vent its fury against the most prominent local Dissenters, lay and clerical, and against members of the Lunar Society. Three Unitarian meeting houses and one Baptist chapel were seriously damaged or destroyed and the houses of at least twenty-seven persons were attacked, looted, or burnt to the ground.[51] Priestley, who had been playing backgammon with his wife at home after entertaining a visiting lecturer, was hurried away by his friends when the alarm was raised and made good his escape in a post-chaise and later on horseback.[52] His house at Fair Hill, Sparkbrook, was, however, ransacked and burnt and his manuscripts, books and scientific apparatus

48. R. B. Rose, 'The Priestley riots of 1791', *Past and Present*, no. 18 (Nov. 1960), p. 84. The latest account is J. Money, *Experience and Identity: Birmingham and the West Midlands, 1760–1810* (Manchester, 1977).

59. Rose, p. 80.

50. *Parl. Hist.*, vol. 29, cols. 1437, 1443. The affidavits, which were originally taken out by William Russell, on the advice of the Treasury Solicitor, are in PRO HO 42/19.

51. Rose, p. 76. One of the worst sufferers was William Russell (1740–1818), the wealthy merchant and reformer, who had promoted the Bastille day dinner, largely for commercial reasons, in the interests of Birmingham's trade with France.

52. J. T. Rutt (ed.), *Life and Correspondence of Joseph Priestley* (London, 1832), vol. 2, p. 127.

perished in the flames. Although evidence was collected against about fifty rioters, only seventeen were tried at the Summer Assizes at Warwick and Worcester. Four were found guilty, one later being reprieved, and three were hanged.[53]

This was not toleration, nor was it justice: it hardly inspired belief in the reality, or even in the existence, of the constitution. If 'Church and King' meant anything at this point, as the redoubtable Dr Parr was bold enough to say publicly in Birmingham after the riots were over, it signified 'a Church without the gospel and a King above the law'.[54] Local prejudice had culminated in the persecution and expulsion of some of the town's most distinguished and influential citizens. Dissenters, in general, had been given notice that in future they would advertise their pro-French sympathies at their peril. Many heeded the warning, dissociated themselves from Painite radicalism and, in December 1792, publicly declared their firm attachment to the constitution of which they had earlier been so critical.[55] The riots did not put an end to the Lunar Society, nor did they prevent a Birmingham Society for Constitutional Information from struggling into precarious existence in November 1792, alongside of the quaintly named local Association for preserving Liberty and Property against Republicans and Levellers.[56] This explosion of local reaction nevertheless prevented Birmingham from becoming the regional centre of Midlands radicalism and ensured that the hard core of unrepentant reformers in the town should confine their activities to 'the quiet diffusion of principles'.[57]

The wholesale propagation of Painite doctrine by the resuscitated Society for Constitutional Information and the celebration of the anniversary of the fall of the Bastille, not only in England, but also in Scotland and Ireland, gave Burke the incentive to resume and intensify his attacks on the metropolitan reform societies in his *Appeal from the New to the Old Whigs* in August 1791. This was, in effect, Part II of the *Reflections*, written in the context of Burke's open parliamentary breach with the Whig leaders Fox and Sheridan,

53. Rose, p. 82.

54. W. Derry, *Dr. Parr* (Oxford, 1966), p. 137.

55. e.g. the Declaration of Loyalty of the Deputies of the London Protestant Dissenters of 12 December 1792, which spoke of the constitution as 'excellent in its principles, and widely framed for the extension of solid happiness and real liberty'. *Gentleman's Magazine*, vol. 62, Pt. 2 (1792), p. 1070.

56. R. B. Rose, 'The origins of working-class radicalism in Birmingham', *Labour History* (Canberra), no. 9 (Nov. 1965), p. 12.

57. Williams, p. 65.

and in response to the publication of Part I of *The Rights of Man*.[58] The pamphlet was, however, less an answer to Paine than an assault on the 'New' or Foxite Whigs. Burke's quarrel with Sheridan and Fox sprang from his conviction that they were leading the Whig grandees in the direction of reform and flirting with French principles.[59] He now accused them of 'daily going out of their way to make public declarations in parliament, which notwithstanding the purity of their intentions, had a tendency to encourage ill designing men in their practices against our constitution'.[60] Burke drove home the heinousness of this crime by accusing the metropolitan reform societies of publicly incorporating themselves 'for the subversion of nothing short of the *whole* constitution of this kingdom' and 'for the utter overthrow of the body of its laws, civil and ecclesiastical, and with them the whole system of its manners, in favour of the new constitution, of the modern usages of the French nation'.[61] Burke had now evidently decided that the Society for Constitutional Information was just as insidious and dangerous as the London Revolution Society. The correspondence of the latter with the French National Assembly and the Parisian and provincial Jacobin clubs had fully demonstrated, in his view, that 'Great Britain was a principal object of their machinations'.[62] There can be little doubt, either, that Burke had the Society for Constitutional Information in mind when he suggested that 'those who circulate operative poisons, and give, to whatever force they have by their nature, the further operation of their authority and adoption, are to be censured, watched, and, if possible, repressed'.[63] The gravamen of his charges against the radical leaders was that they were 'active in spreading mischievous opinions, in giving sanction to seditious writings, in promoting seditious anniversaries'.[64] Neither the Whig grandees, the 'men of great hereditary estates', nor the general public seemed to have grasped the dangers implicit in the evolving situation. Burke warned that ministerial blunders or aristocratic miscalculations

58. The *Appeal* states, at length, the arguments which he had been prevented from making in the debates on the Quebec Bill on 6 May 1791.

59. For this see Mitchell, pp. 169–70, and F. O'Gorman, *The Whig Party and the French Revolution* (London, 1967), pp. 75–6.

60. E. Burke, *Works* (Bohn ed., 1878), vol. 3, p. 7.

61. *Ibid.* This, however, involved resort to 'the horrid doctrine of constructive treason'. *A Vindication of the London Revolution Society* (London, 1792), p. 49.

62. Burke, vol. 3, p. 11.

63. *Ibid.*, vol. 3, p. 105.

64. *Ibid.*, vol. 3, p. 101.

might well precipitate a crisis of order in Britain in which men of property would be unable to count on the political inactivity of a populace intent not on 'a change of actors', but on 'an alteration in the machinery'.[65]

It was at this point that Burke forecast the nature of the next phase of British radicalism – the incursion of the working class into political life.

Then will be felt the full effect of encouraging doctrines which tend to make the citizens despise their constitution. Then will be felt the plenitude of the mischief of teaching the people to believe, that all ancient institutions are the results of ignorance; and that all prescriptive government is in its nature usurpation. Then will be felt, in all its energy, the danger of encouraging a spirit of litigation in persons of that immature and imperfect state of knowledge which serves to render them susceptible of doubts, but incapable of their solution. Then will be felt, in all its aggravation, the pernicious consequence of destroying all docility in the minds of those who are not formed for finding their own way in the labyrinths of political theory, and are made to reject the clue, and to disdain the guide.[66]

For the moment these words fell on deaf ears, but in 1792 they were seen to have been prophetic.

Shortly after, however, a Painite counterblast appeared in print – in the form of an *Address and Declaration of the Friends of Universal Peace and Liberty, Held at the Thatched House Tavern, St. James St., August 20th 1791*.[67] Like Burke's *Appeal*, this was to be one of the most significant, though least noticed, contributions to the great debate that was now dividing the country. Though only a short pamphlet, it expressed for the first time some of the seminal ideas which were to make the second part of *The Rights of Man* such a landmark in political and social theory – and it also had important repercussions on the evolution of provincial radicalism. In one sense it was just another radical apologia in response to the campaign of wilful misrepresentation conducted by Burke and the 'Church and King' faction. Paine explained that the radicals had welcomed the French revolution as men but more particularly as Englishmen.

As men they had congratulated the French nation for having laid the axe to the root of tyranny and for erecting Government on the sacred HEREDITARY Rights of Man: they had also adopted as their own the

65. *Ibid.*, vol. 3, p. 106.
66. *Ibid.*, vol. 3, p. 106.
67. Reprinted in M. D. Conway, *Life of Thomas Paine* (New York and London, 1892), vol. 1, pp. 315–19.

principle 'that every nation has at all times, an inherent, indefeasible right to constitute and establish such government for itself as best accords with its disposition, interest and happiness'

– in other words the right of self-determination.[68] Among the benefits which Britain might derive from the French revolution Paine listed the chance of reducing the enormous burden of taxation as the prospects of war with France receded, the opportunity for greater state expenditure on poor relief, and the inducement to get rid of the remaining relics of feudalism – 'the game laws, borough tenures and tyrannical monopolies of various kinds'.[69] When Paine showed this apologetic to Horne Tooke, they had decided to make it public at a meeting at the Crown and Anchor Tavern on 4 August 1791 and, incidentally, to commemorate on that date the anniversary of the 'overthrow' of French feudalism in 1789.[70] This intention was frustrated when the landlord of the inn withheld his permission for the meeting to be held on such a 'seditious' occasion.[71] Undeterred, the 'Friends of Universal Peace and Liberty', under the chairmanship of Horne Tooke, met at the Thatched House Tavern on 20 August and decided to publish the Declaration.

This outlined two of the leading concepts which Paine was to elaborate in Part II of *The Rights of Man* – the emphasis laid on excessive taxation as the root cause of chronic pauperism and the claim that the state had a 'moral obligation' to provide for 'old age, helpless infancy and poverty'.[72]

Paine's *Address and Declaration of the Friends of Universal Peace and Liberty*, signed by J. H. Tooke as chairman, was also the indirect means by which the Sheffield Constitutional Society, shortly after its formation, attained a significant and rewarding connection with the London Society for Constitutional Information. By invoking the help of the editor of the *English Chronicle*, the committee of the Sheffield society was able to get in touch with Horne Tooke, who it assumed from the *Address* was chairman of a metropolitan reform society with headquarters at the Thatched House Tavern.[73] In his reply Tooke having corrected this misconception, commended the

68. T. Paine, *Address and Declaration of the Friends of Universal Peace and Liberty* (London, 1791), p. 1.

69. *Ibid.*, p. 5.

70. *Ibid.*

71. *Ibid.*, p. 6.

72. *Ibid.*, p. 3.

73. John Alcock to Editor of the *English Chronicle*, 15 Jan. 1792. PRO TS 11/952/3496(ii).

Sheffield society's efforts to disseminate Painite principles, and recommended its organization by divisions to the London Corresponding Society.[74] He also welcomed the idea put forward by the Sheffield society that, in order to ensure 'a regular communication', certain of its members should be incorporated as associate members in one of the metropolitan radical societies. In due course Tooke was able to persuade the Society for Constitutional Information to accede to this request by accepting the nomination of a dozen Sheffield reformers as associate members.[75] When despatching copies of Part II of *The Rights of Man* to the Sheffield society, Tooke also successfully recommended that it should adopt as its own a set of resolutions eulogizing the whole work which had been drafted by the Society for Constitutional Information.[76] This concerted action, when noticed in the London newspapers, would, he considered,

very much tend to promote the general cause and shew to the Public at large that we are closely united together and are going forward in a systematical manner to obtain for the whole Nation a Restoration of our Rights and a Relief from that Oppression and Plunder of the People which we have already endured too long.[77]

The year 1791 had thus been remarkable for the public and parliamentary discussion of the principles of 1789, for the pamphlet controversy on the fundamental issues of government and for a series of Anglo-French commemorative anniversaries. One further such anniversary remained – that of 4 November – and this too was to influence the momentous developments that helped to make 1792 the climax of Painite radicalism and French Jacobinism. The presence at this annual dinner of the London Revolution Society of Thomas Paine and Jérome Pétion, one of the foremost of the French democrats, and the remarkably Francophile spirit of the proceedings made the occasion a memorable one.

The invitation to Pétion appears to have been very much a last-minute afterthought. Pétion's stay in London from 30 October to 8 November was partly accidental and partly a matter of personal discovery for an ex-member of the Constituent Assembly on the eve of the municipal elections which were to make him mayor of

74. J. H. Tooke to Sheffield Constitutional Society, 2 March 1792. PRO TS 11/951/3495.
75. Minutes. 30 March 1792. PRO TS 11/962/3508.
76. 2 March 1792. PRO TS/951/3495.
77. *Ibid.*

Paris in mid-November, in succession to Bailly.[78] He had, however, also been commissioned by the duc d'Orléans in a personal capacity to accompany his young daughter Adèle, his putative daughter Pamela – the famous beauty who later married Lord Edward Fitzgerald – their governess and his own mistress, the celebrated Madame de Genlis on their journey to England, ostensibly to take the cure at Bath.[79] Pétion, who had accompanied the French royal family in their coach on their return from Varennes in the summer, had agreed to the suggestion because it offered him the opportunity to visit London at Orléans's expense, to become acquainted with English judicial institutions at first hand and, incidentally, to make contact with the leaders of the English democratic movement.[80] Armed with letters of introduction and with the help of an interpreter, Pétion had, on his arrival in London, managed to have preliminary discussions on law and current English and French political problems with Samuel Romilly, the criminal law reformer, Lord Stanhope, David Williams, the Welsh radical political theorist, and J. H. Stone, a wealthy Unitarian London merchant, who in 1792 became a member of the circle of British exiles in Paris.

From his own contemporary account of the anniversary dinner at the London Tavern, attended by about 350 guests, it appears that the enthusiasm generated by the presence of a small number of French visitors, including himself, converted the anniversary into a demonstration of Anglo-French radical solidarity.[81] Pétion was treated as guest of honour, placed next to the chairman for the occasion – Thomas Walker of the Manchester Constitutional Society – and was delighted to meet both Paine and Dr Priestley, on the eve of the latter's election to succeed Dr Price at the Gravel Pit chapel at Hackney.[82] He noticed that the royal toast was drunk 'in gloomy silence', that several of the diners wore tricolour cockades and that all their enthusiasm was reserved, not for the traditional

78. For the whole of this episode in Anglo-French radical relations see M. Reinhard, 'Le Voyage de Pétion à Londres, 24 Octobre–11 Novembre 1791', *Revue d'Histoire Diplomatique* (Jan.–June, 1970), pp. 1–60.

79. *Ibid.*, pp. 11–12.

80. *Ibid.*, pp. 6–8.

81. *Ibid.*, pp. 50–1.

82. Priestley was elected as Price's successor on Sunday, 6 November 1791. McLachlan, p. 118. Lindsey's own account of the proceedings, ascribing much of the credit for the success of the celebration to 'our worthy chairman, Mr. Walker of Manchester', appears at p. 89.

toast to the revolution of 1688, but for that to the French nation.[83] Other signs of an *entente cordiale* between English and French democrats were that the national colours of the two countries were displayed intertwined and surmounted by a crown and that the orchestra punctuated the proceedings with spirited and repeated renderings of the revolutionary refrain, '*Ça ira*'.[84] In replying to the toast of the French guests, coupled with his own name, Pétion briefly thanked the society and proposed a toast to the sincere and lasting friendship which he hoped would unite England and France in the future.[85] He did not mention that Paine's response to a similar invitation was to offer the more challenging toast – 'The Revolution of the World'.[86] Events had indeed already revealed that its mover had cast himself for the role of international revolutionary.

Pétion stayed on a few more days in the capital, visiting St Paul's in the November fog, the Tower of London, a museum full of Captain Cook's acquisitions in the Antipodes, and concluding his hasty tour, in time to be back in Paris for his election as mayor, with a not entirely enjoyable evening out at the theatre.[87] Though Farquhar's Restoration comedy *The Recruiting Officer* struck Pétion as in bad taste, the audience's lack of response to the outmoded jibes against his compatriots supplied him with further reassuring evidence that Anglo-French amity might not, after all, be a mere mirage conjured up by the members of the London Revolution Society.[88] The significance of his visit and of the anniversary dinner which he attended was, however, that it helped to foster the feeling of solidarity between the English and French democrats and provided, in his own person, a channel of direct communication with the Jacobin club of Paris and the French National Assembly.

The winter months of 1791 also marked a decisive turning point

83. Reinhard, p. 50.

84. Lindsey wrote of 'the music being happily intermixed with the toasts, with some excellent songs, and the famous French Revolution tune '*Ça ira*', seemed to inspire the whole company with a portion of their spirit'. McLachlan, p. 89.

85. Reinhard, p. 51.

86. C. B. Cone's account of this anniversary meeting (*The English Jacobins* (New York, 1968), pp. 112–13) is inaccurate and misleading. It does not mention the presence of Pétion, it suggests that this was the last occasion when the society celebrated the anniversary of 1688, and implies that the society was collapsing.

87. Reinhard, pp. 55–7.

88. *Ibid.*, p. 58.

in the life of Thomas Hardy, the Scottish shoemaker who was to found the most famous of all the radical societies of this period – the London Corresponding Society – early in 1792.[89] Hardy had arrived in London from Scotland in 1774 at the age of twenty-two with a few introductions and eighteen pence in his pocket, after being brought up and taught his trade by his maternal grandfather, Thomas Walker. In 1781 he had married a Miss Priest, youngest daughter of a carpenter and builder of Chesham in Buckinghamshire. Ten years later he had prospered sufficiently to be able to set up on his own as a master bootmaker with five or six journeymen at No. 9 Piccadilly.[90] In November and December 1791 Hardy spent some of his leisure hours rereading a number of political tracts issued by the Society for Constitutional Information in its early years, which had been presented to him by one of its founder-members, Thomas Brand Hollis. Hardy's interest in politics, originally aroused during the war of American Independence by Price's work on *Civil Liberty*, was in this way rekindled.[91] Two tracts in particular seem to have influenced the nature and scope of his initial political activity. The first was the Duke of Richmond's celebrated letter to Lt-Col Sharman of the Irish Volunteers of 15 August 1783, and the second was Major Cartwright's pamphlet *Give Us Our Rights*, which had first appeared as an appendix to the Society for Constitutional Information's *Second Address to the Public* in 1780.[92] The former was the classic contemporary exposition of the right to universal male suffrage as the sole means of evoking that body of popular support necessary to ensure success for the policy of parliamentary reform. The latter not only outlined the main arguments, historical and political, in support of the radical programme of universal suffrage and annual parliaments, but also claimed that, on the basis of its population, the metropolitan area was entitled to have its parliamentary representation increased from ten to fifty seats.[93]

89. H. Collins's essay on the London Corresponding Society in J. Saville (ed.), *Democracy and the Labour Movement* (London, 1954), pp. 103–34, contains too many factual errors to make it a satisfactory secondary source.

90. The short biographical sketch in the *Dictionary of National Biography* is worth consulting.

91. BL, Add. MSS. 27814, fo. 18. 'A Narrative of the Origin & Progress of the London Corresponding Society' by Thomas Hardy.

92. F. D. Cartwright, *Life and Correspondence of Major Cartwright* (London, 1826), vol. 1, p. 135.

93. SCI, *Second Address to the Public* (1782 ed.), pp. 58–9.

The loss of the right to vote in parliamentary elections, so Cartwright argued, had resulted from the operation of 'one unconstitutional statute' (8 Henry VI c.7),[94] which fell with particular hardship on the poor.[95] Universal suffrage and annual parliaments, moreover, went hand in hand, for where parliaments were allowed to sit for longer periods than one session, those who came of age subsequently were deprived for a number of years of their best inheritance, their entitlement to 'the actual exercise of their elective franchise'.[96] Whereas a thousand years (!) of annual parliaments, from the time of 'the immortal Alfred' to the reign of Charles I, had resulted in 'not a single disadvantage to liberty', a mere one hundred years of longer parliaments after 1688 had left the nation 'nothing of liberty but the name'. Cartwright had even invoked in his tract the biblical parable – 'watch ye in the night season' – to point out that Englishmen had been robbed, whilst they slumbered, of their electoral rights and their freedom by boroughmongers and corrupt politicians.[97] In this way the radical programme of the 1780s had been presented as merely a plea for a restitution of ancestral rights, 'without which no Englishman can be a free man, nor the English nation a free nation'. 'An Englishman's Liberty or Freedom', the pamphlet insisted,

consists in having an *actual share*, either in legislation itself, or in the appointing of those who are to frame the laws; which, although they ought to protect him in the full enjoyment of those absolute rights, that are vested in him by the immutable Laws of Nature, may yet be fabricated to the destruction of his Person, his Property, his religious Freedom, Family and Fame.[98]

In this manuscript account of the origins of the London Corresponding Society Hardy specifically tells us that he 'took the idea' of forming a society 'to correspond with individuals and societies of men who wished for a reformation' from 'that admirable letter of the Duke of Richmond to Col. Sharman, Chairman of the Com-

94. This statute of 1430 had restricted the county franchise to freeholders worth 40s. per annum. J. Cannon, *Parliamentary Reform, 1640–1832* (Cambridge, 1973), p. 2.

95. 'Since the *all* of one man is as dear to him as the all of another, the *poor* man has an *equal* right, but more *need*, to have a representative in parliament than a rich one.' *Give Us Our Rights* (London, 1782), p. 8.

96. *Ibid.*

97. *Ibid.*, pp. 51–3.

98. *Ibid.*, p. 7.

mittee of Correspondence at Lisborn in Ireland'.[99] His original plan had envisaged a society consisting exclusively of the unenfranchised, but he had abandoned this as 'too narrow' in favour of a wider association of 'all classes and descriptions of men (criminals, insane and infants excepted)' – according to the plans of the radicals of 1780.[100] Two of the elements in that original concept which were retained in the final version have been regarded by historians as marking a new departure in radical politics. The first was the low weekly subscription of one penny, the second was the provision, 'That the number of our Members be unlimited.' It seems probable, however, that neither of these rules was original – the first being 'a standard device of the early trade organizations which combined the functions of friendly and trade societies',[101] while the second seems to have been borrowed from the original regulations of the Society for Constitutional Information.[102]

99. BL, Add. MSS. 27814, fo. 22. One of the main reasons for Hardy's acquittal in the treason trials of 1794 was that he proved conclusively 'that he uniformly acted upon the Duke of Richmond's plan, that he pursued that only which the Duke of Richmond wished to be carried into effect, that he promoted it by the means by which the Duke of Richmond wished to see it accomplished'. A. G. Olson, *The Radical Duke* (Oxford, 1961), p. 62.

100. BL, Add. MSS. 27814, fo. 20. The draft rules of 'The Corresponding Society of the unrepresented part of the people of Great Britain' as originally conceived by Hardy are in the original letter book of the society. Add. MSS. 27811, fo. 2.

101. E. C. Black, *The Association: British Extra-Parliamentary Political Organization, 1769–1793* (Cambridge, Mass., 1963), p. 226, fn. 29.

102. 'April 1780 – Resolved. That this Society be unlimited in its Number.' Minute Book of the Society for Constitutional Information. 1780–1783. PRO TS 11/1133/1. According to the latest biographer of the society's founder Major Cartwright, this provision 'was meant to include the higher rather than the lower social ranks', i.e. the dukes rather than the dustmen. J. Osborne, *John Cartwright* (Cambridge, 1972), p. 25. A similar interpretation, *mutatis mutandis*, could be put on the rule in the case of the London Corresponding Society, for its force was to admit the propertied and enfranchised class as well as the disfranchised working men who, according to Hardy's original notions, would alone have been members. Alternatively, it may have meant that the society contemplated the indefinite expansion of its numbers until the objective of universal suffrage had been obtained. Cf. rule 2 of Hardy's original draft – 'That this Society be unlimited in its numbers while there is one in Great Britain unrepresented. . . .' Add. MSS. 27811, fo. 2. It is surely misleading to suggest, however, that this rule 'was one of the hinges upon which history turns', that 'it implied a new notion of democracy' and that 'such a revolutionary challenge . . . was bound to lead on to the charge of high treason'. E. P. Thompson, *The Making of the English Working Class* (London, 1965), pp. 21–2. The rule was, in fact, both unprovocative and derivative.

Like the cutlers and tradesmen of Sheffield who had preceded him in taking a similar political initiative, Hardy was understandably diffident in his attempt 'to form a society of another class of the people, to effect that most desirable and necessary Reform, which had baffled the united associations of men of the greatest talents, worth and consequence in the nation'.[103] The Associators of 1780 had, however, lacked popular support and had announced their intention of refraining from further agitation so long as the mass of the people remained politically inert.[104] By 1791 the politically underprivileged tradesmen and artisans of the metropolis had found, like their counterparts in Sheffield, that the high cost of living and their continued pauperism provided them with the incentive publicly to condemn 'the want of a fair and equal representation in the Commons house of parliament' which the men of 1780 had taught was the mainspring of popular grievances.[105] In these changed circumstances, Hardy had felt emboldened to try out a political experiment. If, he calculated, a society were formed 'on the principle of the representative system', there might be a good prospect that 'the friends of freedom who had been active in 1780–2 would again come forward'. He seems to have thought that once the unenfranchised had given the impetus,

men of talents who had time to devote for promoting the cause would step forward, and we who were the framers of it, who had neither time to spare from our daily employments, nor talents for conducting so important an undertaking, would draw into the background.[106]

The principle of unlimited membership, combined with the low weekly subscription, would allow Hardy's projected society to recruit the 'journeymen, tradesmen and mechanics' of the metropolis and yet admit those whose means, accomplishments and commitment

103. BL, Add. MSS. 27814, fo. 20.
104. *Ibid.*, fo. 35.
105. *Ibid.*, fo. 24.
106. LCS, *Memoir of Thomas Hardy* (London, 1832), pp. 100–1. Cf. the same attitude taken by the Sheffield Constitutional Society in its letter of 14 May 1792 to the Association of the Friends of the People – emphasizing that it had never attempted to prescribe any particular plan of parliamentary reform, 'believing that, in due time, men of more respectable characters and great abilities would step forward; to such we have always had an eye, and upon such we have ever meant to rely for our government'. *ST*, vol. 24, col. 1026. This attitude was, however, quickly abandoned when the FOP made plain its anti-Painite principles.

might provide the practical assistance and political experience so necessary to guide the society in its infancy.

Such were the ideas which Hardy discussed with a few friends and associates in the winter of 1791. Having received their encouragement, he drew up outline plans for a metropolitan reform society which were approved at a meeting at the Bell tavern in Exeter St off the Strand on 25 January 1792.[107] Hardy documented the general case for parliamentary reform by reading extracts from various pamphlets published in the Society for Constitutional Information and particularly impressed his hearers by quoting the figures of 'mock representation' from Cartwright's *Give Us Our Rights*. After discussion of other alternatives, the title of London Corresponding Society, as suggested by Hardy, was adopted, Hardy was elected secretary and treasurer and eight of those present joined on the spot by making a penny deposit each in return for a membership ticket.[108] A week later, at the next meeting, eight more joined, a chairman was appointed, and a formal agenda drafted for the next meeting. This time the membership of the society increased to a total of twenty-five. When an animated discussion arose on the general necessity of a reform in the representation of the House of Commons, the members were beset by the conscientious scruple – 'Have we who are Tradesmen, Shopkeepers and mechanics any right to seek to obtain a parliamentary reform.'[109] It was only after protracted debate spread over 'five consecutive nights' that this doubt in the minds of these London artisans was dispelled.

Having overcome this initial obstacle, Hardy then concentrated his attention on three main priorities – the initiation of correspondence with other and particularly provincial reform societies, the conduct of the society's public relations, and the drafting of a constitution for the regulation of its own business.

The successful fulfilment of these items on the society's agenda required all Hardy's considerable powers of independent initiative as well as his willingness to seek and accept advice from all who were as eager as himself to make possible the 'Grand Design' of radical parliamentary reform. The most fruitful early contacts made by Hardy were with the Sheffield Constitutional Society and with Horne Tooke, the grand vizier of the Society for Constitutional Infor-

107. BL, Add. MSS. 27814, fo. 20.
108. *Ibid.*, fo. 24.
109. *Ibid.*, fo. 26.

mation.[110] A tentative approach early in March 1792 to the Sheffield reformers, through the Reverend William Bryant, brought a reply informing Hardy of their system of integrated divisional organization and their successful application to the Society for Constitutional Information for associate membership.[111] Both these devices were adopted and used by the London Corresponding Society, which also made formal contact with the Society for Constitutional Information before the end of the month.[112] Hardy, however, had been in personal touch with Horne Tooke since the beginning of March and had consulted him at every stage of the difficult and protracted discussions within the Corresponding Society on the rival drafts of its first *Address to the Public*.[113]

It was, however, the reply from Sheffield which put fresh heart into Hardy's society and led it to appoint a committee to draft both a declaration of its principles and a formal constitution.[114] On a request from Hardy the Society for Constitutional Information gave its imprimatur to the final draft of the *Address* and Horne Tooke ensured its publication in the newspapers by signing it with Hardy's name when its author Maurice Margarot, and Hardy as secretary, had shown reluctance to do so.[115] The London Corre-

110. It is strange that Hardy only made contact with the Revolution Society at Norwich in the autumn of 1792, shortly before the dispatch of the London Corresponding Society's address to the French National Convention. PRO TS 11/952/3496.

111. BL, Add. MSS. 27811, fos. 4–5. PRO TS 11/952/3496(ii).

112. PRO TS 11/962/3508: minute-book of SCI, 30 March 1792.

113. BL, Add. MSS. 27811, fo. 6. Hardy to Horne Tooke, 27 March 1792. Apparently Paine had offered to draft an Address for the LCS but could not find the time to do so.

114. 'It animated them with additional ardour when they were informed that others in a distant part of the nation had *thought* and had also *begun to act* in the same way with themselves' – 'a committee of six was that night appointed to revise, alter or amend the laws and regulations – and to prepare something to be published as an address to the nation'. BL, Add. MSS. 27814, fo. 29 (Hardy's *Memoir*).

115. Hardy had hesitated from modesty, Margarot from fear of losing prospective employment with city merchants connected with the government. Margarot, soon to be elected Chairman of the LCS, had been born in 1745. His father was a wine and general merchant operating in Portugal and France. A home in London frequented by the supporters of Wilkes, an education in Geneva, and residence in France on family business between 1789 and 1792 had made Margarot a radical, and his first action on returning to England in the spring of 1792 had been to join Hardy's society. M. Roe, 'Maurice Margarot: A Radical in Two Hermispheres, 1792–1815', *Bulletin of the Institute of Historical Research*, vol. 31 (1958), pp. 68–78.

sponding Society, however, undertook the separate publication and
dissemination of the *Address* and this enabled Hardy to initiate
formal correspondence with existing metropolitan and radical
societies and to stimulate the foundation of new ones.[116] Hardy's
memory was, however, at fault when he later asserted in his printed
Memoir that this proliferation of reform societies in 1792 was the
reason why Burke 'in one of his mad rants in the House of Commons' called the London Corresponding Society 'the Mother of all
Mischief'.[117] Though the *Address*, dated 2 April 1792, reasserted the
radical claim to universal male suffrage as Cartwright had formulated it, proclaimed the need for eternal vigilance against all abuses
of power, and complained bitterly of 'oppressive taxes, unjust laws,
restrictions of liberty, and wasting of the public money', it did not
attempt to prescribe detailed remedies. If the end in view was 'a
fair, equal and impartial Representation of the People in Parliament',
the means were to be 'reason, firmness and unanimity' alone.[118]
This first *Address* revealed its authors as the disciples of Cartwright
rather than the pupils of Paine.

April and May of 1792 were taken up with the drafting and discussion of the society's constitution. By the second week in April
its membership had increased to seventy[119] and Hardy soon found it
expedient to adopt the Sheffield form of organization in divisions
to allow further expansion without compromising the orderly conduct of business. By the end of April nine such divisions had been
established, and on Thursday 3 May their delegates formed themselves into a committee which elected Margarot as the president of
the society and confirmed Hardy in office as secretary and treasurer.[120]
Tooke acted as unofficial consultant and adviser, and it was probably at his instigation that the radical barrister Felix Vaughan was
appointed a delegate in order to help in the drafting of the regulations.[121] These largely reflected existing practices, and were

116. Hardy to the Manchester and Sheffield Constitutional Societies, enclosing
a copy of the address and resolutions, 7 April 1792. BL, Add. MSS. 27811, fo. 7.
117. *Memoir* (1832), p. 109. Burke's dictum was in fact made on 9 April 1793
in the debate on the third reading of Pitt's Traitorous Correspondence Bill and
it referred *not* to the London Corresponding Society, but to the London Revolution Society. *Parl. Hist.*, vol. 30, col. 645. This error has not hitherto been
noticed by historians.
118. BL, Add. MSS. 27814, fos. 2–3. *ST*, vol. 24, cols. 377–8.
119. Hardy to T. B. Hollis, 10 April 1792. BL, Add. MSS. 27811, fo. 8.
120. *Ibid.*, Add. MSS. 27812, fo. 4.
121. PRO TS 11/958/3504: Treasury Solicitor's brief against Horne Tooke,

approved and published on 24 May in the form of an address *To the Nation at Large*.[122] The title of the association was settled as 'The London Corresponding Society united for the reform of parliamentary representation', admission to which was thrown open to all adults, proposed and seconded, after taking a preliminary test asserting their belief in, and willingness to promote, 'by all justifiable means', parliamentary reform, combined with universal suffrage. Membership also entailed the payment of one penny a week subscription (or one shilling and a penny per quarter) for which the divisional secretaries had to account monthly to the treasurer, who reported quarterly to the committee of delegates. The revenue from this source was to be used partly for postage and stationery, and partly for printing the society's publications. Each division was to consist initially of thirty members and was to form another division as soon as its numbers rose to sixty. Divisions were to meet weekly and to appoint their own officials, including a delegate. The divisional delegates were also to meet weekly on Thursdays in what was later called the General Committee – the effective governing body of the society.[123] Their main function was to act as links between the General Committee and the divisions, reporting the business transacted at the centre to the local branches and keeping the General Committee informed of the wishes and views of their constituents. As a body they were authorized 'to answer any correspondence which may require immediate attention' and two-thirds of their number were to constitute an Executive Committee for the general despatch of business.[124] Appointed quarterly, the delegates were subject to recall by their divisions before their term had expired, if it was considered necessary.[125]

It is clear from these regulations, and from Hardy's own reminiscences, that the society's business was conducted from the start in an orderly, methodical but, above all, in a thoroughly democratic manner. Although professional and business men and even nobility were admitted, their offers to pay higher admission fees than ordinary

---

1794. In this Tooke is roundly accused of having 'set up the L.C.S.' and as proof reference is made to 'a plan for the original formation of the L.C.S. with corrections in Mr. Tooke's handwriting – found among the papers of Mr. Hardy, the Secretary, which were seized by the messengers'.
122. PRO TS 11/957/3502(i): *ST*, vol. 24, cols. 378–82.
123. *ST*, vol. 24, col. 380.
124. *Ibid.*
125. *Ibid.*

members were scrupulously refused and within the society they were kept firmly in their place.[126] Hardy was adamant that the radical Lord Daer, former pupil of Dr Parr, and eldest son of the Earl of Selkirk, should not, as was suggested, be elected chairman shortly after his admission on the strength of his social position.[127] He was afraid such a move would 'discourage the people exerting themselves in their own cause' or make them revert to their former implicit 'dependence on the mere ipse dixit of some nobleman or great man without the least trouble of examining for themselves'.[128] Whereas, initially, some members, as artisans or tradesmen, had been doubtful whether they were competent to concern themselves in a struggle for parliamentary reform, the conclusion of the May address *To the Nation at Large* was more confident.

But as Providence has kindly furnished men in every station, with faculties necessary for judging of what concerns themselves, shall we the multitude suffer a few, with no better right than ourselves to usurp the power of governing us without control? Surely not! Let us rather unite in one common cause, to cast away our bondage: being assured, that in so doing, we are protected by a jury of our countrymen, while we are discharging a duty to ourselves, to our country and to mankind.[129]

Hardy himself in his *Memoir* later recorded the suspicion and distrust felt in the society for some of the aristocratic 'friends of freedom'. 'The higher class as they are called have at all times made use of the middling and lower orders as a ladder to raise themselves into power, then kick it away.'[130] This seemed a judgement on the Whig parliamentary Opposition. He even felt disenchanted with Wyvill's Yorkshire Association which, he thought, had 'broken their faith with the people', when they failed to resume their campaign for parliamentary reform after popular support had at last shown itself.[131]

Though wishing to correspond on friendly terms with the Society for Constitutional Information and even with the aristocratic Association of the Friends of the People, the leaders of the London Corresponding Society preferred to maintain the relationship at

126. BL, Add. MSS. 27814, fo. 37.
127. *Ibid.*, fo. 36.
128. *Ibid.*
129. *ST*, vol. 24, col. 382.
130. BL, Add. MSS. 27814, fo. 36.
131. *Ibid.*, fo. 35.

arm's length.[132] They gladly welcomed advice and help from such sources, but never at the cost of their own independence. It was this greater self-reliance, their indignant and critical appraisal of the blemishes and injustices of the political establishment, and their fierce determination to assert the rights of which they felt they had been dispossessed by self-interested and corrupt politicians which made Hardy and his 'industrious' associates of the London Corresponding Society real political innovators. Just as there were members of all social classes inside the society so, Hardy informs us, there were men of 'almost all religious opinions' and indeed 'some who cared for none of those things'. Hence it was found necessary to prohibit all discussion of theological issues in the society in order to preserve harmony and good order.[133] Despite such social and religious differences, however, what united the members and gave them their determination to persist in their struggle against all difficulties was the feeling 'that they were oppressed, that the fruits of their honest industry were taken from them either by force or fraud to support *idle drones* in *useless* places and unmerited pensions'.[134] Their demands were for social justice as well as for equal political rights.

Meanwhile, a more strident and revolutionary challenge had been formulated in Thomas Paine's *Rights of Man*, Part II, published on 16 February 1792. It was this pamphlet which was to be the Bible of the English democrats. Characteristically, the London Corresponding Society did not announce its conversion to the new revelation till the publication of its Third *Address* on 6 August 1792.[135] Once again it was Horne Tooke, in the name of the Society for Constitutional Information, who both prompted and publicized the formal resolutions of the main provincial reform societies in mid March welcoming the appearance of the book.[136] Unitarian 'enthusiasts' like Thomas Cooper of the Manchester Constitutional Society

132. *Ibid.*, fo. 36.
133. *Ibid.*, fo. 30 v.
134. *Ibid.*
135. It has often been observed that this address, also drafted by Margarot, was virtually a summary of Part II of the *Rights of Man*. Williams, p. 68. Hardy rightly commented that the address was 'well calculated for giving political information to those whose occupations in life made it impossible for them to spare time to read large works'. BL, Add. MSS. 27816, fo. 218.
136. The Manchester society's resolution of 13 March 1792 spoke in praise of the work's 'excellent and practical plans' for 'the immediate and considerable' reduction of both public expenditure and taxation and its social welfare schemes. PRO TS 11/952/3496(ii). The Sheffield society, on 14 March 1792, resolved its

and the Reverend Theophilus Lindsey of the Exeter St chapel in London needed no nudging – the one to exclaim that *The Rights of Man* had made him 'more politically mad then ever I was', and the other to confess that he was an 'idolator' of the work.[137] There is no mystery either about the reasons why Part II of *The Rights of Man* found such receptive audiences among the artisans, journeymen and shopkeepers of the British radical societies and why its booming circulation statistics so far exceeded those of Part I.[138]

Brushing aside Paine's criticism of the futility of petitioning Parliament for reform, ignoring his rejection of Anglo-Saxon historicism, and tolerating his republicanism as an intelligible personal eccentricity, they shared his millenary aspirations for universal peace, for a liberal alliance between the United States, Britain and France, and enthusiastically welcomed his views on the reduction of taxation, the abolition of primogeniture, his condemnation of enclosures, borough-mongering and state sinecures. What more nearly affected them was Paine's emphasis on the need for public education, his humanitarianism, his compassionate concern for the poor and his prophetic blue-print of a modern welfare state.[139] The total abolition of the poor rate, bonuses for newly married couples, maternity and family allowances, education grants for children under fourteen, old-age pensions starting at the age of fifty and increasing in amount over sixty, even grants, in certain cases, in aid of funeral expenses – such were the social benefits which Paine thought could easily be financed by cutting the costs of defence and central administration, by the abolition of unjustifiable pensions and sinecures and by the introduction of a form of progressive income tax.[140] Paine's uncompromising assault on

---

thanks to Paine for 'the affectionate concern he has shown in behalf of the poor, the infant and the aged' and stated that it had 'derived more true knowledge' from Parts I and II of the *Rights of Man* 'than from any other author on the subject.' WWM, MD 251.

137. F. Knight, *The Strange Case of Thomas Walker* (London, 1957), p. 63; McLachlan, p. 131.

138. Sales of the book are difficult to establish, owing to the number of cheap or abbreviated editions and the number given away. 50,000 copies of Part I at 3s. and 150,000 copies of Part II by the end of 1793 are figures which modern scholars have accepted as probable. Thompson, p. 108.

139. T. Paine, *Rights of Man*, Part II, ch. 5.

140. N. Sykes, 'Thomas Paine', in *The Social and Political Ideas of Some Representative Thinkers of the Revolutionary Era*, ed. F. J. C. Hearnshaw (London, 1931), p. 122.

Parliament as the citadel of aristocratic privilege, the Augean stables of borough-mongering corruption, and the centre of financial mismanagement vindicated the radical approach to the problem of reform.[141] Once this stronghold was carried by the sovereign people in a constitutional convention the economic injustices which plagued the poor would disappear. It was a beguiling prospect and at one point even Paine professed to believe that, in his scheme for tax remission, he had made a convert of the Younger Pitt.[142] Those, however, who feared the advent of British democracy recalled with enhanced apprehension what Burke had foretold in his *Appeal from the New to the Old Whigs*. Before the autumn of 1792 was out French republicanism and the September Massacres had imparted a new and more sinister connotation to the term 'convention' which made any talk of the possible summons of such an assembly in Britain tantamount to treason.

Early in May 1792 the London Revolution Society inadvertently added further fuel to this gathering alarm by publishing its correspondence with the French National Assembly and the Parisian and provincial Jacobin clubs.[143] It did so partly to refute Burke's malicious insinuations, but partly also as a contribution to that 'peace and amity' between England and France which it regarded as 'essential to the prosperity of the commerce of this kingdom, to the relief of the burthens of the state, and the general cause of humanity'.[144] Trusting somewhat naively that the correspondence published *in extenso* would 'speak for itself', the society appealed in self-justification to the 'friends of justice, of truth and of freedom'.[145] Many felt, however, that the Anglo-French correspondence vindicated, not so much the motives of the Revolution Society as

141. For an interesting analysis of the economic ideas of the *Rights of Man* see Patricia Hollis, *The Pauper Press – A Study in Working Class Radicalism of the 1830s* (Oxford, 1970), pp. 203–6.

142. In the appendix of Part II of the *Rights of Man* Paine insinuated that Pitt had borrowed the idea of his tax remissions mentioned in his speech of 31 January 1792 (and incorporated in his budget proposals of 17 February) from the proofs of the pamphlet purloined before publication from the printer by a government agent. Pitt himself acknowledged his indebtedness to Adam Smith. Stanhope, *Life of Pitt* (London, 1861), vol. 2, p. 141.

143. The decision to publish the correspondence had been taken at a general meeting of the society on 22 July 1791. *Correspondence*, p. 233. For the actual date of publication see J. Gifford, *A Second Letter to the Hon. Thomas Erskine . . . on his 'View of the causes and consequences of the war'* (London, 1797), p. 5.

144. *Correspondence of the London Revolution Society*, p. vii.

145. *Ibid.*, p. vi.

the imputations of Burke – an impression which was strengthened when the society claimed credit for 'that cordial reception, which every Englishman who had lately visited France has experienced throughout that Kingdom'.[146] The allusion was general, but opponents saw it as having relevance to a recent and highly controversial visit paid to the Jacobin club in Paris by James Watt Jnr and Thomas Cooper of Manchester.

Both were close personal friends, who had resigned from the Manchester Literary and Philosophical Society in 1791 in protest against its refusal to follow the example of the Derby Philosophical Society, which had sent a message of sympathy to Dr Priestley after the Birmingham riots.[147] Watt, son of the inventor, had recently taken up an appointment as travelling representative of the Manchester textile firm of Thomas Walker, and he had also joined the local Constitutional Society. His visit to Paris had been arranged to promote Walker's and his own father's business interests in France, but his friend had joined him, hoping to combine pleasure with the chance to observe the revolution at close quarters.[148] Walker supplied them with a personal letter of introduction to Pétion, now mayor of Paris, reminding him of his cordial reception at the anniversary dinner of the London Revolution Society the previous year, and invoking his good offices on their behalf.[149] Walker's assessment in this letter of the probable political consequences of the recent appearance of the second part of *The Rights of Man* is not without interest. He was confident that it would 'produce some material alteration in our system, and that, I hope, at no distant period'.

Aristocracy he [Paine] has wounded mortally, war he has put an end to; Taxes can go no further, and monarchy will not, I think, continue long in fashion; in a word, he has pointed out to the people that their own interest is so closely connected with the principles he lays down that these cannot fail to act upon them ere long.[150]

Walker had also anticipated that the visit of Watt and Cooper

146. *Ibid.*

147. E. Robinson, 'An English Jacobin: James Watt, Junior, 1769–1848', *Cambridge Historical Journal* (1955), pp. 349–55.

148. Malone, p. 34.

149. AN, F[7]4774[70]. I am indebted for this reference to my friend Professor Marcel Reinhard of the Sorbonne.

150. This file also contains Pétion's correspondence with other English radicals, such as J. H. Stone David Williams and Thomas Christie.

to France would afford an opportunity for the Manchester Constitutional Society to follow in the steps of the London Revolution Society by establishing a regular correspondence with a number of French patriotic clubs. Writing from St Omer on 6 March 1792, Watt reminded Walker of this project and asked him to obtain authorization from the Manchester society for himself and Cooper to act as delegates to the Jacobin club in Paris and to similar societies at Nantes and Bordeaux. Watt announced, at the same time, that he and Cooper would, immediately on arriving in Paris, assume the character of delegates, without waiting for formal authorization.[151] In that capacity Watt and Cooper were presented to the Paris Jacobin club by Robespierre on 13 April 1792 and delivered an address, probably drafted by Cooper, reiterating the need to banish national prejudices between peoples and invoking once more the principle of international fraternity.[152] As a preliminary step towards an ultimate federation of European patriotic societies, the delegates had suggested that a regular correspondence should be established between their own society and the Jacobin club in Paris. The proposal was welcomed in a warm-hearted and generous response by the vice-president of the Jacobins, M. Carra, who paid tribute to the example set by England in 1688 and pledged support for a universal alliance between nations.[153]

The two delegates were also prevailed upon, no doubt by Pétion, to take part, on 15 April, in a massive patriotic fête organized by the Parisian democrats. This demonstration was intended to honour the 'martyred' Swiss mercenary troops of the regiment of Châteauvieux whose mutiny at Nancy in 1790 had been savagely repressed by the royalist General Bouillé, with the support of Lafayette. Several of the mutineers had been hanged, many had been sent to the galleys, and, despite the terms of a general amnesty proclaimed at the end of the Constitutional Assembly, the rest had been kept in prison.[154] They had, however, been released in February 1792 by the Legislative Assembly. The public recognition of their 'martyrdom' was seen by Collot d'Herbois, Tallien and other radical extremists as a way of expiating the 'massacre' of popular demonstrators carried out,

151. T. Walker, *The Original*, ed. Blanchard Jerrold (London, 1874), p. 82.

152. F. A. Aulard, *La Societe des Jacobins* (6 vols. Paris, 1889–97), vol. 3, p. 496.

153. *Ibid.*, pp. 500–2. T. Cooper, *A Reply to Mr. Burke's Invective against Mr. Cooper and Mr. Watt in the House of Commons on 30th April, 1792* (Manchester, 1792), appendix, pp. 86–8.

154. M. Reinhard, *La Chute de la Royauté* (Paris, 1969), pp. 34–5.

on Lafayette's orders, on the Champ de Mars in July 1791.[155] The fête itself was the culmination of a series of civic banquets and federations of provincial Jacobin societies and was the first to be entrusted to the neo-classical painter Louis David – soon to win wide acclaim as 'pageant-master' of the revolution.[156] On this occasion between 200,000 and 300,000 spectators lined the Champ de Mars to see Watt proudly bearing the British flag and Cooper a bust of Algernon Sydney in the monster procession.[157] Five days later France was at war with Austria and, on 30 April, in a virulent tirade in the House of Commons, Burke named Cooper and Watt as agents in a conspiracy to promote a federation with the Jacobin 'regicides' of Paris. He read their address to the Jacobin club and concluded, from Carra's reply, that the 'worthies of Manchester' had engaged, 'from what authority he knew not . . . to represent all England'. Among others who 'avowed similar principles' Burke cited 'Mr. Walker of Manchester'.[158] In his celebrated reply Cooper later maintained that such accusations were the result of Burke's disturbed imagination – 'mere Burkisms without proof and invective without argument'.[159] But the evidence shows that, though exaggerated, they were not entirely without foundation.

While Burke had thus characteristically emphasized the Manchester society's much publicized association with the Parisian Jacobins, the government itself had been more concerned at the spread of Painite doctrines at home and also at the recent formation of the Whig Association of the Friends of the People. The decision to form such an association to press for parliamentary reform, taken on 11 April 1792, had arisen from renewed concern at ministerial malpractices in the Westminster election contest of 1788.[160] The

155. *Ibid.*, p. 274.
156. *Ibid.*, p. 275; D. L. Dowd, *Pageant Master of the Republic* (Nebraska, 1948).
157. A. Mathiez, *La Révolution et les étrangers* (Paris, n.d.), p. 22. Cooper in a letter to Walker on 25 April 1792, described the celebration as 'the first festival truly civic that Europe has seen'. Walker, pp. 85–6. For a detailed report of the proceedings see *Manchester Herald*, 28 April and 5 May 1792.
158. *Parl. Hist.*, vol. 24, col. 1323.
159. Cooper, p. 7.
160. George Rose, Secretary to the Treasury, had been ordered by the Court of King's Bench to discharge a debt of £100 incurred to a publican named Smith for services rendered on behalf of the court candidate, Lord Hood, in the Westminster election. A motion for an enquiry into further charges against Rose was negatived in the House of Commons on 13 March 1792. *Parl. Hist.*, vol. 29, cols. 1014–33.

204   *The Friends of Liberty*

habitués of Holland House attempted to ridicule the new departure
as a madcap post-prandial escapade of the wilder spirits inside the
Whig party, encouraged by the irresponsible Earl of Lauderdale.[161]
An equally distorted view of the association was taken by ministerial
'Alarmists', such as Bland Burges, who portrayed it as 'a club for
propagating Democratical principles in this country' under the
direction of Sheridan, and 'composed of a few foolish Boys and silly
Country Squires, and a larger proportion of Presbyterian parsons
and desperate Revolutionists'.[162] So far from being an after-dinner
prank, the move was the result of long and anxious consideration
by a younger generation of Whig MPs, led by Charles Grey, Mackintosh, Maitland, Courtenay and Sheridan, who had become pro-
gressively dissatisfied with the Whig 'agreement to differ' on the
issue of parliamentary reform since the disastrous General Election
of 1784.[163] Ever since Pitt's mishandling of the Russian armament
issue in 1791, when ministry and Parliament had both shown themselves so badly out of touch with public opinion in the country,[164]
this group of liberal-minded and ambitious politicians had become
more convinced of the need for parliamentary reform and more
optimistic about Whig prospects of being able to form a ministry.
In effect, Grey and his colleagues had for some time been acting as
a 'ginger-group' within the Whig Opposition and the Association
of the Friends of the People may be regarded as an attempt to
broaden the basis of their support in the country at large. It was,
nevertheless, very much an exclusive society – with an entrance fee
of two and a half guineas and an annual subscription of the same
amount.[165]

In one respect, the association represented a development which
both the Sheffield Constitutional Society and the London Corresponding Society had eagerly anticipated – namely a return to the
Wyvillite tradition of moderate reform under the auspices of the
'respectable' and propertied classes. These were the natural political
leaders to whose judgement and discretion they had declared their

161. *Journal of Elizabeth, Lady Holland* (London, 1908), vol. 1, p. 101.
162. J.B.B. to Edward Thornton, 9 May 1792. Transcripts of political papers
of Sir James Bland Burges, Bodleian Library, Oxford.
163. P. J. Brunsdon, 'The Association of the Friends of the People'. Unpublished MA thesis, Manchester (1961).
164. On this see J. P. W. Ehrman's article, 'The Younger Pitt and the Ochakov
Affair', *History Today*, vol. 9 (July 1959), pp. 462–72.
165. Cannon, p. 122.

willingness to defer.[166] Secondly, the association was an attempt to stem the growing ascendancy of Burkian conservatism in the Whig Opposition and of Painite extremism in radical politics by occupying an intermediate position in support of liberal parliamentary reform.[167] With this objective the Friends of the People set out to make parliamentary reform respectable by making it moderate and by rigidly repudiating Painite principles. Initially their objects were 1) 'To restore the freedom of election, and a more equal representation of the people in parliament, 2) to secure to the people a more frequent exercise of their right of electing their representatives.'[168] Thirdly, Grey and his friends made it plain, from the outset, that they wished to disentangle the issue of reform from its French associations. They announced in their *Address to the Nation* (26 April 1792) that they were convinced of the irrelevance of recent French political innovations in an English context. Having denied 'the existence of any resemblance whatever between the cases of the two kingdoms', they utterly disclaimed 'the necessity of resorting to similar remedies'. They asserted their determination 'to avert for ever from our own country the calamities inseparable from such convulsions'.[169] Like the radicals they defined their intention as 'not to change, but to restore; not to displace, but to re-instate the constitution upon its true principles and original ground'.[170]

In so far as the new society marked a return to the methods and objectives of the Yorkshire Association movement, however, it came too late to be effective – for Wyvill's supporters had either melted away, or become more conservative, and he himself was sceptical of his latter-day imitators.[171] Similarly, the attempt to compromise between the Burkian and Painite extremes ignored the polarization of English politics that had resulted from the unsuccessful campaign for the 'complete toleration' of Protestant Dissenters, the great debate on the fundamental issues of government, and the celebration of the anniversaries of 4 November 1688 and 14 July 1789 as though

166. S. Ashton, Secretary, Sheffield Constitutional Society to the Committee of the Friends of the People, 14 May 1792. *ST*, vol. 24, cols 1026–8. BL, Add. MSS. 27814, fos. 32–5.

167. Mitchell, p. 176; O'Gorman, p. 82.

168. *Declaration. Parl. Hist.*, vol. 29, col. 1303.

169. *Ibid.*, vol. 29, col. 1307.

170. *Ibid.*, vol. 29, col. 1306.

171. J. R. Dinwiddy, 'Christopher Wyvill and Reform, 1790–1820', *Borthwick Papers*, no. 39 (1971), pp. 2–10. (Publications of the Borthwick Institute of Historical Research, University of York.)

they were one and the same.[172] Finally, events themselves were increasingly to demonstrate that the French revolution, so far from being irrelevant, had already become the real touchstone of English domestic politics.

Though Charles James Fox – the effective leader of the Whig Opposition in Parliament – had not been consulted about the formation of the society, and though he did not join it, neither did he repudiate its objectives or discourage its sponsors.[173] It was left to Charles Grey, as the 'orator' of the group, to give notice on 30 April 1792 of a motion for parliamentary reform to be made in the following session.[174] In doing so Grey gave no hint of the society's specific proposals and thus allowed his opponents to insinuate that the association's plans were unconstitutional, or even subversive.[175] It was also alleged that the reform motion had been deferred for a year to give the association time to work up popular discontent in the country in the interim.[176] Pitt anxiously observed that prominent MPs in the association

were concerned with others, who preferred not reform only, but direct hostility to the very form of our government. This afforded suspicion, that the motion for a reform was nothing more than the preliminary to the overthrow of the whole system of our present government.[177]

Burke ridiculed the whole idea of moderate or temperate reform, stressed the radical societies' commendation of Paine's *Rights of Man* as evidence of their subversive intentions, and focused attention on the recent fraternization of Cooper and Watt with the Jacobins of Paris. In order to succeed in their objectives Burke concluded that the members of the association, however patriotic

172. Thomas Cooper, not unnaturally, denounced the Friends of the People as 'half-measured Reformers – Men of Rank and Respectability, as they sometimes call themselves: who desire no farther reform than to extend the aristocratic monopoly of power to that in which themselves are included'. Cooper, p. 74.

173. Mitchell, p. 179.

174. *Parl. Hist.*, vol. 29, cols. 1300–1.

175. Erskine later recalled that, as soon as Grey gave notice of his intentions in the Commons, 'there was an instantaneous motion among Ministers, as if a great national conspiracy had been discovered'. *A View of the Causes and Consequences of the present war with France* (London, 1797), p. 14. On a point of procedure, Grey in giving notice of his motion was not allowed to go into details. It seems as if, however, the Friends of the People had not, at that stage, any agreed plans on reform.

176. Dundas accused both Fox and Erskine of having made speeches intended 'to excite the people'. *Parl. Hist.*, vol. 29, col. 1337.

177. *Ibid.*, cols. 1311–12.

their motives, would be compelled 'to unite themselves with some of the worst men in the kingdom'.[178]

Though Philip Francis rightly exposed this tactic of smearing the 'Friends' for their supposed radical affiliations,[179] there can be no doubt that ministerialists and conservative Whigs alike viewed the association with real suspicion and alarm.[180] There is solid evidence in support of the contemporary view that the government's decision to issue a Royal Proclamation against Seditious Writings and Publications on 21 May 1792, was precipitated by, and was specifically directed against, the association.[181] In inaugurating the policy of ministerial repression Pitt no doubt had the ulterior motive of wishing to play on the conservative fears of the Portland Whigs in order to draw them into a coalition ministry and thus split the Whig Opposition.[182] That manoeuvre temporarily misfired and the efforts of Pitt and Dundas to 'dish' the Whig friends of liberty and to check both the spread of Painite principles and the expansion of the radical societies had only a limited success in temporarily intimidating the Whig associators.[183] The Royal Proclamation, however, did little to check the progress of radicalism, and the simultaneous initiation of a prosecution against Paine did much to stimulate a wider public curiosity in the contents of *The Rights of Man*.

178. *Ibid.*, col. 1323.

179. In addressing the critics of the Association, he made the effective point that: 'You look for our principles not in our declarations, but in the supposed views and projects of other men, whose views and projects, if any such exist, we have expressly renounced and disclaimed.' *Ibid.*, p. 1340.

180. Windham, for example, viewed the Association 'as nothing but the first big drops of that storm, which having already deluged France, is driving fast to this country.' *The Windham Papers*, ed. Lord Roseberry (London, 1913), vol. 1, p. 100.

181. Earl Fitzwilliam to the Rev. Henry Zouch, 5 June 1792. WWM, E 234/25. Sir Herbert Butterfield, 'Charles James Fox and the Whig Opposition in 1792', *Cambridge Historical Journal* (1949), pp. 293–330.

182. For Pitt's negotiations with Loughborough and the Duke of Leeds in the summer of 1792 see O'Gorman, pp. 91–100.

183. The severed relations between the Association and the radical societies which occurred in the latter part of May 1792 may be partly attributed to this cause.

7 English radicalism in the wake of the French revolution and the Loyalist reaction, 1792–3

L'isle heureuse qui a vu l'aurore de la liberté est digne de recevoir le bienfait de l'égalité.

J. P. R. RABAUT DE SAINT-ÉTIENNE TO M. MARGAROT, 8 November 1792[1]

The cause of liberty can never be endangered by the assault of its enemies, but may sometimes be exposed by the indiscretions of its friends.[2]

1792 – a year of destiny for British artisans and working men as well as for Parisian *sans-culottes* – was notable, less for literary controversy or commemorative anniversaries, than for the spread of Painite radicalism, the advent of the first French republic and the triumph of English conservatism. English working-class radicalism came of age at a time when French liberty and independence were both threatened by a Continental counter-revolutionary coalition, but its development was soon arrested by a rapidly growing reaction, fuelled by revulsion from the September Massacres, suspicion of French metaphysical proselytism and fears of revolutionary aggrandizement in the Netherlands. It was this French dimension of English radicalism, rather than its Painite overtones, which allowed the conservative 'Alarmists' to brand those who were prepared to fraternize with the French with the evocative label of 'English Jacobins'.[3] It may well have been, as Francis Place later suggested, that the Alarmists were secretly more afraid of English liberty than of French democracy.[4] If so, they would hardly have confessed as

1. PRO TS 11/965/3510A, pt. 2.
2. Charles Grey to S. Ashton, secretary to Sheffield Constitutional Society, 24 May 1792, *ST*, vol. 24, col. 1029.
3. This stigma, like the corresponding term of abuse applied to the Parisian democrats – *sans-culottes* – those who wore trousers and not breeches – lost much of its sting by its indiscriminating use and ended by endearing itself to the radicals.
4. BL, Add. MSS. 35154, fo. 32. Place concluded that the real motive behind the Royal Proclamation of 21 May 1791 and the subsequent repression was fear of English liberty.

much, and the radicals were certainly more plausible scapegoats when depicted as 'Atheists' and 'Jacobins' than as 'Republicans and Levellers'. The continued use of the latter slur, as an alternative term of abuse, probably indicates how much the Reevite Loyalist associations in the winter of 1792 still felt it necessary to endorse the anti-Commonwealth prejudices of their precursors and collaborators – the Church and King clubs. As, however, Britain and France moved closer to war, the ambivalent attitude unwisely adopted by the English radicals made the anti-Jacobin jibes of their opponents more credible, and the outbreak of hostilities early in 1793 not only fatally compromised the immediate prospects of any campaign for parliamentary reform, but also confirmed the status of the radicals as an alienated and unpopular minority of political malcontents, whose pro-French sentiments could easily be misrepresented as rooted in constructive treason.

According to Hardy, the formation of the Whig Association of the Friends of the People caused an immediate and 'astonishing' increase in the membership of the London Corresponding Society and somewhat diluted its working-class composition.[5] The initial diffidence of the metropolitan radical artisans appears to have been overcome and their hopes of success stimulated by the spectacle of so many Opposition MPs throwing in their lot with the association in the interests of reform.[6] Following the example set by Lord Daer, Colonel Maitland, Christie and others, members of the new association and 'all ranks and classes of men began now to join the London Corresponding Society or to give their countenance and support to their measures'.[7] Despite the abstention of Wyvill and the Yorkshire committee, Hardy saw this accession of strength as 'only a second edition' of the County Association movement of the 1780s.[8] Such was the influx into the society in the summer months of 1792, when, according to Hardy, three or four hundred members were admitted every week, that printed membership tickets were issued with the motto – 'Unite, persevere and be free'.[9] As had been intended, the principle of 'unlimited membership' operated without

5. BL, Add. MSS. 27814, fo. 34.

6. *Ibid.* Of the hundred signatories of the Association's *Declaration* (11 April 1792) twenty-eight were MPs. *Parl. Hist.*, vol. 29, col. 1304. A few radicals – Lord Daer, Cartwright, J. H. Stone and Thomas Christie, for example – were also members of the Friends of the People.

7. BL, Add. MSS. 27814, fo. 35.

8. *Ibid.*

9. *Ibid.*, fo. 37.

discrimination upwards as well as downwards in the social scale. Though these new recruits from the professional, commercial or leisured classes were welcomed as a reserve of ability which could be drawn on to fill the responsible and elected posts of divisional delegates, there was, nevertheless, real concern that the identity and independence of the working-class element in the society might be affected. Hardy himself was determined that this should not happen, but it remained to be seen what the attitude of the Friends of the People would be to the radical movement in the metropolis and the provinces.

This issue was put to the test when Major Cartwright, as chairman of the Society for Constitutional Information, and Samuel Ashton, as secretary of the Sheffield Constitutional Society, wrote on 27 April and 14 May 1792 respectively to welcome the new association to the ranks of committed reformers. As an elder statesman of the radical movement, however, Major Cartwright was very much on his guard against the aristocratic connections, the untried and dubious sincerity of reforming MPs and the credibility of the society's commitment to the popular cause.[10] These anxieties were frankly expressed by Cartwright when he solemnly warned the Friends of the People of their need to live up to their self-chosen title by committing themselves publicly to 'a substantial reform in the representation of the people' and by sponsoring a 'Declaration of Rights' similar to that adopted by the Society for Constitutional Information.[11] This was a summons to the new association to model its objectives, its attitudes and its behaviour on those of the senior reform society.

The committee of the Sheffield Constitutional Society was, understandably, less demanding and far more deferential in its approach. It expressed its willingness to surrender the lead in the work of reform to 'men of more respectable characters, and great abilities', whose support it had, indeed, eagerly anticipated.[12] Nor had it any wish to 'adopt, or point out any particular mode' of obtaining 'a more free and equal representation in the House of Commons'.[13] Despite the misrepresentations of its enemies, its firm intention was 'strictly to adhere to, maintain and be governed by', the principles laid down in the Declaration issued by the Friends of

10. PRO TS 11/962/3508, fo. 63.
11. *Ibid.*
12. *ST*, vol. 24, col. 1026.
13. *Ibid.*

the People. The committee quoted its successful organization of the booming membership of the society as proof of its ability 'to introduce useful knowledge, good order and regularity into the minds and morals of the common, or lower orders of the people'.[14] The one suggestion it ventured to make to the metropolitan association was that, as a means of obtaining the general sense of the nation on reform in the interim period before Grey made his motion in the House of Commons, a convention of delegates from each county or district should be held in London.[15] This was no doubt meant as a reversion to the radical precedent of 1780, rather than advocacy of the sort of convention for the framing of a new constitution, as prescribed by Paine.

In his reply to Cartwright, dated 12 May 1792, the chairman of the Friends of the People, Lord John Russell MP, justifiably protested: 'Your letter appears to us to be written with a view to create distrust of our designs, to insinuate doubts of sincerity and to excite an early suspicion of our principles in the minds of the People.'[16] In words reminiscent of Burke's, Russell contemptuously dismissed Paine's social welfare schemes as recommended by the SCI and Cartwright's promise to 'obtain the full extent of the Rights of the People' as the 'indefinite language of delusion'. This would merely open up 'unbounded prospects of political adventure' and 'excite a spirit of innovation of which no wisdom can foresee the effects and no skill direct the course'.[17] The reason why the Friends of the People wished to reform the constitution was their desire to preserve it. The views of the two societies on such topics were completely irreconcilable and Russell, therefore, categorically declined 'all future intercourse' with the Society for Constitutional Information. This excommunication was pronounced even before the publication of the Royal Proclamation against Seditious Writings.

After that event the fears expressed by the association were even more revealing. The cause of liberty it felt, would be more 'exposed by the indiscretion of its friends' than 'endangered by the assault of its enemies'.[18] It was in this vein that Grey, as the association's new chairman, exhorted the Sheffield society, in his reply to Ashton on

14. *Ibid.*, col. 1027.
15. *Ibid.*
16. PRO TS 11/952/3496(ii).
17. *Ibid.*
18. *ST*, vol. 24, col. 1028. Charles Grey, chairman to Samuel Ashton, secretary to Sheffield Constitutional Society, 24 May 1792.

24 May, to 'imitate the wariness of our language and conduct' in order that it could rebut the charge now levelled against all reform societies – 'of meditating one object and holding forth another'.[19] If the Sheffield society would follow the Friends of the People in declaring the preservation of the constitution as 'the foundation of all their proceedings and the measure of all their reforms, it would conciliate many to the cause of a reform who are now held in honest neutrality by their fears' and disarm 'the interested supporters of the present abuses'. This union of 'moderation of principles' with 'wariness of language' was, indeed, the test which the association intended to exact of all societies which wished to correspond and co-operate with it.[20] It had already declined all intercourse with Cartwright's society on precisely such grounds. As regards the suggested summons of a delegate convention of reformers in London, while not rejecting it outright, Grey considered its discussion, for the moment, premature.[21]

Though this reply was not reported to a general meeting of the Sheffield society until 28 May, and then only in an edited version,[22] a copy of Russell's earlier rebuff to the Society for Constitutional Information had reached the Sheffield committee on 19 May and had shattered its previous hopes and expectations of a fruitful co-operation with the Whig association. Secretary Ashton indicated as much when writing sympathetically to the Society for Constitutional Information on 26 May to criticize the attitude of the new metropolitan society. He assured Cartwright that the Sheffield committee would make no further effort to communicate with the Friends of the People until it had received his 'sentiments on the subject' or until its own doubts had been resolved.[23] Grey's letter of 24 May did nothing to dispel those doubts and the breach was slow to heal.

What this and other correspondence indicates is that the title 'Friends of the People' had misled the provincial radical societies into thinking that the Whig association might be prepared to underwrite a wide range of popular grievances and to give practical assistance in their solution by incorporating them in its demands for parliamentary reform. On 3 May 1792, for example, a delegate

19. *Ibid.*
20. *Ibid.*
21. *Ibid.*, col. 1030.
22. WWM F 44a(16).
23. PRO TS 11/952/3496(ii). *ST*, vol. 24, col. 1112.

meeting of several Norwich working-class reform societies, in welcoming the formation of the association in a widely publicized set of resolutions, had

humbly recommended the said gentlemen to use their utmost endeavours towards the procuring, as speedily as may be, a smaller and more equal division of all the lands of the kingdom, as a reasonable means both of lowering the price of provisions, and also furnishing employment, and a decent maintenance for a multitude of labourers and mechanics, who are at present groaning under hard labour and the want of necessaries.[24]

This revolutionary panacea undoubtedly owed something to Paine's onslaught on the institution of primogeniture as 'a law of brutal injustice'.[25] Such dangerous Painite 'delusions', however, only made the Friends of the People as apprehensive of the radicals' potential extremism as the Alarmists themselves.[26] The consequent division in the ranks of the reformers was serious – it hamstrung the association from the outset, but it also deprived the popular societies of the moderate and far-sighted leadership which might have saved them from the later indiscretions and miscalculations which discredited the radical movement at a crucial stage of its development.

By a curious irony, however, both the government and the conservative Whigs seem to have felt more anxiety at the fresh impetus given to parliamentary reform by the Friends of the People than at the spread of working-class radicalism.[27] Grey and his colleagues were quick to represent the Royal Proclamation against Seditious Writings as aimed particularly against their association,[28] and this suggestion is confirmed by the correspondence of Earl Fitzwilliam, one of the most prominent of the Whig Alarmists. In a letter of 5 June 1792 to the West Riding magistrate, the Rev. Henry

24. Manchester Central Reference Library. MS 942.073 (newspaper cuttings from Nov. 1792 to Aug. 1793). 2000 copies of these resolutions were printed.

25. T. Paine, *The Rights of Man*, Part II, ed. H. Collins (Harmondsworth, 1969), p. 250.

26. Grenville referred to this 'demand', in the House of Lords, as one for 'an Agrarian law'. *Parl. Hist.*, vol. 29, col. 1529.

27. 'The Proclamation would probably never have appeared if the late Association of many of the Members of Parliament and others had not made these other publications more talked of and more alarming.' Lord Spencer to Dowager Lady Spencer, 22 May 1792, quoted by L. G. Mitchell, *Charles James Fox and the Disintegration of the Whig Party, 1782–1794* (Oxford, 1971), p. 180.

28. *Parl. Hist.*, vol. 29, cols. 1486, 1506.

Zouch, Fitzwilliam succinctly analysed the political motivation behind the Royal Proclamation and the reasons why the Portland Whigs had supported it. 'Undoubtedly', he wrote,

this Association has been the real cause of it – the Revolution Society, the Constitutional Society, both in London, the Sheffield society, that of Manchester, that of Norwich, existed before, and perhaps some few others (tho' I know of none) – but all together, composed as they were, though objects deserving the attention of Prudence, *still were held in contempt*: but they took a very different aspect, when they were to be headed by a new Association, formed of some of the first men in the Kingdom in point of rank, ability and activity. – When members of Parlt. began to tell the lowest orders of the people that they had rights, of wh. they were bereaved by others; to recover these rights, they had only to collect together, and to unite: that if they were anxious to vindicate those rights, they had the power of doing so, and to effect this, advocates and leaders were ready at their call – it became no longer a matter of indifference and grave men felt the necessity of making a stand in the outset, even against those, with whom they had been in constant habits of acting – it was a matter not to be play'd with: it was a business of the most serious cast, if it was anything.[29]

Contrasting the existing situation with that in 1780, 'when Parliamentary Reform first rear'd its head', Fitzwilliam noted two important and ominous differences. Whereas in 1780 pressure for reform had originated with the country gentlemen, 'men of property and of great stake in general tranquillity' and application had been made to Parliament, in 1792 the agitation had begun 'with members of parliament, in parliament, and the appeal is made from parlt. to the people, and to the very lowest orders of the people'. Whereas earlier

the general state of Europe was settled, now there is nothing but Revolutions, and in that of France, is an example of the turbulent and factious, instigating the numbers to exercise that right, which is incontrovertibly in the numbers, namely that of power, which they have exercised with a vengeance, that is to the subversion of the first principle of civil society, its primary, I had almost said, its only object, the protection of the individual against the multitude.

While recognizing that Pitt had ulterior party motives in seeking to divide the Old from the New Whigs, Fitzwilliam stressed

29. In this Burkian assessment, Fitzwilliam attributes to the Friends of the People attitudes and policies which were more characteristic of the Society for Constitutional Information, the London Corresponding Society and Painite radicalism in general.

that was no reason for us [the Portland Whigs], who wished to prevent mischief by foresight, from not agreeing with Ministers in such measures as were fit for the purpose of calling the attention of the grave, the good, and the prudent, to circumstances at least of suspicion, and that ought to lead to circumspection and prevention – in hopes that it will put all men upon their guard.[30]

The actual issue of the Royal Proclamation on 21 May 1792, calling all loyal subjects to resist attempts to subvert all regular government and on all magistrates to make diligent enquiries to discover the authors, printers and disseminators of seditious writings, did little, however, to stem the rising tide of Painite radicalism.[31] The simultaneous decision to prosecute the author of *The Rights of Man* for seditious libel, also recoiled on the head of the government by persuading Paine of the need to publish cheap editions of his work.[32] The London Corresponding Society, which had not hitherto publicly declared its support for Paine's principles, soon took the initiative of raising a subscription for his legal defence.[33] The Sheffield Constitutional Society adversely criticized the Proclamation as an unjustifiable infringement of free speech and called for copies of the cheap editions of *The Rights of Man* as soon as they were available.[34] Above all, the gauntlet thrown down by Dundas as Home Secretary was taken up by the Society for Constitutional Information, which now emerged as the effective leader of the whole democratic movement.

This ascendancy, which was to prove only temporary, may be ascribed to several causes. First, in the spring of 1792, there was a sudden increase in its membership and a change in its character. Several of the new recruits, who were to become prominent in metropolitan radical politics, were men of humble origins, who had achieved a degree of 'respectability' by their professional skills or ability. William Sharp (1749–1824), for example, whose father had been a gunsmith, had won for himself a European reputation as an engraver.[35] The Rev. Jeremiah Joyce (1763–1816) had started life

30. WWM E 234/25.
31. For the text of the Proclamation see *Parl. Hist.*, vol. 29, cols. 1476–7.
32. See letter of Paine to chairman of the SCI, 18 May 1792. PRO TS 11/962/3508.
33. *Ibid.*, fo. 86.
34. J. Gales to Daniel Adams, secretary of the SCI, 11 July 1792, calling for 500 copies of the second part of the *Rights of Man*, as soon as it was published. PRO TS 11/952/3496(ii).
35. He was elected an honorary member of the Imperial Academy at Vienna and of the Royal Academy in Munich.

as a journeyman glazier, but had risen to become tutor to the sons of Earl Stanhope, after acquiring a sound knowledge of mathematics and Latin, when studying for the Unitarian ministry. Thomas Holcroft (1745–1809), whose most famous and successful play, *The Road to Ruin*, had been performed for the first time at Covent Garden on 18 February 1792, had himself played many parts – not only as a strolling actor, prompter, journalist, novelist and translator from the French, but also as a schoolteacher, pedlar, stableboy at Newmarket and cobbler in his father's shoe shop. Dr William Maxwell, who achieved notoriety shortly after the September Massacres by attempting to raise a subscription for the French and was hounded out of the country for his pains, also joined the society in May 1792. A more conventional figure was John Frost (1750–1842), educated at Winchester, trained as an attorney, who had been an ally of the Younger Pitt in his reforming days in 1782.[36] All of these men may be described as 'enthusiasts' – Sharp, a personal friend of Paine, held republican views and later became a devotee of the religious delusions of Richard Brothers and Joanna Southcott. The others were outspoken in their pro-French sympathies. All of them, and especially Frost and Holcroft, were intimate friends of Horne Tooke and all, except Frost and Maxwell, were to be defendants in the treason trials of 1794.

Secondly, in the spring of 1792 the Society for Constitutional Information seems to have taken over from the London Revolution Society as the chief channel of communication between the English radicals and their French counterparts.[37] On 9 March, for example, the society gratefully accepted the dedication to it by Oswald, a British democrat living in exile in Paris, of his English translation of Collot d'Herbois's popular revolutionary handbook *L'Almanach du Père Gérard*.[38] Following letters received from Cooper and Watt Jnr reporting their reception by the Paris Jacobin club in April, a fraternal address to that society was voted on 11 May, transmitted by Horne Tooke and read by Watt on 27 May. It was a message of sympathy and encouragement to the French nation which had recently found itself embroiled in war with Francis II, 'King of

36. The article on Frost in the *Dictionary of National Biography* is, as Veitch first pointed out, full of serious errors.
37. So far as can be discovered, no messages passed between the London Revolution Society and the French political clubs between February and November 1792.
38. PRO TS 11/962/3508 (9 March 1792).

Hungary and Bohemia'. Regretting that the principles of the revolution had not been accepted by France's neighbours and that the spirit of international concord had been stifled by monarchical conspiracy, the society announced its support for French efforts in 'self-defence'.

> We have beheld your peaceable principles insulted by despotic Ignorance. We have seen the right hand of Fellowship which you held out to the world rejected by those who riot in its Plunder: We now behold you a Nation provoked into Defence: and we can see no mode of Defence equal to that of establishing the general freedom of *Europe*. In this best of causes we wish you success. Our Hearts go with you: and in saying this we believe we utter the Voice of Millions.[39]

France had not yet embarked on a policy of revolutionary proselytism, but this address later appeared as an incitement to do so from the leading English radical society.[40] Even more unguarded was the further statement that:

> The principles we now declare are not peculiar to the society that addresses you: they are extending themselves, with accumulating force, through every part of our country, and derive strength from an union of causes, which no other principles admit.[41]

Thirdly, both metropolitan and provincial popular societies had, by this time, clearly acknowledged the political leadership of the most senior reform society. No effective rivals existed, for the London Revolution Society met too infrequently to influence events, and the Association of the Friends of the People had been exposed as 'popular' only in name. The initiative which the Society for Constitutional Information had taken in spreading Painite principles, the practical advice which it had given to the London Corresponding Society and the provincial clubs in the drafting of their rules and regulations, and the help it was soon to give in the establishment of local radical newspapers – all this consolidated its hold on the allegiance of its disciples and supporters. Equally important in the aftermath of the Royal Proclamation was the stand taken by the society as the most vocal and effective critic of the whole policy of governmental repression initiated by Dundas.[42]

39. *ST*, vol. 25, cols. 150–1.
40. Sir John Mitford, Solicitor General, made particular use of this argument in opening the case for the prosecution against Horne Tooke in 1794. *ST*, vol. 25, col. 43.
41. *Ibid.*
42. See, especially, the uncompromising set of resolutions in defence of the

All these policies were epitomized in the person of John Horne Tooke, who now dominated the society which he had done so much to revitalize. 'The principal ornament and support of the English Jacobins',[43] the patron of the rising generation of metropolitan reformers, and the political mentor of the provincial democrats, Tooke held a unique but ambiguous position in the reform movement. Much earlier in life he had shown that he could get the better of Junius in political controversy and was able later to discountenance the most eminent law officers of the Crown in the treason trials of 1794. He could drink the celebrated and cantankerous Greek scholar Porson under the table after a dispute which it was agreed to settle by a drinking contest[44] and yet maintain the highest notions of the 'aristocracy of learning'. He was both a noted philologist and an acute and powerful logician.[45]

The 'treason' that he talked at his Sunday evening dinner parties at his home in Wimbledon was convivial rather than conspiratorial and owed as much to the port that he so liberally circulated among his guests as to his delight in disconcerting his next-door neighbour – the Home Secretary, Dundas. In the same provocative spirit Tooke transferred the meetings of the society, in the summer of 1792, to the Crown and Anchor Tavern, the headquarters of the Association for the Preservation of Life and Liberty against Republicans and Levellers, where he could entertain visitors in a dining club as a preliminary to the formal business of the society later in the evening.[46]

His youthful sympathies and correspondence with John Wilkes deprived him for some time of the degree of MA at Cambridge, and his clerical status, of which he could not divest himself, precluded his admission to the bar and cost him, in 1801, the parliamentary seat for the pocket borough of Old Sarum, which he owed to the

---

principles of free speech and right of association passed on 25 May 1792, in defiance of the Royal Proclamation. PRO TS 11/952/3496(ii).

43. *Quarterly Review*, vol. 7 (1812), p. 314.

44. This was in response to Porson's threat to 'kick and cuff' his host after a quarrel had developed. A. Stephens, *Memoirs of John Horne Tooke*, vol. 2, (London, 1813), pp. 315–16.

45. Tooke's major achievement as philologist was *The Diversions of Purley* (1786–1805). For Hazlitt's tribute see E. D. Mackerness (ed.), *The Spirit of the Age* (London, 1969), pp. 90–6.

46. Visitors were, however, not admitted to the society's meetings. Earlier meetings had been held at the secretary's house. The first meeting at the Crown and Anchor was held on 1 June 1792. *ST*, vol. 25, col. 150. PRO TS 11/962/3508.

influence of Lord Camelford.[47] Tooke nevertheless remained a consistent champion of the privileges of the established church and an inveterate defender of the monarchy and the House of Lords.[48] Completely at his ease in eighteenth-century society, he brought to the Society for Constitutional Information, at the height of its influence, the polished wit and personal assurance of a man of the world, a long experience of the arts of political management and manoeuvre, and a characteristic caution which won for him the unmerited reputation of being the Machiavelli of the popular movement.[49] Distrustful of the political judgement of the masses, Tooke was as consistent an opponent of universal suffrage as Charles James Fox.[50] He was also sharply critical of the passages of *The Rights of Man* in which Paine attacked the hereditary principle in British institutions.[51] He was, however, a committed, though discriminating, supporter of revolutionary France, especially when it was beset by the combined powers of reactionary Europe, and throughout his chequered and turbulent career, he proved himself a 'patriot' and 'friend of liberty'.[52] He did much to train and develop the political talents of Felix Vaughan, John Thelwall and Sir Francis Burdett, all of whom were proud to acknowledge their debt to him and to be his disciples.[53] He would have been the last to man the barricades, and never sought or approved outright confrontation with the government, but in the crisis of 1794 he displayed a moral courage, despite his accumulating physical infirmities, which inspired

47. In 1771 Tooke re-applied for the MA degree at Cambridge, and despite Paley's opposition, the grace was granted by a large majority. Tooke was excluded from the House of Commons under the terms of the Clergy Incapacitation Act 1801 – a declaratory act of which he was the occasion. He was thus the last Anglican clergyman to sit as a member of the house. W. H. Reid, *Memoirs of the Public Life of John Horne Tooke* (London, 1812), pp. 167–8.

48. Stephens, vol. 2, p. 477.

49. At his trial in 1794 the prosecution made much of the corrections and emendations which Tooke made in the phraseology of the public addresses and resolutions of the London Corresponding Society as evidence of his occult influence in its proceedings. Tooke stoutly maintained, however, that his alterations were to protect the drafters of the documents from charges of sedition.

50. Stephens, vol. 2, p. 482.

51. *ST*, vol. 25, col. 318.

52. He always kept a stone from the Bastille in a prominent position in his study. On the occasion of the Crown and Anchor dinner on 14 July 1790, however, Tooke had 'moderated the Moderator' by revising the Francophile toast moved by Sheridan in order to prevent misunderstanding. See above, p. 123.

53. Stephens, vol. 2, col. 306.

his humbler companions in the Tower with confidence and resolution.[54]

Second only to the spread of Painite doctrines and the renewed vitality of the Society for Constitutional Information in the rapid evolution of the popular movement in 1792 was the rise of a radical newspaper and periodical press. Some of the most active and influential leaders of the radical reform societies in the provinces were liberal-minded printers, publishers and newspaper proprietors. Many of the provincial societies, influenced by the advice and example of the Society for Constitutional Information, regarded it as one of their primary functions to provide the working and middle classes with some knowledge of their constitutional liberties and current affairs as their essential passport to an extended or universal electoral franchise.[55] For this purpose the newspaper was as vital a means of communication as the pamphlet or handbill. Improved and speedier communications with the capital, the inroads on illiteracy in the larger industrial towns made by the Sunday School movement, the rise of subscription reading rooms, and the passage of Fox's Libel Act in 1792 were all factors fostering the development of a newspaper press, hitherto restricted by heavy taxation and the disapproving attitude of the political establishment.[56]

The early reform societies were, moreover, fully persuaded of the need for their proceedings to be 'open' or public, in order to rob their opponents of the opportunity to misrepresent their views or to misconstrue their immediate plans or ultimate intentions.[57] This

54. A few days before the prisoners were removed to Newgate for their trial, Tooke had made a great impression on Thelwall by announcing his determination 'to live to be useful or to die usefully'. Thelwall thought this a maxim for all seasons. J. Thelwall, the *Tribune*, vol. 3, p. 238.

55. The Manchester and Sheffield Constitutional Societies and the Norwich Revolution Society all stressed this educational aspect of their activities.

56. For these topics see R. K. Webb, *The British working-class reader, 1790–1848: Literacy and Social Tension* (London, 1955), *passim*; A. Aspinall, *Politics and the Press, c. 1780–1850* (London, 1949), p. 25; D. Read, *Press and People, 1790–1850* (London, 1961). So long as highly conservative judges, and not juries, decided whether publications were libellous, the expression of novel or radical political opinion was severely handicapped. By allowing juries to pass general verdicts, on both the law and fact of publication, of alleged libel, Fox's act redressed this situation. H. M. Lubasz, 'Public opinion comes of age: reform of the libel law in the eighteenth century', *History Today*, vol. 8 (1958), pp. 453–61.

57. G. S. Veitch, *Genesis of Parliamentary Reform* (London, 1965 reprint), p. 204.

natural concern for their public relations required the publication of their more important 'Resolutions', 'Addresses' or 'Declarations', either as separate handbills, or more expeditiously, by their insertion in local newspapers. For this, however, the societies were dependent on the goodwill of the editors or proprietors of existing journals, and as local hostility to the radicals mounted and as governmental repression intensified, the continued acquiescence of such editors became problematical. It was, indeed, the refusal of Charles Wheeler, editor of the moderate *Manchester Chronicle* to print the Painite *Address and Declaration of the Friends of Universal Peace and Liberty*, forwarded to Thomas Cooper by Horne Tooke in August 1791, which convinced the Manchester radicals of the necessity to establish their own independent weekly journal.[58] Fair and regular reporting of their main activities in local newspapers was also regarded by the radicals as an effective means of recruiting new members and attracting the notice and support of the established metropolitan reform societies.[59] Notice of the times and places of the fortnightly divisional and monthly general meetings of the societies organized on the Sheffield model could also be conveniently and cheaply given in the form of newspaper advertisements.[60] Counter-petitions or emergency 'protest' meetings representative of local opposition to government policy could also be promoted in the same way.[61] Once such radical journals had become well established and had achieved wide regional circulations, they enabled provincial reform societies in different parts of the country to maintain contact, to render each other mutual assistance, and, if necessary, to concert action on a national scale. Public opinion in the country as a whole could hardly, as yet, be converted to the need for radical parliamentary reform by such means, but the provincial newspaper press, at least in the North-West, soon proved itself a vital part of the democratic process, and a valuable ally of popular radicalism. That was why it was singled out by local reactionaries for violent repression and why its leading

58. For the *Address and Declaration* see above, pp. 184–5. D. Malone, *The public life of Thomas Cooper, 1783–1839* (New Haven, 1926), p. 31.

59. For the early relations of the Sheffield Constitutional Society with the Society for Constitutional Information see *ST*, vol. 24, col. 284 and *ST*, vol. 25, col. 135.

60. For the complicated arrangements made for a general meeting of the Sheffield society on 27 February 1792 see *Sheffield Register*, 24 Feb. 1792. A. W. L. Seaman, 'Reform politics at Sheffield, 1791–98', *Transactions of the Hunter Archaeological Society*, vol. 7 (1957), p. 218.

61. F. Knight, *The Strange Case of Thomas Walker* (London, 1957), p. 76.

editors or proprietors were driven, by threatened prosecution or repeated physical intimidation, to seek refuge in exile.

Once again Sheffield was to be a pioneer – mainly owing to the public spirit, varied talents and radical commitment of Joseph Gales, editor and proprietor, since 1787, of the *Sheffield Register*, and one of the promoters of and contributors to the fortnightly periodical, the *Patriot*, started in April 1792.[62] Son of Thomas Gales, parish clerk and schoolmaster of the village of Eckington, the domain of the Sitwell family, Joseph had learnt typography at Newark, married a novelist connected with the peerage and arrived in Sheffield in 1786 as a master printer and bookbinder at the age of twenty-five. Soon after he set up a printer's and stationer's shop in the Hartshead in the centre of the town. From there on 8 June 1787, in partnership with an engraver, David Martin, he brought out the first number of his *Sheffield Register*. Gales himself, as a leading Unitarian, promoter of the Sunday School and abolitionist movements, friend of Paine and member of a small literary and scientific group meeting at the Bull Inn in the Wicker,[63] soon became a prominent figure in the local community. His business activities were diverse – he was a successful auctioneer, vendor of patent medicines, agent of the Royal Exchange Fire Office, music, map and print-seller.[64] Owing to its arrangements for the early receipt of news from London, and the enlightened views of its proprietor, the *Register* prospered, and within a few years of its foundation had achieved a circulation not only in the counties of York, Derby and Nottingham but also 'in some of the principal towns of Lincolnshire, Cheshire, Lancashire, Warwickshire, Durham and Northumberland'.[65]

As a reformer with a strongly developed social conscience and radical leanings, Gales ventilated in his weekly journal the grievances of the journeymen cutlers against their masters and the resentment of the townspeople against the enclosing activities of the agents of

62. W. H. G. Armytage's article, 'The editorial experience of Joseph Gales, 1786–1794', *North Carolina Historical Review*, vol. 28 (1951), pp. 332–61, is invaluable. W. E. Smith's article in the *Dictionary of American Biography*, vol. 7 (1943), is also useful.

63. I. Inkster, 'The development of a scientific community in Sheffield, 1790–1850: a network of people and interests', *Transactions of the Hunter Archaeological Society*, vol. 10 (1973), pp. 99–131.

64. PRO HO 42/30. Contains Gales's business description on a bill head dated 27 May 1794.

65. *Ibid.* In May 1794 its circulation reached 2025 copies. J. Holland and J. Everett, *Memoirs of James Montgomery* (London, 1854), vol. 1, p. 163.

the Duke of Norfolk.[66] Besides this sympathetic reporting, Gales opened his columns impartially to correspondents who wished to air their own views on political issues of national or local importance, but made clear his own attitude to reform by printing extracts from the various replies to Burke's *Reflections*, including the first part of *The Rights of Man*.[67] In the winter of 1791, along with his former partner, David Martin, Gales helped to organize the Sheffield Constitutional Society and to secure for it the active support or benevolent neutrality of liberal minded patrons, who had been prominent members of Wyvill's Yorkshire Association.[68] He served on the society's committee, inserted notices of its meetings and public declarations in the *Register* and acted as chairman of its large open-air meetings. In April 1792 his expanding business and increasing involvement in the radical movement led Gales to engage as his accounting clerk and assistant in his printing office the twenty-one year-old son of a Moravian minister – James Montgomery, a man of some literary and poetical talent.[69]

Almost simultaneously with his appointment there appeared on 3 April 1792 the first number of a new radical periodical with the title of the *Patriot, or Political, Moral and Philosophical Repository* – a fortnightly publication which Gales printed in response to a suggestion originally made to provincial reformers by the Society for Constitutional Information.[70] Gales no doubt served on its editorial board, but its editor-in-chief was Matthew Campbell Brown – 'a barber turned advocate', who, in 1793, became secretary of the Sheffield Constitutional Society and its delegate to the British Reform Convention in Edinburgh.

This periodical was the most original and significant radical

66. *Sheffield Register*, 27 August 1790, 5 August 1791.

67. *Ibid.*, 19 Nov. 1790, for an unfavourable review of the *Reflections*; 7 June 1791 for extracts from Paine.

68. The chief of these was a fellow Unitarian steelmaster, Samuel Shore III (1738–1828), whose sister Hannah had married Thomas Walker, the Manchester radical. Shore was a generous benefactor of local charities. He had served, while still young, as high sheriff of Derbyshire, and later acted for some years as a West Riding magistrate. He had also been a member of the committee of Wyvill's Yorkshire Association and was a member of the Society for Constitutional Information. Lady Stephen, 'The Shores of Sheffield and the Offleys of Norton Hall', *Transactions of the Hunter Archaeological Society*, vol. 5 (1937–43), pp. 1–17. Also *Sheffield Independent*, 26 Nov. 1828 for biographical notice. Sheffield Central Library, Local Pamphlets, vol. 41(11).

69. Holland and Everett, vol. 1.

70. PRO TS 11/952/3496(ii). Editors of the *Patriot* to the SCI, 11 June 1792.

publication to issue from the provincial press.[71] It found its way to Scotland, Ireland and America and was even translated into Welsh.[72] Its editors also maintained close contact with their colleagues on the *Doncaster Journal*, the *Manchester Herald*, the *Chester Chronicle* and the *Leicester Chronicle*.[73] Its editorial preface, dated 20 March 1792, made clear that it was aimed at 'the middle and lower ranks of the people' and that its general purpose was 'to induce the people at large to examine and think for themselves'. The style and presentation would make it intelligible to 'the meanest capacity' and the price of 3d. per copy would bring it 'within the compass of everyone's purchase'. Its object would be 'to show what it is that constitutes LIBERTY by a delineation of government in general and our own excellent Constitution, or form of Government, in particular'. Interest in 'the fundamental principles of government in general and the secret or mainsprings by which they are actuated' had been aroused by the momentous revolutionary changes in America and France. The public and private liberties enshrined in the British constitution had also been impaired by 'the destructive hand of time' and the secret influence of the court. Its defects would, therefore, be examined and 'the proper and natural' means of correcting them by a 'reform of abuses and an equal Representation of the People' would be indicated. Readers were informed that their time would not be wasted on 'mere controversies or personalities'.[74]

Its contents fell into three main categories. As was to be expected, each issue contained longer or shorter extracts from the main eighteenth-century classics of liberal political theory – Locke, Bolingbroke, Montesquieu and Junius, Rousseau's *Social Contract*, David Williams's *Letters on Political Liberty*, Obadiah Hulme's anonymous *Essay on the English Constitution*, Burgh's *Political Disquisitions* and Volney's *Ruines ou méditations sur les révolutions des empires* (1791).[75] Secondly, there were editorial articles, letters and texts bearing on the various aspects of reform politics – instances of

71. It is usually found in bound form – vol. 1, containing 13 fortnightly numbers, covering the period from 3 April to 18 September 1792; vol. 2, with the same number of issues, from 2 October 1792 to 26 March 1793; and vol. 3 with eleven issues, extending from 23 April 1793 to mid-September 1793.

72. G. A. Williams, *Artisans and Sans-Culottes* (London, 1968), p. 59.

73. PRO TS 11/952/3496(ii). Editors of the *Patriot* to SCI, 11 June 1792.

74. *Patriot*, vol. 1, pp. 3–10.

75. *Patriot*, vol. 3, pp. 103–7. It was the free-thinking tone of the comte de Volney's Utopian prose-poem rather than its anti-colonialism which appealed to later radicals.

corrupt borough representation, the merits of short parliaments, the *Addresses* and *Declarations* of the radical and reform societies, the famous reports on the *State of the Representation* issued by the Association of the Friends of the People in 1793 and its petition for parliamentary reform.[76] Thirdly, there was a series of articles on Anglo-French relations and translations of the fundamental legislative decrees of the French National Assemblies.[77] All the topics were seasoned with pungent editorial comment and enlivened by the controversial views of correspondents.

Although the title of *Patriot* aroused some uneasiness in ministerial circles, the prevailing polemical tone of the periodical was moderate. If the extension of the popular reform societies was encouraged, their members were exhorted, at the same time, to be 'very circumspect and prudent in all their proceedings' – even before the issue of the Royal Proclamation.[78] When the timeliness of parliamentary reform was reasserted even after the outbreak of war with revolutionary France, it was because it appeared as a more preferable alternative than either republicanism or monarchical tyranny.

Against the prevalence of both extremes there only exists one remedy. It is to invigorate the democratic part of the constitution; it is to render the House of Commons so honestly and substantially the representative of the people, that Republicans may no longer have topics of invective, nor Ministers the means of corruption. . . . The same reform will preserve the English constitution from the sap of Royal influence and from the storm of tumultuous democracy.[79]

Though Burke would not have agreed, the sentiment might well have been endorsed by the Association of the Friends of the People. As would also the virtual absence of all Painite propaganda.[80] Though

76. For the FOP reports see *Patriot*, vol. 3, pp. 136–41; 206–13; 335–48; 382–413. The article on 'Short Parliaments' by 'Harrington' in April 1793 is well worth consulting. *Ibid.*, vol. 3, pp. 214–16.

77. E.g. 'Philanthropus' on 'the probable influence of the French Revolution on Great Britain'. *Ibid.*, vol. 1, pp. 86–93 and 'Alfred' on 'An alliance with France' (15 May 1792), vol. 1, pp. 122–6. Translation of the Declaration of the Rights of Man, vol. 1, pp. 229–34, on the ground that 'it had been frequently abused, vilified and misrepresented in many of the public prints'. Translation of the Constitution of 1793. *Ibid.*, vol. 3, pp. 313–26.

78. Editorial comment, 17 April 1792. *Ibid.*, vol. 1, p. 46.

79. *Ibid.*, vol. 2, pp. 349–50 (5 Feb. 1793).

80. The only quotation from Paine's works is in vol. 2, pp. 331–4 – Paine's letter to Lord Onslow June 1792. A letter from 'Candidus' (5 Sept. 1792), however, takes up the cudgels in Paine's defence. *Ibid.*, vol. 2, pp. 194–5. 'If we

prudential restraint was, no doubt, enforced on the *Patriot* at a time of general reaction, no one could question its perseverance in the cause of parliamentary reform, even when the chances of success had dwindled to vanishing point.

How the editors of the *Patriot* envisaged their self-chosen task of inducing 'the people at large to examine and think for themselves' is revealed in their correspondence with the Society for Constitutional Information and with other reform societies in the provinces. Convinced that no reform could be achieved without 'the powerful interposition of the great Body of the People', their first concern had been to inform the mass of the people of their constitutional rights, of which they appeared to be 'so universally, and so fatally ignorant'. Writing on 11 June 1792 to the Society for Constitutional Information, the editors enclosed copies of the issues of the *Patriot* so far published with a request for a candid opinion on their contents and for any 'hints' which might enhance their utility. They also asked for the metropolitan society's moral support and practical help in view of the difficulties they were encountering from 'a strong, a powerful, and a well disciplined Phalanx' of opponents – 'long enured [*sic*] to every possible mode of attack; thoroughly skilled in the science of defence' – and in 'circumventing and smothering every attempt that may be made against them while in its Infancy'. They complained of their inability to insert advertisements in the London journals circulating in the provinces, since nine out of ten were in the interest of government. Opposition to the circulation of the *Patriot* had come particularly from the clergy, who 'had great influence everywhere, equal leisure to exert it and . . . a never failing inclination'. Almost as disconcerting was the inertia of the rural population and its lack of interest in any form of political discussion.[81]

Besides requesting the members of the SCI to use their individual and collective influence to recommend every new publication which might 'serve the glorious cause of liberty', the editors of the *Patriot* made their own critical appraisal of how the provincial reform societies could best checkmate the manoeuvres of their enemies. Their first need was to maintain 'equal Discipline, Activity and strict

---

consider the book as an essay on civil government, Paine has said no more than what many have said before him; and if we consider it as a defence of religious liberty, he has said more in one single page on this most interesting subject, than other writers of first-rate abilities have been able to say in a whole volume.'

81. PRO TS 11/952/3496(ii).

Adherence together of the Friends of the People' in the face of their opponents' efforts to 'divide and dominate' them. Solidarity was what they meant and this was to be a significant watchword for the future. To offset the influence of the government-controlled metropolitan journals in the regions, the editors ventured to suggest that a better popular response might be ensured by encouraging the sale of small and cheap publications (such as the *Patriot*) in preference to the policy of distributing reform literature free, which was favoured by the Society for Constitutional Information. They pointed out that the general public was often sceptical of the motivation behind such free propaganda and that the policy was, therefore, often counter-productive.

Thirdly, in order to overcome the apathy of the farming community, and incidentally to embarrass their clerical opponents, the editors called on both the metropolitan reform societies and the other regional centres of radicalism – in Manchester and Norwich – to follow the example of Sheffield by engaging in aggressive missionary propaganda in surrounding country districts against the evils and injustices of ecclesiastical tithes. This was the only way in which the farmers and 'husbandmen' could be brought over to the reform camp. The latter were 'so sunk in Ignorance and absorbed in the *Amor sceleratus habendi*' that

an Angel might exhaust his eloquence in vain in talking to *them* of the importance of *Rights, Liberties, Franchises* and *Privileges*, it would be as useless as if wasted on the Desart [*sic*] air. But let the poorest D– that ever wagged his tongue but mention tythes – tho' it was in the hoarse and discordant Accents of the raven – it wld. appear more mellifluous in their ears than the sweetest strains of the Nightingale – would awaken and rivet their attention and rouse them to any measures and any resolves by which it might appear they wd. rid themselves of those Hay and Straw chains in which the tenth of the produce of their Fields is bound to and carried away *pro bono Ecclesiae*.

This issue had been raised in Devonshire, why should not an agitation become general throughout the country?[82]

Similarly, John Andrew, who encountered much local hostility when launching the Stockport Society of the Friends of Universal Peace and the Rights of Man in the autumn of 1792, was given a complete lesson in the art and psychology of political persuasion.[83]

82. *Ibid.*
83. SCI to J. Andrew, 13 October 1792. *Ibid.*

He too had suggested the need to evangelize the country districts,[84] but was warned that missionaries for the purpose would have to be carefully chosen and instructed in the best methods of approach. Just as the farmers could be roused by the mention of tithes and shoemakers by emphasis on the 'excessive dearness of leather', so innkeepers could be brought to listen if the burdens of 'a numerous and unnecessary standing army' were underlined.

A temperate and dispassionate relation of the immense number of sinecure places and useless offices, in which the corrupt and prostituted favourites, Agents and Dependents of the rich and Great, riot in the spoils and plunder, wrested from the sweat of the Brow, and continual labour of body, of the Husbandman, the Mechanic, the Labourer and Artificer

– would, in itself, be sufficient to incite the resentment and indignation of the general public quite apart from its more specific grievances. Advice was also given how best to counter insinuations that the reformers were Levellers and how best to enlighten those prejudiced in favour of abuses. Those who were still unconvinced by such arguments or by explanations of the aims and purposes of the reform societies should be invited to attend their meetings and judge for themselves.[85]

The maturity and sophistication of this lesson in the art of political persuasion are remarkable. The Manchester, Norwich, Stockport and other societies moved their missionaries into the rural areas and even the Society for Constitutional Information could only recommend the insertion in the *Patriot* of 'proverbial axioms' as used by Franklin in his *Poor Richard's Almanack* – appealing to 'the real wants, grievances, and affections of the people'.[86]

In contrast with the moderation of the Sheffield *Patriot*, the *Manchester Herald*, the first issue of which appeared on 31 March 1792, was unequivocally radical in its commitment to 'the cause of the public'. Printed by Matthew Falkner and Samuel Birch, both booksellers and members of the Manchester Constitutional Society, the *Herald* soon became the organ of the radical movement through-

---

84. J. Andrew to Editors of the *Patriot*, 4 Oct. 1792, in reply to their letter of 5 September. *Ibid.* 'I have observed that a principal thing wanting among the People is spirit; they do not sufficiently venerate themselves as Men; they are broken with Taxes; they are lulled asleep by Ministerial Prints and in many places seem to be quietly sinking into slavery.'

85. SCI to Andrew. 13 Oct. 1792. *Ibid.*

86. *ST*, vol. 24, cols. 829–31. Draft answer, undated, but sometime in October 1792.

out the industrial North-West. Rejecting 'that lukewarm caution and prudent moderation which casts a veil over political delinquency, and conceals from the public *what the public ought to know*', the editorial preface announced that, short of incurring the penalties of libel, 'no fear or favour shall prevent us from making our publication *decidedly* the PAPER OF THE PEOPLE'.[87] It repudiated mere party politics – either ministerial or Whig – and scorned social gossip or 'articles of *fashionable* intent', though snobbery was not excluded from its remunerative advertisements.[88] The journal concentrated its attention on serious issues – the cause of Negro emancipation, the condemnation of the Royal Proclamation, eulogy of the second part of *The Rights of Man*, concern for the plight of Manchester's poor, and the promotion of radical concepts of parliamentary reform. Detailed advice on the formation and organization of popular societies was provided and full reports given of their principles and transactions.[89] Priced at $1\frac{1}{2}$d. for each weekly copy, the *Manchester Herald*, like the *Sheffield Register*, achieved a wide regional circulation, aided by the trenchant articles contributed by Thomas Cooper, under the pseudonym of 'Sydney'.[90] The whole tone of the journal was Painite, in its scurrilous attacks on the Crown, the aristocracy and the House of Commons and in its unrestrained admiration for the French revolution.[91] Its strongly Francophile bias survived the September Massacres, the overthrow

87. 31 March 1792.

88. Typical advertisements were for 'genteel Lodgings and Post-Chaises, Cures for Corns', the 'famous Parisian vegetable syrup', guaranteed to cure anything, or 'a Variety of Silke Florentines, Armazeens, Bombazeens, Morettas, Russels, Wildbotes, Durants and Blankets.' Knight, p. 72.

89. 'A plan for associations of good citizens, for the purpose of obtaining political information, and for promoting an effectual reform of Parliament' appeared on 16 June 1792. E.g. notices of the formation and principles of the Manchester 'Patriotic' (24 May 1792) and 'Reformation' Societies (6 June 1792), of the Stockport 'Friends of Universal Peace and the Rights of Man' (1 September), the Warrington 'Amicable Society for Free Representation and Political Information' and the Newton 'Friends of Freedom, Peace and Free Enquiry' (10 November 1792).

90. One of the most incisive of these articles dealt unmercifully with the Royal Proclamation against Seditious Writings. *Manchester Herald*, 2 June 1792. See also D. Read, *Press and People, 1790–1850* (London, 1961), pp. 71–2, and D. Clare, 'The growth and importance of the newspaper press in Manchester, Liverpool, Sheffield and Leeds, 1780–1800', unpublished MA thesis, Manchester (1960).

91. Its first issue contained a glowing assessment of the effect of the French revolution in undermining aristocracy and making possible universal liberty.

of the Bourbon monarchy, and the expansionist policy of the National Convention.[92] This feeling had been rekindled by the heroic defence of the fatherland by the republican volunteer troops against the combined armies of Habsburg and Hohenzollern. An editorial article of 28 April 1792 had seen the interests of British, and indeed of Universal, Liberty at stake in that conflict[93] and, even on the eve of Anglo-French hostilities, Cooper was fearless in his condemnation of the manifold evils of war and its consequences both for the Manchester merchants and for the manufacturing poor.[94]

Similar roles in the evolution of provincial radicalism were performed by the editors of other local journals, notably at Derby and Leicester. William Ward, editor of the *Derby Mercury* from 1789 to 1791, was one of the prime movers, along with Joseph Strutt, Samuel Fox and Erasmus Darwin, in the formation of the Derby Society for Political Information early in 1792. Son of a builder of Burton-on-Trent, he had been brought up by his mother as a devout Methodist and had cultivated his oratorical gifts as a youthful lay preacher.[95] Like Gales and Cooper, Ward used his position on the *Derby Mercury* to print editorial articles on current politics instead of extracts from the London journals. His early views as a moderate reformer were reflected by his support for the French revolution, his fervent advocacy of relief for Protestant Dissenters and his reasoned pleas for parliamentary reform. The rapid evolution of his own opinions and of the members of the Derby society, under the stimulus received from Paine, can, however, be traced in the society's *Address to the Friends of Free Enquiry and the General Good* of 16 July 1792.[96] This had been agreed to at the society's first public meeting which had been held at the Talbot inn, instead of a dinner to commemorate the fall of the Bastille. It was the work, not of Erasmus Darwin, but of Ward. Instead of calling, as the society's original rules had done, for 'full, free and frequently elected repre-

92. The editors of the *Herald* put out a special apology for and defence of the September Massacres on 10 September 1792 – based on eye-witness reports from correspondents in Paris. It was also circulated in handbill form. A copy was delated to the Home Office. PRO HO 42/21, fo. 560.

93. The article was headed 'THE WAR OF FREEDOM'.

94. Pamphlet on 'WAR', 10 December 1792.

95. S. Stennet, *Memoirs of the Life of William Ward* (London, 1825), p. 237. E. Fearn, 'Reform movements in Derby and Derbyshire, 1790–1832', unpublished MA thesis, University of Manchester (1964).

96. J. C. Marshman, *The Story of Carey, Marshman and Ward*, vol. 1, p. 94.

sentation',[97] the *Address* based the case for universal suffrage, not on the theory of individual rights, but on more specific economic grounds. It also attacked the political establishment from the standpoint of its evil social consequences and outlined a wide-ranging programme of social welfare benefits derived directly from the second part of *The Rights of Man*.[98] Though the Derby society, along with the other provincial reform societies, continued to be fed with Painite publications by the Society for Constitutional Information, it experienced increasing difficulty in circulating them. When William Strutt, the main cotton manufacturer in Belper and leader of the Derby society, attempted to distribute copies among his workpeople in November 1792, his mills were flooded and the books were burnt.[99] Despite the adoption of the Sheffield model of organization, the divisions of the Derby society did not attract large numbers of working men and its total membership never exceeded one hundred.[100] The society at Belper was even smaller. Middle-class leadership recoiled at the strength of local opposition, and, after the rejection of its petition for reform by the House of Commons in May 1793, the Derby Society for Political Information ceased to meet.[101] Its main contribution to the radical cause was to have fostered the budding demagogic talents of Henry Redhead Yorke, of whom more will be heard later.[102]

At Leicester, too, the establishment of an independent newspaper by a radically disposed bookseller contributed, along with other factors, to the formation in November 1792 of a local reform society. Leicester was a borough with parliamentary representation dominated in the late eighteenth century by feuds between the Tory Anglican corporation and an opposition grouping of Dissenters, wealthy hosiery manufacturers and Whig county families, led by the Duke of Rutland.[103] Since 1774 these opposing factions, in order

97. *Rules of the Derby Society for Political Information*, Derby Central Library.

98. The *Morning Chronicle* published the *Address* in December 1792 and was prosecuted for a seditious libel, unsuccessfully, however. *ST*, vol. 22, cols. 953–1023. Fearn, pp. 89–91.

99. *Manchester Mercury*, 13 Nov. 1792.

100. Fearn, p. 112.

101. Its moderate petition was presented on 6 May 1793. *Commons Journal*, vol. 48, p. 734.

102. See below, p. 253.

103. A. Temple Patterson, *Radical Leicester: A History of Leicester, 1780–1850* (Leicester, 1954), ch. 4. R. W. Greaves, *The Corporation of Leicester, 1689–1836* (Oxford, 1939), p. 97. J. Thompson, *History of Leicester in the Eighteenth Century* (Leicester, 1871).

to avoid the expense of contested elections, had agreed to divide the borough representation between them. Though sectarian strife over the repeal campaign in 1789 led to a confrontation between the local Whig Revolution Society and a newly established Tory Constitutional Club, and though further violent divisions occurred during the General Election of 1790, mounting local Alarmism in 1792 induced the Whig borough member Thomas Parkyns to unite forces with the Tory representative, Samuel Smith, as a supporter of Pitt's administration.[104] Led by the Rutland interest, the Whig grandees and gentry of Leicestershire also defected en bloc to the Tory side. The closure of the Tory Constitutional Club after the General Election of 1790 and of the Revolution Society after a final anniversary dinner early in November 1792 removed the final obstacles to the formation of an independent and more unified reform party.[105] The way was thus opened for the establishment, shortly afterwards, of the Leicester Constitutional Society for Promoting an Equal Representation of the People in Parliament.

This Leicester radicalism can, however, also be associated with the activities of Richard Phillips, the vegetarian bookseller and eccentric newspaper proprietor, whose early career was strongly reminiscent of that of Joseph Gales.[106] The son of a Leicestershire farmer, born and educated in London, Phillips had arrived in the town in 1788 aged twenty-one with small means, which he nevertheless invested in a commercial academy. In 1789, with borrowed capital, he opened a hosier's shop but, in the following year, after acquiring a bookseller's business, he diversified his interests by selling pamphlets, pianofortes, prints and music. He was also a vendor of patent medicines and canal shares. He was far, however, from being a mere mountebank. In 1790 he revealed his more serious interests by founding a literary society and by joining a group of young intellectuals interested in science called the Adelphi Society.[107] Early in May 1792 Phillips established a new local journal, the *Leicester Herald*, to compete with the existing Tory newspaper, the *Leicester Journal*, but soon encountered a further rival in the shape of the *Leicester Chronicle*. Though Phillips announced his support

104. Patterson, p. 67.

105. Greaves, p. 108.

106. F. S. Hearne, 'An old Leicester bookseller', *Transactions of the Leicester Literary and Philosophical Society* (Leicester, 1873). *Dictionary of National Biography*.

107. Patterson, p. 68.

for parliamentary reform, the calculated moderation of his public pronouncements and the unbiased opinions of his newspaper correspondents enabled him to make a success of this latest business venture.[108]

The aims and principles of the new radical society, whose secretary George Bown had been a member of the Adelphi group, as set out in the *Leicester Herald*, appeared innocuously Whiggish.[109] But Phillips' business interests as a bookseller and his own radical commitment had led him in July 1792 to request from the Society for Constitutional Information supplies of the cheap edition of Paine's *Rights of Man* and to offer to open up his newspaper columns to any of Paine's writings.[110] It was as a distributor of seditious publications that he attracted the attention of the government and was sentenced, after trial, in April 1793 to eighteen months' imprisonment.[111] Though he continued to edit the *Herald* from prison, Phillips did not venture on further criticism of the government until 1794. Early in 1793, however, the Leicester Constitutional Society collapsed and even the members of the Adelphi group, 'whose experiments with electricity had become confounded in the public mind with the construction of infernal machines', thought it advisable to disband also.[112] The *Leicester Herald* survived till November 1795 when a disastrous fire destroyed Phillips's bookshop and newspaper offices.[113] His migration to London in 1796 robbed Leicester's already virtually extinct radicalism of its sole surviving supporter of any consequence.

If the Royal Proclamation of May 1792 did nothing immediately to check Painite propaganda or to prevent the spread of radical societies, it nevertheless created an atmosphere in which local or ministerial repression could claim to be strengthening the defences of ordered society against what were regarded as the forces of disorder. Public opinion had been alerted to the dangers of 'subversive' propaganda. 'Church and King' activity against Dissenting and radical minorities was rekindled, and local authorities were encouraged to send in addresses of thanks to the sovereign for having issued the proclamation – mainly as a means of mobilizing sentiment

108. *Ibid.*, p. 69.
109. The political principles of the Leicester society almost exactly mirrored those of the Manchester Constitutional Society. *Leicester Herald*, 15 Dec. 1792.
110. PRO TS 11/952/3496(ii). R. Phillips to D. Adams, 11 July 1792.
111. BL, Add. MSS. 27809, fo. 208.
112. Patterson, p. 73.
113. Patterson, p. 77.

against the reformers and indicating areas where loyalty was lukewarm.[114] The anxieties of the government as to security in the manufacturing towns, where few local magistrates were actually resident, and where troops billeted in alehouses were exposed to seditious influences, were real enough. In the summer of 1792 the Secretary at War despatched Colonel de Lancey, Deputy Adjutant General, on a special mission to the Midlands and North-West to report on the disposition of the troops and their reliability in case of emergency.

Arriving in Manchester towards the end of May to investigate the alleged growth of 'the spirit of combination and discontent' among the men of the Second Regiment of Dragoons, who had bolstered their claims to higher wages by electing four committees from the rank and file to negotiate with their commanding officer, de Lancey took the opportunity also to survey the state of public opinion in the town. His reports to the War Department and the Home Office on both counts were, on the whole, reassuring. No attempts had been made to tamper with the soldiers' loyalty, their claims to higher wages, given the higher cost of living in Manchester and previous promises made to them when in Scotland, were not unreasonable, and had not been prompted from outside. Discipline had been restored by the dissolution of the mens' committees.[115] On 13 June, in a long and well-informed letter to Dundas, de Lancey reported that public discontent in Manchester, particularly among 'the lower class of the inhabitants', was not as prevalent as he had been led to expect. The Church and King faction was in the ascendant and the reformers were on the defensive.[116] A note of warning, however, followed.

There is a set of people of a higher description associated for purposes very subversive of good order and tending to destroy the peace and government of the country, to whose operations I think it is necessary that some attention should be paid, as it is impossible to tell the moment when they may acquire a sufficient ascendancy over the minds of the lower class of people to be able to lead them to any extremities.[117]

This comment had probably been prompted by the recent formation of two working-class clubs – the Manchester Patriotic

114. T. Walker, *A Review of Some of the Political Events in Manchester* (London, 1794), pp. 34–7.
115. PRO HO 42/20. De Lancey to Dundas, 22 May 1792.
116. PRO HO 42/20. De Lancey to Dundas, 13 June 1792.
117. *Ibid.*

Society and the Manchester Reformation Society under the patronage and protection of the middle-class leaders of the local Constitutional Society.[118]

Much more serious, however, was the situation at Sheffield – a natural centre of sedition – where troops of the Sixth Regiment of Dragoons had recently clashed in street disturbances with the local inhabitants.[119] Here public order appeared to be endangered by the inroads made by Painite principles among the townspeople and by the riotous behaviour of the journeymen cutlers whose high wages led them to work for only half the week and to spend the rest of it in dissipation.[120] Industrial discipline among the "small masters" was non-existent and in de Lancey's view, "the magistracy of the place scarcely deserved the name'.[121] Even more disturbing was the rapid expansion in the membership of the local Constitutional Society – which had now risen to about 2500 – the seditious influence it was exerting over the towns and villages of the surrounding countryside, its extensive correspondence with similar reform associations in other parts of the kingdom, and the priority it had given to attempts to subvert the allegiance of the troops of the Sixth and Seventh Regiments of Light Dragoons.[122]

Similar bad blood between townsmen and troops was reported by de Lancey from Birmingham, where resentment against the military repression of the Priestley riots still lingered. Liverpool, however,

118. The Manchester Patriotic Society was formed on 24 May 1792, and its declaration was approved by a meeting at the Windmill Tavern in Dolefield. Walker, pp. 34–6. The declaration is of interest because it stated a case for the parliamentary representation of the commercial and manufacturing interest and because of its distrust of party politicians. The Manchester Reformation Society's declaration was dated 6 June 1792 and followed closely on that adopted by the Manchester Constitutional Society. *Ibid.*, p. 37. A. Goodwin, 'A comparative study of regionalism in politics in Lancashire and Normandy during the French Revolution', *Annales de Normandie* (May, 1958), pp. 235–55, and P. Handforth, 'Manchester radical politics, 1789–1794', *Transactions of the Lancashire and Cheshire Antiquarian Society*, vol. 66 (1956), pp. 87–106.

119. The riots lasted from 7 to 9 May and a pacification was only obtained by some Dissenting ministers on the 10th, on the basis that the military should temporarily withdraw from the town within four days. PRO TS 11/952/3496(ii).

120. PRO HO 42/20. De Lancey to Dundas, 13 June 1792.

121. *Ibid.* Two non-resident magistrates, Samuel Tooker and Francis Edwards, had to be specially summoned to part the townsmen and troops. *Ibid.*, 10 May 1792.

122. PRO HO 42/20. De Lancey to Dundas, 13 June 1792.

236   *The Friends of Liberty*

was conspicuous for its loyalty,[123] and though the inhabitants of Chesterfield, Nottingham, Leicester and Loughborough were all 'disposed to riot', this regrettable tendency arose, according to de Lancey, from 'dissipation' rather than from 'disaffection'.[124] The dilemma facing military commanders in the industrial areas could only be resolved, in the short run, by quartering the troops needed for police duties outside, but within easy reach of, the large towns affected by radical influences, and in the long run by building barracks to isolate the troops from close contact with disaffected civilians.[125] Pitt took immediate steps to implement this advice and, despite the long-standing objections to the maintenance of standing armies in peacetime, put in hand an extended programme of barrack-building in the industrial districts.[126] It is not surprising that in Pitt's subsequent 'Reign of Terror' these barracks were usually designated as English 'Bastilles' by the radicals whom they were meant to overawe.

More broadly, however, de Lancey considered that if the spirit of disaffection abroad in the provinces were to be contained, the gentlemen of property, who had so far 'held it in too great contempt', would need to unite and to exert themselves in self-defence. The danger was that they might delay too long and that the mischief might take too great a hold for it to be successfully eliminated.[127] Burke had given the same warning in his *Appeal from the New to the Old Whigs* in 1791, but it was not until these fears of civil disorder were transformed into an actual fear of revolution in the autumn of 1792 that the message was heeded.[128]

By mid-summer, however, the radical societies were operating in

123. It appears that 'the Liverpool working class was almost entirely, if not entirely, unaffected by the current of reform engendered by the events of 1789'. R. B. Rose, 'The "Jacobins" of Liverpool', *Liverpool Libraries, Museums, and Arts Committee Bulletin*, vol. 9 (1960–1), pp. 35–49.
124. PRO HO 42/20. 13 June 1792.
125. *Ibid.*
126. Barracks for small detachments of cavalry were built at Birmingham, Nottingham, Northampton, Sheffield, Manchester, Coventry and York. Infantry were stationed at Newcastle, Sunderland, Tynemouth, Carlisle, Chester and Liverpool. J. L. and B. Hammond, *The Town Labourer, 1760–1832* (London, 1949 reprint), vol. 1, p. 92.
127. PRO HO 42/20. De Lancey to Dundas, 13 June 1792.
128. A. Mitchell, 'The Association movement of 1792–3', *The Historical Journal*, vol. 4, no. 1 (1961), pp. 56–77. E. C. Black, *The Association: British Extraparliamentary Political Organization, 1769–1793* (Cambridge, Mass., 1963), ch. 7.

an increasingly hostile environment. The meetings held up and down the country to approve addresses of loyalty to the sovereign and of support for the constitution gave the 'Church and King' associations the chance to vent their spleen against the radicals and to inflame local feeling against them as Dissenters and disciples of Paine. As Thomas Walker later complained, 'all the bad passions of party were let loose, and political rancour against the friends of reform became a virtue of the first magnitude'.[129] During the May riots in Sheffield, egged on by reactionary clergy, the men and officers of the Sixth Regiment of Dragoons had provoked the townsfolk into retaliation by insulting their women in the streets and inflicting injury on harmless bystanders.[130] Towards the end of August magistrates and police officers at Stockport even resorted to threats of physical violence in the effort to intimidate the officials of a recently formed radical society.[131] Innkeepers who allowed such popular reform clubs to meet on their premises were threatened by magistrates with the loss of their licences – a form of economic blackmail which few of them could resist.[132] It was interference of this kind which, in mid June, forced Division 2 (Hardy's) and the General Committee of the London Corresponding Society to move from the Bell Inn in Exeter St, to the Unicorn in Henrietta St, Covent Garden, while its several divisions were kept constantly on the move.[133] Eventually the branches were compelled to withdraw to private houses and the society had to hire large auction rooms to accommodate its general meetings.[134] When, eventually, this policy of harassment was carried to its logical conclusion and the radicals were prevented from holding large indoor meetings of any kind, it proved self-defeating. The response of the radical societies was to organize large, and well-disciplined, open-air meetings with their own numbers swollen by curious but receptive members of the general public and with talented 'stump' orators as the voice of radical

129. Walker, p. 34.

130. S. Ashton, secretary to the Sheffield Constitutional Society to Daniel Adams of the SCI, 3 July 1792. PRO TS 11/952/3496a.

131. J. Andrews, secretary to the Stockport Society of the Friends of Universal Peace and the Rights of Man to the Editors of the *Patriot*, 4 Oct. 1792. *Ibid.*

132. The landlord of the Bell in Exeter St reckoned that the loss of his licence would have cost him about £1000. BL, Add. MSS. 27811, fos. 14–15.

133. BL, Add. MSS. 27812, fo. 10.

134. The decision that divisions should hire private rooms was taken on 6 December 1792. *Ibid.*, fos. 29–30.

protest.[135] Where, however, in 1792, radical meetings contrived to be held in public, local solicitors, such as James Wheat at Sheffield, were able to obtain detailed and, on the whole, reliable reports of the proceedings from paid 'observers', though the Home Office itself does not appear to have resorted to the regular use of spies inside the metropolitan societies till the winter of 1792.[136]

In the effort to counter a mounting campaign of misrepresentation, the reform societies found it expedient, especially when they were first established, to publish declarations of the essential moderation of their principles, the legality of their methods and objectives and their repudiation of all forms of civil disorder.[137] Caution, as well as altruism, no doubt led a committee of the Society for Constitutional Information early in July to refuse Paine's generous offer of £1000 – the proceeds of the sales of *The Rights of Man* – despite the society's continuing financial difficulties.[138] The number of public dinners held by the more sedate reform societies to celebrate the anniversary of the fall of the Bastille in July 1792 dropped dramatically both in the metropolis and the provinces. Those which were held were often not advertised in advance and the proceedings were usually restrained rather than provocative.[139] Thomas Hardy's comment on the closing of the ranks against the reformers that the aristocracy was 'trembling in every joint for their exclusive privileges' was, characteristically, over-sanguine.[140] The attitude of Margarot,

135. See Chapter 10 below.

136. Abstracts of the proceedings of the general monthly meetings of the Sheffield Constitutional Society on 30 January, 27 February, 26 March and 28 May 1792 were sent by Wheat to the Rev. Henry Zouch, West Riding magistrate, who communicated them to Earl Fitzwilliam with his comments. WWM, F 44a.

137. For statements of the Manchester Patriotic and Reformation Societies on 24 May and 6 June 1792, see Walker, pp. 34–6, 37. The Sheffield declaration, drafted by its select committee on 1 June and approved by the whole society on 4 June 1792, was printed by the *Manchester Herald* on 16 June.

138. Paine's letter of 4 July 1792 offering to make the SCI trustees of the profits is in PRO TS 11/952/3496(ii). The society's final refusal dated 20 July is in TS 11/962/3508, fo. 101.

139. For the LCS's decision, on 5 July 1792, not to hold a dinner see BL, Add. MSS. 27812, fo. 13. The SCI, on 4 July, passed a draft resolution to advertise its celebration of 14 July, along with the borough society and to celebrate the occasion as publicly as possible. On 6 July this draft resolution was not approved. PRO TS 11/955/3500. Horne Tooke, however, presided over an uneventful dinner of the society at the Shakespeare Tavern. C. B. Cone, *The English Jacobins* (New York, 1968), pp. 132–3.

140. Hardy to Lord Daer, 14 July 1792. BL, Add. MSS. 27811, fo. 14.

chairman of the London Corresponding Society, was more guarded and realistic. In drafting the society's third *Address to the Public*, dated 6 August, he was content to base the case for parliamentary reform on an updated version of the proposals put forward by Pitt and the Duke of Richmond in the 1780s in the conviction that 'an HONEST PARLIAMENT', annually elected, would suffice to extinguish political corruption and remove the main economic and social grievances of the common man without recourse to a constitutional convention or any Painite schemes for extended social benefits.[141] The presentation of parliamentary reform as an economic panacea may have been derived from Paine and was certainly novel,[142] but, in other respects, Margarot had carefully adjusted the sentiments expressed to the prevailing climate of suspicion.[143]

Then, too, on 20 July 1792 the Society for Constitutional Information – the main driving force behind the democratic movement – which had, on Horne Tooke's recommendation, taken to meeting at the Crown and Anchor Tavern since mid May adjourned for its summer recess till the last Friday in September.[144] Much of the impetus behind the agitation for parliamentary reform was lost, the provincial radical movement suddenly found itself rudderless at a time when it had been driven on to the defensive, and as summer turned into autumn, the vital political initiative in the metropolis passed to the London Corresponding Society. A damper descended on the spirits of the reformers and, except in Scotland, most radical societies seemed content to suspend their agitation for the time being, until at least some clear decision had been reached on whether or not to call for the summons of a convention in preference to pressurizing Parliament by means of multiple petitions for reform.

Though the radicals were prepared to wait on events, they did not have to wait long. The events which recharged their energies and imparted a new turn to their activities occurred, however, not in

141. BL, Add. MSS. 27812, fos. 15–19. PRO TS 11/3495; *ST*, vol. 24, cols. 382–7.

142. P. A. Brown, *The French Revolution in English History* (3rd impression, London, 1965), p. 58. Francis Place thought 'it was well calculated for giving political information to those whose occupations in life made it impossible for them to spare time to read large works'. BL, Add. MSS. 27816, fo. 217.

143. Replying to the criticism of the Stockport society that 'the sentiments hardly rise to that height which we expect from men sensible to their full claims to absolute and uncontrollable liberty', Margarot explained that the address had been expressed 'in as strong terms as prudence will permit'. *ST*, vol. 24, col. 389.

144. PRO TS 11/962/3508, fo. 102.

England, but in France and, for the rest of the year, their affairs were closely linked to the fortunes of the Parisian *sans-culottes* and the French republican armies. What fused these democratic forces in both countries into a common front of political solidarity was the issue, on 25 July 1792, of the 'bloody and tyrannous' manifesto reluctantly signed by the Duke of Brunswick as generalissimo of the Austrian and Prussian forces poised for their assault on revolutionary France.[145] This was to prove the most deceptive and counter-productive ultimatum of modern times.[146] Commissioned by the French court in the effort to forestall any *émigré* attempts to resuscitate the *ancien régime*, it had, however, been drafted by the agents of Count Fersen and Calonne with the intention of intimidating the extreme revolutionaries and of thwarting the moderate royalists.[147] It proclaimed that Austrian and Prussian forces were intervening in France to defend the feudal rights of the German princes in Alsace, to suppress anarchy, to prevent further attacks on the French monarchy and to restore Louis XVI to his rightful and legitimate authority. The allied sovereigns repudiated all intentions of enriching themselves at the expense of France or of interfering in its internal government. Offering to protect all loyal subjects of the Crown, they threatened to punish as rebels all National Guards who resisted and to burn or demolish the homes of all civilians who dared to defend themselves. The members of the Legislative Assembly and of the Parisian municipal administration were made answerable for events in the capital. If the mob again invaded the Tuileries palace, as on 20 June, or if the slightest violence was offered to the royal family, the allies promised to exact 'an exemplary and ever memorable vengeance by handing over the city of Paris to a military execution and total destruction'.[148]

The reply given to this manifesto, as the counter-revolutionary

145. The Duke of Brunswick strongly disapproved of the attitudes and manoeuvres of the *émigrés* at Coblentz and also of the terms of the manifesto. He subordinated his own views, however, to those of the King of Prussia. A. Sorel, *L'Europe et la Révolution Française* (Paris, 1908), vol. 2, p. 509.

146. It represented the views neither of Louis XVI, nor of the newly crowned Holy Roman Emperor, Francis II, both of whom were antagonistic to the cause of the *émigrés*. *Ibid.*, vol. 2, pp. 504–5. M. Reinhard, *La Chute de la Royauté* (Paris, 1969), pp. 374–5.

147. The document was drafted by a M. de Limon, under the direction of the Swedish Count Fersen, lover of Marie Antoinette, who had organized the royal flight from Paris in June 1791. Sorel, vol. 2, p. 509.

148. The text is in J. M. Thompson (ed.), *French Revolution Documents, 1789–94* (Oxford, 1933), pp. 186–90.

armies slowly converged on Champagne, was the swift and decisive attack on the Tuileries palace on 10 August by the combined forces of the Parisian *sectionnaires* and the *fédérés* from Marseilles and the overthrow of the Bourbon monarchy. The prediction in some conservative journals in Paris in early July of the issue of the manifesto, the rumours of the King's impending escape from the capital, and the discovery of synchronized plots in Normandy, Brittany and La Vendée,[149] revealed the existence of a wide-ranging royalist conspiracy timed to coincide with the Austrian and Prussian invasion. Suddenly the whole foundations of French liberty and constitutional monarchy seemed likely to crumble, menaced from without by a league of Continental despots and undermined from within by royalist regional conspiracies. The treacherous surrender of the frontier fortresses of Longwy and Verdun at the end of August opened the way to the French capital for the invading forces, and provided a colourable pretext for the September Massacres of priests and aristocrats in the prisons of Paris. The suspension of the King by the Legislative Assembly, the imprisonment of the royal family in the Temple at the insistence of the revolutionary Commune and the transference of power to an elected Provisional Executive Council of six ministers proved only the preliminary stage to the summons of a National Convention elected by universal male suffrage and the proclamation on 21 September 1792 of the first French republic. The organization of national defence under the heroic leadership of Danton similarly paved the way for the victory of Dumouriez and Kellerman at the battle of Valmy on 20 September, which arrested the Austrian and Prussian forces in their tracks.

The impact of these events on the British radicals was profound.[150] In the course of the summer they had been conscious that governmental repression had eroded their constitutional rights and liberties as Britons, but had taken consolation in the reflection that as 'citizens of the world' their human rights were still intact. The Brunswick manifesto convinced them that even these were now menaced and that democracy was indivisible. They would, therefore, need to

149. A Goodwin, 'Counter-revolution in Brittany: the royalist conspiracy of the Marquis de la Rouerie', *Bulletin of the John Rylands Library*, vol. 39 (1957), pp. 326–55.

150. According to Thomas Hardy, the Brunswick manifesto 'was the cause of the friends of liberty in this country addressing the Convention and promising assistance to the friends of freedom in France'. BL, Add. MSS. 27814, fo. 46.

demonstrate their sympathy and solidarity with their French brethren and to provide them with practical assistance if their own liberties were to survive. They were soon to hail the French as the champions of 'Universal Liberty' against the menace of despotic monarchy, the Parisians as the exponents of direct democracy and, as the tide of victory turned in their favour, the republican armies as the potential liberators of oppressed peoples.

Attempts to organize public subscriptions in aid of the French and demonstrations of sympathy with the defenders of Paris and of admiration for the victors of Valmy not only roused the radical societies from their previous apathy, but, unfortunately, led them to become apologists for French revolutionary excesses and apparent converts to French notions of equality and republicanism. There were a few committed radicals, like Dr William Maxwell, whose convictions led them to sacrifice friends, influence and fortune in efforts to assist the French by volunteering to serve in their armies and by providing them with arms.[151] Maxwell was a typical enthusiast whose views may, however, have been influenced, as his family believed, by his residence, near to the French embassy, in Great Portland Street.[152] As France's military situation became desperate, Maxwell had obtained an interview in Paris at the end of August 1792 with Servan, then minister of war, and, according to his own account, had offered to equip a company of sharp-shooters with rifle-bored guns.[153] Servan had agreed and promised to give Maxwell command of the company, on condition that payment for the rifles should be deferred till the end of the war. In the same interview Maxwell had also suggested the utility of a formation of commando-type troops, equipped with pikes, daggers and small shields. One in ten could be given light sporting guns to provide the skirmishers with fire cover, while the daggers were intended for hand-to-hand

151. Another was the eccentric soldier, socialist and vegetarian John Oswald (1755–1793) who, having served in the war of American independence and in India, abandoned his military career and eventually settled in Paris, where he became a member of the Jacobin club. He lost his life serving as a volunteer commander in the Vendée. H. Lichtenberger, 'John Oswald – un précurseur du socialisme en Angleterre', *Revue Encyclopédique, 1896*, pp. 810–11, is a rehash of the article in the *Dictionary of National Biography*. Oswald, too, was an exponent of the pike.

152. PRO HO 42/22, fo. 3 contains extracts of letters from members of Maxwell's family attempting to dissuade him from volunteering for the French service.

153. AN, F^7 4394^1 (Pache's papers). Letter of Maxwell to Pache, 7 November 1792.

combat at close quarters. Such improvised irregular forces could, Maxwell contended, operate with advantage 'in the rain, in the dark, or when disorder had spread to the enemy ranks'. Each man should carry a blanket which could be used with a pike to form a tent, while ship's biscuits would provide the necessary iron rations.

When Servan asked Maxwell to supply him with a specimen of the daggers, such was the suspicion attaching to these weapons in Paris at the time that no workman could be induced to provide a pattern in either wood or iron. Maxwell had, accordingly, returned to England to negotiate in Birmingham for the supply of pikes, guns and daggers.[154] Early in September, Maxwell approached several firms of sword manufacturers in the town who supplied him with patterns for the daggers and quoted him a price of 22s. per dozen for the weapons complete with handles and scabbards.[155] On 10 September he then gave an order for 3000 daggers to another manufacturer Thomas Gill, on the same terms, saying that he expected to be able to follow this up with a further firm order for 20000 in a week's time.[156] This seems, however, to have been dependent on the success of a public subscription in aid of the French, which Maxwell announced in the London press would be opened at his house in Great Portland St on 12 September. When he returned to the capital to launch the appeal, he was obliged to beat a hasty retreat to Paris by the hostile demonstrations of a mob egged on by the police.[157]

This was by no means the end of the incident, for Maxwell became the involuntary means by which first the Society for Constitutional Information, of which he was himself a member, and then the London Corresponding Society became involved in more extensive and momentous efforts to assist the French. Though Maxwell judged it wiser, for the moment, to postpone his plans, he did not abandon them, since his friend Horne Tooke had immediately stepped into his shoes as sponsor of the subscription despite the riot it had provoked.[158] In a matter of days a sum of £1151 was collected, and Horne Tooke lost no time in contacting Pétion in the

154. *Ibid.*

155. J. Brooke, mayor of Birmingham, to Evan Nepean at the Home Office, 21 Sept. 1792. PRO HO 42/21, fo. 590.

156. Letter of T. Gill to Editor, 18 October 1792. *Public Advertiser*, 24 Oct. 1792. BL, Burney Collection of newspapers, p. 844.

157. Veitch, p. 227.

158. *Ibid.*, p. 228.

effort to discover the appropriate means of transmitting it to France.[159] The attempt to remit either money or arms to France in the aftermath of the September Massacres could be seen, however, by wiser heads to be highly dangerous, and it was for this reason that on 15 September, Margarot, president of the London Corresponding Society, wrote privately to Horne Tooke to suggest an alternative means of demonstrating radical sympathy and support for the beleaguered Parisians. His proposal was that all the radical societies throughout the country should be asked to give their assent to 'an Animated (but safe) Declaration', assuring the French of their cordial friendship and their determination to keep the British government to its pledged policy of neutrality. Such a move, while not necessarily impeding the subscription, might ultimately prove 'more useful' by helping to quiet French fears of British intervention and by encouraging them in their arduous struggle with the invading forces of the Continental coalition. It would have the additional merit that many more radicals might be prepared to add their mere signatures to such a declaration rather than contribute to a subscription.[160] In this way an impressive demonstration of radical strength in the country might be staged which would 'give a most severe check to all open or even underhand Ministerial attempts' (at further repression).[161]

Such was the origin of the series of radical addresses presented to the French National Convention in the course of November and December 1792, which had precisely the opposite effects on Pitt's domestic and foreign policy to those which had been anticipated by Margarot.

As might have been anticipated, the sentiments expressed in some of these addresses did not rise above the commonplaces of fraternal felicitation already familiar in the polite exchanges which had already taken place between the London Revolution Society, the French National Assembly and the Jacobin clubs.[162] Nor, despite the

159. PRO TS 11/951/3495. List of subscriptions dated 13 Sept. 1792. Pétion replied on 1 Oct. 1792, promising to send the name of a confidential agent to whom the money could be remitted. PRO TS 11/955/3500.

160. In a letter to Horne Tooke of 16 September 1792 supporting the idea put forward by Margarot, Thomas Hardy argued that: 'Ten or Twenty thousand signatures would have more weight than as many thousand pounds for ten men might subscribe that sum.' PRO TS 11/951/3495.

161. *Ibid.* Margarot to Horne Tooke, 15 September 1792.

162. Cf. the exordium of the address of the Society for Constitutional Information (adopted 9 Nov. 1792): 'Go on, legislators, in the work of human happiness.

Alarmists' attempts to do so, is it possible to establish any direct connection between the reception of these addresses in the National Convention and its passage of the provocative Edict of Fraternity on 19 November 1792.[163] That source of continuing misunderstanding and suspicion between the British and French governments was in fact, the response to a totally different kind of petition emanating from the Rhineland.[164] The address of the London Corresponding Society, signed by Margarot and Hardy on 27 September 1792, was drafted by the former at a time when it still appeared likely that the armies of the Duke of Brunswick would carry all before them and could hardly, in any case, have affected the situation of France one way or the other. As the radicals themselves later contended in self-defence, technically there was nothing unconstitutional or treasonable in despatching such a communication to the French national assembly in peacetime, especially when its message was their determination to hold the British government to its official policy of strict neutrality.

The radical addresses of 1792, however, differed essentially from the earlier congratulatory messages of the London Revolution Society. They were, firstly, more representative, if not of national, certainly of radical opinion. The London Corresponding Society's joint address, subscribed by the chairmen and secretaries of the

---

The benefits will in parts be ours, but the glory shall be all your own – it is the reward of your perseverance! it is the prize of virtue. The sparks of Liberty preserved in England for ages, like the corruscations of the Northern Aurora, served but to show the darkness visible in the rest of Europe. The lustre of the American Republic, like an effulgent morning, arose with increasing vigour, but still too distant to enlighten our hemisphere, till the splendour of the French Revolution burst forth upon the nations in the full fervour of a meridian sun, and displayed in the midst of the European world the practical result of principles, which philosophy had sought in the shade of speculation and which experience every where must confirm. It dispels the clouds of prejudice from all people, reveals the secrets of all despotism, and creates a new character in man. In this career of improvement your example will soon be followed; for nations, rising from their lethargy, will reclaim the Rights of Man with a voice which man cannot resist.'

163. In fact only two addresses had been presented in the convention before 19 November – the joint address from the LCS, Manchester, Norwich and Constitutional Whigs on 7 November, and one from Newington on 10 November. For an attempt to connect the radical addresses with the passage of the Edict of Fraternity see J. Bowles, *The Real Grounds of the Present War with France*, 6th ed. (London, 1794), p. 15.

164. These were petitions soliciting French protection against their former rulers from groups of liberals who had espoused French principles.

Manchester Constitutional and Reformation Societies, the Norwich Revolution Society and the London Constitutional Whigs, represented the signatures of over 5000, while the address promoted by the Sheffield Constitutional Society was said to have received the approval of about 20000 'merchants, manufacturers, workmen and artisans'.[165] In all there were over a dozen separate addresses including one from Belfast.[166] It should be noted, however, that the suggestion of a joint address was rejected by the Scottish reform societies as likely to be 'productive of mischief and misconstruction at home', while the Friends of the People in London also criticized the initiative as likely to 'serve the purposes and strengthen the pretexts' of the French government.[167] Both these misgivings were amply justified by what followed. Secondly, all the radical addresses were sent to a sovereign constituent assembly in France whose first act had been to establish a republic. This gesture was made after the British government had recalled its ambassador from Paris, following the suspension of Louis XVI, and despite Pitt's stubborn and continuing refusal to recognize the new republic. Thirdly, the addresses contained severe and pointed criticisms of both the domestic and foreign policies of the British government and commendations of the actions of the French executive at a time when the diplomatic relations between the two countries were steadily deteriorating.[168] It is important to recognize that for these and other reasons, the addresses influenced the respective attitudes and conduct of both the French and British governments in the disputes that led to open hostilities. At home they were speciously misinterpreted by the Alarmists and the government to convince an already partly converted public of the reality of that subversive English 'Jacobin conspiracy' which had hitherto subsisted only in the imaginations of Edmund Burke and the more extreme 'Church and King' fanatics.

It was, perhaps, only natural that when the London Revolution Society met on Monday 5 November 1792 to hold its annual com-

165. For the LCS address, dated 27 Sept. 1792, see Appendix 1. There is a French translation of the Sheffield address, completed in late October 1792, in the Archives Nationales, Paris (C 240, liasse 275/6).

166. For a list of these see Appendix 2.

167. W. Johnson, chairman of the Associated Friends of the People, Edinburgh, to T. Hardy, 31 Oct. 1792. PRO TS 11/954/3498. Committee of the Friends of the People to the Secretary of the LCS, 15 Feb. 1793. *Parl. Hist.*, vol. 31, col. 806.

168. J. T. Murley, 'The origins and outbreak of the Anglo-French war of 1793', unpublished D.Phil. thesis, Oxford (1959), Bodleian Library, treats the subject in detail.

memorative dinner at the London Tavern, it should have wished, not so much to respond to the call of the London Corresponding Society, as to follow the precedent which its own most distinguished former member, Dr Price, had set in 1789. Once again the occasion was a notable one – upwards of 500 assorted 'friends of liberty' were present and 1000 more were turned away. Mr Rutt, in the chair, was supported by noted Francophiles in the persons of Mr Thomas Christie, on his right, and the Reverend Horne Tooke, on his left.[169] Although Chauvelin, the former French ambassador, had thought it prudent to decline an invitation, Lebrun, the French Minister of Foreign Affairs, had, a few days earlier, sent over copies of the new revolutionary marching song – the *Marseillaise* – as a tribute to the Revolution Society, and this had been sung during the dinner with enthusiasm.[170] Of the forty toasts proposed and drunk, almost half saluted the recent legislative, constitutional and military achievements of the French and one expressed the confident hope that the new republican constitution, when available, would 'be a model for all nations'.[171] After the formal business had been completed, a motion was proposed and carried with acclamation that the society should despatch an 'Address of Congratulation' to the French National Convention.

While expressing the joy of the 'friends of liberty in all countries' at the ignominious retreat of France's invaders, the address was remarkable in seeking to defend the overthrow of the Bourbon monarchy on 10 August, the proclamation of the French republic and the plans for a new and more democratic constitution by reference to the rights of resistance and of self-determination which had 'formed the ground work of the revolution' of 1688.[172] This effort to assimilate the principles, not merely of 1789, but also of 1792, to those of the English revolution of 1688 may have been called for by the occasion of the commemorative dinner itself, but the specific apologia for 10 August and the encomium of French republican institutions must have seemed, to less biased observers, unnecessarily provocative of English conservative opinion, and was certainly open

169. *Manchester Herald*, 10 Nov. 1792. Veitch says the meeting was presided over by Dr Towers, but this seems an error. It was Towers who signed the address as chairman of the society. Veitch, p. 229.

170. AAE, CPA, 583, fo. 94, Lebrun to Noël, 26 Oct. 1792; *Ibid.*, fo. 134, Lebrun to Chauvelin, 31 Oct. 1792; *Ibid.*, fo. 193, Chauvelin to Lebrun, 7 Nov. 1792.

171. Dr Robinet, *Danton Émigré* (Paris, 1887), p. 50.

172. *Annual Register* 1792(2), p. 349.

to misconstruction by the French when the address was read in the National Convention on 1 December 1792.[173] The gesture, however, seems to have been the swan song of the society, for no further traces of its activities or even of its continued existence have survived.[174]

One feature common to several or indeed to most of the English radical addresses to the National Convention in 1792 was their messages of congratulation to the French on their military victories over the hated 'matador' the Duke of Brunswick, whose effigy was burnt in London and several provincial towns in the course of November.[175] Not only the London Revolution Society, but also the Constitutional Societies of Sheffield and Derby, that of the Friends of the People at Newington, and the Belfast Volunteers all saluted the feats of the French volunteer forces at Valmy and later in emancipating French territory from the invader by the latter part of October.[176] The proclamation by the Convention on 19 October that the 'fatherland was no longer in danger' seemed to mark the end of the national emergency and allayed much of the anxiety previously felt and expressed by the English radicals.[177] So, too, Dumouriez's decisive rout of the Austrians at the battle of Jemappes, near Mons, on 6 November, was warmly welcomed by the Society of Friends of the People at Aldgate in its address of 12 November to the Convention.[178]

173. *Procès-verbal de la Convention Nationale*, 1 Dec. 1792.

174. C. B. Cone thought that the last meeting of the Revolution Society had been its commemorative dinner of 4 November 1791! *The English Jacobins* (New York, 1968), pp. 112–13. The outbreak of war with France in February 1793 would provide a satisfactory reason for the discontinuation of such annual festivities which, ever since 1790, had been celebrations of 1789 rather than of 1688.

175. An effigy of Brunswick 'filled with combustible matter', was fired on and committed to the flames during a patriotic fête held at Sheffield on 15 October 1792 to celebrate the expulsion of the invading troops from France. *Manchester Herald*, 27 Oct. 1792. An effigy of the duke, along with that of the Pope, was burnt in London on 5 November. F. Noël to Lebrun, 7 Nov. 1792. AAE Correspondance Politique Angleterre (CPA) 583, fo. 189.

176. Addresses of London Revolution Society (5 Nov. 1792), of the Sheffield Constitutional Society (25 Oct. 1792), of the Derby Constitutional Society (20 Nov. 1792), Newington (31 Oct. 1792) and the Belfast Volunteers (6 Nov. 1792). *Collection of Addresses transmitted . . . to the National Convention of France* (1793), *passim*.

177. The proclamation of '*la patrie en danger*' had been made on 22 July 1792. Sorel, vol. 2, p. 511.

178. AN, C 242, 289/90, fo. 19. There is a French copy of this address in AAE CPA 583, fos. 373–4.

Language fails us to describe the lively emotions of Joy and Admiration with which it hath inspired us, but the sensibility of every True Frenchman may qualify him to judge of Our Transports by those which he himself must feel – May the Blood of the Brave Citizens shed on this occasion, while it shews the Despots the Energy and Magnanimity which Liberty alone can give, spring up in an abundant Harvest of Peace and Freedom throughout the World, and Reason supersede the necessity of Military Conquest![179]

This spate of congratulations may have slowed down, but it did not entirely dry up even when the French armies under 'Citizen General' Dumouriez passed over to the offensive, conquered the Low Countries in a month, and seemed poised for an invasion of Britain's ally, the United Provinces. Dumouriez's entry into Brussels on 14 November, for example, was celebrated on Sunday 18 November at White's Hotel in Paris by a dinner attended by about eighty English, Irish and Scottish residents, who appear to have held advanced democratic or republican views. Captain George Monro, a Scottish spy in the pay of the English government who arrived in the French capital on the following day, reported that the moving spirits in this heterogeneous group of enthusiasts were a future leader of the United Irishmen – Lord Edward Fitzgerald, a disgruntled former MP for Colchester – Sir Robert Smyth and J. H. Stone, now settled in Paris as a manufacturer and printer.[180] Dr Maxwell, who had brought with him a first consignment of 'rifle-barrelled guns' from Birmingham, was also present.[181] The toasts drunk at this dinner were chivalrous, egalitarian and treasonable – to the 'lady defenders of the Revolution, particularly Mrs Charlotte Smith, Miss Williams and Mrs Barbauld';[182] 'the speedy abolition

179. *Ibid.*
180. 'Notes on English democrats in Paris in 1792' (dated 6 Dec. 1792). PRO TS 11/959/3505(ii). Fitzgerald had come over to Paris to enlist Paine's aid in fomenting a revolution in Ireland. A. O. Aldridge, *Man of Reason: The Life of Thomas Paine* (London, 1960), p. 177. Sir Robert Smyth (1744–1802), fifth Baronet, on ceasing to represent Colchester in 1790, had settled in Paris as a banker. He was imprisoned during the Terror, and, though released in 1796, never returned to his native country. L. Namier and J. Brooke, *History of Parliament: The House of Commons, 1754–1790*, vol. 3, pp. 456–7.
181. Monro reported that Maxwell, 'a man of violent principles', was still negotiating with the War Minister for the command of a company in the French service.
182. Mrs Charlotte Smith had achieved contemporary fame as the author of a two-volume novel – *Desmond* – exhibiting radical leanings. For Helen Maria Williams (1762–1827), author of *Letters containing a Sketch of the Politics of*

of titles and feudal distinctions in England'; and 'the coming Convention of Great Britain and Ireland'. The address from these expatriate extremists, dated 24 November, encouraged the National Convention in its self-assumed mission of enfranchising Europe – catching some of the heady enthusiasm which had been generated in that assembly by the passing of the Edict of Fraternity on the 19th. Its signatories wrote of their joy in seeing France 'fulfilling its great destinies'. The conquest, or rather emancipation, of Belgium by Dumouriez was, for them, only the first instalment in the developing drama of liberation. The group even expressed the hope that 'the victorious troops of liberty will lay down their arms only when there are no more tyrants or slaves'. Only thus would Europe as a whole enjoy the rights of man and the blessings of universal peace. Among the anticipated benefits would be 'the formation of a close union between the French republic and the English, Scotch and Irish nations'.[183]

Variations on the same theme occurred in several other radical addresses to the Convention. Whereas the London Revolution Society at an earlier stage had been content to extol the blessings of Anglo-French concord, the London Corresponding Society in a more provocative mood now looked forward to the conclusion of a Triple Alliance 'not of crowns, but of the people of America, France and Britain'.[184] The addresses also echoed Painite pacifism – the wars of the past were condemned as the work of 'weak or ambitious kings, and corrupt ministers' and were contrasted with France's heroic struggle in defence of her own independence and her efforts solely 'to make reason and truth triumph'.[185] Even when French aggression seemed to threaten the independence of weaker neighbouring states, the radicals were still not disposed to question the French renunciation of wars of conquest, recently repeated by the National Convention, or its further promise not to interfere in the affairs of other governments.[186] Even as late as 20 November the

---

France (1795) see L. D. Woodward, *Une Adhérente Anglaise de la Révolution Française. Hélène-Maria Williams et ses amis* (Paris, 1930).

183. AN, C 241 (278). The address is reprinted, with notes and commentary, by J. G. Alger in *English Historical Review*, vol. 13 (1898), pp. 673–4.

184. BL, Add. MSS. 27814, fo. 46.

185. *Address of the English, Scotch and Irish resident and domiciled in Paris, 24 Nov. 1792.* AN, C 241 (278).

186. Address of the Aldgate Society of Friends of the People, 12 Nov. 1792. *Ibid.*, C 242 (289).

address of the Derby Society for Constitutional Information spoke of 'renovated France' – 'directing her brave legions against the despotism of neighbouring Tyrants' and conquering 'only to make free'.[187] When the Sheffield radicals celebrated Dumouriez's military triumphs a week later by holding a public fête, accompanied by ox-roasting and the firing of cannon in the streets, thronged by 5000–6000 spectators, two of their banners borne in procession proclaimed the significance of the latest French victories. The legend on one read 'The glorious conquest of Brussels, in which Life, Liberty and Property were secured even to the Vanquished'; on the other was the message, 'The French by their arms have conquered tyrants; and by just Laws, Liberty and Reason will conquer the world.'[188]

The radical addresses also assured the National Convention that the British government would not easily repudiate its solemn and repeated pledges of neutrality. Both the London and Sheffield Constitutional Societies regretted their inability to engage actively in the defence of liberty alongside the French, but expressed their firm conviction that reactionary forces would not dare to play fast and loose with the promises given by the government in the name of the British people.[189] If a perfidious breach of faith were nevertheless committed, the Sheffield Society asserted roundly that its own members and those of other radical societies, forming between them the most numerous and useful parts of the state, would regard such action as a declaration of war upon their own liberties. They would not only defend themselves, but would use all their influence and all legal means at their disposal to resist any hostile measures directed against the French.[190]

Even more irresponsibly outspoken, though perhaps less meaningful, was the condemnation by a small radical society at Rochester, late in November, of Grenville's refusal to recognize the French republic.[191] This called on the 'friends of equality' and on all the

187. Address of the Derby Society for Constitutional Information, 20 Nov. 1792. BL, Place newspaper cuttings 36, fo. 15.

188. *Sheffield Register*, 30 Nov. 1792.

189. The French text of the address of the Sheffield Constitutional Society presented in the National Convention on 22 Nov. 1792 is in AN, C 240, fos. 275–6. Veitch was unable to identify this address and attributed it to 'some London society' (p. 228); the *Moniteur* of 23 Nov. 1792 ascribed it to the London Revolution Society, while Dr Robinet plumped for the Society for Constitutional Information. Robinet, pp. 53–4. See Appendix 2.

190. AN, C 240, fo. 276.

191. AAE, CPA 583, fo. 263.

corresponding societies in France to bring pressure to bear on the French executive to break off communications with the British cabinet until it had 'acknowledged the sovereignty of the French people'.[192] Its address, motivated by the rumoured despatch of Lindsay as a replacement for the British ambassador without official status, was sent direct to the French foreign minister Lebrun with a covering letter from the society's French-born president, La Chesnaye, on 20 November.[193] In this letter, too, Lebrun was assured that 'a great part of this generous nation is ready to make common cause (with France), if the British Ministry dares to declare itself against our liberty'.[194]

The mere content of these messages to the National Convention was enough to convince the Alarmists that the radicals were only the dupes and secondhand dispensers of French propaganda. The channel by which the addresses were transmitted to Paris, the manner of their presentation in the French national assembly, and the response they elicited seemed to offer proof positive of the existence of an Anglo-French radical conspiracy. It is true that the London Corresponding Society regarded the transmission of its address through the French embassy in London as necessary to guarantee its authenticity. Hardy also believed that this channel of communication could be concealed from the British government. When revealed, however, it was natural to assume that Chauvelin had himself inspired the initiative and that the addresses were the work of French agents.[195] For various other reasons the addresses of the Sheffield Constitutional Society, of the Aldgate Society of the Friends of the People and possibly others too were remitted in the same way.[196] Even more suspect, however, was the decision of the Society for Constitutional Information and the Derby reform society to

192. *Ibid.*

193. AAE, CPA 583, fo. 263.

194. *Ibid.* PRO HO 42/43, fo. 263 supplies further details about La Chesnaye. He had formerly been a subaltern in the French army who had escaped his creditors by emigrating to England.

195. BL, Add. MSS. 27814, fo. 47. For the attribution of the addresses to the promoting of French secret agents in England see Jenkinson's speech in the House of Commons on the second reading of the Alien Bill on 28 Dec. 1792. *Parl. Hist.*, vol. 30, col. 204. Government-controlled newspapers, like the *Sun*, also carried similar suggestions.

196. James Horsfield, secretary of the Sheffield Constitutional Society to Thomas Hardy, 3 Nov. 1792, enclosing copies of the Sheffield address and suggesting that they should be entrusted to Chauvelin for onward transmission to the Convention. PRO TS 11/965/3510A, pt. 2.

despatch their own delegates to Paris to present their addresses in person.[197] Those chosen for this mission were almost inevitably extremists – the strident American republican propagandist Joel Barlow, friend and associate of Paine, and the radical attorney John Frost in the case of the Society for Constitutional Information; and the mulatto demagogue Henry Redhead Yorke and a Dr William Brooks Johnson who represented the Derby society.[198] Away from the control of their constituents, and in the passionate and turbulent atmosphere of the French republican assembly, it is not surprising that such delegates exaggerated the pro-French sentiments and revolutionary sympathies of the English radical societies.

Chance also played its part – for the address of the Society for Constitutional Information was presented on 28 November – almost immediately after the delegates of the English, Irish and Scottish expatriates had claimed that 'if public opinion were consulted, as it ought to be, in a National Convention', their views would be shared by the great majority of their countrymen.[199] Owing also to Frost's inability to speak French, the role of spokesman devolved on Barlow, who showed no disposition to be outdone in his assessment of the strength of the radical movement in Britain.[200] 'Innumerable societies' of the sort he represented, 'were at present forming', he said, in all parts of England, 'thereby increasing the interest in and demand for parliamentary reform'. 'After the example given by France', he went on, 'revolutions will become easy; reason will make rapid progress, and it would not be surprising if, in a shorter time than we should venture to predict, there were to arrive from the continent addresses of congratulation to a National Convention in England.'[201] Barlow was, at this point, clearly indulging in wishful thinking and certainly not reflecting the views of his constituents or obeying their instructions. It seems more than likely that he was embroidering on the theme which had just been

197. TS 11/962/3508. BL, Place newspaper cuttings 36, fo. 15, for the Derby address.

198. For Barlow see V. C. Miller, *Joel Barlow, Revolutionist, London 1791–92* (Hamburg, 1932).

199. *Address of the English, Scotch, and Irish resident and domiciled in Paris. English Historical Review*, vol. 13 (1898), p. 674.

200. Captain G. Monro, 'Notes on English democrats in Paris in 1792'. PRO TS 11/959/3505(ii).

201. *ST*, vol. 24, col. 530. *Moniteur*, vol. 14, col. 593.

outlined before the Convention in the address from the English, Scottish and Irish exiles.[202]

Barlow then informed his audience that, in response to advice received from France, the Society for Constitutional Information had decided to apply the proceeds of the public subscription which it had taken over from Dr Maxwell in the purchase, not of arms, but of much needed footwear for the republican armies.[203] A thousand pairs (provided incidentally through Thomas Hardy, the shoemaking secretary of the London Corresponding Society) had, he announced, already reached Calais and further supplies would, he hoped, follow at the rate of 1000 pairs a week for the next six weeks.[204] The preliminary announcement of this 'patriotic gift' had been entrusted to Frost, but owing to his difficulty with the French language, he seems to have had trouble in convincing the War Minister Pache that he was not one of the infamous band of foreign war contractors trying to dispose of his wares.[205] Less inclined than the minister to look this gift horse in the mouth, the assembly applauded this announcement, if we are to believe Monro, more enthusiastically than the address itself.[206]

After gracefully acknowledging this practical gesture of goodwill, the president of the assembly, the abbé Grégoire, then reverted to the theme of a British Convention. In doing so he swept away all conjecture and suggestion of delay by commenting that 'doubtless the moment is near when Frenchmen will bear their congratulations to the National Convention of Great Britain'. He greeted Barlow and Frost as 'generous republicans'.[207] For its part, the Convention

202. Some English radical societies, however, had already expressed interest in the possibility of calling a Convention, e.g. the Stockport society's enquiry to the LCS (27 Sept. 1792): 'Would not all the evil be done away at once by the people assembled in convention?' *ST*, vol. 24, col. 388.

203. The suggestion had come from a M. Audibert of Calais, one of Paine's constituents, who had accompanied him across the Channel in September. It had been relayed to Horne Tooke by Robert Merry, one of the English exiles in Paris, on 29 Oct. 1792. PRO TS 11/951/3495.

204. *Procès-verbal de la Convention Nationale*, 28 Nov. 1792, p. 381.

205. Monro's 'Notes on the English democrats in Paris', 6 Dec. 1792. PRO TS 11/959/3505(ii).

206. *Ibid.* Though some of the members of the SCI received their money back, after Hardy had sold off surplus stocks of the shoes, there is evidence that more than one consignment of shoes reached France. PRO TS 11/954/3498. See Appendix 2.

207. *Moniteur*, 29 Nov. 1792. *ST*, vol. 24, col. 530.

voted them 'the honours of the session' and ordered that their address should be printed, circulated to all France's eighty-three departments and to her generals in the field and translated into other European languages.[208] Grégoire's reference to the possibility of an early summons of a British Convention and the presence in the assembly of Paine as a deputy for the department of the Pas de Calais, gave added resonance and significance to this revolutionary threat to English parliamentary institutions.[209] If the radicals were seriously contemplating recourse to such an assembly with the active encouragement of the French, then their opponents could reasonably contend that they were involved in a treasonable conspiracy.

In this respect passages from some of the earlier radical addresses seemed to assume greater relevance and to take on a more sinister meaning. If the members of the London Corresponding Society really regarded themselves as 'an oppressed part of mankind', subjected to an 'abhorrent system of inquisition', how did their situation differ from that of other minorities to whom the French appeared to have offered their armed assistance under the terms of the Edict of Fraternity?[210] For the moment, however, the metropolitan radicals had to rest content with the reflection that their views were rapidly becoming more representative of large sections of the British people. 'We can', their address had asserted,

with confidence assure you Freemen and Friends, that knowledge makes a rapid progress among us; that curiosity has taken possession of the minds of the public; that the reign of Ignorance, inseparable from that of Despotism, is vanishing; and that, at present, all men ask each other, What is Liberty? What are our Rights? Frenchmen you are already free, but Britons are preparing to be so.[211]

The question was how and when?

Just as the military successes of Dumouriez had revived the

208. *Procès-verbal de la Convention Nationale*, 28 Nov. 1792, p. 381.
209. Paine took his seat in the Convention on 20 Sept. 1792. According to Frost, who witnessed his reception in the assembly, Paine was in good spirits, but 'rather fatigued with the kissing'. Frost to Horne Tooke, 20 Sept. 1792. PRO TS 11/951/3495.
210. The difference was, according to Lebrun's subsequent explanations, that they were subjects of a neutral state and that the offer of assistance had not been made to small minorities, who happened to have grievances against the established government.
211. BL, Add. MSS. 27814, fo. 45.

flagging fortunes of English radicalism, so the English radical addresses may be said to have strengthened the resolve of the members of the National Convention, despite the opposition of the British government, to persist in the Brissotin policy of armed revolutionary propaganda. This was used, if not to mask, at least to rationalize an aggressive and expansionist foreign policy, which would, otherwise, have been patently incompatible with the French government's previous assurances.[212] Thus the concept of 'national frontiers' was casually formulated by the abbé Grégoire on 28 September 1792 to accommodate the assembly's decision to annex Savoy. Similarly, the decree of 16 November, liberating the navigation of the Scheldt, involved the unilateral breach of an international treaty, of which France was a signatory, but this action was justified on the principles of natural law.[213] Even the promise in the edict of 19 November of 'fraternity and assistance' to all peoples wishing to recover their liberty could be rendered less suspect by recourse to the principles of national sovereignty and the general will. To British Alarmists this decree appeared to have been designed 'to extend universally the new principles of government adopted in France, and to encourage disorder and revolt in all countries, even in those which are neutral'.[214] Lebrun, however, as foreign minister, despatched a further secret envoy, H. B. Maret, to Britain early in December to rebut this construction and to explain to Pitt that the decree, so far from being 'an advertisement for sedition', could only be invoked by the 'solemn and unequivocal expression of the general will' by nations which had emancipated themselves from tyrannical rule and yet needed French protection against their former rulers.[215] It did not, therefore, apply to neutral countries such as Britain. Although Pitt expressed his gratification at this restrictive interpretation, it is worth remarking that the specific reason later given by the British Foreign Secretary, Lord Grenville, for its rejection as implausible and unacceptable was 'the public reception given to

212. Lebrun, however, as Foreign Minister, saw no necessity to carry on active propaganda in Britain, since he was convinced that revolutionary principles were self-generating and irresistible. Any attempts to repress them would, he thought, only recoil on the government. Lebrun to Noël, 11 Nov. 1792. AAE, CPA 583, fos. 210–12.
213. Burke put this point neatly in the House of Commons on 15 Dec. 1792 by observing that: 'Thus the laws of nature superseded the law of nations.' *Parl. Hist.*, vol. 30, col. 112.
214. Lord Grenville to Chauvelin, 31 Dec. 1792. *Parl. Hist.*, vol. 30, col. 253.
215. AAE, CPA 584, fos. 19–22. Maret to Lebrun, 2 Dec. 1792.

the promoters of sedition in this country, and by the speeches made to them precisely at the time of this decree, and since on several occasions'.[216] This response to the British addresses had shown 'unequivocally' that the Edict of Fraternity had been considered by the National Convention as both relevant and applicable to Britain.[217]

It also seems probable that the radical addresses did much to reinforce the impression made on Lebrun's mind by the reports of his agents in England that in November 1792 the whole country was on the verge of a revolutionary crisis.[218] Though some of these reports were untrustworthy, and though both Noël and Chauvelin altered their previous views and gave repeated warnings in late November and December that the situation had completely altered, Lebrun and his colleagues on the diplomatic committee of the Convention retained their revolutionary illusions that the British government was on the edge of 'a volcano'.[219] Lebrun knew that the radical addresses had not been provoked by French secret agents, and he, therefore, accepted at face value their description of the inroads which radical principles had made in large areas of Britain. From the severe strictures which some of the addresses passed on George III, the English aristocracy and the privileged political establishment, it was perhaps reasonable for him to infer that a wide gulf separated the people from their governors and that this situation could, if necessary, be exploited. From these premises Lebrun concluded that, if Anglo-French differences threatened to culminate in open rupture, the British government would be subjected to intolerable pressures from outside Parliament.[220] He continued to credit the earlier conjectures of his observers that if Pitt resorted to the repression of radicalism the tocsin of revolt would be sounded – though facts were later to disprove the

216. Grenville to Chauvelin, 31 Dec. 1792. *Parl. Hist.*, vol. 30, col. 253.

217. *Ibid.*

218. Cf. the reports of Lebrun's chief secret agent Noël, 9 Oct. 1792, suggesting that a declaration of war by Britain would precipitate a revolution. AAE, CPA 582, fo. 312, and 2 Nov. 1792 reporting that 'Ireland was ripe for revolution'. Scotland was causing much anxiety, French principles were rapidly spreading in England and 'the government was now suspended on a volcano'. *Ibid.*, CPA 583, fos. 153–5.

219. *Ibid.*

220. On 21 Oct. 1792 Chauvelin had committed himself to the view that a British declaration of war on France would cause an immediate fall in government stock of 10 per cent, would antagonize the mercantile interest and 'perhaps' entail the overthrow of the monarchy. AAE, CPA 583, fo. 45.

hypothesis.[221] He also accepted the assurances in the addresses that if the British government attempted to repudiate its repeated pledges of strict neutrality, it would have to face the formidable resistance of the organized radical movement. Banking, no doubt, on the widespread pacifism in radical circles, Lebrun also comforted himself with the reflection that, if Pitt indulged in hostile preparations against France, large-scale anti-war demonstrations could be fomented.[222] In the final resort, if hostilities appeared imminent, the population might be split down the middle by an appeal to the British nation over the head of its corrupt and reactionary government.[223] Other evidence convinced Lebrun that a French declaration of war on Britain would also be the signal for rebellion in Ireland, separation in Scotland and civil war in England.[224]

Almost a year later the Jacobin foreign minister Deforgues, in a written indictment of the Brissotin responsibility for the outbreak of war with Britain, frankly attributed the revolutionary illusions of Lebrun and his colleagues to their failure to appreciate the attachment of the British people to their own constitution, their misreading of the political attitudes of the Whig Opposition, but, above all, to their mistaken assumption that the English radicals were thinking in terms of a revolution.[225] All that the radicals had then wanted was reform, and no one, surely, would have bothered to repair a political edifice if it had been decided to demolish it. 'An equal representation in the House of Commons, the repeal of the Test Acts and the reduction of taxation would have satisfied all the demands of the discontented.'[226] Failure to understand the non-revolutionary character of the English reform movement must, indeed, be rated as the fundamental misconception inherent in the Brissotin willingness to extend the war – for even the radical addresses had not concealed that their real political objectives were con-

221. Lebrun himself was, however, more inclined to think that Pitt's position was so weak that he would not dare to resort to repression and that his inactivity would allow French principles to develop unchecked. Lebrun to Noël, 11 Nov. 1792. AAE, CPA 583, fos. 210–12.

222. Lebrun to Chauvelin, 26 Nov. 1792. AAE, CPA 583, fos. 321–3. In his reply dated 5 December, Chauvelin reported that, on 4 December, he had received several London and Manchester merchants at his house and that they had promised that anti-war addresses would shortly be sent to the Convention from all parts of England. AAE, CPA 584, fo. 58.

223. Lebrun made this threat in a speech of 19 December in the Convention.

224. Murley.

225. AAE, CPA 588, fos. 142–3.

226. *Ibid.*, fo. 143.

fined to an effective reform of the House of Commons.[227] Lebrun's individual responsibility for the decree of 16 November 1792 throwing open the navigation of the Scheldt, which his indictment blandly admitted had provided Pitt with plausible pretexts for joining the European anti-revolutionary coalition, was brought home to him in December 1793 and was sufficient to ensure the death penalty.[228]

There had, however, also been misunderstanding, or possibly intentional misinterpretation, of the radical addresses by the English Alarmists and the British government. These were regarded, at the time and later in 1794, as having been promoted by French secret agents operating in Britain.[229] In the autumn of 1792 the metropolitan area had, indeed, been flooded with French official and secret agents of various kinds. That situation had resulted not only from the national emergency in Paris, but also from the decision of the British government virtually to break off diplomatic relations with the French Provisional Executive Council after the overthrow of the Bourbon monarchy.[230] The appointment by Lebrun of his former associate Noël to be the chief French secret agent in London and as a possible replacement for Chauvelin, at the end of August 1792, had been designed to keep open the channels of communication between the two governments in what would otherwise have been a complete diplomatic vacuum.[231] Noël's instructions, dated 28

227. A more cool and objective analysis of the prospects of a radical upheaval in England had been given in a report from Reinhard, second-in-command at the French Embassy in London on 20 September 1792. This suggested that a revolution could only be anticipated in consequence of financial collapse at the end of a long war or of a successful parliamentary reform. AAE, Mémoires et documents, 48, fos. 184–9.

228. Indictment before the Revolutionary Tribunal, 7 Nivôse an II (27 Dec. 1793). AN, W 305, carton 365.

229. The *Sun* newspaper, started on 1 October 1792 by George Rose and Charles Long, under-secretaries at the Treasury, devoted itself to alarming the public about this danger. On 9 October it reported the presence of French agents 'in every quarter of the kingdom', 'who were endeavouring to stir up a spirit of sedition'.

230. For a semi-official explanation of the motives for the recall of Lord Gower from Paris, see H. Marsh, *The History of the Politicks of Great Britain and France from the time of the Conference at Pillnitz to the Declaration of War against Great Britain* (London, 1800), vol. 1, ch. 9.

231. François Noël, a defrocked priest, co-founder of Condorcet's *Chronique de Paris*, a confidant of Danton, who had entered the ministry of Foreign Affairs in April 1792 as first secretary in the department concerned with German and Belgian affairs.

August 1792, moreover, made it quite clear that he had no authority to negotiate, and that his real role was that of go-between and observer.[232] He was specifically warned against any attempts to resuscitate the Whig Association of Friends of the People, which was described as 'paralysed', and against flirting with the Opposition Whigs as Chauvelin had done – to the discredit of the French Legation.[233] Noël's role throughout the five months that he continued as Lebrun's chief informant on British affairs was to endeavour to keep Pitt's government to its policy of neutrality – even after the conquest of Belgium – and to explain, if necessary through friendly intermediaries such as W. A. Miles and William Smith MP, how the successive decrees of revolutionary propaganda were still compatible with Anglo-French amicable relations.

It is also fair to say that, though he was occasionally guilty of interpreting situations by invoking erroneous historical analogies,[234] and of accepting too uncritically evidence pointing to the imminence of a revolutionary crisis in Britain, Noël, like Chauvelin, did not conceal from the French government the remarkable change which had occurred in British opinion at the end of November and beginning of December. Both Noël and Chauvelin duly reported that, by that time, Pitt had successfully united the country behind his ministry and that the outbreak of hostilities would not undermine, but rather cement, the newly found national solidarity.[235]

Few of the other French agents in Britain in the autumn of 1792 were commissioned as spies or *agents provocateurs*, though their primary functions did not necessarily exclude such activities. Some agents were on the track of the manufacturers of false *assignats*, subsidized by Calonne as representative of the *émigré* princes;

232. AAE, CPA 582, fos. 72–7.
233. *Ibid.*
234. Noël to Lebrun, 24 Nov. 1792, compared the situation in England with that of France in 1789 – the Duke of Richmond, as a second comte d'Artois, leading the court party of reaction; the fortified Tower of London as an English Bastille, provoking the democratic mobs of the metropolis; Pitt weakly angling for popularity as Necker had done; Lord Lansdowne fishing in troubled waters like the duc d'Orléans. The Reevite Associations appeared to reduplicate the activities of the *Club Monarchique* while the English aristocracy defended its privileges with the same obstinacy as its French counterparts. Noël concluded, 'All the symptoms indicate that revolutionary movements cannot be far off.' AAE, CPA 583, fos. 314–16.
235. Noël to Lebrun, 14, 15, 16 and 22 Dec. 1792. Chauvelin to same, 5 Dec. 1792. AAE, CPA 584.

others were in pursuit of the thieves who had broken into the Tuileries palace and stolen the crown jewels.[236] Some, like Achille Viart, had been sent over to report on the intrigues of the *émigré* counter-revolutionaries.[237] Then, too, there were the members of the various purchasing commissions appointed by the ministers of war, the interior and foreign affairs, who came over to Britain to tender for the supply of guns, ammunition, equipment, horses, shoes, or corn.[238] When, at the beginning of October, a serious conflict developed between Chauvelin and Noël, further agents were despatched to subject them to surveillance.[239] Nevertheless, the mere presence of so many French agents in London, and the large numbers of suspected spies who were thought to have passed themselves off as refugees from the horrors of the September Massacres, helped to give greater credibility to the stories passed on to the Home Office by French *émigré* sources. These spoke confidently of the existence of a French Jacobin conspiracy to revolutionize the capital in concert with the radicals.[240]

The radical addresses also revealed to an apprehensive British government the close contacts which had been established between the metropolitan radical societies and important French politicians. Though the London Revolution Society had been the first to excite suspicion on this account, attention was now focused on the relations between leading members of the Society for Constitutional Information and the London Corresponding Society on the one hand and, on the other, key figures of the French republican regime, such as Danton, Lebrun, Brissot, Pétion and Condorcet.[241] The subscription in aid of the French and the consignment of thousands of pairs of shoes for the benefit of Dumouriez's badly equipped troops had increased the circle of Horne Tooke's French correspondents, while Margarot had induced his friend Rabaut de Saint-Étienne to help with the translation of the address of the London Corresponding Society and its presentation in the National

236. Noël to Lebrun, 13 Sept. 1792. *Ibid.*, CPA 582, fo. 123.
237. AAE, CPA, Supplément 29, fo. 280.
238. Noël to Lebrun, 13 Sept. 1792. AAE, CPA 582, fo. 123.
239. Instructions to X. Aubriet, 3 Oct. 1792. AAE, CPA Supplément 29.
240. PRO HO 1/1. Letters from *émigrés*, 29 Nov./1 Dec. 1792, submitted to Pitt and the Home Office by Lord Sheffield, friend of Gibbon and Burke, and leading Alarmist.
241. Holcroft was friendly with Danton, Cooper and Thomas Walker with Pétion, J. H. Stone with Brissot, Paine with Condorcet.

Convention.[242] Monro's detailed report on the proceedings in the Convention on 28 November argued that the Society for Constitutional Information as well as the English, Scottish and Irish democrats in Paris were intent on 'the subversion of royalty, universal anarchy and the entire overthrow of the present British constitution and of society'. It also disclosed that 'these diabolical schemes' were believed to be receiving support from 'people in power at present in France'.[243] In making these statements Monro, no doubt, had in mind the republican views of Paine and Barlow, both of whom had been honorary members of the SCI and were then helping to lay the foundations of a future French ultra-democratic constitution.[244] But what were Pitt and his colleagues to think when, in the middle of January 1793, and with the country on the brink of hostilities with France, the Society for Constitutional Information conferred the status of 'associated honorary member' on citizens Jean Bon St André, Barère and Roland, and voted that extracts of the speeches of the first two to the Convention, asserting that the historic mission of that body was 'to destroy kings and royalty', should be inserted in its books and published in the newspapers? [245]

During the previous autumn, despite the Royal Proclamation, both Thomas Cooper and Paine had published pamphlets in self-defence which set new standards of plain speaking and uncompromising argument.[246] In reply to Burke's invective Cooper stated the case for 'effectual parliamentary reform', committed himself to William Ogilvie's scheme for 'an Agrarian Progressive Law' designed to control the evils of monopolistic landlordism, and condemned

242. PRO TS 11/965/3510 A, pt. 2. Though Veitch, p. 227, doubted whether the gift of 6000 shoes had 'ever been completed', it is clear from Guyton de Morveau's report to the Convention on 17 Feb. 1793, suggesting the conferment of French citizenship on Barlow, that most of the consignment had, in fact, reached the French armies. AN, F⁷ 4395. See Appendix 2.

243. PRO TS 11/959/3505(ii).

244. Paine was appointed a member of the constitutional committee of the Convention on 11 Oct. 1792. Aldridge, p. 175. Barlow published a *Letter to the National Convention, on the defects of the constitution of France* . . . on 3 Oct. 1792. On Paine's suggestion this was translated into French and referred for the consideration of the constitutional committee.

245. Minute-book, 18 and 25 Jan. 1793. PRO TS 11/962/3508.

246. Cooper's *Reply to Mr. Burke's Invective against Mr. Cooper & Mr. Watt in the House of Commons on 30th April, 1792* was published on 8 Sept. 1792, and Paine's *Letter Addressed to the Addressers on the Late Proclamation* appeared in mid October.

the current treatment of the poor as 'a system of flagrant Iniquity'.[247] Paine's *Letter Addressed to the Addressers on the Late Proclamation* attributed his prosecution to the government's fear 'at the progressive increase in political knowledge' involved in the publication of cheap editions of *The Rights of Man*, denounced the loyal addresses as emanating from corporations and rotten boroughs, which he had previously exposed as 'august monopolies and public nuisances' and called for the summons of a popular convention to put in hand a 'representative' or republican government.[248] Both Cooper and Paine delivered frontal attacks on the moderation and political hypocrisy of the Whig Association of Friends of the People, both rehearsed the theoretical and practical arguments against hereditary monarchy and aristocracy and both directed attention to the fundamental social, economic and educational grievances which required urgent and radical redress.[249] 'There is among us', wrote Cooper 'too much Inequality of Rank – too much Inequality of Riches – too much inequality of labour.'[250] Paine also suggested that the reason for the alarm generated by the second part of his *Rights of Man* was that his social welfare schemes could only be financed even more at the expense of sinecure placemen and pensioners, than by the reduction of taxes.[251] It is not surprising that such pronouncements were, at the time, regarded as 'Levelling', and that Marxist historians are tempted to see in them evidence of incipient class conflict.

The alarm which spread rapidly throughout the country in the course of November was first felt and communicated to others by the landed aristocracy and gentry.[252] Some of them, such as the Marquis of Buckingham, had themselves already felt the need to conciliate 'the lower ranks of people' by timely concessions, but at the same time had urged the government to prosecute Cooper's and Paine's pamphlets and to tighten up security.[253] The panic spread to

247. Ogilvie appears to have invented the right to forty acres (but not a cow), as a holding, on payment of a rent fixed in perpetuity to the landlord. For an explanation of his scheme see H. W. C. Davis, *The Age of Grey and Peel* (Oxford, 1929), p. 318.

248. Paine, pp. 39–40.

249. Cooper, pp. 71–8; Paine, p. 37.

250. Cooper, p. 75.

251. Paine, p. 36.

252. Lord Sheffield, Earl Fitzwilliam, the Marquis of Buckingham and William Windham, MP for Norwich, were very prominent in this respect.

253. Buckingham to his brother Lord Grenville, 8 Nov. 1792. *Dropmore MSS. Historical Manuscripts Commission, 14th report*, appendix part 5, vol. 2 (1894) pp. 327–8.

members of the local Church and King clubs, always prepared for a witch-hunt among the radical leaders, and to the conservative or Portland Whigs who, under the tuition of Burke, had begun to sniff the polluted breezes from France.[254] When economic discontent at the rising cost of living resulted in seamen's strikes for higher wages in the North-East and widespread rioting in Scotland (where Dundas was at hand to observe it), it was used by those responsible for the maintenance of public order to launch a so-called Association for the Preservation of Liberty and Property against Republicans and Levellers.[255] The object was to strengthen the hands of the government and to unite the country against the threat of radical egalitarianism in league with French republicanism. Founded on 20 November 1792 by John Reeves, a former chief justice of Newfoundland and monopolist, if there ever was one, of lucrative public offices, this association brought about an immediate closing of the ranks against the reformers and sponsored a highly efficient campaign in defence of the social, political and religious establishment.[256] Lord Grenville, in temporary charge of the Home Office in the absence of Dundas, saw the opportunity to recruit the political support of 'merchants and lawyers' in the metropolis and of 'farmers and yeomen' in the country districts, his aim being to unite all sections of the community behind the government and in support of the constitution.[257] By circular letters directed to lords lieutenant, dated 24 November, grand juries were instructed to make presentments of seditious publications at the next quarter sessions, and early in December the Treasury solicitors sent out enquiries to selected firms of solicitors in most of the larger towns asking whether they would agree to act as local agents for the prosecution of the publication or sale of libellous literature.[258] Reeves also sought to counter

254. For Burke's and Windham's activities in alerting the conservative Whigs see F. O'Gorman, *The Whig Party and the French Revolution* (London, 1967), pp. 107–8.

255. For this subject see Black, ch. 7; Mitchell, 'The Association movement of 1792–3', pp. 56–77; and D. Ginter, 'The Loyalist Association movement of 1792–93 and British public opinion', *The Historical Journal*, vol. 9 (1966), pp. 179–90.

256. Reeves's appointments included Receiver of the Public Offices (metropolitan police) 1792; High Steward of the Manor and Liberty of the Savoy, 1793; and King's Printer, 1800.

257. Grenville to Marquis of Buckingham, 25 Nov. 1792. Buckingham, *Memoirs of the Courts and Cabinets of George III* (2 vols, London, 1853), vol. 2, p. 229. This initiative resulted in the influential meeting of merchants, bankers and traders held at the Merchant Taylors' Hall on 5 Dec. 1792.

258. PRO TS 11/954/3498.

the activities of the Society for Constitutional Information by the publication and distribution of short popular tracts in the vernacular designed to refute the 'specious' reasoning of the reformers by the imaginary common sense and caustic wit of ordinary 'mechanics' and day labourers. Hannah More's *Village Politics; A Dialogue between Jack Anvil the Blacksmith and Tom Hod the Mason* set the tone and scored a lasting success.[259] 'Burke in petticoats' she may have been, but her so-called 'Cheap Repository Tracts', full of Evangelical self-satisfaction and fervour, outsold even Paine and long outlasted the Loyalist associations which had sponsored them. Tracts and pamphlets alike were circulated with the help and co-operation of the Post Office.[260]

Reeves's Crown and Anchor Association also urged local magistrates to threaten innkeepers who allowed their premises to be used by radical societies with the non-renewal of their licences, and, in the capital, the various divisions of the London Corresponding Society and its delegate committee were harried from one tavern to another, and were eventually forced to seek refuge in private houses.[261] From one end of the country to the other, corporate towns, public trustees, associations of merchants and manufacturers, parish vestry meetings and private individuals met at the association's behest either to form vigilance committees or to pass resolutions of loyalty to 'the happy constitution' and of support for the government and the guardians of public order.[262] More questionable methods were employed in the work of repression. In early December, with the tacit approval and even encouragement of local magistrates, 'Church and King' mobs were once more directed against the lives and property of prominent reformers. The worst incidence of this renewed bigotry occurred at Manchester when, on 11 December, Thomas Walker's house, then used by the local reform societies for their meetings, and the offices of the *Manchester Herald* were attacked by mobs, and only preserved by Walker's action in firing over the heads of his assailants.[263] Spies and informers were now inserted by the Home Office in the metropolitan

259. M. G. Jones, *Hannah More* (Cambridge, 1952).
260. K. Ellis, *The Post Office in the Eighteenth Century* (London, 1958).
261. BL, Add. MSS. 27814, fo. 43. Half the weekly subscription was allocated for the hire of rooms, fire and candles; the other half being used for printing.
262. Mitchell, 'The Association movement of 1792–3', pp. 61–2.
263. Knight, ch. 9.

radical societies and all forms of reform activity were closely supervised.[264]

On 1 December the government issued a second proclamation, deploring the failure to implement the first, stressing the danger from 'evil-disposed persons – acting in concert with persons in foreign parts' and ordering the embodiment of part of the militia.[265] This required the special recall of Parliament a fortnight later, partly to enforce urgent security measures (including an Alien Bill to control the movements of French immigrants), and partly to increase the country's war preparedness.[266] During the rest of the month, despite the relevant but futile criticism of the Foxite minority in the House of Commons and the last-minute efforts of Lebrun to seek an acceptable compromise through secret diplomatic channels,[267] Pitt refused to acknowledge the French republic or its accredited envoy, insisted on the withdrawal of the Convention's decrees of armed propaganda, and clearly asserted his government's determination to uphold the sanctity of international treaties and to implement its treaty of alliance with the United Provinces. With the country united behind him, Pitt had no need to concern himself with the alleged radical threat of a revolution, which, in truth, only existed in the over-heated imagination of Burke and his Alarmists, in the files of the French ministry of foreign affairs, and the illusory calculations of the Brissotin faction in the National Convention.

Not the least of the self-inflicted difficulties with which the radicals were now confronted was their alienation of their former liberal-minded supporters. The noisy demonstrations organized by the reform societies in support of the French, and above all their injudicious addresses to the National Convention not only helped to provoke an overwhelming conservative reaction, but added to the ranks of the associated defenders of the unreformed constitution

264. PRO TS 11/959/3505(ii) contains Captain G. Monro's reports on the various divisions of the London Corresponding Society and the Society for Constitutional Information.

265. *Annual Register* (1792), pp. 196–7.

266. For the famous 'dagger' scene in the House of Commons when Burke flung down one of Maxwell's daggers to the floor of the house in the second reading of the Alien Bill on 28 Dec. 1792, see *Parl. Hist.*, vol. 30, col. 189 and J. Hutton, *Letters and correspondence of Sir James Bland Burges* (London, 1885), p. 203.

267. Mainly through Maret, but also through W. A. Miles and William Smith MP. See Murley.

some of those Protestant Dissenters,[268] many former members of the Yorkshire County Association[269] and most of the progressive merchants and manufacturers who had, in the past, rendered such yeoman service in the cause of reform.[270] The radicals had not only antagonized their conservative opponents and alienated many of their former liberal supporters, they had also now clearly emerged from their contacts with the French with the distorted but intelligible public image of 'English Jacobins'. As the youthful Macaulay was to write in another connection: 'Liberty has no enemies so pernicious as those misguided friends whose ardour in her cause leads them to outrage the moral sense of mankind, and to arm against her the interests and the feelings which are her natural auxiliaries.'[271]

268. Declaration of Loyalty by London Protestant Dissenters, 12 Dec. 1792. *Gentleman's Magazine*, vol. 62, pt. 2 (1792). Declaration of Manchester Nonconformists of their support for the constitution. *Manchester Mercury*, 29 Dec. 1792.

269. A typical example was the Rev. James Wilkinson, vicar of Sheffield, who 'in his triple capacity of parson, squire and magistrate . . . wielded a power more direct and familiar . . . than that of the Duke of Norfolk'. G. P. Jones, 'The political reform movement in Sheffield', *Transactions of the Hunter Archaeological Society*, vol. 4 (1937), p. 57.

270. Several of the more prominent Norwich merchants seem to have withdrawn from the Norwich Revolution Society at this time. B. D. Hayes, 'Politics in Norfolk, 1750–1832', unpublished PhD thesis, Cambridge (1957), p. 241.

271. Trinity College Cambridge Prize Essay on 'King William III' won by Macaulay in 1882. Reprinted in *The Times Literary Supplement* (1 May 1969), pp. 468–9.

8 War, repression and the British Convention, February–December 1793

State trials will always either be impotent or oppressive, a persecution or a farce.

SIR JAMES MACKINTOSH, *Vindiciae Gallicae*[1]

The war which France declared on Great Britain and Holland on 1 February 1793 was, as Lord Lansdowne, Pitt and Burke all agreed, 'a war of principles'.[2] With a mixture of discernment and calculated irresponsibility Charles James Fox preferred to call it 'a war of false hopes and false grounds', having in mind the miscalculations of the French executive council and the British government's refusal to recognize the French republic.[3] For Alarmists like Robert Banks Jenkinson (later Lord Liverpool), it was a war against French aggrandizement, but also against English radicalism.[4] Those radicals, however, who opposed the war in pamphlet or handbill did so mainly on economic grounds – Thomas Cooper, in a bitter address to the inhabitants of Manchester, possibly prompted by Chauvelin, condemned the likely consequences of hostilities with the French as the ruination of overseas trade, the impoverishment of the local weavers and the degradation, oppression and forcible recruitment of the poor into the army or navy.[5]

The same note of passionate concern for the economic plight of

1. J. Mackintosh, *Miscellaneous Works* (London, 1851), p. 615.
2. R. Coupland, *The War Speeches of William Pitt the Younger*, 3rd ed. (Oxford, 1940), pp. 27–8.
3. For Fox's views on the war see J. L. Le B. Hammond, *Charles James Fox: A Political Study* (London, 1903), ch. 12.
4. Speech in House of Commons, 15 Dec. 1792. *Parl. Hist.*, vol. 30, col. 87. Once war had broken out, Jenkinson argued, the radicals would be forced either to emigrate (many in fact did so) or 'to conduct themselves like good citizens'. Their correspondence with the French would either cease, or, if continued, become treasonable.
5. Manchester Central Reference Library, MS. 942.073. The pamphlet, 'WAR', was published on 10 Dec. 1792 under Cooper's usual pseudonym 'Sydney'. In a letter of 5 Dec. 1792 to Lebrun, who had instructed him to provoke such anti-war

the poor in wartime, but in a rural context, was sounded by William Frend, Unitarian Fellow of Queen's College, Cambridge, in a reform pamphlet published in March 1793 – *Peace and Union Recommended*.[6] In the appendix to this work written in late December 1792 as the result of a chance encounter, Frend commiserated with the lot of country women near St Ives, whose earnings as spinners had been reduced by a quarter by local wool staplers in consequence of an anticipated wartime trade recession.[7] 'We are to be scotched three pence in the shilling – a fourth part of our labour. What is all this for?' were poignant cries which left such a vivid impression on Frend's mind that they dimmed and rendered futile all explanations stemming from the alleged necessity of punishing the executioners of Louis XVI and of reclosing the navigation of the Scheldt.[8] Contrasting the economic miseries and physical danger of the poor, bribed or press-ganged into the armed forces, with the glittering fortunes accumulated by war contractors, Frend suggested that rich profiteers and warmongers alone should have their annual income 'scotched' by a quarter to pay for the war and thus relieve the economic injustices being shouldered by the un-comprehending victims of international conflict.[9] This, however, was too strong a medicine for the stomachs of his own colleagues in college and university and Frend found himself in May 1793 ejected from his college and banished from the university.[10]

The war also quickly dimmed the prospects of the English radical

---

demonstrations, Chauvelin reported that, on the previous day at his home in Putney, he had been assured by several 'very rich' London and Manchester merchants of radical views that anti-war addresses 'conceived and drafted precisely in the manner that I had indicated to them' would shortly be published. AAE, CPA 584, fos. 56–8. It seems likely that Cooper had thus informed Chauvelin of the forthcoming publication of his pamphlet, but whether the French envoy had influenced its form or contents in any way must be doubtful.

6. The pamphlet itself contained a fairly innocuous blend of suggested parliamentary, legal and religious reforms devoid of originality. F. Knight, *University Rebel. The Life of William Frend, 1757–1841* (London, 1971), p. 120.

7. Frend met the country women on his way to St Ives, where he was about to check the printing of the finished pamphlet. He was careful to check the fall of spinners' earnings with one of the main wool dealers in Cambridge.

8. W. Frend, *Peace and Union Recommended* (St Ives, 1793), appendix.

9. 'The whole expence [*sic*] of war should be confined to the rich.' *Ibid.*

10. After leaving Cambridge Frend moved to London, where he made a living as an actuary tutor in mathematics. He joined the London Corresponding Society and served as a member of the committee established to defray the legal expenses of the defendants in the treason trials of 1794.

movement as a whole. Any future correspondence with the French after the outbreak of hostilities would, as Jenkinson had foreseen, either become impossible or involve the radicals in treason. All efforts to press forward in wartime with a programme of parliamentary reform would inevitably be represented by the government as 'untimely' and, if such plans were coupled with proposals for the summons of a 'convention', they could reasonably be prosecuted as, at least, seditious. Popular suspicions of and resentment at the biased attitudes which the radical societies had displayed towards the French and British governments in the diplomatic prelude to the war were exacerbated, not only by the misrepresentations of the Reevite associations, but also by the subsequent unrepentant behaviour of the radicals themselves.[11] As Erskine later observed, these mistakes were not quickly forgotten – in particular, the 'ill-timed and extravagant encomiums' of the French revolution just at the period when its practice had temporarily diverged from the principles which deserved them, the severe strictures against European monarchical despotisms 'from which the mixed principles of our own government were not distinctly or prudently separated', and also the acrimonious observations on the defects of the British constitution and the corruption of the House of Commons, 'some of which, according to the just theory of the law, were unquestionably libels'.[12] Not all members of the Society for Constitutional Information had approved the addresses to the National Convention or the subscription in aid of the French, and some had resigned from the society in consequence.[13]

The price which had to be paid for such blunders, both immediately and in the future, was considerable. Lord Sempill who, as chairman of the Society for Constitutional Information, had signed its address to the French assembly, and Lord Edward Fitzgerald, who had negotiated in Paris for French intervention in Ireland, were both summarily cashiered from their army commands without trial or compensation.[14] John Frost, the radical attorney, who had acted

11. The London Corresponding Society considered that the addresses had neither helped to precipitate the war, nor given a handle to the Alarmists. Letter to Friends of the People, Feb. 1793. *ST*, vol. 24, col. 399.

12. T. Erskine, *A View of the Causes and Consequences of the present war with France* (London, 1797), p. 12.

13. 11 Dec. 1792. PRO TS 11/952/3496(i).

14. Sempill, a representative Scottish peer, who had also taken part in the Scottish burgh reform movement, published his vindication and grievances in *Correspondence with the Secretary at War and other official papers* (London, 1792).

as delegate for the Society for Constitutional Information to the National Convention, was in May 1793 convicted of sedition for disloyal expressions made in the public room of a London coffee-house, when under the influence of drink and provocation from Crown witnesses. He was sentenced to six months' imprisonment in Newgate, an hour in the pillory at Charing Cross, to find sureties for good behaviour for five years, and to be struck off the roll of attorneys.[15] His professional career was thus ruined.

These were far from being the only victims of repression for, on 18 December 1792, a special jury had convicted Thomas Paine in his absence for having published a seditious libel – Part II of *The Rights of Man*.[16] He was now an outlaw. This verdict had two serious consequences for the reformers – it robbed them of their single most effective weapon of radical propaganda and it also exposed the printers and publishers of Paine's works to certain prosecution.[17] The Reevite associations and the Treasury solicitors, working in close collaboration, initiated a spate of prosecutions directed against radical booksellers, often in the hope of terminating their activities as proprietors or printers of local radical newspapers. In this campaign of systematic repression the Attorney General resorted to the use of *ex officio* informations, a procedure which allowed the prosecution to dispense with grand juries, to try cases before hand-picked special juries and to keep the threat of proceedings hanging over the heads of the accused for long periods.[18]

The efficacy of such methods of legal intimidation was illustrated when four *ex officio* informations were drawn up by the Treasury Solicitors against Matthew Falkner and Samuel Birch, proprietors of the *Manchester Herald* early in 1793 and filed with the Court of King's Bench.[19] Before these informations could be proceeded with, six indictments were also found at Quarter Sessions against the accused for selling Painite and other seditious literature at their

15. *ST*, vol. 22, cols. 521–2. Although Frost obtained a free pardon in 1813, he was never restored to the roll of attorneys.

16. *Ibid.*, vol. 22, col. 472.

17. R. R. Rea, 'The "liberty of the press", as an issue in English politics, 1792–1793', *The Historian: A Journal of History* (Phi Alpha Theta), vol. 24 (1961), p. 34.

18. On 13 Dec. 1792 the Attorney General (Sir Archibald Macdonald) stated in the House of Commons that he had 200 such informations on his file. *Parl. Hist.*, vol. 30, col. 59.

19. PRO TS 11/668/2141.

bookshop. Rather than face trial and inevitable conviction, these two leading members of the Manchester Constitutional Society fled to the United States of America in March and, before the month was over, their journal – the voice of radical dissent in the North-West, the *Manchester Herald* – had been silenced.[20] It was also on the specific orders of the government that proceedings were started against Richard Phillips, radical newspaper proprietor of Leicester, for similar offences. In April 1793 he was found guilty and given a sentence of eighteen months' imprisonment.[21]

In the Hilary law terms of 1793 two metropolitan printers and one provincial printer were convicted of publishing Painite and other radical literature and were sentenced to long periods of imprisonment. H. D. Symonds, a Paternoster Row bookseller in London, had been marked down as 'the Master Mover of all the libellous matters in Payne's works', the printer of the cheap edition of *The Rights of Man*, Part II, the original publisher of Paine's *Address to the Addressers* and of the *Jockey Club*, Parts I and II. He had also supplied the Society for Constitutional Information with thousands of copies of Paine's works and other radical pamphlets which were then relayed to the provincial reform societies. On conviction Symonds was sentenced to four years' imprisonment and fines amounting to £200, and was also required to give security for good behaviour for five years after release in £500, with two sufficient sureties of £100 each.[22] For publishing the same works James Ridgeway, owner of a pamphlet shop in York St, St James's Square, after withdrawing his original plea of not guilty, was given a similar sentence.[23] Daniel Holt, publisher of the radical *Newark Herald*, printer to the recently founded Nottingham Political Society, had also aroused the hostility of the local Reevite association as a bookseller, when, after warning, he had refused to withdraw from sale Painite and other radical works. Late in December 1792, *ex officio* informations were filed against him for publishing Paine's *Address to the Addressers* and also for republishing one of

20. These *ex officio* informations had been drawn up at the suggestion of the 'committee of papers' of the Manchester Association for Preserving Liberty, Order and Property, formed on 11 Dec. 1792. F. Knight, *The Strange Case of Thomas Walker* (London, 1957), p. 119. A. V. Mitchell's Manchester MA thesis (1958), 'Radicalism and repression in the north of England, 1791–1797', is particularly valuable on this subject.

21. BL, Add. MSS. 27809, fo. 208.

22. PRO TS 11/944/3419.

23. PRO TS 11/41/151.

Above left: Dr. Richard Price (1723-
1791) From an engraving by T.
Holloway after Benjamin West
National Portrait Gallery Engravings
Reserve

Above right: Dr. Joseph Priestley
(1733-1804) From a portrait in oils by
William Artaud. Dr. Williams's
Library, London

Left: John Horne Tooke (1736-1812)
From a portrait in oils by Richard
Brompton. Heaton Park Hall, nr.
Manchester

Above left: Thomas Paine (1737-
1809) From a portrait in oils by A.
Millière from an engraving by
William Sharp, after Romney National Portrait Gallery

Above right: Thomas Hardy (1752-
1832) Engraving from an original
drawing formerly in the possession of
Mrs. Hardy. John Baxter's *A New
and Impartial History of England*,
1796

Left: John Thelwall (1764-1834)
From a portrait in oils attributed to
William Hazlitt. National Portrait
Gallery

Above left: Amelia Opie, nee Alderson (1769-1853) From a portrait in oils by John Opie. National Portrait Gallery

Above right: Thomas Holcroft, on left, and William Godwin, on right, at the Treason Trials of 1794. From a pencil sketch by Thomas Lawrence, Oxford. Holcroft, who was a prisoner in Newgate during the trials of Hardy and Horne Tooke, was released without trial on 1 December 1794, after Tooke's acquittal on 22 November (S.T.xxv,476). Lawrence must, therefore, have made this drawing of the two friends in the court room of the Old Bailey between 1 and 5 December 1794 during the trial of John Thelwall, the third and last of the so-called 'Twelve Apostles' to sustain trial for high treason. It is rarely that an eighteenth century drawing can be dated so precisely.

Left: Profiles of Mr. Erskine and Mr. Gibbs. Engraving by Williams, 1795. Place Newspaper Collection, vol. 36 (fol 243) British Library

Above: "An Address from the Citizens of N-----h to the National Convention." Caricature by F. Sayers from his *Outlines of the Opposition in 1795. Collected from the works of the most Capital Jacobin artists.* Colman Collection. Central Public Library, Norwich. This print satirizes (i) the pacifist and "unpatriotic" opposition of the local Dissenting interest to the re-election of William Windham as M.P. for Norwich in the bye-election of 1794, occasioned by his appointment as Secretary at War in Pitt's Coalition with the Portland Whigs, (ii) the support given by the Norwich Revolution Society in November 1792 to the joint radical Address to the French National Convention sponsored by the London Corresponding Society.

Left: "British Butcher" (i.e. William Pitt). Caricature by James Gillray, 1795 Department of Prints and Drawings, British Museum. Gillray's portrayal of the British *crise des subsistances* of 1795.

Major Cartwright's reform pamphlets of 1782 – an *Address to the* *Inhabitants of Leeds, Sheffield, Birmingham, Manchester and other* *unrepresented towns on a Parliamentary Reform.* He was found guilty on both counts and sentenced to four years' imprisonment in Newgate and fines totalling £100, and was also required to provide security for good behaviour for five years in £200 and two sureties of £50 each.[24] Besides their fines, the three prisoners had to face bills for their legal defence amounting in all to £800 and the heavy costs of maintaining their respective businesses during the period of their confinement. In January 1795 the three printers collectively estimated that their total expenses by the time of their ultimate release would amount to £3800.[25]

Some of these difficulties had been foreseen by members of the Whig Association of Friends of the People and, after the conviction of Paine for seditious libel, steps had been taken to form an Association for Preserving the Liberty of the Press. The first meeting had been held at the Freemason's Tavern on 22 December 1792 and subsequent meetings, early in 1793, had attracted such large numbers that they could only be accommodated at the Crown and Anchor Tavern – the home of the metropolitan Reevite association.[26] On 19 January Erskine delivered a frontal attack on the Loyalist associations, condemning them as 'doubtful in law, and unconstitutional in principle – a sort of partnership of authority with the executive power – supported by the subscriptions of opulent men, for the avowed object of suppressing and prosecuting writings'. These superfluous and insidious societies posed threats to the three main safeguards of English liberty under the constitution – 'the monopoly of the power of accusation by the chief executive magistrate, the office of the Grand Jury, interposed as a shield between the people and the very laws enacted by themselves, and trial by jury'. These threats were particularly conspicuous in the courts of Quarter Sessions

where the Judges were the very gentlemen who lead these Associations in every county and city in the Kingdom, and where Juries are either their

24. PRO TS 11/836/2820. *ST*, vol. 23, cols. 63, 70. D. Holt, *A Vindication of the Conduct and Principles of the Printer of the Newark Herald*, 2nd ed. (Newark, 1794).

25. G. Dyer, *Dissertation on the Theory and Practice of Benevolence* (London, 1795), pp. 88–90. Appeal to the Public, 3 Jan. 1795. This appeal was not circulated – in the expectation that some relief might be forthcoming from the fund raised on behalf of the defendants in the State Trials of 1794.

26. Rea, p. 35.

tenants and dependents, or their neighbours in the country, justly looking up to them, with confidence and affection, as their friends and protectors in the direction of their affairs.[27]

If the exertions of these combinations were to extend, beyond the suppression of books already condemned by the judgements of the courts,

to whatever does not happen to fall in with their private judgements – if no man is to write but upon their principles, nor can read with safety, except what they have written – no man will venture either to write or speak upon the topics of government or its administration.[28]

These were powerful arguments and 10,000 copies of the speech itself were circulated in the country. But the Friends of the Liberty of the Press were too heterogeneous a body – consisting of members of the Whig club, the Association of Friends of the People, the Society for Constitutional Information and other radical societies – not to be rent by dissension from the beginning. The fund which was opened on 9 March 1793 for the relief of victims of the legal prosecutions hardly survived a division of opinion on 20 April between Erskine and Horne Tooke on the propriety of affording assistance to those who had been successfully prosecuted in the courts.[29] The very success of the proceedings against the Painite printers in the Hilary term of 1793 severely weakened the credibility of the Friends of Liberty of the Press and its final meeting was held on 15 June, when Sheridan blandly explained its demise by claiming that its objects had been achieved.[30] That claim, however, could have been made with more justice by the Association for the Preservation of Liberty and Property against Republicans and Levellers when it virtually suspended its activities earlier in the spring.[31]

A further attempt of the radical societies to co-operate with the Whig Association of the Friends of the People, this time in support of Grey's long-awaited motion for parliamentary reform in May 1793, also foundered – with important consequences for the British

27. *Speech at the Thatched House Tavern* (19 Jan. 1793), p. 18.

28. *Ibid.*, p. 21.

29. F. O'Gorman, *The Whig Party and the French Revolution* (London, 1967), p. 133.

30. Rea, p. 42.

31. E. C. Black, *The Association: British Extraparliamentary Political Organization, 1769–1793* (Cambridge, Mass., 1963), pp. 253–5.

democratic movement in both Scotland and England. Despite their accumulating difficulties, the radicals spent the early months of 1793 deliberating how best to launch a nation-wide campaign in the interest of radical reform. This debate had been sparked off, on the one hand by the perplexities, on the other by the impatience, of some of the provincial societies. At Norwich, where the reform societies in and around the city had increased, by November 1792, to over forty with a total estimated membership of about 2000 and where artisans, weavers and shopkeepers were tending to displace the wealthy Dissenting merchants and manufacturers in the administration and control of the affiliated clubs, the need had been felt for advice and guidance from the metropolis.[32] The problem was that both the provincial and metropolitan societies appeared to be undecided in their reform objectives – the Sheffield Constitutional Society, having originally declared its adherence to the Duke of Richmond's plan, had recently shown signs of being content with a moderate programme of parliamentary reform to be proposed by the Friends of the People; the latter association and the Society for Constitutional Information were, however, at cross purposes, while 'the Manchester people' seemed 'intent upon Republican principles only'. Unsettled by these conflicting views, the officials of a Norwich 'Society for Political Information' had written, on 11 November 1792, to the London Corresponding Society to ask 'whether the generality of the societies mean to rest satisfied with the Duke of Richmond's plan only; or whether it is their private design to rip up Monarchy by the roots, and place democracy in its stead?'[33]

This unguarded enquiry from an hitherto unknown reform society somewhat embarrassed the delegate committee of the London Corresponding Society. Their undated reply, signed by Margarot, as chairman, patently revealed the anxiety of the metropolitan society to preserve at all costs the unity of the radical movement.[34] It played down the current differences between the societies as 'trifling'. It suggested that general topics, likely to foment dissension, such as 'monarchy, democracy and even religion' should be avoided

32. John Cozens, secretary of the Norwich Revolution Society to T. Hardy, 6 Oct. 1792. PRO TS 11/965/3510 A2. This first contact with the LCS had been effected through Thomas Goff, one of the twelve associated members of the society accredited to the SCI who had recently returned from London.
33. PRO TS 11/965/3510 A, pt. 2 and *ST*, vol. 24, col. 392.
34. *ST*, vol. 24, cols. 393–5.

and that provincial societies should not seek to elaborate their reform objectives beyond the agreed demand for universal suffrage and annual parliaments. The removal of existing abuses should be left to 'a parliament so chosen' and if expectations were disappointed at the year's end fresh representatives would be elected. The Sheffield model for the organization of proliferating reform societies was recommended and a single delegate committee representative of all the Norwich clubs should be given the responsibility of corresponding with other societies, metropolitan or otherwise. Such a co-ordinating role at Norwich, however, originally fulfilled by the Revolution Society, had already been taken over by the delegate committee of the Norwich United Constitutional (or Political) Societies, which had been in touch with the SCI since May 1792.[35] Though ignorance of this situation pointed to the need for closer links between the LCS and the Norwich societies, Margarot's advice that discussion should be concentrated on 'the methods of obtaining a reform in parliament' helped to provide the key to the ensuing discussion of the various alternatives open to the reformers.

A more urgent plea for united and effective action had come from the Sheffield radicals on 16 January 1793. Having resolved that a circular letter should be immediately sent to every reform society in Great Britain asking them to specify how they intended to implement their several declarations in the current session of Parliament, the Sheffield committee impressed on the Society for Constitutional Information that concerted action should be taken without delay to bring agreed proposals before the public. The restoration of the rights to universal suffrage and annual parliaments would be indispensable. For its own part, the Sheffield society announced its intention of petitioning the House of Commons 'to take into their most serious consideration' such speedy and effectual measures as seemed appropriate to remove the evils and remedy the grievances resulting from the system of inadequate popular representation. It would also be desirable that the reform societies should immediately inquire what were 'the express views and plans of the Society of Friends of the People', so that they could know how far they could support Grey's proposed motion in the House of Commons.[36]

When, however, the last suggestion was followed up by the

35. PRO TS 11/952/3496(ii).
36. Appendix E, *Second Report of the House of Commons Committee of Secrecy 1794. Parl. Hist.*, vol. 31, col. 803.

London Corresponding Society, the Friends of the People declined, on 15 February, to disclose either the extent of its reform proposals or the time when they would be brought forward in Parliament, insisting that to do so would be to surrender its discretion to outside influences and give the opponents of reform their chance of motivating their objections in advance.³⁷ The undertone of distrust of the London Corresponding Society's lack of political judgement can be inferred not only from the association's insistence on 'the peculiar necessity of circumspection and moderation', but also from its renewed criticism of the society's previous indiscretions in its addresses to the National Convention.³⁸ This concern no doubt derived from the association's desire not to be compromised by any radical blunders in the preparation it was making for the presentation of its own petition to Parliament. Late in February 1793 the Friends of the People published two well documented reports on *The State of the Representation in England & Wales*³⁹ and, on 16 March, it authorized Grey to bring his motion before the Commons.⁴⁰

Meanwhile the London Corresponding Society, in an effort to ascertain the reactions of the radical societies in the provinces, had circulated a questionnaire, in which they were asked to state their preference for one of three alternatives – a petition to Parliament, a petition to the Crown, or a Convention.⁴¹ From the replies received there was a clear consensus that a petition to the Crown would prove 'futile'. Though the Norwich societies and the Society for Constitutional Information favoured the summons of a convention, both recognized that the majority preference was for a petition to Parliament.⁴² Both the metropolitan societies, however, no less

37. *ST*, vol. 24, col. 397.
38. *Ibid.*, cols. 398–9. The FOP had given the LCS 'a friendly admonition' on 6 Dec. 1792 to 'abstain from the Intermixture of Foreign Correspondence and Domestic Reform'. BL, Add. MSS. 27812, fo. 30.
39. The reports, compiled by George Tierney, were a virtual abridgement of Thomas Oldfield's *History of the Boroughs* (2 vols., London, 1792). Black, appendix A. Three hundred copies of the reports were presented by the FOP to the LCS which circulated them to its divisions for weekly discussions. BL, Add. MSS. 27814, fo. 55.
40. O'Gorman, p. 134.
41. PRO TS 11/953/3497. United Societies at Norwich to SCI, 5 March 1793.
42. *Ibid.* The SCI's letter of 16 April 1793 to Norwich stated that: 'As to a Convention, we regard it as a plan the most desirable and most practical as soon as the great body of the people shall be courageous and virtuous enough to join us in the attempt. Hitherto, we have no reason to believe that the moment is arrived for that purpose.' PRO TS 11/955/3500.

clearly recognized that such an approach could only result in 'an absolute negative'.[43] Both seem to have 'acquiesced' in the idea of multiple petitions to Parliament in deference to the views of the majority. Both confessed to having ulterior motives for doing so. On 4 March 1793, in response to the Sheffield Constitutional Society's original suggestion, the London Corresponding Society took the view that, although a petition could not be expected to produce a reform, a general petitioning movement would oblige MPs to discuss the subject frequently and that newspaper reports of such parliamentary deliberations would be bound to have favourable repercussions on public opinion. If each society petitioned Parliament separately, following the example already set by Nottingham, and if such petitions were similarly rejected, the eyes of the general public would be opened.[44] The attitude of the SCI was even more revealing. In reply to an enquiry of 5 March 1793 from the United Political Societies of Norwich it described the 'policy' of petitioning Parliament as 'well worth considering as a warning voice to our present legislators and as a signal for imitation to the majority of the people'. If the petitioning movement became general it might well bring to light the reforming views of the silent majority and thus prove to the country as a whole that the radicals were 'not a handful of individuals unworthy of attention'.[45] Extra-parliamentary pressure was thus clearly envisaged as an exercise in public relations, but a suspicious government later concluded that the real, though unavowed, motive behind a petitioning movement which was not expected to succeed could only have been to enforce the logic of a resort to a convention.[46] As we have seen, some radical societies had held Painite views of the ways and means of constitutional revision from the beginning – while others were, indeed, content to let a decision rest on the fate of the reform petitions in Parliament.

43. *Ibid.*
44. *ST*, vol. 24, cols. 406–7. The petition from Nottingham, signed by about 2500 inhabitants, was rejected by the House of Commons on 21 February 1793 as 'disrespectful'. *Parl. Hist.*, vol. 30, cols. 460–7.
45. PRO TS 11/955/3500.
46. *Ibid.* This file is labelled, 'Proofs of the case and indictment That the Persons so to be assembled in a Convention (in 1794) were to assume to themselves all the powers of legislation and Government in and over the kingdom without and in defiance of and against the will of the Parliament thereof and that the meeting such Convention was to be supported by an Armed Force.' It contains the main documents in support of the prosecution's case in the treason trials of 1794.

The difficulties, however, involved in an organized petitioning movement, sponsored by the Association of the Friends of the People in an uneasy and unnatural alliance with the radical societies, were not long in revealing themselves. From the radical standpoint, the very drafting, signature and presentation of reform petitions in sufficient numbers to impress both public and Parliament was no easy task.[47] The petition promoted by the London Corresponding Society illustrated some of the practical problems confronting the supporters of the campaign. Prompted by the circular letter from Sheffield and stimulated by the receipt of a dozen copies of Tierney's reports on the state of the representation, the London Corresponding Society resolved, on 23 February 1793, that the radical societies in the provinces should be encouraged to initiate separate petitions to Parliament and that it should do so itself, 'but not precipitately'.[48] A draft produced by one of its rising delegates, Joseph Gerrald, was approved by the General Committee and, on 7 March, after revision, was ordered to be printed for submission to the several divisions.[49] By early April about 1300 signatures had been obtained, but it was later decided to advertise it in the newspapers as open for signature by the general public.[50] Despite aggressive canvassing on the part of Gerrald, who enrolled signatures from the inmates of the King's Bench prison, the delegates of the LCS encountered considerable resistance in their efforts to boost the number of signatories. 'Ignorance, Interest and Timidity' were said by Hardy in his minute of 2 May 1793 to have prevented many from signing the petition.[51] Many well-wishers 'in the subordinate situations of life' who had been intimidated by their employers into signing the Loyalist addresses of the Reevite associations, felt themselves precluded from signifying their approval 'on both sides of the question'.[52] Publicans were afraid to commit themselves for fear of losing their licences and workmen were similarly afraid of forfeiting their employment.[53] Nevertheless, by the beginning of May between 5000 and 6000 signatures to the petition had been obtained.[54]

47. For the growth of public petitioning see P. Fraser, 'Public petitioning and Parliament before 1832', *History*, vol. 46 (1961), pp. 195–211.
48. BL, Add. MSS. 27812, fo. 36.
49. *Ibid.*, fo. 38.
50. *Ibid.*, fo. 39.
51. *Ibid.*, fo. 42.
52. *Ibid.*
53. *Ibid.*
54. *Ibid.*

It had been hoped that Charles James Fox, as MP for Westminster, would agree to present the petition in the Commons and that he would be supported by George Byng, MP for Middlesex, and Alder-man Sawbridge for the City.[55] Fox, however, after some delay, declined on the ground that he had always been 'an avowed enemy of Universal Suffrage' and his place was taken at the last moment by Philip Francis, who presented the petition in the Commons on 6 May – when it was ordered to 'lie on the table'.[56] Though nomi-nally representing the views of subscribers resident in the metropolis, it was quickly identified in the debate as emanating from the London Corresponding Society and discredited on that account alone.[57]

Other radical petitions, from Sheffield and Nottingham, were rejected outright as disrespectful in their language and derogatory to the dignity of the Commons, while a petition from Norwich, signed by 3700 inhabitants, was disqualified as a printed submission.[58] Mainly as a result of the hold exercised by Reevite associations over local corporations and communities, no petitions were forthcoming from the counties. In the event thirty-six petitions in all were received, of which twenty-four came, significantly, from Scotland.[59] It could hardly be pretended that public opinion in the country as a whole had registered its support even for moderate, much less for radical, reform.

All these submissions were intended to prepare the way for the petition to be presented on 6 May 1793 by Grey when moving for parliamentary reform in accordance with the pledge he had given in 1792. This obligation Grey now carried out more from a sense of duty than with real enthusiasm.[60] In doing so he was careful to repudiate the principle of universal suffrage, to make clear that the Association of the Friends of the People had disclaimed all idea of

55. *Ibid.*, fo. 41.
56. *Ibid.*, fo. 43.
57. *Parl. Hist.*, vol. 30, col. 804.
58. For the Sheffield petition, presented on 2 May 1793 by one of the Yorkshire county members, Mr Duncombe, see *Parl. Hist.*, vol. 30, cols. 775–7. The Norwich petition introduced by one of the city's representatives, Mr Hobart, was rejected on 6 May 1793. *Ibid.*, col. 786.
59. J. Cannon, *Parliamentary Reform, 1640–1832* (Cambridge, 1973), p. 125.
60. Some pressure was exerted on Grey by reformers such as Lord Daer to keep him to his pledge. Daer to Grey, 17 Jan. 1793. E. Hughes, 'The Scottish reform movement and Charles Grey, 1792–4', *Scottish Historical Review*, vol. 35 (1956), pp. 39–41.

a convention and, in line with current practice, refrained from putting forward any specific plan of reform.[61] Instead Grey rested his case on the evidence contained in the petition drafted by Tierney and submitted, nominally as from inhabitants of the metropolitan area, though in reality by the Whig association of the Friends of the People.[62] This he moved should be referred for consideration to a committee of the Commons.

Although Grey had intentionally not referred to his radical allies, he was obliged to concede, when questioned by Pitt on the point, that he wished their petitions also to be considered in the same way.[63] This admission gravely compromised Grey's whole argument in favour of moderate reform. It was, indeed, on the radicals' insistence on universal suffrage (on which Pitt announced his firm refusal even to deliberate), on the proved inability of the Whig association to control the demands or influence the behaviour of the radical societies, and particularly on the danger accruing from their French principles that the opponents of reform, such as Windham, the Earl of Mornington and Pitt himself, so eagerly fastened in debate and so successfully exploited.[64] Despite the disclaimers of both Grey and Francis that the French dimension of English reform politics had now lost whatever relevance it had once possessed,[65] the defence priorities of the French war, the horrific consequences of universal suffrage in the French republic, and repeated references to the radical addresses to the French National Convention were the most telling arguments in precipitating the decisive defeat of Grey's motion on 7 May 1793 by the enormous majority of 282 votes to 41.[66]

Though this reverse did not destroy the conviction of the Friends of the People that something might yet be achieved by petitioning, it left the radicals with the sole remaining option – if further agitation for parliamentary reform were to be resumed – of resort to a national

61. *Parl. Hist.*, vol. 30, cols. 804, 808.
62. This petition was noteworthy for the emphasis it laid on the extent of private parliamentary patronage, on the extraordinary deficiencies of the Scottish representative system, the grossly disproportionate distribution of the parliamentary franchise and the prohibitive cost of contesting parliamentary seats. *Ibid.*, cols. 788–99.
63. *Ibid.*, col. 897.
64. *Ibid.*, cols. 822–6 (Windham); cols. 850–78 (Mornington); cols. 890–902 (Pitt).
65. *Ibid.*, col. 802 (Grey); cols. 844–6 (Francis).
66. Most of these points were made by Pitt. For the list of the minority see *Parl. Hist.*, vol. 30, col. 925.

convention.[67] For the moment, however, their discouragement was such that several of the provincial clubs – the Manchester Patriotic and Reformation Societies and the Derby Political Society, for example – gave up the unequal struggle and passed quietly out of existence.[68] Even Hardy thought seriously of moving that the London Corresponding Society should be suspended for three months.[69] The only outlet for radical activity seemed to be the organization of public meetings of protest against the economic privations of the poor resulting from the war against France.[70]

One unexpected but important by-product of the petitioning movement was, however, that the London Corresponding Society and some of the provincial societies were brought into renewed contact with Scottish reformers, just at the time when changing circumstances north of the border were causing the latter, at long last, to think in terms of closer collaboration with the English radicals. Owing to the legacy of ill-will left by Wilkes's anti-Scottish propaganda in the 1760s, Scottish reformers had hitherto tended to hold aloof from their English counterparts. Scottish Protestants had been lukewarm in the campaign for the repeal of the Test Acts, nor had the Scots displayed any interest in the agitation for 'economical' reform, and, when Wyvill had solicited Scottish support for his County Association movement, the response had been negligible.[71] Though both had a common origin in the aftermath of the disastrous American war, Scottish reform movements had run parallel to, rather than fused with, English extra-parliamentary agitation. Whereas, also, in England social and economic discontent usually culminated in pressure for parliamentary reform, in Scotland priority had been given to attempts to redress the flagrant and more pervasive defects of local government. Two separate movements had arisen – the first directed against the abuses and oligarchical nature

67. G. S. Veitch, *Genesis of Parliamentary Reform* (London, 1965 reprint), p. 282.

68. The last recorded statement of the Manchester Reformation Society appeared in the *Manchester Mercury* of 23 March 1793 – reaffirming their support for 'Peace & Good Order'. Knight, *The Strange Case of Thomas Walker*, p. 111. For the demise of the Derby Society see evidence of J. Strutt in treason trial of T. Hardy in 1794. *ST*, vol. 24, col. 1099.

69. *ST*, vol. 24 (30 May 1793).

70. Once again the Sheffield Constitutional Society gave a lead in this respect by a series of spirited anti-war resolutions, forwarded to the LCS. BL, Add. MSS. 27812, fo. 37 (23 Feb. 1793).

71. Cannon, pp. 108–11.

of the Scottish parliamentary franchise in the counties[72] and the second against the administrative and financial abuses prevalent in the royal burghs.[73] Neither of these movements had made a bid for popular support, and neither had made much progress, even though the burgh reformers had enlisted the assistance of the English Whig Opposition in 1787. In 1788 pressure had been stepped up when forty-six of the sixty-four royal burghs had petitioned Westminster, but Sheridan, who had been deputed by his colleagues to oversee proceedings in Parliament, had been too dilatory in promoting remedial proposals in 1788 and 1790 and had not resumed his conduct of Scottish burgh reform, in the commons until the spring of 1792.[74] Though Robert Dundas, as Lord Advocate, admitted in debate that Scottish municipal officers should be made accountable at law for dishonest mismanagement of burghal revenues,[75] Sheridan had spoilt his case for wider reforms by rhapsodizing about the beneficial effects of the French revolution on English domestic politics in a House of Commons which had greeted the recent formation of Grey's Association of the Friends of the People with unconcealed distrust.[76] The motion for an enquiry on 18 April 1792 was lost by 69 votes to 27.[77]

Economic changes in the Highlands leading to large-scale evictions of subtenants and cotters to make way for Lowland sheep farmers,[78] the rapid progress of Painite opinions in the larger towns, the evils of the excise administration, hatred of the rule of Robert and Henry

72. The main abuse associated with the county franchise, based on feudal tenure, was the creation of nominal or fictitious votes by peers or wealthy landholders who conveyed the necessary amounts of land held directly from the Crown (i.e. in so-called 'Superiority') to friends or dependants in trust. The nominal votes of these 'parchment-barons' in some counties had come to outnumber those of legally qualified voters. H. W. Meikle, *Scotland and the French Revolution* (Glasgow, 1912), pp. 8–11.

73. Most of the local magistrates were self-elected, and being unaccountable at law usually diverted public funds into their own pockets.

74. Cannon, pp. 113–14.

75. *Parl. Hist.*, vol. 29, col. 1193.

76. 'It infused its benign influence through all our avocations of life; it mingled with the light which we enjoyed; it floated in the air which we breathed; it made part of the contemplation of the studious; the conversation of the social and communicative. It formed part of the taste of our public entertainments, and mingled in our melody.' *Ibid.*, cols. 1188–9.

77. *Ibid.*, col. 1203.

78. J. Prebble, *The Highland Clearances* (Harmondsworth, 1969), ch. 1, and E. Richards, 'Patterns of Highland discontent' in R. Quinalt and J. Stevenson (eds.), *Popular Protest and Public Order* (London, 1974), pp. 75–109.

Dundas, widespread rioting and strikes in Perth, Dundee and Aberdeen, associated with French revolutionary slogans and the planting of Trees of Liberty, heralded, in November 1792, the advent of a new form of Scottish democracy. Already in the summer and autumn numerous popular societies had been formed in and around Edinburgh and Glasgow to press for parliamentary reform.[79] Most of these clubs had assumed the title of 'Friends of the People' and, though their social composition resembled more closely that of the London Corresponding Society, they had modelled their political attitudes and programmes on those of Grey's association in London. Characteristically cautious in the thickening climate of Scottish governmental and judicial Alarmism, these societies had rejected the London Corresponding Society's invitation to join in addressing the French Convention.[80] When 160 of their delegates, representing eighty societies, met in their first General Convention in Edinburgh early in December 1792, the resolutions passed in favour of parliamentary reform had all the generality and moderation which Grey had claimed as the attributes of the parent association in London.[81] Before the convention adjourned, however, till April 1793, it established precedents which were to have important political overtones. Its proceedings had brought to the forefront two men of advanced political views – William Skirving, the secretary, and Thomas Muir, the vice-president, of the Associated Societies of Friends of the People in and around Edinburgh;[82] a new note of solidarity with other and more radical reformers had been sounded when Muir insisted on reading what some regarded as a seditious address from the Society of United Irishmen at Dublin;[83] and the convention's adjournment had been marked by a conscious

79. Meikle, ch. 5.

80. W. Johnson, chairman of the Associated Societies of Friends of the People at Edinburgh to T. Hardy, 31 Oct. 1792, considered that an address to the convention at that stage 'might be productive of mischief and misconstruction at home'. PRO TS 11/954/3498.

81. Meikle, pp. 108–9.

82. Skirving, son of a farmer at Liberton near Edinburgh, after education at the University of Edinburgh, had taken to farming, rejecting his original purpose of entering the ministry. He was mainly responsible for the summons of the British Convention in Nov. 1793. Thomas Muir was the son of a Glasgow merchant, who had a small property at Huntershill. After studying at Glasgow and Edinburgh universities, he had become an advocate in 1787. He was the founder of the first Scottish reform society and the best known of the 'Scottish martyrs'.

83. This action almost caused a schism in the convention. Meikle, p. 108.

imitation of French revolutionary procedures when the assembled delegates, rising to their feet and holding up their right hands, had taken the Jacobin oath to 'live free or die'.[84]

The second General Convention of the Scottish reformers met at Edinburgh on 30 April 1793 on the eve of the petitioning movement at Westminster. The delegates were of lower social standing than their predecessors, but the division of opinion between moderates and radicals persisted.[85] The failure of the Scottish petitions and the rejection of Grey's motion for an enquiry into the state of the representation, however, formed the real watershed in Scottish democratic politics. These setbacks caused the burgh reform agitation to be suspended and virtually terminated the county reform movement.[86] The Scottish radicals also repudiated the aristocratic and temporizing patronage of Grey's association in London. It was these political displacements and the need for new and like-thinking allies which led William Skirving to welcome the approach now made to him by the officials of the London Corresponding Society. In their letter of 17 May 1793 Margarot and Hardy requested 'a renewal of correspondence and a more intimate cooperation' with Skirving's society in Edinburgh. The failure of the petitioning movement had, they noted, demonstrated the need for greater solidarity between the radical societies throughout the country and for the adoption of 'some more effectual means' of achieving their purpose. It was advice on this crucial problem which the Londoners now sought, in their perplexity, from their Scottish brethren, pledging themselves, in return, to 'adopt the firmest measures provided they are constitutional'.[87] In their hopes for increased popular backing the London Corresponding Society looked confidently to mounting opposition to the war with France.

In his reply of 25 May Skirving agreed that the common danger confronting the reformers and 'the ennobling principle of universal benevolence' both enforced the need for fraternization. He also argued that, reason and weight of numbers behind the petitions having failed to make any converts to the cause of reform, it would be pointless to repeat the experiment. In accepting the proffered leadership of the radical cause with modest assurance, Skirving

84. Meikle, p. 272. For the full minutes of the convention see Meikle, pp. 239–73.
85. *Ibid.*, pp. 125–6.
86. *Ibid.*, pp. 126–7.
87. *ST*, vol. 24, col. 36.

stated that the Scottish reformers had already 'in great wisdom' perfected their plan of organization. The lessons he himself had drawn from the recent reverse at Westminster were the need to rely on the judgement and resolve of the people themselves in their popular societies rather than on the Whig association in London, the necessity to decide on 'the extent of the reform we ought to seek'. and the indispensable agreement of all reformers 'to affiliate in one great and indivisible family'.[88]

What Skirving had in mind was undoubtedly the reconvening of the delegate convention of the Scottish radical societies at Edinburgh to announce their adoption of the full democratic programme of universal suffrage and annual parliaments. Through earlier correspondence with the Sheffield reformers Skirving had secured the support and blessing of several recently formed societies in Yorkshire and the Midlands[89] and he may also have been aware that the federated Norwich societies and the Society for Constitutional Information in London had expressed a preference for the summons of a national convention. The rejection even of a convention of delegates by the metropolitan Friends of the People in July[90] merely confirmed Skirving's view that the Whig association was 'an aristocracy for the good of the people' and that the time had arrived for the Edinburgh popular societies to initiate a new departure in the Scottish democratic movement themselves.[91] Events in the summer and autumn were to provide the Scots with still other incentives to do so.

In Scotland resentment against the unpopular and costly Anglo-French war was then fuelled, as in England, by a sudden stagnation of trade and credit and consequent unemployment.[92] Rising prices bore with increasing severity upon the poor, while the victims of the Highland clearances, as in 1792, resorted in their desperation to

88. *ST*, vol. 24, cols. 37–40. *Parl. Hist.*, vol. 31, cols. 816–18.

89. The Leeds Constitutional Society had received 'directions' from the Sheffield society to correspond with 'all the societies in England and Scotland'. Leeds to LCS, 30 May 1793, *Parl. Hist.*, vol. 31, col. 819. Skirving had written to Sheffield on 10 May 1793 to report on the proceedings of the second Scottish convention; for the reply, dated 27 May, with its president's assertion that parliamentary reform would only be achieved 'by the powerful interposition of the great body of the people', see *Ibid.*, cols. 836–41.

90. *Ibid.*, col. 842.

91. *Ibid.*, col. 817.

92. Comments of the Rev. James Lapslie of Campsie to R. Dundas on the origins of the Edinburgh convention, 6 Dec. 1793. PRO HO 102/9, fos. 268–73.

riot and civil disturbances.[93] The ranks of the radical societies thus filled with new recruits prepared to listen to Painite propaganda, to engage in anti-war demonstrations, and to throw their weight behind demands for radical parliamentary reform and universal suffrage. The Scottish government, in the person of Robert Dundas as Lord Advocate, and the Scottish judiciary, epitomized by the prejudiced and brutal Lord Braxfield, saw to it, moreover, that the radicals were now supplied with a further powerful stimulus and source of emotional commitment in the shape of political martyrs. Thomas Muir, founder of the first society of the Friends of the People in Edinburgh, and the Reverend Thomas Fyshe Palmer, Unitarian minister of Dundee, had been marked men ever since the time of the first radical convention – Muir for his sponsorship of the alleged seditious 'Address of the United Irishmen', Palmer for his advocacy of the idea of petitioning Parliament.[94] Within a fortnight of each other, at the end of August and early in September, they were both tried for sedition, found guilty and sentenced to transportation to Botany Bay – Muir for fourteen years and Palmer for seven. Muir had been charged with having excited disaffection by seditious speeches, by circulating Painite literature and by his support of the Irish address at the first General Convention of the Friends of the People.[95]

The evidence was far from substantiating these charges, but Muir had prejudiced his case by breaking bail to cross to Paris on the eve of hostilities with France, and had returned through Ireland, where he had been enrolled as a member of the Society of United Irishmen in January 1793.[96] For failing to present himself in time for his original trial fixed for 11 February, he had been declared an outlaw and his name had been removed from the roll of advocates.[97] He was in fact regarded by the High Court of Justiciary, which eventually tried him at the end of August, as well as by the

93. J. Prebble, ch. 1.
94. Palmer came from an old Bedfordshire family and had been educated at Eton and Cambridge where he became a Fellow of Queen's College. Like Frend, he had forfeited preferment in the University on account of his Unitarian beliefs and had served a congregation at Dundee.
95. The passage of the address which was incriminated referred to Scotland's resurgence 'not by a calm, contented, secret wish for a reform in Parliament, but by openly, actively, and urgently willing it, with the unity and energy of an embodied nation'. *ST*, vol. 23, col. 124.
96. Meikle, p. 131.
97. *Ibid.*, p. 130.

Lord Advocate, who prosecuted him, as 'an emissary from France or the disaffected in Ireland'.[98] For the presiding judge, the Lord Justice Clerk, Lord Braxfield, it was, however, sufficient – although this was not part of the indictment – that Muir was an advocate of parliamentary reform. Agitation for such an object in such dangerous times was, according to Braxfield, the very definition of sedition. Speaking as the foremost authority on Scottish feudal law, and echoing the panic fears of his class and professional colleagues, Braxfield informed the jury – every member of which had been hand-picked by the judicial bench, without the possibility of challenge from the accused,[99] from the reactionary Edinburgh Goldsmiths' Hall Association[100] – that

a government in every country should be just like a corporation; and in this country, it is made up of the landed interest, which alone has a right to be represented. As for the rabble, who have nothing but personal property, what hold has the nation on them? What security for the payment of their taxes? They may pack up all their property on their backs, and leave the country in the twinkling of an eye.[101]

When Muir, in self-defence, contended that he had advocated reform only by legal and constitutional means, and when this was confirmed by the prosecution witnesses, this did not deter the Lord Advocate from suggesting that Muir was thereby merely 'sowing the seeds of discontent and sedition'.[102]

The whole judicial proceedings, even by Scottish standards, were highly irregular. Only one of the charges in the indictment – the reading of the 'Address from the United Irish' at the first General Convention of the Friends of the People – was established, and the verdict of guilty only served to show that, in the minds of both the bench and the jury, the case had been prejudged. The reactionary statements of the judges and the intimidating behaviour of Braxfield – the Scottish Jeffreys, whom R. L. Stevenson pilloried as 'Weir of Hermiston' – warranted their impeachment.[103] The sentence

98. Robert to Henry Dundas, 2 Aug. 1793. PRO HO 102/8.
99. Meikle, p. 132.
100. The Goldsmiths' Hall Association was an anti-reform society modelled on Reeves's Association against Levellers and Republicans.
101. *ST*, vol. 23, col. 231.
102. C. B. Cone, *The English Jacobins* (New York, 1968), p. 173.
103. The prime authority for the legal issues involved in the Scottish trials is Lord Cockburn's *Examination of the Trials for sedition in Scotland* (2 vols., Edinburgh, 1888).

imposed was so savage and so unexpected that even the jurors themselves were appalled. And yet, as things stood, there existed no appeal from the Scottish High Court of Justiciary to superior English courts.[104]

Palmer was tried before the Circuit Court of Justiciary at Perth in September.[105] He was accused of having written and disseminated an inflammatory address from a reform society at Perth blaming the war on 'a wicked ministry and a compliant parliament' who wished to 'form chains for a free people and eventually to rivet them for ever' on the British people.[106] In fact the pamphlet was the work of one George Mealmaker, and Palmer had only helped to revise it for the society by toning down some of its more virulent passages.[107] The decision to circulate the address had been taken, against his advice, by the Dundee society, and his agreement to supervise publication had been intended to curtail the risks involved in that decision. Although the conduct of the bench was, on this occasion, more circumspect, the trial itself was clearly a political one, and Palmer's real crime was that, like Muir, he was a supporter of parliamentary reform and also that he had engaged in missionary propaganda in and around Edinburgh.[108] The Lord Advocate had determined, in advance of the trial, to secure his conviction as 'the most determined *Rebel* in Scotland'.[109]

The response to these flagrant and vindictive trials in Scotland was immediate and widespread. Public indignation was expressed even in France and America.[110] When the news of Muir's sentence reached Robert Burns in remote Galloway in the first days of September it inspired his famous invocation to Scottish patriotic resurgence – '*Scots wha hae*'.[111] Reporting to William Scott, Procurator Fiscal, on 6 September, the government spy 'J. B.' noted that 'the severity of Mr Muir's sentence, instead of extinguishing the

104. There was no recourse to the appellate jurisdiction of the English House of Lords because the Scottish Justiciary and Circuit courts were supreme courts. *ST*, vol. 23, col. 115; *Parl. Hist.*, vol. 30, col. 1487.

105. *ST*, vol. 23, cols. 237 ff.

106. *Ibid.*, col. 311.

107. *Ibid.*, cols. 301–4, 306.

108. Cone, p. 172.

109. Robert to Henry Dundas, 2 Aug. 1793. PRO HO 102/8.

110. Muir's address to the jury is said to have become a set piece for declamation in New England schools. Cone, p. 174.

111. P. A. Brown, *The French Revolution in English History* (London, 1965 reprint), p. 97.

spirit of the associations, seems to have given new life and vigour to them'.[112] On the previous evening between 200 and 300 members attended the monthly meeting of the General Committee of the Societies of the Friends of the People in Edinburgh. Inspired by the heroic stand of Muir in vindication of the cause of reform, the committee solemnly declared that they would 'not part with their rights and liberty but with their lives' and prayed that 'they may never be driven to that awful point, at which resistance becomes duty, when the voice of reason is no longer heard; when complaining and remonstrating are interdicted and when the will of the ruler is made the Law to an enslaved people'.[113]

The meeting also resolved to make 'another application for re-dress of grievances and restoration of rights' in anticipation of the resumption of Parliament, to 'cultivate a more intimate correspon-dence with all the societies of Parliamentary reform in the kingdom', and to 'concert measures for the forthcoming General Convention of delegates in Edinburgh by means of a regular committee of correspondence'.[114]

'God help the people who have such judges' was the characteristic exclamation of Charles James Fox who, together with the Earl of Lauderdale and Sheridan, attempted, unsuccessfully, to question the legality of the sentences of transportation for the alleged crime of 'leasing-making', or verbal sedition.[115] The London Corresponding Society paid its generous tribute to the heroism of the Scottish 'martyrs'[116] and readily identified itself with the actions and attitudes of Palmer, for most of its efforts during the summer and autumn of 1793 had been concentrated on the holding of its first general meet-ings – in protest against Parliament's continued refusal to concede reform and the economic and social impact of the war.[117] Skirving's tentative suggestion to Hardy that the London Corresponding

112. PRO HO 102/9, fo. 52.

113. *Ibid.*

114. PRO HO 102/9, fos. 63–4.

115. After Lauderdale had seen Muir in prison in October, all three had inter-viewed Dundas on 11 December 1793 and had submitted a case based on a statute of 1703 which had limited the punishment for 'verbal sedition' to 'fine, imprisonment or banishment'. PRO HO 102/9, fos. 282–3. Their arguments were rebutted by Braxfield, summarizing the opinions of the Scottish judges, on 27 Dec. *Ibid.*, fo. 303.

116. BL, Place newspaper cuttings, vol. 36, fo. 72. *ST*, vol. 24, col. 39.

117. For the society's first general meeting of 8 July 1793, and the subsequent attempts to petition the King in September see BL, Add. MSS. 27812, fos. 50–5 and fos. 63–73.

Society should send two delegates to the forthcoming General Convention in Edinburgh, and the formal invitation to do so which followed, dated 5 October, therefore met a ready response, though final approval had to be given by the several divisions.[118] Preparations to hold a general meeting of the society, the drafting of instructions for the delegates and other necessary business delayed the formal election of Margarot and Gerrald till 24 October. This took place at the society's first open-air meeting, chaired by Richard Hodgson, in a field lent for the occasion by Thomas Briellat, a pump-maker on the Hackney Road.[119] The meeting, which had been advertised in the newspapers a fortnight previously, drew large crowds of spectators, but many casual passers-by had gathered on the spot without knowing the reason. Some rumoured that Tom Paine had come over to plant the Tree of Liberty, others that the French Jacobins were at the bottom of it. A kinder and more popular conjecture among the women and poor working people was that the society had met to lower the price of provisions.[120] Three hundred police under the orders of a high constable, and the presence of one of the Treasury solicitors and three local magistrates ensconced in the Nag's Head, indicated that security was tight. The organizing committee, meeting in a nearby house, was, however, threatened and insulted by the crowd and had to ask for protection from the magistrates. Despite the unsympathetic behaviour of the police constables, the meeting passed off quietly, thanks to speeches in explanation of the business and the society's objectives made by the two candidates who were eventually elected – Margarot and Gerrald. Their articles of instruction from the society were unanimously approved and a sum of £6. 2s. 0d. was collected for defraying their expenses. Votes of thanks to the magistrates and in particular to the high constable and to 'our fellow citizens the spectators (in number about 4,000)' brought the proceedings to an uneventful close.[121] About an hour after the crowds had dispersed the magistrates issued a warrant for the arrest of Briellat, the owner of the meeting place, on a charge of having spoken seditious words against the King ten months before – on the sworn testimony of a Jewish butcher's boy. On conviction for

118. *ST*, vol. 24, cols. 39–40.
119. BL, Add. MSS. 27812, fos. 76–8.
120. BL, Add. MSS. 27814, fo. 57.
121. E. Smith, *The Story of the English Jacobins* (London, 1881), pp. 83–5, quoting at length Hardy's own account of the meeting in BL, Add. MSS. 27814, fos. 56–60.

this offence Briellat was imprisoned for two years in Newgate and fined £100. He celebrated his release by emigrating to America.[122]

Four days later, on 28 October, a more discreet gathering of members of the Society for Constitutional Information at the Crown and Anchor Tavern chose as their delegates to the Scottish convention – Charles Sinclair of Edinburgh and Henry Redhead Yorke of Derby.[123] It was an unfortunate choice, for Yorke gave up the mission, on grounds of ill-health or for financial reasons, and Sinclair later turned King's evidence. All the indications are that this society committed itself with some reluctance to the Scottish enterprise, and that its hands may even have been forced and its instructions to its delegates radically altered by the presence at this meeting of four members of the London Corresponding Society.[124] The original draft instructions had required the delegates to promote the work of parliamentary reform by petitions for an inquiry into the state of the representation in the Commons and by demanding a specific remedy for the prevalent abuses.[125] In specifying the principles upon which redress was to be demanded, the delegates were to derive them from Pitt's speeches ('before he was a placeman'), the Duke of Richmond's letter to Colonel Sharman, Flood's motion for reform in the House of Commons and the defence of Horne Tooke at the suit of Charles James Fox in an action for debt.[126] In the final version of the instructions, all these moderate submissions, the procedure by petition and the demand for a specific remedy were omitted and the delegates were sharply reminded that they would need to insist on 'general suffrage and annual representation, together with the unalienable right in the people to reform'. They were also to support the case for the payment of MPs 'by a national contribution' and punctually to correspond with the society to keep

122. BL, Add. MSS. 27809, fo. 269.

123. *ST*, vol. 24, col. 556.

124. The four were Margarot, Hardy, Martin and Richter – all of whom had been elected as honorary members of the SCI on 13 July 1793. Only fourteen other members were present.

125. PRO TS 11/957/3502(i) – deposition of G. Williams before R. Ford, 5 July 1794. The original draft instructions also appear in *ST*, vol. 24, cols. 557–8. These points had been included to meet some of the criticisms made by Pitt of Grey's motion for reform in May.

126. *Ibid.* Fox's suit for his costs related to Tooke's petition against the Westminster election return of 1790 at which Tooke had been a candidate. Veitch, p. 117.

it informed of their activity and to receive such further instructions as circumstances might require.[127]

If these final instructions are compared with those already approved by the London Corresponding Society, the reason for these amendments will be apparent – to bring them into line with those issued by Margarot and Gerrald. It is significant, too, that Horne Tooke, whose hand may be detected in the original draft, purposely stayed away from the meeting at the Crown and Anchor in order to register his opposition to the convention.[128] The main instructions given to the LCS delegates were, indeed, that they should 'on no account whatever, depart from the original object and principles, namely the obtaining annual parliaments and Universal Suffrage by rational and lawful means', that they should 'support the opinion that representatives in Parliament ought to be paid by their constituents' and that 'it is the Duty of the People to resist any Act of Parliament repugnant to the original principles of the Constitution; as would be every attempt to prohibit Associations for the purpose of Reform'.[129]

The invitations to the English provincial reform societies reached them so late that it was doubtful whether any of them would be able to send delegates to the northern capital. Sheffield's first reaction was to express its inability to do so and to suggest that the convention should be postponed till the spring of 1794.[130] Eventually it elected Matthew Campbell Brown as its delegate on 13 November, but too late to attend the opening ceremonies.[131] The Norwich societies first approached the Rev. Mark Wilks – minister of St Paul's Baptist chapel – and, on his refusal, agreed to ask Margarot to represent them as well as the London Corresponding Society.[132] Brown of Sheffield similarly was induced to act as delegate for the Leeds Constitutional Society.[133]

Though the number of English delegates to the Scottish conven-

127. PRO TS 11/962/3508, fo. 152. *ST*, vol. 24, cols. 556–7.

128. See Tooke's cross examination of D. Adams, secretary of the SCI, at his trial in 1794. *ST*, vol. 25, col. 87.

129. BL, Add. MSS. 27814, fos. 75–6. This clause had no doubt been prompted by the restrictions placed on the holding of quasi-representative assemblies by the Irish parliament in the Convention Act of 1793.

130. *Parl. Hist.*, vol. 31, cols. 832–3.

131. J. Brookfield to Evan Nepean, 13 Nov. 1793. PRO HO 42/27.

132. For the offer to Wilks see WWM F 44a/37. The Norwich societies elected Margarot to serve as their delegate on 16 Nov. 1793. PRO TS 11/953/3497.

133. Brown, p. 104.

tion was thus quite small, their political experience and the weight of radical opinion for which they claimed to act as spokesmen enabled them to play a prominent and decisive role in the assembly's deliberations and decisions. They took the lead in devising its committee system and its regulations for the conduct of business; they suggested the change in its title and, in so doing, profoundly altered its political significance. They initiated its policies and presided in turn over its daily sessions. By their radical harangues, the adoption of French revolutionary terminology and procedures and uncompromising defiance of established authority, they provoked its premature suppression, their own trials for sedition and the confrontation between the radical movement and the government in both Scotland and England.

Margarot, who had virtually controlled the affairs of the London Corresponding Society from the beginning as its chairman or president, was to prove himself in Scotland an enterprising, resourceful but incalculable and somewhat devious politician.[134] Sinclair, in his native environment, became a clever intrepreter of the moods of the assembly in the capacity of assistant secretary.[135] Gerrald was to leave behind him a legendary reputation as a fiery orator, scholarly custodian of the Anglo-Saxon radical tradition and sympathetic champion of Irish constitutional liberties.[136] M. C. Brown, although overshadowed by his colleagues, showed his resolution in a crisis and proved an effective link with radical opinion in Yorkshire.[137]

134. Margarot had drafted most of the printed addresses of the LCS, took a considerable part in its correspondence with the provincial radical societies, and had first mooted the joint address to the French National Convention. There is no doubt that he was the dominating influence in shaping the resolutions and procedures of the British Convention.

135. Sinclair was the nephew of Sir John Sinclair (1754–1835), first president of the board of agriculture, and author of the *History of the Public Revenue of the British Empire* (1784).

136. Gerrald (1763–1796), a descendant of an old Irish family, had been born in the West Indies but had been the favourite pupil of Dr Parr at Stanmore. After practising at the bar in Pennsylvania, he returned to England in 1788 and plunged into reform politics.

137. Brown was the editor of the Sheffield *Patriot*, and immediately before his election as delegate to the Edinburgh convention had been secretary of the Sheffield Constitutional Society. He appears to have been an actor, had married an Irish lady whose fortune he had squandered, and had only been released from the debtors' jail in Sheffield by having his debts paid by local business men with radical views. Anonymous Sheffield informer to W. Scott, Procurator Fiscal 24 Dec. 1793. PRO HO 102/9, fo. 303.

Even before these English representatives arrived in Edinburgh early in November, Skirving's General Convention of the Scottish Friends of the People, attended by about 160 delegates, had thrown down the gauntlet to authority by declaring its support for universal suffrage and annual parliaments – an action which the Scottish judiciary had already equated with sedition.[138] Its subsequent determination to petition Parliament for redress of grievances and to address the Crown against the war, showed, nevertheless, that it did not intend to claim for itself any unconstitutional authority.[139] Its decision, after four days, and in the absence of the English deputations, to adjourn till April 1794 also indicated that it did not overrate the part it might play in the approaching crisis.

Shortly after the convention had dissolved the English delegates at length arrived in the Scottish capital and, on 6 November, attended a meeting of the General Committee of the Edinburgh associations, which sanctioned Skirving's action in recalling the General Convention for 19 November.[140] Two members of the United Irishmen – Archibald Hamilton Rowan and the Hon. Simon Butler – who had come over to lodge protests at the Lord Advocate's disparaging references to their members as 'wretches' during Muir's trial, were also present, though they shortly returned to Ireland without attending the convention.[141] When questioned on the progress of the radical societies in England, Margarot assumed a confident air and talked in terms of their proliferating membership in the metropolis and of whole provincial communities as given over to reform, where, as in Sheffield and district, the radicals could count on 50,000 adherents and, as at Norwich, where they were organized in thirty federated clubs. He suggested that if a convention representing England and Scotland could be brought into existence the reformers might claim the support of between 600,000 and 700,000 males – a majority of all those in the kingdom – and that, confronted with

138. Meikle, p. 139.
139. *Ibid.*
140. *Ibid.*, p. 140.
141. Though they were not delegates to the Edinburgh convention, their discussions with the Scottish and English reformers on their grievances as a result of the passage of the Irish Convention Act in the summer of 1793 vitally influenced the most provocative resolution of the British Convention, see below p. 301. For Hamilton Rowan see H. Nicholson, *The Desire to Please: A Study of Hamilton Rowan and the United Irishmen* (London, 1943). Rowan's fine collection of French revolutionary tracts is on deposit in the John Rylands Library at Manchester.

such a situation, 'the ministry would not dare refuse our rights'.[142] It was this will-o'-the-wisp vision of ministry and Parliament yielding to the commanding voice of organized and united radical majorities in England, Scotland and Ireland which was to obsess Margarot throughout his stay in the North. While waiting for the convention to reassemble, Margarot and Gerrald took this message to the surrounding Scottish countryside, rekindling the enthusiasm for reform, founding new radical societies on the model of the LCS and confirming Margarot's own private conviction that Scotland could become the decisive fulcrum in the forward thrust of the democratic movement as a whole.[143]

On 17 October 1793, in a letter to the Norwich Constitutional Societies informing them of Skirving's general invitation to the English radical clubs to send delegates to the Edinburgh assembly, Hardy had referred to it as 'a kind of convention'.[144] The almost metaphysical terms which Skirving had used in his earlier correspondence, when emphasizing the need for contingent planning by the associated reformers in case the system of 'Old Corruption' collapsed in general confusion, and his reference to the necessity of replacing 'the tabernacles of oppression' by 'our tabernacle of righteousness' had no doubt confused, rather than clarified, Hardy's notions as to what exactly Skirving had in mind.[145] Later historians have laboured under a similar difficulty and most have, besides evading this particular issue, given a very inadequate and summary treatment of the actual proceedings of the Edinburgh convention, taking as their excuse the defects and ambiguity of the surviving official minutes.[146] It is impossible, however, properly to understand the real nature of the confrontation which occurred between the English radical movement and the British government in the spring

142. *ST*, vol. 23, col. 414. Trial of William Skirving.

143. W. Scott (Procurator Fiscal) to R. Dundas, 16 Nov. 1793. PRO HO 102/9, fos. 154–5.

144. PRO TS 11/953/3497.

145. Skirving to Hardy, 25 May 1793. *ST*, vol. 24, cols. 37–8.

146. Veitch, p. 288, devotes only a single paragraph to the actual proceedings; E. P. Thompson, *Making of the English Working Class* (London, 1965 reprint), p. 126, does the same, while even Meikle, pp. 139–44, covers the subject in five and a half pages. The minutes are available in *ST*, vol. 23, cols. 391–471 (trial of Skirving), or, less fully, in *Parl. Hist.*, vol. 31, cols. 844–53. Although the minutes themselves are meagre and unsatisfactory, they can be supplemented from the very detailed and reliable daily reports of the government informer 'J.B.' and the files of the *Edinburgh Gazetteer*, and other material in the Scottish Correspondence at the PRO HO 102, vols. 9 and 10.

of 1794 and the ensuing treason trials, unless its origin in this crisis of Scottish reform at Edinburgh is clearly recognized.

Though Skirving himself may have had an apocalyptic vision of the eventual summons of 'an assembly of commissioners from all countries of the world',[147] the convention of 180 delegates which met at the Masons' lodge in Edinburgh on Tuesday 19 November 1793, was, originally, no more and no less than an adjourned meeting of earlier conventions of the delegates of the Scottish Societies of the Friends of the People – afforced by a sprinkling of English delegates.[148] It was clearly no Painite convention of popularly elected representatives with full powers to draft a written republican constitution. Neither was Thomas Erskine, as defence counsel in the treason trial of Thomas Hardy, justified in contending that the convention's sole concern was to frame a reform petition to Parliament,[149] nor was Scott, for the prosecution, in arguing that it was a copy of the French National Convention, intent on displacing the legitimate authority of Parliament and on exercising complete popular sovereignty.[150] A closer examination of the actual proceedings of this short-lived assembly suggests that the English delegates sought to change its character so as to demonstrate the strength of radical opinion on which it might rely for support, if it chose to exert further extra-parliamentary pressure on the government. Secondly, they sought power to convert the convention into a formal bastion of popular resistance against any prospective government encroachments on, or restrictions of, public and private liberties, and to reconvene it as a permanent 'emergency convention', if it were illegally or forcibly dissolved. Thirdly, they spent considerable time in elaborating the organization and procedures of the assembly, so as to allow them to be used in future joint conventions of the English and Scottish peoples. All such 'innovations' were inevitably regarded by the opponents of reform as challenges to established constitutional authority. The first was viewed as a disorderly resort to public 'clamour' in order to overawe Parliament; the second, as an attempt to restrict Parliament's legislative omnicompetence; and the third as providing machinery for the summons of unconstitutional rival popular assemblies. It is not surprising that the Scottish High Courts condemned such activities as seditious or even bordering on treason.

147. Skirving to Hardy, 25 May 1793. *ST*, vol. 24, col. 39.
148. Meikle, p. 140.
149. *ST*, vol. 24, cols. 940–6.
150. *Ibid.*, col. 1203.

These far-reaching claims and pretensions, which were voiced predominantly by the English delegates, and above all by Margarot, sprang from the latter's overriding concern to achieve a union of English and Scottish reformers in what would, nowadays, be termed a 'popular front'.[151] In the opening session of the convention on 19 November, Margarot took a first step in this direction by moving that, before an 'Address to the Public' was published, as suggested by Skirving, a committee should forthwith be appointed to 'consider the means and draw up the outlines of a plan of General Union between Scotland and England in their constitutional efforts for a thorough reform of Parliament'.[152] After Gerrald had seconded this proposition it was passed unanimously, and a committee of thirteen, including all four of the English delegates, was immediately appointed.[153] On 21 November the plan was discussed at length in the convention, sitting as a committee of the whole house, the major intervention being an hour-long excursus by Gerrald on the origins, progress and current state of the British constitution.[154] In this, the familiar radical myth of the extinction of Anglo-Saxon 'democracy' by the bastard Norman conqueror and the erosion of the constitutional liberties acquired in 1688 were rehearsed. The only way of recovering this lost inheritance would be by a democratic union of England and Scotland in the work of reform and by Scots and English mutually instructing each other in political knowledge. Only when the general public had been so educated would it be unanimous, and only then would *vox populi* be, in truth, *vox dei*. In the meantime it was the duty of the friends of the constitution in both parts of the kingdom to demand their rights in an orderly, constitutional, but firm and determined manner, which would brook no resistance. In conclusion, Gerrald stressed the necessity of the Scottish and English peoples uniting in a general convention to be held in some central place, preferably in England. He suggested York as a possibility – 'even though it was the seat of an Archbishopric and of a swarm of aristocracy'. 'Our Saviour went about among publicans and sinners that he might convert them – Perhaps we might convert the sinners of York by meeting there.' The suggestion

151. Writing to his Norwich constituents from his prison in the Edinburgh Tolbooth on 18 Jan. 1794 after his trial, Margarot stated that: 'My greatest crime [in the eyes of Ministry] was the attempt to promote an Union between the people of both nations.' PRO TS 11/953/3497.

152. Report of informer 'J.B.', 19 Nov. 1793. PRO HO 102/9, fo. 203.

153. *Ibid.*, fo. 210.

154. *Ibid.*, fos. 214–16.

was warmly endorsed and the whole speech repeatedly applauded.[155]

While these thoughts were still in the minds of his hearers, Gerrald, as temporary president of the assembly, reported, on Saturday 23 November, that he had just received a letter from the federated Norwich societies, nominating Margarot as their delegate, and expressing their willingness to contribute their share of the convention's expenses.[156] This announcement provoked a resolution that the assembly should assert the unity of the delegates from South and North.[157] On the motion of 'Citizen Scott', all the members then stood up and joined hands in solemn token of their solidarity. It remained, however, for the delegate of the Society for Constitutional Information – the young Charles Sinclair – to capitalize on these emotional gestures of mutual commitment by moving that, henceforth, the assembly should assume the title of 'The British Convention of the Delegates of the People, associated to obtain Universal Suffrage and Annual Parliaments'.[158] This 'revolutionary' change of style and status was approved unanimously in a thinly attended meeting, with not more than fifty delegates present.[159] As a further contribution to this growing solidarity, Sinclair also sponsored a motion on the same day that, in view of the passage of the Convention Act, which had recently made such assemblies illegal in Ireland, any members of the Society of United Irishmen should be allowed to speak and vote in the British Convention if they were delegated.[160] This motion was allowed to lie on the table over the week-end for the consideration of the various committees ('sections') into which the convention now separated for the consideration of business. On Monday 25 November, however, with M. C. Brown, the delegate from Sheffield, in the chair, this resolution was carried. In the course of the debate some concern was expressed that the English ministry might follow the example of the Irish parliament and restrict the right of public assembly. One of the most active of the Scottish members, A. Callender, of the Canongate society, sought to allay such fears by moving that any attempt to do so should be the signal for the delegates to meet in convention to assert their rights.[161] This proposal gave rise to a three-day

155. *Ibid.*, fo. 216.
156. *ST*, vol. 23, col. 426.
157. *Ibid.*, cols. 426–7.
158. *Ibid.*, col. 427.
159. 'J.B.'s report, 23 Nov. 1793. PRO HO 102/9, fo. 226.
160. *Ibid.*
161. *ST*, vol. 23, col. 454.

discussion, in which its scope was greatly extended and the practical details settled for the summons of an emergency convention. In welcoming Callender's motion on the 26th, Margarot drew attention however, to its omission to specify either the place or timing of such an assembly and asked the delegates to consider, as an alternative, a proposal sponsored by the committee of regulations for an 'interim' committee of the convention invested with powers to reconvene the delegates in a number of other circumstances.[162] This suggestion of a standing committee to function in the intervals between conventions was reminiscent of, and was probably copied from, French administrative procedures.[163] It implied that radical conventions would meet at regular intervals in the future. Margarot explained that the committee should be 'appointed for the particular purpose of watching every act which may militate against the rights of the People' and that it should be secret.[164] On 27 November, Sinclair and Gerrald and two Scottish delegates moved further amendments. With Callender stubbornly defending his own original motion and being supported by others, including M. C. Brown, the convention was threatened by a serious internal schism.[165] From this danger the assembly was saved by Gerrald's success in assuaging the wounded feelings of Callender and by Margarot's compromise proposal that the delegates should approve the spirit of the original motion, while condemning its phraseology and remit it, along with the several amendments, to a committee consisting of the mover and seconder and those who had suggested amendments.[166] This committee was ordered to prepare a single composite motion, and to submit it for the consideration of the convention on the following day.[167]

Thursday 28 November was decisive. Sinclair acted as *rapporteur* for the revising committee and, on his motion, the convention resolved itself into a general committee to consider its report. After a protracted and animated debate, in which M. C. Brown treated his audience to a potted, not to say garbled, history of the Habeas Corpus Act, the substance of the report was adopted unanimously by the convention, the delegates standing and with hands joined in

162. *Ibid.*

163. Such 'interim committees' were familiar features of the organization of the Gallican clerical assemblies in the eighteenth century and were also used when Calonne and de Brienne established provincial assemblies in 1787–8.

164. *Edinburgh Gazetteer*, 3 Dec. 1793. PRO HO 102/9.

165. 'J.B.'s report, 28 Nov. 1793. *Ibid.*, fo. 235.

166. 29 Nov. *Ibid.*, fos. 239–40.

167. *Edinburgh Gazetteer*, 3 Dec. 1793.

solemn testimony of their united resolve.[168] The final resolution, moved by Margarot, took the form of a firm declaration of intent.

That this convention, considering the calamitous consequences of any act of the legislature, which may tend to deprive the whole, or any part of the people, of their undoubted right to meet, either by themselves, or by delegation, to discuss any matter relative to their common interest, whether of a public or private nature, and holding the same to be totally inconsistent with the first principles and safety of society, and also subversive of our known and acknowledged Constitutional Liberties, do hereby declare before God and the World, that we shall follow the wholesome example of former times, by paying no regard to any act which shall militate against the constitution of our country, and shall continue to assemble and to consider of the best means by which we can accomplish a real representation of the people and annual election, until compelled to desist by superior force. And we do resolve, that the first notice given for the introduction of a Convention Bill, or any bill of a similar tendency to that passed in Ireland, in the last session of their parliament, or any bill for the suspension of the Habeas Corpus Act, or the act for preventing wrongous imprisonment,[169] and against undue delays in trials, in North Britain; or in case of an invasion, or the admission of any foreign troops whatsoever into Great Britain or Ireland; all or any of these calamitous circumstances, shall be a signal to the several delegates to repair to such place as the *Secret Committee* of this convention shall appoint.[170]

Margarot had thus got his way on the main issue and the secret committee of four which was then approved to determine the venue of any such emergency convention was, in fact, the interim committee which he had also proposed. The delegates elected to this committee were Skirving (*ex officio*), J. Clark, Margarot and M. C. Brown.[171] These resolutions were deferred for incorporation in the official record as an appendix on the termination of the session, and a blank was thus left in the minutes of the day's proceedings.[172]

168. *Ibid.*
169. 1701.
170. *ST*, vol, 24, cols. 1257–8.
171. *ST*, vol. 23, cols. 433–4. The place decided on was to remain secret. At the break up of the convention each delegate was to be entrusted with a sealed letter containing the place of meeting. This letter was to be delivered unopened to the delegate's constituents and its receipt acknowledged to the secretary of the convention. It was only to be opened when the Emergency Committee was summoned.
172. It was Margarot who caused this suspicious circumstance by insisting that these provisions formed part of the formal regulations of the convention.

Gerrald then justified these resolutions by commenting at length on the Irish Convention Act, which he maintained had been passed 'to feel the pulse of the people of Britain, that our rulers might know if it beat high with indignation, or if the blood run coldly in our veins, and we are willing to bow our necks to the yoke and suffer in fear and silence'. He congratulated the convention on its determined declaration and expressed his conviction that it would be 'not only a Resolution of words, but a rule of action'.[173] In order to ensure this, J. Clark and M. C. Brown, both members of the secret committee, moved that a committee of observation should be appointed in London to give the earliest intimation of any governmental repressive action of the kind condemned in the main resolution.[174] On the following day, the 29th, however, Margarot argued that such a committee would be superfluous, since there were several thousand people in that city 'on the look out'. His allusion was understood and it was agreed that the convention should request the London Corresponding Society's committee of correspondence 'to give the earliest intelligence of what passes in parliament'.[175]

Meanwhile, in its daily business and proceedings the convention had seen fit to adopt French revolutionary forms of address and procedures. Delegates addressed each other as 'Citizens', visitors and petitioners were voted 'the honours of the session', 'honourable mention' was made in the minutes of 'patriotic donations', however insignificant.[176] From 29 November the convention began to date its proceedings 'the First Year of the British Convention'.[177] It referred all proposals and resolutions for detailed discussion to its separate 'divisions', renamed 'sections', it appointed committees of 'instructions', secrecy and finance and reports from these sources were sometimes headed '*Vive la Convention*' and subscribed '*Ça ira*'.[178] The suggestion that the 'Address to the British People', which the convention had commissioned its Committee of Union to draft, should be prefixed by a Declaration of Rights betrayed the same disposition to imitate French revolutionary models wherever possible.[179] The use of such phraseology and the resort to such

173. *Edinburgh Gazetteer*, 3 Dec. 1793.
174. *ST*, vol. 23, col. 434.
175. *Ibid.*, col. 435.
176. Meikle, p. 144.
177. *ST*, vol. 23, col. 815.
178. Meikle, p. 144. *Parl. Hist.*, vol. 31, col. 731.
179. *ST*, vol. 23, col. 426 (22 Nov. 1793).

procedures was probably not so intentionally provocative or so insidiously revealing of an intention to assume the status or powers of a French republican convention as was suggested by the prosecution in the subsequent sedition and treason trials.[180] Such symbolism may even have been thought fitting by leaders who were fond of striking attitudes and who were inclined to be histrionic in their speeches and behaviour. Nevertheless, its use was bound to be counterproductive in its effect on contemporary public opinion and was a gratuitous indiscretion, for which Skirving, Margarot and Gerrald were to pay dearly.

On 4 December signs of impending action by the authorities prompted Margarot to move, and the assembly to resolve, that any illegal dispersion of the convention should be considered as the signal for the delegates and the secret committee to proceed without delay to the place of meeting to be appointed for the emergency convention.[181] This culminating provocation provided the excuse for which the Lord Advocate had been waiting to terminate the convention's existence.[182]

On Thursday 5 December the 'order of the day' was a motion for the convention to consider a petition to Parliament for reform.[183] Even if this belated action was designed as a conciliatory gesture, or merely as a resumption of unfinished business left over by the convention before the arrival of the English delegates, it came too late. It may, however, have been a tactical move to substantiate the legality of the assembly's proceedings on the eve of its anticipated dissolution. When the delegates assembled for the usual evening's session they learned from Skirving, who had been released on bail, that he, Margarot, Gerrald, A. Scott and W. and G. Ross had been arrested early that morning and their papers confiscated.[184] Several members were about to leave to offer bail for the release of the remaining prisoners when the Lord Provost of Edinburgh, accompanied by fellow magistrates, entered to dissolve the meeting

180. See argument of Solicitor General in Hardy's trial. *ST*, vol. 24, cols. 1251–3. Lord Cockburn in his *Examinations of the Trials for sedition in Scotland*, vol. 1, p. 225, suggests that this mimicry of the National Convention was partly intended for 'the culpable purpose of terrifying their adversaries'.

181. *Edinburgh Gazetteer*, 10 Dec. 1793. *ST*, vol. 23, cols. 464–5.

182. R. Dundas had apparently decided to act, however, on the strength of the account of the proceedings contained in the *Edinburgh Gazetteer* of 3 Dec. Dundas to Home Office, 6 Dec. 1793. PRO HO 102/9, fo. 250.

183. *Edinburgh Gazetteer*, 10 Dec. 1793.

184. *Ibid. ST*, vol. 23, col. 465.

as illegal and unconstitutional.[185] In this crisis Brown, who was called to the post of president, proved a worthy champion of the convention's legal status and, before adjourning the meeting to a lodge in Canongate, obliged the Lord Provost, as Chief Constable, to pull him from the chair. Later in the evening, with Brown still presiding, it was resolved that the convention be 'instantly declared permanent'.[186]

This scenario was re-enacted the following night, 6 December. Just as Margarot and Gerrald, released on bail, were recounting the manner of their arrest and examination, the sheriff substitute for the county, attended by the magistrates and a posse of constables, carrying what Gerrald described as 'the funeral torches of liberty', arrived to dissolve the meeting. One after the other Margarot and Gerrald were voted to the chair. Vigorously protesting against the illegality of the sheriff's action, they demonstrated its forcible character by having to be pulled from their places as presiding officers. Gerrald closed the meeting with the customary prayer.[187]

As Gerrald had anticipated, most of the Scottish popular societies did not long survive the dissolution of the British Convention. Their cohesion as an organized movement for reform in association with the English radicals was compromised and the few members who persisted found themselves committed to real, rather than imaginary, treason.[188] Skirving's attempt to recall the convention on 12 December only led to his re-imprisonment, and though Gerrald, Margarot and Brown resumed their missionary tours – Gerrald in Perth, Margarot and Brown in East Lothian – they were hampered by lack of funds and discouragement from London.[189] A plan to carry political education to the Highlands, sponsored by the convention, also foundered.[190] In these circumstances Gerrald's pamphlet *A Convention the only means of saving us from Ruin*, which was published early in the new year, seemed ludicrously inappropriate in its

185. *Ibid.*

186. *ST*, vol. 23, cols. 467–8. By the term 'permanent', the delegates probably meant 'to meet in daily session' – again a French usage.

187. *ST*, vol. 23, cols. 469–70.

188. See below, p. 305.

189. Margarot to Hardy, 22 Dec. 1793. PRO TS 11/954/3498.

190. The motion proposed by a Scottish delegate called Wright was carried on 29 Nov. 1793. Wright publicly declared that though he had had the project in his mind for some time previously, he would not have brought it forward in the convention 'had it not also been suggested by our brethren from the South'. *Edinburgh Gazetteer*, 3 Dec. 1793.

nomenclature and timing, while his *Address of the British Convention . . . to the People of Great Britain* merely carried the unconvincing message that the sole objects of the united reformers was the restoration of annual parliaments and universal suffrage.[191] Both publications contained passages which were inevitably regarded as inflammatory. Gerrald's scheme for the indirect popular election of a convention consisting of 250 English and 125 Scottish delegates was grounded on the conviction that 'in this awful season of national calamity' – 'no other resource' remained but 'the interposition of the great body of the people themselves, electing deputies in whom they can confide, and imparting instructions which they must enjoin to be executed'.[192] To his own constituents the final words of Gerrald's Address must have seemed both prophetic and disquieting.

We must ever regard the suppression of the meetings of the people, (by the interference of power, however elevated), of which the guide is order, the object knowledge, and the end peace, as establishing principles, and deducing consequences, that must EXTINGUISH FOR EVER THE LIBERTIES OF OUR COUNTRY.[193]

Skirving, Margarot, Gerrald, Sinclair, and Alexander Scott, editor of the *Edinburgh Gazetteer*, were all indicted on charges of sedition, though Sinclair saved his skin by turning King's evidence and Scott sought safety in flight. Skirving was tried in the first week of January 1794 and Margarot a week later – Gerrald being allowed to return, for the time being, to London to attend to urgent private business.[194] Skirving and Margarot were found guilty, mainly, as the prosecution alleged because, as leading members of the convention, they had promoted 'a determined and systematic plan to subvert the limited monarchy and free constitution of Britain, and substitute in its place, by intimidation, force and violence, a republic or democracy . . .'.[195] The irregularities of the legal proceedings, the prejudiced

191. For the date of publication of Gerrald's *Convention . . .* see R. Dundas to E. Nepean, 27 Jan. 1794. PRO HO 102/10, fo. 116. For the *Address* see *ST*, vol. 23, col. 964.

192. J. Gerrald, *A Convention the only means of saving us from Ruin, in a letter addressed to the People of England* (London, 1793), p. 85.

193. *Address of the British Convention assembled at Edinburgh, November 19, 1793 to the People of Great Britain*, p. 24.

194. For Skirving's trial see *ST*, vol. 23, cols. 391–471; for Margarot's, *ibid.*, cols. 604–778; for Gerrald's, *ibid.*, cols. 803–1012. The *locus classicus* for a critical analysis of these trials is Lord Cockburn, *Examination of the Trials for sedition in Scotland*.

195. *ST*, vol. 23, col. 545.

and bullying behaviour of Braxfield, and the sentences of fourteen years' transportation merely repeated the general pattern set in the previous sedition trials – though Skirving's defence had been over-confident and Margarot's unnecessarily provocative and insolent.[196] Both had acted as martyrs in the democratic cause, and while Skirving was the darling, Margarot was the idol of the Edinburgh 'rabble'. Gerrald returned from London in mid March, less willingly perhaps than his admirers and radical tradition maintain, not, as he said, to stand trial, but to receive sentence.[197] His spirited and eloquent defence inspired his audience in court and posterity alike, but provoked only the withering cynicism and brutal contempt of Braxfield.[198] The verdict of guilty and the sentence of fourteen years' transportation closed one of the most shameful pages of Scottish judicial history and helped to precipitate the crisis of confrontation in England.

196. The Lord Advocate in a letter to the Home Office during Margarot's trial described him as 'the most daring and impudent villain of the whole gang'. PRO HO 102/10, fo. 76.

197. For Gerrald's apparent reluctance to return to Edinburgh to stand trial see below, p. 311.

198. *ST*, vol. 23, cols. 947–97. When Gerrald argued that Christ himself had been a reformer, Braxfield commented: 'Muckle he made o' that, he was hanget.' Lord Cockburn, *Memorials of His Times (1779–1850)* (Edinburgh, 1909), p. 117.

9 Confrontation and the treason trials of 1794

This trial is certainly one of the most memorable epochs in the history of English liberty.

WILLIAM GODWIN, November 1794

Just as the open resistance of the Edinburgh assembly had been sparked off by the Irish Convention Act, so the confrontation between the English radicals and the government in the spring of 1794 stemmed directly from the dissolution of the British Convention and the ensuing Scottish sedition trials. The response of the London radicals to these events was, to some extent, predictable. They could hardly repudiate the 'grand federation' with their Scottish allies which had been so publicly and solemnly proclaimed by the British Convention on the initiative of Margarot. Nor would they be likely to submit tamely to the 'martyrdom' of their delegates by the packed juries and prejudiced judges of the Scottish High Courts. But would they go further by giving their public approval to the transactions of the British Convention, which the Lord Advocate and the Scottish judges had not hesitated to condemn as tantamount to treason, even though they had lacked the evidence to support such a charge? Would they also attempt to implement the programme of resistance devised by their own deputies in Edinburgh by passing strongly worded resolutions of protest against anticipated threats to constitutional liberties, by exercising a watching brief over the legislative enactments of Parliament, and, if necessary, by summoning an emergency convention of popularly elected delegates in England? The answer to the last question depended largely on the attitude adopted by the government and on events. It was not long, however, before the Society for Constitutional Information and the London Corresponding Society made plain their fullest sympathy with, and support for, their former leaders and identified themselves with the proclaimed objectives and policies of the British Convention.

In response to 'important letters' received from its delegate Sinclair, and under the direct impact of the sentences of transportation passed on Skirving and Margarot, the Society for Constitutional Information held a general meeting at the Crown and Anchor Tavern on Friday, 17 January 1794 to publicize its sense of outraged indignation.[1] Encouraged by the presence of Gerrald in their midst, the members carried a set of incautious and defiant resolutions verging on sedition.[2] The first three resolutions, passed when Horne Tooke was presiding, summarized the society's reactions to the behaviour of the Scottish judges.

Resolved, That law ceases to be an object of obedience whenever it becomes an instrument of oppression. Resolved, That we recall to mind, with the deepest satisfaction, the merited fate of the infamous Jeffreys, once lord chief justice of England, who at the era of the glorious revolution, for the many iniquitous sentences which he had passed, was torn to pieces by a brave and injured people. Resolved, That those who imitate his example, deserve his fate.[3]

At this point, overcome by the prompting of his native caution, Tooke vacated the chair in favour of Gerrald.[4] The rest of the resolutions emphasized the identity of interest of English and Scots in the face of blatant injustice, the resolve to resist and approbation of the British Convention. The terms of these resolutions were uncompromising, not to say provocative, and served to show that, however lukewarm the society had been in its initial commitment to the Scottish assembly, it had now identified itself with the victims of Scottish judicial intemperance and with the conduct of the convention. The penultimate resolution contained a thinly disguised menace to resort, if necessary, to open violence.

Resolved, That we see with regret, but we see without fear, that the period is fast approaching when the liberties of Britons must depend not upon reason, to which they have long appealed, nor on their powers of expressing it, but on their firm and undaunted resolution to oppose tyranny by the same means by which it is exercised.[5]

1. PRO TS 11/962/3508 (SCI Minute-book).

2. Gerrald had been elected an associate member of the society in the summer of 1793.

3. PRO TS 11/962/3508. *ST*, vol. 24, cols. 558–9.

4. This action was mentioned by Erskine and Gibbs in Tooke's trial for treason as evidence of his moderation. *ST*, vol. 25, cols. 298, 476–7.

5. *ST*, vol. 24, col. 559.

On 20 January 1794 the London Corresponding Society also held a crowded general meeting followed by an anniversary dinner at the Globe Tavern in Fleet Street.[6] Presided over by John Martin, an attorney, and attended by over 1000 members or sympathizers,[7] the meeting approved a spirited *Address to the People of Great Britain and Ireland* and passed a set of emphatic resolutions providing for action in the confrontation with the government which then appeared imminent. The purpose of the address was to proclaim the society's continued solidarity with the Scottish reformers and its perseverance in its plans for radical parliamentary reform. Drafted partly by Martin and partly by Horne Tooke,[8] the address rehearsed popular complaints against the sacrifice of blood and treasure in the 'fruitless crusade to re-establish the odious despotism in France', which, in the course of a single campaign, had almost ruined British trade, commerce and industry and impoverished the families of countless operatives and artisans. A melancholy survey of the political situation in Great Britain and Ireland demonstrated that virtually all the public and private liberties contained in Magna Carta, the Bill of Rights and the revolution settlement of 1688 had been eroded. The consequences had been seen with the passage of the Convention Act in Ireland, and also in Scotland, where, despite 'the wisdom and good conduct of the British Convention in Edinburgh', 'infamous and illegal sentences of transportation' had been imposed on innocent and deserving delegates who had been 'fettered into dungeons among felons in the hulks'. English reformers were now facing similar threats and it was their 'duty and interest to stand or fall together'. The blame for these assaults on ancestral rights and constitutional liberties and for the ensuing political crisis was squarely placed on the Irish parliament and the Scottish judges, actuated by the 'corrupt and corrupting influence' of the English executive.[9] Stark alternatives now confronted the radicals. 'We are at issue. We must now choose at once either liberty or slavery for ourselves and our posterity.' 'Will you wait', the address asked, 'till *barracks* are erected in every village and till *subsidized* Hessians and Hanoverians are upon

6. *ST*, vol. 24, cols. 442–6.

7. Estimates of the attendance varied between 1000 and 1500. The weight of numbers on the first floor caused one of the principal beams to give way about a foot and carpenters had to be called in to effect repairs and the meeting transferred to an upper floor. BL, Add. MSS. 27814, fo. 69.

8. Thelwall to 'Citizen Jack Vellam', 23 Jan. 1794. PRO TS 11/955/3499. *ST*, vol. 25, cols. 221–2.

9. *ST*, vol. 24, col. 444.

us?'[10] Just as Christ had taught that no one should expect to gather grapes from thorns or figs from thistles, so the redress of popular injuries through a 'fair, free and full Representation of the People' could only result 'from our own laws, and not from the laws of our plunderers, enemies, and oppressors'.[11] If this meant anything at all, it implied that the radicals did not intend, in future, to seek reform by petitions to a corrupt and unyielding Parliament.

The resolutions which followed, read one by one by a young man named Richter,[12] and passed unanimously, served notice upon a Parliament about to reassemble for a new session and upon a government which had not yet publicly disclosed its attitude to the sentences passed by the Scottish judges, that the society intended to implement the emergency procedures laid down by the English and Scottish delegates in Edinburgh. The General Committee of the society was accordingly instructed, during the ensuing session of Parliament, to meet daily to watch its proceedings and those of the executive.[13] 'On the first introduction of any bill or motion inimical to the liberties of the people' the General Committee was 'forthwith' to summon a *'General Convention* of the *People'*. Such action would follow if the government attempted to land foreign troops in Great Britain or Ireland, to suspend the Habeas Corpus Act, to proclaim martial law or 'to prevent the people from meeting in societies for constitutional information'. Except that it omitted any reference to the possibility of a foreign invasion, this list of emergencies which would automatically precipitate the summons of a convention, was identical with that in the British Convention's main resolution.[14]

These proceedings also marked the rise to political leadership of John Thelwall, one of Horne Tooke's protégés, lecturer extraordinary, orator, poet and talented publicist.[15] Though we may well believe

10. *Ibid.* The rumours about the landing of Hessian mercenary troops appear to have stemmed from the temporary disembarkation of a corps of such troops recruited for foreign service from troopships stationed off the Isle of Wight because of sickness. King's message to the Commons, 27 Jan. 1794. *Parl. Hist.*, vol. 30, col. 1310.

11. *ST*, vol. 24, col. 444.

12. *Ibid.*, col. 26.

13. *Ibid.*, col. 445.

14. See above, p. 301.

15. Born in 1764, the son of a London silk mercer, Thelwall had tried his hand at acting, the law and the family business before taking to journalism. A voracious reader, his interest in politics had been stimulated by his membership of the Society for Free Debate at Coachmakers' Hall in Southwark. With Gerrald as his sponsor, Thelwall had joined division no. 25 of the LCS (Spitalfields) in

that Thelwall had used 'very bold and strong language' to commend the above resolutions, it is doubtful if he actually advocated the use of force to resist the landing of foreign mercenaries, as a government spy alleged.[16] After the anniversary dinner was over and the cloth removed, Thelwall had taken the chair for the formal toasts. He himself had proposed 'The Rights of Man' and had also enlivened the occasion by singing republican songs which he later printed and sold to members of the society and the audiences at his political lectures. Most of the toasts embodied enthusiastic support for the English and Scottish 'martyrs' and for the conduct of the Edinburgh convention. Among the diners was a further prospective 'martyr' – Gerrald himself, fulfilling his last engagement before returning to the northern capital for trial.[17] When the toast to Margarot had been proposed Gerrald had delivered an eloquent tribute, concluding with the wish that he and his audience too would 'rather die the last of British freemen, than live the first of slaves'.[18] Three days later the society resolved to print and distribute 100,000 copies of the proceedings, and the Society for Constitutional Information resolved that they should stand in its own records and that the LCS had, in French revolutionary parlance, 'deserved well of their country'.[19]

The immediate aims of the metropolitan reform societies were thus to impress on the government the widespread popular demand for peace with France, to campaign for the reversal of the sentences of transportation on the Scottish and English radicals, and to deter the executive from further repression by threatening to resort to the emergency procedures elaborated by the British Convention. In these objectives the radicals could count on the parliamentary support of

---

the autumn of 1793, and as from 21 October 1793 had become its delegate on the General Committee. Mrs Thelwall, *Life of Thelwall* (London, 1837), and C. Cestre, *John Thelwall: A Pioneer of Democracy and Social Reform in England during the French Revolution* (London, 1906).

16. Evidence of John Taylor, *ST*, vol. 24, col. 26.

17. For Gerrald's 'appearance of reluctance' to return to Edinburgh to stand trial (despite contemporary tradition), see a draft, undated and unsigned, letter to him from several members of the LCS. PRO TS 11/954/3498. It appears that, at the meeting on 20 January 1794, many sympathizers had urged him not to return to Edinburgh to face certain conviction, and in his precarious state of health, what would also be a death sentence.

18. The above-mentioned letter, urging Gerrald to stand trial in the interests of the radical cause, reminded him of this sentiment and fixes its date as sometime after 20 January.

19. PRO TS 11/962/3508 (24 Jan. 1794).

the Foxite Whigs. The Whig reformers had bitterly opposed the war from the outset; Lauderdale, Fox, Grey and Sheridan had exerted themselves, though without success, to convince Dundas of the illegality of the sentences passed on Muir and Palmer,[20] and they would also strongly oppose any attempt to suspend Habeas Corpus. On the other hand, it could hardly be expected that the Association of the Friends of the People, which had repudiated any idea of sending delegates to the Edinburgh convention, would support, or even countenance, the summons of a second British Convention. In any case the Foxites were, by this time only the rump of a Whig Opposition on the point of disintegration.[21] Though the conservative Whigs did not join Pitt's administration till July, Portland and his supporters were already undeviating in their determination to prosecute the war vigorously, to resist parliamentary reform at all costs and to strengthen the government's hands against French republicanism and English 'Jacobinism'.[22]

It was not, therefore, surprising that the government was not deflected from its war policy either by radical demonstrations or by Foxite criticisms. All efforts in Parliament between the end of January and the beginning of March 1794 to carry motions in favour of peace proved abortive. Earl Stanhope's motion in the House of Lords on 23 January to acknowledge the French republic and 'thereby to lay the foundation for a speedy reconciliation and a lasting peace' only provoked the derisive comment of the Earl of Abingdon that the sole response it called for was 'a good loud horse-laugh'. It was, in fact, negatived without a division.[23] The Marquess of Landsowne's motion in the Lords for a separate peace with France on 21 February was rejected by the comfortable majority of ninety, while Whitbread's similar motion in the Commons on 6 March was lost by 138 votes to 26.[24] The impression left by such defeats on the provincial radicals was indicated by the concluding resolutions carried on 28 February – a day set aside by the government for a general fast – at a large

20. PRO HO 102/9, fos. 282–3.
21. The Foxite Whigs, nevertheless, outnumbered the Portland Whigs at this stage. F. O'Gorman, *The Whig Party and the French Revolution* (London, 1967), appendices 3, 4.
22. By a curious coincidence the conservative Whigs had met at Burlington House on 20 January 1794, on the same day as the LCS general meeting, to 'consider the means of giving the most effectual support to a vigorous prosecution of the war'. *Ibid.*, p. 178.
23. *Parl. Hist.*, vol. 30, col. 1297.
24. *Ibid.*, cols. 1424, 1486.

public meeting in Sheffield.[25] Such decisions, it was stated, merely demonstrated 'the total inefficacy of *argument* against a *Ministerial Majority*' and proved that the only remedy for popular grievances was 'a REFORM IN PARLIAMENT – a measure which we determine never to relinquish, though we follow our Brethren in the same glorious cause to Botany Bay'.[26]

Nor were Foxite attempts to pave the way for a possible revision of the sentences on Muir and Palmer by allowing the House of Lords an appellate jurisdiction in certain specified Scottish criminal cases, although repeatedly pressed between early February and the middle of March, any more successful.[27] They only revealed that Pitt was firmly behind the Lord Advocate in his support of the Scottish judicial sentences and that Dundas was adamant in his refusal to contemplate any reform of Scottish criminal procedure.[28]

Meanwhile the anxieties of the radicals had been alerted by measures which the government had taken to increase its inadequate security forces. Towards the end of January accounts of the landing of Hessian mercenary troops on the Isle of Wight and at Portland inspired conjectures that they were to be quartered in the barracks which Pitt had constructed in the main industrial areas where, it was supposed, they would be used to overawe local radicals.[29] A bill to recruit and arm French *émigré* regiments in Britain and to take them into government pay was interpreted in a similar fashion and was opposed by the Foxite Whigs as an abuse of the royal prerogative.[30] Though radical fears in both these respects were exaggerated, the formation of Volunteer Corps in the spring of 1794, nominally to step up the nation's preparedness against the dangers of French invasion, had undoubtedly been partly inspired by the desire to place

25. *A Serious Lecture delivered at Sheffield February 28 1794 . . . to which are added a Hymn and Resolutions*, 6th ed. (London, 1794). *ST*, vol. 24, cols. 636–8.

26. *Ibid.*, resolutions 10 and 11.

27. Debates were held on 4 Feb. on Adams's motion for criminal law reform in Scotland; on 24 and 27 Feb. on Palmer's petition to the House of Commons against his sentence; on 10 and 25 March on Adams's motion for the exercise of royal pardon for Muir and Palmer and the reform of Scottish criminal procedure. *Parl. Hist.*, vol. 30, cols. 1346, 1449, 1460, 1486, and *ibid.*, vol. 31, col. 54.

28. *Ibid.*, vol. 30, cols. 1572–6, and vol. 31, cols. 62–5.

29. Margarot, writing to Hardy from his Tolbooth prison in Edinburgh on 24 Jan. 1794 concluded, 'Armed associations are I perceive, now set on foot by the rich, wherefore should not the poor do the same? Are you to wait patiently until 20,000 Hessians and Hanoverians come to cut your throats?' *ST*, vol. 24, col. 480.

30. *Parl. Hist.*, vol. 31, cols. 373–432 (11 April, 1794).

a further instrument of repression in the hands of the government.[31] The Volunteer movement was also, as the late Professor J. R. Western rightly emphasized, 'an integral part of the government's campaign to break up the Foxite Opposition, form a national conservative coalition, and harass and discredit the Radicals by judicial persecution'.[32] The part played by the clergy and Reevite Loyalist associations in the formation of Volunteer companies at local level was, in itself, sufficient to proclaim their purpose as the safeguarding of the social and political establishment. Though exemption from the unpopular militia service and monetary compensation for days spent on drill drew in many poor recruits, the government saw to it that a proportion of the corps formed was composed of, and officered by, reliable men of property and social standing. The main ballast of the corps was provided by richer middle-class members, attracted by the brilliant uniforms, and by the opportunities for displays of patriotic conviviality and of local patronage. The elite of the corps was the Yeomanry (or Volunteer cavalry) who paid for most of their equipment and mounts, though they were also sometimes assisted by local subscriptions. Though this new form of internal security force was not, in the spring of 1794, strong enough to overwhelm the radical societies, its potentialities in the hands of the conservative and governing classes were not lost on men who were already convinced that they were to be the next victims of governmental repression. To avert that danger before it became too great, or to ward off further assaults on leading radicals by 'Church and King' mobs, perhaps it might be necessary, in self-defence, to secure arms and to train in their use?

The Hessian scare, the least substantial of all such threats, but vivid enough in popular memories of the use to which such mercenaries had been put in the American conflict, triggered off the mechanism for the summons of an emergency convention.[33] On 30 January,

---

31. J. R. Western, 'The Volunteer movement as an anti-revolutionary force, 1793–1801', *English Historical Review*, vol. 71 (1956), pp. 603–14.

32. *Ibid.*, p. 605. For the defence situation in 1794 see also J. R. Western, 'The county fencibles and the militia augmentation of 1794', *Army Historical Review*, vol. 34, pp. 3–11.

33. It was also used as an excuse for the suggestion that the radicals should arm themselves. Richard Hodgson was the author of a placard advocating this in mid-April 1794. 'The Ins tell us that we are in danger of invasion from the French. The Outs tell us that we are in danger from the Hessians and Hanoverians. In either case we should arm ourselves; get arms and learn how to use them.' *ST*, vol. 24, col. 837.

on the initiative of Thelwall, and following the precedent set by Margarot, the delegate committee of the London Corresponding Society agreed to establish a secret committee to plan the necessary arrangements. This consisted of John Martin, who had chaired the meeting of 20 January, John Baxter and Richard Hodgson, former chairmen of the society and both extremists, Matthew Moore and Thelwall himself.[34] It was given the discretionary power of reporting back to the General Committee of delegates. Little or nothing is known about this secret committee, except that it had no secretary, but was clearly dominated by Thelwall, and that it was renewed on 6 February to conceal the identity of its members from the delegates.[35] In fact the membership remained the same, except that John Richter – a young manservant – was co-opted in place of Martin.[36]

After the failure, on 10 March, of Adams's motion praying for the exercise of the royal pardon for Muir and Palmer, and the condemnation of Gerrald a few days later to fourteen years' transportation, the new secret committee met on Sunday 16 March and called for a general meeting of the whole society.[37] On the 20th the delegate committee approved this recommendation and fixed the date of the meeting for 7 April.[38] The significant decisions, however, were taken on Monday 27 March.[39] The date of the general meeting was then postponed till 14 April to accommodate Thelwall's difficulties in drafting suitable resolutions.[40] To protect itself, in the approaching confrontation, from a 'a repetition of wicked and unjust sentences' as well as to secure the redress of popular grievances 'in a legal and constitutional manner' by 'a full and fair representation of the PEOPLE of Great Britain', the London Corresponding Society also resolved that 'there ought to be *immediately* a CONVENTION of the PEOPLE, by delegates, deputed for that purpose from the different societies of the *Friends* of *Freedom*, assembled in the various parts of

34. Report of George Lynam, government spy. PRO TS 11/954/3498 and *ST*, vol. 24, col. 803.

35. Lynam himself, a member of the delegate committee, was at this time rightly suspected of being a spy, despite his acquittal of such a charge in June 1793. BL, Add. MSS. 27812, fo. 47.

36. PRO TS 11/952/3496(ii).

37. Report of John Taylor, 18 March 1794. PRO TS 11/955/3499.

38. *Ibid.*

39. *ST*, vol. 24, col. 562.

40. Report by J. Ashley, 1 April 1794, in PRO TS 11/952/3496(ii). Thelwall apparently found it 'a matter that required the utmost exertion of mental powers to simplify the business and yet to make known the sentiments of the society in bold and nervous resolutions'.

the kingdom'.[41] The views of the other metropolitan societies and of the provincial associations in both England and Scotland were also to be consulted.

Hardy wrote off the same day to the Society for Constitutional Information, on 4 April to the Whig Association of the Friends of the People and, about the middle of April, despatched circular printed letters to the provincial reform societies. These letters help to clarify the intentions of the London Corresponding Society in promoting the idea of a second British Convention – one of the crucial issues which preoccupied the prosecution and defence counsel in the treason trials of 1794.[42] In urging the necessity of '*a speedy convention*' Hardy informed the Society for Constitutional Information that its purpose would be twofold – to procure the redress of urgent popular grievances and to prepare the way for the long-term objective of 'a full and fair representation of the people'. 'The late illegal and unheard-of prosecutions and sentences' seemed to require from 'all the friends of freedom' 'a full and explicit declaration' of their intentions – whether they would abandon, or persevere in their plans for, radical reform with increased vigour and determination. Presenting this clear alternative to the Society for Constitutional Information, Hardy asked, without further explanation, whether it would be ready, when called on, to unite with the London Corresponding Society and other associations to press, 'in a constitutional and legal method', for redress and reform by means of a convention?[43]

In his letter of 4 April to Sheridan, chairman of the Friends of the People, Hardy specified the abuses needing 'immediate redress' – the government's efforts to introduce foreign mercenaries into the country, the 'intended bill' to embody foreigners into his majesty's service, and the use of public funds to maintain 'a train of spies, more dangerous to society than so many assassins'. In soliciting the co-operation of the Whig association 'in assembling, as speedily as the nature of the business will admit, a Convention of the Friends of Freedom', Hardy was, however, intentionally vague about its composition and purpose. The aim would be 'a full and effectual representation' obtained in 'a legal and constitutional method' and, above all, in a solely peaceful way. The determination of the London Corresponding

41. *ST*, vol. 24, col. 563.
42. For interesting comments on this problem see T. M. Parssinen, 'Association, convention and anti-parliament in British radical politics, 1771–1848', *English Historical Review*, vol. 88 (1973), pp. 513–15.
43. *ST*, vol. 24, cols. 562–3.

Society to persevere in the cause of reform rested on its firm belief that 'as there is no power which *ought*, so there is no power which *can* finally withstand the just and steady demands of a people resolved to be free'.[44]

The clearest and least equivocal exposition of the Corresponding Society's immediate plans was, however, contained in the printed circular letters sent out to the popular societies in England and Scotland in mid April.[45] Nothing was said in these letters about parliamentary or any other reform – the whole stress being placed upon the urgent need to form 'another British Convention' before the government introduced legislation to make such action illegal. What seems to have been envisaged was a demonstration, on a nation-wide basis, of radical solidarity in the face of continuing ministerial repression and the reorientation of 'the future operations of the friends to freedom' in accordance with the views to be expressed by the delegates of the different societies assembled in conference.[46] Time was of the essence – the Hessian threat had not been lifted and the answer of the provincial societies was requested not later than the 20th. The place of meeting could not be revealed till all the replies had been received, but the Corresponding Society had in view 'a central situation convenient for the whole island'.[47] Each society was required to specify its numerical strength and the number of delegates it could send to the convention. Hardy added, in a postscript, that possibly the example of the metropolitan society in forming a secret committee might be followed elsewhere.

Predictably, the society of the Friends of the People politely declined the invitation on the ground that the suggested convention would only give a handle to the opponents of reform and might well alienate potential supporters.[48] The Society for Constitutional Information, however, 'heartily concurred' in the proposals on 28 March, suggesting joint discussions. A joint 'committee of conference', meeting twice weekly at Thelwall's lecture rooms at No. 2 Beaufort Buildings off the Strand, lost no time in recommending that 'a general meeting or convention of the friends of liberty' should be called 'to consider the proper methods of obtaining a full and fair

44. *Ibid.*, col. 736.
45. These circular letters were drafted, not by Hardy, but by the joint 'committee of co-operation and communication' established by the LCS and the SCI on 11 April 1794. PRO TS 11/952/3496(ii).
46. *ST*, vol. 24, col. 481.
47. *Ibid.*, col. 482. Was this York, as Gerrald had suggested?
48. Letter of 11 April 1794. *Ibid.*, col. 737.

representation of the people'.[49] Its other proposals were that 'a regular and pressing correspondence' should be started with those provincial associations which seemed disposed to send delegates and that personal contact with any of their members who happened to be in London from time to time should be made through a joint standing 'committee of co-operation and communication'.[50] These recommendations were approved by the general committee of the London Corresponding Society on 10 April and by the Society for Constitutional Information on the following day.[51]

The government was kept fully informed of these moves by its spies inside the London Corresponding Society – one of whom, George Lynam, a former Walbrook ironmonger and commission agent, had been reporting on the proceedings of its general committee as a delegate for No. 23 division ever since 1792.[52] Another informer, John Taylor, who had joined the society at the end of January 1794, had been instructed to attend regularly and report on the political lectures which Thelwall had been delivering to raise funds towards the expenses and defence costs of the society's delegates to the Edinburgh convention.[53] These lectures were originally held on Wednesday evenings at the Three Kings Tavern in Southwark, where the audiences could not exceed sixty or seventy, and on Friday evenings at No. 3 New Compton Street, Soho.[54] At the end of March 1794 they were transferred to No. 2 Beaufort Buildings off the Strand, where Thelwall became tenant-at-will of a large assembly room rented by a friend.[55] Although the price of admission was kept at 6d.

49. *ST*, vol. 24, col. 564. Some discussion had taken place as to whether the word 'convention' should be used; the delegates from the SCI – the Rev. Jeremiah Joyce, William Sharp, Thomas Holcroft, Thomas Wardle and Stewart Kyd – would have preferred 'general meeting', but Thelwall had insisted on the retention of the term 'convention'. The other LCS members of this committee were Matthew Moore, John Baxter, Richard Hodgson and John Lovett. PRO TS 11/955/3600.

50. *ST*, vol. 24, col. 564. The 'committee of co-operation and communication' was composed of the above-named LCS delegates and Joyce, Sharp, J. A. Bonney, John Pearson, J. H. Tooke and Thomas Wardle of the SCI. PRO TS 11/965/3510A.

51. *ST*, vol. 24, cols. 564–5.

52. Lynam's reports are in PRO TS 11/954/3498.

53. Taylor's reports are in PRO TS 11/955/3499.

54. *Ibid*.

55. The accommodation was leased in the name of George Williams, leather seller, of West Smithfield – a member of both the SCI and the LCS. PRO TS 11/957/3502(i). This accommodation was used for meetings of the secret committee of the LCS and for the deliberations of the joint committees of the LCS and SCI.

to attract large popular audiences, the authorities soon became aware that the lectures were also making an unexpected and disconcerting impact on other types of listeners. Many who had come out of idle curiosity, or for amusement, were observed to leave visibly impressed by Thelwall's considerable powers as a controversialist and his vivid presentation of popular grievances.[56] In these discourses all the well-worn themes of radical protest were exploited – the destructiveness of eighteenth-century wars, the inequalities of the judicial process, the accumulating distress of the poor, the corruption and oppression of magistrates and ministers, and the need to persevere in the cause of parliamentary reform despite increasing opposition. Thelwall also drew, however, on several newer and more potent sources of political enquiry – Daniel Eaton's *Politics for the People, or Hogs' Wash*, Gibbon on 'Superstitious Observances', and Godwin's *Political Justice*.[57] He repeated his own parable of the game-cock 'with ermine-spotted heart' – 'a haughty sanguinary tyrant of the farm yard' which had been beheaded by the teller of the story – for printing which, in *Hogs' Wash*, Eaton had been recently tried and acquitted.[58] On the theme of religious superstition Thelwall took occasion to compliment the French on having emancipated so many potential wives and mothers by throwing open the nunneries and observed, on the custom of touching for the 'King's evil', that it was not the only evil attending the monarch.[59] *Political Justice* was plundered for evidence of 'the abuses of the law', to enforce the notion of equality, to decry religion and to elaborate on the concept of social justice. The discussion of such weighty topics was seasoned with running commentary on current discontents – the Scottish sedition trials, the horrors of transportation, the illegal employment of Hessian mercenaries, the 'idle pageantry' of the Lord Mayor's Show, and Pitt's use of the pension list as his 'Smelling Bottle' to 'revive the spirits of his sycophants'.[60] Despite his harsh voice and embarrassing lisp, Thelwall

56. 'Every popular topic was urged with a seeming force of argument and an enthusiasm of manner scarcely to be resisted, indeed the effect was but too visible on the audience many of whom were by no means to be ranked with the lowest orders of the people.' Anonymous letter to Sir Joseph Banks, 19 April 1794, forwarded on 22 April to Treasury Solicitor. PRO TS 11/959/3505(i).

57. *Political Justice* had been published early in 1793 and had escaped prosecution because its price of three guineas was thought to place it outside the reach of the general public.

58. Reports of J. Taylor, 5 Feb. and 12 March 1794. PRO TS 11/955/3499.

59. *Ibid.*, 28 Feb. 1794.

60. 19 March 1794. Taylor commented: 'This lecture appeared to me to contain the most treasonable and seditious sentiments that could be.' *Ibid.*

managed, in this way, to engage and hold the attention of audiences which, in a few months, rose to over 600. Forced to move from tavern to tavern as their landlords' licences were suspended or withdrawn, constantly beset by spies and informers eager to exaggerate or misrepresent as treasonable statements which occasionally bordered on the seditious, threatened with physical violence by gangs of 'Bludgeon men', hired and led by young aristocrats like Charles Jenkinson, son of the reactionary Lord Hawkesbury, Thelwall courageously stood his ground, relying mainly on the protection of his impromptu bodyguards, but strengthening the crown of his hat to make it cudgelproof and carrying with him a small sword stick 'in case of extremity'.[61]

From Taylor's reports the government learnt of the violence of Thelwall's anti-clericalism, his repeated aspersions on the 'imbecility' of George III, the coarseness of his jibes against the judicial hierarchy, his bitter criticism of the way the laws were administered 'to aggrandize the rich and oppress the poor', his contempt for Pitt and the revolutionary implications and treasonable tendencies of his political commentaries.[62] It was the latter charge which mattered and it was in this respect that the spy betrayed his inability or unwillingness to recognize that Thelwall's words of caution were sincere.[63] In a long report to the government at the end of April on the urgent need to tighten up security measures in the capital, John Reeves, architect of the Association for the Preservation of Liberty and Property against Republicans and Levellers, expressed concern at the proliferation and growing confidence of the radical clubs and the increasing licence of popular pamphleteering after the repeated acquittals of the bookseller Daniel Isaac Eaton.[64] His comment on Thelwall's lectures was brief, but perceptive. 'The mischief of these lectures', he wrote, 'is of a new kind' – all the more insidious, because

61. Mrs Thelwall, vol. 1, p. 135.
62. PRO TS 11/955/3499, *passim*.
63. Cf. 14 Feb. 1794. Taylor reported Thelwall as saying: 'He rejoiced to say that Tyranny and despotism was on the eve of dissolution all over Europe, the undertaker was knocking at the door, and the coffin was already bespoke. He added: Be steady and resolute then, fellow citizens, and your end is accomplished.' From this Taylor insinuated that Thelwall was anticipating 'a Revolution in this country'. PRO TS 11/955/3499.
64. 'Report on Sedition etc.', 29 April 1794. PRO ST 11/965/3510A(ii). In Feb. 1794 Eaton was found not guilty of publishing *Hogs' Wash* (*ST*, vol. 23, col. 1054), after being acquitted in 1793 on charges of publishing an expurgated edition of the *Rights of Man* and Paine's *Address to the Addressers*.

some 'serious people' who had heard them had been oblivious of their consequences.[65] Yet Thelwall was neither an original, nor a subversive, thinker, and in nothing was he more representative of his generation than in the unrestrained violence of his rhetoric and in the temporizing moderation evident in his own conduct and the political advice which he gave to his popular audiences.[66] In this he showed himself the true disciple of Horne Tooke and William Godwin – though the latter frequently attempted to dissuade him from continuing his lectures and bitterly criticized his failure to do so.[67] The spies who listened in smoke-filled taverns to Thelwall's emotive conversational indiscretions and his blasphemous raillery, when emboldened by drink, and the government which discovered from his intercepted correspondence that he proudly claimed to be both a 'Republican' and 'a downright *sans-culotte*', were in no mood, however, to make allowances, or to interpret such views as 'purely speculative'.[68] For them Thelwall was a self-confessed revolutionary. Perhaps, nevertheless, Thelwall was right when he later contended that his real crime was not his alleged treason, but, 'what was infinitely more offensive to the men in power', his conduct of 'a bold and open investigation' of the measures by which 'they were plunging the country into irretrievable destruction'.[69] Thelwall undoubtedly saw himself at this time as 'fighting an important battle – for the right of public investigation upon political subjects'.[70] When a copy of his second lecture was presented to the grand jury at the Court Leet of the Duchy of Savoy on 1 May 1794 with the suggestion that it would serve as a basis of a prosecution for libel, he was quick to present his defence in his lecture on the following day.[71] He had, he said, no plans to pull down the constitution and was not even a particular enemy to monarchy. What he did condemn, however, was the assumption of his opponents that 'the people had no business in discussing political

65. PRO TS 11/965/3510A(ii).
66. Thelwall's advice to his followers at these lectures was to be 'at once *active, vigilant* and *prudent*'. Mrs Thelwall, vol. 1, p. 129.
67. J. Thelwall, *The Tribune*, vol. 2 (London, 1795), p. viii.
68. Thelwall to Allum, 13 Feb. 1794. PRO TS 11/960/3506(i).
69. J. Thelwall, *The Natural and Constitutional Right of Britons to Annual Parliaments, Universal Suffrage and the Freedom of Popular Association* (London, 1795), p. 86.
70. Thelwall to Allum, 13 Feb. 1794. PRO TS 11/960/3506(i).
71. Mrs Thelwall, vol. 1, p. 137. The lecture of 2 May 1794 was entitled, 'The characters and Views of the present Reformers and their opponents, in answer to Mr Mainwaring's charge to the Grand Jury'. PRO TS 11/957/3502(i).

affairs', the despotic powers wielded by the chief minister, the expense, purpose and consequences of the war, and the 'illegal and abominable proceedings of that most abandoned and infamous court – the Court of Justiciary in Scotland'. 'There was', he maintained,

no great mischief in royalty itself, it was in those who, having the Treasury at their back and corruption in their hearts, had introduced a system of spies and informers to stop the free use of man's intellectual faculties, who had introduced an Inquisitor General among us in the person of the immaculate Mr Reeves, and who were endeavouring to wrest from the people their few remaining rights and liberties.[72]

Even so he could not refrain from a rhetorical gesture – a promise that, if Scottish legal procedures were introduced into English courts, 'he would leave off lecturing and would meet them at Charing Cross, where he would mount the Black Horse, and tell them from thence that it was no longer a time for speaking, that the time for action was arrived'.[73] In retrospect, and in more reflective mood, Thelwall, however, came to see himself 'not so much as the reaper who goes into the field to collect the harvest of opinion, as the sower, whose business it is to scatter the seed'. That harvest, he thought, might well prove distant, but it could never be in doubt.[74]

Meanwhile, the government had been following, with some anxiety and mounting suspicion, the activities of a secret emissary of the French Committee of Public Safety – the Reverend William Jackson – a member of the community of Anglo-Irish exiles in Paris, who had landed at Hull from Hamburg on 26 February.[75] On reaching London, Jackson, masquerading as an American, had contacted William Stone, a Nonconformist wholesale coal and coke merchant of Rutland Place, Upper Thames St. He had brought with him messages from the latter's brother John Hurford Stone, a former member of the London Revolution Society, who in the summer of 1792 had established at Paris a concern for the manufacture of sal-ammoniac and other chemical substances and had, more recently, also engaged in the printing and publishing business. As an expatriate admirer of the French revolution, Hurford Stone had presided over the treasonable

72. *Ibid.*
73. *Ibid.* The 'Black Horse' was, presumably, the equestrian statue of Charles I.
74. Thelwall, *Tribune*, vol. 2 (London, 1795), p. xiv.
75. PRO TS 11/555/1793. Brief for prosecution, King *v* William Stone for high treason. Jackson had been born in Ireland, but, after an Oxford education had held Anglican orders in London, where he had been an acquaintance of the notorious Duchess of Kingston.

meetings of the English, Irish and Scottish democrats in Paris in November 1792 and he had also formed confidential connections with several of the Girondin ministers.[76] Jackson's mission was partly to collect evidence from reliable, but sympathetic, English sources as to the probable reception French invasion forces might expect from the general population and partly also to assess the amount of more active support and collaboration which such forces would be likely to obtain if Ireland were invaded. Jackson's projected visit to Dublin to contact the leaders of the United Irish had been prompted by Nicholas Madgett, an Irish exile who was acting as an intelligence officer in the French Admiralty. His preliminary enquiries in England had, however, been suggested by Hurford Stone, who had recently come under some suspicion in Paris because he had contended that the English people were firmly attached to their existing constitution and forms of government.[77] Jackson explained that the prevailing opinion in French government circles was that nine-tenths of the English people would be likely to throw in their lot with any French invasion forces.[78] This view was stoutly rebutted by William Stone, who nevertheless undertook to obtain reliable evidence of the exact state of English public opinion, so that this might be used by his brother to restore his credit in Paris and enable him to dissuade the French government from persevering in its invasion plans. He had, accordingly, put out feelers in radical, nonconformist and Whig Opposition circles and had obtained from Benjamin Vaughan, MP for Lansdowne's pocket borough of Calne, and from William Smith MP, the spokesman for the Unitarian interest in Parliament, written assessments of the likely English response to a French invasion attempt.[79] Despite their pro-French sympathies, both these politicians made it clear in their statements that the majority of the English population would instinctively rally in arms to the defence of the country, that earlier pro-French sentiment had evaporated, and that, despite discontent with the war, Pitt had been successful, as Smith

76. Stone was friendly with Pétion and Kersaint and his opinion on English affairs was much consulted. L. D. Woodward, *Une adhérente Anglaise de la Révolution Française. Hélène-Maria Williams et ses amis* (Paris, 1930), pp. 67–72.

77. PRO TS 11/555/1793. For Madgett see R. Hayes, *Biographical Dictionary of Irishmen in France* (Dublin, 1949), pp. 194–5.

78. PRO TS 11/555/1793.

79. William Stone had also approached Earl Lauderdale, Sheridan, Dr Priestley and Samuel Rogers – without encouragement. Sheridan referred him to Dundas! For Vaughan's analysis see *ST*, vol. 25, cols 1260–2 and for Smith's, *ibid.*, cols. 1262–3.

put it, 'in raising a strong spirit of attachment to every branch; I might almost say, to every abuse of the constitution'.[80] Vaughan added categorically that: 'If France were to invade England, every man would turn out, from good will or fear, and the few who are discontented would be quelled with ease, as the French citizens were by LaFayette in the Champs de Mars'.[81] Smith agreed: 'We should', he wrote, 'only wrap our Cloak tighter around us, like the man in the Storm, and refuse every offer of Fraternity that came to us in so questionable a shape.'[82] When these discouraging reports were sent by Jackson on 18 March to his control in Hamburg for communication to Hurford Stone, they were, however, intercepted by British intelligence agents and were forwarded to Lord Grenville at the Foreign Office and by him to Nepean at the Home Office.[83]

Though William Stone did his best to persuade Jackson to return to Paris immediately without fulfilling his mission to Ireland, the agent set off for Chester on 30 March and arrived at Dublin on 3 April.[84] He was accompanied by his former associate John Cockayne, an attorney who had already betrayed him to Pitt and who, as *agent provocateur*, by introducing him to Hamilton Rowan, Wolfe Tone and other leaders of the United Irish, was to ensure his arrest by the Irish government on 28 April.[85] The English government arrested William Stone on 3 May and on the same night closely questioned both Vaughan and Smith before the Privy Council.[86] Vaughan thought it wise after this experience to cross the Channel to Paris, and to emigrate, after a short stay in Switzerland, to the United States.[87] Smith's reputation was gravely compromised. Owing to the difficulties in procuring defence witnesses from England Jackson was not tried for high treason till April 1795. The verdict of guilty was a foregone conclusion, but Jackson committed suicide by taking poison in the dock.[88] Stone had to wait till the end of January 1796 until he was acquitted on a similar charge as an innocent accessory.[89]

80. *ST*, vol. 25, col. 1262.
81. *Ibid.*, cols. 1260–1.
82. *Ibid.*, col. 1263.
83. *Ibid.*, col. 1258.
84. PRO TS 11/555/1793.
85. For Jackson's negotiations with the leaders of the United Irish see below, Chapter 11.
86. PRO TS 11/555/1793.
87. Woodward, p. 13.
88. For Jackson's trial see *ST*, vol. 25, cols. 783–890.
89. *Ibid.*, col. 1438.

These arrests and the highly charged atmosphere of conspiracy which they created, the evidence of continued French reliance on supposed radical support for their invasion schemes, and the solidarity with the leaders of the United Irish, soon to be publicly reiterated by the London Corresponding Society, help to explain the government's decision in the second week of May 1794 to arrest the English radical leaders on charges of high treason.

Three final acts of defiance from the radicals clinched that decision – the provocative resolutions and address to the British nation approved at a large open-air meeting of the Sheffield Constitutional Society on 7 April; the calm but challenging proceedings at the general meeting of the London Corresponding Society at Chalk Farm on 14 April; and the irresponsible speeches and toasts at the anniversary dinner of the Society for Constitutional Information on 2 May. Though the reformers had been protesting since the end of January that the time for resistance had arrived, it was they rather than the government who precipitated the confrontation.

The meeting of the self-styled 'Friends of Justice, Liberty and Humanity' at Sheffield, was stage-managed by Joseph Gales, editor of the *Sheffield Register*, and Henry 'Redhead' Yorke, the young and bombastic mulatto who, after the dissolution of the Derby Society for Political Information in the spring of 1793, had placed his undoubted demagogic and journalistic talents at the disposal of the northern radicals.[90]

Held on Castle Hill on Monday 7 April and attended, it was claimed, by upwards of 10,000 people, the meeting heard and approved petitions to the King requesting him to exercise his prerogative of mercy on behalf of 'the persecuted patriots' of the British Convention and to procure 'the total and unconditional emancipation of the Negro slaves'.[91] The primary concern of its organizers was, however, to enforce their conclusion that it was useless to petition Parliament further for the redress of grievances or reform. With this end in view Gales and Yorke, in collusion with William Broomhead, the secretary of the society, had induced the latter to propose an 'Aunt Sally'

90. Yorke had, it will be remembered, delivered the Derby society's address to the French National Convention in Paris in December 1792 and had been elected the delegate of the Society for Constitutional Information to the British Convention in October 1793. He had just returned from the trial of Thomas Walker at Lancaster in which he had been a witness.

91. *Proceedings of the Public Meeting held at Sheffield, in the open air, on 7 April, 1794*. Sheffield Central Library, Local Pamphlets, vol. 80(3), pp. 3–10.

motion in favour of petitioning Parliament, in order that it should be rejected.[92] This motion, when made, was greeted with murmurs and not even seconded. This gave Yorke, as chairman of the meeting, his cue for making an hour-long rhetorical speech in justification, in which he mixed hypothetical threats and abuse with more dispassionate arguments derived from eighteenth-century political theory and Anglo-Saxon 'precedents'. In a vein reminiscent of Thelwall or Gerrald, Yorke referred to the ways in which hard contemporary experience could teach 'humanists' how to enkindle 'the combustible elements' in suffering nations so as to produce that 'grand political explosion' which at the same time that 'it buries despotism, already convulsive and agonising, in ruins, may raise up the people to the dignity and sublime grandeur of Freedom'.[93] Such a political revolution, however, he hastily added, would need to be preceded by 'a revolution of sentiment'. Similarly, a doom-laden forecast that 'the commanding voice of the whole people shall recommend the Five Hundred and Fifty-eight Gentlemen in St. Stephen's Chapel to go about their business' would depend on the dawn of an era in which 'the mists of prejudice' had been dispersed, the 'meanest cottager in the country' had been 'enlightened' and 'the sun of Reason shall shine in its fullest meridian over us'.[94] This right of resistance, derived from Locke's *Second Treatise on Civil Government*, was thus deferred, as a later commentator has observed, till the Greek Kalends.[95] At the time, however, it was used as the basis for resolutions that 'the people ought to demand as a *Right*, and not petition as a *Favour*, for Universal Representation' and 'that therefore we will petition the House of Commons no more on this subject'.[96] The grounds for this solemn decision were left to be elaborated by the committee of the Sheffield Constitutional Society, which did so in an *Address to the British Nation*, subsequently published, along with the proceedings of the meeting, by Gales.[97] That resolve stemmed ultimately from the rejection by the House of Commons of the Sheffield petition for parliamentary reform in the spring of 1793 by 108 votes to 29, on account

92. Evidence of Broomhead at Hardy's trial, *ST*, vol. 24, col. 605.
93. *Proceedings of the Public Meeting held at Sheffield*, p. 15.
94. *Ibid.*, p. 18.
95. G. P. Jones, 'The political reform movement in Sheffield', *Transactions of the Hunter Archaeological Society*, vol. 4 (1937), p. 65. Yorke carried out his promise to produce an abbreviated reprint of the Second Treatise, under the title *The Spirit of Locke: Thoughts on Civil Government*, after the meeting.
96. *Proceedings of the Public Meeting, etc.*, p. 21.
97. The address is contained in the *Proceedings*, pp. 27–44.

of the 'unparliamentary' language in which it had been expressed.[98] That dilemma had remained,

for if grievances, abuses, complaints and truth are to be discarded from that House, because not dressed in a gentlemanlike language, how are we, plain mechanics, ever to obtain redress, who are not gentlemen, and who are consequently ignorant of those polite and courtly expressions which are necessary to gain a hearing in that House?[99]

But their opponents, too, could be confronted with a dilemma more logically embarrassing. If MPs were, as was often claimed, the real representatives of the people, then the latter certainly had the right to dictate rather than petition – since the former were, in that case, merely the organs of the public will. If, on the contrary, MPs were not the representatives of the people, to petition them on that assumption would be 'a manifest absurdity, if not an insult and mockery of ourselves'.[100] The popular *right* to representation could, moreover, also be derived from 'the constitutional principles of their Saxon fathers'. The sad decline from the age of 'the immortal Alfred', when 'both the supreme magistrate and the legislative authority were elected by and responsible to the people' – to the age of George III in which the House of Commons had become 'an appendage of the Crown or of the Aristocracy' would need to be reversed.[101] The resurrection of ancestral liberties should therefore be demanded as a right not supplicated from an unheeding and corrupt legislature.

Yorke had not specified the short-run consequences of such a refusal to petition Parliament, but the government concluded, from these proceedings, that they were designed as a curtain-raiser for the second British Convention[102] – a conjecture that seemed to be confirmed, when the seizure of Hardy's papers in May revealed that preparations were in hand to make Sheffield an arsenal for a general distribution of pikes and other weapons to the reformers.[103]

The postponed general meeting of the London Corresponding Society took place on 14 April on the bowling green at Chalk Farm

98. Yorke had been present when the Commons rejected the petition on 2 May 1793.

99. *Proceedings*, p. 35.

100. *Ibid.*

101. *Ibid.*, p. 37.

102. 'The address from Sheffield to the nation . . . was intended to prepare the people for a convention.' *Second Report of the House of Commons Committee of Secrecy, Parl. Hist.*, vol. 31, col. 739.

103. *Ibid.*, cols. 689–91.

by the Hampstead Road at the foot of Primrose Hill. Whereas the Sheffield meeting had been summoned, at least nominally, to consider the presentation of a reform petition to Parliament, the London meeting did not even pretend to have that excuse.[104] On the other hand, although the occasion had been planned as part of the preparations for the eventual summons of a general convention, Thelwall saw to it that no formal resolution calling for such action was put.[105] The meeting was, in fact, remarkable for the sobriety of what Francis Place called 'the immense multitude . . . of *thinking* and *reasoning* men' who were present and the good order of the proceedings.[106] This was partly due to the careful and business-like arrangements made by Thelwall and partly to the invidious refusal of the magistrates, comfortably ensconced in a nearby tavern, to allow the local publican to serve the large crowds with food or drink, though the day was hot and the meeting protracted.[107] The chairman was John Lovett, a hairdresser; the letters exchanged between the society and the Association of Friends of the People on the subject of the proposed convention were read by John Richter; but the virtual director of the proceedings and chief speaker was Thelwall. Closely watched by a number of spies, detachments of troops in the offing and a numerous police force, the organizing committee secured the unanimous approval of the meeting for a lengthy list of resolutions mainly drafted, after careful deliberation, by Thelwall.[108] These expressed the society's indignation at the arbitrary proceedings of the executive and courts in Scotland, the increasing threats to public and private liberties in England and the imprisonment of the leaders of the United Irish in Dublin. The society boldly commended 'the disinterested patriotism' of its condemned delegates Margarot and Gerrald, emphasizing, at the same time, the strict conformity of their conduct with its own 'wishes and instructions'.[109] It stated, unequivocally, that 'the whole proceedings of the late British Convention of the

104. As the law stood, the calling of public meetings without authority and the specific intention of petitioning Parliament was of doubtful legality. H. L. Jephson, *The Platform: Its Rise and Progress* (London, 1892), vol. 1, p. 277.

105. Martin, the attorney, had drafted a provocative set of resolutions for submission to the general meeting, including one for the summons of a convention. *ST*, vol. 24, cols. 870–1. These draft resolutions had, however, been rejected by the organizing committee on the initiative of Thelwall.

106. BL, Add. MSS. 27814, fos. 74–6.

107. *Ibid.*, fo. 75.

108. *Ibid.*, fos. 70–3 and *ST*, vol. 24, cols. 735–41.

109. *ST*, vol. 24, col. 738.

people at Edinburgh' had merited 'its approbation and applause' and
stigmatized 'the arbitrary and flagitious proceedings of the court of
justiciary in Scotland' as reminiscent of 'the doctrines and practices
of the star chamber, in the times of Charles I'.[110] It also passed an
elaborate and moving address 'to our beloved and respected friend
and fellow citizen, a martyr to the glorious cause of equal representation' – Joseph Gerrald.[111] After rehearsing 'the late rapid advances
of despotism in Britain', the society went on to declare, in its most
challenging resolution, that

> any attempt to violate those yet remaining laws, which were intended for
> the security of Englishmen against the Tyranny of Courts and Ministers,
> and the Corruption of dependent Judges, by vesting in such Judges a
> legislative or arbitrary power (such as has lately been exercised by the
> Court of Justiciary in Scotland) ought to be considered as dissolving
> entirely the social compact between the English nation and their Gover-
> nors; and driving them to an immediate appeal to that incontrovertible
> maxim of eternal justice, *that the safety of the people is the* SUPREME, *and
> in cases of necessity, the* ONLY *law*.[112]

It was this resolution, the alleged attempt to incite popular resistance
to measures under active consideration in Parliament, and 'the open
attacks on all branches of the legislature' which aroused the particular censure of both the government and the House of Commons.[113]
All that the spies could contribute to the further discredit of the
society was the report that Thelwall, when quenching his thirst after
the five-hour meeting at a divisional supper in Compton St, had
removed the froth from his tankard with a knife and the comment –
'So should all tyrants be served'. The anecdote was entirely in character and is confirmed by the reliable testimony of Francis Place.[114]

On 2 May the Society for Constitutional Information celebrated

110. *Ibid.*
111. *Ibid.*, cols. 739–40.
112. Resolution 5, *ibid.*, col. 738.
113. *First Report from the Committee of Secrecy of the House of Commons on
Seditious Practices. Parl. Hist.*, vol. 31, col. 496.
114. BL, Add. MSS. 27814, fo. 76. A slightly different version appears in
Grove's report to Nepean, in PRO TS 11/954/3498, where Thelwall was said to
have 'blown' off the head of a pot of porter, remarking: 'This is the way I would
serve Kings.' Contrast with this, however, the last of the resolutions at Chalk
Farm: 'the firm conviction of this society that . . . whatever may be the interested
opinion of *hereditary* senators, or *packed* majorities of *pretended* representatives,
Truth and Liberty, in an age so enlightened as the present, must be Invincible
and Omnipotent.' *ST*, vol. 24, col. 739.

its fourteenth birthday by its traditional anniversary dinner at the Crown and Anchor. This was a purely convivial occasion and its main concern was for all to pass a congenial evening and no resolutions. Politics were to be confined to the toast list and (perhaps) to the incidental music. As a gesture of solidarity with the London Corresponding Society, a generous number of free tickets were distributed to a select group of its members, including, as it turned out, at least a couple of well-accredited government informers.[115] In all, the assembled company totalled upwards of 300. Perhaps the tone of the celebration might have been anticipated from the special invitation to chair the meeting accepted by Mr Wharton, MP for Beverley, who had only recently been informed by letter that he had been elected a member of the society.[116] Almost a year before, however, Wharton had moved in the Commons for a committee to enquire into, and if necessary, to restore the lost civil and constitutional liberties inherited from the Glorious Revolution of 1688.[117] His presence was, therefore, not only unique, but tendentious. Though the general conversation before dinner turned on a run of recent French military victories, and though the diners were electrified from time to time by the strains of the *Carmagnole*, and the *Ça ira*, and, above all, by the *Marseillaise*, the speeches struck a more sober note. Even Horne Tooke pretended not to be inebriated, though this was to impress the informers, who preferred, in fact, to believe their eyes rather than their ears.[118] Ironically, also, Tooke chose as his theme the demise of the constitution, suggesting that the society ought either to dissolve or change its name, since there was no longer a constitution in England to interpret or defend.[119] In bitter and cantankerous mood he lavished the adjective 'scoundrel' indiscriminately on the ministry, Parliament and Opposition, whose combination was for him 'a scoundrel coalition' – 'to betray that poor man the King, to insult and betray the Hereditary nobility of the country, and to abuse the people'. Even the people were 'blind and stupid' – though 'he had no object but their good and

115. 'Citizen' Groves and Taylor.
116. Examination of John Wharton MP before Privy Council, 24 May 1794. PRO PC 1/22/A 36(a). Tooke had told him privately that 'the society was rather falling into disrepute' and that his agreement to join 'might be a credit to it'.
117. *Parl. Hist.*, vol. 30, col. 965 (31 May 1793). Wharton had been thanked for this speech by the SCI on 14 June 1793. PRO TS 11/962/3508, fo. 141.
118. Groves commented: 'I cannot say I think Mr. Tooke was sober, he certainly affected coolness.' PRO TS 11/954/3498.
119. Taylor's report. *Ibid.*

did not care if he was hanged in their service'.[120] It was, indeed, fortunate for Tooke that the constitution, whose demise he had deplored, proved more robust than he was willing to concede – otherwise he might have achieved a more notable martyrdom than even Gerrald or Margarot. The society it was that died.

The Privy Council, however, when examining the informers who had been present and the chairman, showed more interest in, and affected more alarm at, the toasts than the speeches. Wharton confessed he had been doubtful about the toast, 'The armies contending for liberty', and thought the sentiment 'May the abettors of the present war be its victims', improper rather than criminal. He was even prepared to defend the toast 'The persecuted patriots of England'.[121] For the rest the toasts were either merely ironical or traditional, and Ashley of the London Corresponding Society was probably not alone when he later admitted before the Privy Council that he had drunk them with more gusto than understanding.[122] According to Wharton, the toast to Thomas Paine had been an afterthought, not having been in the original toast list, but it was 'called for clamorously at the end of the day and was not formally given from the Chair'.[123] Perhaps, however, it was the proper note on which the society should have ended its existence – for it did not meet again.

Although neither the Sheffield nor the Chalk Farm meeting had called for a general convention, the government could no longer afford to ignore the accumulating signs that the secret committee of the London Corresponding Society was only awaiting a favourable response from the provincial societies before issuing such a summons.[124] Decisive intervention to forestall such action and to terminate the emergency was also considered necessary in order to counter the recently revealed invasion threat from France, enemy intrigues in

120. Groves's report. PRO TS 11/954/3498.

121. Examination of Wharton before Privy Council. 24 May 1794. PRO PC 1/22/A 36(a). For the full list of toasts see *ST*, vol. 24, cols. 571–2.

122. P. A. Brown, *The French Revolution in English History* (London, 1965 reprint), p. 116.

123. PRO PC 1/22/A 36(a). On 16 June Wharton, having read the *Second Report of the House of Commons Committee of Secrecy*, thought it his duty publicly to repudiate the conduct of the radical societies, by voting for the Royal Address. *Parl. Hist.*, vol. 31, col. 931.

124. It is a curious fact that late in April 1794 both the Sheffield and Norwich Constitutional Societies in response to the circular letters from the LCS had begun to have doubts about the expedience or timeliness of a national convention. PRO TS 11/955/3500.

Ireland, and the increasing violence of radical remonstrances. At 6.30 a.m. on Monday 12 May, Thomas Hardy, secretary of the London Corresponding Society and Daniel Adams, secretary of the Society for Constitutional Information were arrested at their homes on charges of treasonable practices and large consignments of their papers, books and documents were also seized.[125] Dundas, as Home Secretary, announced these measures in the Commons, later in the day, quoting from a royal message which referred to the contemplated summons of

a pretended general convention of the people, in contempt and defiance of the authority of parliament, and on principles subversive of the existing laws and constitution, and directly tending to the introduction of that system of anarchy and confusion which has fatally prevailed in France.[126]

On 13 May Pitt moved, and the Commons agreed, that the confiscated papers of the radical societies should be referred to a committee of secrecy of twenty-one members, which was supposedly chosen by ballot on the following day.[127] The committee consisted of ministerialists – Pitt himself and Dundas – Alarmists like Burke, conservative Whigs like Windham and Thomas Grenville,[128] and an official legal element, in the persons of the Attorney and Solicitor General and the Lord Advocate of Scotland – all of whom were committed to repression. Although Pitt was strictly correct in not including any members of the Foxite Opposition, Fox bitterly complained that the committee consisted only of 'men who were either dupes themselves, or men who are willing to dupe others'.[129] A similar secret committee of nine in the Lords also included three of the conservative Whig peers – Portland himself, Carlisle and Mansfield.[130]

In the next few days further arrests were made – mainly of those who had been delegates of the two metropolitan societies on their

125. The MS. journal of the LCS (BL, Add. MSS. 27812) was, at the time of Hardy's arrest, not in his possession, since the latest entries were being made by Pearce, clerk to Martin the attorney, and did not in fact ever come into the hands of the government.

126. *Parl. Hist.*, vol. 31, col. 471.

127. *Ibid.*, col. 474.

128. Technically the conservative or Portland Whigs were still in Opposition and their inclusion marked a further step in Pitt's efforts to make possible that national coalition which was achieved in July 1794. O'Gorman, p. 190.

129. *Parl. Hist.*, vol. 31, col. 555. 'The dupes' were, of course, the conservative (Portland) Whigs.

130. *Ibid.*, col. 573.

joint committee of co-operation and communication.[131] Thelwall and the Reverend Jeremiah Joyce were picked up on 13 May; Horne Tooke, John Lovett, who had chaired the Chalk Farm meeting, John Richter and John Augustus Bonney on the 16th.[132] Not all the wanted men were immediately secured. Thomas Wardle, Matthew Moore and Richard Hodgson – a Westminster hatter whose extremist views earned him the title of 'Jacobin' – all evaded their warrants. The warrant against John Baxter the Shoreditch journeyman silversmith who had succeeded Margarot as chairman of the London Corresponding Society, was only served on him at the end of June. Thomas Holcroft, the dramatist, against whom no warrant had been issued, only surrendered voluntarily to the courts on 7 October, the day after the Grand Jury of Middlesex had found a true bill against himself and the other prisoners for high treason.[133] Of the provincial leaders Joseph Gales of the *Sheffield Register* went into temporary hiding before escaping to Germany late in June and then to the United States in July 1795,[134] while his associate, Henry Yorke, on his way out of the country, was arrested on 16 June at Hull by an astute collector of customs.[135] In Norwich, Isaac Saint, landlord of the Pelican inn in Colgate, was brought to London for examination by the Privy Council, as were also a number of officials and members of the Sheffield Constitutional Society, who were rounded up at the end of May and induced to act as Crown witnesses in the trial of Hardy and later of Henry Yorke.[136]

The sense of urgency and alarm which had meanwhile gripped the Commons showed itself in the first report of its committee of secrecy which was presented to the House on 16 May – the day after its appointment.[137] Burke himself could well have written it the day before its appointment. In a succinct but general survey of the activities of the metropolitan reform societies since 1792, the report insis-

131. 'Names of persons committed for High Treason and on suspicion of Treason'. PRO TS 11/965/3510A.

132. For Thelwall's account of his arrest see the *Tribune* (1795), vol. 1, pp. 85–7; and for Joyce's see '*An Account of Mr. Joyce's Arrest for "Treasonable Practices"* etc.', 2nd ed. (London, 1795).

133. *ST*, vol. 34, col. 212.

134. For Gales's journey to the United States see 'The diary of Joseph Gales, 1794–1795', W. S. Powell (ed.), *North Carolina Historical Review*, vol. 24 (1949), pp. 335–46.

135. PRO TS 11/963/3509.

136. *Norfolk Chronicle and Norwich Gazette*, 17 May 1794. PRO TS 11/957/3502. *ST*, vol. 25, cols. 1121–31.

137. *Parl. Hist.*, vol. 31, col. 475.

ted that, throughout this period, marked by the spread of Painite principles and their addresses to the French National Convention, the radicals had been 'uniformly and systematically pursuing a settled design, which appears to your committee to tend to the subversion of the established constitution, and which has of late been more openly avowed and attempted to be carried into full execution'.[138] The measures recently taken by these societies, acting in concert, to summon a second British Convention – in England – it construed as 'an open attempt to supersede the House of Commons in its representative capacity and to assume to itself all the functions and powers of a national legislature'.[139] In its conclusion the report referred briefly to the steps which had recently been taken to provide and distribute arms to the societies and noted that the arrest of their leaders had not deterred the radicals from continuing their meetings or from persisting in their plans and that they showed every sign of preparing to resist repression by force.[140]

On the strength of this report Pitt immediately introduced a bill for the limited suspension of Habeas Corpus.[141] Though this proposal was bitterly opposed by the Foxite Whigs, who divided the house upon it fourteen times and threatened even to secede from Parliament, the bill passed its third reading in the early hours of 18 May by 146 votes to 28.[142] It passed the Lords on 22 May and received the royal assent on the following day. If the act only applied to those who were suspected of complicity in the alleged treasonable conspiracy and was limited in its duration to about eight months, it nevertheless gave the government the power to hold the radical leaders in prison for a considerable period without bringing them to trial.[143]

It was at this point that the accidental discovery of pikeheads and battleaxes, during the search of a bankrupt's house in Edinburgh, placed in the government's hands evidence of a real treasonable conspiracy, which appeared to have connections with the radical plans for holding a general convention in England.[144] In fact the conspiracy was a legacy of the earlier British Convention and was master-

138. *Ibid.*, cols. 475–6.
139. *Ibid.*, col. 495.
140. *Ibid.*, cols. 496–7.
141. *Parl. Hist.*, vol. 31, cols. 497–505.
142. *Ibid.*, col. 573.
143. Thurlow stressed these limitations on the scope of the act in the Lords on 22 May. *Ibid.*, cols. 587–8.
144. Meikle, *Scotland and the French Revolution* (Glasgow, 1912), pp. 150–2; Brown, pp. 125–6.

minded by Robert Watt – an Edinburgh wine merchant and former
government spy, who may have wished to re-establish his credit by
acting as an unofficial *agent provocateur*, or who may, as he later
confessed, have been converted to radicalism by his earlier activities.[145]
Watt was a member not only of a so-called Committee of Union,
consisting of delegates from four reform societies in the Edinburgh
district which had continued to meet after the dissolution of the convention, but also of a permanent and secret 'Committee of Ways and
Means' which had been elected early in March 1794.[146] It was to this
small executive subcommittee that Watt had disclosed his plans for
an armed insurrection in Edinburgh aimed at forcing the King to
dismiss his ministers and to terminate the war on pain of 'abiding the
consequences'.[147] His plan was to draw the garrison troops of
Edinburgh castle out of their quarters at dead of night by starting a
fire in the Excise Office, and to overcome them in detail by armed
rebels stationed at strategic points, as they passed through the city.[148]
The Lord Provost, the Lord Justice Clerk – the hated Braxfield – and
the judges of the Court of Justiciary were to be seized and held as
hostages and a ready-made treasury was to be acquired by capturing
the city's banking houses.[149] Preparations for this *coup* had begun
with attempts to subvert the local troops and the despatch of a commissioner to the west of Scotland to attract support and to collect
contributions, allegedly for the relief of Skirving's wife.[150] These were
to be diverted to the use of the conspirators by the treasurer of the
Committee of Ways and Means – an Edinburgh goldsmith named
David Downie.[151] Watt had also engaged several blacksmiths, including one called Orrock, to manufacture pikes and other weapons.[152]
As these arrangements were proceeding, copies of Hardy's circular
letters suggesting the summons of a second British Convention on
English soil had been received in Edinburgh and had been passed on

145. Watt's trial is in *ST*, vol. 23.
146. The Committee of Ways and Means was originally established to consider
ways of repaying a debt of £20 due to Skirving from the first British Convention.
ST, vol. 24, col. 857.
147. A proclamation in this sense was to be issued and sent to the King after
the success of the *coup*. *ST*, vol. 24, col. 855.
148. Dundas to Pitt, 23 May 1794. *Second Report of Commons Committee of
Secrecy. Parl. Hist.*, vol. 31, col. 699.
149. *ST*, vol. 24, col. 62.
150. *Ibid.*, cols. 101–2.
151. His trial for high treason appears in *ST*, vol. 24, cols. 2–200.
152. *Ibid.*, col. 90.

to Perth, Paisley, Strathaven and Dundee.[153] All these plans had been frustrated by the accidental discovery of arms caches at Watt's and Orrock's houses on 15 and 16 May and preliminary details of the conspiracy were communicated to Pitt by Dundas on the 19th.[154] Downie and Watt were arrested and imprisoned on charges of high treason.[155]

The second report of the Commons Committee of Secrecy was ready on 6 June and was debated on the 16th. Its purpose was three-fold. First, it set out to demonstrate – from the insurrectionary conspiracy in Scotland, the active preparation and collection of arms in Sheffield, and the training of members of the London Corresponding Society in the use of arms – that the radicals were resolved, when ready, to resort to open violence.[156] Secondly, it argued that the radicals' repeated insistence on the need to achieve parliamentary reform by legal and constitutional methods had always been intended to conceal their preference for revolutionary change by means of a national convention.[157] This conclusion was enforced by retracing the history of the Society for Constitutional Information and its disciple, the London Corresponding Society, from the year 1792, so that their fundamental principles could be attributed to Painite and their ideology to French revolutionary influences.[158] Thirdly, it contended that the avowed attempt to summon a second British Convention had been prompted by the dissolution and conditioned by the resolutions of the first British Convention.[159] The purpose of the convention was, therefore, either to overawe the legislature to secure universal suffrage and annual elections, or to supersede Parliament entirely in order to destroy the whole fabric of the constitution and of society itself.[160] The report rested this thesis on the evidence of intimidated prisoners and witnesses examined by the Privy Council,

153. *Ibid.*, col. 56.

154. *Parl. Hist.*, vol. 31, col. 696.

155. They were tried in September and found guilty – Watt being executed in October while Downie was pardoned.

156. *Parl. Hist.*, vol. 31, cols. 689–96, 740.

157. *Ibid.*, cols. 722–4.

158. *Ibid.*, cols. 710–22. Particular emphasis was placed on the radical addresses to the National Convention in November–December 1792 and Barère's speech on the powers of the Convention in relation to the execution of Louis XVI, which had been incorporated in the records of the SCI. *Ibid.*, cols. 714–16.

159. The proceedings of the British Convention were regarded as so important that the report gave 'a connected account' of them with references to extracts from its minutes in an appendix. *Ibid.*, cols. 727–33.

160. *Ibid.*, cols. 740–1.

on the latest information on the treasonable conspiracies in Scotland and Ireland and on up-to-the-minute details of the continued surreptitious activity and para-military organization of the London Corresponding Society after the arrest of its leaders.[161] Lengthy extracts from the minutes, resolutions and declarations of the metropolitan and provincial radical societies since 1792 were provided in a series of appendices.[162]

The far from objective findings of the report, reflecting substantially the views of the government and the Alarmists, were briefly summarized in an even more tendentious address to the Crown moved in, and approved by, the House of Lords on 13 June.[163] This referred to the existence of 'a seditious and traitorous conspiracy, directed to the subversion of the authority of your majesty and your parliament and to the utter destruction of the established constitution and government of these your majesty's kingdoms'.[164] When this address was debated in the Commons on the 16th, Fox regretted that Parliament should be kept sitting 'to echo back the information received from the privy council', noted that Lord Howe's naval victory of 'the glorious 1st of June' had effectively removed all danger of a French invasion, and suggested that if a convention with such exiguous forces at its command attempted to exercise 'any authority contrary to law' it could, in his view, be easily dispersed by the nearest magistrate.[165] If, he said, Parliament had approved such an address before the recent scandalous trial of his friend Thomas Walker of Manchester for a conspiracy, the jury which had acquitted him might have been prejudiced and misled by such a declaration and might have found him guilty in the teeth of the evidence and in spite of the obvious perjury of the main witness.[166] By asserting its belief in a similar

161. It referred, in particular, to the 'Committee of Emergency' appointed by the society to resist government repressive measures. *Parl. Hist.*, vol. 31, col. 741.

162. *Ibid.*, cols. 744–879.

163. *Ibid.*, cols. 911–13.

164. *Ibid.*, col. 912.

165. *Ibid.*, cols. 923–4.

166. *Ibid.*, col. 926. Thomas Walker had been tried at Lancaster Assizes on 2 April 1794, along with nine other members of the Manchester radical societies, on a charge of conspiring to overthrow the King, constitution and government, and 'to aid and assist the French in case of invasion'. He was acquitted, largely owing to the perjury of the main witness against him, Thomas Dunn, a drunken Irish weaver, who had been encouraged to accuse Walker of high treason by the Rev. Maurice Griffith, of the local 'Church and King' club. Walker had the benefit of Erskine as his defence counsel. F. Knight, *The Strange Case of Thomas Walker* (London, 1957), ch. 15.

'conspiracy' on evidence hardly less suspect, Parliament would be pre-judging the cases of the radical leaders shortly to stand their trial for high treason.[167] This was precisely what Parliament did when it approved the royal address in its unamended form.

This extra-judicial pronouncement of Parliament had a significant bearing on the preparation of the case against the accused. Even before the actual arrests the Attorney General, Sir John Scott, had consulted his legal advisers as to what charges might be preferred against the Society for Constitutional Information, which, at the end of January 1794, had seemed to be taking the lead in the open defiance of government.[168] The past proceedings and recent resolutions of the society were, therefore, submitted for an opinion on the extent of their criminality to Spencer Perceval. Replying on 2 March 1794, in an assessment which paid an unconscious tribute to the restraining influence exerted by Horne Tooke, Perceval noted that 'the same spirit of sedition and mischief seems to show itself in equal degree through the whole, while the same caution is always at work, keeping them within the bounds of misdemeanour, and out of the reach of a heavier charge'.[169] Even their resolutions of 17 January 1794, 'when, if ever, their caution nearly forsook them', would not 'upon examination be thought to amount to high treason'. He also reminded Scott that, in their instructions to their delegates to the British Convention in Edinburgh, the society had been 'particularly cautious to repeat the *constitutional* and *peaceable* methods' by which their objects were to be pursued in that assembly. Nor did Perceval think it at all likely, from their past conduct, that the members of the society would 'proceed to any act of Treason, till they have made themselves believe that they have a very near prospect of its success'.[170]

Mr Lowndes, writing from chambers in the Temple on 29 April 1794, on the very eve of the arrests, also advised Scott that the proceedings of the Society for Constitutional Information still 'fell short of the crime of High Treason'.[171] Even the society's delegation to the French National Convention and its subscription in aid of the French had not directly involved 'concert with the king's enemies' and had occurred before the declaration of war. Since then, he observed, the society 'appears to have been much on their guard'.

167. *Parl. Hist.*, vol. 31, col. 926.
168. PRO TS 11/959/3505(i).
169. *Ibid.*
170. *Ibid.*
171. PRO TS 11/959/3505(ii).

Nor had they, as yet, subscribed to 'the tenets published from Nottingham and Sheffield, which go far beyond any idea of seeking a reform by legal temperate means'.[172] To discover 'the channel of communications', Lowndes advocated the seizure of the society's books and papers, because no reliance, in securing convictions, could be placed on purely parole evidence.

Several considerations, however, caused Scott to indict the prisoners, not for sedition, as he had been advised, but for high treason. Among those whom he had consulted had been the judges who were members of the Privy Council and who had been present at the lengthy examination of the accused, witnesses and government informers during May and June 1794. They had stated, when consulted, that in their considered judgement, the prisoners were guilty of high treason.[173] The trial warrants had also treated the accused as committed for high treason, and the debates in Parliament on the reports of the committees of secrecy of both Lords and Commons had indicated that felony rather than misdemeanour was involved. In view of these weighty pronouncements Scott, as Attorney General and public prosecutor, had not felt himself 'at Liberty in the indictment to let down the character of the offence'.[174] He had also felt himself impaled on the horns of a legal dilemma – for if the radical leaders had been indicted for sedition and the evidence in court had later proved a case of high treason, this would have entitled them to an acquittal for the misdemeanour and would have virtually debarred their subsequent indictment for high treason.[175] Scott's overriding concern, however, was to use the trials to convince the public at large of the full extent of the dangers to which it would have been exposed if the radicals had been allowed to meet in a general convention.[176] This was the reason why, at the risk of exhausting or confusing the jury, Scott decided to lay before the court every scrap of printed or manuscript evidence bearing on the radicals' alleged

172. *Address to the British Nation*, drawn up by the committee of the Sheffield Constitutional Society in accordance with the instructions of the public meeting of 7 April 1794. Sheffield Central Reference Library, Local Pamphlets, vol. 80(3), pp. 27–44. I have not been able to trace any reference to similar declarations from Nottingham.

173. *Lord Eldon's Anecdote Book*, ed. A. L. J. Lincoln and R. L. McEwen (London, 1960), p. 56.

174. *Ibid.*

175. *Ibid.*, p. 56.

176. Eldon referred to his main aim in the prosecution as 'the great object of satisfying the country and making them aware of their danger'. *Ibid.*

treasonable practices since 1792.[177] As he himself subsequently admitted, the purpose behind such a wearisome form of prosecution was, less the conviction of the accused, than the fullest rehearsal of the dangers confronting both government and society at a time of grave national emergency.[178] That being so, Scott had clearly allowed his fears as an 'Alarmist' to dictate his conduct as Attorney General.

Parliament's extra-judicial intervention also influenced a further controversial aspect of legal procedure in the preliminaries to the State Trials. This was the much-criticized charge delivered by Lord Chief Justice, Sir James Eyre, to the grand jury of Middlesex on 2 October 1794.[179] After an impartial exposition of the nature of high treason, as defined by the governing statute of 25 Edward III, and as interpreted by Sir Matthew Hale and Sir Michael Foster, Eyre himself adopted the construction which Parliament had placed on the plans to summon a convention – namely that its purpose was either to usurp the functions and authority of the legislature, and thereby to subvert both the monarchy and the government, or to overawe Parliament in order to extort from it universal suffrage and annual elections.[180] The judge directed that, in either case, the grand jury should return a true bill against the accused as indicated, though he himself regarded it as 'doubtful' whether an attempt solely to overawe Parliament would amount to high treason. In his view, however, it would be as well if this dubious issue were 'put into a judicial course of enquiry, so that it might receive a solemn adjudication'.[181] On 6 October the grand jury returned a true bill for high treason against twelve of the accused – Thomas Hardy, John Richter, Matthew Moore, John Thelwall, Richard Hodgson and John Baxter of the London Corresponding Society, and Horne Tooke, John Augustus Bonney, Stewart Kyd, Jeremiah Joyce, Thomas Wardle and Thomas Holcroft of the Society for Constitutional Information. Lovett was discharged.[182] Four of the accused – Wardle, Moore, Hodgson and Holcroft – were still not in custody, but in a dramatic gesture that redounded to the credit of the reformers, Holcroft appeared in court

177. *Ibid.*, pp. 56–7.

178. 'It appeared to me to be more essential to securing the public safety that the whole of their transactions should be published, than that any of these Individuals should be convicted.' *Ibid.*, p. 56.

179. *ST*, vol. 24, cols. 200–10.

180. *Ibid.*, cols. 207–8.

181. *Ibid.*, col. 210.

182. *Ibid.*, cols. 212–13. After his release, Lovett, like so many other radicals at this time, emigrated to the United States.

on the following day and voluntarily surrendered himself to imprisonment in Newgate.[183] Before doing so, however, Holcroft summoned to his aid his friend William Godwin, then on a visit to Dr Parr in Warwickshire.[184] Returning post haste to the capital, Godwin spent several days considering the full implications of the charge and studying the views expounded by Eyre to the grand jury. On Friday and Saturday 17 and 18 October he 'locked himself up' to write the *Cursory Strictures* which first appeared in the *Morning Chronicle* of the 20th.[185] This contribution represented perhaps the most signal service Godwin ever rendered to the cause of radicalism – in so far as it demonstrated that ministers, Crown lawyers, Privy Counsellors, judges and even parliamentarians had not 'the clear and andoubted grounds' for incriminating the prisoners that they had claimed. It also showed Erskine, the main defence counsel, how vulnerable the doctrine of 'constructive treason' was and how it could be demolished. 'This', Godwin wrote,

is the most important crisis in the history of English liberty, that the world ever saw. If men can be convicted of High Treason, upon such constructions and implications as are contained in this charge, we may look with conscious superiority upon the republican speculations of France, but we shall certainly have reason to envy the milder tyrannies of Turkey and Ispahan.[186]

If a true bill could be returned against the prisoners so that a dubious case of 'constructive' treason should be determined in the courts, Godwin's savage indignation was surely justified. 'According to this method of estimate', the *Strictures* implied, 'laws, precedents, cases and reports are of high value, and the hanging of a few individuals is a very cheap, economical and proper way of purchasing the decision of a doubtful speculation'.[187] The proper method of creating new treasons unknown to the law was not by judicial interpretation but by the passing of special legislation. The rest of the charge Godwin 'cursorily' dismissed as 'made up of hypothesis, presumption, prejudication and conjecture'.[188] It suddenly began to look as if the real

183. *ST*, vol. 24, col. 214.
184. C. Kegan Paul, *William Godwin: His Friends and Contemporaries* (London, 1876), vol. 1, p. 118.
185. *Ibid.*
186. *Cursory Strictures on the charge delivered by Lord Chief Justice Eyre to the Grand Jury, Oct. 2, 1794*, p. 24.
187. *Ibid.*, p. 22.
188. *Ibid.*, p. 10.

'conspiracy' was one against the prisoners and of which Godwin did not hesitate to say that the chief architect was Pitt himself.[189]

This incident was a modest consolation for the prisoners now facing their long-awaited trials. For most of them, but particularly for Hardy, Tooke and Thelwall who had to bear the main burden of the state prosecutions, the period of waiting had been a protracted and painful ordeal. Closely confined in the Tower, guarded by soldiers with fixed bayonets and pried on by churlish wardens, with few privileges or visitors, anxiously aware of the government's attempts to turn popular hostility against them, they had only the consciousness of their own innocence and their courage to sustain them against the petty tyrannies of prison discipline and the daunting prospect of eventual trial for their lives.[190] Hardy was the chief victim, for during the celebrations on 11 June of Lord Howe's famous naval victory, his house and shop in Piccadilly, although patriotically illuminated, had been made the target of rioting crowds and his pregnant wife, in trying to escape, had suffered injuries which in August proved fatal.[191] Her child was stillborn. The unrepentant and normally resilient Tooke was racked with illness and with anxiety about the welfare of his two natural daughters, full of complaints at being kept 'in closer custody than was used in the Bastille', but characteristically managed to keep up a cheerful flow of occasional banter with his fellow prisoners and confined his more sombre thoughts to the diary of his tribulations written on the interleaved pages of his personal copy of the *Diversions of Purley*.[192] His nearby neighbour Thelwall, perplexed by financial worries and his wife's ill health, seething with indignation at the seizure of his valuable collection of prints and engravings, calmed himself by writing occasional verse, reading *Macbeth* and composing improving meditations on Nature, Freedom and Humanity.[193]

At long last the final preparations for the trials were completed.

189. 'The man in whose mind the scheme of this trial was engendered was Pitt.' Paul, vol. 1, p. 118.

190. Entry in Tooke's prison diary for 25 July 1794: 'I cannot find any one Action that I have committed, any word that I have written, any syllable that I have uttered, or any single thought that I have entertained, of a political nature, which I wish either to conceal or recall.' BL, *Diversions of Purley*, vol. 1, pp. 103 ff.

191. Brown, p. 123.

192. Tooke's two-volume work, *The Diversions of Purley*, is called by Hazlitt 'one of the few philosophical works on Grammar that were ever written'. Essay on Tooke, *Spirit of the Age*, ed. E. D. Mackerness (London, 1969).

193. Thelwall, *Tribune*, vol. 1, pp. 306, 318–19.

On 24 October the seven prisoners in the Tower were removed to Newgate to join Holcroft and Baxter.[194] On the following day, after being formally arraigned at the Sessions House in the Old Bailey, all pleaded not guilty. At the request of their defending counsel – Thomas Erskine and Mr Gibbs – it was agreed that they should be tried separately and the Attorney General announced his intention to proceed first against Thomas Hardy.[195] This was because Hardy, as secretary of the London Corresponding Society, could be proved to have been personally concerned in the active preparations for the summons of the proposed English convention by his despatch of circular letters to the provincial radical societies in April 1794, and also because it was thought he might be compromised by correspondence from Sheffield on the question of the provision of arms to the radical societies in London and Norwich.[196] It was also apparent that the effective direction of the whole radical movement during the crisis of confrontation had been assumed by the London Corresponding Society and that some members of the Society for Constitutional Information had only acquiesced in the plans for an English convention with marked reluctance.[197]

Scott, however, soon made it clear that Hardy and the other prisoners were not being prosecuted as individuals, but as responsible members of two closely associated metropolitan societies which, under cover of a lawful campaign for the reform of the House of Commons, had sought to assemble a popular convention intended to usurp the functions of both legislature and executive, subvert the monarchy and bring about the deposition and death of the sovereign, as stated in the indictment.[198] After instructing the jury that they should in no way be influenced by the extra-judicial opinion expressed by Parliament, and categorically repudiating the use of the 'constructive' interpretation of the extent of high treason, the Attorney General embarked on a 100 000-word speech for the prosecution which lasted nine hours.[199] This largely recapitulated the evidence and conclusions

194. *Ibid.*, pp. 311 ff.
195. *ST*, vol. 24, col. 238.
196. See below, pp. 345, 350.
197. When Thelwall first submitted a sketch of a convention to the joint committee of the LCS and SCI on 7 April 1794, the members of the SCI wished to use the term 'meeting' instead. When Thelwall insisted, the compromise solution of 'Convention or meeting' was adopted. PRO TS 11/955/3500.
198. *ST*, vol. 24, cols. 263–5.
199. *Ibid.*, col. 252; for the speech itself see pp. 241–370. Thurlow's comment is well known: 'Nine hours. Then there is no treason, by God!'

set out in the reports of the committee of secrecy of the House of Commons and did, in fact, resort to the use of constructive reasoning to demonstrate that the summons of a convention would necessarily have obliged the King to resist such an attempt to take over political sovereignty and would ultimately have resulted in his deposition and death.[200] Only in this way could the 'overt acts' alleged against Hardy and his colleagues be used as evidence of their treasonable intentions of 'compassing' the death of the King as laid down in the Edwardian statute.[201] This approach involved the rehearsal of every scrap of evidence, not only against Hardy, but against all the radical societies, metropolitan or provincial, engaged in the alleged subversive conspiracy – their minutes and resolutions dating back to 1792, every 'seditious' pamphlet ever presented to them or circulated by them, their messages of sympathy and support to the French Jacobin societies, their addresses to the French National Convention, their slavish adoption of the forms of address and procedures of the French revolutionary assemblies, their toasts to the success of the revolutionary armies, Thelwall's ridicule and denigration of George III, the vilification of Pitt's administration and the public meetings of protest on the eve of confrontation.[202] All these transactions, and in particular the radical addresses to the French National Convention, were depicted as 'the measures of determined Republicans, going out of their way to express their zeal in the cause of Republicanism'.[203] As evidence that the radicals had preached moderate and constitutional reform merely to conceal these treasonable designs against the constitution, Scott instanced their adoption of the ideas of 'representative government' as advocated by Paine.[204] He endeavoured to prove that the radical petitions to Parliament in 1793 had never been genuine and that their concealed motive had merely been to strengthen the case for the subsequent resort to the holding of conventions first in Scotland and then in England.[205] Similarly, Scott interpreted the radical outcries against the persecution of the English delegates to the Scottish convention as a cover for the clandestine preparations

200. *Ibid.*, cols. 264–5.

201. 25 Ed. III. *ST*, vol. 24, col. 250.

202. *ST*, vol. 24, cols. 281–370.

203. This was the imputation placed on the addresses by the prosecution, as Eyre noted in his summing up, leaving it to the jury to judge how far it was merited. *Ibid.*, col. 1366.

204. *Ibid.*, cols. 282, 290.

205. *Ibid.*, cols. 327–8.

for the summons of an English convention.[206] The fact that the Scottish convention had ended without violence and that the English convention never actually met did not indicate that the radicals were either moderates or constitutionalists, but merely that they had been prevented from carrying out their nefarious designs by the vigilance of the authorities.[207] Scott concluded his case against Hardy with a brief 'outline' of the evidence which the Crown witnesses were to give of his complicity in the plans for the wholesale manufacture of pikes at Sheffield and their distribution among the metropolitan and provincial radicals.[208] He also referred to Hardy's dealings with individual members of 'a military society' in Lambeth, who were equipped with muskets and had engaged in drilling. This organization, he implied, was an insurrectionary offshoot of the London Corresponding Society.[209]

After the examination of the Crown witnesses had got under way and midnight approached, the court decided, on Erskine's intervention, to adjourn the sitting till 8 a.m. on the following morning.[210] It also agreed to allow the defence counsel, at Erskine's request, to defer addressing the jury, in order that they might examine the accumulated mass of documentary evidence recited by Scott, the manuscript part of which had not been made available to them.[211] Temporary arrangements were then made for the jury to pass the night at the Old Bailey on mattresses, while Hardy was taken back to Newgate.

The first day's proceedings set the pattern for the rest of the protracted and exhausting trial in the crowded court room. Beginning each morning at 8 or 9 a.m., the prosecution dragged on till long after midnight, Erskine rarely reaching his bed before 2 or 3 a.m.[212] The examination of the Crown witnesses proved even more time-consuming than Scott's opening speech, with Erskine challenging their evidence at every point and employing bullying tactics and innuendo to undermine their credibility.[213] Four days went by in this way in the consideration of still further written and parole evidence,

206. *Ibid.*, cols. 350–2.   207. *Ibid.*, col. 270.   208. *Ibid.*, col. 368.
209. *Ibid.*, cols. 368–9.   210. *Ibid.*, col. 420.   211. *Ibid.*, cols. 419–20.
212. *Ibid.*, col. 861.
213. An example of his domineering cross-examination is that of Henry Alexander, linen draper. 'Erskine: "You need not look at me. I shall hear it well enough; why do you hesitate? – come, cough it up, answer me that upon your oath; are you acquainted with Mr. Dunn of Manchester?" – "No." ' *Ibid.* col. 643. 'Erskine: "Then you do not speak the truth, I suppose, unless when you are upon oath?" – "Yes I do." ' *Ibid.*, col. 645.

with the tension mounting as the exchanges between Erskine and the Attorney and Solicitor Generals, from being formally polite, became steadily more abrupt and abrasive. After the first night the members of the jury were found more comfortable quarters in the Hummums (!) in Covent Garden, where they were accompanied by the under sheriffs and court officers.[214] Each night Hardy returned under guard to Newgate and each morning he left for the Old Bailey, blithely remarking to his fellow prisoners as he passed their cells: 'Farewell, citizens, Death or Liberty.'[215] At that stage there did not seem more than a fifty–fifty chance of his acquittal.

At about one o'clock in the morning of Saturday 1 November the Crown case for the prosecution was drawing to its close, Erskine was exhausted and ill and the court was due to resume to hear his speech for the defence in a few hours. Just as the court was about to adjourn, Erskine again made an urgent plea for further time to consider the vast volume of evidence which had been brought against Hardy and to consult with his colleague as to the best method of defence. Copies of the unprinted material which Scott had used had still not reached him, two days had been consumed in hearing the parole evidence, and illness had prevented him from using the time which the court had previously granted for the review of the documents. He suggested that if a few hours were allowed to the defence counsel to arrange their papers and to select those on which they would base their case for Hardy's acquittal, time would be saved.[216] When Erskine proposed, as an expedient, that the court should be adjourned till noon, the Lord Chief Justice at first offered, out of consideration for the jury, to resume at eleven o'clock, but, on the intervention of a juryman in Erskine's favour, finally agreed to an adjournment as originally proposed.[217] This was to prove a vital tactical advantage for the defence, for the presiding judge had indicated that he did not intend to sit on Sunday and Erskine could, therefore, hope that his opening speech for the defence would remain uppermost in the jury's mind over the weekend.[218]

On Saturday 1 November the court resumed its sitting, as agreed,

214. *Ibid.*, cols. 572–3.
215. Thelwall, *Tribune*, vol. 3, p. 212. '*Vivre libre ou mourir*' was the motto of the French Jacobin society. Erskine himself had returned from Paris in 1790 wearing buttons inscribed with this legend. S. Romilly, *Life of Sir Samuel Romilly* (London, 1842), vol. 1, p. 312.
216. *ST*, vol. 24, cols. 861–3.
217. *Ibid.*, col. 865.
218. C. B. Cone, *The English Jacobins* (New York, 1968), p. 205.

at noon to hear the Attorney General conclude the evidence for the Crown – Gibbs deputizing for Erskine in the cross-examination of the witnesses.[219] Erskine, however, was now ready with the six-hour speech for the defence which he had composed since the court's adjournment. At the end of this speech in his printed copy of Hardy's trial, Horne Tooke added the brief postscript: 'This speech will live for ever.'[220] Holcroft also, among many others, paid tribute.

Your speech in favour of Hardy at the close of the evidence for the Crown, was such that every creature who witnessed it, young or old, never mention it in my hearing but with rapture. Accompanied as it was by that profound sense of the magnitude of the cause you had to defend, and by that almost superhuman energy, for such it is described to have been, with which its momentous consequences inspired you, the words you uttered were engraven upon the hearts of your hearers! Their affections were expanded, and they glowed with that divine enthusiasm, in the behalf of justice, which strength of feeling and genius like yours only could infuse. Sir, *you saved a nation*, and a nation's tears, a nation's blessings, a nation's love, will follow you to the grave.[221]

Erskine began quietly by endorsing the contrast which the Attorney General had drawn between the excellence of the British constitution and the horrors of anarchy in France. For him, however, that contrast was between a settled system of law beyond the reach of arbitrary power or political expediency, in which every subject had a right to 'a trial and judgement by his equals', and a regime, 'where every protection of law is abrogated and destroyed' and where accusation and sentence were the same, 'following one another as the thunder pursues the flash'.[222] 'Let not him,' he urged, 'be hurried away to a pre-doomed execution from an honest enthusiasm for the public safety. – I ask for him a trial by this applauded constitution of our country.'[223] Erskine also protested, at the outset, on Hardy's behalf, against 'all appeals to speculations concerning *consequences*, when the law commands us to look only to INTENTIONS'.[224] It was on this theme that his exposition of the law of treason was based.

In vivid contrast with the procedure adopted by the prosecution, Erskine went straight to the core of the indictment, explaining to the

219. *ST*, vol. 24, cols. 867–9.
220. *Ibid.*, col. 877.
221. T. Holcroft, *A Narrative of Facts relating to a Prosecution for High Treason etc.* (London, 1795), p. 124.
222. *ST*, vol. 24, col. 878.
223. *Ibid.*
224. *Ibid.*

jury that the 'overt acts' there charged against Hardy and the other prisoners were not in themselves treasonable, but were only evidence of their alleged traitorous intention of bringing about the death of the King.[225] The leading charge was, indeed, not the agreement to hold a convention, which, as Erskine said, it was 'notorious, self-evident, and even admitted that they intended to hold',[226] but rather 'the agreement to hold it for the purpose alleged, of assuming all the authority of the state, and in fulfillment of the main intention against the life of the king'. Unless this double intention could be supported by the evidence before the jury the conviction of Hardy as guilty of high treason could not be justified.[227] The same argument also applied to the other 'overt acts' charged in the indictment – the composition and publication of addresses, resolutions and declarations exhorting the King's subjects to send delegates to such a convention and the provision and distribution of arms to maintain it when assembled.[328] These acts, too, would only be treasonable by law if they could be proved to have been committed in fulfilment of the same traitorous intention of bringing the King to death. Such motivation was the touchstone of treason as laid down in the statute of 1351 (25 Edward III) and, as Erskine maintained, this statute, like all criminal statutes, would need to be construed strictly. A further requirement under that act was that the 'proof' of any treasonous intention against the King's life should be 'direct and manifest' and should not rest on 'consequential presumptions and inferences'.[229] Yet it had been by precisely such constructive interpretations, and by what Scott had called 'necessary inferences', that the prosecution had sought to bring the 'overt acts' allegedly committed by Hardy within the scope of treason as laid down by statute. Scott had argued that universal suffrage, if attained, would have as its consequence the destruction of the hereditary nobility, which would, in turn, involve the overthrow of monarchy and the death of the sovereign.[230] Alter-

---

225. Erskine laid much stress on the significance of this term. 'The moment you get right upon the true meaning and signification of this term, the curtain is drawn up, and all is light and certainty.' As the 'compassing' or designing the death of the King was 'a hidden operation of the mind', Erskine explained that an overt act 'is anything which legally proves the existence of such traitorous design and intention'. *Ibid.*, col. 894.

226. *Ibid.*, col. 911.

227. *Ibid.*

228. *Ibid.*, cols. 224–38.

229. *Ibid.*, col. 891.

230. *Ibid.*, col. 906.

natively, the subversion of the King's civil authority by the projected convention would lead, by successive stages, to royal resistance, civil war, the deposition and untimely death of the king.[231] Such a chain of inferred consequences led Erskine to remark to the jury: 'Gentlemen, if the cause were not too serious, I should liken it to the play with which we amuse our children. "This is the cow with the crumpledy horn, which gored the dog, that worried the cat, that ate the rat, etc, ending in the house that Jack built" '.[232] However bemused the jury may have been by 'the labyrinth of matter' laid before them by the prosecution, or by the technicalities of the law of treason as expounded by both prosecuting and defending counsel, they could at least, when the point was put to them, 'distinguish between an intention to kill the king and an intention to reform the House of Commons'.[233]

In the second part of his address Erskine, therefore, set out to convince the jury that the reformers were not, and never had been, crypto-republicans, that they had no intention of attacking the House of Lords, and that they had no ulterior designs beyond their professed aims of universal suffrage, and annual parliaments.[234] To rebut the accusation that their pleas for the reform of the House of Commons were only a cover for treason and rebellion, Erskine reminded the jury that the radicals had never committed themselves to Painite schemes for 'representative government', but had, throughout, restricted their aims to the plans advocated by the Duke of Richmond in 1780 and 1783.[235] Both the Sheffield Constitutional Society and the London Corresponding Society had refused, when pressed, to go beyond the duke's methods and objectives.[236] In considering the London Corresponding Society's attempt to convoke a convention in England, Erskine rightly stressed that this had been precipitated by the dissolution of the Scottish convention and that its character

231. *Ibid.*, cols. 263–5.

232. *Ibid.*, col. 906.

233. T. Holcroft, *Letter to the Rt. Honourable William Windham on the Intemperance and Dangerous Tendency of his Public Conduct* (London, 1795), p. 11.

234. Cross-examination of William Camage, *ST*, vol. 24, col. 596.

235. *Ibid.*, cols. 912–14. Erskine called the Duke of Richmond's plan 'the grand main spring of every proceeding we have to deal with'.

236. When the Sheffield Constitutional Society reprinted in 1792 Richmond's famous letter to Lt.-Col Sharman of the Irish Volunteers of 1783, it said in a preface: 'The principles laid down in that letter comprehend and include all and every object they have in view with respect to a reform in Parliament etc.' Sheffield Central Library, Local Pamphlets, vol. 184(10).

and objectives differed in no respect from those of its forerunner.[237] Yet, as he reminded the jury, those who had been imprisoned, sentenced and transported for their part in the Edinburgh convention had been accused and found guilty of sedition, not treason.[238] Hardy, moreover, could not be proved to have had any knowledge whatsoever of the British Convention's only treasonable legacy – Watt's conspiracy – the forlorn and tragic attempt of a former spy to recapture his credit with the government.[239]

Erskine had less to say about the radical addresses to the French National Convention, treating them in their diplomatic rather than their domestic context. He noted that the latest of them had been made while the issue of war and peace still hung in the balance and that the French government had continued to give the most solemn assurances of friendship for Britain down to the end of 1792, 'subsequent to all the correspondence and addresses complained of'.[240] He thought it worth while, however, to rebut the prosecution's derivation of the emotive terms 'convention' and 'delegates' from the practices of revolutionary France by tracing them back to a pre-revolutionary origin in the Irish and English reform conventions of the 1780s. In Scotland too 'conventions' had been a familiar feature of local politics long before 1789.[241]

In the final part of his speech Erskine dealt with the charges that Hardy had been concerned in the collection and distribution of arms among the radical societies and that he had connived at and facilitated the activities of a small armed organization in London – the Lambeth Loyal Association founded in 1793.[242] The only written evidence relating to arming was a letter of 24 April 1794 to Hardy from one Richard Davison at Sheffield, offering to supply the London Corresponding Society with pikeheads at a shilling a piece and informing him that a plan had been prepared which, if sufficiently supported, would 'no doubt, have the effect of furnishing a quantity of pikes to the patriots, great enough to make them formidable'.[243] A similar letter had been enclosed which Hardy had been requested to forward to Norwich. Erskine was able to show, however, that Hardy had never answered the letter from Sheffield,

237. *ST*, vol. 24, col. 950.
238. *Ibid.*, col. 943.
239. *Ibid.*, cols. 963–4.
240. *Ibid.*, col. 947.
241. *Ibid.*, cols. 914–15.
242. *Ibid.*, cols. 961 ff.
243. *Ibid.*, col. 955.

had never shown it to members of his own society, and had never despatched the unopened letter to Norwich.[244] It also appeared that Davison had wished the radicals to be 'formidable', not in order to revolt against a repressive regime, but in self-defence against threats of violence from local 'Church and King' mobs.

The rest of the charges relating to arming rested so far solely on the parole evidence of Crown witnesses. William Camage and William Broomhead, both former secretaries of the Sheffield Constitutional Society, when cross-examined by Erskine and Gibbs, had spoken of the interference of local magistrates in their meetings and of an inflammatory handbill circulated in the town against their members.[245] Broomhead insisted that in the Sheffield society no suggestion had ever been made of resisting, much less of attacking, the government.[246] Camage admitted that he had obtained a pike, but only for self-defence and had never heard 'a syllable' in the society about using pikes, or other arms, for any other purpose.[247] Hill, a cutler, employed by Davison to make the blades for the pikes, had been victimized by the 'Church and King' faction, who had fired muskets under his door and threatened to pull his house down.[248] Widdison, a turner and hairdresser, who had made a dozen and a half handles for the pikes ordered by Davison and one for himself, revealed that Davison had written his letter to Hardy entirely on his own initiative, and confirmed once more that the Duke of Richmond's plan was the Sheffield society's 'only object'.[249]

Finally, Erskine dealt almost perfunctorily with the prosecution's attempt to connect Hardy with the shadowy Lambeth Loyal Association organized by Franklow, which had carried out surreptitious drilling and military exercises, but which had been recruited by public advertisement, had only a tenuous connection with the London Corresponding Society, and was short of men and equipment. It had come into existence in November 1793 as a cross between a fire brigade and a local riot squad.[250] The uniform of the

244. *Ibid.*, col. 956.
245. *Ibid.*, cols. 956–7.
246. *Ibid.*, col. 957.
247. *Ibid.*
248. *Ibid.*, col. 958.
249. *Ibid.*, col. 957.
250. Article 5 of the rules of the association stated: 'As the protection of public and private property is the object of this association, we hereby engage to step forth in case of fire, tumults, commotions, and riots but not beyond the parish of St. Mary's, Lambeth.' *Ibid.*, col. 696.

association was 'a blue coat lapelled, scarlet collar, plain gilt buttons, white waistcoat, nankeen breeches, white stockings, half-black gaters, black stock, cocked hat and cockade' – but the only member who could afford one was Franklow, who had appeared in it at the Globe Tavern dinner of the London Corresponding Society.[251] Some drilling had occurred in Thomas Spence's pamphlet shop in Little Turnstile off Holborn, but Hardy's only connection with the association was that he had dropped an indiscreet hint to one of his customers, Samuel Williams, a gunsmith, that he might be able to dispose of some of his muskets to its members.[252]

Erskine had almost finished, but by this time he was so exhausted that he could hardly stand and could not speak loud enough for the judges to hear him – so that his words had to be repeated by another.[253] Before sitting down, however, he summoned up enough strength to describe Hardy's character as 'religious, temperate, humane and moderate, and his uniform conduct all that can belong to a good subject and an honest man'.[254]

As he concluded the audience in court broke out into spontaneous and prolonged applause and this was re-echoed by the throng of waiting spectators in the surrounding streets.[255] When the court adjourned shortly after midnight till the following Monday, after hearing some of the evidence for the prisoner, the judges found themselves besieged by excited and hostile demonstrators and unable to get to their carriages. They were the target for much hissing and hooting and were eventually able to leave only after Erskine had pacified the crowd by a personal appeal. He himself had to yield, however, to popular insistence on dragging him and his coach back to Serjeant's Inn.[256] Although the trial lasted for two and a half more days, occupied mainly by the speeches of the Solicitor General for the prosecution, of Gibbs for the defence and by the eminently fair summing up of the presiding judge, even greater crowds continued

251. *ST*, vol. 24, col. 699.

252. *Ibid.*, col. 961. Further information about the association is in an 'intelligence' report of 26 May 1794 in the Home Office papers, PRO HO 42/30. The only other place where drilling occurred was at John Shelmerdine's, a hatter in the borough. Orr, a tailor from Camberwell, who claimed service in the French army, did most of the instruction. The informant thought that 'this despicable set are not of that importance to give government any uneasiness'.

253. *ST*, vol. 24, col. 965. F. D. Cartwright, *Life and Correspondence of Major Cartwright* (London, 1826), vol. 1, p. 206.

254. *ST*, vol. 24, col. 970.

255. *Ibid.*

256. Lord Mayor to Portland, 6 Nov. 1794. PRO HO 42/33.

their demonstrations each night as the court adjourned.[257] The Lord Mayor, who had made special arrangements to keep access to the court clear, increased the number of constables on duty, but was compelled, on 4 November, to call on detachments of the Artillery Company and the Light Horse Volunteers to keep the 'mob' at a safe distance.[258] On Wednesday 5 November (Guy Fawkes Day) Hardy's ordeal was over. The jury retired at 12.30 p.m. and returned three hours later with their verdict of 'Not Guilty'. Hardy spoke from the bar for the first time – turning to the jury. 'My fellow countrymen, I return you my thanks.' More words would have seemed less eloquent and Eyre himself from the bench joined Hardy in his thanks for their patient endurance.[259] That evening Hardy too was drawn in a coach by exultant crowds of supporters from the Strand to St James's, pausing on the return journey for a few minutes' silence by his empty shop in Piccadilly before retiring to his brother-in-law's house in Lancaster Court, where he remained for the next fortnight.[260] The last to leave the Old Bailey were Erskine and Gibbs, and Erskine was once more drawn home by his admirers. By 10.30 all was quiet and the Lord Mayor was able to dismiss the Light Horse Volunteers and the Artillery Company after keeping them on duty in heavy and persistent rain for four hours. They had managed to prevent any rioting, protect the judges from further molestation and to extinguish one solitary illumination in Silver St – a transparency with the words 'The glorious acquittal of Thomas Hardy'.[261]

The next trial – that of Horne Tooke and his associates in the Society for Constitutional Information – took place a fortnight later and lasted from Monday 17 to Saturday 22 November.[262] Despite Hardy's acquittal, the prosecution considered that a charge of high treason against Horne Tooke could still be sustained because the Society for Constitutional Information could be shown to have been mainly instrumental in the dissemination of Paine's works, and because of Tooke's own patent responsibility for the society's addresses to the Paris Jacobin club and the French National Convention. The

257. Major Cartwright reported on Tuesday 4 November: 'Gibbs spoke like an angel. I left the court with the full persuasion that Hardy was safe.' Cartwright, vol. 1, p. 207.

258. PRO HO 42/33. Lord Mayor to Portland, 6 Nov. 1794.

259. *ST*, vol. 24, col. 1384.

260. Cone, p. 206.

261. The illumination was taken down and the owner reprimanded. PRO HO 42/43.

262. For the trial proceedings see *ST*, vol. 25, cols. 2–745.

M

prosecution was also prepared to argue that Tooke's had been the directing intelligence behind both the London Corresponding Society and the provincial radical clubs, and finally that he had been actively engaged in the plans for an English convention. Scott had told J. B. Burges, under-secretary at the Foreign Office, early in October, that if the grand jury found a true bill against Tooke, he would 'undertake to hang him'.[263] This intention may have been reflected in the 'evident marks of management and partiality' in the empanelling of the trial jury which Major Cartwright noticed on the first day and which prompted Erskine's remark to Tooke: 'By God, they are murdering you'.[264] Such was the open dislike displayed by the Lord Chief Justice for the leading defence counsel during the trial that immediately on its conclusion Erskine asked him to repeat some of his remarks and then challenged him.[265] It is a mistake, therefore, to assume that Tooke's trial was a formality and that its result was a foregone conclusion.

Though the indictment against Tooke was virtually the same as against Hardy, both prosecution and defence counsel reshaped their tactics in the later trial as a result of Hardy's acquittal. The chief burden of the prosecution fell this time on the Solicitor General, Sir James Mitford, who was no less determined than Scott to secure a conviction.[266] Nevertheless, Mitford wisely did not press the charge of arming – for which evidence against the accused and the Society for Constitutional Information was completely lacking, and he also refrained from the use of spies and informers as Crown witnesses.[267] This restraint inspired in Erskine neither relief nor surprise – he merely noted, in an aside, that 'the abortive evidence of arms has been abandoned, even the solitary pike that formerly glared rebellion from the corner of the court, no longer makes its appearance; and the knives have retired to their ancient office of carving'.[268] His comment on the withdrawal of parole evidence on arming was that it showed sound discretion – for 'to have attempted it a second time by

263. Bodleian Library, Oxford. Bland Burges papers, box labelled 'Original MS. of Hutton. Bland Burges Papers before excision'.

264. Cartwright, vol. 1, p. 209.

265. Amelia Alderson of Norwich was a witness of the incident. C. L. Brightwell, *Memorials of the life of Amelia Opie*, 2nd ed. (Norwich, 1854), pp. 48–9.

266. *ST*, vol. 25, cols. 27–71.

267. Instead Mitford laid great stress on the addresses of the two metropolitan societies to the National Convention as indicating that the reformers did not mean to confine themselves to parliamentary reform. *Ibid.*, cols. 44–8.

268. *Ibid.*, col. 286.

spies and informers would only have been uselessly bringing up their ragamuffins to be peppered'.[269] Instead the Solicitor General focused the attention of the jury not on Horne Tooke's political principles but on his political conduct – his role as protector and mentor of the London Corresponding Society, as director of his own society and as father confessor to the provincial radicals, his mediation between the English 'friends of liberty' and the leaders of French republicanism, and his participation in the preparations for an English convention.

Erskine also changed his conduct of the defence. By repeated references to the verdict of acquittal in Hardy's trial he succeeded in getting it admitted by the court in evidence in Tooke's case.[270] He attracted the sympathy and concern of the jury for his client by emphasizing his age, infirmities and sufferings in the Tower and by stressing Tooke's insistence that he should not be exculpated by his counsel at the expense of his humbler and less prudent associates.[271] He repaid the Attorney General in his own coin by recapitulating all the evidence on the moderation and fixity of Tooke's political principles ever since 1780, demonstrating how his client had been a consistent critic of the radical panacea of universal suffrage, that he had been a staunch defender of the hereditary principle in monarchy and Parliament, and that he had never been a democrat, much less a republican.[272] He also pointed out that though Tooke had raised a subscription for the legal defence of Paine, he had never approved or defended those parts of *The Rights of Man* which had been prosecuted.[273] He was able to show that Tooke had condemned the delegation of Sinclair and Yorke to the Edinburgh convention and that he had never attended meetings of the joint committees appointed to prepare the summons of the proposed English convention.[274] One argument remained unchanged – that Tooke, like Hardy, could not be proved to have plotted or imagined the death of the King, and since Hardy, 'the chief conspirator', had already been acquitted, Tooke could not reasonably be convicted.

Above all, Erskine allowed Horne Tooke, whose forensic talents were remarkable and whose caustic wit was such a powerful solvent

269. *Ibid.*, col. 307.
270. *Ibid.*, cols. 261–2, 285.
271. *Ibid.*, cols. 293, 325.
272. *Ibid.*, cols. 319–20, 321–3.
273. *Ibid.*, cols. 318–19.
274. *Ibid.*, cols. 291, 308–9.

of legal subterfuge, to play a prominent part in his own defence. Tooke availed himself of the opportunity to the full and in doing so, as Hazlitt later observed, 'he baffled the Judge, dumbfounded the Counsel and outwitted the Jury'.[275] He took particular delight in using Daniel Adams, the former secretary of the Society for Constitutional Information who had escaped prosecution by turning King's evidence, and William Sharp who had also agreed to act as Crown witness, to bolster his defence.[276] He put Major Cartwright founding father of the incriminated society, Charles James Fox, the Duke of Richmond, Sir Philip Francis, Sheridan and even Pitt himself in the witness box – to the sorry discomfiture of the latter and in vindication of the soundness of his constitutional principles.[277] Had he not said on many an occasion that he would rather be governed by St James's than by St Giles's, and had he not, at the Crown and Anchor dinner on 14 July 1790, 'moderated the moderator', by amending the toast proposed by Sheridan in commemoration of the fall of the Bastille?[278] He even persuaded the presiding judge that he had turned the Society for Constitutional Information into 'a mere club' with an exiguous and declining membership, whose meetings he had sought to adjourn and from whose most vital decisions he himself had dissented.[279] In order to demonstrate that he had never gone the whole way with Paine and 'other persons who had speculated upon government', he recounted his own parable that if he found himself on a stage-coach with companions who wished to press on to Windsor, he would always insist on dismounting at Hounslow.[280] His hand-written emendations of the draft resolutions and addresses of the London Corresponding Society did not prove that he had been its Machiavellian manipulator, but merely that he had striven throughout to protect his less sophisticated associates from the consequences of libel.[281] In contrast with Margarot's and Gerrald's

275. Hazlitt, p. 88. This was a general statement of Tooke's legal tactics in court, not necessarily applicable to this trial, but relevant nevertheless.

276. *ST*, vol. 25, cols. 84–98 (Adams), 247–55 (Sharp).

277. *Ibid.*, cols. 325–95.

278. St Giles in the Fields was a London parish noted in the eighteenth century as a thieves' kitchen and turbulent Irish ghetto. M. D. George, *London Life in the Eighteenth Century* (Harmondsworth, 1966), pp. 113, 121. *ST*, vol. 25, col. 391.

279. *ST*, vol. 25, col. 731.

280. *Ibid.*, col. 330. Cartwright cross-examined by Tooke.

281. See Tooke's personal explanation to the court after the verdict of 'Not Guilty'. *Ibid.*, col. 744.

histrionic defiance of the Scottish judicial authorities, Tooke skilfully deferred to the rulings of the court and was careful not to provoke the antagonism of the Crown lawyers. It was an impressive and professional performance which, so far from detracting from the efficacy of Erskine's superb defence, actually enhanced it. The most striking tribute to its success was that the jury, which had been hand-picked to ensure his conviction, took no more than eight minutes to acquit him.[282] They were, moreover, all moved to tears when Tooke thanked them for his life, after the shouted acclamations in court at their verdict had subsided.[283] Tooke also expressed his thanks to the judge and to his defence counsel – Erskine and Gibbs – and his hope that the verdict would be a warning to the Attorney General 'not to attempt to shed men's blood upon lame suspicions and doubtful inferences'. It was a justly deserved rebuke.[284]

Tooke's clerical status had already disqualified him from a potentially successful career at the bar and, in 1801, was to exclude him from the parliamentary seat for the rotten borough of Old Sarum to which he was nominated by the second Lord Camelford, the celebrated duellist.[285] In 1794, however, his legal expertise had enabled him to cheat the hangman, checkmate the Attorney General and, through his own acquittal, to secure also the automatic release of the other accused members of the Society for Constitutional Information. This was some compensation.[286] It was soon to be Tooke's proud boast that he was one of the few Englishmen (there was one Irishman) who had been tried for both sedition and high treason.[287] But then he was a connoisseur with eccentric tastes – and would not, perhaps, have minded overmuch if a more fickle fate had made him the martyr that he had certainly never aspired, nor intended, to become.[288] A martyr to gout he had always been and that was, for him, more than enough.

282. *Ibid.*, col. 743. F. D. Cartwright, vol. 1, p. 209.

283. *Ibid.*

284. *Ibid.*; *ST*, vol. 25, col. 745.

285. W. H. Reid, *Memoirs of the Public Life of J. H. Tooke* (London, 1812), pp. 157–8.

286. Bonney, Joyce, Kyd and Holcroft were acquitted on 1 December. *ST*, vol. 25, col. 746.

287. J. Binns, *Recollections of the Life of J. Binns, written by himself* (Philadelphia, 1854). Binns was the Irishman who had also been so tried.

288. Thelwall, Tooke's near neighbour in the Tower, described how they had, in conversation, both rejected the idea of suicide. Tooke had remarked, 'I will either live to be useful, or die usefully.' Thelwall, *Tribune* (1796), vol. 3, p. 211.

Thelwall, whose trial began on 1 December before Chief Baron Macdonald and finished on the 5th, would, no doubt, have been prepared to try and emulate Tooke's performance. When, however, during the court hearings he indicated his dissatisfaction with the way in which his defence was being conducted by writing a note to Erskine – 'I'll be hanged if I don't plead my own cause', it was only to receive the curt and discouraging reply: 'You'll be hanged if you do.'[289] Fortunately, perhaps, the records of this trial have not survived, for the fragmentary references to the court proceedings suggest that they were very far from reaching the heights of the preceding trials. Major Cartwright, reporting on the opening of the prosecution case on the first day, wrote that it had taken Serjeant Adair seven hours to do so – 'which nearly lulled me to sleep, and I was told that the Chief Justice had been asleep the greatest part of the time'.[290] It seems probable that the prosecution placed great emphasis not only on Thelwall's intercepted letters, in which he had defended the Montagnard system of 'revolutionary government' and claimed to be an English '*sans-culotte*', and on his management of the secret committee of the London Corresponding Society, but also on the alleged subversive character of his political lectures.[291] One shudders to think, however, that the prosecution may have felt it necessary to quote verbatim and at length from Thelwall's demagogic harangues in the effort to give an unwonted piquancy to its own pedestrian and collateral arguments. The trial continued for five days and was probably only redeemed by the legal acumen, combined talents and unwearying exertions of Erskine and Gibbs as defence counsel. Their client was more vulnerable than either Hardy or Tooke, and it took the jury two hours to reach their verdict of 'Not Guilty'.[292]

The government took ten days to consider its position but, on 15 December, decided not to bring any evidence against the two remaining prisoners – Richter and Baxter – and released them.[293] The treason trials were at last over.

---

289. Earl Stanhope, *Life of Pitt* (London, 1861), vol. 2, p. 273.

290. Cartwright, vol. 1, p. 211.

291. J. Thelwall, *The Natural and Constitutional Right of Britons to Annual Parliaments, Universal Suffrage and the Freedom of Popular Association* (London, 1795), p. 85. This was the speech in self-defence which Thelwall had intended to deliver at his trial, if Erskine had not vetoed the suggestion.

292. Cone, p. 209.

293. *ST*, vol. 25, col. 748.

10 The rise of the protest movement; Pitt's 'Reign of Terror' and the decline of the popular societies (1795–7)

These bills are an unwilling homage that the too eager advocates of authority pay to the rising genius of liberty.[1]

Radicalism had always been, inherently, a protest movement – voicing popular resentment against the social and political consequences of an exclusive and insensitive legislature, privilege in the established church and inequality in the law. Its advocates had always urged the need to combat the degradation and helplessness of the poor in a *laissez-faire* economy, the necessity of a system of popular education and of safeguards against crimping, the press gang and the game laws.[2] They had also claimed the democratic right to active participation in politics, to adequate representation in the House of Commons, and to emancipation from a parasitic class of pensioners, sinecurists, court favourites, borough-mongers and government informers.[3] They had given unequivocal and effective support to one of the earliest, and ultimately the most successful of all protest movements – the campaign for the abolition of the slave trade.[4]

1. W. Godwin, *Considerations on Lord Grenville's and Mr Pitt's Bills concerning Treasonable and Seditious Practices and Unlawful Assemblies* (1975), p. 86.
2. 'Crimping' was the forcible enrolment of unwilling recruits into the army. Under the terms of 8 Geo. III c.7.s.70 soldiers 'enlisted' in this way had to be brought before the nearest justice within four days to have their recruitment legally certified as 'voluntary'. Crimping houses were places of rendezvous for the recruiting officers and the magistrates. For the game laws see Chester Kirby, 'The English game law system', *American Historical Review*, vol. 38 (1932–3), pp. 240–62.
3. T. Cooper, *A Reply to Mr Burke's Invective against Mr Cooper and Mr Watt* (London, 1792), pp. 71–8; G. Dyer, *The Complaints of the Poor People of England* (London, 1793); [James Parkinson], *Revolutions without Bloodshed* (London, 1794); J. Baxter, *Resistance to Oppression: The Constitutional Rights of Britons Asserted* (London, 1795), p. 7.
4. For this see R. T. Anstey, *The Atlantic Slave Trade and British Abolition, 1760–1810* (London, 1975) – the latest and most authoritative account.

These pleas for social justice in their eighteenth-century context had, however, been to some extent muted or masked by tactical concentration on the prior need for radical parliamentary reform. It was only when the prospects of achieving political reform receded, as they did after the treason trials of 1794, that radicalism emerged as a serious movement of public protest against a whole range of more urgent popular grievances.[5] The novel feature of this new departure in radical agitation was the organization by the London Corresponding Society of mass general meetings of its members and sympathizers in the metropolis, designed to demonstrate the weight of popular support which could be marshalled behind carefully drafted petitions or remonstrances to King and Parliament, its own resolutions and the formal statement of public grievances in printed addresses to the nation. 1795 was a year of general food shortages, rapidly rising prices of articles of common consumption and acute economic distress among the poor.[6] The large-scale assemblies of popular protest against the war and government inaction on domestic issues were thought of as substitutes for the rioting and price-fixing which were sweeping sporadically across the rest of the country.[7] The meetings were also characterized by the orderly conduct of their proceedings, the moderation of the speakers and the peaceful behaviour of the vast crowds of spectators. Technically, however, they were regarded as in breach of a Caroline statute against 'tumultuous petitioning' and were viewed with apprehension by the government as seditious attempts to overawe the legislature. Though they were temporarily suppressed by Pitt and Grenville's 'Gagging Acts' of December 1795, mass meetings of protest were to become one of the distinguishing features of nineteenth-century radical agitation. The potentialities of 'protest' as a tactical political weapon in situations where reformers were on the defensive were rapidly appreciated and exploited between 1795 and 1797 – for it was used by the radical

5. What made parliamentary reform impractical at this stage was the virtual collapse of provincial radicalism, the demise of the Society for Constitutional Information and the decision of the Association of the Friends of the People to suspend its operations in Feb. 1795. *Parl. Hist.*, vol. 31, col. 1152.

6. N. M. Stern, 'The bread crisis in Britain, 1795–6', *Economica*, new series, vol. 31 (1964), pp. 168–87.

7. Bread riots occurred in July 1795 at Tewkesbury and Mitcheldean in Gloucestershire, at Blakeney, Norwich, Yarmouth and Cambridge in East Anglia, at Berwick-upon-Tweed, Croydon, Newhaven and Bishop's Stortford. See also J. Stevenson, 'Food riots in England, 1792–1818', in R. Quinalt and J. Stevenson (eds.), *Popular Protest and Public Order* (London, 1974).

societies to urge the need for measures to alleviate the economic misery of the poor, by the Foxite Opposition, in association with metropolitan and provincial radicals, to resist Pitt's 'Reign of Terror', and by the leaders of the naval mutinies in 1797 to ventilate the grievances of British sailors.

The acquittal of Hardy, Horne Tooke and Thelwall and the collapse of the treason trials were greeted with relief by moderate but committed reformers in the capital and with demonstrations of widespread joy and satisfaction by the 'friends of liberty' in the provinces.[8] Both Cartwright, who had not attended meetings of the Society for Constitutional Information since May 1792, and Grey, as a founding member of the Association of the Friends of the People, were convinced that the verdicts of 'Not Guilty' in the trials had narrowly averted a general proscription of all who had promoted reform associations or who had expressed pro-French sympathies.[9] As it was, the Duke of Richmond, behind whose political views the radicals had sheltered in the trials, was relieved of his post as Master General of the Ordnance shortly after the acquittals.[10] Horne Tooke was quick to celebrate his own release at a large dinner party given at his Wimbledon home on Sunday 30 November. There was talk of commissioning busts, medals and other commemorative souvenirs, and among the guests were Hoppner, the portrait painter, Banks, the sculptor, and Sharp, the engraver. Tooke no doubt felt malicious pleasure in proposing the King's health, conscious that Pitt and those who had prosecuted him on the capital charge of 'compassing' his sovereign's death were, on the same evening, being entertained to dinner by his next-door neighbour – Dundas.[11] Earl Stanhope's country seat at Chevening (now used by the present Prince of Wales) was the scene of a more lavish celebration in honour of the release of the Reverend Jeremiah Joyce – tutor to Stanhope's sons. Four hundred of the earl's friends and tenants attended a ball and 200 sat down to dinner under variegated lamps arranged in the form of letters pro-

---

8. F. D. Cartwright, *Life and Correspondence of Major Cartwright* (London, 1826), vol. 1, p. 210; C. Kegan Paul, *William Godwin: His Friends and Contemporaries* (London, 1876), vol. 1, pp. 134–7; T. Sadler, *Diary, Reminiscences and Correspondence of Henry Crabb Robinson* (London, 1869), pp. 26–7.

9. Cartwright, vol. 1, p. 210 and G. M. Trevelyan, *Lord Grey of the Reform Bill* (London, 1929), p. 85.

10. A. G. Olson, *The Radical Duke: the Career and Correspondence of Charles Lennox, third Duke of Richmond* (Oxford, 1961), p. 62.

11. Cartwright, vol. 1, p. 211.

claiming 'The Rights of Juries'.[12] These private celebrations were eclipsed by a public dinner at the Crown and Anchor Tavern in the Strand on 4 February 1795, attended by 1300 'respectable Citizens', and presided over by Earl Stanhope.[13] Even the traditional annual commemoration of the revolution of 1688 on 4 November was soon to yield pride of place to a new anniversary in the reformers' calendar – the 'ever memorable' 5 November, when Hardy, unlike Guy Fawkes, had escaped the executioner.[14]

The main causes for the reformers' exultation at the outcome of the State Trials were the refutation by Godwin, Erskine and Gibbs of the doctrine of constructive treason, the vindication of the English jury system, the setback to Pitt's repressive policies, the exposure of the one-sided political bias shown by Privy Councillors, MPs and Crown lawyers in the examination and prosecution of the prisoners, and the continued existence and resilience of the London Corresponding Society.[15] Most of these gains, however, in the aftermath of the trials, proved to be ephemeral and the balance of political advantage came to rest with the government rather than with the radicals. The first casualty was the Society for Constitutional Information. Because its secretary, Daniel Adams, had turned King's evidence after his arrest, and because all its papers, minutes and records had been seized by the government, the society found it impractical to resume its activities and ceased to meet – without, however, being formally dissolved.[16] Horne Tooke, whose increasing infirmities had been aggravated by his long imprisonment, withdrew from active

12. The Rev. J. Joyce, *An Account of Mr Joyce's Arrest for 'Treasonable Practices' etc.*, 2nd ed. (London, 1795), p. 30.

13. *Substance of Earl Stanhope's Speech on the 4th of February 1795 to celebrate the happy event of the late Trials for supposed High Treason* (London, 1795), p. 1.

14. Thelwall was the first to give a 'Civic Oration' to commemorate Hardy's acquittal, on 5 Nov. 1795. The speech is reprinted in Thelwall's *Tribune*, vol. 3, pp. 201–20. The 4 November anniversary had, however, been observed as usual in 1795. *Ibid.*, p. 203.

15. The determination of the LCS to continue its meetings and not to abandon its principles after Hardy's arrest had been asserted in a unanimous resolution of its General Committee on 5 June 1794. PRO TS 11/956/3501(ii). See also *Account of the Seizure of Citizen Thomas Hardy, Secretary to the London Corresponding Society* (London, 1794) and (James Parkinson), *A Vindication of the London Corresponding Society* (London, 1795).

16. G. S. Veitch, *Genesis of Parliamentary Reform* (London, 1965 reprint), p. 324. It seems to have been revived in the autumn of 1795, sufficiently at least to publish a powerful indictment of Pitt and Grenville's repressive legislation.

concern in metropolitan radical politics and, early in 1795, even announced that he had abandoned his parliamentary ambitions.[17] Holcroft, after a final outburst against the excesses of the conservative Whigs, found it expedient to produce his plays under an assumed name and eventually sought immunity from further persecution by voluntary exile on the Continent.[18] Even though Major Cartwright survived to carry on the struggle for parliamentary reform after the Napoleonic wars, little more was heard of the pseudo-historical assumptions of Anglo-Saxon 'democracy' and the classical and re-publican ideology of the early eighteenth-century Commonwealth men, which he had sponsored and popularized in the radical interest.[19] The society had probably outlived its usefulness, but its disappear-ance meant that the London Corresponding Society was left to soldier on alone.

Nor did the London Corresponding Society emerge from the state Trials unscathed. Its precarious finances, which had never properly recovered from the expenditure incurred by sending Margarot and Gerrald as delegates to the Scottish convention, had been further depleted by heavy printing bills, the defence costs of Hardy and Thelwall in the Old Bailey trials, and the calls on the private gener-osity of its members to maintain the families and dependants of their accused colleagues during their imprisonment.[20] Shrinking numbers in the autumn of 1794 meant that the society's only regular income, from membership subscriptions, also declined, so that, early in 1795, its finances were seriously embarrassed, if not in deficit. The treason trials also induced many of the more cautious members of the society to resign, in order to protect themselves from the legal consequences of the ill-judged or seditious behaviour of their less responsible associates.[21] The principle of the collective responsibility of all mem-bers of such popular societies for the words and actions of individual

17. This announcement, made at the Crown and Anchor dinner on 4 Feb. 1795 to celebrate the acquittals, did not, however, prevent Tooke from contesting the Westminster seat, unsuccessfully, in 1796.

18. H. N. Brailsford, *Shelley, Godwin and their Circle* (London, 1936), p. 48.

19. C. B. Cone, *The English Jacobins* (New York, 1968), p. 213.

20. The expenses of the delegates to the British Convention totalled £240. PRO PC 1/23/A 38. By 19 Nov. 1794 over £284 had been spent, of a total of £314.16s.9d. collected, on the families of the LCS prisoners. BL, Add. MSS. 27813, fo. 143. The total defence costs of all the accused amounted to £4000. Mark Wilks, *Athaliah, or the Tocsin sounded by Modern Alarmists: Two Collection Sermons towards defraying the expenses of the Defendants in the late Trials for High Treason . . . 19 April 1795* (Norwich, 1795).

21. J. Binns, *Recollections . . .* (Philadelphia, 1854), p. 43.

members done in pursuance of any order or resolution of the societies or their committees had been laid down during the trials, not only by the law officers of the Crown, but by the judges. The risks attendant upon membership of popular societies were thus too great for many serious but timid reformers willingly to assume. Those moderates who were not deterred by such anxieties from joining the London Corresponding Society during or after the trials, tended, therefore, to favour Fabian, rather than aggressive, tactics in 1795 and to stress the educational rather than the political role of the popular societies.[22] As such moderates were, after 1794, in the minority, resignation from the London Corresponding Society was often their only means of registering their dissent and this meant that open schisms became more frequent.[23]

Gaps also appeared in the leadership of the society. Thomas Hardy, exhausted by his recent bereavement and his ordeal at the Old Bailey, did not resume his political activity and concentrated on the uphill task of reviving his business as a master shoemaker.[24] Thelwall, weighed down by his family responsibilities and anxious not to compromise his colleagues by his political lectures, withdrew from the society for the better part of a year.[25] Fortunately, these and other losses were made good by able and resolute reformers who joined the society as its fortunes ebbed in the summer and autumn of 1794. John Ashley, who replaced Hardy as secretary, was also a shoemaker. It was he who introduced to the society his friend Francis Place – the self-made and self-educated journeyman tailor, who served for long periods in 1795 as chairman of its General Committee and member of its Executive Committee.[26] Thelwall's place as propagandist and itinerant lecturer was filled by John Gale Jones, an apothecary, who captivated popular audiences in the capital by his histrionic manner and flamboyant rhetoric.[27] Another prominent recruit in December 1794 was John Binns, an Irish plumber's mate, recently arrived from Dublin, whose advanced views later led him to forge links with the

22. BL, Add. MSS. 35143, fos. 15, 93.
23. See below, p. 368.
24. He recommenced his business on 29 Nov. 1794 at Tavistock St, Covent Garden, moving in 1797 to Fleet St. He became a Freeman of the Cordwainers' Company and retired in 1815. BL, Add. MSS. 27814, fo. 8.
25. Thelwall, *Tribune*, vol. 1, pp. 332–3 (20 June 1795).
26. G. Wallas, *Life of Francis Place*, 4th ed. (London, 1925); Mary Thale (ed.), *The Autobiography of Francis Place (1771–1854)* (Cambridge, 1972), preface.
27. Veitch, p. 323.

United Irish movement.[28] These new leaders, who came rapidly to the fore, contributed powerfully to the revival of the society in the course of 1795 and largely shaped its policies in the period of repression which followed.

The treason trials also severed the links which had been so carefully forged in 1792 and 1793 between the metropolitan and provincial reform societies. Those members and officials of the Sheffield and Norwich societies, for example, who had been arrested and brought to London to serve as witnesses for the Crown, appear not to have taken any further part in radical activity – other than to celebrate their release on their return home.[29] When they did so, late in 1794 or early in 1795, they found their former leaders dispersed – some like Joseph Gales, the Sheffield printer, in self-chosen exile abroad; others, such as Henry Redhead Yorke, facing charges of conspiracy in prison; or, as in Norwich, no longer prepared to assist the federated popular societies, which, in passing out of middle-class control, had already virtually disintegrated.[30] For Manchester radicalism, Thomas Walker's acquittal at Lancaster Assizes in April 1794 from the trumped-up charges of conspiracy brought against him by his Church and King enemies, proved only a pyrrhic victory – for it involved him in financial ruin and virtually terminated his career as a reformer.[31] When provincial radicalism recovered from these setbacks, it did so under fresh auspices and with altered objectives.

Nor had the State Trials affected the government's resolve to prolong the suspension of Habeas Corpus. This was partly because of the formal coalition which it had contracted in July 1794 with the group of conservative Whigs led by the Duke of Portland.[32] These

28. Binns, p. 41.
29. For the reception given to the Sheffield witnesses on their return (22 Dec. 1794) see BL, Place newspaper cuttings, vol. 36, p. 277.
30. Isaac Saint, the secretary of the Norwich affiliated societies, remained in custody till the beginning of 1795. PRO HO 42/34. By that time the radical clubs in Norwich were completely discredited – though the reforming impulse, thanks to the steadfastness of the Nonconformists, remained strong.
31. Walker's business as a fustian and cotton manufacturer failed and he and his family, living on a small farm at Longford outside Manchester, bequeathed to him by his friend and attorney Felix Vaughan, were only rescued from poverty by a public subscription in 1801. He continued his interest in public affairs till his death on 2 Feb. 1817. F. Knight, *The Strange Case of Thomas Walker* (London, 1957), ch. 16.
32. F. O'Gorman, *The Whig Party and the French Revolution* (London, 1967), ch. 5, and L. G. Mitchell, *Charles James Fox and the Disintegration of the Whig Party, 1782–1794* (Oxford, 1971), ch. 6.

new allies, Alarmists to a man, had joined Pitt's administration, not only to share in ministerial office, but also in order to press for a more vigorous conduct of the war with France, in association with the French *émigrés*, to reinforce the resistance to parliamentary reform and to step up the repression of the English Jacobins.[33] As soon, however, as the new parliamentary session opened at the end of December 1794, the Foxite Whigs attempted to capitalize on the acquittals in the State Trials by moving for an immediate repeal of the act suspending Habeas Corpus, due to expire at the beginning of February 1795. After Sheridan had given notice of this intention even before the Commons debated the King's speech, it was argued in support that 'the practical inference' from the Old Bailey trials was that 'there never existed any such plot as was stated to exist and that there was no occasion for shutting up individuals for six months upon such charges as had been preferred against them'.[34] This was a direct rebuttal of the arguments used by the prosecution in the trials and a challenge to the views of the conservative Whigs, who had identified themselves with 'conspiracy' theories of radicalism. It brought immediate replies from the Solicitor General, Sir John Mitford, and Serjeant Adair, both of whom had taken prominent parts in the state prosecutions. Both were completely unrepentant about the conduct of the trials and both vigorously reasserted their belief in the existence of the conspiracy which the secret committees of both Houses had documented and which Parliament itself had accredited.[35] From this they were led on to assail the view that the acquittal of the prisoners, necessarily established their 'complete innocence'. Mitford argued that 'the only effect of the late verdicts was that the persons acquitted could not be again tried for the same offence', and, as Fox noted, he virtually resurrected the doctrine of constructive treason.[36] Adair noted, in his turn, that mere doubt as to the prisoners' guilt was sufficient in law for the juries to reject the prosecution case for their conviction, so that the verdicts of acquittal did not establish their entire innocence.[37] A far more provocative

33. Portland became Home Secretary (with control of the colonies but not of the war), Earl Spencer was appointed First Lord of the Admiralty, Windham Secretary at War, Earl Fitzwilliam Lord President of the Council with the promise of the Irish Viceroyalty, and the Earl of Mansfield, minister without portfolio.

34. *Parl. Hist.*, vol. 31, cols. 995–6.

35. *Ibid.*, cols. 997, 1000.

36. *Ibid.*, cols. 997, 998.

37. *Ibid.*, col. 1000.

and memorable intervention, however, came from the conservative Whig and minister at war, William Windham, MP for Norwich, and friend and disciple of Burke. Generalizing and extending the arguments of the Crown lawyers, Windham referred to Thomas Hardy as 'an acquitted felon' and contended that the verdicts of 'Not Guilty' on those who had been tried for high treason merely registered the absence of legal proof against them and 'by no means proved that they were free from moral guilt'.[38] Though the label 'acquitted felons' was deprecated at the time by Foxite Whigs and radicals alike, as impugning the constitutional verdicts found by the juries, it proved remarkably adhesive, for it epitomized the widespread distrust of the motivation of the reform societies and 'the lingering doubt' which many people felt about the 'moral', as distinct from the legal, innocence of the liberated prisoners.[39] In the immediate context, however, the main significance of the slur was that it did much to ensure the rejection of Sheridan's motion for the repeal of the act suspending Habeas Corpus on 5 January 1795, by the substantial majority of 185 votes to 41.[40] This meant that Henry Redhead Yorke was kept in prison till the end of July 1795, and William Stone till late January 1796 before being tried respectively for conspiracy and high treason.[41] Yorke had been arrested on 16 June 1794 and Stone in May 1794. Yorke was found guilty and sentenced to a fine of £200 and two years' imprisonment in Dorchester Gaol, where he found a bride in the governor's daughter and recanted his radical views.[42] Stone was acquitted. The suspension of Habeas Corpus was not finally removed until 1801, by which time radicalism had ceased to be a serious political problem.[43]

38. *Ibid.*, col. 1029.

39. For the denunciation of the phrase 'acquitted felons' see T. Holcroft, *A Letter to the Rt. Hon. William Windham on the Intemperance and Dangerous Tendency of his Public Conduct* (London, 1795), pp. 10–11. Earl Stanhope also devoted a major portion of his speech at the Crown and Anchor dinner on 4 Feb. 1795 to the condemnation of Windham's speech. *Substance of Earl Stanhope's speech on 4 Feb. 1795* (London, 1795). Strong resolutions were also passed on this occasion against 'the doctrine that a verdict of *Not Guilty* is no proof of innocence'. BL, Place newspaper cuttings, vol. 37, p. 15.

40. *Parl. Hist.*, vol. 31, col. 1130.

41. For Yorke see above, p. 325; for Stone see above, pp. 323–4.

42. Almost the last we hear of Yorke was as a lieutenant-colonel, second-in. command of a Fencible Regiment on a recruiting drive in Sheffield in Oct. 1798- He was subsequently admitted a member of the Bar. The Rev. J. Wilkinson to Earl Fitzwilliam, 6 Oct. 1798. WWM F 44(C)47.

43. Subsequent acts suspending Habeas Corpus were passed on 21 April 1798,

These and other mounting pressures from a hostile political environment also provoked a series of internal schisms in the London Corresponding Society. Government itself contributed to these differences by making tentative approaches in January 1795 to the society's assistant secretary, Joseph Burks, to persuade him to inform on the activities of one of its spies in the Committee of Correspondence.[44] The terms were tempting – fifty guineas as a down payment and a guinea for each weekly report. Burks, however, remembering the fate of the Scottish informer, Watt, was not tempted.[45] In what he obviously intended to be an ironical letter, on 15 February 1795 Burks invited the Duke of Portland as Home Secretary to nominate someone of proven integrity to be a member of the society's General Committee, so that it could be secured from misrepresentation and the government assured of full and regular intelligence.[46] What Burks did not apparently know was that the acting president of the society – and the co-signatory of his letter – one James Powell – was already fulfilling precisely that role![47]

At the end of March 1795 when Burks's own division made specific charges against No. 12 division of harbouring such a spy in its midst, the latter seceded from the society under the leadership of John Bone, a Holborn bookseller. Though it declared its social compact with the General Committee dissolved,[48] and underlined its independence by adopting the title of the London Reforming Society, this did not prevent it from maintaining a close association with the parent body and offering to contribute to the extinction of its debts.[49] This offshoot of the Corresponding Society channelled its main energies into a 'Book Plan', devised by Bone, which seems to have anticipated,

---

20 May 1799, 28 February 1800, 31 December 1800, and 18 April 1801. E. Halévy, *Histoire du Peuple Anglais au XIXᵉ siècle* (Paris, 1913), vol. 1, p. 146. The suspension was, however, temporarily lifted in the parliamentary recess between June and October 1795.

44. The approach was made by William Metcalfe, himself an attorney and government spy. See letter of 14 Jan. 1795 from Burks in *The Senator, or Clarendon's Parliamentary Chronicle*, vol. 11, col. 288.

45. *Ibid.*, col. 289.

46. *Correspondence of the London Corresponding Society, revised and corrected* (London, 1795), pp. 16–17.

47. Powell's detailed reports to the government on the proceedings of the Executive and General Committees between July 1795 and December 1796 are in PRO PC 1/23/A38 (Privy Council papers).

48. *Correspondence of LCS* (1795), p. 18.

49. *Ibid.*

but on a non-commercial basis, some of the features of modern book-clubs. Its purpose was partly political – 'to produce uniformity of sentiment in the Nation in proportion to the diffusion of knowledge', by inducing the provincial reform societies to purchase as many copies of books so published as they had members – and partly educational – to make it possible for anyone who could not afford to buy even cheap editions of political works to borrow them either from members of the radical societies or from 'patriotic booksellers'.[50] The plan was also intended to reduce the cost of printing and circulating select political texts by increasing the size of editions and dispensing with the cost of advertising.[51] Among the texts suggested for reprinting on this basis were Joseph Gerrald's *A Convention the only Means of Saving Us from Ruin* (1793) and Yorke's *Thoughts on Civil Government* (1794), which was Locke's second treatise on the subject refurbished for a popular audience. Bone himself persuaded the LCS to republish, at the modest price of 3d., the informative *Report on the State of the Representation of England and Wales*, originally printed in 1793 by the Friends of the People.[52]

Differences of opinion within the Corresponding Society on the need for a revised constitution after the State Trials were at the root of a second schism – Joseph Burks's No. 16 division seceding on this issue to form a new association called 'The Friends of Liberty'.[53] Here again amicable relations were maintained between the dissidents and their former associates. Little or nothing is known about their activities, except where they impinged on, or supported, the views and policies of the Corresponding Society itself.[54] A prominent member of the group, however, was John Baxter, one of the 'Twelve Apostles' who had been discharged from prison in December 1794 without being given an opportunity of vindicating his innocence. It has been suggested that the Friends of Liberty, under the 'extremist'

50. London Reforming Society to LCS, 9 May 1795. *Correspondence of LCS* (1795), pp. 23–5.

51. *Ibid.*, p. 23.

52. *Ibid.*, pp. 25–6.

53. *Ibid.*, pp. 19–23.

54. On 23 July 1795 the Friends of Liberty, in a letter to the parent society, conveyed the view that the 'L.C.S. had deserved well of their country', but managed to offend by concluding: 'It is true that we are ranged under *different leaders*. Yet being engaged in the same sacred cause, the same standard must infallibly unite us all.' The LCS replied, on 30 July, that 'they recognize no leaders, depending only on the correlative exertions of each other'. *Correspondence of LCS* (1795), p. 40.

influence of Baxter, were 'probably more anarchist' than the rest of the Corresponding Society.[55] There is, however, room for doubt whether Baxter's views were as republican or revolutionary as the evidence of the spy Gosling in Hardy's trial suggested, or as has been assumed from the mere title of, and certain passages in, his pamphlet *Resistance to Oppression*.[56] Even disregarding the rough handling which Gosling received at the hands of Erskine in the witness box, some of his evidence at the Old Bailey regarding Baxter's 'insurrectionary' views was directly contradicted by another Crown witness, Hillier, and had not appeared in Gosling's reports to the Home Office authorities or in his examination before the Privy Council.[57] If Baxter was as dangerous an anarchist as has been supposed, why was he allowed to remain at large so long before being arrested at the end of June 1794? It is true that, at the height of the food crisis in November 1795, Baxter ascribed much of the current distress among the poor to the 'Pride and Luxury of the Great', and attacked the land monopolists who had, with parliamentary support, converted arable into pasture, exported cattle and grain and rackrented their tenants – thus placing the necessaries of life beyond the reach of the poor. This is what he meant when he stated: 'While the whole power of the State is confined to men of landed property, it may be truly said, they have the *means* of LIFE and DEATH in their hands'.[58] Baxter also made it clear, in this same address, that in defending the popular right of resistance, he was maintaining 'a maxim essential to the constitution', and was not advocating 'the opposition of Force to Force'.[59] Recognizing that the popular societies were bodies unknown to the law and that many were averse to joining them for that reason, Baxter recommended as a means of constitutional redress that parish, town and county meetings should be summoned for the purpose of petitioning King or Parliament.[60] Resort to such legal and traditional machinery for the ventilation of popular grievances implied surely a

55. G. A. Williams, *Artisans and Sans-Culottes* (London, 1968), p. 98.

56. The full title of Baxter's pamphlet was *Resistance to Oppression: The Constitutional Rights of Britons Asserted in a lecture delivered before Section 2 of the Society of the Friends of Liberty on Monday Nov. 9th 1795.*

57. P. A. Brown, *The French Revolution in English History* (3rd impression, London, 1965), pp. 142–3. For Gosling's examination before the Privy Council on 19 May 1794 see PRO PC 1/22A/36A.

58. Baxter, *Resistance to Oppression*, p. 8.

59. *Ibid.*, p. 4.

60. *Ibid.*, p. 5. Pitt's Seditious Meetings Act of 1795 applied no restrictions on parish, town and county meetings.

realistic rather than a revolutionary attitude. When Baxter published in 1796 an 830-page *New and Impartial History of England*, his intention was to provide his fellow countrymen with 'a perpetual memento of their rights and liberties', to ensure that 'every Briton should be well acquainted with our laws and constitution', and 'to secure the subject from being sacrificed to fictitious conspiracies'.[61] The whole of English history was once more depicted as a decline and fall from the golden age of Saxon liberty under Alfred. As a theorist Baxter was as much an eighteenth-century 'patriot' and constitutionalist as Major Cartwright himself – though, when addressing popular audiences, he could be as ambivalent as Thelwall.[62]

The combination of these various strains and stresses drastically reduced the number of the society's active divisions from forty-eight at the time of Hardy's arrest to seventeen by March 1795.[63] In September 1795 the loss of a further six whole divisions was threatened when large numbers of Methodists, after vainly trying to ban atheists and Deists from the society for a year, themselves seceded to form an association called 'The Friends of Religious and Civil Liberty' in protest.[64]

Suddenly, however, the decline in members was arrested and then reversed. By the summer of 1795 the number of divisions had increased to thirty and then to forty.[65] Rumours of the seriousness of the internal divisions and of the continuing paralysis of the London Corresponding Society, however, persisted and led the activists on its Executive and General Committees to press for the summons of a large public meeting, so that its reviving fortunes and its determination to continue the fight for universal suffrage and annual parliaments could be brought to the notice of the general public.[66] According to Place this proposal was also based on the assumption that if sufficient extra-parliamentary pressure were exerted on a tottering and highly unpopular government, it would be forced to concede the

61. Baxter, *New and Impartial History of England*, p. vi.

62. E. P. Thompson, *The Making of the English Working Class* (3rd impression, London, 1965), p. 86. According to a note on the fly-leaf of the Bodleian copy of the *History*, copies of the work 'were bought up and rigidly suppressed by the government of the day'.

63. Thompson, pp. 133, 140.

64. J. Powell's report 24 Sept. 1795. PRO PC1/23/A 38.

65. On 2 July there were twenty-nine divisions and on 6 Aug. forty-one. BL, Add. MSS. 27813.

66. *Ibid.*, Add. MSS. 27808, fo. 27.

reformers' demands.[67] The accumulating military reverses and the unmistakable signs of the approaching disintegration of the European coalition against France seemed to give hope that the government might be induced to conclude a general peace.[68] Considerable anxiety also prevailed among the poor that the wheat harvest might be damaged by exceptional flooding in June and that bread and flour prices, already high, would fail to fall in the autumn, for the second year running, despite the normal pattern of fluctuation.[69] Though the prospects of being able to whip up anti-ministerial protests therefore seemed promising, Place himself considered that large public meetings would further compromise the financial resources of the society and generate fresh government repression.[70] The decision to proceed with the plans for a monster protest meeting was, however, the result of a referendum conducted in the divisions.

Advertisements summoning a general meeting of the society for Monday 29 June in St George's Fields (near the Obelisk) were inserted in the daily papers, and handbills enjoining good order and behaviour were also circulated.[71] On the day before, and on the morning of the meeting, large basket-loads of biscuits were distributed among the poor, stamped on one side with the inscription 'Unanimity, firmness and spirit' and, on the other, 'Freedom and plenty, or slavery and want'.[72] The meeting, attended by vast crowds, variously estimated at between 10,000 and 100,000, began at 3 p.m. under the chairmanship of John Gale Jones, who set the tone by a vigorous and highly charged onslaught on the ministry.[73] Addresses to the nation and to the King were moved and carried, as well as a number of resolutions, the most important of which demanded manhood suffrage and annual parliaments as the undoubted rights of the

67. *Ibid.*, Add. MSS. 35143, fo. 14.

68. The British forces in Holland under the Duke of York were back in this country on 25 May 1795. The Duke of Tuscany had made peace with France on 9 Feb. 1795, the King of Prussia on 6 April, Holland (renamed the Batavian Republic) on 16 May, Sweden on 12 June. Spain followed suit on 22 July. *Histoire des Relations Internationales* (ed. P. Renouvin), vol. 4. A. Fugier, *La Révolution Française et l'Empire Napoléonien* (Paris, 1954), pp. 89–95.

69. Stern.

70. BL, Add. MSS. 35143, fo. 15.

71. As reported in the Tory newspaper the *Sun*, 30 June 1795.

72. *Ibid.*

73. Thompson, p. 140. The LCS estimate of 100,000 is obviously an exaggeration, just as that of J. B. Burges, under-secretary of state at the Foreign Office – of 10,000 – erred in the opposite direction. J. B. Burges to his wife, 29 June 1795. Bodleian Library, Oxford, Bland Burges papers.

people. Other resolutions deplored the high cost of provisions, caused entirely by 'the cruel and unnecessary war', and called on the government 'to acknowledge the brave French republic, and to obtain a speedy and lasting peace' as the sole remedy.[74] Votes of thanks to Citizens Erskine and Gibbs were carried for their eloquent defence of the prisoners in the State Trials and to Citizens Stanhope and Sheridan for their proof that 'the people had at least one honest man in each House of Parliament'.[75] Throughout the proceedings there was no disturbance of any kind, and about 8 p.m. the meeting was brought to a close and the large crowds quietly dispersed.[76]

The peaceful outcome of the meeting, after they had made such dire predictions of riots and disorder, was attributed by ministerialists to the orders given to the magistrates about four o'clock to read the Riot Act and to the concentration on the area of large detachments of guards and cavalry ready for instant intervention.[77] The exhortations given by the society to peaceful behaviour, the issue of 6d. tickets for admission to the enclosure, and the careful preparation of the agenda and Address to the King had, however, contributed not a little to the final result.[78]

As a gesture of public protest the experiment lacked any effective sequel, for the Duke of Portland, as Home Secretary, after receiving the delegation from the Corresponding Society bearing the Address to the King, refused to forward or acknowledge it.[79] As an exercise in public relations, however, the meeting was highly successful. It stimulated an immediate and impressive increase in the number of new recruits to the society, hundreds joining weekly throughout the summer and autumn, so that by October, the number of divisions reached its maximum of between seventy and eighty.[80] It proved that the society could organize large demonstrations of public protest in a legal and constitutional manner in the presence of magistrates,

74. Earl Stanhope, *Life of Pitt* (London, 1861), vol. 2, pp. 325–6.

75. *Summary of the Proceedings . . . Monday, 29 June 1795* and *History of the Two Acts* (London, 1796), pp. 90–108.

76. J. B. Burges, *ut sup.*

77. *Ibid.*

78. The *Sun*, 30 June 1795. *Correspondence of the LCS* (1795), pp. 32–3. Place was, however, highly critical of the *Address to the Nation* as both commonplace in substance and melodramatic in form. The *Address to the King* he thought 'a better drawn paper'. BL, Add. MSS. 27808, fos. 38–40.

79. PRO PC 1/23/A 38.

80. Four hundred new members were counted in June, 800 in July. *Correspondence of LCS* (1795), p. 34.

police and regular troops without precipitating a confrontation or endangering the public peace. It also made possible the resumption of contacts with the provincial radical societies, most of which, like the Corresponding Society itself, had found a fresh impetus in the popular economic grievances thrown up by the war.

In Norwich the resumption of radical activity, signalized by the foundation of the Norwich Patriotic Society on 20 April 1795, stemmed from the strongly rooted tradition of intellectual liberalism among its cultivated professional elite, the persistent loyalty of local Dissent to the democratic cause, and the increasing impact of the war upon the city's export trade with the Continent.

Even before the outbreak of the war with France unemployment and distress among the city's poor were already on the increase.[81] That event, however, imperilled the very source of the worsted manufacture's former prosperity – its trade with the Continent. Writing to the Home Office on 12 March 1793, Robert Harvey Jnr – an important Norwich manufacturer and alderman – noted the plight of the local weavers in wartime.

The consequences of this just and inevitable war visit this poor city severely, and suspend the operations of the Dutch, German and Italian trade and the only lingering employment in the manufactory is the completion of a few Russian orders and the last China cambletts which I hope will find encouragement in the East India charter. This languid trade has doubled our poor rate and a voluntary subscription of above £2000 is found inadequate to the exigencies of the poor.[82]

The printed accounts of receipts and disbursements of the Court of Guardians of the city from 1 April 1793 to 1 April 1794 showed an expenditure of £22,695.[83] Slightly over a year later Thelwall estimated that 25,000 of the city's population of 40,000 had 'been obliged to claim relief from the hand of charity'.[84] A further informed contemporary description, quoted by Holcroft, completes the picture for 1795.

There can be no doubt of the distress of the poor in this city. A comber who used to employ sixty men, now is able to employ only fifteen. A hotpresser whom I know, assured me that all the hotpressers in this city do not now employ so many journeymen as he alone did before the war. The money paid to the villages in the country for spinning, before the

81. *Norwich Chronicle*, 17 Dec. 1792.
82. PRO HO 42/25.
83. Holcroft, p. 41.
84. Thelwall, *Tribune* (23 Sept. 1795), vol. 2, p. 316.

war, was a thousand pounds a week. It is at this time not quite half the sum; and the quantity of spinning that used to be done for one shilling is now done for sixpence; so that the poor spinners are doubly distressed.[85]

The discredit and disarray in which the federated Norwich radical societies had been involved by the State Trials left the victims of the local trade recession without organized spokesmen or champions – until the liberal leanings and charitable concern of the Dissenting clergy and their congregations turned local resentment with the war policy of the government into a movement of political protest. Windham's re-election as MP for Norwich in July 1794, after his elevation to cabinet rank as minister at war in the Portland coalition, thus called into play much local opposition, partly because of his commitment to the policy of no negotiation with the French, and partly because of his alleged condemnation of foreign commerce in the debates on the Traitorous Correspondence Bill in March 1793.[86] The circumstances in which 770 Norwich freemen cast their votes against Windham as 'a man of blood', and 'wrote their protest against the measures of administration and the commencement and continuation of a dreadful war' were recalled by the Reverend Mark Wilks, who had led the campaign, when he preached two collection sermons in St Paul's Chapel on 19 April 1795 in aid of the defence expenses of the prisoners in the State Trials.[87] Wilks had not surrendered his pro-French sympathies and his sustained pacifism enabled him to play as effective a role in the final phase of Norwich 'Jacobinism' as he had done earlier inside the local Revolution Society. The Norwich Patriotic Society came into existence on the day after these sermons were delivered.

In 1794–5, however, the most striking evidence of the resilience of Norwich intellectual 'Jacobinism' in a period of increasing reaction was the appearance of the *Cabinet* – a periodical miscellany of political and literary essays and occasional verse, contributed by a gifted

85. Holcroft, p. 40.

86. The slogan 'Perish commerce, let the constitution live', attributed to Windham, was never used by him, but by a Mr Hardinge. *Parl. Hist.*, vol. 30, col. 622*n.* In 1793, however, the words were printed in pamphlet form and 'stuck up in the workshops of Norwich, to alienate the affections of the people from him, and persuade them that he was their worst enemy'. W. Windham, 5 Jan. 1795. *Parl. Hist.*, vol. 31, col. 1078.

87. *Athaliah, or the Tocsin Sounded by Modern Alarmists . . .*, p. 83. See also *An Address to the Electors of Norwich, being a Vindication of the Principles and Conduct of Mr. Windham's Opponents at the late election, 12 July 1794* (Norwich, 1794).

coterie of local 'friends of liberty'.[88] Its form and presentation were reminiscent of the Sheffield *Patriot*, while its ethos and outlook foreshadowed those of Coleridge's journal, the *Watchman*, of 1796. In the preface, dated 17 January, T. S. Norgate explained that its aim was 'to encourage a spirit of free and dispassionate enquiry, to provide a liberal investigation of the nature and object of civil government and to remind their fellow citizens at once of their duties and their rights' – at a time 'When the public mind, seduced by the base artifices of a designing and profligate administration, rejected with a furious disdain, every effort at rational reform'.[89] While confessing to a Rousseauite (or Godwinian) belief in human perfectibility, the *Cabinet* did not aspire 'to work the complete reformation of mankind by argument' or to overcome popular ignorance and political imposture at the stroke of a pen.[90] Theology was excluded, in order not to offend local religious prejudices, and metaphysics because the journal's aims were practical, not speculative.[91] In line with this policy the contributors restated the case for the revival of the provincial reform societies,[92] attempted to dissuade local radical leaders from emigrating,[93] defended the feasibility of universal suffrage, when combined with indirect elections, and of annual parliaments on the basis of partial renewal of the membership of the House of Commons,[94] and conducted an unrelenting assault on the war as the source of the deepening economic crisis.[95]

88. The discovery of a 'marked' set of the three volumes of the *Cabinet*, formerly the property of Richard Taylor, father of the hymn-writer, in the library of the University of Michigan, has enabled the authorship of many of the anonymous articles to be established. The political contributions were mainly by Charles Marsh, its printer and later MP for Retford, John Pitchford, Dr William Enfield, John Stuart Taylor and William Youngman. Other notable contributors were Henry Crabb Robinson ('On Spies and Reformers'), William Taylor, the Germanist, and Amelia Alderson (Mrs Opie). W. Graham, 'The authorship of the Norwich *Cabinet*, 1794–5', *Notes and Queries*, vol. 162 (Jan–June, 1932), pp. 294–5.
89. *Cabinet*, vol. 1, preface.
90. *Ibid.*, vol. 1, pp. 3–6.
91. *Ibid.*, vol. 1, p. 2.
92. *Ibid.*, vol. 2, pp. 234–7.
93. *Ibid.*, vol. 1, p. 60.
94. *Ibid.*, vol. 2, p. 236.
95. *Ibid.*, vol. 2, pp. 58–63. The war itself was characterized, in Whiggish terms, as 'an unprincipled war, begun for the protection of an ally who dreaded our officious zeal, carried on for the humane purpose of re-establishing an odious despotism on the fertile plains of an independent country, and, at present, madly continued to stop the progress of truth, and arrest the banishment of ignorance'.

An ideal form of government would be based on the principles of 'perfect toleration, equal rights and popular consent'.[96] The role assigned to actual government was, however, paternalistic – 'to guard the weak against the strong, the ignorant against the arts of the more experienced and the poor from being crushed by the ascendancy of the rich'.[97] One contributor noted that the poor rate – 'that barometer of the poor man's misery' – had been driven to excessive heights by the war, and that private charity was no longer adequate to provide the necessary relief for such large numbers. The conclusion was that the problem could only be solved if the state assumed responsibility and sought to eliminate the evil by acts of social justice.[98] Such views were derived from Godwinian socialism, and other writers explored the subject of female emancipation opened up by Mary Wollstone-craft. For the time being all that could be done was to associate – even though popular addresses against the war were unheeded and radical petitions disregarded.

When the Norwich Patriotic Society published its declaration of principles and constitution on 20 April 1795, it was content to conform to the well-established pattern of a provincial reform society. The evils it complained of – 'numerous, burdensome and unnecessary taxes', 'unprincipled, ruinous and unnecessary wars', and the high cost of provisions – were, as usual, attributed to the lack of adequate popular representation in the Commons. The society pledged itself to pursue the remedy – universal suffrage and annual parliaments – with 'reason, firmness and unanimity', repudiating 'tumult and violence' and 'corresponding and co-operating with other societies united for the same objects'.[99] Its organization – with divisions of thirty members each meeting fortnightly and a delegate committee elected quarterly – was identical with that of the London Corresponding Society. A minimum subscription of a penny a fortnight suggests that the membership was intended to consist mainly, but not exclusively, of weavers, cordwainers, artisans and shopkeepers. The rules for admission were, nevertheless, strict – new members had to be sponsored and proposed by existing members, willing to vouch for

96. *Ibid.*, vol. 1, p. 13.
97. *Ibid.*, vol. 1, pp. 187–8.
98. 'A nation is not to relieve the distresses of the poor by acts of charity; it ought to prevent their existence by acts of justice.' *Ibid.*, vol. 1, p. 193.
99. *The Declaration and Constitution of the Norwich Patriotic Society established the twentieth of April 1795 to obtain a reform in the Commons House of Parliament.* Central Library, Norwich, Colman Collection, 25E.

their 'political principles, means of life and good character'.[100] Even so candidates could be black-balled. Its officials were well-known and 'respectable'.[101]

By the end of June 1795 the society was sufficiently well established to write to the London Corresponding Society soliciting a regular correspondence and encouraging it to persist in its efforts 'to obtain that redress of grievances' so loudly demanded by 'the starving manufacturers and neglected peasantry of Great Britain and Ireland'.[102] In its reply of 17 July the London society announced that it had cleared off the debts incurred during the State Trials, that 'upwards of four hundred' new members had joined during the past month, and that, in accordance with Bone's 'Book Plan', and as evidence of its renewed activity, it was despatching copies of the proceedings of the general meeting of 29 June and of the reprinted *Report on the State of the Parliamentary Representation* published by the Friends of the People in 1793.[103] The correspondence thus re-established was continued till late in 1797. By early September 1795 the Norwich society had grown to nineteen divisions and to twenty-seven divisions by October.[104]

At Sheffield the arrest of half a dozen of its members to serve as Crown witnesses in the State Trials, the flight of Joseph Gales, its printer and newspaper editor, and the capture of Henry Yorke, its orator-in-chief, had not broken up or intimidated the Constitutional Society. Before he left for the Continent Gales had printed and circulated a handbill reasserting the society's belief in the necessity of a reform in Parliament, defending it from the charge of 'levelling' or arming, and vindicating the open and orderly conduct of its meetings.[105] Though Alarmism had triumphed for the time being, Gales reminded his fellow countrymen that 'a Nation having once got its Liberties in view will never lose sight of them till obtained'.[106] In a farewell message to his readers in the last issue of the *Sheffield Register* of 27 June

100. B. D. Hayes, 'Politics in Norfolk, 1750–1832'. Unpublished PhD thesis, Cambridge (1957), p. 245.

101. Its first president was J. Stuart Taylor. A successor was John Davey, a man of means and future alderman. Its secretary was John Lightbody, a respected bookbinder.

102. *Correspondence of the London Corresponding Society* (1795), pp. 27–8.

103. *Ibid.*, pp. 28–9.

104. *Ibid.*, p. 63.

105. *An Appeal to Britons*, enclosed in a letter from R. A. Athorpe, magistrate, to Nepean, 25 June 1794. PRO HO 42/31.

106. *Ibid.*

1794, he explained his motives in seeking safety from the accusations of suborned witnesses, repudiated the charge of having written the letter to Hardy offering to supply pikes to the London Corresponding Society, and expressed a modest pride in having printed and edited 'an impartial and truly independent newspaper'.[107] The *Register* itself was continued under a new name, the *Iris*, and a new editor – Gales's former associate, James Montgomery. Temporarily financed by the Reverend Benjamin Naylor, the Unitarian minister of the Upper Chapel in Norfolk St, who entered into partnership, Montgomery eventually acquired the sole ownership of the journal. Though sympathetic to the cause of peace and reform and committed to the charitable support of the families of the State Trials prisoners, Montgomery disclaimed the influence of party spirit, repudiated political controversy, and sought to pursue a middle course between radicalism and reaction.[108] This studied moderation, however, only lost the *Iris* the support of its 'Jacobin' subscribers without attracting the patronage of the 'aristocratic party', who remained loyal to the Tory *Sheffield Courant*.[109] In any case, Montgomery could not have continued to act as printer for the Sheffield radicals since their society's funds for publishing political propaganda had been exhausted.[110] Because his own workmen continued to attend radical meetings and because the Hartshead office of the *Iris* still continued as 'the rendezvous of the disaffected', Montgomery found it impossible to avert the suspicions which his predecessor had aroused.[111] Despite his caution, he seems to have been unable to suppress his own real feelings, or to control the indiscretions of his subordinates.

The receipt of the news of the acquittals in the State Trials, the return of Camage and Hill to Sheffield on the night of 20 December after their release on the 15th, and of the rest of the Sheffield prisoners a few days later were made the occasion of general rejoicing among the radicals. On 25 November at a large meeting at the Bull Tavern

107. *Sheffield Register*, 27 June 1794.

108. J. Holland and J. Everett (eds.), *Memoirs of James Montgomery* (London, 1854), vol. 1, p. 178.

109. According to a conversation, recorded many years later in the *Sheffield Times and Iris* of 30 Aug. 1873, Montgomery lost 1000 subscribers in his first year.

110. William Chow to 'Citizen Hodgson' of the LCS, 3 Dec. 1794. 'The finances of the society have been for the last six months in so feeble a state that we have not been able to publish anything worth sending you.' BL, Add. MSS. 27813, fos. 11–12.

111. Holland and Everett, vol. 1, p. 189.

in the Wicker, the account of Horne Tooke's acquittal brought by the evening mail was read and acclaimed and repeated patriotic toasts were drunk.[112] On the evening of 20 December Camage and Hill were met half a mile outside the town by a coach hired for the occasion and drawn to their homes at the centre of an elaborate torchlight procession by 'an immense crowd of the Swinish Multitude, to the sound of repeated cannon fire.[113] After Broomhead, Widdison and Moody had returned, the heroic five were fêted by the friends of reform at a monster dinner on 26 December in Watson's Walk in celebration, not only of their own release, but also of the part they had played in the acquittals of the London radicals. A hymn composed by Montgomery was sung and the substance of the speeches was reported in the *Iris*.[114]

Montgomery, however, soon after became the victim of a fabricated charge of seditious libel brought against him at the instigation of the Attorney General chiefly with the intention of putting a stop to the meetings of the associated radical clubs in Sheffield, on the false assumption that he had continued his predecessor's practice of publishing their alleged 'inflammatory' resolutions and proceedings.[115] At the end of January 1795, after the chairman of the bench of magistrates at Doncaster Assizes had refused to accept the jury's special verdict, Montgomery was found guilty of having published a seditious libel – a 'Patriotic Song' by the Rev. Scott of Dromore first sung on 14 July 1792 at a Belfast commemoration of the fall of the Bastille.[116] On the eve of the invasion of France by the Prussian and Austrian armies, the song had proclaimed the dangers to the liberties of Europe if the country were conquered. It had been printed by the Belfast *Northern Star*, the *Morning Chronicle* and by Gales in the *Sheffield Register* – eight months before the outbreak of the

112. BL, Place newspaper cuttings, vol. 36, fo. 242.

113. BL, Place newspaper cuttings, vol. 36, fo. 277.

114. *Sheffield Local Register* (1830), 26 Dec. 1794. Holland and Everett, vol. 1, p. 187.

115. This was only revealed when, in 1839, an extract from the brief for the prosecution came into Montgomery's possession when the prosecuting attorney, J. Brookfield, changed his offices. The briefs were marked 'with the Attorney General's compliments' and contained the statement: 'this prosecution is carried on chiefly with a view to put a stop to the Associated Clubs in Sheffield; and it is to be hoped, if we are fortunate enough to succeed in convicting the prisoner, it will go a great way towards curbing the insolence they have uniformly manifested'. R. E. Leader, *Sheffield in the Eighteenth Century* (Sheffield, 1901), pp. 298–9. Holland and Everett, vol. 1, pp. 210–12.

116. *Ibid.*, vol. 1, pp. 189–93. *Patriot*, vol. 1, pp. 338–49.

Anglo-French conflict. Two years later, in August 1794, the foreman in Montgomery's printing office had offered copies of the verses, the type for which had remained intact, to a former acquaintance of his called Jordan – a peripatetic song vendor. At the latter's request Montgomery had eventually agreed to sell him six quires of the verses for eighteen pence – made up, as his defence counsel, Felix Vaughan, put it, of 'sixpennyworth of paper, sixpennyworth of printing and sixpennyworth of profit'.[117] For this venial error Montgomery was sentenced to three months' imprisonment in York Castle and fined £20.[118]

What the Sheffield radicals had uppermost in their minds in 1795, however, was not so much the celebration of the verdicts in the State Trials, or the fresh injustice done to Montgomery, as the lengthening spectre of famine conditions and general poverty. These problems were so acute by early February 1795 that voluntary subscriptions in the town and several of the surrounding villages were organized to subsidize the purchase of meal and bread flour by the poor.[119] The chief anxiety arose, however, from the scarcity of grain during a severe winter and so soon after the last harvest, which had itself been deficient. The normal supplies of corn from Lincolnshire and the eastern parts of the West Riding had not arrived and the local farmers had been forced to complete their threshing operations sooner than usual. Even so, supplies remained as low as they normally were at midsummer, while farm workers joined the ranks of the unemployed.[120] Relief measures temporarily eased this shortage, but at the end of June the necessary supplies to tide the local population over till the harvest could only be procured by the establishment of a municipal corn committee and the raising of a loan of £9000, financed by the Sheffield banks and guaranteed by the Duke of Norfolk, Earl Fitzwilliam and other well-endowed citizens.[121] The sale price of wheat flour and oatmeal was fixed, large quantities of potatoes were bought and sold at prime cost and soup kitchens operated two or three times a week.[122] The committee of charitable subscribers dis-

117. Holland and Everett, vol. 1, pp. 189–204.
118. *Ibid.*, p. 204.
119. The Rev. J. Wilkinson to agent of Earl Fitzwilliam, 7 Feb. 1795 and C. Bowns (agent) to Earl Fitzwilliam, 8 Feb. 1795. WWM F 121/12.
120. *Ibid.*
121. Dr J. Browne, chairman of the Corn Committee, to Earl Fitzwilliam, 1 July 1795. WWM F 47/9.
122. The Rev. J. Wilkinson to R. Ford, 6 Aug. 1795. University of Nottingham Portland papers, PWF 3943.

tributed tickets to the poor to allow them to buy meal, flour and potatoes at half or two-thirds of the ruling prices.[123]

Despite these measures popular fears of continuing food scarcity were not allayed and there is some evidence that the serious riot which broke out on the evening of 4 August in Norfolk St in the centre of the town may have been influenced by plans to seize the available stocks of corn, flour meal and bread with the connivance of the newly raised and disaffected troops of Colonel Cameron's regiment.[124] After the normal evening exercise the privates in this regiment, to press their claims on bounty money and pay in arrears, refused to disband. One local magistrate believed that this mutinous disposition had been encouraged by the radicals.[125] This altercation led to large crowds of curious onlookers gathering on the parade in Norfolk St. The responsibility for the maintenance of public order thus devolved on the force of local Volunteers under the command of Colonel R. A. Athorne – a magistrate from Dinnington, near Worksop.[126] When the townsfolk refused to disperse on his orders, the colonel rode into the crowd brandishing his sword and injuring several bystanders. The crowd retaliated by throwing stones at the Volunteers and stood their ground after the proclamation in the Riot Act had been read. Eventually, with tempers frayed on both sides, and after more than the time limit for the forcible dispersal of the rioters had expired, the Volunteers were ordered to fire on their fellow citizens. Two persons were killed and several others wounded by the 'butchers in blue' as the local poetaster Mather called them.[127] It was several days before tranquillity in the town and discipline in Colonel Cameron's regiment were restored.[128] On 7 August, Montgomery, in the columns of the *Iris*, accused Athorne, though not by name, of having 'wounded with his sword men, women and children promiscuously' and defended the crowd from charges of riotous behaviour or intent.[129] For this he was charged and found guilty of a seditious libel and in January 1796 was sentenced to six months' imprisonment

123. *Ibid.*
124. *Ibid.*
125. *Ibid.*
126. Athorne had been actively concerned in the suppressing of the Sheffield enclosure riots of 1791 and had sat on the magistrates' bench at Doncaster Assizes when Montgomery had received his first sentence.
127. Holland and Everett, vol. 1, pp. 234–5. J. Wilson (ed.), *The Songs of Joseph Mather* (Sheffield, 1862), p. 47.
128. Rev. J. Wilkinson to Duke of Portland, 11 Aug. 1795. PRO HO 42/35.
129. Holland and Everett, vol. 1, p. 235.

in York Castle and fined £30. Montgomery could hardly be blamed if he construed this second prosecution as an attempt to suppress his newspaper out of hand.[130]

Meanwhile, by the end of July, the London Corresponding Society had resumed contact with the Sheffield radicals, who were reported as 'persevering in the cause of liberty', and when their Constitutional Society held a large open-air demonstration on Crooke's Moor on 10 August to petition against the war, the meeting was presided over by 'Citizen Barrow' of the London society of the Friends of Liberty.[131] In the address and petition to the King fears were expressed that famine 'might be added to the innumerable other calamities heaped upon our heads by the war', and the plea for bread was accompanied and justified by the appeal for peace.[132] Since the war had ruined their trade, reduced their wages and starved their families, the petitioners were convinced that royal humanity would respond to their entreaties. 'Let not our prayers for peace be drowned in the thunder of war; when we ask for Bread, let not the Father of his People give us a stone.' After the address had been unanimously adopted, resolutions were carried ascribing the food crisis entirely to the export of supplies to the armies abroad, repudiating all riots and civil disorders and requesting Lord Stanhope to present the petition. The demands for universal suffrage and annual parliaments were half defiantly reasserted and the London Corresponding Society was declared to have 'deserved well of the country'. The meeting was closed by the chairman exhorting all those who were not already members of the Sheffield Constitutional Society to join, as union was the only means of achieving their objectives.[133] He carried back to London a request that the metropolitan societies should help with the defence costs of Henry Yorke, who had recently been found guilty of Conspiracy.[134] Nine days after this demonstration the price of fine flour and bread flour at Sheffield was reduced by the Corn Committee to 2s. 6d. and 2s. per stone respectively, and on 22 August a crowd of women with ribbons and cockades in their hats invaded the Cutlers' Hall to thank the members of the committee; they would have drawn its chairman, Dr Browne, in a chaise through the principal streets of the town, if

130. *Ibid.*, p. 246. *Sheffield Local Register* (1830), 21 Jan. 1796.

131. *Correspondence of the London Corresponding Society*, 1795, p. 33; Sheffield Central Library, Local Pamphlets, vol. 8, no. 5, *Proceedings of the Public Meeting held on Crooke's Moor, at Sheffield, in the Open Air, on Monday August 10, 1795.*

132. *Ibid.*, p. 4.

133. *Ibid.*

134. PRO PC 1/23/A 38.

he had not declined the honour.[135] One protest meeting, at least, had achieved part of its objectives.

Meanwhile, a new cycle of events and a further intensification of the protest movement was started by the large open-air meeting held by the London Corresponding Society at Copenhagen House in Islington on Monday 26 October – a few days before the opening of the new parliamentary session.[136] This was a repeat or 'follow-up' of the meeting in St George's Fields designed to enforce some official response to the society's earlier petition to the King which ministers had stifled or suppressed.[137] The intention was also to reassert the society's perseverance, despite its trials and persecution, in the 'grand and glorious cause of PARLIAMENTARY REFORM'. The rapid succession of military disasters, the neglect of the nation's accumulating grievances and the spectre of famine on the heels of an abundant harvest, were therefore blamed, not only on ministerial incompetence, but also on that debilitating disease of the body politic, 'Parliamentary Corruption'.[138] Lastly, it was planned to announce publicly the positive measures by which the society would seek the peaceable redress of its immediate grievances and the achievement of its long-term objectives. The organization of this meeting set the pattern for a series of subsequent monster public meetings of protest in the metropolis.[139] It was followed by, and was said by the Alarmists to have inspired, the attack on the King's coach on 29 October on the occasion of the state opening of Parliament. It also provoked the repressive legislation restricting the right of public meeting and free speech which led Charles James Fox to refurbish and proclaim in Parliament the popular right of resistance to oppression.

Speaking in the House of Lords on the subject of large public meetings on 9 December 1795, Lord Thurlow, former Lord Chancellor, observed mildly that 'whenever he heard of a speech made before 30,000 persons, the first thing that occurred to him was that it was impossible that one thirtieth part of the audience could hear it'.[140]

135. *Sheffield Local Register* (1830), 19 and 22 Aug. 1795.
136. Copenhagen House was a popular tea-garden of the period.
137. See above, p. 373.
138. *Account of the Proceedings of a meeting of the London Corresponding Society held in a field near Copenhagen House, Monday Oct. 26, 1795. Printed for Citizen Lee, at the TREE OF LIBERTY*, pp. 7–8.
139. These were held on 12 November, 2 and 7 December, in protest against the Treasonable Practices and Seditious Meetings Bills.
140. *Parl. Hist.*, vol. 32, col. 541. Charles James Fox had claimed to have spoken to a crowd of 30,000 at a meeting in Palace Yard Westminster on 17 Nov. 1795.

The enormous crowds which slowly assembled near Copenhagen House in the forenoon of 26 October were said eventually to have numbered over 100,000.[141] The difficulty noted by Thurlow, had, however, been anticipated by the organizing committee and three widely dispersed rostra or tribunes had been erected from which different speakers were detailed to explain the order of proceedings, to read the draft addresses and resolutions and to submit them for approval by means of a popular vote.[142] The committee's nomination of John Binns as chairman and of Thelwall, John Gale Jones and Binns as principal speakers was also ratified. The main business was confined to the reading and explanation of an Address to the Nation, a Remonstrance to the King and a number of resolutions. Comments from the audience were invited without result, the speeches were well received and the address, remonstrance and resolutions were approved *nem. con.* Shortly after five o'clock the meeting was brought to a close. The crowds dispersed in an orderly manner and in the good-humoured persuasion of 'A DAY WELL SPENT'.[143]

Thelwall had taken the opportunity to explain the reasons why, since his release, he had ceased to be a member of the London Corresponding Society without abandoning its principles. He also condemned the popular attacks during the summer on crimping houses and flour mills, and warned his hearers against any resort to tumult or violence.[144] Some other features of the day's proceedings, however, almost inevitably awakened fresh fears and anxieties among the opponents of reform. Chairman Binns, before reading the Address to the Nation, had reminded ministers that 'when the voice of a united people went forth, it was their duty to attend to it' or else incur the guilt of high treason against the people.[145] The address itself reminded the King that 'when he ceased to consult the interests and happiness of the people, he will cease to be respected, and that justice is a debt which the Nation hath a right to demand from the Throne!'[146] After reciting the long catalogue of popular grievances and ministerial misdeeds, it posed the query: 'Why, when we inces-

141. The Remonstrance to the King claimed that the numbers attending the meeting were 200000!
142. *Sun*, 27 Oct. 1795. *Account of the Proceedings . . ., Oct. 26, 1795*, p. 15.
143. *Ibid.*
144. *Speech at the General Meeting of the Friends of Parliamentary Reform – Oct. 26, 1795*, p. 12.
145. *Account of the Proceedings . . ., Oct. 26, 1795*, p. 4.
146. *bid.*, p. 7.

santly toil and labour, must we pine in misery and want?'[147] It warned that the 'Friends of Peace and Reform' might not be able always to 'restrain the aggravated feelings of insulted human nature' and that if ever the British nation should loudly demand strong and decisive measures the members of the reform societies were prepared to dedicate their lives to the salvation of the country.[148] The Remonstrance to the King claimed the right of 'a wearied and afflicted people' to advise as well as to supplicate, and asserted that 'a Reform in the Representation of the People, the removal of your present Ministers, and a speedy PEACE, are the only means by which the country can be saved, or the attachment of the people secured'.[149]

Some of the resolutions also indicated the society's disillusionment both with the executive government and the party politicians, its conviction that 'immediate and effectual redress' of the country's unexampled grievances was called for and that this could only be achieved by direct popular action. The society announced its intention, in the General Election of 1796, of exacting from prospective candidates electoral pledges in favour of radical reform[150] and, in the interim, its decision to despatch special deputies to the principal towns in the kingdom to convince their inhabitants of the need to associate 'as the only means of procuring a Parliamentary Reform'.[151] Nothing was said about a national convention, but some sort of 'a popular front' seems to have been envisaged.

The attack on the King's coach, as the royal procession converged on Palace Yard Westminster on 29 October for the opening of the new parliamentary session, was seized on by the government as an excuse for introducing the so-called Two Acts – one extending the scope of high treason and the other limiting the right of public meeting.[152] A Royal Proclamation of 4 November, however, attributed the attempt on the King's life directly to the '*inflammatory*' discourses delivered at the Copenhagen House meeting, its subversive

147. *Ibid.*, p. 8.
148. *Ibid.*, p. 9.
149. *Ibid.*, p. 12.
150. Resolution No. 8, *Proceedings*, p. 13.
151. Resolution No. 14, *ibid.*, p. 14.
152. As the state procession wound through St James's Park, large crowds had raised cries of 'No Pitt, No War, Bread, Bread, Peace, Peace'. As the royal coach approached the House of Lords, one of its windows was broken by a small stone or ball said to have been shot from an air gun. An alleged attempt to drag the King out of his coach on the return journey to the palace was said by Place to have been an invention. BL, Add. MSS. 27808, fos. 46–7.

proceedings and the seditious pamphlets inciting to regicide said to have been on sale there.[153] Instructions had, accordingly, been issued to all magistrates and law enforcement officers to 'discourage, prevent and suppress all seditious and unlawful assemblies' and to bring to justice 'all persons distributing such seditious and treasonable papers as aforesaid'.[154] This was an emergency measure taken by the Duke of Portland on the initiative and advice of Henry Dundas, his predecessor at the Home Office.[155] It was also a preparatory move towards legislation to restrict the holding of any further large public meetings and to subject subversive speeches and writings to the penalties of high treason. With the memories of the disastrous consequences of the Gordon Riots still fresh in their minds, both statesmen and sovereign were convinced of the immediate need of preventive measures to secure life and property in the capital.[156]

Both the Treasonable Practices Bill, introduced into the House of Lords by Grenville on 6 November 1795 and the Seditious Meetings Bill, moved by Pitt in the Commons on 10 November, were double-barrelled.[157] The former modified the law of treason so as to bring within its scope any who 'compassed or devised' the death, bodily harm, imprisonment or deposition of the King, who exerted pressure on him to change his measures or counsels, who plotted to assist foreign invaders, or to intimidate or overawe both houses or either house of Parliament, whether such intention was expressed, as hitherto, by overt act, or by speech or writing. Two witnesses were to be required for a conviction.[158] These clauses of the act were to remain in force during the life of the King and till the end of the next session after his death. The second main provision of the bill made those who incited the people to hatred or contempt of the King, the established government or constitution by speech or writing liable, on a first conviction, to the penalties of a high misdemeanour, and on a second, to a sentence of transportation for up to seven years.[159]

The Seditious Meetings Bill subjected to the discretionary control of local magistrates all public meetings of over fifty persons convened

153. *Parl. Hist.*, vol. 32, cols. 243–4.

154. *Ibid.*, col. 244.

155. University of Nottingham, Portland papers. H. Dundas to Duke of Portland, 1 Nov. 1795. PWF 3495.

156. George III to Duke of Portland, 13 Nov. 1795. *Ibid.*, PWF 4104.

157. *Parl. Hist.*, vol. 32, cols. 244–5, 272–6.

158. 36 Geo. III c. 7.

159. By an amendment made in committee these clauses were restricted to three years. Stanhope, vol. 2, p. 360.

for the discussion of public grievances or for the consideration of any petition, remonstrance or address to King or Parliament bearing on the 'alteration of matters established in Church or State'.[160] Under the terms of the bill prior notice, specifying the time, place and purpose of such meetings had to be given by at least seven resident householders in a local newspaper and a copy sent to any local justice on demand.[161] Any such public meetings which did not conform to these requirements were made illegal and could be dissolved immediately by one or more magistrates. These were also given the power, at their own discretion, to break up properly convened meetings if speeches were made likely, in their view, to bring the king, government or constitution into contempt. Any popular resistance to the orders of magistrates to disperse at such meetings after due warning was made punishable by death and justices were completely indemnified for any loss of life or injury that might ensue in consequence.[162] Other provisions in the bill were specifically designed to put a stop to the public lectures delivered by Thelwall. All rooms or places where lectures were held concerned with supposed public grievances or 'the government and policy of these kingdoms' and for which an admission charge was made were, unless previously licensed by two magistrates, deemed to be 'disorderly houses'.[163] Their proprietors or lessors were rendered liable to fines of up to £100 for each offence. The exception made in the bill in favour of public lectures at the universities may have been no more than a pious piece of window-dressing, incumbent on Portland as Chancellor of the University of Oxford.[164] The bill was to continue in force for three years only.

Here at last was that 'Convention Bill' which the radicals had been predicting since the clash with the government in the spring of 1794, the new law of treason which the discredit of the 'constructive interpretation' of the Edwardian statute during the Old Bailey trials had made necessary, and the importation from Scotland of the penalty of transportation in cases of misdemeanour which both Dundas and the Lord Advocate had been accused of wishing to incorporate in English law after the Scottish sedition trials.[165] In Pitt's view, how-

160. Certain public meetings were excepted, especially county meetings called by the Lord Lieutenant or Sheriff or, in Scotland, by the Convenors of Counties or Stewartries.
161. 36 Geo. III c. 8.
162. *The Senator*, vol. 13, col. 216.
163. *Ibid.*, col. 218.
164. *Ibid.*, cols. 220–1.
165. For the Lord Advocate's views see *Parl. Hist.*, vol. 30, col. 1553.

ever, preventive legislation of this sort might well check the radical demonstrations which legal prosecution had hitherto so conspicuously failed to suppress.[166] To control the expression of discontent might, moreover, render unnecessary the outright suppression of the radical societies or the complete curtailment, as opposed to the strict regulation, of the right of public meeting.[167] Alarmism had done its work, and by placing large public assemblies under the close surveillance of local magistrates, the government could count on their unquestioning collaboration in the work of internal security. In Parliament Pitt could rely on the unwavering support of large ministerial majorities and the enthusiastic backing of the Portland Whigs to force through these repressive policies, and in the country the propertied, piofessional and middle classes, rallied once more by the Reevite associations, united in self-defence against the renewed threats from reviving radicalism.

The introduction of legislation to restrict the right of free speech and public meeting coincided, however, with the annual celebration of the Whig revolution of 1688 and the first public dinner to commemorate the acquittal of Thomas Hardy.[168] Its timing helped to forge a temporary union of moderate and radical reformers in a vigorously conducted campaign of nation-wide protest against the passage of the so-called 'Gagging Acts' through Parliament. In this 'last, and greatest, period of popular agitation' in the eighteenth century,[169] Thelwall rejoined the London Corresponding Society to become the chief draughtsman of its public remonstrances and Francis Place, from being a cautious critic of the protest movement inside the General Committee, now dedicated his considerable energy and talents to the campaign against the Two Acts.[170] For a brief moment even the Society for Constitutional Information resurfaced to play a significant role in the determination of radical

166. *Parl. Hist.*, vol. 32, col. 273.

167. Pitt was at pains to insist that the bill did nothing to restrict the right of public meeting or of petitioning. *Ibid.*, col. 275.

168. For Thelwall's lecture on 4 November 1795 on the anniversary of the revolution of 1688 and how its principles were threatened by Pitt's 'counter-revolution' see *Tribune*, vol. 3, pp. 143–62. His 'Civic Oration' in commemoration of Hardy's acquittal delivered on the following day, is in *Tribune*, vol. 3, pp. 201–20.

169. Thompson, p. 145.

170. BL, Add. MSS. 35143, fo. 15. Place was constant in his attendance at meetings of the Executive Committee which met every evening, except Thursday, when the General Committee met – during the debates on the Two Acts.

political strategy.[171] The chief animator, however, of resistance to what he melodramatically termed Pitt's 'Reign of Terror', both in and outside Parliament, was Charles James Fox.

On 11 November, the day after the introduction of the Seditious Meetings Bill in the Commons, the Whig Club held a meeting presided over by the Duke of Bedford and attended by all its members who had seats in either house of Parliament.[172] Fox seized the opportunity to call for a nation-wide movement to petition Parliament against the bill, recalling as he did so that the method of protest meetings had been used with great effect during the American war, and that the government had its own 'alliance out of doors'.[173] He also took the chair at, and addressed, a mass protest meeting of over 30,000 people in Palace Yard Westminster on 16 November.[174] Meanwhile, on 10 November, he had insisted on a 'call' of the House of Commons to secure the attendance of independent members for the debate on the Seditious Meetings Bill.[175] On 23 November, after numerous petitions had been presented against the bills, Fox moved for a week's delay on the ground that they repealed the Bill of Rights and subverted the constitution.[176] He also repeated his opinion, in the teeth of Pitt's accusation that he was thereby 'openly advising an appeal to the sword', that

if, in the general opinion of the country, it is conceived that these bills attack the fundamental principles of our constitution . . . that the propriety of resistance instead of remaining any longer a question of morality, will become merely a question of prudence.[177]

On 27 November, followed by most of his supporters, Fox refused to take part in the discussion and amendment of the Seditious Meetings Bill at the committee stage, on the ground that 'it was impossible for any amendment to render it worthy of retaining a place in the statute books of the Kingdom'.[178] Such tactical moves were partly a

171. For resolutions carried at a general meeting of the SCI on 14 December 1795 condemning the bills, see *History of the Two Acts*, p. 767.

172. *Ibid.*, p. 209.

173. J. L. Le B. Hammond, *Charles James Fox: A Political Study* (London, 1903), p. 128.

174. Loren Reid, *Charles James Fox: A Man for the People* (London, 1969), p. 318.

175. For this early form of a whip system see P. D. G. Thomas, *The House of Commons in the Eighteenth Century* (Oxford, 1971), pp. 105–114.

176. *Parl. Hist.*, vol. 32, col. 382.

177. *Parl. Hist.*, vol. 32, col. 385.

178. *Ibid.*, cols. 422, 460.

reflection of Fox's wish to register an impatient protest against Pitt's overwhelming voting strength in the Commons, but were also a further means of exciting opposition to the bills in the country at large.

There can be no doubt of the extent and intensity of the petitioning movement against the bills thus generated. According to the contemporary *History of the Two Acts* ninety-four petitions against the bills, with over 130,000 signatures, were presented to Parliament.[179] Most of these remonstrances were approved at large public meetings in the provinces, whereas the sixty-five petitions in support of the government, with 30,000 signatures, were sponsored by closed corporations, government contractors, established clergy, military and Loyalist associations.[180] Radical protest meetings, such as those held by the Norwich Patriotic Society and the Sheffield Constitutional Society on 17 November, were in response to circular letters addressed to their provincial supporters by the London Corresponding Society on 7 November.[181] The latter held two monster meetings to protest against the repressive legislation, the first on 12 November – in defiance of the prohibitions in the Royal Proclamation of 4 November – in a field near Copenhagen House, and the second on 7 December in Marylebone Fields (Regent's Park). The procedure on both occasions followed closely the pattern set by the original Copenhagen House meeting. On 12 November, the vast crowds assembled to hear 'Citizens' Richard Hodgson, John Thelwall and John Ashley on their separate hustings were said to have numbered between 300,000 and 400,000.[182] Besides a remonstrance addressed to the King, complaining of the proposed restrictions on the expression of popular grievances, the meeting approved petitions to both houses of Parliament, calling on them to spurn ministerial recourse to precedents drawn from the arbitrary reigns of the Tudors and Stuarts, and to reject the

179. *History of the Two Acts*, pp. 826, 827.
180. BL, Add. MSS. 27808, fo. 55. The numbers of petitions for and against quoted in the text are broadly confirmed by the *Commons Journals*, vol. 51 (Oct. 1795–May 1796), which mentions eighty-nine petitions against, and sixty-nine in favour, of the two bills.
181. For the Norwich meeting, see Norwich Central Library, Colman Collection, 31 D; and for the Sheffield meeting, see *Sheffield Local Register* (1830), p. 80. The circular letter to the patriotic societies is noted in *History of the Two Acts*, p. 37. The original is in BL, Add. MSS. 27815, fo. 11.
182. *Account of the Proceedings of a Meeting of the People in a field near Copenhagen House, Thursday November 12 . . . on the subject of the Threatened Invasion of their Rights by a Convention Bill*. The estimate of 400,000 must be reckoned a gross exaggeration.

bills which threatened the stability of the throne as well as the rights and liberties of the people.[183] Resolutions were also passed deploring the attack made on the King's coach, and repudiating, as 'a gross, unfounded, WILFUL, and treacherous calumny', the accusation of 'interested and designing persons' that the assault had stemmed from the previous Copenhagen House meeting.[184] A final resolution, in emphasizing the society's responsible appreciation of 'how much to cherish and practise, in cases of the LAST EXTREMITY, the constitutional right of RESISTANCE TO OPPRESSION', also asserted its determination 'on all occasions to repress all irregularity and excesses, and to bring the authors of such unjustifiable proceedings to the just responsibility of the law'.[185] Some wild talk from John Gale Jones in anticipation of the day 'when the ministers, who had advised such arbitrary measures against the long-established rights and privileges of the people, would answer for it with their heads'[186] – was offset by cautionary and moderate advice from Thelwall. The meeting broke up 'in a manner which shewed that the presence of magistrates was altogether needless'.[187]

When this petition to the House of Commons was presented by Mr Charles Sturt MP on 23 November, he went out of his way to defend the society from fresh accusations made by Lord Mornington that its printer 'Citizen Lee' had published a regicidal tract, *King Killing No Murder*, which had been on sale at the first Copenhagen House meeting.[188] Sturt was able to show that Lee, so far from being the society's printer, was not even a member of it, having been twice expelled. It also appeared, from Lee's own account, that he had merely appropriated the title of a seventeenth-century republican tract in order to promote his pamphlet's sale and that the paragraph on tyrannicide had been borrowed from an issue of the Norwich *Cabinet* of a year earlier.[189] Sturt also made a pointed contrast between the moderate and constitutional views of Thelwall at the original Copenhagen House meeting and the assertion of 'a certain Mufti' in the House of Lords that 'the Mass of the People in every

183. *Ibid.*, p. 12.
184. *Ibid.*, p. 14.
185. *Ibid.*
186. *Ibid.*, p. 16.
187. *Ibid.*
188. For Mornington's speech, 17 Nov., 1795, see *Parl. Hist.*, vol. 32, cols. 332–3.
189. For Sturt's comments and observations see *The Senator*, vol. 3, cols. 363–8, omitted in Cobbett's *Parliamentary History*.

Country had nothing to do with the Laws but to obey them'.[190] Pressing home his advantage, Sturt then quoted extracts from a recent Tory pamphlet, *Thoughts on English Government* by John Reeves, to the effect that Lords and Commons were only branches of the legislature which might be 'lopped off' without essential damage to the main trunk of the constitution, the monarchy – a sentiment reminiscent of Divine Right theory.[191] Though Reeves was subsequently acquitted of a charge of seditious libel, the jury nevertheless thought it appropriate to reprimand his tract as 'very improper'.[192] For the moment honours in the pamphlet warfare seemed nicely balanced.

23 November, however, also saw the publication by the London Corresponding Society of a masterly vindication of its principles and policy addressed to the Parliament and people of Great Britain.[193] In this the society emphasized the distinction between the social equality which it had always advocated (based on the recognition of equal rights, equal laws and equal and actual representation) and the equalization of property, which it had always unreservedly repudiated.[194] In rejecting 'the detestable and delusive doctrines of Passive Obedience and Non Resistance' ('a system which none but *hypocrites* will *profess*, and none but *slaves* will *practise*'), the handbill described 'resistance to oppression', as both 'a natural right' and 'a constitutional duty' – but only in order, explicitly, to differentiate it from the 'promotion of tumult', which it solemnly abjured.[195] The society felt itself in a position impartially to denounce both 'the FANATICAL ENTHUSIASM that would plunge into a sea of anarchy in quest of speculative theories and the VILLAINOUS HYPOCRISY that would destroy the essence of existing institutions, under pretence of preserving them from destruction'.[196] It was a telling counter-blast to Reeves, but there were many other MPs besides Abbot, future Speaker of the

190. The 'Mufti' was, of course, Dr Horsley, Bishop of Rochester. For his speech of 11 Nov. 1795, see *Parl. Hist.*, vol. 32, col. 258.
191. *The Senator*, vol. 13, col. 367. Even Pitt thought it 'a production from the school of Filmer'. *Parl. Hist.*, vol. 32, col. 646.
192. *ST*, vol. 26, col. 594. The trial took place on 20 May 1796, on an *ex officio* Information made by the Attorney General on an address to The King by the House of Commons. *Parl. Hist.*, vol. 32, col. 681.
193. BL, Add. MSS. 27814, fo. 79. Printed handbill, *An Explicit Declaration of the Principles and Views of the London Corresponding Society*.
194. *Ibid.*
195. *Ibid.*
196. *Ibid.*

Commons, who only saw in it a disquieting echo of Fox's declaration that 'resistance to oppression' might well become merely a question of prudence rather than of morality.[197]

The final protest meeting of the London Corresponding Society, on 7 December 1795, was held at a time when it was clear that nothing could stop the Treasonable Practices and Seditious Meetings bills becoming law within a matter of days. Matthew Campbell Brown, who had played a resolute part in the final transactions of the British Convention on the eve of its dissolution, and a former editor of the Sheffield *Patriot*, did not exaggerate when he said that he had been called to preside over 'the last free meeting of the people under the existing constitution.[198] Though the right of resistance to oppression would still remain, Brown begged his audience not to contemplate the 'dreadful and dernier resort' – 'till every other legal, peaceable and constitutional means were tried and found ineffectual'.[199] On this occasion, the approval of the meeting was sought for an Address to the Nation, a Petition and Remonstrance to the King and a number of resolutions. The main speakers were John Gale Jones, Thelwall and William Frend, the latter a quondam Fellow of Jesus College Cambridge, who had been banished from the University and ejected from his Fellowship on account of his Unitarian and radical views.[200] In facing an uncertain future, the Address sought consolation in its persuasion that the protest movement had at least roused the nation from its previous lethargy, that the real objects of the minister had been revealed 'in all their naked deformity', and that the passing of the bills could not render repression permanent.[201] The Remonstrance to the King, however, merely expressed the pious hope that he would refuse his sanction to the two bills, dismiss his ministers and restore the blessings of peace to his 'impoverished and distracted country'.[202] Thelwall who had left his sick-bed to be present, and who appeared 'emaciated and labouring under severe indisposition', contented himself with condemning the bills as unconstitutional and reassuring the crowd that its anxieties about the intervention of the military would not be realized.[203] John

197. *Parl. Hist.*, vol. 32, col. 450.
198. *History of the Two Acts*, p. 644.
199. *Ibid.*, p. 645.
200. F. Knight, *University Rebel. The Life of William Frend, 1757–1841* (London, 1971), p. 187. See above, p. 269.
201. *History of the Two Acts*, p. 649.
202. *Ibid.*, pp. 650–1.
203. *Ibid.*, p. 649.

Gale Jones's repeated threat that Pitt would have to face 'public execution' aroused no comment – though 'an almost constant convulsive twitching of his hands, shoulders and arms' created an unfavourable impression on at least one spectator.[204]

One set of resolutions, moved by Frend, condemned the bills as 'a direct violation' of the thirteen articles of the Declaration of Rights and another, proposed by Richter, expressed the thanks of the society to Charles Sturt and the leading members of the Whig Opposition for their exertions in combatting the bills in Lords and Commons.[205] In obedience to the chairman's concluding recommendations the meeting dissolved, like its predecessors, quietly and in good order, but not until the society had resolved never to deviate from its original principles whatever the conduct of its persecutors.

On 18 December the bills which had given rise to the united opposition of the Foxite Whigs inside, and of the radical societies outside, Parliament became law, after receiving the royal assent. It now remained to be seen whether the much invoked right of resistance to oppression would be exercised and whether the tenuous alliance of Whigs and radicals would long survive the end of the parliamentary contest.

The appeal of the radicals to the right of resistance to oppression had not been envisaged as an insurrectionary or revolutionary threat, and had been made partly in deference to Whig preoccupation with the constitutional safeguards elaborated in 1688 against the recurrence of Stuart despotism.[206] Horne Tooke had characteristically compared the resistance he had in mind with 'the resistance of the anvil to the hammer'.[207] Even Charles James Fox had felt it expedient to offer a more flexible and disarming explanation of his provocative statement in the Commons. He had, he said, 'urged it as an advice to the governors, not an incitement to the governed'.[208] In speaking of resistance, he had not meant 'actual resistance, or the propriety of it at the present time; he only stated it as an argument, to show that it might be just'.[209] Moreover, the vexed issue of whether or not to exercise prudential restraint from the exercise of the right he had 'left

204. J. Greig (ed.), *The Farington Diary* (London, 1922), vol. 1, pp. 118–19.
205. *History of the Two Acts*, pp. 652–3.
206. Place pointed out that Whig arguments in Parliament were 'echoed back by the people'. BL, Add. MSS. 27808, fo. 56.
207. Tooke made this remark on 5 Nov. 1795 on the anniversary of Hardy's acquittal. Thelwall, *Tribune*, vol. 3, p. 265.
208. *Parl. Hist.*, vol. 32, col. 456.
209. *Ibid.*, col. 455.

the people entirely to determine for themselves'.[210] It was soon clear, moreover, once this theoretical deterrent had failed. that Fox and the Whig club could only think in terms of an association, not to resist, but to repeal legislation, which large sections of the general public enthusiastically supported,[211] and in which some of its former opponents were now prepared to acquiesce. Fair-minded critics of government, like Francis Place, were obliged to admit that Pitt and the ministerialists had shown skill, determination and resource in the parliamentary defence of their policy,[212] and once both bills were on the statute book could see no use in prolonging resistance to the point where either sedition or treason was unavoidable.[213]

Instead of following the lead given by the Whig club, the London Corresponding Society preferred to adopt alternative tactics suggested by the Society for Constitutional Information.[214] The new policy was to exploit the loopholes, particularly in the Seditious Meetings Act, in order to pursue radical objectives, even parliamentary reform, whilst remaining strictly within the letter of the law. This involved redrafting the society's constitution; it meant offering fresh advice to radical societies in the provinces as to how the repressive legislation could be evaded, and it also demanded of Thelwall the courage to indulge in legalistic subterfuge in order to be able to continue his political lectures. Thelwall indeed set himself the task 'to shew the Public that if we have discrimination and courage at once to obey the law and persevere in every unprohibited *duty*, it is impossible for Ministers to frame restrictions that can effectually impede the progress of truth; and consequent reform'.[215] His message was one of hope – 'notwithstanding the formidable appearance and ambiguous principle of these Bills, when they are accurately examined, it will be found that there is scarcely a measure important to the cause of freedom which may not still be adopted and pursued, if we have but

210. *Ibid.*, col. 457.

211. Writing to Harrison on 15 Feb. 1842, Place noted: 'Infamous as these laws were, they were popular measures. The people, ay, the mass of the shop-keepers and working people, may be said to have approved them without understanding them. Such was their terror of the French regicides and democrats.' Wallas, p. 25.

212. BL, Add. MSS. 27808, fo. 56.

213. *Ibid.*, fo. 67.

214. The lengthy analysis of the Two Acts approved by the SCI on 23 Dec. 1795, suggesting how they might be evaded, appears in Sampson Perry's *The Argus or General Observer of the Moral, Political and Commercial World* (London, 1796), pp. 185–194

215. Thelwall, *Tribune*, vol. 3, p. 328.

the spirit to exercise with boldness and discretion the privileges that remain'.[216]

A week before the two bills received the royal assent, the General Committee of the London Corresponding Society approved the new organization necessary to ensure that its future proceedings would conform to the requirements of the Seditious Meetings Act.[217] In order to prevent any of its meetings being attended by more than fifty people, a new hierarchy of elected committees was established. London and its suburbs were divided into four sections – East, Middle, Western and Surrey – each of which was restricted to forty-five divisions. The composition of divisions was similarly confined to a maximum of forty-five members. Every division was to elect a delegate to its own district or sectional committee, which in turn was empowered to elect one delegate for every five constituent divisions to the General Committee. The weakest links in this new hierarchy were the sectional committees, which were badly attended because they met merely to hear reports, on the one hand from the divisions, and, on the other, from the General Committee.[218] The latter, however, was left with all the legislative powers it had previously possessed and a small Executive Committee also continued to function.

Although, on paper, this arrangement allowed for an increase in the numbers of the existing divisions and of the over-all membership of the society, after the passage of the Two Acts, as Place tells us, 'the reformers generally conceived it not only dangerous, but also useless to exert themselves any longer'.[219] By the beginning of 1796 sixteen divisions of the London Corresponding Society had ceased to meet at all and there had been a marked slump in attendances at the other divisions.[220] Although this drift away from the divisions was temporarily arrested by an urgent and cogent appeal from the General Committee in the form of printed circular letters addressed to members of the society on 31 December 1795, the ground lost was, according to Place, never subsequently recovered.[221] The General Committee, of which Place was now elected chairman for the next three months, was nevertheless indefatigable in its efforts to stem

216. *Ibid.*, p. 329.
217. For the draft of this new organization approved on 12 Dec. 1795 see PRO PC 1/23/A 38. For Place's account see BL, Add. MSS. 27808, fos. 68–9.
218. *Ibid.* The number of sections was later increased.
219. *Ibid.*, fo. 67.
220. Report of 7 Jan. 1796. PRO PC 1/23/A 38.
221. A copy of the printed circular letter is in PRO PC 1/23/A 38 among Powell's reports. See also BL, Add. MSS. 27808, fo. 67.

this decline in morale – deputing its members to whip up the attendance of divisional delegates at the sectional committees and to encourage the faint-hearted absentees from the divisional meetings.[222]

It was partly with this same motive in mind, i.e. to rekindle the dwindling radical enthusiasm in the metropolis itself, that the decision was taken, early in February 1796, to send selected delegates from the London Corresponding Society on missionary tours to advise and assist newly formed radical societies in the provinces.[223] The original concept of such missionary propaganda tours had been suggested, it may be recalled, by the editors of the Sheffield *Patriot* in the heady days of 1792.[224] Put into practice by Margarot and Gerrald in Scotland before and after the British Convention in 1793, the policy had been resurrected by the fourteenth resolution carried at the original Copenhagen House meeting on 26 October 1795. Appeals for advice and assistance from a newly formed society at Rochester late in October, and early in 1796 from Portsmouth and Birmingham, encouraged the General Committee of the Corresponding Society to implement that resolution, especially when it was realized that the new tactic of evading rather than challenging the provisions of the Two Acts needed to be explained to its provincial clientèle.[225] It was hoped that the latter would agree, as the Rochester society had, to help to defray the travelling and living expenses of the delegates.[226] By keeping the despatch of such agents secret, and by giving them strict instructions to observe the restrictions imposed on public meetings by the new repressive legislation, it was anticipated that they would not run the risk of interference from local magistrates.[227]

Subsequently, Place shamefacedly admitted that the despatch of such missionary delegates was misguided, though he himself did not oppose it. The decline in the membership of the London Corresponding Society since the passage of the Two Acts led him to consider, in retrospect, that the policy had 'lost its purpose'.[228] In fact, the tours failed to sustain the sagging morale of the radicals in the capital; they

222. *Ibid.*, Add. MSS. 27808, fo. 69.
223. PRO PC 1/23/A 38. Place says: 'It was expected that the éclat of the deputies would revive the spirit of reform in London, and send them back to their divisions.' Add. MSS. 27808, fo. 72.
224. See above, p. 227.
225. PRO PC 1/23/A 38.
226. BL, Add. MSS. 27808, fo. 72.
227. PRO PC 1/23/A 38.
228. BL, Add. MSS. 27808, fo. 71.

involved the Corresponding Society in a series of difficulties which absorbed most of its time and energies in the course of 1796; and they helped to make the society dependent on the dubious financial support of its provincial protégés. Owing to the presence in its innermost councils of the government spy James Powell, the society was not able to preserve the secrecy of these missions, so that they were closely watched, or even accompanied by, spies, who either obstructed them, or brought the delegates to justice.[229] When the society itself dubbed these agents '*représentants en mission*', it was not surprising that their Jacobin symbolism was much emphasized by the Alarmists. Though the despatch of such missions to the naval dockyard towns was in response to specific requests from local reformers,[230] opponents were naturally quick to saddle the society with an alleged criminal responsibility for the subsequent outbreak of the naval mutinies of 1797. The presence of other delegates in Lancashire and Yorkshire in the early months of 1796 and their success in supporting the expansion of the newly established Manchester Corresponding Society and in encouraging the formation of radical societies in Bradford and Halifax have usually gone unnoticed.[231] They were, in any case, exceptions to the general rule that the radical missions of 1796 involved the parent society in considerable discredit and severe financial setbacks.

This was perhaps only to be expected when the persons entrusted with these missions – particularly John Binns and John Gale Jones – conspicuously lacked the discretion which would alone have enabled them to evade the attention of local magistrates. The instructions they received from the society were also, to say the least, ambiguous; for while enjoining on the deputies strict conformity to the procedures laid down by statute for the conduct of public meetings, and warning local reform societies against 'violent propositions and illegal measures', the delegates were also told

229. At various times in 1796 Powell was elected a member of the General Committee and also of the Executive Committee of the LCS. His reports to the Home Office in PRO PC 1/23/A 38 are the most detailed source of information about the proceedings of those committees that have survived.

230. Letters from Rochester and Portsmouth were received by the LCS late in January 1796. PRO PC 1/23/A 38.

231. The most active of these was James Shaw, who took a leading part in the formation of the Manchester Corresponding Society and became its chairman in Aug. 1797. BL, Add. MSS. 27815, fo. 27. For the Manchester Corresponding Society see J. Walvin, 'English democratic societies and popular radicalism, 1791–1800', unpublished PhD thesis, University of York (1969).

to call upon our Fellow Citizens to be ready with us to pursue our common object, if it must be to the Scaffold, or rather (if our Enemies are desperate enough to bar up every Avenue of Enquiry and Discussion) to the Field at the Hazard of Extermination; convinced that no Temper, less decided than this will suffice to regain Liberty from a bold and usurping Faction.[232]

Such exhortations may have been no more than the common form of radical rhetoric, but in the hands of extremists like Binns and Jones they were bound to cause the sort of unruly disturbances which the General Committee wished, at all costs, to avoid.

An early indication of the trouble in store for such zealots came when Binns was despatched to Portsmouth on 5 February 1796.[233] He was under surveillance from the outset by agents of the Home Secretary and his arrival in Portsmouth had been anticipated in the local newspapers by defamatory notices.[234] His visits to the dockyards, naval depots and some of the largest ships afloat gave rise to the suspicion that he had been sent to set fire to naval installations.[235] His interviews with the inmates of a large French prisoner-of-war camp at Portchester Castle led the authorities to suppose that he had planned their liberation.[236] His contacts with the local Corresponding Society only confirmed the impression that he was a dangerous subversive. Rumours that he was about to be seized by naval press gangs led the General Committee to send Ashley, its secretary, post-haste to Portsmouth on 12 February to recall Binns to London.[237] Although he had partially completed his mission and escaped arrest, Binns had only succeeded in alerting the Home Office and in arousing suspicion that the London Corresponding Society was engaged in treasonable attempts to subvert the loyalty of naval ratings at Portsmouth and Gosport.

On 6 February 1796 John Gale Jones was despatched on a similar mission to radical societies in and around Rochester and Chatham. According to his own account, he had accepted the mission owing to 'ill-health, a recent disappointment, and an inclination to travel'.[238]

232. *Instructions of the L.C.S. to Citizen John Gale Jones, deputed to visit the societies of Birmingham etc.*, Art. 7. *Report of the Secret Committee of the House of Commons* (1799), appendix no. 4, p. 69.
233. PRO PC 1/23/A 38.
234. Binns, pp. 64–6. J. Dugan, *The Great Mutiny* (London, 1966), p. 68.
235. Binns, p. 65.
236. *Ibid.*
237. PRO PC 1/23/A 38.
238. John Gale Jones, *Sketch of a Political Tour through Rochester, Chatham, Maidstone, Gravesend, etc.*, pt. 1 (London, 1796), p. 1.

On his tour of the region, which lasted over three weeks, Jones found plenty of evidence that local feeling was preponderantly pacifist and anti-ministerialist. Many of his popular audiences, in Kent, he discovered, had attended the large public meetings held by the Corresponding Society in the autumn of 1795 and knew him by sight.[239] An effigy of the Bishop of Rochester, with a Bible in one hand, a lighted taper in the other and a label round its neck bearing the legend: 'the people have nothing to do with the laws but obey them' had recently been paraded through the city accompanied by vast crowds before being committed to the flames.[240] On a visit to a French prisoner-of-war ship anchored in the estuary Jones learnt of the growing discontent among the sailors and their officers and at Chatham he heard how the dockyard workers had refused to sign a loyal address after the attack on the King's coach and had supported, instead, a petition against the 'Convention' bills.[241] Though the Two Acts had temporarily disconcerted the Rochester radical society, they had not affected its zeal for reform. Jones addressed several of its ten divisions, at Rochester, Chatham, Gillingham and other places, recruited new members, and advised on matters of policy and administration. Though he was quickly recognized by an official of the local post office, who attempted to open his correspondence, Jones did not encounter any interference or opposition, even when he was ordered by the General Committee to visit Gravesend and Maidstone, where opinion was more sharply divided. The success of the mission was mainly due to the warm enthusiasm of the local community for the London Corresponding Society and the unpopularity of Pitt's war and repressive policies.

The very success of Jones's mission, however, and the effervescent character of radicalism in the Midlands made the government all the more determined to intervene decisively when both Binns and Jones were despatched to Birmingham on 7 March 1796.[242] For several days each held separate meetings with the divisions of the local reform society in various taverns, their actions and speeches being closely

239. *Ibid.*, p. 37.
240. *Ibid.*, p. 82.
241. *Ibid.*, p. 81. Typical of the naval officers of the time was one who was interviewed by Jones. 'He would not allow that seamen in time of battle were ever stimulated to action by any other motives than a sense of danger or a *fear of punishment*. The idea of patriotism and courage he treated as ridiculous, and attachment to their country as a farce!' *Ibid.*, p. 53.
242. J. Gale Jones's *Farewell Oration to the Westminster Forum, 16 March 1797*. PRO HO 42/40.

scrutinized by government spies. On 11 March they were suddenly arrested and imprisoned, on Treasury warrants, in the town gaol.[243] The charges against them were not disclosed, but the Executive Committee of the Corresponding Society responded quickly by sending Francis Place to Birmingham to assist them.[244] He spent three days attending their examination before the magistrates and attempting, unsuccessfully, to secure bail for them, sacrificing his own employment and endangering his livelihood in the process.[245] The financial securities necessary to procure their release pending trial were, however, subsequently raised in London and arrangements were made for their eventual legal defence.

Once it became clear that the charges against the deputies were alleged breaches of the Two Acts, their prosecution was regarded by both the government and the radicals as a test case. For the government the very credibility of its whole repressive machinery was at stake, while the Corresponding Society saw in it a test of its ability to communicate directly with, and to sustain, its provincial supporters by means of uninhibited personal contact rather than merely by correspondence, subject to all the hazards of official interference.[246] The activists in the society had, by this time, come to regard the missionary tours of its delegates as 'the most powerful and effectual means of raising our brethren to vigilance in the cause of reform',[247] so that adverse verdicts in the courts would endanger the very cohesion and solidarity of the radical cause at a crucial stage of its existence. From the spring of 1796, therefore, the Corresponding Society put in hand an urgent and general appeal to all the provincial radical societies with which it was in contact for financial help towards the heavy costs of their deputies' defence.[248] Its own funds had been exhausted by the large expenditure and indebtedness occasioned by its monster public protest meetings in the previous autumn, by the

243. Binns, p. 66.

244. BL, Add. MSS. 35143, fo. 17.

245. Place temporarily accepted the paid post of assistant secretary of the LCS to tide him over. *Ibid.*, fo. 18. This did not, however, prevent him suffering 'poverty' and 'privation'.

246. Undated letter of LCS to Hereford (? early May 1796). BL, Add. MSS. 27815, fo. 56.

247. *Ibid.*

248. BL, Place newspaper cuttings, vol. 37, fo. 231. The draft appeal was approved by the General Committee on 27 April 1796. One hundred copies were ordered to be printed and despatched immediately. PRO PC 1/23/A 38. Powell's reports to Home Office.

drop in its membership revenue after the passage of the Two Acts, and the financial drain of the tours themselves. Against the better judgement of Place and the interested opposition of Bone, the society simultaneously committed itself to the publication of a monthly journal – the *Moral and Political Magazine*.[249] Since this was intended to be the sole publication of the society in the future, it involved the abandonment of the ambitious 'Book Plan' adopted in 1795. Instead of the former subscription of a penny a week, members were called on to pay 4½d. a month, for which they were to receive a copy of the magazine free.[250] As Place later wrote: 'A better contrivance to prevent the society paying its debts could hardly have been devised.'[251] The first issue was published on 1 July 1796, but disagreements on editorial policy, on the procurement of paper and the costs of printing, advertisement and management caused considerable delay in the subsequent monthly issues and this affected its good will in the provinces.[252] Attempts to raise the subscription rates only resulted in a slump of sales and the continuation of the venture beyond the end of the year was only made possible by raiding the funds raised on behalf of Binns and Jones.[253] This ill-advised experiment, which had to be abandoned in May 1797, not only rendered the prospects of a successful defence of the society's delegates problematical, it also irretrievably compromised the society's financial viability and did much to alienate both Place and Ashley from further responsible concern with its affairs.[254] In the event, Jones, after trial in April 1799, was found guilty, but not sentenced, while Binns, after a successful defence by Samuel Romilly, was acquitted in the following August.[255]

1796 was also a bad year for Thelwall, who made his own independent and courageous attempts to evade the provisions of the

249. Bone opposed the *Magazine* because he thought it would compete with his own periodical, the *Politician. Ibid.*

250. PRO PC 1/23/A 38. 10 March 1796.

251. BL, Add. MSS. 27808, fos. 74–5.

252. These disagreements can be followed in PRO PC 1/23/A 38.

253. £170 raised for the defence of Binns and Jones, as well as some regular membership dues, were diverted to this purpose and general expenses by December 1796. BL, Add. MSS. 27808, fo. 74. A second fund for Binns and Jones had to be raised.

254. Ashley was suspected of mismanaging the affairs of the society and of profiting from advertising the *Magazine*. Both Ashley and Place were finding themselves in disagreement with the policy pursued by the General and Executive Committees at this time.

255. *ST*, vol. 26, cols. 595 ff.

Seditious Meetings Act by preparing a fresh series of lectures nominally concerned with the history of Greece and Rome, but 'the same
in principle' with those he had previously delivered.[256] Though 'this
was not the intention, Thelwall forecast that local magistrates would
'receive a little insight into the facts and principles of ancient history'
without paying for their admission.[257] The audiences he expected in
London were, however, owing to intimidation, insufficient to allow
him to continue the lectures in the capital and he accordingly opted
to move to East Anglia, where he thought he could be sure of a more
sympathetic hearing. After a hard-fought campaign in support of
Horne Tooke's independent candidature at Westminster in the
General Election of that year,[258] Thelwall accepted an invitation
from Miss Amelia Alderson of Norwich. In June he delivered a course
of twenty-two lectures before 'an audience composed of all the different classes of society, and with a degree of impression, surpassing
anything I have ever witnessed before, in any place, or upon any
occasion'.[259] After two short reconnaissances in Yarmouth, where he
was well received by the 'moderates', Thelwall was also persuaded
to return there in mid August, at the height of the watering season,
to deliver a course of six public lectures on classical history in a
warehouse near the sea front belonging to one of the principal merchants of the town. In the effort to dissipate the 'torpor and lethargy'
prevalent in the seaport, Thelwall braced himself to face 'their
reverences of the church, and their worships of the corporation'.[260]
In fact he encountered a highly organized general plan of repression
reminiscent of the Birmingham 'Church and King' faction in the days
of Priestley. The mayor and corporation, the clergy, the militia and
the commander of a naval frigate all united to disrupt his meetings
by riot and physical violence. After clergymen, militia officers in
disguise, and youths under the command of a naval officer had failed
to excite disturbances during the first two lectures, a gang of about
ninety sailors, on instructions from their commander, and armed
with bludgeons, cutlasses and pikestaffs, broke up the third lecture

256. *Tribune*, vol. 3, pp. 329–30.
257. J. Thelwall, *Prospectus of a Course of Lectures, in strict conformity with
the restrictions of Mr Pitt's Convention Act, 1796.*
258. C. Cestre, *John Thelwall: A pioneer of democracy in England* (London,
1906), p. 127.
259. J. Thelwall, *An Appeal to Popular Opinion against Kidnapping and Murder,
including a Narrative of the late atrocious Proceedings at Yarmouth*, 2nd ed.
(London, 1796), p. 13.
260. *Ibid.*, p. 17.

after extinguishing the lights. They partially demolished the building, injured over thirty persons, some seriously, tore up Thelwall's books and papers and threatened him with further assault. It was only his counter-threats to use his pistol and the intervention of a group of his sympathizers which saved him.[261] Appeals for protection to the local magistrates and the mayor were unavailing and only resulted in an acrimonious pamphlet war of mutual recrimination.[262] The incident, however, did not deter Thelwall from continuing his lectures for a second week, concluding on 26 August. On the following day he left Yarmouth for 'the friendly, the intelligent, the beloved society of Norwich', where he composed his own account of the outrages.[263] His conclusion was that 'the bludgeon' had silenced 'what no jury could be expected to condemn, nor crown lawyer could venture to impeach'.[264] He tried again, in September, to deliver a short course of lectures on 'Roman' history at King's Lynn and Wisbech, but only to encounter yet another form of riotous intervention – this time from squads of sailors from merchant ships, egged on, led and, no doubt, terrorized by members of the press gang.[265]

Bitter experiences of this kind eventually convinced Thelwall that 'the petty tyranny of provincial persecution' had, in fact, a sharper edge than metropolitan repression and that in such areas he would not be given a licence to advocate universal suffrage by commentaries on Roman history or to plead for rising living standards under the pretence of explaining the agrarian laws of the Gracchi.[266] Even at the height of the Terror in revolutionary France advocacy of such 'agrarian laws' had been made punishable with death.[267] When it also became clear that his published protests against his treatment would evoke neither public sympathy nor magisterial protection, his disillusionment was almost, but not quite, complete.

The year which had begun badly for Thelwall, with the loss of £400 on the surplus stocks of the *Tribune*, after its suppression by the government in April,[268] ended dismally with his ejection from his

261. *Ibid.*, pp. 22–6.
262. *Ibid.*, p. 26.
263. *Ibid.*, p. 26.
264. *Ibid.*, p. 52.
265. *Ibid.*, pp. 54–5.
266. Cestre, p. 128.
267. Decree of 18 March 1793. G. Lefebvre, *La Révolution Française*, vol. 13 of *Peuples et Civilisations* (Paris, 1951), p. 344.
268. Cestre, p. 125. He had printed the *Tribune* at his own expense.

lecture rooms at Beaufort Buildings off the Strand.[269] He was thus deprived of his political base in the capital and the General Committee of the Corresponding Society, which had been meeting there for the past year, had to accept temporary accommodation at the home of Thomas Evans, secretary of division No. 9, at 14 Plough Court, Fetter Lane.[270] When this was found inadequate the committee moved at the end of December to its last headquarters – an old building with the romantic name of Queen of Bohemia's Palace at No. 8 Wych St, Drury Lane.[271]

The naval officer who had agreed to show John Gale Jones over the French prison ship *La Ville de Paris* in the Medway in Feburary 1796 was himself 'an excellent Democrat, but unable to avow his principles because of his status'.[272] He had, nevertheless, feelingly confessed to the delegate that, in his view, 'the King's service was the most abject slavery'.[273] Those who felt more keenly still their situation and grievances in the Royal Navy at this time were, however, the naval ratings, subjected to the iron discipline of the quarter-deck, defrauded by the pursers of benefits and allowances, unfairly treated in the distribution of prize money, deprived of adequate shore leave at the end of long periods of service at sea, wretchedly fed and abominably paid.[274] Though punishment of offences at sea was probably no more inhuman at the time than the savage criminal code that brutalized life ashore and though bad food was better than relative starvation on land in times of scarcity, resentment at the conditions of their service had become more vocal since 1795 as the result of ships' companies being joined by the 'quota men' levied on the country and urban areas according to their population.[275] This machinery for supplementing the operations of the press gang, introduced into the Navy a new and most unreliable element of former debtors, gaol birds, bankrupts and unemployed ne'er-do-wells,

269. PRO PC 1/23/A 38. Report of General Committee of LCS, 8 Dec. 1796.
270. *Ibid.*
271. *Ibid.* Report of proceedings of General Committee of LCS, 29 Dec. 1796.
272. Jones, p. 42.
273. *Ibid.*, p. 52.
274. C. Gill, *The Naval Mutinies of 1797* (Manchester, 1913), chs. 22, 23; M. Lewis, *The History of the British Navy* (Harmondsworth, 1957), and *A Social History of the British Navy, 1793–1815* (London, 1960); and J. Dugan, *passim.*
275. The Quota Acts of 1795 authorized judges and magistrates to hand over to the fleet 'rogues, vagabonds, smugglers, embezzlers of naval stores and other able-bodied, idle and disorderly persons' who were unemployed. Hitherto the state had only been legally entitled to press 'seafarers' or 'watermen'.

attracted to the service by hopes of high bounty payments and prize money. Among these undesirables was a small but significant minority of professional men of some education, with experience of affairs and often conversant with Painite notions of social justice and the concept of the 'rights of man'.[276] More intolerant of personal degradation and oppression than the ordinary seamen, they were natural protesters and some had the necessary literacy and experience to formulate demands for improvement in the form of petitions and to organize discontent in the fleet both against the brutality of the serving officers and the negligence of their Lordships of the Admiralty. It was these men, some with political vendettas to wage, who provided the leadership of the naval mutinies at Spithead and the Nore in the spring of 1797 – revolts which threatened to paralyse Britain's naval defences against the triple menace from France, Holland and the Irish rebels.[277]

The Channel fleet, under the command of Lord Bridport, moored at the Spithead anchorage off Portsmouth, mutinied first in April, refusing to put to sea until the seamen's demands for a long-overdue increase in pay and the settlement of arrears had been met and the abuses of discipline by junior officers and the peculation of the pursers had been corrected. This revolt has been well described as a modern 'sit-down strike, the first of its kind',[278] conducted with efficiency and restraint by leaders whose patriotism was not in doubt and whose hold over the conduct of the mutineers was inflexible. It was also a highly successful 'protest movement' which may have owed something to the various forms of radical protests against social and political injustice and the financial burdens of the war. By concentrating on the issue of pay, by skilful negotiation with Lord Howe, and by making clear that their actions would not be allowed to prejudice national security against the French, the rebels secured an acceptable improvement of pay and conditions and the grant of a royal pardon.[279]

The Nore mutiny of the North Sea fleet which followed in May 1797 was, however, a less justifiable and more dangerous revolt, led by Richard Parker, a 'quota man' with dubious antecedents and of

276. Paine himself had begun his 'apprenticeship to life' by serving at sea in privateers and he, therefore, was well aware of seamen's grievances at this time. *Rights of Man*, ed. H. Collins (Harmondsworth, 1969), p. 241.

277. Gill, pp. 315–19.

278. M. Lewis, *History of the British Navy*, p. 186.

279. The rise in pay was one shilling a day. The last rise had been in Charles II's reign.

questionable loyalty.[280] After the mutineers had been joined by the majority of Admiral Duncan's squadron from Yarmouth, which should have been maintaining the watch for the Dutch invasion fleet off the Texel, the Thames itself was blockaded, officers were tarred and feathered, effigies of Pitt and Dundas, suspended at the yard-arm, were riddled with shot and some rebels even considered the surrender of their ships to the French.[281] Fortunately for the government and the nation, dissension broke out among the crews on the extent of their demands and the decision whether to accept the proffered pardon, the limit of the concessions then available. Late in June the mutiny at the Nore collapsed. Parker was hanged and many of the rebels were executed or transported.[282]

It is impossible, even now, to be certain whether the London Corresponding Society or its provincial offshoots had helped to precipitate these mutinies. An enquiry on the spot conducted immediately after their collapse, at the request of the Home Office, by two specially chosen London magistrates – A. Graham and D. Williams – indicated that 'no such connection or correspondence ever did exist'.[283] Suggestions to the contrary had also been repeatedly and strenuously denied, on the eve of his execution, by the president of the so-called 'Floating Republic' – Parker himself.[284] The main sources of contemporary suspicion were the missions of Binns to Portsmouth and of Jones to Rochester and Chatham in 1796, the seeming familiarity of the uneducated mutineers with the forms and procedures of the radical societies, and the obvious influence of Painite and French revolutionary principles upon the language and contents of the seamen's petitions and addresses.[285] On the first point,

280. Parker came from Exeter, where his father had been a grain merchant and baker. He had served in the fleet in the American war, and as an officer in the war against France. He had been court-martialled and reduced to the ranks for indiscipline and invalided out of the fleet. He had emerged from a debtors' prison in Perth to become a 'quota man' on HMS *Sandwich* at the Nore in 1797.

281. Dugan, chs. 13–16.

282. *Ibid.*, chs. 17, 18.

283. Report dated 24 June, 1797. PRO HO 42/41.

284. *Morning Chronicle*, 12 Oct. 1797. BL, Place newspaper cuttings, vol. 38.

285. Cf. the Nore address: 'Shall we, who in the battle's sanguinary rage, confound, terrify and subdue your proudest foe, guard your coasts from invasion, your children from slaughter, and your lands from pillage – be the footballs and shuttlecocks of a set of tyrants, who derive from us alone their honours, their titles and their fortunes? No, the Age of Reason has at last revolved. Long have we been endeavouring to find ourselves men. We now find ourselves so. We will be treated as such.' Gill, p. 301.

it has already been seen that the missions to the vital dockland areas had been prompted, not by any treasonable designs on the part of the Executive Committee of the LCS but by the pressing appeals for guidance and assistance from the recently formed societies at Portsmouth and Rochester, apprehensive as to their prospects in the climate of repression created by the passage of the Two Acts.[286] Binns's mission had been short-lived and largely abortive and both visits had provoked close surveillance by agents of the Home Office and local Alarmists. Secondly, the mutineers' use of ships' delegates and committees, the deference of both to the popular will expressed by the ships' companies, and the effective and democratic procedures adopted were ascribed, by Graham and Williams, on reflection, not to the extraneous and treasonable intervention of radical deputies, but to the administrative capacity and 'know-how' of the 'quota men' who had acted as leaders.[287] Thirdly, the influence of human rights theory upon the claims put forward by the seamen's delegates, although powerful, was, at most, indirect.

It is also relevant to note that the virtual take-over of the London Corresponding Society by the small extremist faction of declared republicans did not occur till after the naval mutinies were over.[288] In the spring of 1797 the Corresponding Society was still preoccupied with the problems raised by the defence of Binns and Jones in the courts and its main energies were absorbed by the planned synchronization of mass protest meetings throughout the country on 31 July.

Franco-Irish intrigue in the mutinies is equally difficult to establish – though it is known that certain members of the United Irish society had joined the fleet specifically to incite unrest, and the oath-taking ceremonies of the mutineers no doubt derived from that source.[289] Several of the seamen's leaders, notably Valentine Joyce and Charles McCarthy, and surgeons like McCurdy and Dean were Irish and there were certainly large numbers of Irish in the fleets, though by

286. See above, p. 398.
287. PRO HO 42/41. Report to the Duke of Portland, 24 June 1797.
288. Place and Ashley had resigned as delegates in March 1797 and they ceased to be paid-up members of the LCS at the end of the June quarter. BL, Add. MSS. 35143, fos. 24, 25. After the July arrests the leading members of the society were Thomas Evans, who succeeded Ashley as secretary, a prominent Spencean; Benjamin and John Binns, promoters of the United Englishmen; Dr R. Watson; John Bone; Colonel Despard; Crossfield and Hodgson.
289. A United Irish lawyer called Lee, a recent recruit to the fleet, had attempted to suborn marines at Plymouth and had planned to set fire to the barracks. After exposure, he was condemned by court martial and executed. Dugan, pp. 309–10.

no means as many as Wolfe Tone himself is said to have claimed in his negotiations with the French government.[290] Tone himself had called on his compatriots in the British fleet in a proclamation of 1796 to overpower their officers and to take their ships into Irish ports.[291] But the actual outbreak of the mutinies seems to have taken both him and the French government by surprise.[292] The British government's concern to conceal the identity and activities of the double-agent Samuel Turner at Hamburg also caused it to suppress in the report of the secret committee of the House of Commons in 1799 the intelligence it possessed of the fire-raising projects of the United Irishman William Duckett for the destruction of British naval dockyards.[293] Nor can these be easily pieced together from the archives of the French ministry of foreign affairs, which only serve for the most part to illustrate the total lack of co-ordination and real understanding at this time between the rival representatives of the Dublin United Irish Executive in Paris and the French Executive Directory.[294] Nor, so far as is known, was there at the time of the mutinies, any direct channel of communication between the French government and the English radical societies.[295]

The mutinies, however, form an important link with the Irish rebellion of 1798 in at least two respects. Firstly, they revealed to the French government the plausibility of the Irish claims that discontent in the British fleet could be worked on to paralyse the country's naval strength, and that, if Irish independence were achieved with French help, that too might well destroy the naval superiority that alone stood in the way of French hegemony on the Continent.[296] Secondly, after the collapse of the mutinies, the Irish militants who had sought to synchronize an Irish rising with the Spithead and Nore

290. Since the start of the war 15,500 rebel prisoners – exclusive of volunteers or pressed men – had been sent to the British fleet by the Irish executive. In putting the figure of Irish seamen in the fleet as high as 80,000 Tone was clearly exaggerating. W. J. Fitzpatrick, *Secret Service under Pitt* (London, 1892), p. 113.

291. Gill, p. 331.

292. Fitzpatrick, pp. 108–9.

293. For Samuel Turner see Fitzpatrick and below, p. 438. For Duckett's letters from Hamburg, urging a renewed French invasion in the autumn of 1797, see AAE, CPA 592, fos. 80, 84, 129.

294. This documentation is mostly contained in AAE CPA 592.

295. The flight of John Ashley to Paris late in 1797 provided a means of direct contact, though this does not appear to have been used by the French government.

296. These points are well brought out in Marianne Elliott's unpublished DPhil thesis (Oxford, 1975), 'The United Irishmen and France, 1793–1806'.

revolts turned their attention to cultivating closer relations with the extremist members of the London Corresponding Society and of the radical societies in the North-West and thus stimulated the rise of the republican faction of the clandestine United Englishmen, closely identified with, and serving the political objectives of, the Society of United Irish.[297]

It was precisely these developments which the government sought to prevent, and succeeded at least in neutralizing, by two acts carried in response to the mutinies. The first made it possible to inflict the death penalty on anyone found guilty of inciting His Majesty's naval or land forces to mutiny.[298] The second sought to frustrate the formation of secret societies for political agitation by forbidding the administration of unlawful oaths on pain of death or transportation.[299]

The summer of 1797 also witnessed the last attempt by the London Corresponding Society to organize a co-ordinated series of mass public meetings across the country to enforce the conclusion of peace and the concession of radical political reform.[300] The idea had been revived, as early as 23 March, by the Executive Committee, in the shadow of the suspension of cash payments by the Bank of England.[301] Printed handbills were circulated to the provincial radical societies, calling on them to summon general meetings on the same day as the metropolitan society. They were asked to support a remonstrance to the King demanding the dismissal of his ministers and the conclusion of peace. The real objective was less 'a change of men' than 'a change of measures' and, notably, the concession of universal suffrage and annual parliaments.[302] The proposal, however, did not meet with the unanimous support of the leading members of the society, for it was strenuously opposed by both Francis Place and John Ashley.[303] Nor did it evoke a wholly sympathetic welcome from all the provincial reform societies. In particular the Sheffield radicals were highly

297. See below, Chapter 11.

298. 37 Geo. III c. 70.

299. 37 Geo. III c. 123. This was the act under the terms of which the Tolpuddle Martyrs were transported in 1834.

300. Dr Robert Watson, a former member of the Executive Committee of the LCS, in a pretentious memorial to the French Directory dated 10 July 1799, stated that the secret motive behind this project was to prepare the ground for a general insurrection timed to coincide with the French invasion. AAE, Mémoires et documents, 53, fos. 261–5.

301. BL, Place newspaper cuttings, vol. 38, fo. 33.

302. *Ibid.*

303. BL, Add. MSS. 35143, fos. 24–5.

critical of the initiative, arguing forcibly that a mere removal of ministers would effect no useful purpose, that Parliament would never agree to reform itself and that even the restoration of peace would still leave the country saddled with a crushing burden of taxation. Mass meetings calling for such ends would be patently futile and it would, therefore, be advisable to wait patiently for the inevitable national crisis in which both ministerial and parliamentary corruption would be engulfed.[304]

Despite this opposition, and the crushing defeat of Grey's scheme for the introduction of a householder franchise on 26 May,[305] the London Corresponding Society went ahead with its plans for a public meeting on 31 July. Even the warning by the Bow St magistrates that the meeting, as advertised, would be illegal, without specifying the reason why, did not deter the organizers.[306] The meeting was held in a field near the Veterinary College at St Pancras, each of the three rostra being surrounded by a group of magistrates, some on horseback. Two thousand constables and as many soldiers were posted on the spot and between 6000 and 8000 troops were held in reserve in the vicinity. Shortly after the proceedings had begun the organizers were unable to prevent the assembled magistrates from proclaiming the meeting as an illegal assembly – even though the proposed Address to the Nation was referred back for further consideration to the divisions and the demand for the dismissal of ministers was dropped.[307] Once it had become clear that the proclamation calling on the crowd to disperse had in fact been read, the meeting broke up without a show of resistance. Six of the speakers on the various platforms – Benjamin Binns, Fergusson, Galloway, Barrow, Stuckey and Richard Hodgson – were arrested, though they were released on bail and drawn through the streets of the metropolis by enthusiastic supporters. They found further satisfaction when no bill was ever found against them by the grand jury.[308] This challenge to the authorities, however, only served to show that the repressive machinery of the Seditious Meetings Act, when used with a show of force, was an effective means of preventing the ventilation of strongly felt public grievances. G. S. Veitch's verdict that the meeting was

304. Dated 15 May 1797. BL, Place newspaper cuttings, vol. 38, fo. 67.
305. Grey's motion for leave to introduce a reform bill along these lines was defeated by 256 votes to 91. Veitch, p. 331.
306. *A Narrative of the Proceedings at the General Meeting of the L.C.S. held on Monday, July 31, 1797 . . .*, pp. 3–4.
307. *Ibid.*, pp. 8 and 27.
308. BL, Add. MSS. 35143, fo. 26.

'the death-blow of the real London Corresponding Society' still stands.[309]

One by one the arguments used by Thelwall to try and convince radicalism's wavering supporters that courage and persistence could frustrate the successful implementation of the Two Acts had been shown to be untenable. One after another the provincial radical societies succumbed to persistent pressure from 'Church and King' clubs, Reevite associations, Volunteer companies or local magistrates. It was only here and there and, significantly, in Manchester, Sheffield and Norwich, that a few defiant spirits continued to keep in touch with the London Corresponding Society and to profess their democratic faith in public.[310] Increasing numbers of committed radicals found no alternative but to seek a new life across the Atlantic or a fresh start among friends in the French capital.[311]

The withdrawal of the moderate leaders from active concern in the affairs of the London Corresponding Society was also a feature of the decline and fall of the democratic movement. By the end of 1796 Ashley and Place, who had taken the place of Hardy and Margarot in the inner councils of the society, had become totally disenchanted by the irresponsible behaviour of its Executive and General Committees. Ashley, whose efficiency and integrity had recently come under unfavourable scrutiny, resigned as secretary of the society late in December 1796.[312] About the same time Place, who had been critical of the holding of large public meetings, the despatch of delegates on missionary tours, and the publication of the *Moral and Political Magazine*, refused in future to be re-elected as chairman of the General Committee.[313] In the spring of 1797 both Ashley and Place dissociated themselves still further from the policies of which they disapproved by resigning as delegates of their respective

309. Veitch, p. 335.

310. E.g. Norwich Patriotic Society assured the LCS on 10 July 1797: 'We continue firm at our Post, prepared for the worst of events, determined rather to make a Public exit than to abandon the object of our association.' BL, Add. MSS. 27815, fo. 159. On 18 Aug. 1797 the same society published an address to the inhabitants of Norwich concurring in the views expressed in Paine's *First Principles of Government* (1795) and defending Thelwall's recent visit. Norwich Central Library, Colman collection, N.306.

311. Williams, p. 103.

312. BL, Add. MSS. 27808, fo. 76. He was succeeded as secretary by J. Bone and then by Thomas Evans.

313. *Ibid.*

divisions and, at the end of the June quarter, ceased to be members of the society.[314] Sometime in the autumn Ashley, increasingly distracted by his amorous indiscretions, resolved to abandon both his shrewish wife and over-demanding mistress. After selling up his once prosperous but now ailing business, he emigrated to Paris.[315] Place's poverty at this time was such that he was tempted to accept Ashley's invitation to accompany him and was only dissuaded from doing so by his wife.[316]

Even Thelwall, the most indomitable of all the radical leaders, finally acquiesced in the inevitable and withdrew from political lecturing. At the end of May 1797 he had returned to the scene of his former triumphs at Norwich, but only to receive the same treatment that he had suffered the year before at Yarmouth and other places.[317] In July, smarting from this unexpected reverse, he had moved across country to seek consolation and renewed poetic stimulus from his correspondents Samuel Taylor Coleridge and William Wordsworth, then engaged in planning their *Lyrical Ballads* in the heart of north Somerset.[318] Wordsworth had recently moved from Racedown in Dorset to become tenant of Alfoxden House near Nether Stowey, where Coleridge was living under the patronage and protection of Thomas Poole – a well-endowed but democratic tanner.[319] Even there, however, Thelwall's passionate outbursts at his host's dinner-table terrified the servants and the nocturnal reconnaissances of the neighbourhood by the philosopher poets and their enquiries about the navigability of the local river from the sea drew down upon the group the attention, but fortunately not the interference, of a Home Office informer.[320] The rural retreat and decent oblivion which Thelwall had sought in the West Country he eventually found in Wales, where the generosity of a few friends enabled him to stock a

314. BL, Add. MSS. 35143, fos. 24–5.

315. *Ibid*, fo. 28. Ashley who, according to Place, had hitherto been 'a sedate, sober, steady man', fell violently in love with a sub-tenant of his, a Mrs Lambert, a fine tall handsome woman who had previously been 'in high keeping'. Ashley prospered in business in Paris and never returned. He died in 1829.

316. Place was so poor that his children were fed by Ashley. *Ibid*., fo. 29.

317. For the extensive damage done by the Inniskilling Dragoons at the Shakespeare Inn, the Rose Tavern and the King's Arms during the riots of 29 May 1797 see the documents in Norfolk and Norwich Record Office, Case 6.h.

318. Brown, p. 155.

319. For Poole see M. E. Poole (Mrs Sandford), *Thomas Poole and his Friends* (2 vols., London, 1888).

320. J. Walsh to J. King, 15 Aug. 1797. PRO HO 42/41; same to same, 16 Aug. 1797. *Ibid*.

small farm at Llys-Wen. Here he was shielded from the insidious attacks of the local curate by a well-to-do sympathizer.[321]

After the defeat of Grey's reform proposals in July 1797 the Foxite Whigs similarly opted out of parliamentary politics by seceding *en bloc* from the House of Commons – as Opposition Whigs had done during the American war. Fox, it appears, had encouraged Grey to move for parliamentary reform in 1797, not with any hope or expectation of success, but mainly as a protest against the government's whole domestic and foreign policy.[322] Secession was only the logical outcome of that gesture and was itself the ultimate protest of which the Foxite Whigs were then capable.

The second half of 1797 thus saw the popular societies in total disarray – either preparing to give up the unequal struggle in the suffocating climate of anti-Jacobin reaction, or on the verge of metamorphosis into clandestine republican cells, infiltrated by the treasonable emissaries of the United Irish Executive in Dublin.

321. Cestre, p. 148.
322. Mitchell, p. 268.

11 The Irish dimension and Anglo-Irish clandestine radicalism, 1797–8

We will not buy or borrow freedom from America or France, but manufacture it ourselves.

Address from the Society of United Irishmen in Dublin to the Delegates for promoting a Reform in Scotland, 23 November 1792[1]

In its final phase, from 1797 to 1799, what remained of English radicalism committed itself to the pursuit of those subversive, clandestine and republican objectives which its more moderate leaders had hitherto consistently repudiated. In this way the Burkian concept of an English Jacobin conspiracy at length gained some of the credibility which it had earlier so conspicuously lacked. As such, however, it was a fringe movement of extremists and fanatics, small in numbers and, in its organized form, restricted to the destitute Irish ghettos in the capital and the industrial North-West. It was at this period that the surviving elements of the London Corresponding Society and its provincial associates dabbled in treasonable activities such as attempts to subvert the armed forces, and clandestine preparations to assist Irish republicans in open rebellion and the French government in its invasion plans. This change in the character and purpose of the radical movement no doubt partly derived from the retirement from active politics of those 'acquitted felons' of the London Corresponding Society and the Society for Constitutional Information, whose livelihoods had been compromised, or whose commitment to reform had been undermined, by the treason trials of 1794. Further government repression in 1795 and 1796 under the regime of the Two Acts had also rendered the public activities of even law-abiding radical societies increasingly difficult and had put a premium upon clandestine organization in the case of those who had been converted to republicanism. The most potent factor of change, however, was the increasing influence inside the radical societies exerted by members

1. *Parl. Hist.*, vol. 34, col. 616.

of the United Irish movement, working in association with their resident representatives in Paris and the French government itself. This phase of English radicalism cannot, therefore, be divorced from, and can only be properly understood in, its Irish and French dimensions.

The shift, indeed, from earlier constitutional methods in the pursuit of radical parliamentary reform and Catholic emancipation to an uncompromising policy of complete Irish separatism and republicanism had occurred earlier in the history of the United Irish movement and to some extent, prepared the way for the analogous change in the nature of English radicalism.

Although in November 1792 the Dublin Society of United Irishmen had proudly boasted to the Scottish Reform Convention in Edinburgh that 'it would not buy or borrow freedom from America of France' but manufacture it for itself, this had been, not so much a repudiation of its debt to the democratic impulse from abroad, as a cautious rejection of revolutionary extremism at a time when Britain was on the verge of a breach with republican France.[2] The truth was, however, that the ultimate origins of the United Irish movement derived from the political aftermath of the American revolution in Ireland while its character and principles as well as its actual foundation were, in large part, determined by the reformist, universalist and republican ideals of the French revolution.[3] To Wolfe Tone himself the French revolution was, indeed, to be 'that morning star to liberty in Ireland'.[4]

The insecurity of Ireland during the war of American Independence, especially after the draining away of men from the Irish military establishment and the entry of France and Spain into the conflict on the side of the colonists, had forced the government to tolerate the rise and spread of independent Volunteer companies, raised and officered by the landed gentry and consisting mainly, but not exclusively, of Protestants.[5] These armed associations on which the govern-

2. *Parl. Hist.*, vol. 34, col. 616.
3. See particularly M. Wall, 'The United Irish movement' in *Historical Studies* (papers read before the biennial Irish conference of historians), vol. 5 (1965), pp. 122–40; J. C. Beckett, *The Making of Modern Ireland, 1603–1923* (London, 1971), ch. 13; E. M. Johnston, *Ireland in the Eighteenth Century* (Dublin, 1974), ch. 7; and Gearóid ó Tuathaigh, *Ireland before the Famine, 1798–1848* (Dublin, 1972), ch. 1.
4. *Report from the Secret Committee of the [Irish] House of Commons* (17 July 1798), appendix 2.
5. H. Butterfield, *George III, Lord North and the People, 1779–80* (London, 1949), pp. 79–83.

ment found itself compelled to rely for home defence, but impotent
to control, had been the means of extorting from the British government under Lord North essential trade concessions in December
1779. These had removed the penal restrictions on the export of
Irish woollens and provisions and had admitted Ireland to the
benefit of direct trade with British colonial possessions in America
and the West Indies.[6] In 1780 similar extra-parliamentary pressure
resulted in the removal of the sacramental test which had hitherto
imposed on Irish Protestant Dissenters the same qualification for
public office as excluded from municipal and other offices so many
English Dissenters.[7] Other long-standing grievances were also remedied – in 1782 a Habeas Corpus Act was passed for Ireland and the
independence of judicial tenure was conceded.[8]

The culmination of these reforms was the establishment, again as
a direct result of the American war, of the legislative independence
of the Irish parliament. In 1782, after the whole country had been
roused by the challenging resolutions of the Convention of Ulster
Volunteer Companies at Dungannon in February,[9] the solution of
the constitutional crisis had been made possible by the overthrow of
Lord North's ministry on 24 March and the accession to power of
Lord Rockingham.[10] Poyning's law was then so amended as to remove all restraints on Irish legislation except the royal veto, and the
sole right of the Irish parliament to legislate for Ireland and the
appellate jurisdiction of the Irish House of Lords were established
by the repeal of the Declaratory Act of 1719.[11]

From that point onwards, however, the prospects of further concessions to the Irish 'patriots' had been clouded by the personal
vendetta between Grattan, the architect of independence, and Flood,

6. *Ibid.*, p. 175. Beckett, p. 218.

7. Beckett, pp. 160, 219.

8. Johnston, pp. 151–2. The best account of this crisis is M. R. O'Connell's
Irish Politics and Social Conflict in the Age of the American Revolution (Philadelphia, 1965).

9. Among the resolutions were the assertion of the legislative independence of
Ireland, the condemnation of Poyning's law and a perpetual mutiny act as
unconstitutional, the demand that judges should have the same security of
tenure in Ireland as in England and a guarded approval of religious equality.
Beckett, p. 222.

10. *Ibid.*, p. 223.

11. Johnston, p. 152. The act of 1719 declared the right of the British Parliament
to legislate for Ireland and to act as the final court of judicature for Irish law-
suits. That right was explicitly renounced, on Flood's insistence, by a special
act in 1783.

the champion of parliamentary reform;[12] by the division inside the Volunteer movement on the need to grant political as well as property rights to the Roman Catholics, and by the confrontation between the national Volunteer Convention in Dublin and the Irish parliament in November 1783, on the issue of parliamentary reform. The years 1782 to 1784 thus registered a series of setbacks for the 'patriot' cause. Catholic relief was confined to an act of 1782 allowing Roman Catholics to purchase land as freely as Protestants, but excluding them from the political franchise, while Flood's bill for parliamentary reform, sponsored by the Dublin Volunteer Convention, was rejected on 30 November 1783 by an Irish House of Commons which expressed its 'perfect satisfaction' with 'the present happy constitution'.[13] Both the rivals for the leadership of the 'patriots' had shown some political lukewarmness – Flood for the cause of further Catholic relief, and Grattan for parliamentary reform at the behest of outside pressure groups – while the Dublin Volunteer Convention retired from the political stage by adjourning *sine die*.[14] It was thus that the United Irish movement, during its constitutional phase from 1791 to 1795, came to adopt as its twin objectives – Catholic emancipation and parliamentary reform.

Its birth-place was in Ulster, the home of eighteenth-century Irish radicalism. This was because in Ireland the 3,000,000 Roman Catholics, in a population of about 4,750,000, were excluded from political life by the operation of the penal laws.[15] In the northern counties, however, the bulk of the population consisted of transplanted Scottish Presbyterians, Covenanters and other Protestant Dissenters, who were highly critical of all forms of established authority.[16] Until 1780 they too had been excluded from public office, like their English counterparts, by the sacramental test and, within the comfortable security provided by their majority position in Ulster, they could afford to deplore the depressed political status of their Catholic neighbours. Initially also the United Irish society was a middle-class

12. Beckett, p. 228.
13. *Ibid.*, pp. 230, 232.
14. *Ibid.*, p. 232.
15. M. Wall, *The Penal Laws, 1691–1790*, Dublin Historical Association pamphlet (Dublin, 1961). See also R. Jacob, *The Rise of the United Irishmen, 1791–1794* (London, 1931).
16. Tone noted that the Dissenters were 'the first to stand forward in the most decided and unqualified manner in support of the principles of the French revolution'. W. T. W. Tone (ed.), *Life of Theobald Wolfe Tone . . .* (Washington, 1826), p. 42.

urban movement of prosperous northern Dissenters. Its leaders, both in Belfast and Dublin, were well-connected local councillors, lawyers, clothiers and linen manufacturers or members of the medical profession.[17]

Before 1789, however, the way ahead for liberal reform in Ireland had been blocked by the refusal of the great Irish office-holders and borough-mongers[18] to share their political monopoly with Protestant reformers of the middle class, by the analogous reluctance of the aristocratic and episcopal members of the Catholic Committee to press forward with the political enfranchisement of their co-religionists,[19] and by the growing distrust of the northern Whigs on the part of the Belfast radicals. In Dublin the Protestant reformers were, therefore, driven to seek the support of the middle-class Catholics, who were coming to the fore inside the central Catholic Committee under the leadership of John Keogh, while the need for such a re-alignment of political forces had also become clear to some at least of the northern Dissenters.[20] With the Catholic Committee in disarray, the Volunteer companies devitalized, and the parliamentary opposition, led by Grattan and Ponsonby, distrustful of radical reform, the way was open for a 'new departure' in Irish politics. What the radicals needed in this situation was a new form of extra-parliamentary organization and the mass support of the Catholic peasantry.

It was to supply these needs that the original branch of the Society of United Irishmen was formed in Belfast in October 1790 on the basis of the equality of rights for all, irrespective of religious belief, and the need for 'a complete and radical reform of the representation of the people in parliament'.[21] Despite the republican aspirations of some of its leaders (notably of Dr William Drennan, the chief publicist of the Dublin branch), the society limited its political objectives to moderate constitutional reform, in order not to alienate

17. R. B. McDowell, 'The personnel of the Dublin Society of United Irishmen, 1791–4', *Irish Historical Studies*, vol. 2 (1940), pp. 12–53.

18. In particular John FitzGibbon, Attorney General (later Lord Clare), John Foster, Chancellor of the Exchequer, and John Beresford, first Commissioner of Revenue.

19. The Catholic Committee had been established in 1760 to promote Roman Catholic political interests – until 1791 it was dominated by Lord Kenmare and other nobles who, under government influence, seceded from the committee in 1790 in protest against a renewed application for Catholic relief. M. Wall, 'The United Irish movement', p. 123.

20. It took some time, however, for the idea of an alliance with the Catholics to gain general consent in Belfast. *Ibid.*, p. 127.

21. *Ibid.*, p. 129.

the conservative views of its Catholic members. Even Theobald Wolfe Tone, the young Dublin Protestant barrister who had outlined the policy of reconciliation with the Catholic majority in an influential pamphlet addressed to the Belfast Dissenters in September 1790, and whose lode-star was the complete separation of Ireland from England, did not originally contemplate the establishment of a republic.[22] On 9 November 1791 a branch of the United Irish society was formed in Dublin, of which the Honourable Simon Butler was the first chairman and James Napper Tandy, a veteran reformer, was the first secretary. This branch was immediately joined by many prominent members of the general Catholic Committee, though no formal links between the two organizations were established.[23] The meetings of the society, like those of the radical societies in Britain, were open and its test for membership, initially pledged only support for 'an impartial and adequate representation of the Irish nation in parliament' and, as a means to that end, the promotion of 'a brotherhood of affection, an identity of interests, a communion of rights, and an union of power among Irishmen of all religious persuasions'.[24] Thomas Collins, the government spy inside the society, was unable to report any illegality in its proceedings or even the presence in its midst of working men.[25] When its subcommittee on reform adopted the principle of universal suffrage, by a narrow majority, a considerable proportion of the members seceded.[26]

Although parliamentary reform was regarded as having priority over the extension of Catholic relief,[27] little or no progress was made during the first phase of the society's existence. It was not until December 1792 that the Dublin branch outlined a programme of

22. The pamphlet was entitled *An argument on behalf of the Catholics of Ireland* and it led the Belfast radicals to invite its author to help in the establishment of the Belfast society of United Irishmen.

23. In the spring of 1792, however, Wolfe Tone was appointed assistant secretary and agent to the Catholic Committee, in place of Richard Burke.

24. *Report from the Committee of Secrecy of the [Irish] House of Commons* (17 July 1798), appendix 5.

25. McDowell, p. 17. The annual subscription was one guinea and there was an entrance fee of the same amount.

26. *Ibid.*, p. 18.

27. 'We, therefore, wish for Catholic emancipation without any modification, but still we consider this necessary enfranchisement as merely the portal to the temple of national freedom . . . The Catholic cause is subordinate to our cause and is included in it.' *Address of the Dublin Society of United Irish to the Volunteers of Ireland, 14 Dec. 1792.*

specific reforms. These were almost a duplicate of those advocated by the English radical societies. Universal male suffrage at the age of twenty-one, annual parliaments, payment of members, no property qualification, disqualification of MPs convicted of the use of bribery in elections, and the division of the country into 300 single-member constituencies – such were the plans recommended to the Irish nation and, in particular, to 'the poorer classes of the community' by the Dublin society on 25 January 1793.[28] One particular proposal – 'that the votes of all electors should be given by voice and not by ballot'– registered a significant division of opinion between the Protestant Dissenters and the Roman Catholic members of the society. Since more than 90 per cent of the land in Ireland in the eighteenth century was owned by Protestants, and since the majority of the Catholic population was dependent on the land for subsistence, the Catholics had favoured the adoption of the secret ballot. The policy of equal rights for all was, indeed, not without its disadvantages for those who were thinking in terms of 'a grand incorporation of the Irish people' – for each section of the community had its own fears – the Protestants of the numerical dominance of Catholic voters, if these were fully and equally enfranchised, and the Catholics of eviction from their holdings by their Protestant landlords, if electoral votes were not protected by the secret ballot.[29]

The main concerns of the mass of the Catholic peasantry were, however, the burden of tithes, the security of their holdings and the eventual recovery of their ancestral lands. Painite propaganda, French revolutionary notions of equal rights and even the prospect of political emancipation left them indifferent. The United Irish societies never really penetrated the country districts before 1795 and the radicals were thus unable to exert the same sort of outside pressure on Parliament as the Volunteers had done in 1783.

Steady and substantial gains, on the other hand, were made before 1794 in the way of Catholic emancipation. The credit for this lay, not so much with the United Irish, as with a revitalized central Catholic Committee and the British government itself. As the result of an internal schism, the Catholic Committee, under the more democratic and committed leadership of John Keogh, Richard McCormick and Edward Byrne, had resolved to press forward with its demands for

28. *Report of Secret Committee of the [Irish] House of Commons* (17 July, 1798), pp. 79–85.
29. Wall, 'The United Irish movement', p. 134.

the abolition of the penal code.[30] Early in 1792 a moderate measure of Catholic relief, introduced by a private member, Sir Hercules Langrishe, repealed the disabilities attached to 'mixed' marriages, the remaining restrictions on the education of Catholics and the prohibition of their entry into the legal profession.[31] The act, however, failed to satisfy the reformers, mainly because it had only been carried as the result of English pressure on the Irish executive and also because a clause admitting Catholics to the county franchise had been rejected.[32]

In order to continue the pressure for further concessions and to meet the criticism that it was not representative of the views of its co-religionists in the country at large, the Catholic Committee provided for itself a wider basis of popular support and summoned to Dublin in early December 1792 a delegate Catholic Convention. This body, with a membership intentionally equal to that of the Irish parliament itself, and representing, not the Protestant ascendancy, but the entire Catholic population, drafted a petition calling for the redress of its grievances and appointed a special delegation to present it to George III in person, instead of forwarding it through the Lord Lieutenant.[33] At the virtual dictation of Pitt, the Irish government itself promoted and carried an extensive measure of Catholic relief in April 1793.[34] This act gave the Catholics the right, under special circumstances, to bear arms, threw open to them, with certain important exceptions, careers in the civil and military services, and admitted them to the parliamentary and municipal franchise on the same terms as Protestants. It still, however, excluded them from membership of the Irish parliament.[35]

This high-water mark in the tide of English concessions registered less a capitulation to the moral force of organized Catholic opinion than the British government's concern to ensure Catholic loyalty in the war which had recently broken out with France. Though the

30. Johnston, p. 166.
31. 32 Geo. III c. 21.
32. Beckett, p. 249.
33. *Ibid.*
34. 33 Geo. III c. 21.
35. The draft petition by the Dublin Catholic Committee had only asked for a limited share in the franchise at a higher qualification than Protestants. The demand for complete emancipation (including the right of representation in Parliament) had been adopted on the insistence of the delegate from County Antrim, Luke Teeling, representing the views of the inner circle of Belfast United Irishmen. Wall, 'The United Irish movement', p. 132.

Catholic Committee received the act with gratitude, it soon appreciated that the political power it apparently conferred on the Catholics
would not become a reality unless it were followed by an instalment
of effective parliamentary reform. Events, however, were soon to
demonstrate that this indispensable prerequisite in the United Irish
programme would not, in the new situation of anti-Jacobin reaction,
be conceded to public agitation, even if this were conducted in a
legal and constitutional manner. The so-called 'Back Lane Parliament' of the Dublin Catholic Convention, when followed by the
meeting of an Ulster Reform Convention at Dungannon on 15
February 1793, convinced the Irish government of the urgent need
to prevent the summons of a Convention of United Irishmen, whose
leaders had already proclaimed their conversion to Painite doctrines,
if not as yet to republicanism.[36] Early in February the Volunteer
companies were, therefore, disarmed and disbanded, and in
July 1793 a Convention Act was passed, prohibiting the summons
of any representative or delegate assemblies other than Parliament.[37]

The outbreak of hostilities with France in February 1793 was only
the first of a series of events which transformed the United Irish
society from a small and ineffectual group of radical reformers
first into a secret, oath-bound and hierarchical organization led by
ardent republicans and, finally, into an armed and mass insurrectionary levy, prepared to act in an auxiliary role to French
invasion forces.

In this process the year 1794 proved a crucial turning point. In the
spring of that year the French government, at the instigation of the
resident Anglo-Irish radicals in Paris, resumed those earlier contacts
with the United Irish which the repressive measures of the previous
year had rendered futile.[38] This time the Reverend William Jackson,
an Anglican clergyman with dubious antecedents and of Irish extraction, was entrusted with a mission intended to clarify the likely
response of the English public to a projected French invasion and

36. Beckett, p. 252.
37. 33 Geo. III c. 29.
38. The first agent sent by France to Ireland was Colonel Eleazer Oswald who,
at the instigation of Lord Edward Fitzgerald and with the support of Paine, had
been commissioned by Lebrun as Foreign Minister early in 1793 to explore and
report on the chances of a successful rebellion. Though he contacted the main
leaders of the United Irish in Dublin in May, Oswald had reported that the
radicals were then quite unprepared. Written report dated 11 June 1793. AAE
CPA, vol. 587, fo. 167/8.

also to test the strength of pro-French sentiment in Ireland.[39] The mission had been suggested by Nicholas Madgett, an Irish exile, who had been in French government employment before 1789 and who, since 1793, had held an intelligence post in the French Admiralty, nominally concerned with the translation of English documents and newspapers, but unofficially, with the despatch of secret agents to the British isles.[40]

The English aspects of Jackson's mission have already been noticed as bearing on the government's decision to institute the State Trials of 1794.[41] Jackson's ill-fated visit to Dublin and his contacts with the United Irish leaders had, however, more lasting and significant consequences. After receiving discouraging reports on the hostility which any French invasion would be likely to encounter in England, Jackson had travelled on to Dublin in the company of the double agent who was to betray him – a former associate and attorney called Cockayne. This man had already revealed Jackson's presence in London to Pitt, who had commissioned him to maintain a close watch on his negotiations with the Irish radicals.[42]

Soon after his arrival in Dublin early in April 1794, Jackson had secured introductions to the leading United Irishmen through a former law student of Cockayne's, Leonard McNally. His initial reception had been guarded. Lord Edward Fitzgerald refused to meet him. Simon Butler and McNally expressed scepticism, while Wolfe Tone was more than half-inclined to suspect that Jackson was either an English spy or an *agent provocateur*.[43] Edward Lewins, later to be appointed the accredited representative of the United Irish in Paris, was, however, more receptive to Jackson's overtures and arranged for him and Cockayne to meet the influential United Irish leader Alexander Hamilton Rowan, who was then in Newgate prison.[44] Despite Jackson's lack of any official credentials from the

39. Jackson had been educated at Oxford and had held a curacy in London where his taste for high society had brought him into the circle of the notorious Duchess of Kingston. In 1791 he had travelled to Paris on the Duchess's business and had become prominent in the colony of British radicals there. He had been a signatory of the address of the resident Irish and English radicals to the National Convention in November 1792.

40. For Madgett see Richard Hayes, *Biographical Dictionary of Irishmen in France* (Dublin, 1949), pp. 194–5.

41. See above, pp. 322–4.

42. For his evidence on this point at Jackson's trial in 1795 see *ST*, vol. 25, col. 828.

43. Tone, p. 83.

44. *ST*, vol. 25, col. 818.

French government,[45] Hamilton Rowan treated him with every mark of confidence, and by exaggerating the strength of republicanism in the United Irish society and the depth of the Irish desire for independence, gave Jackson an opening to proffer firm assurances of French support for any Irish attempt at open rebellion.[46]

After Wolfe Tone had overcome his earlier misgivings about Jackson and had asserted his own strong views on the necessity and inevitability of an eventual Irish bid for independence, it was agreed among the conspirators that he should draft a memorandum on the state of Ireland for the French Committee of Public Safety.[47] This would stress Irish grievances under English rule and the country's willingness to welcome liberation at the hands of French invasion forces. According to Wolfe Tone's own account, this draft memorandum (of which he made no copy) was entrusted to Hamilton Rowan on condition that, if a copy was taken of it, the original would be destroyed. In Tone's temporary absence at the Drogheda Assizes Rowan had made three copies of the document in his own handwriting and, after burning the original, had handed these over to Jackson with the warning not to despatch them by post. Despite this, Jackson posted two copies of the memorandum on 24 April, one addressed to the Hamburg merchant house of Chapeaurouge and the other to the French minister at The Hague.[48] On information from Cockayne, both letters were intercepted in the post and, on 28 April 1794, Jackson was arrested. His trial did not come on till April of the following year, but when it did so the verdict of 'Guilty' on the charge of high treason was a foregone conclusion. The testimony of Cockayne, the intercepted correspondence and the implied admission of complicity suggested by the flight of several of the leading conspirators left Jackson with no chance of acquittal, though he managed to cheat the executioner by taking arsenic in the dock.[49]

Although Hamilton Rowan managed to effect a dramatic escape

45. All that Jackson could produce were two letters from J. H. Stone at Paris, who had arranged the details of his mission to London, one to J. Horne Tooke and the other to Dr Crawford. *Ibid.*, col. 846.

46. Rowan's own account of these interviews is contained in his letter of 2 October 1794 to the Committee of Public Safety. AAE CPA, vol. 588, fos. 262 ff.

47. Tone, p. 80. For the memorandum itself see *ST*, vol. 25, cols. 841–3. For the English memorandum drawn up by Benjamin Vaughan see *Ibid.*, col. 844.

48. *ST*, vol. 25, col. 832.

49. *Ibid.*, col. 889. The poison is said to have been administered by Jackson's wife.

from prison and found a temporary refuge in Paris,[50] and though Wolfe Tone evaded the full consequences of his involvement by agreeing to go into voluntary exile in America,[51] the discovery of the conspiracy led to the immediate suppression of the Dublin Society of United Irishmen on 4 May 1794. By driving the more conservative members out of the movement, it left the control of the society as a whole in the hands of a small group of determined republicans, who henceforward were totally committed to the policy of soliciting a French invasion of Ireland. The missions of Oswald in 1793 and of Jackson in 1794, both officially sponsored, seemed to indicate that future pleas from the United Irish for armed assistance would be assured of a warm response from the French government.[52] Such a conclusion, however, overlooked the fact that both missions had been purely exploratory, both had been abortive and that a French invasion would be dependent not only on better guarantees of Irish determination and ability to organize a successful revolt, but also upon the internal situation in France itself and upon the exigencies of its military commitments elsewhere.[53]

The end of the United Irish society's existence as a reform association and its transition to a clandestine republican organization bent on complete Irish separation from Britain was also the result of the rejection in March 1794 of Grattan's moderate measure of parliamentary reform and the subsequent failure, early in 1795, of Earl Fitzwilliam's attempt as viceroy to liberalize the Irish administration

50. Faced by a certain charge of high treason, Rowan had persuaded his jailor to allow him to spend his wedding anniversary at home and had escaped to France in a small fishing vessel manned by three sailors on 5 May. After landing at Roscoff in Brittany, he was imprisoned for two months until he was allowed to go to Paris through the intervention of Sullivan, Madgett's nephew. His petition to the Committee of Public Safety for financial support dated 2 October 1794 is in AAE CPA, vol. 588, fos. 262–4. He left France for America in April 1795.

51. He left Ireland for Philadelphia on 13 June 1795 and landed in France on 2 February 1796. Henceforth he concentrated on the task of persuading the French government to send substantial invasion forces to Ireland.

52. In fact the main effect of the Jackson episode in France was that it resulted in the recognition of Wolfe Tone as the accredited representative of the United Irish in Paris.

53. Under the Executive Directory, France's main military commitment still remained the conquest of the 'natural frontiers' and all plans for an invasion of Ireland were regarded as strategical diversions meant to compromise Britain's chances of Continental intervention or to force her to the conference table. A. Sorel, *L'Europe et la Révolution Française* (Paris, 1910), vol. 5, pp. 47–51.

in association with the Irish Whigs and to concede to the Roman Catholics full membership in the Irish legislature.[54] These failures registered the Younger Pitt's abandonment of his policy of conciliation towards the Irish Catholics, the impregnable position of the reactionary regime at Dublin Castle and the futility of working for Catholic emancipation or parliamentary reform in alliance with the Whig Opposition or by purely legal and constitutional methods.

In the course of 1794 and 1795 the United Irish society, whose numbers had declined sharply as a result of the Jackson episode, and which had even been officially suppressed, was reconstituted on a new hierarchical and territorial basis. The number of societies was increased by reducing their membership from thirty-six to twelve and each elected a secretary and treasurer. The secretaries of five of these societies were constituted as a 'lower baronial committee', one member of which was delegated to an 'upper baronial committee'. Above these, district committees were established in the urban areas and county committees in the country districts. A superior echelon was provided by four provincial directories – one each for Ulster, Leinster, Munster and Connaught. All of these committees met at least once a month and kept in regular touch with their constituent branches. The apex of the organization was a General Executive Directory, composed of five persons elected by secret ballot from the provincial directories.[55] This body had 'the supreme and uncontrolled command of the whole body of the union'.[56] A new oath was exacted from all members which omitted from the original test the words 'Parliament' and 'reform' and a further innovation was the attempt to conceal the identity of the members of the several committees from their constituents in the interest of security.[57]

Secrecy was also imposed on the new society by its absorption in 1796 of the illegal and widespread Catholic agrarian organization – the so-called 'Defenders'. Paradoxically it was sectarian strife be-

54. G. C. Bolton, *The Passing of the Irish Act of Union* (Oxford, 1966), pp. 15–19.

55. *Report of the Secret Committee of the House of Commons* (15 March 1799), *Parl. Hist.*, vol. 34, cols. 582–3.

56. *Report from the Committee of Secrecy of the House of Lords in Ireland* (30 Aug. 1798), p. 7.

57. *Report from the Committee of Secrecy of the House of Commons of Ireland* (17 July 1798), appendix 30, p. 225. The purpose of the omission in the new test, according to Dr McNevin, was 'to reconcile reformers and republicans, and because they had given up all idea of reform, and were determined on republicanism'.

tween Catholic Defenders and Protestant 'Peep O'day Boys' in Ulster which was to make possible the temporary and elusive union of Catholic and Protestant within the depleted ranks of the United Irish society. At the root of this local rivalry had been increased pressure of population on the land and the consequent competition for holdings.[58] This often took the form of agrarian outrages and it was a skirmish between these factions at a cross-roads in county Armagh, later known as the Battle of the Diamond, which had led to the formation of the Protestant Orange Order in 1795.[59] In the following year the fusion of the Orange lodges with units of the Yeomanry, a part-time home defence unit, recently instituted by the Irish government and recruited by local landlords from their tenantry, resulted in the intensification of the persecution against the Defenders in Ulster. In the winter of 1796 thousands of Defenders fled from their homes to the security of the Catholic south and west of Ireland, where they were absorbed more or less sporadically into the cadres of the reorganized United Irish society.[60] They brought to the society a deeply rooted tradition of agrarian violence, and an intense hatred of the established government. Entirely devoid of political sophistication, they nevertheless helped to reinforce the society's growing republicanism. Their sheer numbers offered the radical leaders of the United Irishmen the ultimate prospect of being able to call on the support of a mass movement of peasant irregulars prepared to massacre their landlords and to subvert the established government. Their affiliation with the society was to be an important bargaining tool in the hands of those who were commissioned, after 1795, to solicit the military and financial assistance of the French government in the fulfilment of the cherished dream of an independent Irish republic.[61]

As a result of protracted and difficult negotiations with the French Executive Directory conducted mainly by the official representatives of the United Irish in Paris, Wolfe Tone and later Edward Lewins, four French naval expeditions with accompanying land forces were, in fact, despatched between 1796 and 1798 to assist in the task of

58. K. H. Connell, *The Population of Ireland, 1750–1845* (Oxford, 1950). and L. M. Cullen, *An Economic History of Ireland since 1660* (1972).

59. H. Senior, *Orangeism in Ireland and Britain, 1795–1836* (London and Toronto, 1966).

60. Beckett, p. 257.

61. Carnot anticipated that the Defenders could be employed to conduct a *chouannerie* in reverse, though Hoche would have preferred to transport former Vendéen rebels to Ireland for the purpose. Sorel, vol. 5, p. 50.

liberating Ireland.[62] All of these expeditions were, however, tragic failures. The first of these, after many delays, sailed from Brest, in mid December 1796 under the military command of one of France's most brilliant generals – Lazare Hoche. Though successful in evading the British fleet, the expedition was scattered by winter storms and forced to seek temporary refuge in Bantry Bay. Instead of pressing forward to land their troops in the north of Ireland, where alone they could have expected effective support, the subordinate commanders, separated from Hoche, retreated to French ports with their mission uncompleted.[63] The three later expeditions, all hurriedly improvised in the effort to resuscitate the Irish rebellion, which had already collapsed in the spring and summer of 1798, were on a small scale, were not synchronized as originally intended and were misdirected to areas in the far north-west and north of Ireland where their chances of success were dubious in the extreme.[64] After landing at Killala Bay in north Connaught on 23 August, an expedition commanded by General Humbert penetrated inland as far as county Longford, but was then obliged to surrender to the vastly superior forces of Lord Cornwallis and General Lake at Ballinamuck on 8 September. This led to the prompt withdrawal of Napper Tandy's 'Northern Army of Avengers' which had put ashore on the island of Raghlin a week later. The third force under General Hardy was intercepted on 12 October off Lough Swilly in Donegal and virtually captured outright.[65] Among the prisoners in the flagship was Wolfe Tone, who had been given the rank of colonel (*chef de brigade*) in the French army. He was taken to Dublin, tried and condemned to death by court martial, although he had never held a commission in either the British or Irish forces and although the Court of King's Bench was then sitting. An attempt by Curran to obtain his release by a writ of Habeas Corpus and retrial was frustrated by his suicide in his prison cell on 19 November.[66]

It was, however, in the preparation of the rebellion of 1798, and in the wake of its failure, that the United Irish movement became, for a brief period, the centre of British radical politics. The misun-

62. See E. Guillon, *La France et l'Irlande pendant la Révolution* (Paris, 1888). H. L. Calkin, *Les Invasions d'Irlande pendant la Révolution Française* (Paris, 1956).

63. E. H. Stuart-Jones, *The Invasion that failed: the French expedition to Ireland, 1796* (Oxford, 1950).

64. Thomas Pakenham, *The Year of Liberty: The great Irish Rebellion of 1798* (London, 1969).

65. *Ibid.*, p. 338.

66. *Ibid.*, p. 345.

derstandings and miscalculations that precipitated the outbreak of that rebellion and did so much to ensure its collapse stemmed from the events of 1796. The disastrous expeditions of that year not only discouraged the French from launching any future invasion forces until the Irish had committed themselves to outright rebellion, but had divided the leadership of the United Irish on the timing of such open defiance.[67] By doing so it complicated the political and strategical options open to both the French and Irish in 1798 and made the synchronization of their operations impossible. By seeking also to link their separatist aspirations with those of the disintegrating British radical societies, the United Irish agents only exposed them to the scrutiny of English Home Office spies and stimulated the revelations of renegade Irish informers.[68]

Irish co-operation with France nevertheless inevitably involved an attempt, sooner or later, to make political use of the large pockets of Irish immigrants in the industrial North-West of England and in the capital.[69] French insistence that the United Irish should actively assist their invasion schemes in England as the price of French military support in Ireland made inevitable Irish attempts to penetrate the existing cadres of the English radical movement. By 1797 or 1798 republican sentiment in the London Corresponding Society and its provincial offshoots had made considerable progress and the remaining nuclei of active leaders were committed to the expediency of violence and the consequent necessity of clandestine organization.[70] All these shifts in political attitudes facilitated the infiltration of

67. A militant minority, including Arthur O'Connor and Lord Edward Fitzgerald, wished to capitalize on the increasing membership of the United Irish early in 1797, by precipitating an armed rising as soon as possible to assure France of their good intentions. When these proposals were considered in Dublin they were, however, rejected by the moderates. T. A. Emmet and McCormick, *Report of the Secret Committee of the Irish House of Commons* (Dublin, 1798), p. 21.

68. The main informer was Samuel Turner LLD a former member of the Northern Executive of United Irishmen, who had left Ireland as a result of the schism between the extremists and moderates and had escaped to Hamburg in the autumn of 1797. W. J. Fitzpatrick, *Secret Service under Pitt* (London, 1892).

69. For Irish immigration see B. M. Kerr, 'Irish immigration into Great Britain, 1798–1838', unpublished BLitt thesis (Oxford, 1938).

70. Deposition of J. Powell, 12 March 1798. PRO HO 42/42. This was one of the reasons why Francis Place considered that from the beginning of January 1798, 'what remained of the society was its refuse, with the exception of Galloway, Hodgson, Lemaître and a few others, who from what they considered conscientious motives, still adhered to it'. BL, Add. MSS. 27808, fo. 106.

select English radical groups by important agents of the United Irish on their way through Liverpool, Manchester and London to Hamburg and Paris. Orange terrorism in Ulster had, moreover, driven large numbers of Irish Catholics to Lancashire where they kept open the lines of communication with the Belfast United Irish and brought with them the methods and obsessions of the Irish extremists. It is not, therefore, surprising that willingness to resort to political assassination, plans for armed risings in strategic areas, systematic attempts to subvert the armed forces of the Crown and secret preparations to assist an Irish rebellion or French invasion forces became the stock-in-trade of the United Irish societies in Britain and were surreptitiously recommended to English sympathizers with the cause of Irish independence and French republicanism. Disagreements both in Dublin and in Paris between the moderate and extremist elements of the United Irish leadership as to the timing of the Irish revolt also increased Irish reliance on English radical support as a means of ensuring adequate French military assistance. Small but dangerous groups of English radicals were thus involuntarily drawn into a complicated web of clandestine international intrigue, the secrets of which, fortunately, came into the possession of the English government almost from the outset.

At the centre of this conspiracy was the flamboyant but tragic figure of the Reverend James Coigley – a characteristic product of the eighteenth-century Irish penal laws.[71] A native of county Armagh in Ulster and born in 1762, Coigley had, from 1785, been educated for the priesthood at the Collège des Lombards in Paris. After quarrelling with the college authorities he had returned to Ireland in 1791 and had joined first the illegal Defender organization and then the United Irish society. His own activities as a recruiting agent for the latter soon made him a marked man and the systematic campaign of terrorism conducted by the Orange lodges against the Catholics in Armagh in 1796 had singled out his aged parents for victimization.[72] For these reasons Coigley had been compelled to flee in disguise from Ireland in the summer of 1797. Henceforth he played the precarious and dual role of secret messenger between the extremist factions of the United Irish in Dublin and Paris and of link man with English republican groups in Lancashire and London.

At Whitsun 1797, on his way to the Continent, Coigley stayed

71. S. Simms, *The Rev. James Coigley, United Irishman* (Belfast, 1937).
72. *The Life of the Rev. James Coigley, as written by himself* (Maidstone Gaol, 30 April 1798). *ST*, vol. 27, col. 148.

three days in Manchester, lodging at the sign of the Fire Engine, kept by Isaac Perrins.[73] Here he met and discussed his plans with James Dixon, a young Irish immigrant weaver and cotton spinner from Belfast who had lived in Manchester since 1788. In January 1797, when about to revisit Ulster, Dixon had been commissioned by a special meeting of the Manchester Corresponding Society to obtain copies of the constitution of the United Irish and of their secret oath and test.[74] By doing so Dixon had helped to convert some members of the Manchester Corresponding Society into secret, oath-bound members of the new republican society – the United Englishmen. Through Dixon Coigley also got in touch with Robert Gray, an auctioneer's clerk and leading figure in local radical politics who, in March 1798, was to become a government informer. After an exchange of secret signs Coigley told Gray that he was on a second diplomatic mission to Paris as representative of the United Irish executive, seeking French military assistance for a planned revolt of 300,000 insurgents.[75] His immediate need was for cash to defray his personal expenses and for this he appealed to members of the United Irish in Manchester and Stockport. A meeting attended by thirty-five of the sixty-seven divisional secretaries of the Manchester Corresponding Society summoned by Gray at the lower Ship Inn on Strude Hill, Manchester, and chaired by William Chetham, agreed to organize a collection in aid of Coigley's mission, knowing it was a traitorous one.[76] The proceeds amounting to just over £10 helped to swell the total collected for this purpose to £60.[77]

Coigley also further stimulated the growth of societies of United Englishmen in the Manchester region, urging the radicals to penetrate the local militia units, to subvert the regular troops and even to resort to the Irish practice of killing unpopular local magistrates.[78]

In the autumn of 1797 Coigley effected more significant contacts in London – with John and Benjamin Binns, the main advocates inside the London Corresponding Society of its conversion into a society of United Englishmen, with Valentine Lawless, son of the first Viscount Cloncurry, who had recently settled in the capital as

73. Examination of James Dixon, April 1798, PRO PC 1/42/A 140. Examination of Mary, wife of Isaac Perrin, 14 April 1798, PRO HO 42/45.

74. Examination of James Dixon, 5 May 1798. *Ibid.* For a copy of the constitution and test of the United Irish see *ST*, vol. 27, cols. 1367–73.

75. Deposition of Robert Gray, 19 March 1798. PRO HO 42/45.

76. Further evidence of Robert Gray, 12 April 1798. *Ibid.*

77. Deposition of Robert Gray, 19 March 1798. *Ibid.*

78. *Ibid.* Sworn deposition of Robert Gray, 19 March 1798.

the resident representative of the United Irish; and with Colonel Despard, who was already one of the most important links between the Irish, English and French republicans.[79] At secret meetings with these and other extremists in Furnival's Inn cellar in Holborn, Coigley cemented his relations with English and Irish republicans and also met with 'a Delegate from the United Scotch, sent expressly to London to know how far the English Patriots were willing to assist their brethren in Scotland and Ireland in the great work of overthrowing Tyranny'.[80] Some serious discussion of the consequences of a successful French invasion appears to have taken place, for Coigley took with him to France a document, in Benjamin Binns's handwriting, outlining English popular grievances – political, economic, legal and religious – depicting the serious disaffection in both the army and the fleet, and setting out the terms and conditions on which radical support for a French invasion could be guaranteed.[81] According to Coigley the document emanated from 'the chief revolutionary committee of England'.[82] In the prevailing uncertainty as to French intentions Coigley, in communicating the information to the French government, later explained that, if an expedition were despatched to Ireland, the members of the committee solemnly pledged themselves 'to secure the leading members of the Privy Council (the king only excepted) and thus paralyse the Government at least for a time'.[83] If, on the other hand, the French attacked England alone, they could count on 'the most effectual support' from British 'patriots', provided they first agreed to observe 'the following terms':

1st That the British Isles shall form distinct republicks, 2. That the republicks shall choose their own form of Government. 3. That no contribution shall be exacted, except the actual expences of invasion . . . and

79. For Lawless see *Personal Recollections of the Life and Times of Valentine, Lord Cloncurry* (Dublin, 1849), and W. J. Fitzpatrick, *The Life, Times and Contemporaries of Lord Cloncurry* (London, 1855).

80. AAE CPA, vol. 592, fo. 43. Memorandum of James Coigley and Arthur McMahon to the French Executive Directory, 4 October 1797. H. W. Meikle, in *Scotland and the French Revolution* (Glasgow, 1912), p. 191, suggests that the Scot in question may have been the Angus Cameron who had been outlawed for his part in the Scottish militia riots of September 1797.

81. PRO PC 1/43/A 152.

82. AAE CPA, vol. 592, fo. 43. 4 Oct. 1797.

83. No mention of this intention is made in the original document (PC 1/43/A 152) which Coigley purported to be summarizing, but such a move would probably have been recommended by Colonel Despard.

finally that the French shall require only the ships and possessions taken from them and their allies.[84]

Accompanied by the Reverend Arthur McMahon, a refugee Presbyterian minister from county Down, Coigley took ship first to Cuxhaven, then boarded the Dutch invasion fleet assembled in the Texel, and, early in October 1797, made his way to Paris. After communicating the message from the English republicans, both Coigley and McMahon took sides with the United Irish faction led by Napper Tandy, which in November arraigned both Wolfe Tone and Edward Lewins – the accredited representatives in Paris of the United Irish executive – before a meeting of their compatriots for their alleged supine conduct of negotiations with the French government. After Lewins had refused to attend this meeting and Wolfe Tone had treated it with disdain, their opponents decided to send Coigley back to Ireland to secure the replacement of Lewins at Paris by a more impressive and determined leader in the shape of Arthur O'Connor.[85]

Coigley arrived back in London on 30 November 1797 when his every movement was followed by Bow Street constables – the secret of the tripartite republican conspiracy having been betrayed to the English government by the renegade United Irish representative at Hamburg, Samuel Turner.[86] After lodging with the Binns brothers, borrowing money from Valentine Lawless and procuring an address of sympathy and support from the central committee of the 'United Britons' to the United Irish on 5 January 1798, Coigley crossed to Dublin, accompanied by Benjamin Binns and William Bailey.[87] Here he learnt from Lord Edward Fitzgerald of the latest schism in the

84. A further stipulation, contained in PC 1/43/A 152, 'that those who will join the Invaders shall have arms provided', was quietly dropped by Coigley in his letter to the Directory.

85. *Autobiography of Wolfe Tone.*

86. Although Turner had left Ireland as a result of the rift with the moderates, he seems as a northern Irish Protestant to have been alienated from the cause of Irish independence largely by his conviction that the southern Catholics had determined to use it to put through large-scale confiscations of landed property. He pretended that his withdrawal to Hamburg was flight, infiltrated the Irish *émigré* colony there and became the confidant of Lord Edward Fitzgerald's wife, Pamela – hence his alias of 'Richardson' or 'Mr R' in government correspondence. Turner began reporting to the government through Lord Downshire from early October 1797. PRO HO 100/75, fos. 7–9.

87. For the address see *Report of the Committee of Secrecy of the Irish House of Lords* (30 August 1798), appendix 2. This is the first time that the name of 'United Britons' appears to have been publicly assumed. PRO HO 42/45.

United Irish leadership – the militant wing of which, under O'Connor, had been frustrated in its plans for an immediate rising under cover of the midnight Christmas Eve mass. The moderates, led by Thomas Addis Emmet, more distrustful of French intentions, had preferred to await the arrival of a French expedition promised for April 1798.[88] Coigley had immediately returned to London, where O'Connor had sought refuge early in January 1798 from the prospect of a second term of imprisonment in the congenial and sympathetic company of the Opposition Whigs.[89] After being advised by Erskine and Sheridan to beat a further retreat to the Continent, O'Connor readily agreed to accompany Coigley back to Paris in order to supersede Lewins as resident representative of the United Irish executive.

Ever since he had quitted Ireland in the previous summer, Coigley, masquerading as 'Captain Jones', had dressed the part in a conspicuous military uniform of blue pantaloons seamed with red, a blue top coat and red cape. Not to be outdone, and with a slightly better claim to the status, as a former Volunteer officer, O'Connor adopted the alias of 'Colonel Morris'. The need for disguise in the move across the Channel was, indeed, imperative, for Coigley had agreed to deliver to the French government a second address from the 'Secret Committee of England', dated 25 January 1798, revealing the alliance between the English, Irish and Scottish republicans and promising enthusiastic support for French invasion forces from the 'friends of liberty'.[90] 'Already', the document stated,

have the English fraternized with the Irish and Scots, and a delegate from each now sits with us. The sacred flame of liberty is rekindled: the holy obligation of brotherhood is received with enthusiasm: even in the fleets and the armies it makes some progress: disaffection prevails in both and united Britain burns to break her chains. . . . United as we are, we only

88. F. MacDermot, 'Arthur O'Connor', *Irish Historical Studies*, vol. 15 (1966), p. 57.

89. He had been imprisoned in Dublin Castle on 2 February 1797 for a seditious address published in the Belfast *Northern Star*. After his release on bail in early August, O'Connor took the initiative in founding the Dublin *Press* – an extremist United Irish newspaper designed to replace the *Northern Star*, which had been suppressed. After its nominal editor, Finerty, had been convicted for seditious libel on 22 December 1797, O'Connor announced that he was the real publisher and promptly left for England. Brian Inglis, *The Freedom of the Press in Ireland, 1754–1841* (London, 1954), pp. 98–102.

90. *Report of the Committee of Secrecy of the House of Commons* (March, 1799), appendix 10. *Parl. Hist.*, vol. 34, cols. 645–7. See also *ST*, vol. 26, cols. 1250–2.

wait with impatience to see the hero of Italy, and the brave veterans of the great nation: myriads will hail their arrival with shouts of joy.[91]

In a memorandum submitted to the French Foreign Minister, Talleyrand, early in April 1798, John Ashley, former secretary of the London Corresponding Society, then resident in Paris, attempted to quantify the 'myriads' of pro-French sympathizers in the London area by suggesting that they amounted at least to 100,000 and that, of these, 30,000 were 'active and decided men ... ready to co-operate against the Government when opportunity shall present itself'.[92] What form 'co-operation' might have taken at that stage was later indicated by Dr Robert Watson, a more ardent and committed republican, a self-styled former member of the Executive Committee of the London Corresponding Society and close associate of Colonel Despard.[93] According to Watson's subsequent testimony to the French government, plans had been made at the time of the French invasion preparations to stage a diversion in favour of the military operations by a general insurrection of the radical 'friends of liberty' throughout the country. Undercover preparations for this intervention had taken the form of circular letters addressed to all the affiliated societies, purporting to renew the agitation for radical parliamentary reform and the conclusion of peace with France. Once the French had invaded, the provincial radicals would have been summoned by proclamations issued on the same day in all the important towns to rise in hostile demonstrations against the establishment. This manoeuvre would, it was thought, compel the government to disperse its troops to the localities, thus leaving the capital open to the assaults of the French. If, on the other hand, government forces were concentrated in large army corps in the regions, the radicals themselves could attempt a successful *coup* in the capital.[94]

91. *Ibid.*
92. AAE, Mémoires et documents, vol. 53, fo. 161 (verso). Earlier in this document Ashley estimated that the numbers attending the LCS public meetings in 1795 had amounted to 100,000 and that the total membership of the LCS since its foundation was about 30,000. The coincidence of these figures with those quoted for pro-French sympathizers and militant activists is significant.
93. See article in *Dictionary of National Biography*. In 1797 he was arrested for relaying intelligence to France via Hamburg. On his release, in 1799, he escaped to France.
94. AAE, Mémoires et documents, vol. 53, fos. 263–4. This long memorandum dated 22 Messidor, an VII (10 July 1799) reflects the exaggerated views of the republican clique surrounding Colonel Despard. Watson offered the Directory a

Bonaparte, however, had not been impressed by the factious behaviour of the United Irish in Paris and was soon to leave for Egypt, committing the veterans of his Italian campaigns to the will o' wisp of Eastern conquest rather than the gamble of an Irish or English invasion.[95] Even if French troops had effected a Channel crossing, they would have been greeted, not by 'myriads' of British 'patriots' but by thousands of armed and patriotic Volunteers.[96]

Coigley and his ill-assorted companions, however, found the problem of hiring cross-Channel transport at the height of an invasion scare equally insuperable. Preliminary inquiries made by John Binns, posing as a smuggler, at Whistable and Deal for a boat to Flushing or a French Channel port proved abortive. Returning to London on 25 February to warn his colleagues, he found that they had already set out for Whitstable and he only succeeded in rejoining them at Margate on 27 February. Here on the 28th the whole party, consisting of O'Connor, Coigley, their 'servants', Allen and Leary, and Binns, was arrested at the King's Head Tavern by the two Bow Street constables who had kept Coigley under surveillance since his return to London in January. Thanks to the detailed and accurate information passed to it by Samuel Turner from Hamburg, the British government was, in fact, now in full possession of the main aspects of the conspiracy – its precise motivation, its timing in relation to the projected Irish rebellion, its connection with the extremist wing of the London Corresponding Society and even the day-to-day movements of the leading participants.[97] When the incriminating document from the 'Secret Committee of England' was found in the pocket of Coigley's greatcoat at the time of his arrest, the chain of evidence to support the charge of high treason against him and his companions seemed complete.

Meanwhile, a report had reached the Home Office which pointed to the existence in Manchester of a numerous and expanding society

---

sum of £20 million and the payment of the French forces on the same basis as English troops if it would commit itself to invade! He did not explain where the money was going to come from.

95. Bonaparte sailed for Egypt on 19 May 1798 a few days before the outbreak of the Irish rebellion, though the decision not to invade England or Ireland had been taken on 25 March.

96. See J. R. Western, 'The Volunteer Movement as an anti-revolutionary force', *English Historical Review*, vol. 71 (1956), pp. 603–14.

97. PRO HO 42/45. 'Proofs of the connection between the London Corresponding Society, the United Irish and the Irish rebels.'

of United Englishmen, modelled on the United Irish. Writing from Stonyhurst on 15 February 1798, an Irish Roman Catholic priest, the Reverend John Waring, informed the Duke of Portland that, a fortnight before, he had been visited at his home in Thornley, near Preston, by a young muslin weaver, a native of Armagh, named Kerr. Besides being a Freemason and 'Knight Templar', Kerr also belonged to the society of United Englishmen, the total membership of which in Manchester alone he estimated at 20,000. All these, he maintained, were ready to join the French in case of an invasion.[98] In order to check on the credibility of this claim, Portland invoked the assistance, on 21 February, of the most senior and respected of the Manchester magistrates, Thomas Butterworth Bayley.[99] After an initial failure to discover any traces of United English activity in the Manchester area, Bayley was soon able to draw on a prolific, though not wholly trustworthy, source of information in the person of Robert Gray, a prominent member of the local Corresponding Society, who agreed, partly from scruples of conscience, and partly from baser motives, to become a paid informer of the Home Office.[100] In this way Bayley learnt how the divisions of the Manchester Corresponding Society, formed in 1796, had been infiltrated by members of the resident United Irish and how these had actively canvassed the establishment of secret, oath-bound societies of United Englishmen. Gray revealed the names of those who had assisted Coigley on his visits to Manchester, cited those actively involved in the collection raised for Coigley's personal expenses, and named the ringleaders of the new republican society. He also asserted that no less than eighty divisions of the United English society had already been formed in the Manchester area, each containing between fifteen and thirty men, organized into twelve districts, and that a county committee, then sitting at Manchester, was shortly to be transferred to Liverpool to facilitate closer contact with Ireland. Finally, he deposed that the

98. PRO., PC 1/43/A 152.

99. PRO HO 43/10, fo. 288. Born in 1744 and educated at the University of Edinburgh, Bayley had served as magistrate in the Manchester area before being appointed High Sheriff. A prison reformer, and supporter of the abolition of the slave trade, he was an elected member of the Manchester Board of Health and one of the early vice-presidents of the Manchester Literary and Philosophical Society. W. E. Axon, *The Bayley Family* (Manchester, 1890), pp. 12–13.

100. Gray contended that his conscience as a Methodist had been affronted by the deistic and atheistical tendencies of the local radicals, though it soon appeared that 'he was disappointed about money matters' as Bayley reported to W. Wickham at the Home Office on 12 July 1798. PRO HO 42/44.

loyalty of the troops in the Manchester barracks had been tampered with and that some members of the Lancashire supplementary militia had also been won over.[101]

Though these revelations were received with some scepticism both in London and Dublin, they were naturally followed by the precautionary arrest of those whom Gray had delated.[102] The examination of the prisoners, accused of the suspicion of high treason, enabled the government to make a more balanced assessment of the extent and state of readiness of the United English organization in the North-West.[103] The most important of the witnesses was the Irish immigrant James Dixon, who, according to Gray, was the leading activist in the Anglo-Irish conspiracy. Arrested on 10 April 1798, Dixon contended that only twenty-five divisions of the United English had so far been organized in Manchester, but disclosed that the town was the effective hub of an extensive underground movement which had ramifications in Yorkshire, the Midlands, Cornwall, London and Scotland.[104] At his second examination, on 7 May, he also reported that the last of the monthly delegate meetings before his arrest had 'settled how the correspondence with Scotland was to be effected'. This was to be by means of special messengers, moving in relays and by successive stages, from Manchester to Bolton, Preston, Kendal, Carlisle and then to Glasgow. According to Dixon it was in Glasgow that the Executive Committee of Scotland and England held its meetings and it was from there that a similar relay system for the transmission of secret messages operated via Huddersfield, Halifax, Leeds, Sheffield, Nottingham, Norwich to London.[105] Supplementary evidence from Gray also indicated that special dele-

101. Sworn deposition before Bayley, 19 March 1798. PRO HO 42/45.

102. Enclosing Gray's deposition in a letter to Edward Cooke, under-secretary at Dublin, dated 24 March 1798, Wickham stated, 'As yet I am afraid to give much credit to his story, though there are certainly many facts stated in it that carry an appearance of truth.' In his reply, 27 March 1798, Cooke agreed: 'I should think Gray overcharges. It is a common vice of informers: but parts of what he says are probable and of the system of intimidating the gentry by assassination, would Quigley, who is a sharp man, open so much to a stranger all at once?' PRO HO 100/75. Gray was, therefore, brought down to London and cross-questioned further by Portland and Wickham.

103. Eleven United men were arrested in Manchester in the course of March 1798 – William Chetham and James Dixon, as ringleaders, were detained till 1801. Five were still in custody in October 1799 and four were bailed in the course of 1799. PRO PC 1/44/A 161.

104. Examination of Dixon by R. Ford, 5 May 1798. PRO HO 42/45.

105. Examination of Dixon, 7 May 1798. PRO PC 1/42/A 143.

gates from Manchester had been despatched to proselytize in Cheshire, Derbyshire, Yorkshire, Nottinghamshire and throughout Lancashire.[106]

These disclosures of the wide-ranging coverage of the clandestine movement were, however, offset by evidence that the network had not, in fact, progressed much beyond its preparatory stages, that the society of United English in the North-West consisted mainly of destitute Irish weavers, spinners, tailors, shoemakers and labourers and was dependent for arms on the uncertain chance of procuring a few pistols from the Manchester barracks.[107] It also became clear from the examination of the other Manchester radicals who were taken into custody that several had been drawn into the clandestine organization on the strength of their Freemasonry, or in response to offers of liquid refreshment.[108] Attempts to swear in isolated soldiers as members of the United English could be traced back either to Dixon or to Gray, especially after the latter had agreed to act as an *agent provocateur*. The evidence as to the inroads made on the loyalty of the troops in Manchester was, however, far from impressive. James Murdoch, for example, a private in the Princess Royal's Own Fencible Cavalry, had been 'put up' for membership of the United English Society at the festive Christmas season, when he was 'a little in liquor', by his own cousin.[109] William Simmons, a militiaman from Preston, had been given subversive literature by James Hughes, an Irish weaver from, Ulster on the prompting of Gray, but had not bothered to attend a meeting in Manchester to which he had been summoned.[110] Sergeant Joseph Tankard, of the Eleventh Regiment of Light Dragoons stationed in Manchester, testified before Bayley on 4 April 1798 that he had just been admitted to a branch of the United English society by Andrew Donahey, an Irish weaver, after taking the prescribed oath. The copy of the oath in the Privy Council records re-echoes the Irish brogue of the man who administered it.

106. Examination of Gray, 15 April 1798. PRO PC 1/41/A 139.
107. James Dixon, Moses Fry and James Hughes – were all from Northern Ireland – Dixon and Hughes being cotton weavers and Fry a tailor. Two other prisoners, Andrew Donahey and John Dodds, accused of administering illegal oaths, were also Irish weavers. For the procurement of pistols see deposition of Gray, 19 March 1798, PRO HO 42/45.
108. Dixon, Hughes and Fry were all Freemasons.
109. Evidence of Murdoch, 14 April 1798. PRO HO 42/45.
110. Sworn testimony of Joseph Tankard, 4 April 1798. Examination of Gray, 17 April 1798. *Ibid.*

In a ful Presence of God, I a b doo swear not to abay the Cornall but the Peapell. Not the officers but the Committey of United Inglashmen then sitten in Ingland an Scotland, and to assist with arms as fare as lise in my power to astablish a Republican Government in this country and others and to asist the french on ther landing to free this contray. So helpe my God. G.S.I.U.[111]

Although he had repeated these words 'in his full regimentals', there was, however, no question of Tankard's loyalty, since he had done so on the instructions of his commanding officer, Colonel MacDowall, and of Mr Bayley, in collusion with Gray, at whose house the ceremony had been performed.[112] This manoeuvre enabled the authorities to bring home to Dixon a larger share of responsibility for the attempted subversion of troops in the Manchester barracks than he had been willing to admit in his examination. He was also exposed by Gray and other witnesses as having urged the adoption by the United English of the military formations of the United Irish and having expressed his determination, on Coigley's recommendation, to assassinate one of the well-known anti-Jacobin local magistrates – Mr Leaf.[113] All this evidence also strengthened the hands of the government in preparing its case against the conspirators who had been arrested at Margate.

The further disclosures which were made in the preparation of those trials, together with the imminence of the Irish rebellion and the renewed French invasion scare, meant that confidential and circumstantial reports of the involvement of the London Corresponding Society in these treasonable activities had to be acted on.[114] On 18 April thirteen members of the society, including their secretary, were arrested at the George Inn in Clerkenwell, while debating a proposal that they should form a branch of the United English society. On the 19th sixteen delegates attending a meeting of the General Committee of the society in Wych St were arrested and held without trial under powers conferred by the further suspension of

111. PRO PC 1/43/A 152.
112. Sworn testimony of Tankard, confirmed by Gray, 15 April 1798. *Ibid.*
113. *Ibid.*
114. The LCS had not concealed its sympathies with the Irish demand for self-determination. Its published address to the Irish nation, dated 30 January 1798, drafted by Benjamin Binns, and signed by R. T. Crossfield, himself an Irishman, as president, and by Thomas Evans as secretary, was clearly seditious. *Report of the Secret Committee of the House of Commons* (March 1799). *Parl. Hist.*, vol. 34, cols. 642–5. The original MS. copy is in PRO PC 1/44/155.

Habeas Corpus on the following day.[115] In all at least seventy-four suspects found themselves in jail from London and the provinces; some, however, for a matter of weeks only.[116] Francis Place's later assessment of the significance of these proceedings in his autobiography cannot now be accepted without question.[117] As has been seen earlier, Place had been critical of the society's policy of large public meetings of protest in 1795, he had disapproved of the dispatch of delegates to the provinces after the passage of the Two Acts, and he had also condemned the publication of the society's political magazine as financially inexpedient. Disquieted at the increasing extremism of the society's leadership, its mounting indebtedness, and the deterioration in the quality of its members, Place had withdrawn by stages from active participation in its affairs and had finally resigned from it in July 1797.[118] In the early part of 1798 Place was, therefore, only on the periphery of the society, and it is unlikely that, as an inveterate moderate, he would have been taken into the confidence of the handful of republicans who were then dabbling in treasonable practices. His effort to dissociate the London Corresponding Society from all complicity in the Coigley conspiracy does not, therefore, carry conviction. It turns partly on the debating point that John Binns, who was so obviously involved, had, according to Place, ceased to belong to the society 'soon after his trial at Warwick in August 1797'.[119] Secondly, if Place himself, when introduced to Coigley, did not know that he was on his way to France as a United Irish delegate, this did not mean that all members of the society were similarly ignorant of the precise nature of his mission.[120] Even if, as seems likely, Place was correct in maintaining that John Ashley, acting as representative of the society in Paris, had not been in written communication with his former colleagues at this period and could not, therefore, have promised them the military assistance of

115. The title of the act, initiated in the Lords, was significantly – 'An Act to empower his Majesty to secure and detain such persons as his Majesty shall suspect to conspire against his Person and Government.'

116. List of prisoners presented by Dundas, 19 Dec. 1798. PRO PC 1/43/A 150.

117. BL, Add. MSS. 27808, fos. 91–105; Add. MSS. 35143, fos. 60–5.

118. Add. MSS. 27808, fo. 76.

119. BL, Add. MSS. 27808, fo. 105.

120. *Ibid.*, fo. 91. Place saw Coigley 'three or four times, and liked him much. He was a good-looking man, of remarkably mild manners, kind and benevolent. He was supposed to be a man of some property.'

the French in case of a general rising[121] (as was later asserted in the report of the secret committee of the House of Commons in March 1799), documentary proof nevertheless exists in the archives of the French Ministry of Foreign Affairs that Ashley was memorializing the French government at precisely that time (April 1798) in order to try and provoke an invasion.[122]

Place's denial of the existence of any effective United English movement in the capital was based on ignorance, and his effort to ridicule its objectives should be seen mainly as an expression of his impatience with the misguided extremists who, in his view, had led the London Corresponding Society to disaster. He may also have been provoked into asserting that not a single division of the United English society existed in London in April 1798 by the claim of the secret committee of the House of Commons in 1799 that forty such divisions had already been formed in the capital, about twenty of which had their regular places and days of meeting.[123] Though this latter assertion had been based on the papers seized at the delegate meeting on 19 April 1798, Place countered it with a description of the dismal failure of the attempt to establish a society of United Englishmen at the meeting held the previous day.

According to Place, the initiative for this meeting had been taken by Thomas Evans, secretary of the London Corresponding Society – 'a strange creature, with very contemptible reasoning powers, a sort of absurd fanatic, continually operated upon by impulses' – by Benjamin Binns – 'a man of much meaner understanding than his brother' – and by 'an easy silly fellow, their coadjutor, named James Powell'.[124] These had been instructed in the rules and regulations of the United Irish Society by 'a man who was constantly about Quigley' (no doubt a reference to the Reverend Arthur McMahon). They had then undertaken to form an association whose aim was 'to promote a revolution'. Place considered that 'a more ridiculous project was never entered into by the imaginations of men out of Bedlam'.[125] He had done his best to persuade these fanatics of the

121. *Ibid.*, fo. 109. 'At the time the General Committee was seized', Place writes, 'Ashley had never written a line to any person in England, not even to his own family.'

122. AAE, Mémoires et documents, vol. 53, fos. 159–62. Sent to French government, 3 April 1798. AAE CPA, vol. 592, fo. 171.

123. BL, Add. MSS. 27808, fo. 92. *Report of Secret Committee* (1799), *Parl. Hist.*, vol. 34, col. 602.

124. BL, Add. MSS. 35143, fos. 62–3.

125. BL, Add. MSS. 27808, fo. 91.

'extreme folly of their proceedings' and, as a last resort, in order to protect the interests of the saner members of the London Corresponding Society, had even threatened to inform the chief Bow Street magistrate, Sir Richard Ford,[126] of what was afoot. When this move had been condemned by Colonel Despard as 'dishonourable', Place had to be content with an agreement that critics of the proposal should attend the meeting summoned for 18 April 1798 'in order to prove its mischievous tendency'.[127] Having exhausted his arguments (and patience) but not his caution, Place himself did not attend and thus escaped the imprisonment of those who did. His conclusion was 'that government had nursed the United Englishmen, and when it was found that they could not be pushed on to any actual breach of the law, seized them as conspirators'.[128] On Evans, who chaired the meeting, was found a copy of the oath proposed for the United Englishmen and also a printed constitution of the society.[129] This involved his arrest on a charge of high treason and his imprisonment till the expiry of the suspension of Habeas Corpus in March 1801.[130] With one other exception all the rest were released on bail – some before the end of April and the others at the beginning of August.[131]

Place appears to have had no knowledge of any other attempts to form societies of United Englishmen in the capital – hence his mistaken view that not a single division had actually been established.[132] Nor did he know that James Powell, whom he had recognized as one of the offending ringleaders, but whom he sheltered after he had escaped from arrest, and smuggled off to Harwich (en route for the Continent) in order to prevent him from making any disclosures to the authorities, was a government spy of long standing![133] Powell was soon to embark from Yarmouth on the track of other Anglo-Irish conspirators, bearing a bogus letter addressed to John Ashley in

126. Chiefly memorable as founder of the London Mounted police and father of Richard Ford, author of the celebrated *Handbook for Travellers in Spain* (2 vols., 1845).

127. *Ibid.*, fo. 93.

128. BL, Add. MSS. 35143, fo. 65.

129. *Ibid.*, fo. 64. A copy of the 'Declaration, Resolutions and Constitution of the Society of United Englishmen' is in PRO PC 1/42/A 144.

130. PRO PC 1/44/A 161.

131. *Ibid.*

132. BL, Add. MSS. 35143, fo. 63.

133. Place says, 'I made him a suit of half military cloaths, got him a cocked hat, and sent him to Harwich.' BL, Add. MSS. 27808, fo. 94. Powell, however, had been reporting on the activities of the LCS since 1795. PRO PC 1/23/A 38.

Paris – which was designed to establish his *bona fides* with the French resident at Hamburg – Léonard Bourdon, the main co-ordinator of the activities of the refugee United Irish.[134]

By contrast, Place's account of the circumstances and events which led to the final arrest of the General Committee of the London Corresponding Society on 19 April 1798 at Craven House, Wych St, is more informed, partly because it was based directly on Richard Hodgson's contemporary printed record.[135] The background was the crisis in national defence, which Dundas had sought to meet by making provision in a bill introduced into the House of Commons on 27 March, for the introduction of various forms of military and non-combatant voluntary service.[136] One of the bill's essential objectives was to afford ministers the means of maintaining a national register of men between the ages of sixteen and sixty, who, if not already members of a Volunteer corps or of the militia, were 'willing to engage themselves . . . to be armed, arrayed, trained and exercised for the defence of the kingdom, and upon what terms'.[137] The administration of the new Volunteer services was entrusted to the Lord Lieutenants of the counties and their subordinates. The bill passed its third reading in the Commons on 2 April.[138]

The ready response which the act evoked from all sides led some members of the London Corresponding Society to wish for a clarification of the society's policy in the event of a French invasion. On a motion from division Nos. 3 and 7, the matter was first raised at a meeting of the General or Delegate Committee on 4 April.[139] In the discussion which followed, Evans, as secretary, strongly condemned the record of the French Executive Directory. It had, he said, 'suppressed civil liberties at home and pursued aggressive policies abroad'. It had also seemed 'more desirous of establishing an extensive military despotism, than of propagating republican principles'.[140] He, therefore, proposed, in response to the government's initiative, that the society should offer its services in repelling invasion and that the members should collectively engage to form themselves into a

134. PRO PC 1/42/A 143. Powell to Home Office, Yarmouth, 4 May 1798.

135. *Proceedings of the General Committee of the London Corresponding Society . . . on the 5th, 12th and 19th April 1798* (Newgate, 1798).

136. *The Senator or Parliamentary Chronicle*, vol. 20, pp. 699–707.

137. *Ibid.*, p. 761.

138. *Ibid.*, p. 759.

139. H. Collins, 'The London Corresponding Society', in J. Saville (ed.), *Democracy and the Labour Movement* (London, 1954), p. 132.

140. *Ibid.*

Volunteer corps. Whether this attitude reflected his own disillusionment with the French, a desire to hedge his bets, or an attempt to cover up treasonable and secret designs, is hard to determine. On the face of it Evans's behaviour on this issue seems impossible to reconcile with the encouragement he was giving to the United Englishmen. His proposal, however, met with heated opposition in the committee and the discussion was adjourned first to the 12th and then to the 19th. At the final meeting, and in the absence of Evans, arrested the previous day, the tide of argument went against his motion, mainly on the ground that the government would not agree to put arms into the hands of the society organized as a volunteer corps,[141] and also because the government could not be trusted in view of its record of brutality in Ireland.[142] On the other hand, according to Place, all the delegates remonstrated against a French invasion and eventually agreed to recommend the members of the society to volunteer individually by joining some corps or association in their own immediate neighbourhood.[143] It was at that point in the discussion that Bow Street officers and King's messengers burst into the room, arrested the committee *en bloc* on a general warrant and seized all its books and papers. After a brief examination before the Privy Council, the sixteen delegates were committed to various prisons – Tothill Fields, Newgate and the notorious House of Correction at Cold Bath Fields. All were charged with treasonable practices, one was discharged and twelve were released on bail in the course of the summer and autumn. Three, however, who had incurred suspicion on other accounts – Richard Hodgson, Paul Thomas Lemaître and Alexander Davidson – were detailed in prison without trial until 1801.

For Place, in retrospect, these precautionary moves on the part of the government were panic measures justified only by the gross exaggeration of the dangers of French invasion. The fact that no further treason trials were held, after those at Maidstone, indicated to him that the government had no effective evidence on which to proceed against the imprisoned members of the London Corresponding Society. This, however, was to disregard the Irish dimension which motivated so many of the government's measures and to

141. This argument was proved to be a correct estimate of the government's reaction to collective demonstrations of radical 'loyalty', when Lord Onslow, as Lord Lieutenant, refused a similar offer from an association in the Borough of Southwark. For the debate on this refusal initiated by Tierney, as MP for the borough, see *Senator*, vol. 20, pp. 960–88.

142. Collins, in ed. Saville, p. 132.

143. BL, Add. MSS. 27808, fo. 90.

deny the existence of evidence which Pitt thought it expedient to conceal.

The Maidstone trials of Coigley, O'Connor and their companions for high treason were delayed till mid May 1798 partly by the difficulty which the government anticipated in 'bringing such evidence of guilt as will suffice to convict them in the ordinary course of law'[144] (though it well knew that the prisoners were traitors) and partly by the prior need to paralyse the radical leadership. After some hesitation the government proceeded with the trials mainly out of consideration for the urgent desire of the Dublin executive to secure convictions.[145] The trials themselves, however, did not attain the high judicial standards which had been reached in 1794. Attempts on the part of Arthur Young's clergyman son to persuade three prospective jurymen to convict the prisoners 'no matter what the evidence' showed the extent to which anti-Jacobin prejudice had been aroused,[146] while, on the other side, the testimony offered by Fox, Sheridan, Whitbread and other prominent Opposition Whigs as to O'Connor's immaculate political principles and unblemished character, though later revealed as completely false, was allowed by the presiding judge to weigh unduly in his favour.[147] O'Connor himself resorted to equivocation and downright perjury, attempted to bribe a jailor to secure his release, wrote anonymous 'threatening' letters to the government and, in the opinion of some, saved his own skin at the expense of Coigley.[148] Though the government had enough evidence to convict all five of the accused, it refrained from its use in open court in order not to expose and thus destroy its source in the reports of its Hamburg informer. The whole of the prosecution case was thus confined to the one piece of tangible evidence of treason – the second address from the 'Secret Committee of England' to the French Directory found in Coigley's greatcoat.[149] The disparaging terms in which the address referred to the Opposition Whigs, who had come forward in O'Connor's defence, redounded to his advantage and helped to isolate him both

144. That is to say without recourse to the secret disclosures of Samuel Turner, which were too precious to reveal in open court. PRO HO 100/75/283, Portland to Camden, 24 March 1798.

145. *Ibid.*

146. *ST*, vol. 26, col. 1220. Young had exerted 'all his eloquence' to convince the jurors how 'absolutely necessary' it was 'at the present moment for the security of the realm, that the felons should swing'.

147. *Ibid.*, vol. 27, cols. 42–53.

148. *Ibid.*, vol. 26, col. 1220.

149. Quoted in full in *ST*, vol. 26, cols. 1250–2.

from the Anglo-Irish republicans and from Coigley.[150] The full significance of the secret code kept by O'Connor in his razor-case only became clear after the seizure of Lord Edward Fitzgerald's papers on the eve of the Irish rebellion.[151] The government also did not uncover in court the full extent of the tripartite conspiracy, and the general public had to wait till the confessions of John Hughes, O'Connor, Dr McNevin, Samuel Neilson and Thomas Addis Emmet in Dublin in August 1798 for further, and not wholly satisfactory, evidence as to the extent of English radical commitment to the cause of Irish independence.[152]

The prosecution failed to bring home to any of the accused, except Coigley, knowledge of the existence and contents of the address and all, except the priest, were therefore acquitted.[153] Although he repudiated his contacts with the London radical societies and protested his innocence to the last, Coigley was undoubtedly guilty. He did, however, refuse to procure a reprieve for himself by incriminating his companions and, in his final moments, conducted himself with courage and composure on the scaffold.[154] James Mackintosh, who had long since recanted his earlier enthusiasm for the French revolution, incautiously expressed the view at a Whig gathering that one could hardly conceive of a greater scoundrel that Coigley, who had deserved his fate. The unrepentant Whig Dr Parr, who had recently become alienated from his former friend, thought otherwise and observed, tartly, to Mackintosh's acute discomfort, that Coigley after all had been an Irishman, a priest and a traitor, though he might well have been a Scotchman, a lawyer and an apostate![155]

150. The relevant passage reads: 'Parliamentary declaimers have been the bane of our freedom; national plunder was the object of every faction, and . . . the very men who, under the semblance of moderate reform, only wish to climb into power, are now glad to fall into the ranks of the people . . . and there must for ever remain, for Englishmen can never place confidence in them.' *Ibid.*, col. 1251.

151. MacDermot, p. 59.

152. *Report from the Committee of Secrecy of the House of Lords in Ireland* (30 Aug. 1798), appendices 1–6. When asked whether there was any connection between the United Irish in Dublin and the English or Scottish radical societies, O'Connor replied: 'Any connexion with them was merely between individuals. The Irish Executive Directory wished to keep clear of them.' *Ibid.*, p. 41.

153. The government, however, ordered the immediate rearrest of O'Connor and his dispatch to Ireland to answer the charges against him there. PRO HO 100/76/252–3. Wickham to Castlereagh, 24 May 1798.

154. Coigley was hanged on 7 June 1798, aged 36. For his speech, reasserting his innocence see *ST*, vol. 27, cols. 250–2.

155. P. W. Clayden, *The early life of Samuel Rogers* (London, 1887), p. 381.

The real significance of the trials, for the government at least, was to throw into sharp relief the merger of the United Irish in London and Lancashire with the English republicans, and to uncover the existence of a Jacobin underground movement which, however immature in the spring of 1798, outlived the collapse of the Irish rebellion and the formal suppression of the radical societies in 1799. It was to resurface in 1802 with the abortive conspiracy of Colonel Despard and the Irish insurrection of Robert Emmet in 1803.[156]

---

156. Despard was arrested shortly after the trial, under the Habeas Corpus Suspension Act and remained in prison till the winter of 1801. John Binns was also rearrested and confined till March 1801.

12 The suppression of the radical societies, the opposition to the Combination Laws, and the radical legacy

Whatever presses men together, therefore, though it may generate some vices, is favourable to the diffusion of knowledge, and ultimately promotive of human liberty. Hence every large workshop and manufactory is a sort of political society, which no act of parliament can silence, and no magistrate disperse.

> J. THELWALL, *The Rights of Nature against the Usurpations of Establishments* (1796)

Horne Tooke once said that Hume wrote his *History* as witches say their prayers – backwards.[1] He might well have made the same remark about the report of the secret committee of the House of Commons of 1799 which, in the aftermath of the Irish rebellion, analysed the whole evolution of the radical movement in Britain since the early 1790s as if it had always been the clandestine, treasonable and republican conspiracy that it only became on the eve of its dissolution. The intelligence reports of the Home Office spies and the revelations of the Hamburg informer which had led to the arrest and trial of Coigley, O'Connor and John Binns and to the ultimate collapse of the rebellion had been referred for consideration to a secret committee of the House of Commons on 23 January 1799.[2] The report, printed in the middle of March, was debated in the Commons on 19 April.[3] Its immediate purpose was to make public sufficient evidence to justify the government's determination to achieve, at all costs, a formal legislative union with Ireland, to secure parliamentary approval for a further prolongation of the suspension of Habeas Corpus, and to suppress the British and Irish radical societies out of hand. Before publication the evidence was, therefore, carefully

1. G. H. Powell, *Table Talk of Samuel Rogers* (London, 1903), p. 86.
2. *Parl. Hist.*, vol. 34, col. 208.
3. *Ibid.*, cols. 984–98. The report itself appears on cols. 579–656.

452 The Friends of Liberty

selected and some of it, in the interest of national security, was suppressed.[4]

The report summarized its conclusions in its opening paragraph by stating that 'in the whole course of their enquiry' the committee had found

the clearest proofs of a systematic design (long since adopted and acted upon by France, in conjunction with domestic traitors, and pursued up to the present moment with unabated perseverance), to overturn the laws, constitution and government and every existing establishment, civil or ecclesiastical, both in Great Britain and Ireland; as well as to dissolve the connection between the two Kingdoms, so necessary to the security and prosperity of both.[5]

This thesis was supported by citing the outbreak of the Irish rebellion and the subsequent confessions of O'Connor, Emmet and McNevin as proof that the United Irish society had, since its foundation mounted its campaign for Catholic emancipation and parliamentary reform to – divert attention from its real objective – the winning of complete Irish independence, if possible, with the military and financial help of the French.[6] The recent infiltration of the London Corresponding Society and the provincial radical societies in Lancashire and Yorkshire by the United Irish, and their complicity in the plans to precipitate French invasion projects were also evidence that British radicals had concealed a far-ranging Jacobin and republican conspiracy under the cover of an agitation for universal suffrage and annual parliaments.[7] The treason confessed by O'Connor in Ireland after his acquittal in the Maidstone trials was urged in the report as contingent proof that the acquittals of Hardy, Horne Tooke and Thelwall by the Old Bailey juries by no means disproved the existence of the revolutionary conspiracy proclaimed by the earlier secret committees of both Lords and Commons and by Parliament

4. In view of the continuing emergency the committee regarded it as 'their particular duty to abstain from disclosing, in its full extent, the particular information, of which they have stated to the House the general result, and on which their judgment is founded'. *Ibid.*, col. 614.

5. *Parl. Hist.*, vol. 34, cols. 579–80.

6. *Ibid.*, col. 597. Cf. T. A. Emmet's statement under examination (11 Aug. 1798): 'I believe the mass of the people do not care a feather for Catholic emancipation; neither did they care for parliamentary reform till it was explained to them as leading to other objects, which they looked to, principally the abolition of tythes.' *Report of the Secret Committee of the Irish House of Commons* (17 July 1798), appendix 31.

7. *Parl. Hist.*, vol. 34, cols. 601–6.

itself.[8] Later events and further intelligence had confirmed that the Anglo-Irish conspiracy of 1798 was merely an extension of the radical conspiracy mooted at the time of the addresses to the French National Convention in 1792 and of which the implementation was narrowly averted by the dissolution of the Scottish convention in 1793 and by the arrest and trial of the English radical leaders in 1794.[9]

Several features of this 'systematic' conspiracy were singled out as causing the government's continuing anxiety and alarm – the 'destructive' French revolutionary principles which the radicals had propagated so assiduously, the growth of their political societies, now deemed 'inconsistent with public tranquillity and with the existence of regular government',[10] and, above all, the extension of the paramilitary organization and secret procedures of the United Irish to England, Scotland and the Continent. It was, indeed, this 'principle of secrecy, generally enforced by unlawful oaths', adopted from the United Irish by the United English and the United Britons, which represented the most disquieting threat to the maintenance of public order and settled monarchical government.[11] By offering the conspirators some prospect of security the clandestine nature of the new societies 'peculiarly fitted them for the most desperate enterprises' and, at the same time, served 'to defeat subsequent legal inquiry'.[12] The report also briefly drew attention to the establishment of a committee of United Irish at the neutral port of Hamburg to facilitate communications between Ireland and France and the activities of a clandestine international 'Philanthropic Society', devoted to the spreading of republican principles throughout Europe.[13]

To curb these continuing dangers the committee thought it essential that the government's 'power of arresting and detaining suspected persons' should be prolonged.[14] They also expressed

their unanimous opinion, that the system of secret societies, the establishment of which, in other countries, uniformly preceded the aggression of France, and, by facilitating the progress of her principles, has prepared the way for her arms, cannot be suffered to exist in these kingdoms, compatibly with the safety of their government and constitution, and with their security against foreign force and domestic treason.[15]

When commending these recommendations to the House of

8. *Ibid.*, col. 581.   9. *Ibid.*, col. 585.
10. *Ibid.*, col. 580.   11. *Ibid.*, col. 613.
12. *Ibid.*   13. *Ibid.*, col. 612.
14. *Ibid.*, col. 613.   15. *Ibid.*, col. 614.

Commons on 19 April 1799 Pitt also claimed for the executive the power to transfer from the metropolis to less strategically important areas those who had been detained for treasonable or seditious practices and authority to remove those confined in Ireland for similar crimes to places of better security in the United Kingdom.[16] In support of the conclusions of the secret committee the Attorney General suggested that, since the members of the radical societies were now bound by oath not to give evidence against each other, it would be preferable to abolish the societies which resorted to such practices rather than to bring forward useless prosecutions.[17] In the virtual absence of the Foxite Opposition from Parliament, these policies were approved without difficulty and the appropriate bills to continue the suspension of Habeas Corpus and to suppress the offending secret societies by name became law on 20 May and 12 July respectively.[18] The United Englishmen, the United Scotsmen, the United Britons, the United Irish and the London Corresponding Society thus found a common legislative grave as a result of their collaboration in the Irish rebellion. 12 July marked the end of the parliamentary session and royal approval was also given on the same day to a further piece of analogous legislative repression in the form of the Combination Act of 1799.[19]

This act had been prompted initially by a petition from the master millwrights of London to the House of Commons on 5 April 1799, requesting Parliament to make illegal the combinations of their own journeymen.[20] A more general measure to make all combinations illegal was, however, substituted on the suggestion of Wilberforce, and was moved by Pitt on 17 June, after news had been received of a wide-ranging Association of Weavers in Lancashire and Cheshire, extending from Oldham to Stockport and from Blackburn to Wigan.[21] The bill was rushed through Parliament during the last four weeks of the session – the only criticisms coming from Hobhouse in the Commons and Lord Holland in the Lords. Despite the mildness of

16. *Ibid.*, col. 985. Nineteen Irish state prisoners were transferred from Ireland to Fort George in Scotland – where A. O'Connor, T. A. Emmet, Neilson and others were mostly detained till the peace of Amiens, and then released on condition that they should expatriate themselves for ever. W. J. Fitzpatrick, *Secret Service under Pitt* (London, 1892), p. 101.

17. *Parl. Hist.*, vol. 34, col. 994.

18. 39 Geo. III c. 44 and 39 Geo. III c. 79 respectively.

19. 39 Geo. III c. 81.

20. *House of Commons Journals*, vol. 54, cols. 405–6.

21. A. Aspinall, *The Early English Trade Unions* (London, 1949), p. xi. For the address of the weavers forwarded to the Home Office on 27 May 1799 see Aspinall, pp. 21–4.

the penalties enacted, its provisions were manifestly biased in favour of the employers and even in its amended form (1800), it has been termed an 'odious piece of class legislation'.[22] Class interest, however, was not the only factor involved. The act reflected also the government's concern to maintain industrial discipline in time of war and its conviction that workmen's associations, which were already illegal both by common law and under existing statutes, needed more effective suppression because of their increasing proliferation, their clandestine activities and Jacobin overtones. Industrial associations which were tending to model their organization and procedure on those of the radical political societies needed to be prevented or suppressed.

Although the acts of 1799 and 1800 were the first to prohibit all combinations whatsoever, whether of working men to raise wages and restrict hours or of employers to do the opposite, the policy they enshrined was of long standing.[23] The novel features of the act of 1799 were the introduction of a summary procedure for the trial of offenders and the withdrawal of certain of their common law rights. The act allowed offenders to be tried by a single magistrate, even if the latter was himself an employer in the same industry, and also provided that no writ of *certiorari* should be granted to remove any conviction, or other proceeding under the act, to the high courts at Westminster.[24] An even more serious infringement of existing law was the withdrawal of the accused's right to trial by jury and not to be convicted upon his own confession.[25] By comparison with the loss of these constitutional liberties, the maximum penalties imposed – three months' imprisonment or two months' hard labour – were not severe.[26]

Owing to the haste with which the bill was rushed through Parliament there was no chance of collective protests being lodged against it until after it had become law.[27] It was not long, however, before signs of organized opposition to its enforcement in Lancashire and Yorkshire gave Church and King loyalists and local magistrates

22. *Ibid.*, p. xvii.
23. *Ibid.*, p. x. H. Pelling, *A History of British Trade Unionism*, 3rd ed. (London, 1976), p. 16. See also R. Y. Hedges and A. Winterbottom, *The Legal History of Trade Unionism* (London, 1930), ch. 3.
24. Aspinall, p. xvi. This was remedied in the act of 1800.
25. S. 2 of the act of 1799.
26. Hedges and Winterbottom, p. 28.
27. J. L. and B. Hammond, *The Town Labourer (1760–1832)* (London, 1949 reprint), vol. 1, p. 128.

cause for serious concern. At the beginning of August Mr James Harrop – 'the loyal and worthy postmaster of Manchester', printer of the Tory *Manchester Mercury* – persuaded the Home Office to accept the proferred services of William Barlow – a plausible but impecunious informer – who was more interested in escaping the attentions of his creditors and former associates than in the problems of internal security.[28] In the effort to establish his credit with the government, however, Barlow had submitted to Harrop an apparently circumstantial report on the secret activities of groups of United English radicals and *émigré* United Irish in Liverpool, at the head of whom, he claimed, were 'men of Talents, Intelligence and Wealth'.[29] He had also 'uncovered' the existence in Liverpool for the past two years of a blasphemous 'Jesus Christ club' and drawn attention to a recent plan promoted by one James Davis – a Stockport tailor and author of a 'Scripturions Creed' – for the establishment of an Atheistical Corresponding Society.[30] For refusing to join this society Barlow had himself been denounced by its adherents. He now 'retaliated' by giving Harrop the names, occupations and habitual meeting places of the Liverpool 'Jacobins'. In doing so, however, Barlow had stipulated that no use should be made of the information until he had received from authority a written promise that he would not be called upon to substantiate his allegations in a court of law.[31] What the situation demanded, and what Barlow himself suggested, was that the machinations of these assorted republican groups should be kept under surveillance by a specially appointed government agent assuming the guise of an *émigré* United Irishman with landed property in Wexford.[32] This report was sufficiently detailed and disquieting for the government to follow Barlow's advice by bringing over from Ireland a secret agent, George Orr, to investigate the ramifications of the alleged conspiracy.[33]

28. T. B. Bayley to J. King, 21 Dec. 1799. PRO PC 1/45/A 164, pt. 1.

29. PRO PC 1/44/A 161. 'Secret information respecting suspicious persons at Liverpool. Aug. 1799'. R. B. Rose's article, 'The Jacobins of Liverpool, 1789–1793', *The Liverpool Libraries, Museums and Arts Committee Bulletin*, vol. 9 (1960–1), pp. 35–49, is helpful on the Liverpool liberal intelligentsia.

30. PRO PC 1/44/A 161.

31. *Ibid.*

32. Barlow suggested that the agent should claim acquaintance with a certain Cod of Wexford who had been in Liverpool the previous year to purchase arms for the rebels, in order to establish his *bona fides*. *Ibid.*

33. Initially the home government was not convinced that Orr would be the best man for the investigation, but appear to have ultimately agreed to use him.

Hardly had Barlow moved from Liverpool to Manchester in the first week of August 1799, in the interests of his own safety, than he acquainted his prospective employers with the existence of a fully fledged 'secret combination of a very extraordinary nature' aimed against the Combination Act.[34] This association, he alleged, had 'originated' in the 'republican society at Sheffield' and had fanned out from there to the principal towns in Yorkshire and then to Manchester, Stockport and Bury.[35] Contact was maintained between the various small local groups by means of delegates and many of the conspirators were said to belong to the Volunteers and had, therefore, access to arms. The gravamen of the workers' complaints against the act was, briefly, that it made 'Masters Tyrants and Servants Slaves'.[36] In further reports forwarded to the Home Office, Barlow gave estimated statistics of the numbers affected by the provisions of the act in the North-West and the Midlands – 60,000 in Lancashire, 50,000 in Yorkshire and 30,000 in Derbyshire. These were the numbers of workers, he suggested, who would give their support to any petition to Parliament asking for repeal.[37]

By 8 August the Duke of Portland, as Home Secretary, had authorized Harrop to enlist Barlow's services and pay him a regular salary.[38] The Duke's correspondents in Manchester then informed him that Barlow had moved on to Sheffield to try and discover whether the conspiracy, now 'under the immediate direction of Republicans', was to establish its headquarters there or in Derby.[39] Meanwhile consultations between delegates from Sheffield and Hull had been held in Manchester at which it had been resolved that the Lancashire Weavers' Association should not be dissolved and that 'general combinations be made throughout the Kingdom to petition parliament against the Bill and to resist every attempt to enforce it'. If the act was not repealed they also resolved 'to employ what force they have against it'.[40]

In his early reports to the Home Office authorities Barlow confirmed that the Sheffield democrats were engaged in turning local resentment against the Combination Act to their political advantage by exaggerating its restrictions. In this they had largely succeeded

34. R. F(oxley) to Viscount Belgrave MP, Aug. 1799. PRO PC 1/44/A 161.
35. *Ibid.*
36. *Ibid.*
37. R.F. to Viscount Belgrave, Aug. 1799. *Ibid.*
38. R.F. to the Duke of Portland, 8 Aug. 1799. *Ibid.*
39. *Ibid.*
40. *Ibid.*

and Barlow soon gave his opinion that 'there has been more persons turned Jacobins within the little time which has elapsed since the Bill was passed than for a year before'.[41] Taking his time to insinuate himself into the tavern societies of the Sheffield radicals, Barlow pretended, at first, 'to rather shun than court their company'.[42] Masquerading as a tradesman, he confined his activities for several weeks to delating to the authorities the pamphlets published by the local Jacobins.[43] By the first fortnight of September, however, Barlow was spending 'every evening in company with the most determined democrats of this place', though he was conscious that he had not yet penetrated their reserve. He was disconcerted to discover that though the radicals did not conceal their contempt for the government, or their admiration for the French, they never referred to their political activities.[44] They appeared to make no use of secret signs, and Barlow even inclined to the belief that they had either suspended or dissolved the meetings of their political societies. A few crumbs of comfort came his way: Joseph Gales's uncle Timothy disclosed that in mid September there had been a 'business' meeting at Castleton in Derbyshire of four radical delegates from Manchester and four from Sheffield.[45] Despite assiduous attendance in the evenings at the most notorious 'Jacobin' taverns in the Wicker, where he stayed on hopefully till his companions were intoxicated, the informer drew a blank. He was soon reporting back to Manchester that he did not intend 'to fabricate plots to have the merit of discovering them' and to the Home Office that the radicals appeared to be 'saturated with politics', and that the government's repressive measures had probably resulted in the discontinuation of the Sheffield 'primary' or divisional meetings.[46] For the moment he had to be content with reporting his 'strong suspicion' that the Sheffield radicals still maintained an executive or general committee and his renewed conviction that atheism had taken a firm root among the local democrats owing to the numerous reading societies and subscription libraries which

41. W. Barlow to R. Ford, 14 Aug. 1799. PRO PC 1/44/A 161.
42. *Ibid.*
43. Among these Barlow forwarded to T. B. Bayley, chairman of magistrates at Manchester, copies of John Crome's radical periodical, the *Spy, or Political Inspector* (1795), *Address to the Public* by Benjamin Damm (former member of the Sheffield Constitutional Society) and *Rhapsody on Burke* by J. Sharpe. Barlow to Ford, 9 Sept. 1799. PRO PC 1/44/A 161.
44. *Ibid.*
45. Barlow to T. B. Bayley, 19 Sept. 1799. *Ibid.*
46. Barlow to Bayley and Ford, 19 Sept. 1799. *Ibid.*

flourished in the town.[47] The formation in 1798 of the Amicable United Lodge of Oddfellows had no doubt tended in the same direction.[48]

Desperately short of funds for inducing further revelations, Barlow began to retail in his reports local gossip that all the Quakers in the district were in the Jacobin interest and that the Sheffield militants had secreted away for future use 'a vast number of pikes'.[49] One of the contacts he made in Sheffield radical circles at this time was Bonington, lately dismissed from his post as keeper of Nottingham gaol on account of his advanced political views and widely regarded as 'a kind of martyr to the cause'. Soon to become the father of Richard Parkes Bonington (1801–28), the famous landscape artist and lithographer, Bonington himself was then eking out a living as a drawing master in Nottingham, Chesterfield and Sheffield. This allowed him, according to Barlow, to promote the cause of republicanism over a wide area in the Midlands and south Yorkshire without provoking suspicion.[50]

In the third week of October, feeling that he was at last on the point of breaking down the studied reserve of his Sheffield drinking companions, Barlow became less frustrated.[51] A week later he was reporting how the local population had recently responded to a run of French military successes. He wrote of large crowds parading the streets wearing French cockades and singing French marching songs. 'Some bought fireworks, others procured musicians and for three days and nights they continued their excesses. I am informed by several persons that what they expended in cash and lost in time exceeds two thousand pounds!!'[52] Even the grinders, not to be outdone, were said to have written on their lathes the Jacobin slogan 'Death or Liberty'.[53]

47. The works specially mentioned as available in the Sheffield subscription libraries were those by Godwin (*Political Justice*), Volney (*Ruins of Empires*, 1791), Helvétius (? *De L'Esprit*, 1758), and Voltaire (? *Candide*, 1759), all in translation. Barlow to R. Ford, 19 Oct. 1799. *Ibid.*

48. Founded by William Todd and Charles Sylvester, the Sheffield radical poet. Ian Inkster, 'The development of a scientific community in Sheffield, 1790–1850', *Transactions of the Hunter Archaeological Society*, vol. 10, pt. 2 (1973), pp. 120–1.

49. Barlow to Ford, 26 Sept. 1799. PRO PC 1/44/A 161.

50. Barlow to Ford, 28 Sept. 1799. *Ibid.*

51. Barlow to Ford, 19 Oct. 1799. *Ibid.*

52. *Ibid.*

53. Barlow to Ford, 27 Oct. 1799. *Ibid.*

This time, however, Barlow had overshot the mark. The Duke of Portland at the Home Office was frankly sceptical and in the beginning of November felt it necessary to appoint another agent, John Thompson, to oversee Barlow's activities and to check the veracity of his reports. Acting in close touch with a number of local magistrates, Thompson was soon able to verify that the picture of Sheffield as given over to Francophile demonstrations was wildly overdrawn and that the town was in no sense the security risk that Barlow had implied.[54] The story about the Sheffield grinders proved, on investigation, to be baseless rumour.[55] Further enquiry enabled Thompson to report that the radicals still continued to meet, not secretly, but in a small number of local taverns. These meetings, however, were in his opinion so innocuous that any attempt to disturb them might well prove counter-productive.[56] After conversing with Barlow, Thompson had no compunction in describing him as 'a complete Alarmist'.[57] Under cross-examination Barlow was obliged to concede that the pro-French parades had been confined to one district in the town (West Bar) and that the cockades had not been worn in public. When pressed he also admitted that he 'did not apprehend any real danger immediately', but plunged deeper into conjecture by warning that, if the French invaded the country, the local Jacobins 'would murder all the Volunteers in their houses'.[58] The latter, however, appeared to Thompson to be quite capable of looking after themselves and the town. As recently as 5 November the Sheffield Volunteers, about 300 strong, had been reviewed in public by their colonel, the Earl of Effingham, with every sign of strong local support. Thompson commented that they were 'a fine body of men, who together with the inhabitants in general, appear to be completely loyal'.[59]

Barlow was by now completely discredited – his lurid reports of Anglo-Irish conspiracy in Liverpool having been exploded by the investigations of George Orr.[60] His continuing expostulations about his inadequate pay and a final desperate suggestion that he should be

54. J. Thompson to Ford, 5 Nov. 1799. PRO PC 1/45/A 164.
55. Same to same, 8 Nov. 1799. *Ibid.*
56. Same to same, 5 Nov. 1799. *Ibid.*
57. *Ibid.*
58. *Ibid.*
59. *Ibid.*
60. George Orr (Liverpool) to J. King, secretary to Duke of Portland, 12 Sept. 1799. 'I do not find that any attempts are making in this country at a reorganization of the United Irish or of the disaffected.' PRO PC 1/44/A 161.

allowed to follow up the trail of a dangerous group of Jacobins in Leicester led to his dismissal early in December.[61]

Barlow's story has been recounted at some length because it illustrates the temptations and trials of a casual informer in need of hard cash, the critical attitude displayed by the Home Office towards such polluted sources of secret intelligence, and the manner in which a man like Barlow was able to embroider detailed factual information until it lost all semblance of credibility. How little the Lancashire workers' association against the Combination Act was under the direction and control of 'republicans', as alleged by Barlow, and how unreal the further suggestion that it was part and parcel of a widespread Jacobin 'underground' movement may be judged from other and less questionable sources.[62]

On 7 November 1799 T. B. Bayley, chairman of the Manchester bench of magistrates, wrote to J. King, secretary of the Duke of Portland at the Home Office, to draw the attention of ministers to the increasing seriousness of the accumulating security problems with which local JPs were confronted.[63] He enclosed two printed handbills to show the nature of the complaints raised by the Lancashire textile and other workers against the Combination Act and the measures being proposed to prevent its implementation. The first of these – *On Combinations* – urged that the workers 'must either have positive laws to protect them from imposition', or else be permitted to associate in defence of their interests. Otherwise they would be 'reduced to a state of slavery and subject to the capricious dispositions of those who employ them'. For the government to forbid workmen to combine and then to urge masters and men to settle their own differences independently was 'like binding the hands of a dwarf upon his back and telling him to contend with a Goliah, who, without fettering the dwarf, is by far too great a match for him'.[64] The second handbill consisted of a set of printed resolutions carried at a delegate meeting of 'labourers, mechanics and artificers of Manchester' late in October. These gave a reasoned and coherent analysis of

61. Barlow to Duke of Portland, 16 Nov. 1799 and to Ford, 20 Nov. 1799. PRO PC 1/45/A 164, pt. 1. Barlow to Ford, 27 Nov. 1799. *Ibid.* Barlow to Duke of Portland, 4 Dec. 1799. *Ibid.*

62. E. P. Thompson suggests that, in Lancashire and Yorkshire, the act of 1799 'jolted the Jacobins and trade unionists into a widespread secret combination, half political, half industrial, in emphasis'. *The Making of the English Working Class*, 3rd ed. (London, 1965), pp. 500–1.

63. PRO PC 1/45/A 164, pt. 1.

64. *Ibid.*

the workers' grievances – firstly, their general economic disabilities in conducting wage negotiations with their employers, secondly, the inequality of treatment of workers and masters in the detailed provisions of the act, and thirdly, the withdrawal of the common law liberties of the workmen accused of offences under the act. It was represented that, in times of inflation, workmen had 'never had any lawful means of making the price of labour equal to the price of the necessaries of life'.[65] In times of trade depression, on the other hand, they were defenceless in the face of the inveterate practice of employers in reducing wages or in dismissing redundant labour.[66] The act itself was said to increase these disabilities by allowing masters, in times of difficulty, to employ unqualified journeymen or even those who had never served a proper apprenticeship.[67] By making workmen liable to severe penalties for unguarded advice to their fellows to seek an increase of wages or to stop work, it destroyed all trust and confidence between them. By rendering respectable magistrates 'the passive instruments of oppression', the act also reduced workers to the condition of absolute slaves to their masters.[68] Lastly, the resolutions urged, in accordance with the settled principles of English law, that no man should answer on examination such questions as might incriminate him and that ordinary workers had 'the same right to trial by jury that any Nobleman or Gentleman has to his Honours or Estates'.[69] The final resolutions expressed the intention of the workmen 'as men and Englishmen earnestly to petition Parliament to repeal a law, which can be productive of nothing but mischief and distress to ourselves, our families, and posterity' and their decision to transmit printed copies of their resolutions to those MPs whose addresses they had procured.[70]

Bayley had stressed in his letter to King that the mounting industrial discontent in Lancashire had sprung from a temporary increase in the price of bread and from rising unemployment.[71] Both the handbills he had enclosed made it plain that the local workmen had not acted in a clandestine or illegal manner, that they were perfectly loyal in their behaviour, and that their grievances would be set out

65. Resolution 2.
66. Resolution 3.
67. Resolution 9.
68. Resolution 10.
69. Resolutions 6 and 7.
70. Resolutions 13 and 14.
71. PRO PC 1/45/A 164, pt. 1.

in a petition to Parliament praying for the repeal of the act.[72] It subsequently appeared that the only one of the fourteen resolutions voted at the meeting which was signed by all the five delegates of the various trades represented was the decision to forward printed copies of their resolutions to individual MPs.[73] The opinion of the law officers of the Crown on the handbills which were referred to them was, moreover, that they were perfectly legal.[74]

In these circumstances the advice given to the chairman of the Manchester magistrates by the Home Office authorities was to call a general meeting of the bench in order to explain to the weavers their readiness to give every consideration to their temporary economic difficulties, to warn them against the attempts of 'ill-disposed and seditious persons' to mislead them into breaches of public order, to assert their determination to suppress and punish 'in the most effectual and exemplary manner' every break of the public peace.[75]

This action was taken by the assembled magistrates on 28 November 1799 and seems to have had its effect, in combination with resolute measures to disperse food rioters with the aid of the Volunteers, in allaying the current local discontent.[76] In reply to these admonitions, however, the trade delegates who had published the resolutions of the October meeting resolutely denied having attempted to incite any illegal opposition to the act. They had, they maintained, published their views on the assumption that 'this national issue' would involve the widest public discussion and that the masters themselves would wish to be informed of the case their workmen intended to bring before Parliament. They took their stand as loyal subjects, seeking no alteration in church or state, and they also repudiated any connection with seditious radical societies.[77]

In all these proceedings there was no hint of the surreptitious illegal

72. '. . . above all our complaint must be made in a legal manner, which will be easily done by presenting a Petition, praying for the repeal of the aforesaid Act'. *Ibid. On Combinations.*

73. I.e. Resolution 14. 15,000 copies of the resolutions had been printed and paid for by the Society of Fustian Cutters, whose delegate, John Higginbottam of Bailey Croft, Salford, was mainly responsible for the publicity. The other trades represented by delegates were the cotton spinners, calico printers, shoemakers and machine-makers. PRO PC 1/45/A 164, pt. 1.

74. PRO HO 43/11/305. Quoted by Aspinall, p. 30, fn. 2.

75. J. King to T. B. Bayley, 11 Nov. 1799. PRO PC 1/45/A 164, pt. 1, printed in Aspinall, pp. 28–30.

76. *Ibid.*, pp. 31–2.

77. 9 Dec. 1799. PRO PC 1/45/A 164, pt. 1.

conspiracy under republican auspices adumbrated by Barlow, no reference to any regional network of underground Jacobin societies prompting the Lancashire workmen to transform their economic grievances into political demands, hardly an allusion to the prospect of direct revolutionary action. The initiative taken by the Manchester operatives in October 1799 was, however, widely imitated throughout the country in the summer of 1800 – petitions of protest requesting the repeal of the Combination Act flooding into Parliament from London, Bristol, Plymouth, Bath, Derby, Nottingham, Newcastle upon Tyne, as well as from Manchester, Liverpool, Lancaster and Leeds.[78] The result was the amending Act of 1800, promoted by the Tory and Whig MPs for Liverpool and eloquently supported by Sheridan, which removed some, but not all, of the objectionable features of the act of 1799.[79] It is safe to say that if the campaign of protest had been in the hands of republicans and had taken the form of combined militant action on the part of trade unionists and local Jacobins, Parliament would not have been persuaded to alleviate its repressive measures against illegal workers' combinations. Traces of clandestine Jacobin associations can, however, be detected in south Yorkshire in 1800–1 and these mark the trend that culminated in militant Luddism a decade later as well as the changes that were already overtaking radicalism in the industrial areas of the North and North-West.[80]

The secret and treasonable aspects of eighteenth-century radicalism in its final phase were, however, more accurately mirrored in the Anglo-Irish paramilitary conspiracy of Colonel Despard and the futile insurrection of Robert Emmet. These tragic episodes, once regarded as the isolated and demented products of Despard's 'injured vanity and rancorous megalomania' and of Emmet's impractical heroism, are now more properly viewed as connected and significant phases in the transition from eighteenth-century constitutionalism to nineteenth-century 'Physical Force' extremism.[81] In essence both

78. J. L. and B. Hammond, p. 128.

79. 39 and 40 Geo. III c. 106. Instead of one magistrate, two or more Justices were now required to constitute a court of summary jurisdiction. No magistrate was now empowered to act if he was an employer in the same trade as the accused. Provision was also made for appeals and the resort to arbitration in disputes about wages or conditions. *Ibid.*, p. 129. Aspinall, pp. xvi–xvii.

80. Thompson, pp. 476–8.

81. Both Sir Charles Oman and H. W. C. Davis thought that the folly of Despard's conspiracy could only be explained on the supposition that his mind was disordered. Oman, *Colonel Despard and Other Studies* (London, 1922), p. 2,

incidents marked the resurgence of the United Irish separatist conspiracy which had failed so miserably in 1798, which had been temporarily disrupted by the consequent arrest and imprisonment of its leading participants, and which was revived by the passing of the Act of Union.[82] Both Despard's projected *coup* in London in 1802 and Emmet's forlorn rising in Ireland in July 1803 were intended to be synchronized not only with each other, but also, if possible, with a further French attempt at an Irish invasion.[83] But the British government intervened to forestall Despard's madcap plans for military subversion and assassination before Emmet's designs had properly matured and the United Irish negotiations with Bonaparte for military assistance were stultified by the French desire to achieve a peace settlement with Britain at Amiens.[84] In the persons of Despard and his ill-fated followers the purely Irish nationalist cause was merged for a brief moment, as in 1798–9, with that of the secret English revolutionary faction. In its planned method of execution – by the seizure of the Bank of England and the Tower of London and the assassination of George III – Despard's conspiracy also marked a reversion to the earlier designs of Watt in Edinburgh and those which Dr Robert Watson communicated to the French government in 1799.[85] At the same time it provided a link with the capital's East End radical tavern society, with the 'Free and Easy Club' and the post-war revolutionary 'Society of Spencean Philanthropists'.[86] It

---

and Davis, *Age of Grey and Peel* (Oxford, 1929), p. 95. For more recent interpretations see Thompson, pp. 478–83; A. W. Smith, 'Irish rebels and English radicals, 1798–1820', *Past and Present*, no. 7 (April, 1955), pp. 78–85. Two recent Oxford DPhil theses, one by Mrs M. Elliott, 'The United Irishmen and France, 1793–1806', and the other by Miss J. A. Horne, 'The ways and means of London radicalism, 1796–1821', have also thrown fresh light on the subject.

82. Most of the London leaders who were released in March 1801, and notably J. Binns, took the opportunity to emigrate. Despard was an exception.

83. Mrs Elliott, while emphasizing the tripartite nature of the conspiracy, contends that the projected *coup* of 1802 was not of Despard's making and was never intended to precede either an Irish rising or a French invasion. 'The "Despard conspiracy" reconsidered', *Past and Present*, no. 75 (May 1977), pp. 46–61.

84. These points are elaborated in Elliott, 'United Irishmen and France, 1793–1806'.

85. Watson's lengthy memorandum, dated 22 Messidor, an VII (10 July 1799) in the French Foreign Office Archives, Paris, AAE Mémoires et documents, vol. 53, fos. 261–5, contains a section on the Tower of London, comparing it with the Hôtel des Invalides – with a feeble garrison of 500 troops, 200 guns and 120,000 rifles.

86. Smith, pp. 80–1.

was in this way that both these dismal and, at first sight, meaningless failures became part of the indigenous revolutionary tradition of the early nineteenth century.[87]

Colonel Despard (1751–1803), a member of an old Irish landowning family, had spent most of his career in the army abroad.[88] After eighteen years' continuous soldiering as an officer in the West Indies and British Honduras, where he had served alongside Nelson, he had been recalled in 1790 on half pay. Starved of promotion and indignant at his treatment by the War Office, Despard had, on his return, joined the London Corresponding Society and for a time had been a member of its General Committee. Later he had been deeply involved in Coigley's United Irish conspiracy in 1798. After his arrest he had been held in prison without trial until March 1801 – when he had emerged unrepentant and eager to resume his place in a reconstituted society of United Irish and United English in London.[89] Obsessed with the idea of Irish independence, Despard threw in his lot with an already existing insurrectionary intrigue in the summer of 1802. He concerted operations with a fellow conspirator of 1798 recently released from Fort George in Scotland – William Dowdall.[90] When Dowdall returned to Dublin in the autumn of 1802 to plan for an Irish insurrection in 1803, Despard pressed on with preparations for a simultaneous military mutiny and civilian revolt on London. Through the indiscretions of Dowdall in Dublin and the revelations of its own spies in London, however, the government got wind of Despard's plans long before they had fully matured, and on 16 November 1802 arrested him and a large batch of his accomplices.[91]

No evidence, however, of extensive preparations for a rising in London were discovered: no papers were found on Despard at the time of his arrest, and the principal witness at the trial, the guardsman Windsor, probably exaggerated both the imminence of the *coup*

87. T. M. Parssinen, 'The Revolutionary Party in London, 1816–1820', *Bulletin of the Institute of Historical Research*, vol. 45 (1972), pp. 266–82.

88. Oman, 'The unfortunate Colonel Despard' in *Colonel Despard and Other Studies*, ch. 1.

89. Despard had benefited, among others, from the 'No Bastille' agitation led by Sir Francis Burdett. For Despard's obsession with Irish affairs see *Personal Recollections of the Life and Times of Valentine, Lord Cloncurry* (Dublin, 1849), p. 47.

90. Elliott, 'The United Irishmen and France, 1796–1806', pp. 233–4.

91. Thomas Windsor, a private soldier of the Third Battalion of Grenadier Guards turned informer after having taken the illegal oath and gave the authorities regular intelligence of the progress of the conspiracy.

and the part played by Despard.[92] The intervention of the government to forestall the *coup* deprived it of the opportunity to reveal the full extent of the conspiracy or to produce conclusive evidence of Despard's connection with the subsequent Irish rising.[93] The details of the London plot which came to light during the trial appeared so hare-brained and improbable that the Attorney General, Spencer Perceval, spent much time at the outset of the prosecution case trying to establish its credibility on general grounds.[94]

Despard was no Bonaparte and the 40,000 Irish estimated to be living in London at the time had not been organized into a revolutionary army.[95] Stopping the departure of the mail coaches from Piccadilly as a signal for the start of provincial revolts would hardly have produced an extensive nation-wide insurrection – for, with the dubious exception of the secret 'Black Lamp' revolutionary association in Yorkshire, there were no signs of even problematical provincial support.[96] The intention, nevertheless, was to stage a *coup d'état* in the capital with the help of disaffected soldiers in the First and Third Battalions of the Guards, who had been enrolled in the conspiracy by secret oaths.[97] Day-labourers, journeymen, former members of the London Corresponding Society and Irish dockers had also been formed into a paramilitary organization, directed by a secret executive.[98] The aim of the conspiracy, as set out in papers found on the prisoners, was 'the independence of Ireland'; an 'equalization of civil, political and religious rights'; an ample provision for the families of the 'heroes who shall fall in the contest', and 'a liberal reward for distinguished merit'.[99] During the autumn

92. For Windsor's evidence at Despard's trial see *ST*, vol. 28, cols. 392–404; PRO HO 42/46 and TS 11/121/332, examination of Windsor 21 Jan. 1803.

93. In fact the government itself only discovered the connection with Emmet's rising in July 1803.

94. *ST*, vol. 28, cols. 378–80. He represented Despard and his followers as 'political enthusiasts' – 'misled by all the nonsense, and all the villainy which the French revolution has set afloat in men's minds'.

95. PRO PC 1/44/A 153. Information, dated (?) 1799.

96. For the debate on the extent of a secret revolutionary movement in Yorkshire in 1801–2 see a series of articles by J. R. Dinwiddy, critical of E. P. Thompson's exposition, and by J. L. Baxter and F. K. Donnelly, in support of Thompson's views, in *Past and Present*, no. 64 (August 1974), pp. 113–35.

97. The recruiting among the military was conducted mainly by two Irishmen – James Farrell (alias Macnamara) and William Bacon.

98. Ten men were formed into a 'company', under the command of a 'captain'; five companies were grouped together as a 'deputy division' under a colonel. The commander-in-chief was Despard, *ST*, vol. 28, cols. 394–5.

99. *Ibid.*, col. 370.

Despard and his associates had made their plans at a series of secret meetings, moving from one tavern to another in working-class London – the Two Bells and the Coach and Horses in Whitechapel, the Running Horse and the Brown Bear in St Giles's, the Bleeding Heart in Hatton Garden, the Hoop and Ram in the Mint, the Flying Horse at Newington and the Tiger on Tower Hill.[100] News was received at the Home Office on 15 November of a meeting called for the following day at the Oakley Arms in Lambeth at which final arrangements were to be made for the assassination of the King on 23 November on his way to open Parliament.[101] The government, which had known about the conspiracy since September, could delay no longer. On the night of the 16th Despard and forty others were arrested at the Oakley Arms. Twenty were almost immediately discharged and, of the thirteen who were subsequently tried early in February 1803, only Despard and six others were found guilty and subsequently executed, three were acquitted and three others were pronounced guilty but pardoned.[102] All had been charged not only with high treason but also under the act of 1795 'for the safety of his majesty's person and government' and the acts of 1797 against attempts to subvert the armed forces and the taking and administering of illegal oaths'.[103] Though Lord Chief Justice Ellenborough referred, in his summing up in the case of Despard's accomplices, to the disclosure of a 'treasonable conspiracy ... of enormous extent and most alarming magnitude', most contemporaries thought the dangers to the state had been overrated and that the mind of the 'unfortunate' Colonel Despard had been unhinged.[104] This was because so few verdicts of 'Guilty' had been handed down, because the jury had recommended that Despard himself should be pardoned in view of his 'former good character and eminent services', and because the government had purposely refrained from revealing the full ramifications of the intrigue. The Treasury magistrate Sir Richard Ford and the spy John Moody were well aware at the time that Dr Crossfield, William Curry, J. Hartley, Thomas Pemberton, John Heron, Nicholls,

100. *Ibid.*, cols. 394–400.
101. PRO HO 42/66. *Précis* of evidence.
102. PRO TS 11/122/333. Case of Despard *et al. ST*, vol. 28, cols. 524–7. Despard was tried on 7 February 1803, twelve of his accomplices on 9 February. Despard and six others, who had been found guilty, were executed on 21 February 1803.
103. *ST*, vol. 28, cols. 359–62.
104. Ellenborough's summing up. *Ibid.*, col. 525. There was a widespread contemporary belief in Despard's innocence.

Wallis Eastburn and Pendrill – all former members of the London Corresponding Society and of the Society of United Englishmen – were 'deeply in the business', but of these only Pendrill was arrested, and even he was not tried.[105] Once again the government seemed more concerned to preserve intact its sources of secret intelligence than to uncover the full extent of the treasonable conspiracy, or to bring into its net many against whom the evidence was not over-whelming. It may be that the government had reason to know that Anglo-Irish Jacobinism had been effectively killed and not merely scotched. This judgement was borne out in July 1803 with the miser-able failure of Robert Emmet's attempted rising in Ireland.

The process of radical decline had now gone even further than in 1797, when Horne Tooke had expressed the view that the cause of reform was already 'dead and buried'.[106] The 'resurrection' that Cartwright, in reply, had then optimistically predicted came before the long war with France was over, thanks to the electoral exertions of Sir Francis Burdett, Tooke's acknowledged disciple.[107] But before the attempt is made, in conclusion, to assess the legacy of eighteenth-century radicalism to later generations of reformers and to the labour movements of the nineteenth century, its essential and unique charac-ter may perhaps be better appreciated if its social implications and claims are first clarified. So far the democratic movement has been depicted primarily as a political struggle for a political panacea or cure-all radical parliamentary reform. Universal male suffrage had initially been demanded as part of a long-lost inheritance of British liberties dating back to Anglo-Saxon times. The claim had been buttressed by the doctrine of human rights as expounded by the English Rational Dissenters and the American colonists, even before that theory had been given added impetus by the French revolution. But in the 1790s, parliamentary reform was demanded as the in-dispensable tool that would make the redress of pressing social and economic grievances both possible and inevitable.[108] How radical

105. PRO PC 1/3117. Ford to Notary (Moody), Nov. 1802. Pendrill was also concerned in concealing a younger Watson after the Spa Fields riots of 1817. PRO HO 40/6.

106. F. D. Cartwright, *Life and Correspondence of Major Cartwright* (London, 1826), vol. 1, p. 240.

107. His success in the Westminster election of 1807 was largely the result of the efficiency of Francis Place's Westminster Committee. G. Wallas, *Life of Francis Place*, 4th ed. (London, 1925), pp. 43–7.

108. G. Whale, 'The influence of the industrial revolution (1760–90) on the demand for parliamentary reform', *TRHS*, 4th series, vol. 15 (1922), pp. 101–31.

then were the reformers' demands for social justice and 'equality', how original were the 'solutions' for social ills and economic discontents put forward in this revolutionary period, and how revolutionary were the Utopian blue-prints offered for the future by Godwin and Spence? How 'Jacobin' were the 'English Jacobins' and how well-founded were the accusations of the anti-Jacobins?

The last issue may be dealt with first. The catalogue of crimes which Burke had taught the 'Church and King' clubs, the Reevite associations and the secret committees of Lords and Commons to include in their indictments of the radical societies is well known. The 'English Jacobins' were, he alleged, the dupes of the French eighteenth-century rationalists and revolutionists: they were republicans, the sworn enemies of aristocracy, fomenters of tumult and disorder, innovators, atheists, would-be confiscators and redistributors of private and ecclesiastical property, and men who had assumed the spurious title of 'patriots' to champion the claims of the American colonists and the principles and pretensions of Britain's hereditary enemy, the French. In his *Letters on a Regicide Peace* (1796–7), Burke attempted not only to discredit and vilify the 'regicide' Executive Directory of France, with which peace negotiations were currently being conducted, but also to refurbish his attacks on the 'Jacobins of England'. He estimated that of the 400,000 mature 'political citizens' of the United Kingdom, no less than one fifth – or 80,000 – were 'pure Jacobins, utterly incapable of amendment; objects of eternal vigilance, and, when they break out, of legal constraint'.[109] They formed a great and formidable minority, more than a mere faction and yet small enough in numbers to be easily disciplined and directed.

In a reply purporting to reassure an anxious reader of Burke's diatribe, R. Dinmore Jnr. of the Norwich Patriotic Society published in 1797 an *Exposition of the Principles of the English Jacobins*, in which he sought to expose the Alarmist slurs against the reformers by explaining the social and political objectives of his associates. The latter were, he insisted, 'men of strong sense and some reading', who had acquiesced in the title of Jacobins, not because they approved the acts of 'that fell monster Robespierre', but because acceptance of the

---

109. E. Burke, *Works* (Bohn ed., 1877), vol. 5, p. 190. This 'British public' consisted of 'those of adult age, not declining in life, of tolerable leisure for such discussions, and of some means of information, more or less, and who are above menial dependence'.

nickname 'rendered the malice of their enemies pointless'.[110] Their political principles were, however, of pure English growth, derived from Locke, Sydney, Marvell and Milton, and their aims were essentially humanitarian – 'to assist the poor and needy; to lessen the horrors of the dungeon; to uprear the olive branch of peace; and to teach men to do to others as they should do unto them'. It was only popular credulity which allowed Burke to label the 80,000 English Jacobins as 'atheists' – some atheists there were among them, but these were few and far between.[111] So far from being enemies to all law and order, the Jacobins 'held the laws in the most complete veneration'. Bad laws they would seek to repeal, but only by legal and peacable means, and any appeal to the general right of resistance would be prompted only by 'hard necessity'. The exercise of such a right would be superfluous once universal suffrage had been conceded. They did not seek the death of the King – 'for they may lose, but cannot gain, by having George the Third converted into George the Fourth'.[112] Nor did their claim to be 'Citizens of the World' and friends of French liberty necessarily mean that they were unpatriotic. Nevertheless they would not 'strain a point' to assist the prosecution of a 'mad, murderous war', unjustly entered into by the government.[113]

In examining the implications of the reformers' 'grand principle of equality', Dinmore outlined their main criticisms of the country's existing social structure, the injustices of its economic institutions, the parasitic dependence of the younger sons of the aristocracy on public employment and the gross inequalities arising from the inordinate financial rewards given to powerful state functionaries. The English Jacobins had no desire to 'equalize all property', but considered nevertheless that 'the laws ought to have a tendency' in that direction, since the great wealth of the few was only compatible with 'the corresponding misery in the many'.[114] Clerical and state emoluments thus stood in need of revision: the enormous salaries of the prince bishops of the church, such as the Bishop of Durham, should be pruned for the benefit of the impoverished country curates.[115] Generals and naval commanders should have less so that the pay of the private soldier and ordinary seaman could be raised. For the

110. Dinmore, *Exposition* . . ., 3rd ed. (Norwich, 1797), pp. 4–5.
111. *Ibid.*, pp. 8–9.
112. *Ibid.*, p. 11.
113. *Ibid.*, p. 18.
114. *Ibid.*, p. 6.
115. *Ibid.*, p. 6.

same reason the reformers were enemies to the system of primogeniture, all entails, all copyhold tenures and the chartered rights of corporations.[116] They deplored the game laws and held that 'the little as well as the great occupier should possess an equal right to the game on his own land which he has maintained'.[117] The tithe laws were also inequitable for they merely diverted the 'labour of the industrious' . . . 'to pamper fat bishops, lazy deans, idle prebendaries or drowsy rectors'. From these sentiments it may be assumed that many members of the Norwich Patriotic Society in its final phase were Dissenters. They were content to differ with friends and opponents on religious dogma, but were convinced that the principle of church establishment was wrong and that every denomination ought to maintain its own clergy.[118] Their social concern concentrated, however, on the problem of poverty – as a source of crime, imprisonment for debt and inequality before the law, and as the consequence of unjust taxation, social discrimination and callous public indifference.[119] Capital punishment should be abolished, but the real solution for poverty should be sought in the establishment of national schools: 'not to teach boys senseless dogmas, and to bow to every spruce coat they meet; but where they may learn useful knowledge, sound morality and rational principles of government.'[120] Such views were entirely representative of those expressed in the Norwich *Cabinet* and were reminiscent of the social and economic attitudes of both Paine and Cooper.[121]

Thelwall also took up the cudgels on behalf of those whom Burke sought to exclude from his narrowly drawn circle of the British 'political public', and eloquently expressed their rising social and economic expectations.

I, indeed, affirm – that *every* man, and every *woman*, and every *child*, ought to obtain something more, in the general distribution of the fruits of

116. *Ibid.*, p. 6.
117. *Ibid.*, p. 6. The exclusive right of landed proprietors to hunt game was protected by a long series of statutes, culminating in an act of 1671 confining the taking of game to certain specified categories of persons and allowing offenders to be convicted on the oath of a single witness before a single JP. In 1796 J. C. Curwen's effort to reform the system was defeated. Chester King, 'The English game law system', *American Historical Review*, vol. 38, pp. 240–62.
118. Dinmore, p. 8.
119. *Ibid.*, p. 12.
120. *Ibid.*, p. 14.
121. T. Cooper, *A Reply to Mr. Burke's Invective against Mr. Cooper and Mr. Watt* . . . (London, 1792), p. 75. T. Paine, *Rights of Man*, Part II.

labour, than food, and rags, and a wretched hammock, with a poor rug to cover it; and that without working twelve or fourteen hours a day, six days out of seven, from six to sixty. They have a claim, a sacred inviolable claim, growing out of that fundamental maxim, upon which alone all property can be supported, to some comforts and enjoyments, in addition to the necessaries of life; and [quoting Burke's own words] tolerable leisure for such discussions and some means of information as may lead to an understanding of their rights; without which they can never understand their duties.[122]

This did not quite echo the claim of the Parisian *sans-culottes* to '*l'égalité des jouissances*', but it was an advance to think in terms, not of a minimum, but of a rising standard of living.[123]

Nor was it tolerable that the virtuous, intelligent and well-informed *sansculotterie* of Sheffield should be banished from the charmed circle of politically competent citizenry, merely because of its alleged 'menial dependence'.[124] Thelwall was able to show that in popular constituencies, where poor workmen already possessed the vote, there were increasing signs, as at Nottingham, that they were able to use the franchise both responsibly and independently.[125]

Like Dinmore, Thelwall had also endeavoured to persuade large popular audiences that the idea of equalizing property was 'totally impossible in the present state of human intellect and industry'.[126] He was not averse, however, to having legal limits set to 'land monopoly' and the 'accumulation of capital', for he cherished a Rousseauite ideal of a community of small cultivators and producers.[127] What made capitalism acceptable for him was the prospect it held out for profit-sharing in industry and its guarantee that the factory workshop would provide an alternative and involuntary form of political society 'which no act of Parliament could silence and no magistrate disperse'.[128] The answer he gave to Burke's immediate threat of the use of force against the English Jacobins was to impress on the radicals the need for 'fresh vigilance, fresh exertion, close intercourse and intrepid

122. J. Thelwall, *The Rights of Nature against the Usurpations of Establishments* (London, 1796), p. 18.

123. For the concept of 'the equality of enjoyments' see A. Soboul, *Les Sans-Culottes Parisiens en l'an II* (Paris, 1958), p. 459 ff.

124. Thelwall, *The Rights of Nature* . . ., p. 21.

125. *Ibid.*, pp. 25–6.

126. *Speech at the General Meeting of the Friends of Parliamentary Reform – October 26, 1795*, 3rd ed., p. 14.

127. C. Cestre, *J. Thelwall: A Pioneer of Democracy in England* (London, 1906), pp. 185–6.

128. Thelwall, *The Rights of Nature* . . ., p. 21.

unanimity'.[129] A determined champion of 'innovation' as the condition of progress, Thelwall had no use for revolutionary change and no belief either that the corruption of the existing political system would work its own cure.[130] He saw no need to resort to a strategy of clandestine conspiracy. His hopes were pinned rather on 'vigilant, discussion and well-grounded principles', and on the workers' right to self-improvement through education.[131]

Just as Dinmore had not repudiated the tag of English Jacobin, so Thelwall was not ashamed to own that he himself was a *sans-culotte* – though by this he merely meant that he was 'an advocate for the rights and happiness of those who are languishing in want and nakedness . . . the thing in REALITY which Whigs pretend to be'.[132] It was not the men nor the events of the French revolution which he admired, but its principles.

That which I glory in, in the revolution of France, is this. That it has been upheld and propagated as a principle of that revolution, that ancient abuses are not by their antiquity converted into virtues; that it has been affirmed and established that man has rights which no statutes or usages can take away; that intellectual beings are entitled to the use of their intellects; that the object of society is the promotion of the general happiness of mankind; that thought ought to be free, and that the propagation of thought is the duty of every individual; that one order of society has no right, how many years soever they have been guilty of the pillage, to plunder and oppress the other parts of the community, whose persons are entitled to equal respect, and whose exertions have been much more beneficial to mankind.[133]

These were no more, perhaps, than the humanitarian and political principles of the eighteenth-century Enlightenment, but since 1789 they had not only been proclaimed but established as the fundamental axioms of French revolutionary society and government.

129. *Ibid.*, p. 89.
130. 'All that is requisite for the remedy of abuses, the resistance of encroachments, and the overthrow of that corruption which exhausts the *cornucopia* of British industry to pamper luxurious usurpation, and glut the dogs of war, is, that we learn to understand our rights, peaceably associate to maintain them, and firmly assert our opinions.' Thelwall, *Tribune*, vol. 1, p. 162.
131. *The Rights of Nature . . .* , p. 89.
132. *The Natural and Constitutional Right of Britons to Annual Parliaments, Universal Suffrage and the Freedom of Popular Association . . .* (London, 1795), p. 85. This pamphlet purported to be the defence to the charge of high treason which Thelwall had been persuaded by Erskine not to deliver before the Old Bailey jury.
133. *Tribune*, vol. 1, pp. 155–6.

Enlightenment thought had also shaped William Godwin's ideas on human perfectibility, and the revolution of 1789 had stimulated the composition of his treatise on how the human mind could be finally emancipated and the ideal society established. His *Enquiry concerning the Principles of Political Justice, and its influence on General Virtue and Happiness*, commenced in 1791, had been written for the most part as the forces of reaction were gathering strength behind Pitt's policy of repression.[134] Its publication in two quarto volumes early in 1793 raised the immediate question whether it would fall under the ban. It had, however, been designed as 'an appeal to men of study and reflection' and 'one of its express objects' was the condemnation of tumult and violence.[135] The book was also saved from legal prosecution by its metaphysical framework, which was thought to place its message beyond the comprehension of the ordinary artisan, and by its high price of three guineas, which Pitt considered would keep it out of the reach of those 'who had not three shillings to spare'.[136] This estimate was not wholly erroneous, for Godwin's impact was undoubtedly greatest on what Hazlitt called 'the most sanguine and fearless understandings of the time' – the Romantic poets – Coleridge, Wordsworth, Blake, Southey and, above all, his son-in-law, Shelley – and the English socialist thinkers of the early nineteenth century.[137] The book, however, did reach a working-class audience in the large towns through reading clubs and subscription libraries and, if we can believe the informer Barlow, it did much, along with Paine's *Age of Reason* and the translated works of Mirabaud, Helvétius and Volney, to promote the spread of atheism and free thought among the Sheffield cutlers.[138] Such was Godwin's extraordinary prestige among contemporary men of letters

134. Godwin, *Political Justice . . .* (London, 1793), preface, p. ix.
135. *Ibid.*, p. xi.
136. C. Kegan Paul, *William Godwin: His Friends and Contemporaries* (London, 1876), vol. 1, p. 80.
137. W. Hazlitt, *Spirit of the Age*, ed. E. D. Mackerness (London, 1969), p. 37. For the response of the poets to Godwin, see P. A. Brown, *The French Revolution in English History* (London, 1965 reprint), pp. 207–15; H. N. Brailsford, *Shelley, Godwin and their Circle*, 6th ed. (London, 1936); W. J. B. Owen and J. W. Smysen (eds.), *The Prose Works of William Wordsworth* (Oxford, 1974), vol. 1, pp. 35–44. As the editor of Charles Lamb's letters later remarked of Godwin: 'There was nothing better calculated to at once feed and make steady the enthusiasm of youthful patriots than the high speculations, in which he taught them to engage on the nature of social evils and the great destiny of his species.' *Letters of Charles Lamb*, ed. W. C. Hazlitt (London, 1886), vol. 1, p. 209.
138. Barlow to T. B. Bayley, 19 Sept. 1799. PRO PC 1/44/A 161.

that, as Hazlitt also reminds us, 'Tom Paine was considered for a time as Tom Fool to him, Paley an old woman, Edmund Burke a flashy sophist'.[139] In some respects his stature as a Utopian thinker and critic of contemporary society may perhaps be compared with that of Tolstoy in the Russia of the mid nineteenth century.

Godwin differed from Thelwall and most other radical publicists of the time in rejecting the concept of inherent natural rights, in questioning the utility of the political societies and in renouncing, even in a period of reaction, the popular right of resistance.[140] His *Political Justice* was, however, unsparing in its condemnation of the existing political, legal, social and ecclesiastical institutions of eighteenth-century Britain. In it Godwin propounded his system of philosophic anarchism, delivered a frontal attack on the hallowed principle of private property, argued the case for a 'permissive' society and depicted his ideal community as that in which justice as between rich and poor and between citizens and the state would be fully realized through the operation of 'universal benevolence'.[141] As used by Godwin, the latter concept may be said to have affinities with the modern ideal of voluntary social service – a moral obligation which he thought rested on all men – since no one had a right to dispose of his wealth or talents solely for his own advantage. No one should be denied the means to perfect his moral character or intellectual attainments and, since all men have the same common nature, they are capable of the same indefinite improvement.[142] The withering away of the twin evils of law and government and the advent of Utopia would be dependent, however, upon the permeation of the whole community by this spirit of 'universal benevolence' and the redistribution of wealth and property more equitably among the members of society. In the interim period, except for its responsibilities in the fields of internal security and external defence, government could be devolved to a series of autonomous parochial republics. These would be small enough to allow crime, injustice and disorder to be effectively controlled by public opinion, but large enough to provide juries for their suppression if necessary.[143] For the transaction of other common

139. Hazlitt, pp. 36–7.

140. C. H. Driver, 'William Godwin', in F. J. C. Hearnshaw (ed.), *The Social and Political Ideas of Some Representative Thinkers of the Revolutionary Era* (London, 1931), p. 159; Godwin, *Political Justice*, vol. 1, bk. 4, ch. 3.

141. Hearnshaw, pp. 150, 156. Brailsford, pp. 131–3.

142. Godwin, *Political Justice*, vol. 1, p. 90.

143. Hearnshaw, p. 175.

affairs delegates from the parishes could be sent to a national assembly, whose legislative authority would be so severely restricted that it would be pointless for it to meet more than once a year. The stability of this new Utopia would be ensured, not through its political organization, which would be both rudimentary and transitory, but through a new system of property based on individual needs and social justice. Property would be made available to those who stood in need of it and land, no longer monopolized by the few, would be at the disposal of those who wished to cultivate it.[144] The result would be greater productivity and the elimination of waste, so that all the needs of the community could be met if every able-bodied citizen performed only half an hour's work a day.[145] It was on these notions that Coleridge based his famous scheme for the establishment of his so-called Pantisocracy – a commune of freely associated men and women on the banks of the Susquehannah, the funds for which were never forthcoming.[146]

Until the foundations of this Utopia were undermined by Malthus's theory of population and the growing crescendo of anti-Jacobinism, it acted as a powerful beacon, picking out and illuminating the fundamental problems of both the contemporary political world and the society of the future. Godwin's insistence that property posed the fundamental practical problem confronting human society caused the justification and distribution of private property to become the central issue of social speculation and reforming activity in the post-war period.[147] He had less sympathy with one other aspect of radicalism at this period – the cause of feminism – but Mary Wollstonecraft's pioneering and systematic exposition of the theme in her *Vindication of the Rights of Woman* (1792) did not deter him from marrying her in March 1797 after she had become his pregnant mistress, despite his previous strictures on the domestic affections and on marriage itself.[148] In the September following, Mary died after giving birth to the daughter who later became Shelley's wife. Thereafter, as Hazlitt

144. *Ibid.*, p. 176.
145. In a later essay, *The Enquirer*, Godwin conceded that two hours a day would probably be needed.
146. Coleridge hoped to establish 'Pantisocracy' in Pennsylvania as a 'liberty settlement' in the wake of Priestley on land belonging to Benjamin Rush. Mary C. Pack, *Joseph Priestley and the Problem of Pantisocracy* (Philadelphia, 1947).
147. Hearnshaw, p. 150.
148. Claire Tomalin, *The Life and Death of Mary Wollstonecraft* (London, 1974), chs. 9, 18.

put it, Godwin 'sank below the horizon' under the attacks of Malthus Mackintosh and Dr Parr and ended his career as a sponger on the friends whose intellectual development he had fostered, and as a pensioner on the state whose foundations he had sought to undermine.[149]

Whereas Godwin had speculated on the Utopian overtones of 'political justice', Paine in one of his later pamphlets, published in 1797, argued the case for what he called *Agrarian Justice*. This was meant to stand in contrast, on the one hand with 'agrarian law' (or rural communism) and, on the other, with 'agrarian monopoly'. It was a scheme to compensate all men (rich or poor) for having been deprived of their original rights of ownership in the land by the institution of private property consequent upon its cultivation. It was not a proposal for the expropriation of existing landed proprietors or for land nationalization, but for the introduction of a 10 per cent inheritance tax on all real or personal property to endow all those coming of age with a lump sum of £15 to start them on their careers and those of, or over, the age of fifty with an annual pension of £10. In that sense *Agrarian Justice* was an appendix to the blue-print of a welfare state in Part II of his *Rights of Man*, rather than an experiment in 'levelling'.[150]

It may, at first sight, appear curious that the most radical plan for the complete redistribution of landed property in the country had been conceived as early as 1775 by an impoverished and eccentric Newcastle schoolmaster – Thomas Spence.[151] Such an impression, would, however, be erroneous, for it was not the original concept but its subsequent modification in the 1790s which gave Spence's agrarian Utopia its revolutionary overtones. Its author, the son of an Aberdeen netmaker, was, according to Francis Place,

a very simple, very honest, single-minded man, querulous in his disposition and odd in his manners . . . soured by adverse circumstances, and at enmity with the world. Still he loved mankind, and firmly believed that the time would come when they would be wise, virtuous and happy. He was perfectly sincere and unpractised in the ways of the world to an

149. Hazlitt, p. 36.
150. A. O. Aldridge, *Man of Reason: The Life of Thomas Paine* (London, 1960), p. 241.
151. O. Rudkin, *Thomas Spence and His Connections* (London, 1927); T. M. Parssinen, 'Thomas Spence and the origins of English land nationalization', *Journal of the History of Ideas*, vol. 34 (1973), pp. 135–41; BL, Add. MSS. 27808.

extent few could imagine in a man who had been pushed about in it as he had been.[152]

Spence's ideas had stemmed from a dispute between the corporation and freemen of Newcastle about the rents of the Town Moor and had originally been formulated in a lecture which he delivered to the local Literary and Philosophical Society in 1775.[153] For publishing this address under the title of *The Rights of Man* and hawking it about the streets as a cheap broadside, Spence was expelled from the society and his school was boycotted.[154] On the death of his wife, he escaped from this local ostracism by moving, in December 1792, to London, where he set up as a printer and retailer of radical tracts at the 'Hive of Liberty', 8 Little Turnstile, near the top of Chancery Lane. Later he moved his shop to Oxford St and finally sold his wares from a street barrow. Between 1793 and 1796, after joining the London Corresponding Society, Spence had been in and out of prison firstly for publishing Paine's *Rights of Man* and, secondly, for allegedly allowing the Lambeth Loyal Association to drill its members in the use of arms at his shop in 1794.[155] During these years he had printed a radical periodical, *A Pennyworth of Pig's Meat; or Lessons from the Swinish Multitude*, and had modified his original scheme for land nationalization. He reluctantly conceded that, although the actual transfer of land from private to community ownership could be managed on a parochial basis, the 'beautiful and powerful New Republic' that he had envisaged would need a national assembly to provide for the country's defence and the regulation of inter-parochial disputes, as well as some form of executive government.[156] According to his revised proposals, the delegates to the national assembly were to be annually elected by the parishes and were then to choose the twenty-four members of an executive council once every two years. Both institutions were to be strictly subordin-

152. BL, Add. MSS. 27808, fos. 152–3. Thomas Bewick, the celebrated wood-engraver, who was Spence's intimate friend, described him as 'one of the warmest Philanthropists in the world – the happiness of Mankind seemed with him to absorb every other consideration'. T. Bewick, *A Memoir written by himself*, ed. I Bain (London, 1975), p. 52.

153. Wallas, *Life of Francis Place*, p. 61.

154. It was one of the rules of the society that each member should read a written lecture to the members but that none of these should be published. Bewick, p. 52.

155. *ST*, vol. 24, col. 693.

156. T. M, Parssinen, 'The Revolutionary Party in London, 1816–20'. *Bulletin of the Institute of Historical Research* (1972), p. 268.

ated to parochial control. The powers of the council were virtually confined to the administration of the laws passed by the assembly and all such legislation could be vetoed by 5 per cent of the parishes.[157] The essential character of the plan as 'a parochial partnership in land without private landlordism' thus remained intact.

Secondly, the experience of land 'nationalization' in revolutionary France obliged Spence to recognize that private landlords would not acquiesce in the confiscation of their property without demur and that their resistance would, therefore, need to be overcome, if necessary, by their 'root and branch' elimination by forcible means.[158] It was this more clear-sighted realism which commended Spence's projects to the extremist and republican wing of the London Corresponding Society at the time when it had committed itself not only to clandestine conspiracy but also to the tactics of the *coup d'état*.

Under various titles – such as *The Meridian Sun of Liberty* (1796); *Constitution of Spensonea – a country in Fairyland* (1801); *The Restorer of Society to its Natural State* (1801) (for publishing which he was fined £50 and imprisoned for a year); and *The World Turned Upside Down* (1805) (dedicated to Earl Stanhope) – Spence continued to keep his views of a propertyless millennium before the public.[159] From 1807 a group of dedicated enthusiasts in the tavern society of East London met regularly to discuss these final touches to the plan in the Free and Easy Club.[160] On his death in September 1814, his followers commemorated his life's work by continuing to meet as the Society of Spencean Philanthropists.[161] It was as virtual founder and librarian of this society that Thomas Evans (formerly secretary of the London Corresponding Society) published its manifesto – *Christian Policy the Salvation of the Empire* – in 1816.

This was the final version of the Spencean Utopia, and though it gave agrarian communism 'a more general application', in other respects it registered a surprising retreat from Spence's earlier political objectives. The manifesto emphasized that the principle of co-partnership in land, as advocated by the Spenceans, had been based on three historical precedents – the agrarian republican commonwealth of the Mosaic law, the communal holding of property under primitive Christianity and the division of land between units of the families

157. *Ibid.*, p. 268.
158. *Ibid.*, p. 269.
159. *Dictionary of National Biography*.
160. Parssinen, 'The Revolutionary Party in London', p. 269.
161. Wallas, p. 62. You did not have to be wealthy in the eighteenth century to be called a 'philanthropist' – which merely meant – 'a lover of mankind'.

by 'the third saviour of the world' – King Alfred.[162] Confronted by national bankruptcy and economic dislocation in the aftermath of the long French wars, Evans recommended the adoption of the Spencean formula as 'true and genuine Christian policy', but defended the principle of co-partnership also on the analogy of the great joint-stock companies.[163] All ideas of fundamental social or political change were abandoned. The monarchy, the nobility and the established system of government were to be preserved and the only specific political demand was for a written constitution 'to define the forms and powers of government, the rights of the people, and the security of their persons and properties'.[164]

The second noticeable deviation from traditional radical propaganda in the eighteenth century was the transference of the odium of responsibility for the country's current financial plight from the system of political corruption and the parasitic interest group of pensioners and placemen exclusively to the class of agrarian malefactors – 'the landlords and stocklords'.[165] The proposed remedy was correspondingly drastic – 'that all feudality be abolished and the territory of these realms be declared to be the people's farm'. All the 'land, waters, mines, houses and all permanent feudal property' should be transferred to the people to be held in parochial (or other small) partnerships as 'part of the general national estate'.[166] Nothing was said as to how the change was to be effected or whether the use of force was contemplated. Parochial boards or committees were to let the property on leasehold tenure only and, after deducting from the rents thus received their share of governmental expenses (for the support of the state) and all parish charges, were to divide the balance remaining among all the people having settlements in the parish as the profit arising from their natural estate.[167] Evans's calculations suggested that the net proceeds would work out at near £4 a head annually.[168] The financial inducement seemed meagre but the more general benefits of co-partnership were not underestimated:

162. T. Evans, *Christian Policy*, 2nd ed. (London, 1816), pp. 8–13.

163. *Ibid.*, p. 14.

164. *Ibid.*, p. 25.

165. 'Landlords, then, and landlords only are the oppressors of the people.' *Ibid.*, p. 15.

166. *Ibid.*, p. 25.

167. *Ibid.*, pp. 26–7.

168. Evans reckoned the total rental of land, houses and mines of the three kingdoms at £150 million, the expenditure at £75 million, which left a balance of £75 million to be divided between every man, woman and child – or £20 million.

Q

it would remove the cause of war among kings and landlords for acquisitions of territory, of law-suits, contentions and ruin among communities, families and individuals, about titles and inheritance; would lay the foundations of peace, happiness and security; would establish all that the scriptures command, all that religion enjoins; all that the established Christian church, by their policy, practise and enjoy.[169]

The financial salvation of the country would lie in the cancellation of the national debt and the happiness of the people in the abolition of all taxes and tolls.

This brief retrospect of the social and economic thought of the English Jacobins indicates that the responsible spokesmen of the popular societies, like Thelwall and Dinmore, had specifically repudiated all ideas of 'equalizing' property or nationalizing the land and that the true 'Levellers' were harmless Utopian speculators, like Godwin, or impractical 'philanthropists', like Spence.[170] The committed republicans (as distinct from the numerous believers in Painite 'representative government') were usually members or auxiliaries of the United Irish, the minority of the London Corresponding Society which had adopted Spencean principles, or adherents of the provincial Jacobin underground in Yorkshire and Lancashire. The only democrats who were prepared to provoke tumult and disorder or engage in the subversion of the troops were the misguided adherents of Colonel Despard, members of the clandestine insurrectionary wing of the London revolutionary party, or expatriate radical leaders who had sought safety in Paris, such as Dr Watson or John Ashley. When Spence of Thomas Evans invoked the experience of the French revolution it was often to warn against the adoption of policies or courses of which they disapproved.[171] It is not, however, so easy to rebut the accusations of Burke and the anti-Jacobins that the members of the popular societies were deists or atheists for, despite the special case of the Norwich Dissenters noticed by Dinmore, one of the most significant aspects of the final phase of English

169. *Ibid.*, p. 16.

170. Writing of Godwin, the editor of Charles Lamb's letters noted: 'No one would have suspected the author of those wild theories, which startled the wise and shocked the prudent, in the calm, gentlemanly person who rarely said anything above commonplace and took interest in little beyond the whist-table.' *Letters of Charles Lamb*, vol. 1, p. 209.

171. In recommending the Spencean policy of transferring private property in land to collective ownership and the abolition of freehold tenure, Evans made a particular critique of the speculation that had disfigured the sales of the *biens nationaux* during the French revolution to individual owners. Evans, p. 15.

eighteenth-century radicalism was a pronounced shift of minority opinion away from the tenets of revealed religion.

The sourccs of potential working class infidelity in the last decade of the eighteenth century were, of course, embedded in the contemporary social and political environment and in popular experience of the failures and inadequacies of the established church. These are well known: the church's spiritual neglect of the proliferating urban populations of the metropolis and North West; the unpopularity of the clergy as tithe owners, privileged monopolists of ecclesiastical endowments and deferential nominees of their lay patrons the local squirearchy; clerical unconcern for, or even hostility to, the spread of popular education; the reactionary behaviour of clerical magistrates and their entrenched bigotry as 'Church and King' activists and Reevite Loyalists. Rational Dissent and Unitarianism, on the other hand, had taken free thought to the verge of atheism,[172] whilst the hasty retreat of the main body of Dissent from the ranks of the reformers in the winter of 1792 had bred in the radicals both distrust of, and cynicism towards, such fair-weather allies.[173] Society's ability to resist the intellectual solvents of the Old Order had also been drastically weakened, as Burke had correctly predicted, by the French revolution. It was, however, the publication in 1794 of Paine's *Age of Reason* and the London Corresponding Society's promotion of a cheap edition of the book which was the immediate cause of the spread of deism and free thought in the popular societies. Although Paine claimed that he had written the work as a counterblast to the materialism of Condorcet and to deter the French people from 'running headlong into atheism', it was his attack on Christianity and his denial that the Bible was the word of God in Part II of the book, rather than its defence of 'natural religion', which gave such widespread offence in Britain.[174]

We have it on the contemporary authority of W. H. Reid, author of *The Rise and Dissolution of the Infidel Societies in this Metropolis*

172. For a useful discussion of the changing face of Unitarianism between 1795 and 1815 see I. Sellers, 'Unitarians and social change', *Hibbert Journal*, vol. 61 (1962), pp. 16–22.

173. Thomas Walker of Manchester, an Anglican himself, bitterly complained that the Dissenters had 'constantly fallen short of their principles' and that their 'over-strained moderation' had made them 'rather the enemies than the friends of those who have ventured the most, and effected the most for the rights of the people'. *A Review of some of the Political Events which have occurred in Manchester during the last five years* (London, 1794), p. 125.

174. Aldridge, ch. 19.

(1800), that 'the early predilection of the London Corresponding Society for this performance was the sole medium which, for the first time, made infidelity as familiar as possible with the lower orders'.[175] It was, he observed, 'the heads of the party' – an allusion no doubt to Francis Place – who persuaded a bookseller, Thomas Williams, to bring out a cheap edition of the *Age of Reason* – to promote its more ready dissemination throughout the rapidly expanding divisions of the society.[176] Reid also scored a neat point by observing that 'while the infatuated disciples of the new philosophy were declaiming against their clergy, for mingling politics with religion, they themselves employed missionaries to add deism to the democracy of their converts'.[177] Three other devices for the dissemination of deism were also employed: the translation from the French and publication in cheap weekly parts of the more learned and elaborate classics of Enlightenment free thought – Mirabaud's *Système de la Nature* and Volney's *Ruines*; the supply of penny, twopenny and threepenny tracts which were scattered on the tables of the society's divisional clubrooms – 'as it were so many swivels against established opinions'; and, 'to enable the members to furnish themselves with the heavy Artillery of Voltaire, Godwin, etc.', the formation of reading clubs and subscription libraries.[178] To own a copy of the *Age of Reason* was now accepted as 'a collateral proof of the *civism* of the possessor', and to become an elected delegate on the General Committee of the society it was almost a prerequisite to be a non-Christian.[179]

The energetic implementation of this policy of deism in a society whose original regulations had debarred the discussion of religious issues, and despite the lack of agreement either among the members of its General Committee or in the divisions, produced a series of schisms in 1795 – notably that of a numerous body of Methodists.[180] It also seems that the two booksellers, John Bone and 'Citizen' Richard Lee, who seceded for other reasons, were proscribed for having refused to sell Paine's *Age of Reason* and Volney's *Ruines*.[181] Retaliation against the secessionists in the summer of 1797 took the

175. Reid, *Rise and Dissolution of Infidel Societies*, p. 4.
176. Reid, p. 5. For Place's own account of the incident see BL, Add. MSS. 35143, fo. 34.
177. Reid, p. 4.
178. *Ibid.*, pp. 6–8.
179. *Ibid.*, pp. 5, 9.
180. See above, p. 198.
181. Reid, p. 6.

form of harassing Methodist itinerant preachers near the City Road on Sunday mornings.[182] The public disputations in the presence of large crowds obliged the city magistrates to put a partial stop to field preaching in the following year. Not, however, that the deists were without their own difficulties, for Reid notes that one of the first of the metropolitan 'infidel' societies, which met at the Green Dragon in Cripplegate on Wednesdays and Sundays, was obliged to move its quarters four times between the spring of 1795 and the winter of 1797, before it eventually found sanctuary at the British Wine House near Hoxton, beyond the limits of the City officers.[183] Similar societies, nevertheless, managed to meet at this period in Shoreditch, Whitechapel, Spitalfields and Bunhill Row and some success was achieved in infiltrating the benefit societies more generally in the capital.[184] These groups no doubt included some freaks, such as the 'singular character' who attended these gatherings in a 'large round hat, nearly the size of an umbrella, bordered with gold lace',[185] or the members of the Jesus Christ Club in Liverpool who, according to the informer Barlow, blasphemously impersonated the Trinity by wearing different coloured wigs, while others made a bonfire of their Bibles and prayer-books.[186] Such eccentricities should not lead us to suppose that the secularist cult was a superficial or merely ephemeral facet of eighteenth-century radicalism in decline. Free thought was, indeed, to establish itself, alongside the tradition of liberal Dissent, as an abiding element in the working-class mentality of the nineteenth century. For the moment, however, it was only the radical intelligentsia who had felt the impulse of the Continental rational Enlightenment, or who had imbibed such notions at second hand from Paine or Godwin, who passed beyond deism to atheism. Those who, like Francis Place, were self-confessed agnostics were only a minority of a minority.[187]

By the time the radical societies were suppressed in 1799 the designation 'friends of the people' had almost ceased to be a part of the radical vocabulary and had certainly lost much of its relevance. Ever since Rational Dissent had been intimidated by 'Church and King' mobs in 1791, the number of those prepared to profess radical

182. *Ibid.*, p. 17.
183. *Ibid.*, pp. 10–11.
184. *Ibid.*, pp. 12, 20.
185. *Ibid.*, p. 14.
186. Barlow to Harrop, Aug. 1799. PRO PC 1/44/A 161.
187. BL, Add. MSS. 35143, fo. 93. Thompson, p. 726.

sympathies had steadily declined. The September Massacres, the execution of Louis XVI and the rise of the Jacobin and Bonapartist dictatorships had gradually transformed some of the early 'enthusiasts' for French democracy, and most, but not all, of the Romantic poets into Burkian conservatives.[188] Radically minded merchants and manufacturers had themselves decided, or been persuaded by the Reevite associations, to withdraw their financial and moral support from the provincial reform societies, whose growth they had previously encouraged. Those who, like Thomas Walker of Manchester, successfully contested the witch-hunt of their radicalism in the courts, did so only at the expense of their personal and business fortunes.[189] The sedition and treason trials of 1793–4 had crippled the political leadership of the London Corresponding Society, liquidated the Society for Constitutional Information, and paralysed the whole Scottish movement for democratic reform.[190] The 'Gagging Acts' of 1795 had convinced some radicals, despite Thelwall's arguments to the contrary, that it would be dangerous or even pointless to continue their activities.[191] Those who did so only succeeded in offering a token, and increasingly meaningless, resistance to the rigours of governmental and local repression.[192] 1797 deprived the radical cause, on the point of collapse, of its last remaining political prop when the Foxite Opposition, frustrated by successive humiliating reverses in the Commons and the failure of Grey's renewed reform proposals, seceded *en bloc* from parliament. The rump of the London Corresponding Society only survived long enough to precipitate its suppression and the imprisonment of its leaders by complicity in the clandestine and traitorous conspiracies of the United Irish. All that Hardy, Place and Frend had been able to do since 1796 had been to help

188. In the case of Wordsworth and Coleridge it was their disillusionment with German politics in 1798 during their visit to Goslar that helped to revive their patriotic loyalties. F. M. Todd, *Politics and the Poet* (London, 1957), pp. 104–5.

189. Walker was only able to support himself in his last years – he died in Feb. 1817 – owing to a legacy from his friend and defence counsel, Felix Vaughan. F. Knight, *The Strange Case of Thomas Walker* (London, 1957), p. 181.

190. According to H. W. Meikle, the organization of the United Scotsmen 'existed largely on paper'. *Scotland and the French Revolution* (Glasgow, 1912), p. 192.

191. BL, Add. MSS. 27808, fo. 67.

192. There were, of course, exceptions such as the 'staunch old republicans' of Merthyr Tydfil, who continued, at the height of the repression, to read Paine and Voltaire in their reading clubs. G. A. Williams, *Artisans and Sans-Culottes* (London, 1968), p. 66.

the distressed families of such prisoners confined without trial under the suspension of Habeas Corpus.[193]

To avoid further victimization or certain imprisonment, some 'friends of liberty' had, since 1794 or even earlier, sought asylum abroad in America or France. Between 1795 and 1802 the tide of emigration from the United Kingdom to North America rose steadily. Most of those who went were artisans, literate and free thinking, seeking a more prosperous future in the back country of the Monongahela, Kentucky and Ohio valleys. Some of the settlers in these areas, especially the Welsh Baptist ministers and their congregations, were spurred on by the prospect of missionary activity among the Indians of the frontier.[194] Those, however, who had left the homeland for political reasons tended to favour the 'liberty settlements' of Welsh 'Beula' in Pennsylvania, the English republican 'Sparta' in New York State, or the 'new Scotland' projected by the son of the social philosopher John Millar.[195] The more eminent religious or political exiles who found their way to the new world included Dr Joseph Priestley, Thomas Cooper of the Manchester Constitutional Society, Joseph Gales, proprietor and editor of the *Sheffield Register*, Benjamin Vaughan, the protégé of Lord Lansdowne, the radical printers Daniel Isaac Eaton and 'Citizen' Richard Lee, and John Binns and Jasper Moore of the London Corresponding Society. Hardly less impressive was the list of those who, at various times – some temporarily, others permanently – joined the British expatriate colony in Paris: John Hurford Stone, radical industrialist and printer, his mistress the poetess Helen Maria Williams, Mary Wollstonecraft, Thomas Christie, Thomas Paine, David Williams, founder of the Royal Literary Fund, who was granted honorary French citizenship and asked to help with the drafting of the republican constitution of 1793.[196] Among the contingent of former members of the London Corresponding Society who opted for Paris as

193. BL, Add. MSS. 35143, fos. 67–75.

194. G. A. Williams, 'Morgan John Rhees and his Beula', *Welsh History Review*, vol. 3, no. 4 (1967), p. 447.

195. *Ibid.*, p. 444. The attitude of the radicals on emigration was divided, as evidenced by Horne Tooke's remark: 'They are good men who leave, but they are better who stay in England.' Dinmore, p. 24.

196. Williams's liturgical views are also said to have influenced the rise of Theophilanthropy in France under the Directory. A. Mathiez, *La Théophilanthropie et le Culte Décadaire* (Paris, 1903), p. 394. The MS. of his autobiography, 'Incidents in my Own Life which had been thought of some Importance', is in the Cardiff Public Library.

a political refuge were John Ashley, Dr Robert Watson, Richard Hodgson and John Stuckey.[197]

There were, finally, those memorable but involuntary exiles who had been transported to Botany Bay after the Scottish sedition trials. Of these the only one to return to Britain – in 1809 – was Maurice Margarot.[198] William Skirving and Joseph Gerrald had died within days of each other in March 1796. Thomas Muir had escaped from captivity on an American vessel and, after several remarkable vicissitudes on his return journey via Mexico and Havana, had eventually landed at Bordeaux to receive a hero's welcome and a pension from the French government. He died at Chantilly in 1798. The Reverend Thomas Fyshe Palmer, having served his time, died on his way home from Botany Bay, as a Spanish prisoner of war on the island of Guam in mid Pacific in June 1802. These 'Scottish martyrs' were commemorated by an obelisk on Calton Hill, Edinburgh, erected by the friends of parliamentary reform between 1844 and 1846.[199]

197. Both Hodgson and Stuckey had taken prominent parts in the mass protest meetings organized by the LCS in 1795.

198. He landed at Liverpool with three guineas in his pocket. Failing health and impaired eyesight made him dependent on the financial generosity of his few remaining friends. He continued to plead for what he called 'a loyal and constitutional revolution' for the recovery of the nation's constitutional rights (*Thoughts on Revolutions*, 1812). He also propounded a plan to induce fundholders to accept a cut of 25 per cent of their holdings in the National Debt and for the rest of the debt to be extinguished by the surrender of part of their property by the great landholders to the fundholders according to a scale of graduated quotas. *Proposal for a Grand National Jubilee: Restoring to Every Man his Own, and thereby extinguishing both Want and War* (Sheffield, n.d.). On his death on 11 Nov. 1815, his friends raised £200 for the support of his widow. BL, Add. MSS. 27816. See also M. Roe, 'Maurice Margarot: a radical in two hemispheres, 1792–1815', *Bulletin of the Institute of Historical Research*, vol. 31 (1958), pp. 68–78.

199. The proposal for a memorial had been initiated by Joseph Hume in 1837 and had been taken up by the other parliamentary radicals of the period. It had, however, run into difficulties raised by some reformers who considered that Margarot's name should not appear on the monument because he had been guilty of treachery to his fellow prisoners Skirving and Palmer, who had been placed in irons on board the *Surprize* transport on the outward voyage to Botany Bay on the charge that they had conspired to organize a mutiny, and because he had long been suspected of acting as a government spy inside the London Corresponding Society. Francis Place, who had also been the subject of similar suspicions, and who was, along with Sir Richard Phillips – the former radical editor of the *Leicester Herald* – completely convinced of Margarot's integrity, was, however, able to produce documentary evidence refuting both the accusations,

To what extent and in what ways had eighteenth-century radicalism contributed to the formation of a politically conscious working-class in a pre-industrial society and in a period of prolonged war and general reaction? Though much popular animosity had been aroused against the aristocracy as monopolists of land, rotten boroughs and state sinecures, and though invidious comparisons were sometimes drawn between the lot of the rich and the poor under the system of 'Old Corruption',[200] the limitations of pre-industrialism and the survival of the traditional paternalist relationship between the gentry and their dependents in a *laissez-faire* economy had precluded the development of any militant class-consciousness among working people.[201] Painite theory, however, had done much to undermine the habitual political deference of the disfranchised to their social superiors and the increasingly capitalistic exploitation of the land and the high price of wheat generated by the war and the Corn Laws of 1815 finally alienated the urban and rural poor from their former protectors.[202]

As yet the solidarity that had been evoked by reforming radicalism had a political rather than an economic significance. It is impossible

---

so that the memorial was able to go forward as planned. It was characteristic of Macaulay, then MP for Edinburgh, that he should have postponed a visit to his constituency for a week in August 1844 to avoid having to attend the laying of the foundation-stone of the memorial by Hume. Although he 'by no means approved' the severity with which the government had treated the prisoners, neither did he admire the 'proceedings' of men whom he regarded as 'Republicans'. His real motive seems to have been to avoid 'another disagreeable controversy' with his constituents. G. O. Trevelyan, *Life and Letters of Lord Macaulay* (London, 1895), p. 468. For the whole controversy and the charges made against Margarot by Palmer in his *Narrative of the Sufferings of T. F. Palmer and W. Skirving* (Cambridge, 1797), see BL, Add. MSS. 27816.

200. 'Who make the laws? The rich – Who alone can, with probable impunity, break the laws? The rich – Who are impelled by want and misery to break them, and afterwards are imprisoned, transported and hanged? The poor – Who do the work? The poor – Who reap the fruits? The rich – Who pay the taxes? The poor, for their labours pay everything. Who impose the taxes? The rich, whose luxury devours what the labours of the poor produce. On what do the rich feed? On the product of the poor's misery. On what do the rich ride? – On the bent and half broken back of the poor – What supports the fine houses, parks and palaces of the rich? – The hunger and thirst of the poor. . . .' T. Holcroft, *Letter to the Rt. Hon. W. Windham on the intemperance and dangerous tendency of his public conduct* (London, 1795), p. 47.

201. For the evolution of class consciousness see Thompson, ch. 16.

202. E. P. Thompson, 'Working-class culture – the transition to industrialism', *Society for the Study of Labour History*, bulletin no. 8 (1964), p. 5.

to detect, at this period, any trace of the nineteenth-century consciousness of the identity of interest between working men of different occupations, though there were glimmerings of the common interests of workers as 'producers' as against their richer 'taskmasters'.[203] What had contributed to the political solidarity of working-class reformers in England and Scotland in the crisis of confrontation in 1793–4 was a common belief in the 'rights of man' and a determination to strengthen their resistance to the encroachment of reactionary forces on popular and constitutional liberties. The feeling of working-class solidarity and suspicion of the political stance adopted by the higher echelons of the 'friends of liberty' had also been enhanced by the exclusiveness and caution of the aristocratic Association of the Friends of the People in its approach to parliamentary reform and by the withdrawal of the middle-class industrialists from the political struggle between 1792 and 1795. The members of the London Corresponding Society at least had come a long way from their initial doubts of their right, as 'poor mechanics', even to associate, when in 1794 they were prepared to commit the English popular societies to a trial of strength with the government out of sympathy with the victims of Scottish judicial intemperance and in defence of the constitutional right of resistance. One other example of the enhanced self-confidence which went with the growing solidarity of the working-class reformers was the refusal of the popular societies to support the unrealistic efforts of the Whig clubs in 1796 to secure the repeal of the Two Acts, and their determination to work within the legal limits of the restricted but still acknowledged right of public meeting. But it took all the persuasiveness of Thelwall and all the legal acumen of the revived Society for Constitutional Information to enable the metropolitan radicals to maintain such a stand.

Such mature self-confidence and the no less necessary discretion were, however, also the product of the popular societies' concern with the political education of their members, whose exclusion from the electoral franchise was often justified as much by their ignorance of public affairs and of their own civic responsibilities as by their lack of property qualifications. Consciousness of the imperative need to remedy this acknowledged defect, when advocating universal suffrage, had been the driving force behind the Society for Constitutional Information from its earliest days, and from 1794 this role had automatically been assumed by the London Corresponding Society.

203. Holcroft, p. 47 and G. Dyer, *The Complaints of the Poor People of England* (London, 1793), p. 2.

In default of a 'well-digested system of NATIONAL EDUCATION', which he regarded as an essential ingredient in any 'effectual' (i.e. radical) parliamentary reform, Thomas Cooper had in 1792 advised 'the middling and poor classes of society' to establish meetings and clubs

not for riot or revelling, nor yet for Treason or Sedition, but for reading and conversation; that they may gradually become informed what are the rights and what are the duties of a Citizen; what privileges they are deprived of, to which they are fairly entitled; and in what respects their several situations require to be ameliorated by a more wise and equitable system of legislation.[204]

This advice had been part of the radical response to Dundas's Royal Proclamation against Seditious Writings and Publications, but it had also been directed against 'the time-serving, compromising, half-measured plan of reformation', advocated by the Whig Association of the Friends of the People.[205] 'Constitutional information' of the sort recommended by Cooper would enable those whom Burke had called 'a Swinish Multitude' to discern the total inadequacy of the plans for moderate reform canvassed by their pretended allies – the aristocratic Whig Opposition or by the Reverend Christopher Wyvill and his hesitant followers among the county freeholders of Yorkshire.[206]

In retrospect Francis Place mentioned other practical reasons why he had attached such cardinal importance to the educational role of the London Corresponding Society. Among the leaders of the society were some sanguine advocates of radical parliamentary reform who, in his view, needed to be disabused of the idea 'that Parliament might be induced to make a reform as extensive as that which they desired'.[207] Uncompromising exponents of Painite doctrine would have to recognize that Parliament would not readily agree to abolish either the hereditary monarchy or the House of Lords. Such views might well be altered as the result of discussion in the General Committee or in the democratic divisional meetings of the society. In the dark days of 1797 the opinion had grown that the system of 'Old Corruption' would continue unchanged 'until corruption had exhausted the means of corrupting' and that it would then collapse in chaos. Those

204. T. Cooper, *A Reply to Mr. Burke's Invective against Mr. Cooper and Mr. Watt in the House of Commons on 30 April, 1792* (Manchester, 1792), p. 78.
205. *Ibid.*, p. 79.
206. *Ibid.*, p. 74.
207. BL, Add. MSS. 35143, fo. 90.

who thought in this way considered, reasonably enough, that such a disaster would clear the way for the establishment of a system of representative government as outlined by Paine but that, before this happened, the people would have to be instructed in the principles and administrative implications of the new order.[208] Acquaintance with the conventions of the existing constitution and with the loopholes in Pitt's repressive legislation would also enable the radicals to refrain from collective acts which might involve their imprisonment without trial under the suspension of Habeas Corpus. Place rightly emphasized that after the State Trials of 1794 this policy had paid off, since the government had 'never dared to commence legal proceedings against it [the London Corresponding Society] or its officers – either for sedition or libel'.[209] Not all the popular societies had been so successful in this respect for, as Thomas Walker had reason to know from his own experience at Manchester, some had 'failed in the phraseological caution necessary in critical times'.[210] But he too gave it as his belief that

the sum and substance of all the hazard which the friends of freedom run, of all the evils which the people suffer, and of all the political iniquity, past, present and to come, is founded upon, and comprized in, the want of a complete and universal system of public education.[211]

Because neither church nor state had lived up to its responsibilities in this respect, the radical societies, in their own self interest, felt that they had to help to fill the gap themselves.

In the long run, however, Place was concerned to stress the material and moral benefits which had been won for the individual members of the London Corresponding Society. Education was then highly valued for the 'respectability' which it conferred on the journeymen and artisans who needed it to feel secure in their employment and to give them the chance of self-improvement.[212] The moral benefits, though less tangible, were even more formative.

208. *Ibid.*
209. *Ibid.*, fo. 92.
210. Walker, p. 126.
211. *Ibid.*, p. 127.
212. Place was more than gratified to learn, at the anniversary dinner of the acquittal of Hardy on 5 Nov. 1822, that of the twenty-four members then present who had been members of the LCS General Committee when he had been chairman no less than twenty had prospered in business and that some had attained a position of wealth and influence. Most of those with families were giving them a good education. BL, Add. MSS. 35143, fo. 95.

It induced men to read books, instead of wasting their time in public houses, it taught them to respect themselves, and to desire to educate their children. It elevated them in their own opinion. It taught them the great moral lesson '*to bear and to forbear*'. . . . The discussions in the divisions, in the Sunday evening readings, and in the small debating meetings, opened to them views which they had never before taken. They were compelled by these discussions to find reasons for their opinions, and to tolerate others. It gave a new stimulus to an immense number of men who had been but in too many instances incapable of any but the grossest pursuits, and seeking nothing beyond mere sensual enjoyments.[213]

Even the small number of 'benefit' societies which then existed in the metropolis always met in public houses and, according to Place, were essentially 'drinking clubs'.[214]

At the dawn of the new century, however, few of these advantages had been fully reaped – the popular societies were things of the past and the uncomplicated political tenets of Horne Tooke, Major Cartwright and Thelwall seemed old-fashioned and somehow irrelevant in the new and harsher environment created by the industrial revolution and the advent of peace. Whether we attribute their origins to fluctuations in the trade cycle, the difficulties of the 'take-off' in a period of rapid industrial expansion, the unprecedented growth and redistribution of the population, the economic dislocations inseparable from post-war depression, or to increasing capitalist exploitation of the labour force, the problems then demanding solution were both intricate and novel.[215] The condition of the domestic outworkers – the hand-loom weavers of the North-West, the framework knitters of the Midlands and the silk-weavers of Spitalfields – the need to regulate the employment of women and children in mines and factories, the fate of the impoverished field labourers and Poor Law reform: these were the issues which underlay the grave unrest and discontent among the industrial workers and agricultural labourers in the pre-Reform Bill period and which helped to shape the new and more class-conscious radicalism of the future.[216]

Until the thirties, however, when disillusionment with the failure to win the electoral franchise for the workers during the Reform Bill crisis caused popular interest to be transferred from political agita-

213. *Ibid.*, fo. 94.
214. BL, Place newspaper cuttings, vol. 36. 'A Retrospect of the last fifty or sixty years' (dated 21 Aug. 1847), introduction.
215. Thompson, *The Making of the English Working Class*, chs. 6–10.
216. Thompson, 'Working-class culture – the transition to industrialism'.

tion to Owenite socialism and the trade union movement, the various forms taken by post-war radicalism were still largely conditioned by tendencies and techniques inherited from the democratic movement of the 1790s. Even before 1815 moderate radicals had resumed the struggle for parliamentary reform, while a metropolitan group of Spencean republicans strove to precipitate a popular revolution and the acuteness of provincial distress resulted in large-scale demonstrations of public protest, or futile attempts to bring direct pressure to bear on Parliament. The short-lived movement for political reform confining its demands to the enfranchisement of all direct taxpayers and annual parliaments, was launched under the aristocratic auspices of Sir Francis Burdett, MP for Westminster. It marked a partial reversion to the political ideals of the Whig Association of the Friends of the People. The Hampden Clubs (1811–17),[217] which were designed to provide the movement with popular support in the provinces, owed something, on the other hand, to the earlier loose federation of local radical reform groups with the Society for Constitutional Information and their chief manager and publicist was the irrepressible Major Cartwright.[218] The links between the Revolutionary Party in London (1816–20) and the associates of Colonel Despard and the extremist faction of Spencean republicans were even closer.[219] The latter had maintained a continuous existence throughout the period of repression since the dissolution of the London Corresponding Society and among its members were Arthur Thistlewood, Thomas Preston and Charles Pendrill, who were the leading conspirators in the Cato St assassination plot of 1820.[220] The march of the Manchester Blanketeers (March 1817), the abortive Pentridge rising of Jeremiah Brandreth and his 'Regenerators' (June 1817), and the demonstration that led to the 'massacre of Peterloo' (August 1819), were examples of the diverse forms of radical activity, some legal and others insurrectionary, which derived their driving force from the grievances of the handloom weavers of Lancashire and the unemployed stockingers of the Midlands.[221]

217. The London Hampden Club was a gathering of 'men of wealth and influence' and was confined to owners of, or heirs to, a £300 rental from landed property – the qualification for candidature for the House of Commons.

218. It is worth noting that Cartwright's tours were the response to requests from local Hampden Clubs for contact with the London club in the days of Luddism. R. J. White, *Waterloo to Peterloo* (London, 1957), p. 135.

219. Parssinen, 'The Revolutionary Party in London', pp. 262–82.

220. *Ibid.*, p. 270.

221. On 9 June 1817 Brandreth led a small army of about 300 poorly armed

Each of these types of post-war radicalism absorbed and employed the techniques of organization, proselytism and agitation which had been pioneered in the 1790s – the summons of mass public meetings in the metropolis, the 'missionary tours' to tap and exploit popular support in the provinces, and the attempt to give a national or regional focus to such agitations by the holding of conventions of local delegates. The first of these devices to be deployed – the missionary tour – originally devised by the editors of the Sheffield *Patriot* – was revived by Major Cartwright in January and February 1813 when he visited no less than thirty-five towns in the north, Midlands and the west of England on behalf of the Hampden Club and collected over 400 reform petitions.[222] In July 1815 the club also despatched Thomas Cleary, who later became its secretary, on a tour of Wales, while Cartwright extended his propaganda activities to Scotland.[223] In 1816 the precedent was followed by an out-of-work Lancastrial printer, Joseph Mitchell, a self-appointed political evangelist of the society operating in south Lancashire, who managed to maintain himself by the sale of Cartwright's pamphlets and his own manual, *The A.B.C. of Politics*. On these tours Mitchell was accompanied by an eager 'apprentice' – the man who was to achieve notoriety as 'Oliver the Spy' at the time of the Pentridge rising.[224] All the leading demagogues of the first half of the nineteenth century – Cobbett, 'Orator Hunt' and the Chartist George Julian Harney – used this same means of taking radical issues and policies to the 'grass-roots' of provincial radicalism, or to effect contact with working-class movements, such as Chartism, whose origins were regional.[225]

Perhaps the best known, though hardly the most effective, method used by nineteenth-century 'agitators' to ventilate popular grievances,

---

men from the Derbyshire peak on a march to Nottingham – a stage on the route to the capital where it was hoped a 'provisional government' would be formed, the National Debt extinguished and relief measures undertaken. The party was dispersed on the outskirts of Nottingham by hussars and Brandreth and a few others were hanged. The rising was betrayed to the Home Office by Oliver the Spy. The best account is in Thompson, *Making of the English Working Class*, pp. 656–69.

222. G. S. Veitch, *The Genesis of Parliamentary Reform* (London, 1965 reprint), p. 346.

223. *Ibid.*, p. 345.

224. Thompson, *Making of the English Working Class*, pp. 651–3.

225. For the regional aspects of Chartism see Asa Briggs (ed.), *Chartist Studies* (London, 1959).

or to demonstrate the weight of public support behind their demands, was the holding of mass public meetings. These gatherings were, however, adapted to new needs and used for different purposes. Whereas the large 'general meetings' of the London Corresponding Society in 1795 had been primarily 'protest' meetings, those held after 1815 were also used for propaganda and promotional purposes and as the culmination of prolonged public debate on issues which had reached the point of decision – as in the 'May days' of 1832 or the Chartist crisis of 1848.[226] Such demonstrations called into existence a new brand of popular demagogues whose advent had been anticipated less by Thelwall than by John Gale Jones, though the latter was quickly eclipsed by 'Orator Hunt' and William Cobbett. The earliest resort to such mass meetings in the autumn of 1816 in Spa Fields, however, by the leaders of the Spencean republican party showed that they could not be employed with success to promote and precipitate clandestine revolutionary ends.[227] After that their purpose reverted to what it had been in the 1790s – the orderly and business-like discussion of radical resolutions on terms allowed by the law, to forward necessary changes in a legal and constitutional manner, though invoking at the same time the imposing moral force of a resolute, united and massive body of petitioners seeking redress from Parliament or King.[228]

The last device – the summons of general conventions of regional or national delegates – suffered from a number of practical disadvantages which crippled its effectiveness as a means of bringing pressure to bear on the executive. It was beset by a fundamental division of opinion between moderates who wished to confine its scope to that of the Wyvillite National Association of 1780, and Chartist extremists such as O'Connor, O'Brien and Harney who considered that a national convention of their delegates should, if the need arose, assume and exercise the sovereign power of an 'anti-Parliament'.[229] Apart from Paine's advocacy of a national convention to draft a written republican constitution, it had been the decision to declare

226. For the 'May days' of 1832 see J. R. M. Butler, *The Passing of the Great Reform Bill* (1964 reprint), ch. 9, and M. Brock, *The Great Reform Act* (London, 1973), ch. 8. For the Chartist crisis of 1848 see A. R. Schoyen, *The Chartist Challenge* (London, 1958), ch. 7, and F. C. Mather, *Public Order in the Age of the Chartists* (Manchester, 1959).

227. Parssinen, 'The Revolutionary Party in London', pp. 270–1.

228. Thompson, *The Making of the English Working Class*, p. 670.

229. T. M. Parssinen, 'Association, convention and anti-parliament in British radical politics, 1771–1848', *English Historical Review*, vol. 88 (1973), p. 528.

the sessions of the British Convention at Edinburgh 'permanent', on the eve of its forcible dissolution in December 1793, which had furnished a precedent for the latter concept.[230] Its acceptance was later facilitated by the appeal made by James Watson, a metropolitan Spencean in 1818 to the 'non-represented people' of Britain and the attempted usurpation of the powers and functions of MPs by so-called 'legislational attorneys'.[231] The election of such phantom representatives by large numbers of unqualified voters in a few great industrial centres was clearly illegal and might, if generally followed, have given birth to a rival assembly, though with dubious prospects and problematical finances. The fear that the Manchester radicals might, despite their disclaimers, follow the example of Birmingham, where 50,000 'non-represented' supporters had 'elected' Sir Charles Wolesley as their 'legislational attorney' on 12 July 1819 helped, however, to precipitate the Peterloo Massacre on 16 August.[232]

A further incentive for the adoption of such 'revolutionary' expedients was provided by the radical economists of the 1820s, who developed the theory of the capitalistic exploitation of labour.[233] This was utilized by William Benbow to justify his proposal for the calling of a general strike (or 'national holiday') of the 'productive classes' and the election of an omnicompetent 'National Congress'.[234] All such attempts to circumvent the legal processes of parliamentary General Elections were, however, always subject to proclamation by the executive and this, when supported by the forcible dispersion of preparatory meetings or assemblies, was usually sufficient to render them abortive.[235]

The specific weaknesses of this questionable means of extorting

230. See above, p. 304. On 23 April 1839 O'Connor stated that if the petition for the charter were rejected, the Chartists Convention should also 'declare its sittings permanent'.

231. Parssinen, 'Association, convention and anti-parliament', pp. 516–17.

232. *Ibid.*, p. 516.

233. Thomas Hodgkin, William Thompson and John Gray in particular used Ricardo's labour theory of value and Colquhoun's distinction between the productive and non-productive classes to formulate the theory of exploitation. H. L. Beales, *The Early English Socialists* (London, 1933), ch. 5.

234. W. Benbow, *Grand National Holiday and Congress of the Productive Classes*. Benbow was a leading member of the ultra-radical National Union of Working Classes.

235. The 'Battle of Cold Bath Fields' (13 May 1833), when an attempt was made by a mass meeting to convene a National Congress and organize a general strike was broken up by the police. Parssinen, 'Association, convention and anti-Parliament', pp. 520–1.

concessions from the government were highlighted by the meeting of the Chartist General Convention of the Industrious Classes in London in February 1839.[236] A firm stand by the ministry of Lord Melbourne quickly exposed the advocates of confrontation to all the perplexities, pressures and irresolution inseparable from their unpreparedness for personal martyrdom. 'Brinkmanship' – the essence of O'Connor's tactical approach – did not pay off, and the failure of the extremists to secure adequate backing for a series of 'ulterior measures' with revolutionary implications rendered inevitable successive strategic retreats which ended in a debacle.[237] In May the Chartist convention was transferred from London to Birmingham, then regarded as a radical arsenal, but in June it was adjourned till September, to allow its constituents to be consulted on the implementation of the proposed general strike if the Chartist petition were rejected. But when Parliament rejected the petition on 12 July and the government arrested Dr Taylor, McDougall, Lovett and Collins, and when it became clear that their provincial supporters had no appetite for a general strike, the delegates decided, amid general recrimination, to dissolve the convention.[238] After this setback the experiment was not renewed until May 1848, when a Chartist National Assembly in London, convened to organize resistance against the repeated rejection of the Charter, encountered similar difficulties.[239] The consequent fiasco resulted in the final abandonment of the idea of a convention as an institution of last resort in a crisis of confrontation. The concept had, in fact, come to be as much a radical myth as Cartwright's invocation of Anglo-Saxon constitutionalism – a powerful morale-booster, but powerless as a weapon of intimidation.[240]

Francis Place, who had helped to draft the People's Charter in 1838, had himself been the foremost critic of all these devices during his apprenticeship to radical politics as chairman of the General Committee of the London Corresponding Society.[241] Despite his outstanding services to Westminster electoral radicalism between 1807

236. Schoyen, ch. 3.
237. Parssinen, 'Association, convention and anti-parliament', pp. 521–8.
238. *Ibid.*, p. 527.
239. *Ibid.*; p. 531. Dr I. Prothero, in his important article, 'Chartism in London', *Past and Present* (Aug. 1969), pp. 76–105, makes the point that it was only after the arrival of this convention in London that Chartism attained significance in the capital. He also traces the traditions of artisan radicalism in the metropolis back to the 1790s. *Ibid.*, pp. 85–97.
240. *Ibid.*, p. 532.
241. See above, p. 372.

and 1827, his marshalling of popular pressure on Parliament in the Reform Bill crisis and his active sponsorship of 'Moral Force' Chartism, Place's reputation as a champion of the working class rests securely on his sustained and many-sided contribution to the cause of popular and adult education, the successful campaign for the repeal of the Combination Laws, which he masterminded in 1824, and his spirited leadership in the fight for an unstamped press, which triumphed in 1836.[242] His lifelong conviction that the people would only achieve their full political objectives by co-operating with middle-class radicals and sympathizers was corroborated by the failure of the working classes to benefit from the extension of the franchise in 1832 and even more by the Chartist discomfiture in 1848.[243] Once radical leaders had recognized the need for such assistance, the way for further parliamentary reform and the eventual attainment of the Chartist programme lay open. It was this lesson which the failure of Chartism in 1848 enforced.[244]

The ultimate consequences were as extensive as the early parliamentary reformers had led their followers to expect. The welfare state, the deep-seated concern for social justice, civic and legal equality, full religious toleration, the continuing insistence on human rights, the right of association, public meeting and free speech, national self-determination, the freedom of trade unions from state regulation or legal repression, the solidarity of the working class in industrial disputes and across national frontiers, the right to protest and participate, female emancipation and the right to strike – all these policies and principles had been conceived and pioneered by the eighteenth-century 'friends of liberty'. As Thelwall had anticipated, the harvest sown by the democratic impulse, postponed in his own day, was at length safely gathered in. Even the sceptical Horne Tooke, who died in March 1812, before any radical Utopias had been fulfilled or instalments of reform conceded, in choosing for himself the comforting epitaph 'Content and Grateful', may have felt that time was on the side of those who were then still being persecuted as English Jacobins.[245]

242. Wallas; Patricia Hollis, *The Pauper Press: A Study in Working Class Radicalism of the 1830s* (Oxford, 1970), ch. 3.

243. F. C. Mather, *Chartism*, Historical Association pamphlet, general series, no. 61 (1965), pp. 18–23.

244. *Ibid.*, p. 27.

245. BL. Add. MSS. 27818, fo. 12.

Appendix 1   Three versions of the London Corresponding Society's *Joint Address to the French National Convention, 27 September 1792*

The original[1]

Address to the French National Convention from the following societies of Britons, united in one common cause; namely the obtaining a fair, equal, and impartial Representation in Parliament.

Manchester Constitutional Society	{ Tho. Walker, Pres. { Sam. Jackson, Sec.
Manchester Reformation Society	John Stacey, Sec.
Norwich Revolution Society	{ Tho. Goff, Pres. { John Cozens, Sec.
London Constitutional Whigs, Independent and Friends of the People.[2]	{ Geo. Puller, Chair. { James Bly, Sec.

Authorized by our United Brethren above named, We the London Corresponding Society, for them as well as for ourselves, thus address you:
FRENCHMEN,

While foreign robbers are ravaging your Territories under the specious pretext of Justice, cruelty and devastation lead on their van, while perfidy with treachery bring up their rear, yet mercy and friendship are impudently held forth to the world as the sole motives of their incursions; the oppressed part of mankind, forgetting for a while their own sufferings, feel only for yours, and with an anxious eye watch the ultimate event, fervently supplicating the Supreme Ruler of the Universe to be favourable to your cause, so intimately blended with their own.

Frowned upon by an oppressive system of controul, whose gradual but

1. BL, Add. MSS. 27814, fos. 45–6. Annotated in Hardy's hand: 'The following printed Address to the French National Convention is a true copy, written by Mr. Margarot.'
2. In his notes on the English radical societies in the Metropolis in November 1792 Captain Monro noted that the members of this society had been 'particularly industrious in endeavouring to corrupt the soldiery'. It was said to be 'united for obtaining equal liberty and a Parliamentary reform'. PRO TS 11/959/3505(ii).

continual encroachments have deprived this Nation of nearly all its boasted liberty, and brought us almost to that abject state of slavery from which you have so gloriously emerged, a few thousands of British Citizens indignant, manfully step forward to rescue their country from the opprobrium brought upon it by the supine conduct of those in power; they conceive it to be the duty of Britons to countenance and to assist to the utmost of their power, the champions of human happiness, and to swear to a Nation proceeding on the plan which you have adopted, an inviolable Friendship, – sacred from this day be that friendship between us! and may vengeance to the uttermost overtake the man who shall hereafter attempt to cause a rupture!

Though we appear comparatively so few at present, be assured Frenchmen, that our number encreases daily – it is true that the stern uplifted arm of authority at present keeps back the timid, that busily circulated impostures hourly mislead the credulous, and that court intimacy with avowed French Traitors has some effect on the unwary and ambitious. But with certainty we can inform you, Friends and Freemen, that information makes a rapid progress among us; Curiosity has taken possession of the public mind; the conjoint reign of ignorance and despotism passes away. Men now ask each other, what is Freedom? What are our Rights? Frenchmen, you are already free, and Britons are preparing to become so.

Casting far from us the criminal prejudices artfully inculcated by evil-minded men and wily Courtiers, we, instead of natural enemies, at length discover in Frenchmen our Fellow Citizens of the World, and our Brethren by the same heavenly Father, who created us for the purposes of loving, and mutually assisting each other; but not to hate, and to be ever ready to cut each other's throats at the command of weak or ambitious Kings, and corrupt Ministers.

Seeking our real enemies, we find them in our bosoms. We feel ourselves inwardly torn by, and ever the victims of a restless, all-consuming Aristocracy, hitherto the bane of every Nation under the Sun: – Wisely have you acted in expelling it from France.

Warm as are our wishes for your success, eager as we are to behold Freedom triumphant, and Man everywhere restored to the enjoyment of his just rights, a sense of our duty as orderly Citizens forbids our flying in arms to your assistance; Our government has pledged the National Faith to remain neutral. In a struggle of Liberty against Despotism, Britons remain neutral. O shame! But we have entrusted our King with discretionary powers, we therefore must obey. Our hands are bound, but our hearts are free, and they are with you.

Let German Despots act as they please, we shall rejoice at their fall; compassionating, however, their enslaved subjects, we hope this tyranny of their Masters will prove the means of reinstating, in the full possession of their Rights and Liberties, millions of our Fellow Creatures. With unconcern, therefore, we might view the Elector of

Hanover join his troops to Traitors and Robbers: But the King of Great Britain will do well to remember that this country is not Hanover – should he forget this distinction, we will not.

While you enjoy the envied glory of being the unaided Defenders of Freedom, we fondly anticipate in idea the numerous blessings, which mankind will enjoy, if you succeed, as we ardently wish. The Triple Alliance not of crowns, but of the people of America, France and Britain, will give Freedom to Europe and Peace to the World! Dear Friends, you combat for the advantage of the Human Race! how well purchased will be, though at the expence of much blood, the glorious, the unprecedented privilege of saying, 'Mankind is free! Tyrants and Tyranny are no more! Peace reigns on the Earth! and this is the work of Frenchmen.'

The desire of having the concurrence of different Country Societies to this Address, has occasioned a month's delay in presenting it. Success unparalleled has now attended your arms. We congratulate you thereon – that success has removed our anxiety, but it has no otherways influenced our sentiments in your behalf.

Remember, Frenchmen, that although this testimony of friendship only now reaches your Assembly, it bears date the 27th of September 1792.

(Signed by order)

> MAURICE MARGAROT, President
> THOMAS HARDY, Secretary.

French text as read in the National Convention, 7 November 1792[3]

This text is, on the whole, an accurate and faithful translation of the original, with no forced constructions, and is as literal a rendering, consistent with the observance of the more formal conventions of French grammatical usage, as could be desired.

Its opening paragraph is enough to demonstrate this:

Tandis que des brigands étrangers, sous le spécieux prétexte de venger la justice, ravagent votre territoire, portent partout la désolation et la mort; tandis qu'aussi traîtres que perfides, ils ont l'imprudence de proclamer que la compassion et l'amitié sont les seuls motifs de leurs incursions, la partie opprimée de l'humanité, oubliant ses propres maux, ne sent que les vôtres, et contemplant d'un oeil inquiet les événements, adresse au Dieu de l'univers les prières les plus ferventes pour qu'ils soient favorables à votre cause, à laquelle la leur est si intimement liée.

In a very few instances there are clear divergences, e.g. in the second paragraph 'a few thousands of British citizens' appears as

3. Reproduced in *Moniteur*, vol. 14, p. 411.

'*cinq milles citoyens anglais*', probably reflecting further information supplied at the time when the address was presented.

More interesting, however, are the differences which are in no sense intentional distortions, but efforts to tighten up the logical imprecision or grammatical incoherence of the original. The final effect, nevertheless, is to make a rather vague or innocuous phrase appear more challenging or rhetorically abrasive. For example, the opening of the second paragraph – 'Frowned upon by an oppressive system of controul' – becomes '*Avilis par un système oppresseur d'inquisition*'. The conclusion of the same paragraph – 'Sacred from this day be that friendship between us! and may vengeance to the uttermost overtake the man who shall hereafter attempt to cause a rupture!' – is rendered, quite accurately, but rather more stridently, as: '*Puisse dès ce jour cette amitié être sacrée entre nous, et puisse la vengeance la plus éclatante tomber sur la tête de l'homme qui tentera d'occasionner une rupture!*'

Similarly, paragraph five in the original: 'Seeking our real enemies, we find them in our bosoms. We feel ourselves inwardly torn by, and ever the victims of a restless, all-consuming Aristocracy, hitherto the bane of every Nation under the Sun: – Wisely have you acted in expelling it from France.' Literally translated this would be meaningless in French, and so the sense is given as: '*En cherchant nos ennemis cruels, nous les trouvons dans les partisans de cette aristocratie dévorante qui déchire notre sein, aristocratie qui, jusqu'à présent, a été le poison de tous les pays sur la terre. Vous avez agi sagement en la banissant de la France.*'

Cumulatively, such slight alterations in the phraseology, besides making the Address more intelligible to its French audience, involved some distortion of the original English, sufficient, at least, to make it sound more uncompromisingly caustic or implacable in tone, and more Gallic in sentiment.

The English version printed in 'A Collection of Addresses transmitted by certain English Clubs and Societies to the National Convention of France'[4]

This *Collection* was published, probably at Treasury expense, by Reeves's Association for the Preservation of Liberty and Property against Republicans and Levellers, and was intended to provide the government and public with proof positive of the extent of radical

4. (London, 1793), pp. 6–8.

commitment to the cause of French republicanism. According to Sheridan's evidence in cross-examination at the Old Bailey on the occasion of the trial of Thomas Hardy for high treason on 3 November 1794, copies of this publication had been made available to all members of both houses of parliament shortly before 28 February 1793, when he had moved in the Commons for the appointment of a committee to inquire into the alleged seditious proceedings of the reform societies.[5] He had shown Hardy the *Collection* and sought his opinion of it. Hardy had replied that 'it calumniated the society he belonged to, and its proceedings' in so far as it mis-stated its object, which was simply 'a parliamentary reform according to the plan of the Duke of Richmond'.[6]

The English text of the LCS's joint address to the National Convention, as given in this publication, is an almost literal retranslation from the French version, as it appears in the *Moniteur*. The result is that all the revolutionary rhetorical overtones of the French text are reproduced. It is, perhaps, a moot point whether this final product of double translation gave a more accurate representation of what the members of the French National Convention actually heard than the original English version. It certainly served the purpose of the Reevite association better.

The passages of the original text and of the French version previously discussed appear in the *Collection of Addresses* as follows, with the opening of the second paragraph reading: 'Degraded by an oppressive system of Inquisition' ('*Avilis par un système oppresseur d'inquisition*' in the French translation); and its close as 'May that friendship be from this day sacred between us – may the most exemplary vengeance fall on the head of that man who shall attempt to dissolve it.' Here again the French version is literally rendered back into English with the consequent distortion.

As paragraph five we find in the *Collection*: 'Endeavouring to discover our cruel enemies, we have found them in that destructive Aristocracy by which our bosom is torn, an Aristocracy which has hitherto been the bane of all the Countries of the Earth. You have acted wisely in banishing it from France.'

It is also noticeable that the figure of 'five thousand' instead of 'a few thousands' appears in the English version of the *Collection* – being again imported from the French text.

One slightly more suspect alteration occurs in the first paragraph of

5. *ST*, vol. 24, cols. 1100–2.
6. *ST*, vol. 24, col. 1101.

the Address – where Margarot's 'the oppressed part of mankind' (*'la partie opprimée de l'humanité'* in the French version) is given in the *Collection* as 'an oppressed part of mankind'. If the alteration is intentional – as seems probable – an attempt is being made here to suggest that the phrase alludes to the condition of the English radicals rather than to that of the victims of repression in general – a slight, but significant and loaded, variation of the original.

Finally, Hardy's complaint that the *Collection of Addresses* misrepresented the object of the London Corresponding Society would seem to be borne out by its omission of the prelude to the Address – i.e. all the words in the original English text defining its political purpose as 'the obtaining a fair, equal, and impartial Representation in Parliament'.

Appendix 2   List of addresses from English reform societies to the French National Convention (November, December 1792)

Notes to the table overleaf appear on pages 510–12

Abbreviations: BL (British Library); PRO (Public Record Office); *EHR* (*English Historical Review*); *Collection of Addresses* (*Collection of Addresses transmitted by certain English Clubs and Societies to the National Convention of France* (1793); AN (Archives Nationales, Paris); AAE (Archives du Ministère des Affaires Étrangères, Paris); CPA (Correspondence Politique, Angleterre).

Origin	Date	Transmitted	Read in National Convention	Versions	Source
London Corresponding Society (see Note 1 overleaf)	27/9/1792	via Chauvelin	7/11/1792	a Copy of original b French reprint c Retranslation	BL Add. MSS. 27814, fo. 45 Moniteur, vol. 14 (411) Collection of Addresses pp. 6–8
Newington Friends of the People	31/10/1792	?	10/11/1792	a Original b French version c Retranslation	AN C240 (275) Ibid. Collection of Addresses, pp. 1–2
Sheffield Constitutional Society (see Note 2 overleaf)	Undated ? 31/10/1792	via LCS and Chauvelin	22/11/1792	a Original not known b French Ms. version of original	AN C.240 (275–6)
London Revolution Society	5/11/1792	? Via Chauvelin	1/12/1792	a Original not known b English reprint c English version	Annual Register, 1792, p. 349 Collection of Addresses, pp. 3–4
Society for Constitutional Information (see Note 3 overleaf)	9/11/1792	by Frost and Barlow as delegates	28/11/1792	a MS. copy of original b French MS. version c Retranslation	PRO TS11/962/3508, fos. 116–17 AN C241 (278) Collection of Addresses, pp. 12–15

Assembly of Volunteers and Inhabitants of Belfast	6/11/1792	?	29/11/1792	*a* Original not known *b* French version *c* Retranslation	*Moniteur* *Collection of Addresses* pp. 11–12
Aldgate Friends of the People	12/11/1792	via Chauvelin	3/12/1792	*a* Original *b* French version *c* French version	AN C242 289–90, fo. 19 *Ibid.*, fo. 18 AAE (CPA) 583, fos. 373–4
Rochester	20/11/1792	via Lebrun French Foreign Minister	29/11/1792	*a* Copy of French original *b* Retranslation	AAE (CPA) 583, fo. 263 *Collection of Addresses*, pp. 18–19
English, Irish and Scottish Residents in Paris	24/11/1792	by delegates	28/11/1792	*a* Original *b* French version *c* Reprint of original	ANC 241 (278) *Ibid.* *EHR*, vol. 13 (1898), pp. 673–4
Derby	20/11/1792	by delegates H. Yorke and Dr W. Brooks Johnson	? early Dec. 1792	*a* Reprint	BL Place newspaper cuttings, vol. 36, fo. 15
Nottingham (see Note 4, p. 511)	early Nov. 1792	by delegates Yorke and Johnson	? early Dec. 1792	No text available but in support of LCS address	PRO TS11/965/3510A.
Friends of the Rights of Man Associated at Paris (see Note 5, p. 512)	? late Dec. 1792	? direct	? 10/1/1793	No text available	O. Browning (ed.), *Despatches of Lord Gower 1790–1792*, p. 277

(1) This was the joint address originally suggested by Margarot as president of the LCS on 15 September 1792. It was approved and countersigned by the officials of the Manchester Constitutional and Reformation Societies, the Norwich Revolution Society and London Constitutional Whigs, Independent and Friends of the People. It represented the signatures of 5000 (including 2000 from Norwich). It was subsequently approved by the newly instituted societies at Nottingham and Stockport.

(2) The Sheffield Address, perhaps the most outspoken and un-compromising of the whole series, and supposedly representing the signatures of over 20,000 merchants, manufacturers, workmen and artisans, has so far not been properly identified. The *Moniteur* (vol. 14, col. 543) mistakenly attributed it to the London Revolution Society; Dr Robinet fathered it on the Society for Constitutional Information (*Danton Émigré* (Paris, 1887), p. 53) and even Veitch thought it must have come from some London society other than the LCS or SCI (*Genesis of Parliamentary Reform* (London, 1965), p. 228).

(3) Holland Rose mistakenly asserted that Barlow and Frost were delegates for the LCS! (*Pitt and the Great War* (London 1912), p. 80) and also that the SCI had approved the idea of a joint address (p. 66), whereas it had insisted on drafting its own address. These slips were repeated by H. W. C. Davis in his *Age of Grey and Peel* (London, 1929), p. 80. It would also seem worth while correcting Veitch's tentative and conjectural account of the SCI's 'patriotic gift' of several thousand pairs of shoes to the French armies, about the completion of which he remained sceptical.[1] As has been seen earlier (page 254), the suggestion that the proceeds of subscriptions raised in England in support of the French should be used for the despatch of shoes, rather than arms, had come, indirectly, from France, where the government was receiving constant complaints from Dumouriez of the defects of army clothing and equipment resulting from the peculation and corruption of war contractors.[2]

1. Veitch, pp. 226–7.
2. Ch. 7 above, p. 254. A petition from the General Assembly of the Section du Louvre to the President of the National Convention, dated 9 November 1792, drew his attention to the shoddy condition of some of the soldiers' shoes and requested him to ensure that French deputies should not content themselves with speeches on the futility of monarchy, but realize that the Republic would need to be established on firmer foundations than on cardboard! AN C240 (275/6).

This information was already in the hands of the SCI when, on 9 November 1792, it decided to launch a new subscription of its own 'for the purpose of assisting the efforts of France in the cause of Freedom'.[3] A week later, on 16 November, the society appointed an executive committee of twelve, with Christopher Hull as treasurer, to organize the subscription which was also thrown open to the public.[4] From Hull's account-book as treasurer found among papers seized from Secretary Adams at the time of his arrest in 1794, it appears that this second subscription realized just over £820 and that the whole amount was used to purchase shoes from Thomas Hardy at the rate of £3 per dozen pairs.[5] A thousand pairs would thus have cost about £250 and at least 3000 pairs must have been bought for £750. Assuming that the proceeds of the earlier subscription (which had stood at £1151. 1s. 6d. on 13 September 1792) had been utilized in the same way, a further 4000 pairs would have been available for despatch to France.[6]

At the time when the SCI subscription was wound up in April 1793 the society still had 1098 pairs of shoes on its hands, so that about 2000 pairs had been despatched.[7] In all, it would seem probable that 7000 pairs had been bought, of which 6000 pairs reached their destination. Some confirmation of this was given when the National Convention approved a recommendation from its diplomatic committee, on 17 February 1793, that the honour of French citizenship should be conferred on Joel Barlow. Among the reasons for this recognition was that Barlow had been concerned in the SCI's 'don patriotique' of 6000 pairs of shoes which, the citation noted, *'ont passé de Calais à l'armée'*.[8]

About half of the shoes which had not been sent were sold by Hardy on behalf of the contributors and the rest purchased for his own business at a small loss to the society. Though Hardy still owed the SCI £148 on this account at the time of his arrest, the society was able to repay the smaller contributors to the subscription in full in accordance with its resolution of 13 April 1793.[9]

(4) Veitch said 'no trace' of this address, and another from Man-

3. PRO TS11/962/3508.
4. *Ibid.*
5. PRO TS11/952/3496(ii).
6. PRO TS11/951/3495.
7. PRO TS11/952/3496(ii).
8. AN F⁷4395.
9. PRO TS11/962/3508.

chester referred to in Monro's despatches from Paris, had been found (p. 230).

(5) Little or nothing is known about this address except that it provoked a schism in the society. The articles and declaration of the society dated 'December 4, FIRST YEAR OF THE FRENCH REPUBLIC' are reprinted in British Library, *Political Broadsides*, 648 C 26 (50).

Appendix 3 Numbers and location of provincial radical societies in Great Britain in 1797

Some idea of the approximate numbers and geographical distribution of the provincial radical societies in England, Scotland and Wales in 1797 may be gained from two lists printed in the *Report of the Lords' Committee of Secrecy relative to a Treasonable Conspiracy, May 27, 1799 (Parl. Hist.* XXXIV, 1005–6). The first is described as a 'list of the United Corresponding Societies of Great Britain in the year 1797, found in the possession of a person, sometime a member of the Executive Committee'. The societies are listed as follows:

Portsmouth √	Bristol √	Gravesend √	Hull
Newcastle-under-Lyme	Loughborough √	Maidstone √	Grantham
	Wolver-	Rochester √	Southampton
Salford √	hampton	Chatham	Kendal
Manchester √	Stourbridge √	Bromley √	Wooton
Sheffield √	Wakefield √	Cardiff √	Kegworth
Norwich √	Melbourne √	Woodchurch √	Banbury √
Bradford √	Leicester √	Truro	Adderbury √
Nottingham √	Edinburgh √	Derby √	Tamworth
Birmingham √	Glasgow √	Litchfield	Stockport √
Halifax √	Perth √	Redbridge	Warrington √
St Albans √	Dundee √	Leeds √	Gosport
Exeter √	Paisley √	Chichester	Ipswich
Chester √	Helstone √	Liverpool √	Philips-Norton
High Wycombe	Berwick √	Jedburgh	Ashton-under-
Whitchurch √	Newcastle	Sunbury	Lyne √
Leominster	upon Tyne √	Kilmarnock	Coventry √
York √	Oxford √	Stranraer	Tunbridge √
Bath √	Chevening √	Rowley	Rochdale √

According to the second list, the London Corresponding Society had corresponded with forty-seven of the seventy-two societies in the first list (those marked with a tick), and also with Cradley, Deptford,

Ashton, Trowbridge, Aston, Dudley, Battle, Woolwich, Linsfield, Finsbury, Crawley, Craley, Framlingham, Garstang, Sevenoaks and Chevinam.[1] Assuming that reform societies also existed in these places, the two lists would indicate a total of eighty-eight societies, or eighty-nine with the London Corresponding Society.

1797, however, marked the nadir of the British democratic movement, many societies having ceased to meet as a result of the Seditious Meetings and Treasonable Practices Acts of 1795 and, in 1798, a final decline set in, hardly compensated for by the sporadic growth in the North-West and in London of the clandestine United English societies.

Although reliable statistics for 1795 – the peak year – are difficult to come by, a total of over 100 societies may be taken as probable, not reckoning the separate divisions of the Sheffield and Norwich societies and those of the London Corresponding Society and its 'break-away' offshoots.[2]

With a total 'paper' membership of 10,000 at the end of 1795, the LCS registered weekly attendance figures in the divisions of from 700 to 1100. The figure of 10,000, however, included all who had joined the society since its inception, though 'vast numbers' had resigned in the aftermath of the treason trials, or had ceased to attend meetings after the passage of the Two Acts.[3] What the effective, as distinct from the nominal, membership of the society was at any particular date has remained largely a matter of conjecture.[4]

1. 'As appears by the papers found in the possession of their secretary and at the General Committee room at the Queen of Bohemia's Head' (April, 1798). *Parl. Hist.*, vol. 34, cols. 1005–6.

2. A similar conclusion is reached by W. A. L. Seaman in 'British democratic societies in the period of the French revolution', unpublished PhD thesis, London (1954), p. 20.

3. Report of James Powell, government spy, to the Home Office, 6 Jan. 1796. PRO PC 1/23/A 38.

4. E. P. Thompson, *The Making of the English Working Class* (London, 1965), pp. 153–4.

Select bibliography

Primary sources: manuscripts

The British Library, Additional Manuscripts

Place papers
27808: Notes on the London Corresponding Society (LCS); the 'Pop-Gun' plot and documents for a memoir of Spence
27809: Place collections on political societies, 1792–1832
27811: Letter-book of the LCS, 27 Oct. 1791–23 March 1793.
27812: Minute and letter-book of the LCS, 2 April 1792–2 Jan. 1794
27813: Minute and letter-book of the LCS, 23 April–10 Sept. 1795
N.B: there are no minutes of the LCS extant from 2 Jan 1794–23 April 1795.
27814: Sketch of the history of the LCS by Thomas Hardy
27815: Correspondence of the LCS, 2 July 1795–30 Nov. 1797
27816: Public prosecutions, 1793, 1794 and 1798
27818: Draft letters of Thomas Hardy
35142: Autobiography of Francis Place
35143: Autobiography of Francis Place
35154: Autobiography of Francis Place

Association for the Preservation of Liberty and Property against Republicans and Levellers
16919–31

Public Record Office

Home Office papers
HO 42 (domestic): 18–48 (Jan. 1791–June 1799); 61–70 (Feb. 1801–Dec. 1802)

HO 43 (out letters): 3–11 (1791–1800)
HO 102 (Scotland): 5–11 (Jan. 1792–Dec. 1794)
HO 100 (Ireland): 37–86 (March 1792–Dec. 1800)

Assize papers, NE Circuit
45/37: Trials of Sheffield rioters, 1791

Privy Council papers
PC 1 19 A 23: Birmingham riots 1791
PC 1 19 A 27: J. H. Stone correspondence from Paris, 1792
PC 1 22 A 35(a): LCS papers marked 'Treason', 1794
PC 1 22 A 35(b): LCS papers marked 'Treason', 1794
PC 1 22 A 36(a): Examination of witnesses 1794. Draft minutes
PC 1 22 A 36(b): Examination of witnesses 1794. Draft minutes
PC 1 22 1 36(c): Examination of witnesses 1794. Draft minutes
PC 1 22 A 37: 'Treason'. Corresponding Societies, Oct./Dec. 1794
PC 1 23 A 38: Powell's reports on LCS Executive and General
    Committees. July 1795–Dec. 1796
PC 1 28 A 62: 'Treason'. Corresponding Societies, Jan.–July 1795
PC 1 31 A 77
PC 1 34 A 90: 'Treason', 1796
PC 1 38 A 117
PC 1 38 A 123: Barlow's reports on radical societies, 1797
PC 1 40 A 129: Corresponding Societies, 1797
PC 1 40 A 132: Corresponding Societies, 1797
PC 1 40 A 133: Corresponding Societies, 1797
PC 1 41 A 136: United English society in Manchester
PC 1 41 A 138: Papers of the LCS seized at Wych St, Clerkenwell,
    19 April 1798
PC 1 41 A 139: Seizure of Manchester radicals, 1798
PC 1 42 A 140: Seizure of Manchester radicals, 1798
PC 1 42 A 143: Papers relating to O'Connor, 1798
PC 1 42 A 144: United Englishmen, 1798
PC 1 43 A 150: 'Treason'. Corresponding Societies, Oct./Dec. 1798
PC 1 43 A 152: LCS, United Irish and Jacobin societies in London,
    Jan. 1799
PC 1 44 A 153: Corresponding Societies. Depositions, Feb.–March
    1799
PC 1 44 A 155: Corresponding Societies. Depositions, Feb.–March
    1799. Papers relating to Ireland, April 1799
PC 1 44 A 158: Depositions, May–July 1799

PC 1 44 A 161: Depositions, Aug–Oct. 1799. Col. Despard
PC 1 44 A 164   (Pt. 1): Reports. Corresponding Societies, Nov.–
Dec. 1799

PC 1 3514
PC 1 3526
PC 1 3528
PC 1 3535 ⎬ 'Treason' and Corresponding Societies, 1800–2
PC 1 3536A
PC 1 3582

Treasury Solicitor's Papers

TS11/1133: Minute-book of the Society for Constitutional Informa-
tion (SCI), 1780–3
TS11/961/3507: Minute-book of the SCI, 14 March 1783–7 Oct. 1791
TS11/962/3508: Minute-book of the SCI, 9 Dec. 1791–9 May 1794
TS11/41/150: (1792) Outlawry of Sampson Perry for publishing *Argus*
TS11/41/151: (1792) Ridgeway prosecution for publishing Painite
literature
TS11/541/1755: (1796–7) Prosecution for treason. Gale Jones and
Binns
TS11/547/1777: (1794) 'Pop-Gun' plot
TS11/555/1793: (1795/6) Trial of W. Stone for High Treason
TS11/689/2187: (1798) Trial of O'Coigley for High Treason
TS11/836/2820: (1792) Prosecution of D. Holt for Painite publica-
tions
TS11/892/3035: (1794) Indictment and trial of T. Walker for con-
spiracy, Manchester
TS11/932/3304: (1791) Priestley riots, Birmingham
TS11/944/3430: (1795) Riots (food)
TS11/951/3495: (1794) Sheffield Constitutional Society. LCS Address
to National Convention
TS11/952/3496(i): (1794)
TS11/952/3496(ii): (1794) SCI papers. Norwich. Thelwall
TS11/953/3497: (1794) LCS correspondence with British Conven-
tion, Edinburgh, 1793
TS11/954/3498: (1794) Spy reports on LCS and the SCI, 1794.
Hardy's correspondence with Scottish radicals
TS11/955/3499: (1794) Spy reports on Thelwall's lectures, Jan.–May
1794
TS11/955/3500: (1794) Summons of radical convention
TS11/956/3501: (1793) Relations of LCS with Scotland

TS11/956/3501(ii): (1794) Secret Committee of England. Address to French Executive Directory

TS11/957/3502: (1794) Examinations of radicals before Privy Council

TS11/958/3504: (1794) Prosecution of Horne Tooke for High Treason

TS11/959/3505(i): (1794) Spencer Perceval's opinion on prosecution of the SCI. Spy reports on the LCS divisions

TS11/959/3505(ii): (1794)

TS11/960/3506(i): (1794) Thelwall. Baxter and SCI attitude to summons of a convention

TS11/963/3509: (1794) Hardy's examination before Privy Council

TS11/964/3510: (1794) Index of correspondence of officials of radical societies

TS11/965/3510A: (1794)

TS11/966/3510B: (1794)

TS11/978/3560: Proceedings against Daniel Isaac Eaton

Foreign Office papers
France
FO 27/40: Spy reports on English residents in Paris, Aug.–Dec. 1792
Hamburg and Hanse Towns
FO 33/15: Correspondence with Sir James Crauford, March–Aug. 1798
FO 33/16: Correspondence with Sir James Crauford, Aug.–Dec. 1798

Manchester

Chetham's Library
Constitution and Minutes of Committee. Manchester Association for Preserving Constitutional Order and Liberty, as well as Property, against the various efforts of Republicans and Levellers, 1792

John Rylands University Library
Spencer pamphlets

Sheffield City Libraries   Local History section

Wentworth Woodhouse Muniments: Fitzwilliam papers
F 44 a/1–18: Correspondence of informants with local magistrates

and Earl Fitzwilliam on activities and proceedings of the Sheffield Constitutional Society, Dec. 1791–Oct. 1792

F 33 b/38, 39, 41, 44: Correspondence of local magistrates with Earl Fitzwilliam on Sheffield radicalism, Dec. 1792

F 44 c/–: Correspondence on food riots, 1795

E234/23, 24, 26–8: Correspondence of Earl Fitzwilliam and the Rev. H. Zouch on Sheffield radicalism, April–June, 1792

F 47/9: Corn Committee at Sheffield, 1795

F 121/12: Measures for Poor Relief, Feb. 1795

MD 251: Declaration of the Sheffield Constitutional Society, 14 March 1792

Norfolk and Norwich Record Office, Central Library, Norwich

MS. 502: Records of the Castle Corporation Club, afterwards Pitt Club, 1764–1820

MS. Minute-book of the Norwich Tusculan School, 27 Sept. 1793–2 May 1794. Norfolk Archaeological Society

Minute-book of Quarter Sessions, 1786–94

Court books of the Guardians of the Poor, Jan. 1787–April 1796

Rules of Friendly Societies, 1788. 1799. Four boxes

Documents relating to riots in Norwich occasioned by Thelwall's lectures, Nov. 1797

University of Nottingham, MSS. Dept.

Portland papers (correspondence of third Duke, as Home Secretary)

PWF 3038, 3039, 3040: with P. Colquhoun, 1795

PWF 3929, 3934, 3937: with R. Ford, 1794–5

PWF 3495, 4104, 4106: with Dundas and George III, 1795

PWF 3942, 3943: Sheffield food riots, 1795

PWF 7701–7717: with William Pitt

PWF 10511–10516: Papers on legal aspects of High Treason, 1795

Bodleian Library, Oxford

Bland Burges papers

Box labelled 'Correspondence with Anne, Lady Burges, 1789–94'

Box labelled 'Transcripts of political papers of Sir James Bland Burges, 1789–92'

Box labelled 'Political Transcripts, 1792–8'

Box labelled 'Letters of Sir James Bland Burges about foreign affairs.'
Box labelled 'Letters mainly about foreign affairs, 1793'
Box labelled 'Original letters – foreign affairs, 1794'
Box labelled 'Letters about foreign affairs, 1789–1796'

Archives Nationales, Paris

Série C (Proceedings of revolutionary National Assemblies and annexed papers: 36, 42, 238, 240, 241, 242, 243 (Radical addresses); 359 Dossier 1906 (Dumouriez correspondence, Feb. 1793)
AF II*1: Register of proceedings of Provisional Executive Council
AF II 29: Committee of Public Safety
AF II*288: Register of Committee of General Security
AF III 52–5, 57, 58: Executive Directory: Foreign relations
F^7 (Papers of Committee of General Security. *Police Générale*)
F^7 4368
F^7 4390^2
F^7 4394^1 Pache papers
F^7 4395: Papers of Diplomatic Committee of National Convention, 15 Oct. 1792–15 May 1793
F^7 4398: England
F^7 4748: W. Jackson
F^7 4774^{40}: W. Maxwell
F^7 4774^{49}: G. Monro
F^7 4774^{60}: J. Oswald
F^7 4774^{70}: Pétion's correspondence with English radicals
F^7 4775: White
W 305 (365): Revolutionary Tribunal. Proceedings against Lebrun, 7 Nivôse an 2

Archives du Ministère des Affaires Étrangères (AAE), Paris

Mémoires et documents (fonds divers)
2
  6: Angleterre 5
 19: Angleterre 17
 48: Angleterre 45
 53: Angleterre 50

Correspondance Politique, Angleterre (*CPA*)
582: Aug.–Oct. 1792
583: Oct.–Nov. 1792
584: Dec. 1792
585: 1792, Supplément
586: Jan.–Feb. 1793
587: March–Sept. 1793
588: Sept. 1793–Sept. 1795
589: Sept. 1795–Sept. 1796
590: Sept. 1796–June 1797
591: June–Sept. 1797
592: Sept. 1797–Sept. 1799
593: Sept. 1799–Sept. 1800
    Suppléments 29–30

Printed sources

Parliamentary, official and legal records

The Parliamentary History of England, ed. William Cobbett, 1st series, vols. 27–35 (London, 1813–19)

The Senator; or Clarendon's Parliamentary Chronicle, vols 1–20 (London–1790–8)

A Complete Collection of State Trials, ed. T. B. Howell and T. J. Howell, vols. 23–28 (London, 1813–1820)

Committee of Secrecy of the House of Commons respecting Seditious Practices: First Report (16 May 1794), *Parl. Hist.*, vol. 31, cols. 475–97; *Second Report* (6 June 1794), *Parl. Hist.*, vol. 31, cols. 688–879

Committee of Secrecy of the House of Lords respecting Seditious Practices: First Report (22 May 1794), *Parl. Hist.*, vol. 31, cols. 573–4; *Second Report* (7 June 1794), *Parl. Hist.*, vol. 31, cols. 886–903

Committee of Secrecy of the House of Commons of Ireland: Report (17 July 1798)

Committee of Secrecy of the House of Lords in Ireland: Report (30 Aug. 1798)

Committee of Secrecy of the House of Commons relative to the proceedings of different persons and societies in Great Britain and Ireland engaged in a treasonable conspiracy: Report (15 March 1799), *Parl. Hist.*, vol. 34, cols. 579–656

*Committee of Secrecy of the House of Lords relative to a treasonable
conspiracy: Report* (27 May 1799), *Parl. Hist.*, vol. 34, cols. 1000–6

Periodicals and newspapers

Place Newspaper Cuttings. British Library, vols. 36–40

Periodicals

The Annual Register
The New Annual Register
The Gentleman's Magazine
The Patriot, ed. M. C. Brown, 3 vols. (1792–3)
The Cabinet, 3 vols. Norwich (1794–5)
Hog's Wash: Politics for the People
Pig's Meat (1793–6)
The Anti-Jacobin

Newspapers

The Manchester Chronicle
The Manchester Mercury
The Manchester Herald (31 March 1792–23 March 1793)

The Sheffield Register
The Sheffield Iris
The Sheffield Courant

The Norfolk Chronicle and Norwich Gazette
The Norwich Mercury

Aris's Birmingham Gazette

Leicester Journal
Leicester Chronicle
Leicester Herald

Derby Mercury
The Edinburgh Gazetteer
The English Chronicle
The Morning Chronicle
The Sun
The True Briton

General works

E. Smith, *The Story of the English Jacobins* (London, 1881). An early attempt to write the history of the London Corresponding Society, based largely on printed sources and in particular on Hardy's *Memoir* (London, 1832)

J. B. Daly, *Radical Pioneers of the Eighteenth Century* (London, 1886)

C. B. R. Kent, *The English Radicals* (London, 1899)

E. and A. G. Porritt, *The Unreformed House of Commons* (2 vols, London, 1903). The classic account of the representative system before 1832. Vol. 1 deals with England and Wales; vol. 2 with Scotland and Ireland

W. T. Laprade, *England in the French Revolution* (Baltimore, Md, 1909). A rather biased analysis of Pitt's use of 'Alarmism' to split the Whigs

J. H. Rose, *William Pitt and the National Revival* (London, 1912).

J. H. Rose, *William Pitt and the Great War* (London, 1911). For long the standard life of Pitt the Younger, now superseded

W. P. Hall, *British Radicalism 1791–1797* (New York, 1912). Inaccurate in detail and faulty in interpretation

G. S. Veitch, *The Genesis of Parliamentary Reform* (London, 1913; reprinted 1965). The first scholarly account of British eighteenth-century radicalism. Particularly good on the relations of English and Irish reform societies with their French counterparts. Did not, however, have access to the Treasury Solicitor's papers in the Public Record Office. A pioneering work of permanent value

P. A. Brown, *The French Revolution in English History* (London, 1965 reprint). Brief, brilliant and, still in many ways, the most balanced treatment of the subject. The first to use the Treasury Solicitor's files

E. Halévy, *History of the English People in the Nineteenth Century*, vol. 1: *England in 1815* (London, 1924). In a class of its own. Indispensable

R. Birley, *The English Jacobins from 1789 to 1802* (Oxford, 1924). An undergraduate university prize essay, based partly on MS. sources by a former Headmaster of Eton

H. W. C. Davis, *The Age of Grey and Peel* (Oxford, 1929). The Ford Lectures for 1926. Excellent on the relations of the popular societies with the Whigs, also on social and political thought

S. Maccoby, *English radicalism*, vol. 1: *1762–1785: The origins*; vol. 2: *1786–1832. From Paine to Cobbett* (London, 1954–5)

Detailed narrative, based mainly on parliamentary sources

Sir Lewis Namier, *The Structure of Politics at the accession of George III*, 2nd ed. (London, 1957). Essential

E. J. Hobsbawm, *Primitive Rebels* (Manchester, 1959)

E. J. Hobsbawm, *Labouring Men* (London, 1964). Stimulating analysis of 'pre-industrial' protest and other studies

R. R. Palmer, *The Age of the Democratic Revolution*. vol. 1: *The Challenge*; vol. 2: *The Struggle* (Princeton, N.J., 1959 and 1964). Studies the American and French revolutions and the English, Irish and Scottish democratic movements in the wider context of an emergent eighteenth-century 'Atlantic community'

Sir Lewis Namier and J. Brooke, *The House of Commons, 1754–90* (3 vols., London, 1964) [Volumes in the official *History of Parliament*]

E. P. Thompson, *The Making of the English Working Class* (3rd reprint, London, 1964). A 'grass-roots' vision of English radicalism, particularly valuable on the Dissenting interest and on the economic background to provincial radicalism. Almost makes 'English Jacobinism' credible, but is weak on the French dimension. Essentially a study in the emergence of working-class consciousness

Gwyn A. Williams, *Artisans and Sans-Culottes: Popular Movements in France and Britain during the French Revolution* (London, 1968). A brilliant, but somewhat breathless, synthesis of the work of Lefebvre, Soboul and Cobb, and of Rudé and Thompson on the popular mentality of French and English radicals

C. B. Cone, *The English Jacobins, Reformers in Late Eighteenth Century England* (New York, 1968). An off-shoot of the author's researches on Burke. No critical apparatus or footnotes

J. Ehrmann, *The Younger Pitt*, vol. 1: *The Years of Acclaim* (London, 1969). Vol. 2, not yet published, will also contain new material

Political and social thought

English Commonwealthmen in the eighteenth century

Primary
Robert Molesworth, *An Account of Denmark as it was in the year 1692* (London, 1694)

Robert Molesworth, *The Principles of a Real Whig* (London, 1705; reprinted 1775)

William Molyneux, *Case of Ireland's being bound by Acts of Parliament stated* (Dublin, 1698)

Walter Moyle and John Trenchard, *An Argument showing that a Standing Army is inconsistent with a Free Government* (London, 1697)

John Toland, *Anglia Libera* (Hamburg, 1701).

John Toland, *Christianity Not Mysterious* (London, 1696)

Thomas Gordon, *The Independent Whig* (London, 1724)

F. Blackburne (ed.), *Memoirs of Thomas Hollis* (2 vols., London, 1780)

Secondary

Zera S. Fink, *The Classical Republicans: An Essay in the recovery of a pattern of thought in seventeenth-century England* (Evanston, Ill., 1945)

C. Robbins, *The Eighteenth-Century Commonwealthman* (Cambridge, Mass., 1959)

F. Venturi, *Utopia and Reform in the Enlightenment* (Cambridge, 1971)

J. R. Jones, *The First Whigs* (Oxford, 1961)

J. G. A. Pocock, *The Ancient Constitution and the Feudal Law* (1967)

J. H. Plumb, *The Growth of Political Stability in England, 1675–1725* (London, 1967)

Articles

C. Robbins, 'The strenuous Whig; Thomas Hollis of Lincoln's Inn', *William and Mary Quarterly*, 3rd Series, vol. 7 (1950), pp. 406–53

A. T. P. Cooper, 'The good Mr. Hollis, Dorset's greatest Democrat', *The Dorset Year Book, 1964–5* (Weymouth), pp. 11–21

Wilkes, the American conflict and parliamentary reform

Primary

The Controversial Letters of John Wilkes and the Rev. J. Horne (London, 1771)

Obadiah Hulme, *Historical Essay on the English Constitution* (London, 1771)

James Burgh, *Political Disquisitions* (3 vols., London, 1774–5)

J. Priestley, *Essay on the First Principles of Government, and on the Nature of Civil and Religious Liberty* (London, 1768)

R. Price, *Observations on the Nature of Civil Liberty* (London, 1776).

B. Cozens-Hardy (ed.), *The Diary of Silas Neville, 1768–1788* (London, 1950)

J. Cartwright, *American Independence the Interest and Glory of Great Britain* (London, 1774)

J. Cartwright, *The Legislative Rights of the Commonalty Vindicated, or Take Your Choice* (London, 1776)

J. Cartwright, *Give us our Rights* (London, 1782)

J. Jebb, *Address to the Freeholders of Middlesex, Dec. 1779*

Duke of Richmond, *Letter to Lt. Col. Sharman* (London, 1783; reprinted 1792)

Sir William Jones, *The Principles of Government in a Dialogue between a scholar and a peasant* (London, 1782)

Society for Constitutional Information, *Constitutional Tracts* (2 vols., London, 1783)

C. Wyvill, *Political Papers* (6 vols., York, 1794–1806)

D. Williams, *Lectures on Political Principles* (1789)

B. Bailyn (ed.), *Pamphlets of the American Revolution, 1750–1775*, vol. I: *1750–65* (Cambridge, Mass., 1965)

Secondary

C. G. Rossiter, *Seedtime of the Republic* (New York, 1953)

C. B. Cone, *Burke and the Nature of Politics: The Age of the American Revolution* (Lexington, Ky., 1959)

Sir Leslie Stephen, *History of English Thought in the Eighteenth Century* (2 vols., London, 1881)

C. Hill, *Puritanism and Revolution* (London, 1968)

H. Butterfield, *George III, Lord North, and the People, 1779–1780* (London, 1949)

I. R. Christie, *Wilkes, Wyvill and Reform: The Parliamentary Reform Movement in British Politics, 1760–1785* (London, 1962)

W. J. Shelton, *English Hunger and Industrial Disorders* (Toronto, 1973)

G. Rudé, *Wilkes and Liberty: A Social Study of 1763 to 1774* (London, 1962)

G. S. Veitch, *Genesis of Parliamentary Reform* (reprint with introduction by I. R. Christie, London, 1965)

R. R. Palmer, *The Age of the American Revolution*, vol. 1: *The Challenge* (Princeton, N.J., 1959)

G. H. Guttridge, *English Whiggism and the American Revolution* (Berkeley and Los Angeles, 1966 reprint)

E. C. Black, *The Association: British Extraparliamentary Political Organization, 1769–1793* (Cambridge, Mass., 1963)

B. Bailyn, *The Ideological Origins of the American Revolution* (Cambridge, Mass., 1967)

Staughton Lynd, *Intellectual Origins of American Radicalism* London, 1973)

J. T. Boulton, *The Language of Politics in the Age of Wilkes and Burke* (London, 1963)

J. R. Pole, *Political Representation in England and the Origins of the American Republic* (1966)

C. Bonwick, *English Radicals and the American Revolution* (Chapel Hill, N.C., 1977)

Articles

L. M. Donnelly, 'The celebrated Mrs. Macaulay', *William and Mary Quarterly*, 3rd series, vol. 6 (1949), pp. 173–207

P. Maier, 'John Wilkes and American disillusionment with Britain', *William and Mary Quarterly*, 3rd series, vol. 20 (1963), pp. 373–95

V. W. Crane, 'The Club of Honest Whigs: friends of science and liberty', *William and Mary Quarterly*, 3rd series, vol. 23 (1966), pp. 210–33

J. H. Plumb, 'British attitudes to the American Revolution' in *In the Light of History* (London, 1972), pp. 71–87

The debate on the French revolution

Primary

R. Price, *A Discourse on the Love of our Country*, 4th ed. (London, 1790)

E. Burke, *Reflections on the Revolution in France* (London, 1790)

E. Burke, *Appeal from the New to the Old Whigs* (London, 1791)

E. Burke, *Letters on a Regicide Peace* (London, 1795–6)

M. Wollstonecraft, *A Vindication of the Rights of Man* (London, 1790)

Sir James Mackintosh, *Vindiciae Gallicae: A Defence of the French Revolution and its English admirers* (London, 1792)

Earl Stanhope, *A Letter to the Rt. Hon. Edmund Burke containing a short answer to his late speech on the French Revolution, Feb. 24, 1790* (London, 1790).

Capel Lofft, *Remarks on the letter of the Rt. Hon. Edmund Burke concerning the Revolution in France* (London, 1790)

Joseph Priestley, *Letters to the Rt. Hon. Edmund Burke occasioned by his Reflections on the Revolution in France* (Birmingham, 1791)

A Letter to the Rt. Hon. Edmund Burke in reply to his Reflections – By a Member of the Revolution Society (London, 1790)

Answer of M. Dupont to the Reflections of the Rt. Hon. Edmund Burke (London, 1791)

Thomas Paine, *The Rights of Man: Part I* (London, 1791); *Part II* (London, 1792)

Secondary

E. Halévy, *The Growth of Philosophical Radicalism* (London, 1928).

T. W. Copeland, *Edmund Burke: Six Essays* (London, 1950)

C. Parkin, *The Moral Basis of Burke's Political Thought* (Cambridge, 1956)

P. J. Stanlis, *The Relevance of Edmund Burke* (New York, 1964)

R. R. Fennesy, *Burke, Paine and the Rights of Man* (The Hague, 1963)

B. T. Wilkins, *The Problem of Burke's Political Philosophy* (Oxford, 1967)

C. B. Cone, *Burke and the Nature of Politics: The Age of the French Revolution* (Lexington, Ky., 1964)

Articles

J. T. Boulton, 'The *Reflections*: Burke's preliminary draft and methods of composition', *Durham University Journal*, new series, no. 14 (1958), pp. 114–19

A. Goodwin, 'The political genesis of Edmund Burke's *Reflections on the Revolution in France*', *Bulletin of the John Rylands Library*, vol. 50 (1968), pp. 336–64

Utopian thought

Primary

W. Godwin, *An Enquiry concerning Political Justice and its influence on General Virtue and Happiness* (2 vols., London, 1793)

Mary Wollstonecraft, *A Vindication of the Rights of Woman* (London, 1792)

Thomas Paine, *The Rights of Man*, Part II (London, 1792)

Thomas Paine, *Agrarian Justice* (London, 1797)

T. Spence, *The Real Rights of Man* (London, 1793)

T. Spence, *The Meridian Sun of Liberty* (London, 1796)

T. Spence, *Constitution of Spensonea – a country in Fairyland* (London, 1801)

T. Spence, *The Restorer of Society to its Natural State* (London, 1801)

T. Spence, *The World Turned Upside Down* (London, 1805)

Thomas Evans, *Christian Policy the Salvation of the Empire*, 2nd ed (London, 1816)

Maurice Margarot, *Thoughts on Revolutions* (Harlow, 1812)

Maurice Margarot, *Proposal for a Grand National Jubilee: Restoring to Every Man his Own, and thereby extinguishing both Want and War* (Sheffield, 1812)

Secondary

C. K. Paul, *William Godwin, his friends and contemporaries* (2 vols, London, 1876)

H. N. Brailsford, *Shelley, Godwin and their Circle* (London, 1913)

C. Tomalin, *The Life and Death of Mary Wollstonecraft* (London, 1974)

E. Halévy, *The Growth of Philosophic Radicalism* (London, 1928)

O. D. Rudkin, *Thomas Spence and his Connections* (London, 1927)

Melvin J. Laski, *Utopia and Revolution* (London, 1977)

Articles

T. M. Parssinen, 'Thomas Spence and the progress of English land nationalisation', *Journal of the History of Ideas*, vol. 34 (1973), pp. 135–41

T. M. Parssinen, 'The Revolutionary Party in London, 1816–1820', *Bulletin of the Institute of Historical Research*, vol. 14 (1972), pp. 266–82

The radicalism of Dissent

Primary

Richard Price, *Observations on the Nature of Civil Liberty* (London, 1776

Richard Price, *Observations on the Importance of the American Revolution* (London, 1784)

Richard Price, *A Discourse on the Love of our Country*, 4th ed. (London, 1790)

Joseph Priestley, *Doctrine of Philosophical Necessity* (London, 1777)

Joseph Priestley, *Essay on the First Principles of Government* (2nd ed, London, 1771)

Joseph Priestley, *Lectures on History and General Policy* (Birmingham, 1788)

Joseph Priestley, *Familiar letters addressed to the Inhabitants of the town of Birmingham* (Birmingham, 1790)

Joseph Priestley, *Letters to the Rt. Hon. Edmund Burke occasioned by his Reflections on the Revolution in France* (Birmingham, 1791)

J. T. Rutt (ed.), *Memoirs of Joseph Priestley* (2 vols., London, 1832)

James Burgh, *Political Disquisitions* (3 vols., London, 1774–5)

S. Palmer, *The Protestant Dissenters' Catechism* (London, 1775)

The Case of the Protestant Dissenters (London, 1787)

H. McLachlan (ed.), *Letters of Theophilus Lindsey* (Manchester, 1920)

Thomas Belsham, *Memoirs of the Rev. Theophilus Lindsey,* 2nd ed., (London, 1820)

Joseph Towers, *An Oration delivered at the London Tavern on the Fourth of November 1788 on the occasion of the commemoration of the Revolution* (London, 1788)

S. Heywood, *The Right of Protestant Dissenters to a Compleat Toleration Asserted,* 2nd ed. (London, 1789)

S. Heywood, *High Church Politics* (London, 1792)

J. Towers, *Thoughts on the commencement of a new Parliament* (London, 1790)

Capel Lofft, *Remarks on the Letter of the Rt. Hon. Edmund Burke concerning the Revolution in France* (London, 1790)

Capel Lofft, *History of the Corporation and Test Acts* (Bury St Edmunds, 1790)

Half an hour's conversation between a Clergyman and a Dissenter on the Test Laws (London, 1789)

C. Wyvill, *Defence of Dr. Price and the Reformers of England* (London, 1792)

[J. Parkinson], *A Vindication of the London Revolution Society* (London, 1792)

The Correspondence of the Revolution Society in London with the National Assembly and with various societies of the Friends of Liberty in France and England (London, 1792)

W. Belsham, *Nature and Necessity of a Parliamentary Reform* (London, 1793)

W. Frend, *Peace and Union recommended to the Associated Bodies of Republicans and Anti-Republicans* (St Ives, 1793)

G. Dyer, *The Complaints of the Poor People of England*, 2nd ed. (London, 1793)

G. Dyer, *Dissertation on the Theory and Practice of Benevolence* (London, 1795)

G. Wakefield, *Reply to Llandaff* (London, 1798)

Secondary

D. Bogue and J. Bennett, *History of the Dissenters* (4 vols., London, 1808–12)

I. Parker, *Dissenting Academies in England* (Cambridge, 1914).

E. Halévy, *A History of the English People in the Nineteenth Century*, vol. 1 (London, 1924)

H. McLachlan, *English Education under the Test Acts* (Manchester, 1931)

H. McLachlan, *The Unitarian Movement in the Religious Life of England* (London, 1934)

O. M. Griffiths, *Religion and Learning: A Study in English Presbyterian Thought from the Bartholomew Ejections to the foundation of the Unitarian Movement* (Cambridge, 1935)

H. Gow, *The Unitarians* (London, 1928)

A. Lincoln, *Some Social and Political Ideas of English Dissent, 1763–1800* (Cambridge, 1938)

R. V. Holt, *The Unitarian Contribution to Social Progress in England*, 2nd ed. (London, 1952)

B. L. Manning, *The Protestant Dissenting Deputies* (Cambridge, 1952)

R. Stromberg, *Religious Liberalism in Eighteenth-Century England* (1954)

C. B. Cone, *Torchbearer of Freedom: The Influence of Richard Price on Eighteenth-Century Thought* (Lexington, Ky., 1954)

R. K. Webb, *Harriet Martineau: A Radical Victorian* (London, 1960)

C. Robbins, *The Eighteenth-Century Commonwealthman* (Cambridge, Mass., 1959)

P. Brown, *The Chathamites* (London, 1961)

U. Henriques, *Religious Toleration in England, 1787–1833* (London, 1961)

C. Bridenbaugh, *Mitre and Sceptre: Transatlantic Faiths, Ideas, Personalities and Politics, 1689–1775* (New York, 1962)

P. G. Barlow, *Citizenship and Conscience* (Philadelphia, 1962)

F. Knight, *University Rebel: The Life of William Frend, 1757–1841* (London, 1971)

R. W. Davis, *Dissent in Politics, 1780–1830: The Political Life of William Smith M.P.* (London, 1971)

W. R. Ward, *Religion and Society in England, 1790–1850* (London, 1972)

R. T. Anstey, *The Atlantic Slave Trade and British Abolition, 1760–1810* (London, 1975)

M. R. Watts, *The Dissenters from the Reformation to the French Revolution* (Oxford, 1978)

Articles

T. Bennett, 'Hallam and the Indemnity Acts', *Law Quarterly Review*, vol. 26 (1910), pp. 400ff.

H. Butterfield, *Historical development of the principle of toleration in British life*, Robert Waley Cohen Memorial Lecture (London, 1956)

R. B. Rose, 'The Priestley riots of 1791', *Past and Present*, no. 18 (1960), pp. 68–88

E. J. Hobsbawm, 'Methodism and the threat of revolution in Britain' in *Labouring Men: Studies in the History of Labour* (London, 1964), pp. 23–33

I. Sellers, 'Unitarians and social Change, pt. 1: varieties of radicalism, 1795–1815', *Hibbert Journal*, vol. 61 (1962), pp. 16–22

V. W. Crane, 'The Club of Honest Whigs: friends of science and liberty', *William and Mary Quarterly*, 3rd series, vol. 23 (1966), pp. 210–33

C. M. Elliott, 'The political economy of English dissent, 1780–1840' in R. M. Hartwell (ed.), *The Industrial Revolution* (Oxford, 1970)

B. Semmel, 'The Halévy thesis', *Encounter* (July 1971), pp. 44–55

R. C. E. Richey, 'The origins of British radicalism: the changing rationale for dissent', *Eighteenth-Century Studies*, vol. 7 (1973–4), pp. 179–92

G. M. Ditchfield, 'The parliamentary struggle on the repeal of the Test and Corporation Acts, 1787–1790', *English Historical Review*, vol. 89 (1974), pp. 551–77

Metropolitan radicalism

Before 1789

Secondary

G. S. Veitch, *The Genesis of Parliamentary Reform* (London, 1965 reprint)

W. P. Treloar, *Wilkes and the City* (London, 1917)

H. Butterfield, *George III, Lord North and the People, 1779–80* (London, 1949)

C. Robbins, *The Eighteenth-Century Commonwealthman* (Cambridge, Mass., 1959)

A. G. Olson, *The Radical Duke: Career and Correspondence of Charles Lennox, Third Duke of Richmond* (Oxford, 1961)

I. R. Christie, *Wilkes, Wyvill and Reform: The Parliamentary Reform Movement in British Politics, 1760–1785* (London, 1962)

G. Rudé, *Wilkes and Liberty: A Social Study of 1763 to 1774* (Oxford, 1962)

E. C. Black, *The Association: British Extraparliamentary Political Organization, 1769–1793* (Cambridge, Mass., 1963)

M. D. George, *London Life in the Eighteenth Century* (Harmondsworth, 1966)

C. B. Cone, *The English Jacobins: Reformers in late eighteenth-century England* (New York, 1968)

L. S. Sutherland, *The City of London and the Opposition to Government 1768–1774: A Study in the Rise of Metropolitan Radicalism* (London, 1969)

J. W. Osborne, *John Cartwright* (Cambridge, 1972)

Articles

G. Rudé, 'The Gordon Riots: a study of the rioters and their victims', *Transactions of the Royal Historical Society*, 5th series, vol. 6 (1956), pp. 93–114

G. Rudé, 'The London "Mob" of the eighteenth-century', *The Historical Journal*, vol. 2 (1959), pp. 1–18

L. S. Sutherland, 'The City of London in eighteenth-century politics', in R. Pares and A. J. P. Taylor (eds.), *Essays presented to Sir Lewis Namier* (London, 1956), pp. 49–74

P. D. G. Thomas, 'John Wilkes and the freedom of the press, 1771', *Bulletin of the Institute of Historical Research*, vol. 33, no 87 (1960), pp. 86–98

V. W. Crane, 'The Club of Honest Whigs: friends of science and liberty', *William and Mary Quarterly*, 3rd series, vol. 23 (1966), pp. 210–33

C. Hill, 'The Norman Yoke', ch. 3 in *Puritanism and Revolution* (London, 1968)

After 1789

Primary

London Corresponding Society (LCS), *Address and Resolutions*, 2 April 1792 (drafted by Margarot)

LCS, *The London Corresponding Society to the Nation at large*, 24 May 1792

LCS, *Address from the London Corresponding Society to the Inhabitants of Great Britain on the subject of a Parliamentary Reform*, 6 Aug. 1972 (drafted by Margarot)

LCS, *Address to the French National Convention*, 27 Sept. 1792

LCS, *Address of the London Corresponding Society to the other societies in Great Britain united for obtaining a reform in Parliament*, 29 Nov. 1792 (drafted by Felix Vaughan)

LCS, *Address to the Nation*, 8 July 1793 (drafted by Margarot for the first general meeting of the society)

LCS, *Address to the People of Great Britain and Ireland*, 20 Jan. 1794.

LCS, *Resolutions* at Chalk Farm meeting, 14 April 1794 (probably drafted by Thelwall)

LCS, *Resolutions of the General Committee of the London Corresponding Society*, 5 June 1794

LCS, *Account of the seizure of Citizen Thomas Hardy, Secretary to the London Corresponding Society* (1794)

LCS, *Summary of the Proceedings at a meeting of the London Corresponding Society – in St. George's Fields, Monday 29 June, 1795*

LCS, *Account of the Proceedings of a meeting of the London Corresponding Society, held in a field near Copenhagen House, Monday October 26 1795*

LCS, *Account of the Proceedings of a Meeting of the People in a field near Copenhagen House, Thursday November 12, 1795 on the subject of the Threatened Invasion of their Rights by a Convention Bill*

LCS, *To the Parliament and People of Great Britain: An Explicit Declaration of the Principles and Views of the London Corresponding Society, 23 November 1795*

LCS, *Meeting of the London Corresponding Society, Monday 7 December, 1795 in Marylebone Fields, London*

LCS, *Correspondence of the London Corresponding Society, revised and corrected* (London, 1795)

LCS [James Parkinson], *A Vindication of the London Corresponding Society*, (London, 1795)

LCS, *Address of the London Corresponding Society to Scotland*, 16 April 1796

LCS, *Address to the Nation*, 31 July 1797

LCS, *Address of the London Corresponding Society to the Irish Nation*, 30 Jan. 1798

LCS, *Proceedings of the General Committee . . on the 5th, 12th and 19th of April 1798* (by Richard Hodgson)

LCS, *Address of the London Corresponding Society to the British Nation*, 14 June 1798

LCS [P. Mackenzie], *Memoir of Thomas Hardy* (London, 1832), reprinted in D. Vincent (ed.), *Testaments of Radicalism: Memoirs of Working Class Politicians, 1790–1885* (London, 1977), pp. 37–102

Society for Constitutional Information (SCI), *Resolution of thanks to Thomas Paine* (for publication of Part I of *The Rights of Man*), 23 March 1791

SCI, *Address to the Society of Friends of the Constitution at Paris, called the Jacobins*, 11 May 1792

SCI, *Resolutions on the Royal Proclamation against Seditious Publications*, 25 May 1792

SCI, *Address to the National Convention in France*, 9 Nov. 1792

SCI, *Instructions to the Delegates* (to the general convention at Edinburgh), 28 Oct. 1793

SCI, *Resolutions*, 17 Jan. 1794

SCI, *Report on the Treason and Sedition Bills*, 23 Dec. 1795

Secondary

Works by G. S. Veitch, P. A. Brown, R. Birley, S. Maccoby, E. P. Thompson, G. A. Williams, C. B. Cone (*see* General works, above)

H. Collins, 'The London Corresponding Society' in J. Saville (ed.), *Democracy and the Labour Movement* (London, 1954), pp. 103–34

R. K. Webb, *The British Working Class Reader 1790–1848: Literary and Social Tension* (London, 1955)

A. Aspinall, *Politics and the Press, 1780–1850* (London, 1949)

M. D. George, *London Life in the Eighteenth Century* (Harmondsworth, 1965)

G. Rudé, *Paris and London in the Eighteenth Century* (London, 1970)

E. C. Black, *The Association: British Extraparliamentary Political Organization, 1769–1793* (Cambridge, Mass., 1963)

J. W. Osborne, *John Cartwright* (Cambridge, 1972)

F. D. Cartwright (ed.), *Life and Correspondence of Major Cartwright* (2 vols., London, 1826)

J. A. Hone, 'Radicalism in London, 1796–1802: convergencies and continuities', in J. Stevenson (ed.), *London in the Age of Reform* (Oxford, 1977), pp. 79–107

J. L. and L. B. Hammond, *Charles James Fox: A Political Study* (London, 1903)

L. Reid, *Charles James Fox: A Man for the People* (London, 1969)

M. D. Conway, *Life of Thomas Paine* (2 vols., New York and London 1892)

A. Aldridge, *Man of Reason: The Life of Thomas Paine* (London, 1960)

A. Stephens, *Memoirs of John Horne Tooke* (2 vols., London, 1813)

W. H. Reid, *Memoirs of the Public Life of John Horne Tooke* (London, 1812)

V. C. Miller, *Joel Barlow, Revolutionist: London 1791–2* (Hamburg, 1932)

Mrs Thelwall, *Life of Thelwall*, vol. 1 (London, 1837)

C. Cestre, *John Thelwall: A Pioneer of Democracy and Social Reform in England during the French Revolution* (London, 1906)

Graham Wallas, *The Life of Francis Place* (London, 1898)

D. V. Erdman, *Blake: Prophet against Empire* (Princeton, 1954)

Provincial radicalism

1 *Manchester*

Primary

Items marked * are from the collection of newspaper cuttings, 'Politics from Nov. 1792 to Aug. 1793', in the Manchester Central Reference Library.

The Manchester Chronicle, 1789–1794

The Manchester Mercury, 1789–1794

The Manchester Herald, 31 Mar. 1792–21 Mar. 1793*

The Manchester Gazette, 1796

T. B. and T. J. Howell (eds.), *State Trials*, vols. 23, 24, 25

Rules and Orders of the Manchester Constitutional Society instituted Oct. 1790 (Manchester, 1791)

G. Phillips, *The necessity of a speedy and effectual reform in Parliament* (Manchester, 1792)

T. Cooper, *Letters on the Slave Trade* (1787)

T. Cooper, *A Reply to Mr. Burke's invective against Mr. Cooper and Mr. Watt in the House of Commons on the 30th April, 1792* (Manchester, 1792)

T. Cooper, *War!* (Manchester, 10 Dec. 1792, signed 'Sydney' [pseud.])*

T. Cooper, *To the Unemployed Artisans of Manchester* (Manchester, 1793; signed 'A Friend to the Poor')*

Address presented by the delegates of the Constitutional Society of Manchester to the Society of Friends of the Constitution, sitting at the Jacobins in Paris on 13th April, 1792

G. Lloyd, *A Protest against the Resolutions of the Manchester Constitutional Society for publishing the address of Messrs. Cooper and Watt to the Jacobin Club with the answer and Monsieur Carra's letter to the Society* (Manchester, 1792)*

Declaration and Resolutions of the Manchester Patriotic Society, 24 May, 1792

Declaration and Resolutions of the Manchester Reformation Society, 6 June, 1792

Brother Fustian's Advice to the Inhabitants of Manchester and Salford (1792)*

A Caveat against Misrepresentation (Manchester, 1792)*

Manchester Constitutional Society. Reply to the Calumuies of their enemies (1792)*

Declaration and Resolutions of the Friends of Universal Peace and the Rights of Man (Stockport, 25 Aug. 1792)

The Rights of Man Society at Manchester (Manchester, 1792)*

Apology and defence of the September Massacres, 10 Sept. 1792

Declaration of Manchester and Salford innkeepers boycotting meetings of radical societies on their premises (13 Sept. 1792)

Thomas Walker, *Address to the Inhabitants of Manchester* (13 Dec. 1792)*

An Answer to Mr. Walker's address (1792)*

Equality (1792) (handbill)

Loyal Declaration of Protestant Dissenters in Manchester and Salford, 18 Dec. 1792

Manchester Constitutional, Patriotic and Reformation Societies – united Declaration, 20 Dec. 1792

Violent Dissolution, Being the last Exit of Mons. Herald of Manchester, a near relation to Mons. Argus of London, who expired on Saturday last to the great regret of the Jacobin Painites, etc. but particularly to the BLACK CAT (March 1793)*

A Rod for the Burkites (Stockport, 1794)

The Rights of Swine; an Address to the Poor (Stockport, 1794)

Thomas Walker, *A Review of some of the Political Events which have occurred in Manchester during the last five years* (London, 1794)

To all Loyal and Peaceable Inhabitants of Manchester (Manchester, 1795)*

Dr J. Aikin, *A Description of the Country from thirty to forty miles round Manchester* (London, 1795)

Secondary

James Wheeler, *Manchester, its Political, Social and Commercial History, Ancient and Modern* (London, 1836)

Archibald Prentice, *Historical Sketches and Personal Recollections of Manchester, intended to illustrate the Progress of Public opinion from 1792 to 1832* (Manchester, 1851)

Thomas Walker, *The Original*, ed. W. Blanchard Jerrold (London, 1874)

F. Espinasse, *Lancashire Worthies*, 2nd series (London, 1877)

R. Wade, *The Rise of Nonconformity in Manchester, with a brief sketch of Cross St. Chapel* (Manchester, 1880)

W. E. Axon, *The Bayley Family* (Manchester, 1890)

T. Swindells, *Manchester Streets and Manchester Men* (Manchester, 1907)

D. Malone, *The Public Life of Thomas Cooper, 1783–1839* (New Haven, Conn., 1926)

A. Redford, *Labour Migration in England 1800–1850* (Manchester, 1926)

A. Redford, *Manchester Merchants and Foreign Trade*, vol. 1: *1794–1858* (Manchester, 1934)

A. Redford, *The History of Local Government in Manchester*, vol. 1. (London, 1939)

A. P. Wadsworth and Julia de L. Mann, *The Cotton Trade and Industrial Lancashire, 1600–1780* (Manchester, 1931)

F. S. Stancliffe, *John Shaw's, 1738–1938* (Manchester, 1938)

F. Knight, *The Strange Case of Thomas Walker* (London, 1957)

D. Read, *Peterloo: 'The Massacre' and its Background* (Manchester, 1959)

D. Read, *Press and People, 1790–1850* (London, 1961)

D. Read, *The English Provinces, 1760–1960* (London, 1964)

T. S. Ashton, *An Economic History of England: the Eighteenth Century* (London, 1955)

Manchester and its region: A Survey prepared for the British Association (Manchester, 1962)

Articles

G. W. Daniels, 'The cotton trade during the revolutionary and Napoleonic wars', *Transactions of the Manchester Statistical Society* (1915–16)

E. Robinson, 'An English Jacobin: James Watt, Jnr 1769–1848', *Cambridge Historical Journal*, vol. 11 (1953–5), pp. 349–55

D. Read, 'The social and economic background to Peterloo', *Transactions of the Lancashire and Cheshire Antiquarian Society*, vol. 64 (1954), pp. 1–18

W. H. Chaloner, 'Robert Owen, Peter Drinkwater and the early factory system in Manchester, 1788–1800', *Bulletin of the John Rylands Library*, vol. 37 (1954–5), pp. 82–94

W. H. Chaloner, 'Dr. Joseph Priestley, John Wilkinson and the French revolution, 1789–1802', *Transactions of the Royal Historical Society*, 5th series, vol. 8 (1958), pp. 21–40

W. H. Chaloner, 'Manchester in the latter half of the eighteenth century', *Bulletin of the John Rylands Library*, vol. 42 (1959), pp. 40–60

W. H. Brindley, 'The Manchester Literary and Philosophical Society', *Journal of the Royal Institute of Chemistry* (Feb. 1955), pp. 62–9

Pauline Handforth, 'Manchester radical politics, 1789–1794', *Transactions of the Lancashire and Cheshire Antiquarian Society*, vol. 66 (1956), pp. 87–106

A. Goodwin, 'A comparative study of regionalism in politics in Lancashire and Normandy during the French revolution', *Annales de Normandie*, vol. 8 (1958), pp. 235–55

2 *Sheffield*

Primary

The Sheffield Register (1787–1794), owned, edited and published by Joseph Gales

The Sheffield Iris (4 July 1794). Edited and part owned by James Montgomery who, as from 3 July 1795, became sole proprietor

The Sheffield Courant (10 June 1793). Owned and published by J. Northall in Conservative interest

The Patriot, ed. M. C. Brown (3 vols., 3 April 1792–15 Sept. 1793)

Sheffield Local Register (1830)

Address from the Society for Constitutional Information in Sheffield to the public 19 December 1791. Wentworth Woodhouse Muniments, Sheffield Central Library, F 44a (31)

C. Wyvill, *Political Papers*, vols. 2, 3 and 5 (York and Richmond, 1794–1806)

T. B. and T. J. Howell (eds.), *State Trials*, vol. 24 (London, 1818)

Copy of the Duke of Richmond's letter on a Parliamentary Reform, addressed to Lt. Col. Sharman. Printed for the Constitutional Society, Sheffield, June 1792. Local Pamphlets, Sheffield Central Library, vol. 184 (10)

A complete Refutation of the Malevolent Charges exhibited against the Friends of Reform in and about Sheffield with some reflections on the Declaration agreed to at the Cutlers' Hall on Monday, December 31, 1792

Ten Minutes Admonition in answer to Ten Minutes Caution from a Plain Man to his Fellow Citizens. By a Sheffield Razor Maker (Sheffield, 1793)

Second Report of the Committee of Secrecy of the House of Commons, 1794 (Appendix E)

A Proclamation. By Order of the Sovereign Jacobin Club in Sheffield, 30 April 1794, Sheffield Central Library, MP 204

A Letter to the Rt. Hon. Henry Dundas, MP, Secretary of State etc. . . . by Citizen John Harrison, Sheffield (London 1794). Local Pamphlets, Sheffield Central Library, vol. 63 (5)

The Spirit of John Locke on Civil Government, revised by the Constitutional Society of Sheffield (1794), Local Pamphlets, Sheffield Central Library, vol. 80 (4)

Henry Yorke, *Thoughts on Civil Government, addressed to the disfranchised citizens of Sheffield* (1794), Local Pamphlets, Sheffield Central Library, vol. 31 (4)

Fast Day as observed at Sheffield, 28 Feb. 1794. Local Pamphlets, Sheffield Central Library, vol. 184 (11)

A Serious Lecture delivered at Sheffield, Feb. 28, 1794, being the day appointed for a General Fast, to which are added a Hymn, and Resolutions, 6th ed. (London, 1794)

Proceedings of the Public Meeting held at Sheffield in the open air, on 7 April, 1794, Local Pamphlets, Sheffield Central Library, vol. 80 (3)

J. Gales, *An Appeal to Britons* (Sheffield, 1794)

Proceedings of the Public Meeting held on Crooke's Moor at Sheffield in the open air on Monday Aug. 10 1795. Local pamphlets, Jackson collection, vol. 8 (5)

An accurate account of the proceedings on the occasion of the laying of the foundation stone of the new Corn Mill, Sheffield, 1795. Local pamphlets, vol. 80 (5)

Henry Redhead Yorke, *Trial for conspiracy at York Assizes* (10 July 1795)

H. R. Yorke, *A Letter to the Reformers* (Dorchester, 1798)

J. Wilson (ed.), *The Songs of Joseph Mather* (Sheffield, 1862)

Proposal of Executive Committee of the London Corresponding Society to hold simultaneous public meetings to approve a remonstrance to the King in favour of peace and the dismissal of Ministers (23 March 1797). British Library, Place newspaper cuttings, vol. 38, fo. 33

Executive Committee LCS 24 April 1797: Answer to the Friends of Reform in Sheffield respecting a General Meeting. BL, Place newspaper cuttings, vol. 38, fo. 59

Reply of the Friends of the People in Sheffield (to above) (15 May, 1797) BL, Place newspaper cuttings, vol. 38, fo. 67

Secondary

S. Mitchell, *The Burgery of Sheffield* (Sheffield, 1828)

J. Holland and J. Everett, *Memoirs of the Life and Writings of James Montgomery* (7 vols., London, 1854–6)

Joseph Hunter, *Hallamshire: the history and topography of the parish of Sheffield*, ed. A. Gatty (Sheffield, 1869)

J. D. Leader, *The records of the Burgery of Sheffield, commonly called the Town Trust* (London, 1897)

R. E. Leader, *Sheffield in the Eighteenth Century*, 2nd ed. (Sheffield, 1905)

R. E. Leader, *History of the Company of Cutlers in Hallamshire* (2 vols., Sheffield, 1905–6)

Charles Paul [Carolus Paulus], *Some Forgotten Facts in the History of Sheffield and District* (Sheffield, 1907)

G. I. H. Lloyd, *The Cutlery trades: an historical essay in the economics of small scale production* (London, 1913)

Rev. W. Odom, *Hallamshire Worthies* (Sheffield, 1926)

T. S. Ashton, *Iron and Steel in the Industrial Revolution* (Manchester, 1951)

R. Robson, *The Attorney in Eighteenth-Century England* (Cambridge, 1959)

M. Walton, *Sheffield: Its Story and its Achievements*, 4th ed. (Sheffield, 1968)

Articles

B. Hammond, 'Two towns' enclosures', *Economic History* (1931), pp. 258–66

L. B. Lewis, 'The abolitionist movement in Sheffield, 1823–33', *Bulletin of the John Rylands Library* (July 1934), pp. 377–92

G. P. Jones, 'The political reform movement in Sheffield', *Transactions of the Hunter Archaeological Society*, vol. 4 (1937), pp. 57–68

Lady Stephen, 'The Shores of Sheffield and the Offleys of Norton Hall', *Transactions of the Hunter Archaeological Society*, vol. 5 (1937–43), pp. 1–17

W. S. Powell, 'The diary of Joseph Gales, 1794–1795', *North Carolina Historical Review*, vol. 26 (1949), pp. 335–46

W. H. G. Armytage, 'Joseph Mather: poet of the filesmiths', *Notes and Queries*, vol. 195 (1950), pp. 320–2

W. H. G. Armytage, 'The editorial experience of Joseph Gales, 1786–1794', *North Carolina Historical Review*, vol. 28 (1951), pp. 332–61

A. W. L. Seaman, 'Reform politics at Sheffield, 1791–97', *Transactions of the Hunter Archaeological Society*, vol. 7 (1957), pp. 215–28

J. R. Dinwiddy, 'Christopher Wyvill and reform, 1790–1820', *Borthwick Papers* (University of York, Borthwick Institute of Historical Research), no. 39 (1971), pp. 1–10

I. Inkster, 'The development of a scientific community in Sheffield, 1790–1850: a network of people and interests', *Transactions of the Hunter Archaeological Society*, vol. 10, pt. 2 (1973), pp. 99–131

J. R. Dinwiddy, 'The "Black Lamp" in Yorkshire, 1801–2', *Past and Present*, no. 64 (Aug. 1974), pp. 113–23

J. L. Baxter and F. K. Donnelly, 'The revolutionary "underground" in the West Riding – myth or reality?', *Past and Present*, no. 64 (Aug. 1974), pp. 124–32

J. R. Dinwiddy, 'A rejoinder', *Past and Present*, no. 64 (Aug. 1974), pp. 132–5

J. Taylor, 'The Sheffield Constitutional Society, 1791–1795', *Trans. of the Hunter Archaeological Society*, vol. 5 (1940), pp. 133–46

3 *Norwich*
CC = Colman Collection, Central Library, Norwich

Primary
The Norfolk Chronicle and Norwich Gazette

The Norfolk Mercury
The Cabinet (3 vols. Norwich, 1795)
Dr E. Rigby, *Letters from France . . . in 1789* (ed. Lady Eastlake) (London, 1880)
M. Wilks, *The Origin and Stability of the French Revolution. A Sermon preached at St. Paul's Chapel, Norwich, July 14, 1791* (Norwich, 1791)
The Correspondence of the Revolution Society in London, with the National Assembly, and with various societies of the Friends of Liberty in France and England (London, 1792)
Parliamentary Reform (handbill, 3 May 1792) (report of delegate committee of united Norwich societies)
Committee of Secrecy of the House of Commons respecting Seditious Practices, Second Report (6 June, 1794), appendices C and D
An Address to the Electors of Norwich, being a Vindication of the Principles and conduct of Mr. Windham's opponents at the late election, 12 July 1794, 2nd ed. (Norwich, 1794)
The Declaration and Constitution of the Norwich Patriotic Society established the twentieth of April 1795 to obtain a reform in the Commons House of Parliament (Norwich, 1795), CC 25E
The Correspondence of the London Corresponding Society (London, 1795)
M. Wilks, *Athaliah, or the Tocsin sounded by Modern Alarmists. Two Collection Sermons towards defraying the expense of the Defendants in the late Trials for High Treason, preached on the 19th of April, 1795 in St. Paul's Chapel, Norwich* (Norwich, 1795)
T. Holcroft, *Letter to the Rt. Hon. W. Windham – on the intemperence and dangerous tendency of his public conduct* (London, 1795)
J. Sayers, *Outlines of the Opposition in 1795, collected from the works of the most capital Jacobin Artists* (1795) CC 56C
Proceedings and Speeches at the meeting the seventeenth November 1795 at St. Andrew's Hall, Norwich to petition Parliament against Lord Grenville's and Mr. Pitt's Treason and Sedition Bills, CC 31D
An Address from the Patriotic Society of Norwich to the Inhabitants of that City, 18 Aug. 1797, CC N 306

R. Dinmore Jnr, *Exposition of the Principles of the English Jacobins* . . ., 3rd ed. (Norwich, 1797)

[T.S.N.], *State of Society in Norwich in 1799, Monthly Magazine*, CC 5B

T. Sadler (ed.), *Diary, Reminiscences and Correspondence of Henry Crabb Robinson* (2 vols., London, 1872)

Secondary

Sarah Wilks, *Memoirs of Rev. Mark Wilks* (London, 1821)

W. Taylor, *Collected Works of Dr. Francis Sayers* (Norwich, 1823)

J. Chambers, *General History of the county of Norfolk* (2 vols., Norwich, 1829)

J. W. Robberds, *A Memoir of the Life and Writings of the late William Taylor of Norwich* (2 vols., London, 1843)

J. and E. Taylor, *History of the Octagon Chapel, Norwich* (London, 1848)

C. L. Brightwell, *Memorials of the Life of Amelia Opie*, 2nd ed. (Norwich, 1854)

A. D. Bayne, *A Comprehensive History of Norwich* (London, 1869)

Harriet Martineau, *Autobiography*, vol. 1 (3 vols., London, 1877)

R. H. Mason, *History of Norfolk* (2 vols., 1884–5)

W. Wicks, *Inns and Taverns of Old Norwich* (Norwich, 1925)

S. and B. Webb, *English Local Government from the Revolution to the Municipal Corporation Act*, vol. 7 (London, 1929)

R. K. Webb, *Harriet Martineau: A Radical Victorian* (London, 1960)

B. Green and M. R. Young, *Norwich: the Growth of a City* (City of Norwich Museums, 1968)

R. W. Davis, *Dissent in Politics, 1780–1830: The political life of W. Smith M.P.* (London, 1971)

E. A. Goodwyn, *Selections from Norwich Newspapers: 1760–1790* (Ipswich, 1976)

Articles

'The worthies of Norwich', *Edinburgh Review*, vol. 150 (1879), pp. 41–76

J. H. Clapham, 'The transference of the worsted industry from Norwich to the West Riding', *Economic Journal*, vol. 20 (1910), pp. 195–210

W. Graham, 'The authorship of the Norwich *Cabinet*, 1794–5', *Notes and Queries*, vol. 162 (Jan.–June 1932), pp. 294–5

J. K. Edwards, 'The Gurneys and the Norwich clothing trade in the
s

eighteenth century, *The Journal of the Friends' Historical Society*, vol. 50, no. 3 (1963), pp. 134–52

J. K. Edwards, 'The decline of the Norwich textiles industry', *Yorkshire Bulletin of Economic Social Research*, vol. 16, no. 1 (1964), pp. 31–41

B. D. Hayes, 'Politics in Norfolk, 1750–1832'. Unpublished PhD thesis, Cambridge, 1957 (Cambridge University Library)

4 *Birmingham*

Primary

J. Priestley, *Familiar Letters addressed to the Inhabitants of the town of Birmingham* (Birmingham, 1790)

Birmingham Society for Constitutional Information: Address, Declaration, Rules and Orders (Birmingham, 1792)

Birmingham Society for Constitutional Information: Letter to the English Nation (Birmingham, 1793)

W. Hutton, *A History of Birmingham to the end of the year 1780* (Birmingham, 1781)

Martha Russell, *Journal relating to the Birmingham Riots*

Catherine Hutton, *A Narrative of the Riots in Birmingham, July 1791* (Birmingham, 1875)

Aris's Birmingham Gazette

T. B. and T. J. Howell (eds.), *State Trials*, vol. 24 (London, 1818), for trial of J. Binns (1796)

J. T. Rutt (ed.), *Memoirs of Joseph Priestley to the Year 1795* (London, 1806)

J. T. Rutt (ed.), *Life and Correspondence of Joseph Priestley* (2 vols., London, 1831–2)

Secondary

J. A. Langford, *A Century of Birmingham Life, 1741–1841* (2 vols., Birmingham, 1868)

S. H. Jeyes, *The Russells of Birmingham* (London, 1911)

H. Pearson, *Dr. [Erasmus] Darwin* (London, 1930)

Birmingham and its Regional Setting (British Association, 1950)

H. C. Gill, *History of Birmingham* (Birmingham, 1952)

C. Gill and A. Briggs, *History of Birmingham*, vol. 1 (Birmingham, 1952)

R. E. Schofield, *The Lunar Society of Birmingham* (Oxford, 1963)

Victoria History of the County of Warwick, vol. 7 (London, 1964)

W. Derry, *Dr. Parr* (Oxford, 1966)

J. Money, *Experience and Identity: Birmingham and the West Midlands, 1760–1810* (Manchester, 1977)

Articles

R. B. Rose, 'The Priestley riots', *Past and Present*, no. 18 (1960) pp. 68–88

R. B. Rose, 'The origins of working-class radicalism in Birmingham', *Labour History* (Canberra), no. 9 (Nov. 1965), pp. 6–14

E. Robinson, 'New light on the Priestley riots', *The Historical Journal*, vol. 3 (1960), pp. 73–5

E. Robinson, 'The Lunar Society: its membership and organization', *Transactions of the Newcomen Society*, vol. 35 (1962–3), pp. 153–77

E. Robinson, 'The origins and life-span of the Lunar Society', *University of Birmingham Historical Journal*, vol. 11 (1967), pp. 6–16

5 *Leicester*

Primary
Leicester Journal
Leicester Herald
Leicester Chronicle

Secondary

J. Thompson, *History of Leicester in the Eighteenth Century* (London, 1871)

R. W. Greaves, *The Corporation of Leicester 1689–1836* (Oxford, 1939)

A. Temple Patterson, *Radical Leicester: A History of Leicester 1780– 1850* (Leicester, 1954)

Articles

F. S. Hearne, 'Sir Richard Phillips', *Transactions of the Leicester Literary and Philosophical Society*, vol. 3, pt. 2 (Leicester, 1893)

F. S. Hearne, 'An old Leicester bookseller', *Transactions of the Leicester Literary and Philosophical Society* (Leicester, 1873)

Derby

Primary
The Derby Address to the Friends of Free Enquiry and the General Good, July 16, 1792

Society for Constitutional Information at Derby: Address to the National Convention of France, 20 Nov. 1792. British Library, Place Newspaper Cuttings, vol. 36, fo. 15
Rules of the Derby Society for Political Information (1792)
Derby Mercury

Secondary
A. Seward, *Memoirs of the Life of Dr. Darwin* (London, 1804)
S. Stennet, *Memoirs of the Life of William Ward* (London, 1825)
W. Page (ed.), *Victoria History of the County of Derbyshire*, vol. 2

Articles
E. Robinson, 'The Derby Philosophical Society', *Annals of Science*, vol. 9 (1958), pp. 359–67

English radicalism in its French dimension

Primary
Lord Edward Fitzmaurice (ed.), *Lettres de l'abbé Morellet . . . à Lord Shelburne* (London, 1898)
O. Browning (ed.), *Despatches from Paris, 1784–90* (2 vols., London, 1909–10), *Camden Society*, 3rd series, vols. 16, 19
O. Browning, *Despatches of Earl Gower, 1790–1792* (Cambridge, 1885)
S. Romilly, *Règlements observés dans la Chambre de Communes pour débattre les matières et pour voter* (Paris, 1789)
S. Romilly, *Thoughts on the Probable Influence of the French Revolution on Great Britain* (London, 1790)
S. Romilly, *The Life of Sir Samuel Romilly, written by himself with a selection from his correspondence*, 3rd ed. (2 vols., London, 1842)
Abstract of the History and Proceedings of the Revolution Society in London (London, 1789)
R. Price, *A Discourse on the Love of Our Country*, 4th ed. (London, 1789)
J. Bentham, *Draft of a New Plan for the organization of the Judicial Establishment in France* (London, 1790)
E. Burke, *Reflections on the Revolution in France* (London, 1790)
E. Burke, *Appeal from the New to the Old Whigs* (London, 1791)
A. Cobban and R. A. Smith (eds.), *The Correspondence of Edmund Burke, July 1789–December 1791*, vol. 6 (Chicago/Cambridge, 1967)
J. Mackintosh, *Vindiciae Gallicae* (London and Dublin, 1791)

T. Paine, *The Rights of Man:* Part I (1791), Part II (1792)

E. Dumont, *Souvenirs sur Mirabeau et sur les deux premières Assemblées Législatives,* ed. J. Bénétruy (Paris, 1951)

E. Dumont and S. Romilly, *Letters containing an account of the late revolution in France and observations on the constitution, laws, manners and institutions of the English – translated from the German of Henry Frederic Groenvelt* (London, 1792)

The Correspondence of the Revolution Society in London with the National Assembly and with various societies of the Friends of Liberty in France (London, 1792)

Address presented by the delegates of the Constitutional Society of Manchester to the Society of Friends of the Constitution sitting at the Jacobins in Paris on 13 April 1792.

T. Cooper, *A Reply to Mr. Burke's invective against Mr. Cooper and Mr. Watt in the House of Commons on the 30th April 1792* (Manchester, 1792)

T. Paine, *Letter addressed to the Addressers on the late Proclamation* (London, 1792)

Joel Barlow, *Advice to the privileged orders of Europe* (London, 1793)

Collection of Addresses transmitted by certain English clubs and societies to the National Convention of France, 2nd ed. (London, 1793)

Arthur Young, *The Example of France a Warning to Britain* (London, 1793)

W. Frend, *Peace and Union Recommended* (St Ives, 1793)

W. A. Miles, *The conduct of France towards Great Britain examined* (London, 1793)

W. A. Miles, *Authentic correspondence with M. Le Brun, the French Minister and others* (London, 1796)

J. Bowles, *The Real Grounds of the Present War with France,* 6th ed. (London, 1794)

T. Erskine, *A View of the causes and consequences of the present war with France* (London, 1797)

Edmund Burke, *Letters on a Regicide Peace* (London, 1796)

H. Marsh, *The History of the Politicks of Great Britain and France from the time of the conference at Pillnitz to the Declaration of the war against Great Britain* (2 vols., London, 1800)

Secondary

D. Jarrett, *The Begetters of Revolution: England's involvement with France, 1759–1789* (London, 1973)

R. R. Palmer, *The Age of the Democratic Revolution: A Political History of Europe and America, 1760–1800*, vol. 1: *The Challenge* (Princeton, N.J., 1959)

J. Godechot, *La Grande Nation: expansion révolutionnaire de la France dans le monde de 1789 à 1799* (2 vols., Paris, 1956)

G. Rudé, *Paris and London in the Eighteenth Century* (London, 1970)

Lord Edward Fitzmaurice, *Life of William, Earl of Shelburne*, rev. ed. (2 vols., London, 1912)

J. Norris, *Shelburne and Reform* (London, 1963)

J. Egret, *La Pré-révolution Française, 1787–88* (Paris, 1962)

G. Lefebvre, *Quatre-Vingt-Neuf* (Paris, 1939). English trans., *The Coming of the French Revolution* (London, 1947)

M. Göhring, *Weg und Sieg der Modernen Staatsidee in Frankreich* (Tübingen, 1946)

A. B. Cobban (ed.), *The Debate on the French Revolution* (London, 1950)

P. A. Brown, *The French Revolution in English History* (London, 1918; reprinted 1965)

A. Newman, *The Stanhopes of Chevening* (London, 1969)

G. Stanhope and G. P. Gooch, *Life of Charles, Third Earl of Stanhope* (London, 1914)

J. G. Alger, *Englishmen in the French Revolution* (London, 1889)

J. Bénétruy, *L'Atelier de Mirabeau. Quatre Proscrits Genevois dans la tourmente révolutionnaire* (Geneva, 1962)

A. Aldridge, *Man of Reason; The Life of Thomas Paine* (London, 1960)

V. C. Miller, *Joel Barlow, Revolutionist, London 1791–92* (Hamburg, 1932)

C. B. Todd, *Life and Letters of Joel Barlow* (New York, 1886)

E. D. Woodward, *Une adhérente Anglaise à la Révolution Française: Hélène Maria Williams et ses amis* (Paris, 1929)

M. Reinhard, *La Chute de la Royauté* (Paris, 1969)

A. Mathiez, *La Révolution et les étrangers* (Paris, n.d.)

A. A. Ernouf, *Maret, Duc de Bassano* (Paris, 1878)

Dr Robinet, *Danton Émigré* (Paris, 1887)

A. Sorel, *L' Europe et la Révolution Française*, vol. 2 (Paris, 1908)

A. Saboul, *Les Sans-Culottes Parisiens en l'an II* (Paris, 1958)

W. T. Laprade, *England and the French Revolution, 1789–1797* (Baltimore, 1909)

W. P. Hall, *British Radicalism, 1791–1797* (New York, 1912)

F. O'Gorman, *The Whig Party and the French Revolution* (London, 1967)

L. G. Mitchell, *Charles James Fox and the Disruption of the Whig Party, 1782–1794* (Oxford, 1971)
G. A. Williams, *Artisans and Sans-Culottes: Popular Movements in France and Britain during the French Revolution* (London, 1968)

Articles

J. G. Alger, 'The British colony in Paris, 1792–3', *English Historical Review*, vol. 13 (1898), pp. 672–94
G. Pariset, 'La Société de la Révolution de Londres dans ses rapports avec Burke et l'Assemblée Constituante', *La Révolution Française*, vol. 29 (1895), pp. 297–325
C. Blount, 'Bentham, Dumont and Mirabeau', *University of Birmingham Historical Journal*, vol. 3 (1952), pp. 153–67
J. H. Burns, 'Bentham and the French Revolution', *Transactions of the Royal Historical Society*, 5th series, vol. 16 (1966), pp. 95–114
W. R. Fryer, 'Mirabeau in England, 1784–1785', *Renaissance and Modern Studies* (University of Nottingham), vol. 10 (1966), pp. 34–87
A. Goodwin, 'Counter-revolution in Brittany: the royalist conspiracy of the Marquis de la Rouerie', *Bulletin of the John Rylands Library*, vol. 39 (1957), pp. 326–55
A. Goodwin, 'The political genesis of Edmund Burke's *Reflections on the Revolution in France*', *Bulletin of the John Rylands Library*, vol. 50 (1968), pp. 336–64
A. Goodwin, 'A Comparative study of regionalism in politics in Lancashire and Normandy during the French Revolution', *Annales de Normandie*, vol. 8 (1958), pp. 235–55
M. Reinhard, 'Le voyage de Pétion à Londres, 24 Octobre–11 Novembre 1791', *Revue d'Histoire Diplomatique* (Jan.–June 1970), pp. 1–60

Anti-Jacobinism

Primary
Files of *The Times*, the *True Briton* and the *Sun* newspapers
Edmund Burke, *Reflections on the Revolution in France* (London, 1790)
    Appeal from the New to the Old Whigs (London, 1791)
    Letters on a Regicide Peace (London, 1795–6)
Association for the Preservation of Liberty and Property against

Republicans and Levellers: Association Papers (2 pts., London, 1793)

Hannah More, *Village Politics; a Dialogue between Jack Anvil the Blacksmith and Tom Hod the Mason; Addressed to All the Mechanics, Journeymen and Day-Labourers in Great Britain* (London, 1792)

Mr. Justice Ashurst's Charge to the Grand Jury for the county of Middlesex, 19 Nov. 1792. The Truth addressed to the People at large containing some strictures on the English Jacobins (London, 1792)

A dialogue between an Associator and a well-informed Englishman on the grounds of the late Associations and the Commencement of a War with France (London, 1793)

Collection of Addresses transmitted by certain English clubs and societies to the National Convention of France, 2nd ed. (London, 1793)

A Letter to Mr. Reeves, Chairman of the Association for preserving Liberty and Property. By Thomas Law, Esq. One of the Committee of that society (London, 1792)

William Playfair, *The History of Jacobinism: Its Crimes, Cruelties and Perfidies* (London, 1793)

A. Young, *The Example of France a Warning to Britain*, 2nd ed. (London, 1793)

J. Bowles, *The Real Grounds of the Present War with France*, 6th ed. (London, 1794)

First and Second Reports of the Committee of Secrecy of the House of Commons respecting Seditious Practices (May, June, 1794)

James Sayer, *Outlines of the Opposition in 1795, collected from the works of the most capital Jacobin artists* (London, 1797)

Declaration of the Merchants, Bankers, Traders and other Inhabitants of London (London, 1795)

A History of the Two Acts (London, 1796)

T. J. Mathias, *The Pursuits of Literature, 1794–7: A Satirical Poem in Four Dialogues with notes*, 11th ed. (London, 1801)

The Anti-Jacobin (Nov. 1797–July 1798)

Committee of Secrecy of the House of Commons relative to the proceedings of different persons and societies in Great Britain and Ireland engaged in a treasonable conspiracy (15 March, 1799)

W. H. Reid, *The Rise and Dissolution of the Infidel Societies of this Metropolis* (London, 1800)

T. B. and T. J. Howell (eds.), *State Trials*, vols. 23, 24, 25, 27

Hon. R. Clifford, *Application of Barruel's 'Memoirs of Jacobinism' to*

the secret societies of Ireland and Great Britain by the Translator of
that work (London, 1798)
The Spirit of Anti-Jacobinism for 1802 (London, 1802)
R. E. Prothero (ed.), *Private Letters of Edward Gibbon* (2 vols.,
London, 1896)
J. Hutton (ed.), *Letters and Correspondence of Sir James Bland Burges*
(London, 1885)
Mrs H. Baring (ed.), *The Diary of the Right Hon. William Windham
1784–1810* (London, 1866)
J. P. Gibson, *Correspondence of Edmund Burke and William Windham*
(Cambridge, 1910)
L. S. Benjamin (ed.), *The Windham Papers* (London, 1913)

Secondary
C. Edmonds, *Poetry of the Anti-Jacobin*, 3rd ed. (London, 1890)
J. Bagot, *George Canning and his Friends* (2 vols., London, 1909)
G. M. Trevelyan, *Lord Grey and the Reform Bill* (London, 1920)
D. Marshall, *The Rise of George Canning* (London, 1938)
E. C. Black, *The Association: British Extraparliamentary Political
Organization, 1769–1793* (Cambridge, Mass., 1963)

Articles
M. D. George, 'Political propaganda, 1793–1815: Gillray and
Canning', *History*, new series, vol. 31 (1946), pp. 66–88
J. R. Western, 'The Volunteer Movement as an anti-revolutionary
force, 1793–1801', *English Historical Review*, vol. 71 (1956), pp.
603–14
A. V. Mitchell, 'The Association Movement of 1792–3', *The Historical
Journal*, vol. 4 (1961), pp. 56–71
D. Ginter, 'The Loyalist Association Movement of 1792–93 and
British public opinion', *The Historical Journal*, vol. 9 (1966), 179–
90

The Scottish radical movement

Primary
T. Christie, *Letters on the Revolution of France*, pt. 1 (London, 1791)
J. T. Callender, *The Political Progress of Great Britain* (Edinburgh,
1792)
Hugh Lord Sempill, *A Short address to the Public on the practice of
cashiering Military Officers without a Trial* (London, 1793)

J. Gerrald, *A Convention the only means of saving us from Ruin in a letter addressed to the People of England* (London, 1793)

J. Gerrald, *The Address of the British Convention assembled at Edinburgh, Nov. 19 1793 to the People of Great Britain*

Report of the Committee of the Friends of the People . . . appointed to examine into the state of the Representation of Scotland (1793) in T. H. B. Oldfield, *Representative History of Great Britain*, vol. 6 (London, 1816)

Minutes of the British Convention (Nov.–Dec. 1793) are in the *Second Report from the Committee of Secrecy of the House of Commons respecting Seditious Practices* (June 1794), *Parliamentary History*, vol. 31, col. 844 ff.

C. Wyvill, *Political Papers*, vols. 2, 3 (1795–6)

T. B. and T. J. Howell (eds.), *State Trials* (London, 1813–20), vol. 23

Parliamentary History, vol. 31, for debates on Scottish sedition trials, March 1794

A. Fletcher, *Memoir concerning the Origin and Progress of the Reform Proposed in the internal government of the Royal Burghs of Scotland* (Edinburgh, 1819)

Lord Cockburn, *Memorials of His Times (1779–1850)*, new ed. (Edinburgh, 1909)

Secondary

R. Mackintosh, *Life of Sir James Mackintosh* (2 vols., London, 1835)

Countess of Minto, *Life and Letters of Sir Gilbert Elliott* (3 vols., London, 1874)

G. W. T. Omond, *The Lord Advocates of Scotland*, vol. 2 (Edinburgh, 1883)

G. W. T. Omond, *The Arniston Memoirs: Three Centuries of a Scottish House* (Edinburgh, 1887)

Lord Cockburn, *Examination of the Trials for Sedition in Scotland* (2 vols., Edinburgh, 1888)

P. Mackenzie, *Life of Thomas Muir* (Glasgow, 1831)

H. G. Graham, *Social Life in Scotland in the Eighteenth Century* (new ed., London, 1906)

W. L. Mathieson, *The Awakening of Scotland: A History from 1747 to 1797* (Glasgow, 1910)

H. W. Meikle, *Scotland and the French Revolution* (Glasgow, 1912)

H. Furber, *Henry Dundas* (London, 1931)

C. Matheson, *The Life of Henry Dundas, first Viscount Melville 1742–1811* (London, 1933)

J. D. Mackie, *A History of Scotland* (Edinburgh, 1964)

W. Ferguson, *Scotland 1689 to the present* (Edinburgh, 1968)

T. C. Smout, *A History of the Scottish People, 1560–1830* (London, 1969)

J. Prebble, *The Highland Clearances* (Harmondsworth, 1969)

N. T. Phillipson and R. Mitchison, *Essays in Scottish History in the Eighteenth Century* (Edinburgh, 1970)

J. Cannon, *Parliamentary Reform 1640–1832* (Cambridge, 1973)

Articles

W. P. Ker, 'The politics of Burns', *Scottish Historical Review*, vol. 15 (1917–18), pp. 59–72

Sir James Ferguson, 'Making interest in Scottish county elections', *Scottish Historical Review*, vol. 26 (1947), pp. 119–33

E. Hughes, 'The Scottish reform movement and Charles Grey, 1792–4': some fresh correspondence', *Scottish Historical Review*, vol. 35 (1956), pp. 39–41

E. Richards, 'Patterns of Highland discontent, 1790–1860', in *Popular Protest and Public Order*, ed. R. Quinault and J. Stevenson (London, 1974), pp. 75–114

The treason trials of 1794

Primary

Committee of Secrecy of the House of Commons respecting Seditious practices: *First Report* (16 May 1794), *Parl. Hist.*, vol. 31, cols. 475–97; *Second Report* (6 June 1794), *Ibid.*, cols. 688–879

Committee of Secrecy of the House of Lords respecting Seditious Practices: *First Report* (22 May 1794), *Parl. Hist.*, vol. 31, cols. 573–4; *Second Report* (7 June 1794), *Ibid.*, cols. 886–903

W. Godwin, *Cursory Strictures on the charge delivered by Lord Chief Justice Eyre to the Grand Jury, Oct. 2, 1794*

T. B. and T. J. Howell (eds.), *State Trials*, vols. 24, 25

Lord Eldon's Anecdote Book, ed. Anthony L. J. Lincoln and Robert L. McEwen (London, 1960)

Account of the seizure of Citizen Thomas Hardy, Secretary to the London Corresponding Society, 1794

An Account of Mr. Joyce's Arrest for 'Treasonable Practices, etc.', 2nd ed. (London, 1795)

Horne Tooke's Prison Diary, May–Oct. 1794, Notes and Queries, 8th series, vol. 11 (Jan. and Feb. 1897), pp. 21–2, 61–2, 103–4, 162–3

J. Thelwall, *The Tribune*, vol. 2 (London, 1795)

J. Binns, *Recollections of the Life of J. Binns written by himself* (Philadelphia, 1854)

James Parkinson, *A Vindication of the London Corresponding Society* (London, 1795)

Lord Broughton, *Recollections of a Long Life*, vol. 2 (London, 1909)

J. Hutton (ed.), *Letters and Correspondence of Sir James Bland Burges* (London, 1885)

F. D. Cartwright (ed.), *Life and Correspondence of Major Cartwright* (2 vols., London 1826)

T. Sadler (ed.), *Diary, Reminiscences and Correspondence of H. Crabb Robinson* (2 vols., London, 1872)

T. Holcroft, *A Narrative of Facts relating to a Prosecution for High Treason etc.* (London, 1795)

T. Holcroft, *Letter to the Rt. Hon. William Windham on the Intemperence and Dangerous Tendency of his Public Conduct* (London, 1795)

[P. Mackenzie], *Memoir of Thomas Hardy* (London, 1832)

M. Thale (ed.), *The Autobiography of Francis Place 1771–1854* (Cambridge, 1972)

Secondary

Sir J. F. Stephen, *History of the Criminal Law* (3 vols., London, 1883)

L. Radzinowicz, *History of the English Criminal Law* (3 vols., London, 1948–56)

Sir W. S. Holdsworth, *History of English Law*, vol 10 (17 vols., London, 1903–72)

W. Derry, *Dr. Parr* (Oxford, 1966)

C. K. Paul, *William Godwin, His Friends and Contemporaries* (2 vols., London, 1876)

H. Twiss, *Life of Lord Chancellor Eldon* (3 vols., London, 1844)

Lord John Campbell, *Lives of the Lord Chancellors* (10 vols., London, 1868)

Article

T. M. Parssinen, 'Association, convention and anti-parliament in British radical politics, 1771–1848', *English Historical Review*, vol. 88 (1973), pp. 504–33

The growth of the protest movement

Primary

G. Dyer, *The Complaints of the Poor People of England* (London, 1793)

Rev. David Davies, *The Case of the Labourer in Husbandry* (London, 1795)

Substance of Earl Stanhope's speech on the 4th of February 1795 to celebrate the happy event of the late trials for supposed High Treason (London, 1795)

Correspondence of the London Corresponding Society, revised and corrected (London, 1795)

[James Parkinson], *Revolutions without Bloodshed* (London, 1794)

J. Baxter, *Resistance to Oppression: The Constitutional Rights of Britons Asserted* (London, 1795)

Summary of the Proceedings at a meeting of the London Corresponding Society . . . in St. George's fields, Monday, 29 June 1795

Account of the Proceedings of a meeting of the London Corresponding Society, held in a field near Copenhagen House, Monday October 26, 1795

John Thelwall, *Speech at the General Meeting of the Friends of Parliamentary Reform . . . Oct. 26, 1795*

Account of the Proceedings of a Meeting of the People in a field near Copenhagen House, Thursday November 12, 1795 on the subject of the Threatened Invasion of their Rights by a Convention Bill

To the Parliament and People of Great Britain: An Explicit Declaration of the Principles and views of the London Corresponding Society, 23 November 1795

Meeting of the London Corresponding Society, Monday 7 December, 1795, in Marylebone Fields, London, in *A History of the Two Acts* (1796), pp. 643–53

W. Godwin, *Considerations on Lord Grenville's and Mr. Pitt's Bills concerning Treasonable and Seditious Practices and Unlawful Assemblies, 1795*

London Corresponding Society: A Summary of the Rights of Citizenship (London, 1795)

J. Baxter, *New and Impartial History of England* (London, 1796)

John Gale Jones, *Sketch of a Political Tour through Rochester, Chatham, Maidstone, Gravesend etc.,* pt. 1 (London, 1796)

J. Thelwall, *The Tribune,* vols. 2, 3 (London, 1795–6)

J. Thelwall, *Prospectus of a Course of Lectures in Strict Conformity with the restrictions of Mr. Pitt's Convention Act, 1796*

J. Thelwall, *An Appeal to Popular Opinion against Kidnapping and Murder, including a Narrative of the late atrocious proceedings at Yarmouth*, 2nd ed. (London, 1796)

The History of the Two Acts (London, 1796)

John Gale Jones, *Farewell Oration to the Westminster Forum, 16 March 1797*

A Narrative of the Proceedings at the General Meeting of the London Corresponding Society, July 31, 1797

Committee of Secrecy of the House of Commons . . . Report (15 March 1799)

R. B. MacDowell and J. A. Woods (eds.), *The Correspondence of Edmund Burke*, vol. 9: *May 1796–July 1797* (Cambridge, 1970)

Secondary

H. Jephson, *The Platform: Its Rise and Progress* (2 vols., London, 1892)

M. E. Poole (Mrs Sandford), *Thomas Poole and his Friends* (2 vols., London, 1888)

E. Halévy, *History of the English People in the Nineteenth Century*, vol. 1 (London, 1924)

G. M. Trevelyan, *Lord Grey of the Reform Bill* (London, 1920)

H. N. Brailsford, *Shelley Godwin and their Circle* (London, 1936)

J. Greig (ed.), *The Faringdon Diary*, vol. 1 (London, 1922)

C. Gill, *The Naval Mutinies of 1797* (Manchester, 1913)

M. Lewis, *The History of the British Navy* (Harmondsworth, 1957)

M. Lewis, *A Social History of the British Navy, 1793–1815* (London, 1960)

A. J. Peacock, *Bread or Blood* (London, 1965)

J. D. Marshall, *The Old Poor Law, 1795–1834, Studies in Economic History* (London, 1968)

D. Marshall, *The English Poor in the Eighteenth Century* (London, 1926)

M. W. Finn, *British Population Growth, 1700–1850, Studies in Economic History* (London, 1970)

P. D. G. Thomas, *The House of Commons in the Eighteenth Century* (Oxford, 1971)

R. Quinault and J. Stevenson (eds.), *Popular Protest and Public Order: Six studies in British History, 1790–1920* (London, 1974)

Articles

Chester Kirby, 'The English game law system', *American Historical Review*, vol. 38 (1932–3), pp. 240–62

P. Fraser, 'Public petitioning and Parliament before 1832', *History*, vol. 46 (1961), pp. 195–211

N. M. Stern, 'The bread crisis in Britain, 1795–6', *Economica*, new series, vol. 31 (1964), pp. 168–87

J. Stevenson, 'Food riots in England, 1792–1818', in R. Quinault and I. Stevenson (eds.), *Popular Protest and Public Order* (London, 1974), pp. 33–74

The Irish dimension

Primary

D. A. Chart (ed.), *The Drennan Letters, 1776–1819* (Belfast, 1931)

W. T. W. Tone (ed.), *Life of Theobald Wolfe Tone . . . written by himself and continued by his son* (2 vols., Washington, 1826)

T. B. and T. J. Howell (eds.), *State Trials*, vol. 27

Personal Recollections of the Life and Times of Valentine, Lord Cloncurry (Dublin, 1849)

Hamilton Rowan tracts (John Rylands University Library, Manchester)

Committee of Secrecy of the House of Commons of Ireland, Report (17 July 1798)

Committee of Secrecy of the House of Lords in Ireland, Report (30 August, 1798)

Committee of Secrecy of the House of Commons relative to the proceedings of different persons and societies in Great Britain and Ireland engaged in a treasonable conspiracy, Report (15 March 1799), *Parl. Hist.*, vol. 34, pp. 579–656

Secondary

R. R. Madden, *The United Irishmen, their lives and times*, rev. ed. (4 vols., Dublin, 1857–60)

W. J. Fitzpatrick, *Secret Service under Pitt* (London, 1892)

W. J. Fitzpatrick, *The Life, Times and Contemporaries of Lord Cloncurry* (London, 1855)

W. E. H. Lecky, *History of Ireland in the Eighteenth Century* (5 vols., London, 1892)

W. E. H. Lecky, *Leaders of Public Opinion in Ireland*, 3rd ed., vol. 1 (London, 1903)

J. A. Froude, *The English in Ireland in the eighteenth century*, 2nd ed. (3 vols., London, 1881)

E. Guillon, *La France et l'Irlande pendant la Révolution* (Paris, 1888)

A. Sorel, *L'Europe et la Révolution Française*, vol. 5 (Paris, 1910)

H. L. Calkin, *Les Invasions d'Irlande pendant la Révolution Française* (Paris, 1956)

E. H. Stuart-Jones, *The Invasion that failed: the French expedition to Ireland, 1796* (Oxford, 1950)

R. Jacob, *The Rise of the United Irishmen 1791-4* (London, 1937)

H. Nicolson, *The Desire to please: A Study of Hamilton Rowan and the United Irishmen* (London, 1943)

S. Sims, *The Rev. James Coigley: United Irishman* (Belfast, 1937)

R. B. McDowell, *Irish Public Opinion, 1750-1800* (London, 1944)

H. Butterfield, *George III, Lord North and the People* (London, 1949)

R. Hayes, *Biographical Dictionary of Irishmen in France* (Dublin, 1949)

R. Hayes, *The last invasion of Ireland*, 2nd ed. (Dublin, 1939)

M. Wall, *The Penal Laws, 1691-1760*, Dublin Historical Association pamphlet (1961)

K. H. Connell, *The Population of Ireland, 1750-1845* (Oxford, 1950)

B. Inglis, *The Freedom of the Press in Ireland, 1754-1841* (London, 1954)

E. M. Johnston, *Great Britain and Ireland, 1760-1800: a study in political administration* (Edinburgh, 1963)

E. M. Johnston, *Ireland in the eighteenth century* (Dublin, 1974)

M. R. O'Connell, *Irish Politics and Social Conflict in the Age of the American Revolution* (Philadelphia, 1965)

G. C. Bolton, *The Passing of the Irish Act of Union* (Oxford, 1966)

T. W. Moody and F. X. Martin (eds.), *The Course of Irish History* (Cork, 1967)

T. Pakenham, *The Year of Liberty: The Great Irish Rebellion of 1798* (London, 1968)

J. C. Beckett, *The Making of Modern Ireland, 1603-1923* (London, 1971)

H. Senior, *Orangeism in Ireland and Britain, 1795-1836* (Toronto/ London, 1966)

L. M. Cullen, *An Economic History of Ireland since 1660* (London, 1972)

G. O'Tuathaigh, *Ireland before the Famine, 1798-1848* (Dublin, 1972)

Articles

R. B. McDowell, 'The personnel of the Dublin Society of United Irishmen, 1791–4', *Irish Historical Studies*, vol. 2 (1940), pp. 12–53

F. McDermot, 'Arthur O'Connor', *Irish Historical Studies*, vol. 15 (1966), pp. 48–69

A. W. Smith, 'Irish rebels and English radicals, 1798–1820', *Past and Present*, no. 7 (1955), pp. 78–85

M. Wall, 'The rise of a Catholic middle class in eighteenth century Ireland', *Irish Historical Studies*, vol. 11 (1958), pp. 91–115

M. Wall, 'The United Irish movement', *Historical Studies*, vol. 5 (Dublin, 1965), pp, 122–40

P. Kelly, 'British and Irish politics in 1785', *English Historical Review*, vol. 90 (1975)(pp. 536–63

M. Elliott, 'The "Despard conspiracy" reconsidered', *Past and Present*, no. 75 (May, 1977), pp. 46–61

Decline and Fall (Ch. 12)

Primary

E. Burke, *Letters on a Regicide Peace* (London, 1796–7)

J. Thelwall, *The Natural and Constitutional Right of Britons to Annual Parliaments, Universal Suffrage and the Freedom of Popular Association* (London, 1795)

T. Thelwall, *The Rights of Nature against the Usurpations of Establishments* (London, 1796)

T. Bewick, *A Memoir written by himself*, ed. I. Bain (London, 1975)

R. Dinmore, Jnr, *Exposition of the Principles of the English Jacobins* (Norwich, 1797)

T. F. Palmer, *Narrative of the Sufferings of T. F. Palmer and W. Skirving* (Cambridge, 1797)

Personal Recollections of the Life and Times of Valentine, Lord Cloncurry (Dublin, 1849)

W. J. B. Owen and J. W. Smysen (eds.), *The Prose Works of William Wordsworth* (2 vols., Oxford, 1974)

M. Thale (ed.), *The Autobiography of Francis Place, 1771–1854* (Cambridge, 1972)

W. C. Hazlitt (ed.), *Letters of Charles Lamb* (2 vols. London, 1886)

W. Godwin, *Enquiry concerning the Principles of Political Justice and its influence on General Virtue and Happiness* (2 vols., London, 1793)

T. Spence, *The Rights of Man* (London, 1793)

T. Spence, *A Pennyworth of Pig's Meat; or Lessons from the Swinish Multitude* (London, 1793–4)

T. Spence, *The Meridian Sun of Liberty* (London, 1796)

T. Spence, *Constitution of Spensonea – a country in Fairyland* (London, 1801)

T. Spence, *The Restorer of Society to its Natural State* (London, 1801)

T. Spence, *The World turned upside down* (London, 1805)

T. Evans, *Christian Policy the Salvation of the Empire*, 2nd ed. (London, 1816)

T. Paine, *The Age of Reason* (London, 1794)

M. Margarot, *Thoughts on Revolutions* (Harlow, 1812)

M. Margarot, *Proposals for a Grand National Jubilee: Restoring to every Man his Own, and thereby extinguishing both Want and War* (Sheffield, 1812)

Secondary

R. Y. Hedges and A. Winterbottom, *The Legal History of Trade Unionism* (London, 1930)

A. Aspinall, *The Early English Trade Unions* (London, 1949)

A. E. Musson, *British Trade Unions, 1800–1875, Studies in Economic History* (London, 1972)

H. Pelling, *A History of British Trade Unionism*, 3rd ed. (London, 1976)

J. L. and B. Hammond, *The Town Labourer, 1760–1832* (London, 1949 reprint)

Sir Charles Oman, *Colonel Despard and other Studies* (London, 1922)

A. Soboul, *Les Sans-Culottes Parisiens en l'an II* (Paris, 1958)

M. C. Pack, *Joseph Priestley and the Problem of Pantisocracy* (Philadelphia, 1947)

C. Tomalin, *The Life and Death of Mary Wollstonecraft* (London, 1974)

O. Rudkin, *Thomas Spence and his Connections* (London, 1922)

W. H. Reid, *The Rise and Dissolution of the Infidel Societies in this Metropolis* (London, 1800)

F. M. Todd, *Politics and the Poet: A Study of Wordsworth* (London, 1957)

R. J. White, *Waterloo to Peterloo* (London, 1957)

J. R. M. Butler, *The Passing of the Great Reform Bill* (London, 1964 reprint)

M. Brock, *The Great Reform Act* (London, 1973)

A. Briggs (ed.), *Chartist Studies* (London, 1959)

A. R. Schoyen, *The Chartist Challenge: A Portrait of George Julian Harney* (London, 1958)

F. C. Mather, *Public Order in the Age of the Chartists* (Manchester, 1959)

F. C. Mather, *Chartism*, Historical Association pamphlet G.61 (London, 1965)

H. L. Beales, *The Early English Socialists* (London, 1933)

P. Hollis, *The Pauper Press: A Study in Working Class Radicalism in the 1830s* (Oxford, 1970)

Articles

R. B. Rose, 'The Jacobins of Liverpool, 1789–1793', *The Liverpool Libraries, Museums, and Arts Committee Bulletin*, vol. 9 (1960–1), pp. 35–49

A. W. Smith, 'Irish rebels and English radicals, 1790–1820', *Past and Present*, no. 7 (April 1955), pp. 78–85

M. Elliott, 'The "Despard conspiracy" reconsidered', *Past and Present*, no. 75 (May 1977), pp. 46–61

T. M. Parssinen, 'The Revolutionary Party in London, 1816–1820', *Bulletin of the Institute of Historical Research*, vol. 45 (1972), pp. 266–82

G. Whale, 'The influence of the industrial revolution, 1760–1790, on the demand for parliamentary reform', *Transactions of the Royal Historical Society*, 4th series, vol. 15 (1922), pp. 101–31

C. H. Driver, 'William Godwin', in F. J. C. Hearnshaw (ed.), *The Social and Political Ideas of some Representative Thinkers of the Revolutionary Era* (London, 1931), pp. 141–80

T. M. Parssinen, 'Thomas Spence and the origins of English land nationalisation', *Journal of the History of Ideas*, vol. 34 (1973), pp. 135–41

I. Sellers, 'Unitarians and social change, pt. 1: varieties of radicalism, 1795–1815', *Hibbert Journal*, vol. 61 (1962), pp. 16–22

G. A. Williams, 'Morgan John Rhees and his Beula', *The Welsh History Review*, vol. 3, no. 4 (1967), pp. 441–72

M. Roe, 'Maurice Margarot: a radical in two hemispheres, 1792–1815', *Bulletin of the Institute of Historical Research*, vol. 31 (1958), pp. 68–78

E. P. Thompson, 'Working class culture: the transition to industrialism', *Society for the study of Labour History*, bulletin no. 8 (1964), pp. 4–5.

W. E. S. Thomas, 'Francis Place and working class history', *Historical Journal*, vol. 5 (1962), pp. 61–70

Unpublished university theses

W. A. L. Seaman, 'British democratic societies in the period of the French Revolution', London PhD (1954)

J. Walvin, 'English democratic societies and popular radicalism, 1791–1800', York PhD (1969)

P. J. Brunsdon, 'The Association of the Friends of the People', Manchester MA (1961)

B. D. Hayes, 'Politics in Norfolk, 1750–1832', Cambridge PhD (1957)

A. V. Mitchell, 'Radicalism and repression in the north of England 1791–1797', Manchester MA (1958)

D. Clare, 'The growth and importance of the newspaper press in Manchester, Liverpool, Sheffield and Leeds, 1780–1800', Manchester MA (1960)

E. M. Hunt, 'The north of England agitation for the abolition of the slave trade, 1780–1800', Manchester MA (1959)

E. Fearn, 'Reform movements in Derby and Derbyshire 1790–1832', Manchester MA (1964)

J. Stevenson, 'Disturbance and public order in London, 1790–1821', Oxford DPhil (1972)

D. Drinkwater Lunn, 'John Cartwright – political education and English radicalism, 1774–1794', Oxford DPhil (1971)

J. A. Hone, 'The ways and means of London radicalism, 1796–1821', Oxford DPhil (1975)

I. Sellers, 'Political and social attitudes of representative English Unitarians', Oxford BLitt (1956)

J. T. Murley, 'The origin and outbreak of the Anglo-French war of 1793', Oxford DPhil (1962)

L. Porter, 'Anglo-French relations, Aug. 1792 to Feb. 1793', York PhD (1973)

J. D. Jarrett, 'The Bowood Circle, 1780–1793', Oxford BLitt (1955)

D. Weaver, 'Talleyrand's mission to London in 1792', Cardiff MA (1969)

Marianne Elliott, 'The United Irishmen and France, 1793–1806', Oxford DPhil (1975)

Index

interpretation and its
significance, 58 *n*, 60–2

Daer, Lord Basil William
Douglas, (1763–94), and
LCS, 197, 209
Darwin, Erasmus (1731–1802),
founder member Derby
radical society, 230
Davison, Richard, journeyman
printer, and arming in
Sheffield, 327, 350–1
Declaratory Act, Irish (1719),
repealed, 418
'Defenders', secret Irish
agrarian society, 428–9
Derby Society for Political
Information (1792): *Address
to the Friends of Free
Enquiry and the General
Good* (July 1792), 230;
collapse of (May 1793), 231,
282; delegates present
address to French Convention
(Nov. 1792), 253; origins,
230
Despard, Colonel E. M.
(1751–1803): arrest (16 Nov.
1802), 468; complicity of
former members of LCS
and government reticence,
469; 'conspiracy' reassessed,
465; early career and
significance as a link
between English, Irish and
French republicans, 464–6;
projected *coup d'état* in
London (1802), 467–8
Dinmore, R. Jnr, member
Norwich Patriotic Society:
Exposition of the Principles

of the English Jacobins (1797),
376, 470–2 (*see also* the
Cabinet)
Dissenters, Protestant:
campaign for relief of
disabilities under Test and
Corporation Acts, 72, 74–8;
changes in social and
political attitudes and
'Rational Dissent', 68–72;
early sympathy with French
revolution, 98; significance
in provincial radicalism,
65–7, 145
Dissenting academies, 69–70
Dobden, Sir William, MP for
Oxford University, opponent
of Beaufoy's motion (1787),
84
Dowdall, William, Irish
conspirator, and plans
for insurrection in 1803,
466
Downie, Edward, Edinburgh
goldsmith, and Robert
Watt's conspiracy in 1794,
335
Drennan, Dr William, United
Irishman, republican
aspirations of, 420
Duckett, William, United
Irishman, advises French
government on arson in
fleet, 410
Dumont, Étienne, Genevan
political exile and
collaborator of Bentham:
activities in England and
France as member of
Lansdowne's circle, 104–6
Dundas, Henry, 1st Viscount